# AUDITING PRINCIPLES

Donald L. Hansen
Arnold, NE 69120

## Prentice-Hall Series in Accounting
Charles T. Horngren, Editor

# AUDITING
# PRINCIPLES
## A Systems-Based Approach

**Fifth Edition**

**Howard F. Stettler**

*Professor of Business Administration*
*Peat, Marwick, Mitchell Faculty Fellow*
*University of Kansas*

**PRENTICE-HALL, INC.,** *ENGLEWOOD CLIFFS, NEW JERSEY 07632*

*Library of Congress Cataloging in Publication Data*

STETTLER, HOWARD F.
   Auditing principles.

   Includes index.
   A. Auditing.  I. Title.
HF5667.S815 1982    657'.45     81-15843
ISBN  0-13-051722-4          AACR2

*Editorial/production supervision and interior design by Steven Young*
*Cover design by Miriam Recio*
*Manufacturing buyer: Ray Keating*

Printed in the United States of America

10  9  8  7  6  5  4  3  2  1

ISBN 0-13-051722-4

Prentice-Hall International, Inc., *London*
Prentice-Hall of Australia Pty. Limited, *Sydney*
Prentice-Hall of Canada, Ltd., *Toronto*
Prentice-Hall of India Private Limited, *New Delhi*
Prentice-Hall of Japan, Inc., *Tokyo*
Prentice-Hall of Southeast Asia Pte. Ltd., *Singapore*
Whitehall Books Limited, *Wellington, New Zealand*

# CONTENTS

## Chapter 3

# AUDITORS'
# LEGAL RESPONSIBILITIES
# AND OTHER EXTERNALLY
# IMPOSED REQUIREMENTS    60

## Chapter 4

# INTRAORGANIZATIONAL
# AUDITING    80

## Chapter 5

# ELEMENTS
# OF THE AUDIT PROCESS    106

# Chapter 8

## THE SYSTEM-BASED AUDIT III

### Documenting the Audit: Working Papers    187

# Chapter 9

## SAMPLE SELECTION AND EVALUATION—JUDGMENTAL/ STATISTICAL    208

# Chapter 10

## AUDITS OF AUTOMATED DATA PROCESSING SYSTEMS    251

# Chapter 11

# REVENUES
# AND RECEIVABLES 277

# Chapter 12

# PURCHASES, EXPENSES,
# AND ACCOUNTS PAYABLE 322

# Chapter 13

# COST OF SALES
# AND INVENTORIES 347

# Chapter 17

## MISCELLANEOUS EXPENSES, LOSSES, REVENUES, ASSETS, AND LIABILITIES 500

# Chapter 18

## LONG-TERM DEBT AND OWNERS' EQUITY 532

# Chapter 19

## CAPPING THE AUDIT FIELD WORK 551

Chapter 20

# AUDIT REPORTING STANDARDS I

## The Standard (Short-Form) Report; Circumstances Necessitating Report Modification 576

Chapter 21

# AUDIT REPORTING STANDARDS II

## Special Reports: Compilation and Review Services; Other Special Reports; Long-Form Reports 610

## Chapter 22

## TAX, MANAGEMENT ADVISORY, AND OTHER PUBLIC ACCOUNTING SERVICES 643

## INDEX 671

# PREFACE

In this fully updated edition of *Auditing Principles,* as well as in previous editions of this introductory auditing text, the objectives have been to

- Introduce the reader to the broad aspects of the auditing field, including the role of independent audits in the capital markets of our complex, highly industrialized society, and the role of intraorganizational audits as an aid to management.
- Help the reader to become aware of the public accounting profession and the environment in which it functions.
- Explain how public accounting firms organize to provide customary services to their clients.
- Describe logically the various elements related to the audit process, including

    The functioning of accounting systems and the objectives and features of effective internal controls over those systems.

    The roles of risk and the acquisition and evaluation of evidence as vital aspects of the audit process.

    The nature of audit objectives and the audit procedures through which those objectives are accomplished.
- Help the reader to recognize and understand the reasons that underlie various accounting and auditing procedures.
- Present the increasingly involved and complex aspects of audit reporting.
- Prepare the reader to successfully write the auditing section of the CPA examination. (Here, the extensive use of questions and problems from past CPA examinations should be noted.)

This fifth edition of *Auditing Principles* offers a completely revised introduction to audits and the audit process, with primary emphasis on independent audits of financial statements, but also including extensive material on intraorganizational audits by internal auditors and by government auditors who report to a legislative body. Although the book is designed for use in a first course in auditing at either the undergraduate or the graduate level, it is fully comprehensive of all official pronouncements pertaining to the practice of auditing.

To help readers understand how the auditor assembles in working papers a record of evidence that has been examined in support of an opinion about a set of financial statements, the text gives extensive references to a comprehensive set of illustrative working papers. These are "last year's work papers" in *Practice Case for Auditing* by Sherwood W. Newton and Howard F. Stettler (Prentice-Hall, 1977). Those not using the case as a supplement to the text will find it helpful to obtain the same last year's work papers in the separate pamphlet *Audit Work Papers* (Prentice-Hall, 1977).

This completely new edition of *Auditing Principles* reflects the increasing orientation of independent audits toward reliance on evaluating and testing accounting systems and the internal controls developed by management. *Auditing Principles* now incorporates in an enhanced form the systems approach that I developed in 1967 in preparing *Systems Based Independent Audits,* a text that is currently being phased out.

Beginning with the first edition of *Auditing Principles,* published in 1956, my texts have consistently focused on objectives as the key to effective audits, based on the assumption that recognizing and understanding those objectives leads unerringly to audit procedures that develop the evidence on which an auditor's professional opinion is based. The present edition improves on that approach in two ways:

1. Audit objectives are uniformly expressed throughout the text, in contrast to the former plan of presenting individualized objectives for each financial statement item.

2. Internal control objectives have also been uniformly stated, and the internal control features that will accomplish those objectives are presented and discussed in relation to each objective. Three broad groupings of the objectives are used to facilitate a reader's grasp of internal controls: operating controls, accounting/data processing controls, and monitoring controls, which include internal auditing.

Introductory chapters prepare the reader for the analysis and discussion of the audit process in the "core" chapters, which pertain to each of the accounting subsystems involved in processing the major types of transactions—revenues, expenditures, cost of sales, cash receipts and disbursements, payroll, plant assets, and the long-term capital sources of debt and equity. The eight introductory chapters

- Introduce the reader to the role of audits in our complex economic society.
- Describe the public accounting profession and its continuing efforts to strengthen the standards of practice, including the ethical code of the profession.
- Present the legal and regulatory environment within which the auditing profession operates, and discuss other external influences on auditing practice.
- Discuss standards that have been developed for the segment of auditing practice that is identified as intraorganizational auditing, and which includes internal auditing and auditing within government for the benefit of legislative bodies.
- Show how practitioners organize to perform the audit function.
- Analyze the risks with which auditors must cope.
- Discuss accounting systems and internal control and how those factors affect audit risk.

- Describe in general terms the evidence accumulation process of auditing and the procedures for acquiring the necessary evidence.
- Explain how audit working papers are organized and prepared.
- Introduce the problems of sample selection and evaluation by judgmental and statistical methods, including attribute sampling, statistical estimation, and sampling of monetary units.
- Describe the computer environment of data processing and indicate how auditors cope with computer problems.

The core chapters follow, each displaying a uniform approach to an analysis of the audit process for a particular transaction segment of the accounting system and the related financial statement items. The stated uniform approach deals first with internal control objectives and features and includes a discussion of both the financial and operational audit activities of a highly developed internal audit function. The second portion of each core chapter addresses substantive audit objectives and procedures and includes a summary of key aspects of financial reporting and disclosure standards that must be satisfied.

A chapter on capping the audit discusses a variety of matters involved in the audit process and leads to a comprehensive two-chapter analysis of audit reporting standards. A final chapter discusses other services customarily offered by a public accounting firm, concentrating primarily on management advisory services and some of the controversial aspects of providing that type of service.

Pronouncements of the American Institute of Certified Public Accountants are extensively referred to throughout the text for the reader's benefit and to make the text as authoritative as possible. The cooperation of the Institute in granting permission to quote from its published material, including questions and problems from the Uniform CPA Examination, is gratefully acknowledged.

I would also like to thank the following professors for reviewing the unedited manuscript of this new edition of *Auditing Principles* and for offering many helpful comments and suggestions: William L. Felix, University of Washington; Richard G. File, University of Oklahoma; William L. Kimball, California State University—Northridge; Michael B. Sheffey, University of Wisconsin—Parkside; Jay M. Smith, Jr., Brigham Young University; John Michael Walsh; Bart Ward, University of Oklahoma; and Assistant Professor John Zook, LaSalle College.

Howard F. Stettler

# AUDITING PRINCIPLES

# Chapter 1

# ABOUT AUDITS AND AUDITORS

*[handwritten annotation: most important / Audit Report and 10 Standards]*

Shakespeare noted, "What's past is prologue." Similarly, the significance of the past is recognized by creditors and investors as they rely on the "track record" of businesses in making lending and investment decisions. But information about past operating and financial results communicated by management through financial statements to creditors, investors, or other persons might be of doubtful reliability because bias, carelessness, self-interest, or outright dishonesty could be reflected in the statements. Oversight, for example, might result in the omission from financial statements of liabilities and related expenses that were not yet a matter of book record. Or management might be reluctant to admit that a significant credit sale it had approved had become doubtful of collec-

1

tion. Even worse, inasmuch as financial statements are the representation of management, the figures might be intentionally falsified to present an appearance of improved financial position or operating results in order to support the raising of additional equity capital or the issuance of bonds or other obligations. An alternative reason for inflating reported operating results could be the desire to improve executive incentive compensation based on reported operating results.

### Strengthening Financial Statement Credibility

Given these various possibilities, it is important to assure third party investors and creditors that the information they use in their decisions is reliable; consequently, financial statements are typically subjected to examination by an independent auditor. If the auditor's examination shows that the information is fairly presented, the auditor's report appended to the statements will attest to that fact.

These attestations are important from an overall economic standpoint in a capitalistic society, as well as to individual decision makers, for they help to assure that capital will be directed to the most productive uses, thus producing maximum benefits to both individual investors and to society as a whole. Consider, for example, that investors in their investment decisions seek to maximize return subject to safety constraints. If these decisions are made on a sound basis, they will also result in the optimum allocation of scarce capital resources and maximum benefit to society. But should a firm attract funds by misrepresenting its operating results or financial position, the resulting misallocation of funds would involve a loss to both individual investors and to the overall economy.

An important supplementary effect of the availability of reliable financial information is the fact that investing is consequently more attractive, thus increasing the total supply of capital by reducing fear of potential loss from the use of misleading financial information. Again, the availability of reliable information increases the total output of goods and services.

This book focuses on the independent examinations of financial information that contribute to the salutary results discussed, while also considering other types of audit activity and other services offered by auditors in public practice.

### Chapter Overview

The objective of this chapter is to provide a general introduction to auditing and an overview of the book. With the rationale for independent audits already indicated, the chapter moves to a general definition of auditing that encompasses independent audits and other types of audit activity. Then the discussion returns to independent audits and considers the guidelines known as generally accepted auditing standards. At that point attention is directed to the end product of independent audits: the report on the findings of the audit examination. Following this material on the auditor's report the chapter presents an overview of the succeeding chapters, with the audit process constituting the focal point of the central chapters.

### Auditing Defined

Broadly speaking, auditing may be defined as an objective systematic review process that involves selecting and evaluating evidence for the purpose of either

A. Ascertaining the reliability of reported financial information in terms of its
  1. Correspondence with the underlying economic events being accounted for and reported, and
  2. Conformity with generally accepted principles for recording and reporting such events, or
B. Appraising activities from the standpoint of
  1. The adequacy and effectiveness of controls established over the activities,
  2. The efficiency with which the activities are carried out, and
  3. The effectiveness of the activities in accomplishing stated objectives.

Auditing review activities are performed by auditors who are members of one of the following classes:

A. Independent auditors, who are not employed by the organization being audited. These may be
  1. Public accountants who are independent contractors and are primarily engaged to attest to the reliability of financial information reported to investors, creditors, and other third parties.
  2. Legislative government auditors who report to a legislative body on their audits of the various operating units within the government relative to the aspects of auditing listed above: reliability of financial information, adequacy and effectiveness of controls, efficiency of operations, and effectiveness of activities in accomplishing objectives.
B. Internal auditors, who are employees of the organization being audited but who are independent of the activities that they audit. Most medium and large corporations; not-for-profit organizations such as hospitals, colleges, and universities; and government agencies and departments have internal auditors. These auditors essentially assist management in controlling operations by ascertaining the reliability of internally reported operating and financial information and appraising the adequacy and effectiveness of operating controls and the efficiency with which operations are conducted.

## The Vital Role of Communication

Because auditors are reviewers rather than action takers, they are unlike other professionals, who typically act directly on the basis of their own analysis and findings. Auditors' findings, instead, become a basis for actions to be taken by others, and auditing can usefully fulfill its function only to the extent that the results of the audit are effectively communicated. Thus, although communication is not essentially a part of auditing itself, even the best of audits may be of little or no ultimate value without effective communication of results through the auditor's report, and auditors must remain constantly aware of the vital role of communication.

## Cost/Benefit Considerations and Judgment

Auditing services would not be commissioned if the benefits did not exceed the costs, but it is difficult to place a monetary value on the variety of benefits that auditing produces. Even the direct benefits realized by third-party users of audited financial statements are difficult to value, and there are also the indirect benefits to the economy as a whole plus the benefits associated with the deterrent effect of audits. An employee tempted to defraud an employer might well reconsider if aware that the employer's records are to be audited. A similar deterrent would exist for unscrupulous management who might otherwise consider deliberately deceiving creditors or investors by preparing false or misleading financial statements. Furthermore, audit effectiveness extends beyond examined financial statements to such management representations as unaudited quarterly reports and announcements about future expectations when it is known that these unaudited figures will ultimately be evaluated against audited figures for the period.

In contrast to the indefiniteness of the benefit portion of the cost/benefit relationship, the auditor's fee as the major cost element is readily apparent, although the time that a client's employees devote to responding to auditor requests and inquiries involves hidden costs. Auditors can, however, minimize the resources expended in auditing. The review activities of auditing are normally accomplished through sampling rather than complete inspection, and one obvious way to minimize cost is to use samples that are as small as possible and yet are of sufficient size to produce the desired reliability for the auditor's findings. Therein lies one of the crucial aspects of auditing—the judgment process involved in planning audit procedures so as to obtain evidence sufficient to support the auditor's conclusions while minimizing the costs incurred in arriving at those conclusions. The vital role of judgment in these activities represents one of the principal distinguishing characteristics of any activity that is truly professional.

### Independent Auditors' Reports

An independent auditor's opinion that attests to the fairness of a client's financial statements (thereby accrediting them) is based on an examination of the statements and is presented in the form of a written report. If an auditor has no significant reservations about financial statements after they have been audited, an unqualified opinion is appropriate. An unqualified opinion is expressed in the standard short-form report that consists of two paragraphs: one describing in general terms the scope of the examination that was made and the second giving the auditor's opinion based on that examination. In most cases those two all-important paragraphs accompanying the client's financial statements will constitute the entire report, particularly when the report is primarily for the benefit of third parties, such as stockholders or creditors.

In most instances the wording of the report will follow quite closely the following sample report, referred to as the *standard short-form report,* which is in the form recommended by the Auditing Standards Board of the American Institute of Certified Public Accountants.

Independent Auditor's Report

To the Board of Directors (or To the Stockholders), ABC Company:

We have examined the balance sheet of ABC Company as of December 31, 19X1, and the related statements of operations, retained earnings, and changes in financial position[1] for the year then ended. Our examination was made in accordance with generally accepted auditing standards, and accordingly included such tests of the accounting records and such other auditing procedures as we considered necessary in the circumstances.

In our opinion, the financial statements referred to above present fairly the financial position of ABC Company at December 31, 19X1, and the results of its operations and the changes in its financial position for the year then ended, in conformity with generally accepted accounting principles applied on a basis consistent with that of the preceding year.

Martin, Noll, and Otis
Certified Public Accountants

January 28, 19X2

Although the wording of the report has been carefully developed and studied by the American Institute of Certified Public Accountants, there is no formal requirement that the public accounting profession render reports that are identical in form. For example, one major public ac-

---

[1]Statement titles should be changed, if necessary, to conform to the titles that the client has selected for the statements.

counting firm uses a version that reverses the order of the content of the two paragraphs and combines them into a single paragraph.

*Significance of the Report.* The independent auditor's report is often referred to as the auditor's *opinion,* but a carry-over from previous years is the less preferable term *certificate* as still used in Securities and Exchange Commission regulations. The auditor's report is the principal outward evidence of the major activity of the public accounting profession, and it is heavily relied upon for financial decisions. It is the primary objective of the typical independent audit. *The independent auditor should never lose sight of the fact that the ultimate objective of all auditing procedures is to provide a sufficient basis for the auditor's opinion concerning a set of financial statements.*

The auditor's report is thus the logical place at which to begin the study of independent audits of financial statements, even though in practice the preparation of the report is the last step in an engagement. Each point in the report is carefully considered in the following pages. Through this discussion the reader should strive to obtain a full understanding of the report and to determine exactly what the report says and does not say. Such an understanding, it should be noted, is also important for the person who reads the report and intends to rely on the auditor's opinion.

*Addressing the Report.* The report is normally addressed to the person or group responsible for engaging the auditor. In the case of corporations whose shares of stock are publicly traded, selection and engagement of the auditor is preferably handled by an audit committee of the board of directors. This committee is most effective if composed solely of "outside" directors—that is, those who have no other relationship to the corporation such as officer, employee, or consultant. Audit committees were initially recommended by the SEC in 1939 as a result of problems observed in the McKesson & Robbins fraud perpetrated by the president of that company. In that case the president personally selected the company's auditor and exercised direct control over the scope of the audit. In the report on its investigation of the case the SEC recommended that auditors be nominated by a committee of nonofficer members of the board of directors and that election of the auditors be by vote of the stockholders at the annual meeting of the corporation, but the practices have been extensively followed only in recent years, as is discussed more fully in Chapter 3.

Although the auditor's fee is paid by the company being audited, in all matters and decisions relating to the audit, the auditor must act independently of the client. Only by operating with such independence and by competently performing the necessary work can the auditor look forward to maintaining widespread acceptance of the reports that are prepared. Further discussion of the selection of auditors and the vital matter of independence is deferred to the following chapter.

*Whose Statements Are They?* Because the auditor's report on a client's financial statements is usually given on a separate page rather than on the statements themselves, the report must carefully identify the statements that have been examined. This identification is made in the opening sentence, which gives the name of the business and the names and dates of the statements being reported on.

The question, "Whose statements are they?" also refers to the matter of who is basically responsible for the representations in the statements. Because the statements accompanying the auditor's report are often typed in the auditor's office, many persons reach the conclusion that the auditor is responsible for preparing the statements; however, the client has sole responsibility for maintaining accounting records and preparing financial statements from those records. Professional Standards (AU Sec. 110.2)[2] delineate the respective responsibility of management and auditor for financial statements:

> Management has the responsibility for adopting sound accounting policies, for maintaining an adequate and effective system of accounts, for the safeguarding of assets, and for devising a system of internal control that will, among other things, help assure the production of proper financial statements. The transactions which should be reflected in the accounts and in the financial statements are matters within the direct knowledge and control of management. The auditor's knowledge of such transactions is limited to that acquired through his examination. Accordingly, the fairness of the representations made through financial statements is an implicit and integral part of management's responsibility. The independent auditor may make suggestions as to the form or content of financial statements or he may draft them in whole or in part, based on management's accounts and records. However, his responsibility for the statements he has examined is confined to the expression of his opinion on them. The financial statements remain the representations of management.

[2]This and all subsequent references to "Professional Standards," refer to various official pronouncements that have been codified by Commerce Clearing House and published in its looseleaf reporting service *AICPA Professional Standards.* (Paper bound editions of the service are also available annually as of July 1.) The references show the volume (AU or AC), section, and paragraph number as compiled from the following sources:

AU

    Statements on Auditing Procedure by the AICPA Committee on Auditing Procedure (1939-1972)

    Statements on Auditing Standards by the AICPA Auditing Standards Board (1972 to date, but through 1978 known as Auditing Standards Executive Committee)

AC

    Accounting Research Bulletins by the AICPA Committee on Accounting Procedure (1939-1959)

    Opinions of the AICPA Accounting Principles Board (1962-1973)

    Statements of Financial Accounting Standards by the Financial Accounting Standards Board (1973 to date)

In view of the primary responsibility that management must assume for financial statements, an auditor does not have the prerogative to make changes in those statements. For instance, if management has included in the inventory a substantial amount of obsolete parts valued at their original cost, the auditor has no authority to change the treatment of this item. The auditor's first course of action will normally be to seek to persuade management that its treatment of the item is inappropriate and that a more accurate and realistic treatment would be to recognize the loss that has occurred by reducing the carrying value of the obsolete parts to a realizable figure and making full disclosure by showing the parts with this new valuation as a separate figure on the balance sheet. If management is not willing to follow the auditor's recommendations, the auditor must modify the reported opinion by pointing out that the statements do not present fairly the concern's financial position and results of operations, in that obsolete parts costing X dollars but having a current realizable value of Y dollars are carried at their original cost as a part of the regular inventory. Thus, although management has the final say as to what shall be in the financial statements and how various items are to be displayed, the auditor always has recourse in the report by pointing out matters that might be important to a third party reading the statements. Qualifications, exceptions, and other modifications of the auditor's report are more fully discussed in Chapter 20.

*The Examination.* The report states that the financial statements, which have been appropriately identified as specified above, have been examined by the auditor. The meaning of the phrase, "We have examined the financial statements," involves research to ascertain the reliability of the statements by amassing sufficient competent evidence to support an informed opinion about the statements. In the course of the examination the auditor determines whether accounting records have been maintained under a good system of internal control and whether the various revenues, expenses, assets, and equities shown in the financial statements are properly reported, based on tests of the underlying accounting records and evidence supporting recorded transactions and balances. For example, reported sales should represent actual sales for which the revenue has been earned and realized; the amounts representing uncollected sales should be valid receivables resulting from sales made on or before the balance sheet date; and the receivables should be collectible (or estimated losses should be provided for) and should not have been pledged, discounted, or sold. After all financial statement amounts have been similarly examined and found to be properly reported, the auditor can attest to the fairness of the statements and their conformity with generally accepted accounting principles that have been consistently applied.

*Standards and Procedures.* To inform a reader of the competence of the examination on which an opinion has been based, the report states (if appropriate) that the examination was made in accordance with generally accepted auditing standards and included all procedures that the auditor considered necessary in the circumstances. Complying with generally accepted auditing standards involves compliance with each of ten basic standards that are grouped under three major headings:

General standards (personal attributes of the auditor)
Standards of field work
Standards of reporting.

The ten standards are further elaborated on in the Statements on Auditing Standards issued by the AICPA Auditing Standards Board. Collectively these pronouncements and the underlying standards specify the various aspects of an audit in which an acceptable level of performance must be at all times maintained, such that the resulting audit will be of unquestioned quality. The basic standards are set forth in Professional Standards at AU Sec. 150.02 as follows:

### General Standards

1. The examination is to be performed by a person or persons having adequate technical training and proficiency as an auditor.

2. In all matters relating to the assignment an independence in mental attitude is to be maintained by the auditor or auditors.

3. Due professional care is to be exercised in the performance of the examination and preparation of the report.

### Standards of Field Work

1. The work is to be adequately planned and assistants, if any, are to be properly supervised.

2. There is to be a proper study and evaluation of the existing internal control as a basis for reliance thereon and for the determination of the resultant extent of the tests to which auditing procedures are to be restricted.

3. Sufficient competent evidential matter is to be obtained through inspection, observation, inquiries and confirmations to afford a reasonable basis for an opinion regarding the financial statements under examination.

### Standards of Reporting

1. The report shall state whether the financial statements are presented in accordance with generally accepted principles of accounting.

2. The report shall state whether such principles have been consistently observed in the current period in relation to the preceding period.

*Put disclosures in the report.*

3. Informative disclosures in the financial statements are to be regarded as reasonably adequate unless otherwise stated in the report.

4. The report shall either contain an expression of opinion regarding the financial statements, taken as a whole, or an assertion to the effect that an opinion cannot be expressed. When an overall opinion cannot be expressed, reasons therefor should be stated. In all cases where the auditor's name is associated with financial statements the report should contain a clear-cut indication of the character of the auditor's examination, if any, and the degree of responsibility he is taking.

Although various other pronouncements of the AICPA Auditing Standards Board pertain to the application of certain audit procedures, the pronouncements do not represent the entirety of auditing practices. Most audit procedures, as set forth in textbooks such as this one and as customarily applied in practice, are the result of widespread acceptance of the various procedures that have been developed through the years by practitioners in the field.

In the practice of auditing, judgment is essential in determining what is necessary in order to be in compliance with auditing standards, because meeting the standards involves considering what other competent auditors would conclude is necessary or appropriate given the same facts and circumstances. Thus, the standards involve primarily questions of degree, evaluation, or judgment that should be consistent throughout the profession: Is the auditor's technical training *adequate*? Has *due* professional care been exercised? Has internal control been *properly* evaluated as a basis for determining the *extent* of the tests to be made? Has *sufficient competent* evidential matter been obtained? Are informative disclosures *adequate*?

The standard form of audit report also states that the auditor's examination involves tests of the underlying accounting records (usually applied on a sampling basis) and that the auditor performed all such tests and other auditing procedures that the auditor considered to be necessary in the circumstances. Important in this statement is the assertion that all auditing procedures were performed that the auditor considered to be necessary. By implication the auditor's judgment on these matters was exercised independently, and the auditor's examination was in no way limited by restrictions imposed by the client. Also, all judgmental decisions by the auditor about the scope of the examination were made in conformity with generally accepted auditing standards.

Audit procedures are the methods by which an auditor gains access to evidence supporting the figures reported in the financial statements. Foremost among these procedures is an analysis of the effectiveness of the internal controls that the client has incorporated into the accounting system to safeguard and maintain accountability over assets and to ensure the accuracy of accounting records. The effectiveness of these internal controls has a direct bearing on how much reliance the auditor can place on figures generated by the client's accounting system. Effectiveness of internal control in turn will affect the scope of other aspects of the auditor's examination, primarily in terms of choosing from among alternative procedures used to gather evidence and deciding about the extent of tests of the evidence. Such evidence will include the assets themselves in the case of inventory and plant equipment; acknowledgment from debtors and creditors in the case of receivables and payables; and underlying documents such as customers' purchase orders, shipping orders, bills of lading, and sales invoices—documents that are the source of entries in the accounting records. Key auditing decisions relate to the *sufficiency* and *competence* of the evidence examined as referred to in the third standard of field work.

*The Opinion Paragraph.* The first paragraph of the auditor's report deals primarily with the *scope* of the auditor's examination and is therefore commonly referred to as the *scope paragraph.* The second paragraph, which contains the report of the auditor's findings, is usually referred to as the *opinion paragraph.* The selection and use of the word *opinion* is significant, for the auditor does not certify, guarantee, or give any other such positive indication that the statements are absolutely correct. Any expression stronger than an opinion would be illogical for several reasons. First, the statements themselves involve opinion, as in the case of the provision for depreciation and similar estimated items; consequently it would be illogical to expect the auditor's conclusion concerning the fairness of the statements to be more positive than an expression of opinion. Second, the auditor's findings are not based on a complete examination of all transactions because practical and economic considerations make a complete examination unnecessary. With the typical examination comprised almost entirely of tests involving samples, the auditor's findings obviously cannot reflect certainty. Although the tests will have been carefully selected and the resulting opinion can be expected to be highly reliable, there is always the possibility that discrepancies exist in some of the detailed items not covered by the tests. Consequently, use of the term *opinion,* implying a conclusion based on an informed judgment, is most appropriate.

*Fair Presentation.* Perhaps the single most important aspect of the auditor's opinion is embodied in the words "present fairly." The Auditing Standards Board has stated (AU Sec. 411.03-.04):

> The independent auditor's judgment concerning the "fairness" of the overall presentation of financial statements should be applied within the framework of generally accepted accounting principles. Without that framework the auditor would have no uniform standard for judging the presentation of finan-

cial position, results of operations, and changes in financial position in financial statements.

The auditor's opinion that financial statements present fairly an entity's financial position, results of operations, and changes in financial position in conformity with generally accepted accounting principles should be based on his judgment as to whether (a) the accounting principles selected and applied have general acceptance; (b) the accounting principles are appropriate in the circumstances; (c) the financial statements, including the related notes, are informative of matters that may affect their use, understanding, and interpretation; (d) the information presented in the financial statements is classified and summarized in a reasonable manner, that is, neither too detailed nor too condensed; and (e) the financial statements reflect the underlying events and transactions in a manner that presents the financial position, results of operations, and changes in financial position stated within a range of acceptable limits, that is, limits that are reasonable and practicable to attain in financial statements.

A contrasting view that has not gained general acceptance is that there is an overriding concept of fairness. At one time the report format of one accounting firm emphasized that fairness is a free-standing concept through modification of the report wording to read ". . . present fairly *and* [italics added] in conformity with generally accepted accounting principles . . . ." This notion was presumably subscribed to by the court in *U.S. v. Simon* (425, F. 2d 796; 2d Cir. 1969) involving the audited financial statements of Continental Vending Machine Corporation. In that case the court held that even though there was evidence that the financial statements had been prepared in conformity with generally accepted accounting principles, the crucial question was whether the financial statements presented fairly the financial position and results of operations of the concern, and the audited financial statements were adjudged deficient in that respect. However, the accepted position within the profession, and normally in the courts, is that fairness is meaningful only in the context of generally accepted accounting principles.

A proposed revision of the standard report sought to avoid some of the problems of fairness by eliminating the word *fairly* from the opinion paragraph, but considerable opposition was raised to elimination of the qualifying term, and that and other proposed changes were subsequently dropped.

*Generally Accepted Accounting Principles.* In contrast to the general agreement that has been reached about the composition of *generally accepted auditing standards* (a term that was incorporated in the standard form of audit report in 1941), there has been constant controversy with respect to *generally accepted accounting principles,* a much older term. Most accountants use the term *accounting principles* as the equivalent of *rules of accounting procedure,* and most of the activity of the AICPA's Committee on Accounting Procedure, as well as its successors, the Accounting Principles Board and now the organizationally and financially independent Financial Accounting Standards Board, has been devoted to defining and interpreting such rules rather than to a fundamental statement of generally accepted accounting principles that would be comparable to the statement of generally accepted auditing standards. More general projects have been undertaken, however, notably the FASB's ongoing project to set forth a conceptual framework for accounting and reporting.

In addition to the formal statements of rules and procedures that it issues, the FASB also issues Interpretations and Technical Bulletins, and these too are a part of generally accepted accounting principles. Other official pronouncements that are within the accounting principles domain are AICPA publications, including Industry Audit Guides prepared by the Auditing Standards Board and Industry Accounting Guides and Statements of Position issued by the Accounting Standards Executive Committee, and Statements of the International Accounting Standards Committee. The AICPA publications are, however, undergoing review by the FASB. Pending final decisions by the FASB to accept or modify the positions taken by the AICPA, the AICPA positions have been declared to be official FASB pronouncements with respect to preferability when a firm contemplates a change in accounting principle.

Of primary importance with respect to reporting in conformity with generally accepted accounting principles is the effect of AICPA Rule 203 of the Institute's Rules of Conduct, which states, "A member shall not express an opinion that financial statements are presented in conformity with generally accepted accounting principles if such statements contain any departure from an accounting principle promulgated by the body designated by Council (the governing body of the AICPA) to establish such principles which has a material effect on the statements taken as a whole . . . ." The body presently so designated is, of course, the Financial Accounting Standards Board; and, hence, its Statements of Financial Accounting Standards, the related interpretations, and the official pronouncements of the predecessor Accounting Principles Board of the AICPA that have not been rescinded or modified are all essential parts of "generally accepted accounting principles."

A body of generally accepted accounting principles is especially important in the context of financial reporting and auditing from the standpoint of

- Increasing comparability of financial statements on a company-to-company basis, thus facilitating decision making for investment and credit purposes.
- Strengthening the position of an auditor in opposing a client's preference for an accounting method if the auditor's position has the support of generally accepted accounting principles.

*Consistency.* Despite efforts to "narrow the areas of difference," many alternative accounting methods remain "generally accepted," as, for example, alternative methods of inventory costing or of calculating depreciation. The effect of this situation is to limit the intercompany comparability of financial statements and, to the extent that a company switches from one acceptable method to another, to limit interperiod comparability of that company's financial statements.

The problem of intercompany comparability was attacked by the APB, which stated (Professional Standards AC Sec. 2045.08): "When financial statements are issued purporting to present fairly financial position, changes in financial position, and results of operations in accordance with generally accepted accounting principles, a description of all significant accounting policies of the reporting entity should be included as an integral part of the financial statements." The intent of this requirement is, of course, to put users of financial statements on notice concerning the policies that have been adopted, so that intercompany comparability or the basis for noncomparability of financial statements can be determined.

Interperiod comparability of financial statements of a given company preparing financial statements in accordance with generally accepted accounting principles can be ascertained by reference to the financial statements' notes inasmuch as Professional Standards (AC Sec. 1027.15) require that ". . . changes from period to period in generally accepted accounting principles . . . (be) appropriately disclosed." Generally accepted auditing standards require in the second standard of reporting that, "The report shall state whether such principles have been consistently observed in the current period in relation to the preceding period." When consistency has not been so observed, the opinion paragraph of the auditor's report must be modified by adding a phrase introduced by "except for" and stating the change in accounting principle that has occurred, with reference to the financial statement note that sets forth the change and states the monetary effect of that change on the comparability of the financial statements. A report modified for this or any other reason relating to noncompliance with generally accepted auditing standards or generally accepted accounting principles is referred to as a "qualified opinion." Full discussion of qualifications and other modifications of the auditor's opinion is deferred to Chapter 20.

Despite the possible impact of such qualified opinions some companies have proceeded to change accounting principles on occasion, presumably for the purpose in some instances of increasing or decreasing reported income. The APB sought to constrain such practices by limiting changes to those justifiable on a "preferability" basis, and in Opinion No. 20, "Accounting Changes" (AC Sec. 1051.15-16) stated:

The Board concludes that in the preparation of financial statements there is a presumption that an accounting principle once adopted should not be changed in accounting for events and transactions of a similar type. Consistent use of accounting principles from one accounting period to another enhances the utility of financial statements to users by facilitating analysis and understanding of comparative accounting data.

The presumption that an entity should not change an accounting principle may be overcome only if the enterprise justifies the use of an alternative acceptable accounting principle on the basis that it is preferable.

The auditing profession has not, however, been willing to accept responsibility for a strict interpretation of preferability and has resisted SEC efforts to impose such a responsibility in areas where alternative accounting principles exist. The most common argument offered in opposition to SEC pressure on preferability is that responsibility for developing acceptable standards for ascertaining the preferability of various accounting alternatives should be assumed by the Financial Accounting Standards Board in order to achieve a meaningful or consistent resolution of the issue.

Because the financial statement reporting standards for disclosing changes in the application of generally accepted accounting principles have been so thoroughly spelled out, the Auditing Standards Board concluded that it should no longer be necessary to comment on consistency in the auditor's report. Accordingly the ASB proposed deletion of the second standard of reporting, which requires that the auditor's report state whether accounting principles have been consistently observed, and deletion of the reference to consistency in the standard report. The proposal was withdrawn, however, in response to objection to deleting the reference to consistency in the standard report.

Discussion pertaining to the auditor's standard short-form report is here concluded, but other aspects of this report are examined in Chapter 20. However, to show how the standard report might have been modified by the changes proposed by the Auditing Standards Board in 1980, the standard report form as given in the Board's Proposed Statement on Auditing Standards is presented here:

The accompanying balance sheet of X Company as of [at] December 31, 19XX, and the related statements of income, retained earnings, and changes in financial position for the year then ended are management's representations. An audit is intended to provide reasonable, but not absolute, assurance as to whether financial statements taken as a whole are free of material misstatements. We have audited the financial statements referred to above in accordance with generally accepted auditing standards. Application of those standards requires judgment in determining the nature, timing, and extent of tests and other procedures and in evaluating the results of those procedures.

In our opinion, the financial statements referred to above present the financial position of X Company as of [at] December 31, 19XX and the results of its operations and the changes in its financial position for the year then ended in conformity with generally accepted accounting principles.

Although each of the changes evident in the proposed revision attracted some support, there was sufficient objection to the changes to cause the Board to abandon the proposal.

### Auditors Not in Public Practice

The public accountants who perform the audits described in the preceding discussion of auditors' reports are independent contractors; all other auditors are employees of the organizations that they audit. The organizational status of these auditors as employees should, however, be such as to keep them independent of the activities that they audit, and if that independence is achieved, the credibility of their reports for users within the organization should be comparable to the credibility of the reports of independent auditors for third-party users.

Internal auditors comprise the largest group of employee auditors, and any sizable organization is likely to have one or more internal auditors. Internal auditors have been described as performing ". . . an independent appraisal function . . . within an organization to examine and evaluate its activities as a service to the organization. The objective of internal auditing is to assist members of the organization in the effective discharge of their responsibilities. To this end, internal auditing furnishes them with analyses, appraisals, recommendations, counsel, and information concerning the activities reviewed."[3]

The federal government and many state governments have instituted a form of audit activity that can be described as being somewhere between independent auditing and internal auditing. The auditing groups who carry out such activity, referred to earlier as legislative government auditors, generally report to the legislative arm of the government. They review for that body and its committees 1) the financial compliance of the various government departments and agencies with the budgetary allocations authorized by the legislative body, 2) the efficiency with which department and agency activities are conducted, and 3) the effectiveness of the programs being carried out by those governmental units. The organizational independence of the auditors from the governmental units being audited makes these auditors akin to auditors in public practice, but like internal auditors, they are employees rather than independent contractors, and they are extensively concerned with operating matters as well as financial reporting. Governmental auditing activities are more extensively discussed along with internal auditing in Chapter 4.

---

[3]*Standards for the Professional Practice of Internal Auditing* (Altamonte Springs, Fla.: The Institute of Internal Auditors, Inc., 1978), p. 1.

## *Auditing in Evolution*

The present state of auditing and auditors' reports is the culmination of several centuries of development. Initially audits were performed mostly at the request of business owners who desired assurance that their bookkeeping had been accurately handled and that all cash was properly accounted for. With the development of partnerships, audits also became useful in determining the amount of profits to be distributed to the partners. The Industrial Revolution brought with it large-scale enterprises that needed outside financing to supplement owner-manager capital in order to permit the acquisition of costly machines. At this point the independent audit achieved widespread importance to absentee owners and other third parties who displaced entrepreneurs as the principal beneficiaries of auditing services.

Formal recognition of audits and auditors first occurred with passage of the English Companies Act of 1844. That act of Parliament provided for the registration of joint-stock companies and provided that a certificate of registration be issued only if the shareholders' agreement that formed the company appointed an auditor for the company. Subsequent changes in English Companies law culminated in the Companies Act of 1948, which limited the persons eligible for appointment as auditors to "a member of any body membership of which had been designated by the Board of Trade as qualifying its members to audit the accounts of companies" or to persons "designated by the Board of Trade as qualified to audit the accounts of companies." The principal body so designated was the Institute of Chartered Accountants in England and Wales.

In the United States the first state statute providing for the incorporation of business enterprises was enacted by North Carolina in 1795, but this and the other state corporation statutes that followed were generally silent with respect to auditing requirements. The New York Stock Exchange was the principal motivating force for independent audits, which it encouraged through various listing requirements. But not until 1933 did an audit requirement become mandatory for all listed companies. That action was apparently prompted by the investigations of securities trading and the reporting of financial information triggered by the stock market debacle of 1929. Those investigations culminated in the Securities Act of 1933, which requires that financial statements included in the registration of an offering prospectus be audited by an independent public accountant. The Securities Exchange Act of 1934 requires registration of all companies whose shares are traded on a recognized exchange and requires the registered companies to issue an annual report that must include audited financial statements. (See Chapter 3 for additional information about the audit requirements of the two securities acts.)

Equally interesting changes have occurred in the conduct of audits. Initially auditors concerned themselves primarily with detecting fraud in the accounts and proving the accuracy of clients' records, utilizing internal evidence available within the business being audited. With the subsequent growing demand by third parties for reliable financial information, attention focused more on external evidence to corroborate company figures. Beginning in the 1940s, however, there was a resurgence of interest in internal evidence related to the accounting system and internal control. Without decreasing the importance of external corroborating evidence, auditors began increasingly to recognize the importance of the accounting system in producing accurate and reliable financial statements. As a consequence, auditors are now redirecting more of their attention inward, although at a higher level relating to the functioning of internal control rather than the former preoccupation with bookkeeping accuracy. This emphasis on the accounting system is highlighted by the systems-based approach of this book.

There has also been a resurgence of interest in the detection and prevention of fraud, although on a different basis than in the past. Current interest, stimulated in part by the Foreign Corrupt Practices Act of 1977, is directed toward preventing fraud and deceit—especially by requiring the maintenance of accurate records subject to close internal accounting control. A major purpose of such controls is to ensure that all transactions and events will be accurately and faithfully recorded in the accounting records—a concern prompted by the disclosure in the 1970s that bribes and other illegal or improper payments had been accounted for and reported in ways that concealed the true nature of the activities.

Such efforts at concealment involve deceit, which is the distinguishing characteristic of fraud. Another form of deceit is the intentional misstatement of earnings or financial position for the purpose of concealing operating or financial problems or of attempting to sustain high price/earnings ratios. Concealments or manipulations effected by management are especially difficult for auditors to detect because management can override the controls that it has instituted and can direct employees to take actions that would otherwise be prohibited, or to introduce fraudulent or forged documents designed to present an appearance of authenticity. Some major frauds of this type have caused auditors to reexamine existing audit techniques and to consider ways of detecting such manipulations, as discussed in later chapters.

### Public Sector Auditing

The preceding account of evolutionary developments in auditing considered only the auditing of business organizations. Audits of government-related activities and of voluntary not-for-profit organizations are also of vital importance, and audit activity in the nonbusiness area is expanding at an unprecedented rate, constituting the most rapidly growing segment of auditing.

The current growth of nonbusiness auditing is, of course, a reflection of growth in the volume and scope of activity in the public sector, especially government and not-for-profit educational and health care organizations. Internal and legislative government auditors are obviously affected by such growth, but public accountants also feel results of the growing sphere of government activity and the rising public concern for accountability of public funds. Programs for which audits by independent public accountants are required include revenue-sharing grants to local governments; Medicare, Medicaid, and other aspects of providing health services; and community action programs such as low-rent housing, urban renewal, student aid, Head Start, Comprehensive Employment and Training Act programs, and environmental control programs. The Employee Retirement Income Security Act (ERISA) requires that retirement plans involving one hundred or more participants must file audited annual reports and represents yet another source of increased audit activity.

Interest in audits is also growing with respect to national charitable organizations in order to provide contributors and other interested parties with reliable information about the funds received by the organizations and the way in which those funds have been spent.

### An Overview of Succeeding Chapters

Subsequent chapters consider more fully what auditors do, how they go about doing it, and the responsibilities associated with the performance of independent audits, as enunciated by the profession, the Securities and Exchange Commission, and the courts. Chapter 4 examines the objectives and activities of auditors other than those who are independent public accountants. All other chapters relate primarily to the performance of audits of financial statements by independent public accountants, or in the case of Chapter 22 other services provided by public accountants.

Chapter 2 considers the structure of the public accounting profession and the various ways in which practicing auditors are assisted and regulated by their professional association, the American Institute of Certified Public Accountants. Chapter 3 examines the responsibilities of independent auditors and the influence on those responsibilities exerted by the courts, legislative action, and the Securities and Exchange Commission.

Following Chapter 4 on internal and governmental auditing, the discussion turns to the actual performance of an audit engagement—how the engagement should come about, how the auditor prepares for the examination, the important aspects of reviewing and evaluating the client's system of internal control, and the problems of adapting the scope of the examination to the level of internal control. The role of evidence is especially important. A discussion is included of the various types of evidence available and their reliability and the various techniques for gaining access to the evidence. Chapter 8 discusses preparation of working paper records of the work that has been done. Because most auditing procedures are applied on a sampling basis, Chapter 9 contains an extensive discussion of statistical sampling in audit applications. Chapter 10 relates to another typical audit situation: all but very small companies are likely to make use of an electronic computer in maintaining their accounting records, presenting special problems in auditing those computerized records.

The following section of the book is the "core" that deals with the examination of the various transaction-related accounts that appear in the financial statements: revenues and receivables; purchases and accounts payable; cost of goods sold and inventory; cash receipts, disbursements, and cash balances; depreciation and property, plant, and equipment; payroll expense and liabilities; miscellaneous income, expense, assets, and liabilities; and capital accounts relating to debt and owners' equity.

The discussion then returns in Chapter 20 to consider the auditor's report and the modifications of the report when the scope of the audit or conformity with generally accepted accounting principles necessitate the issuance of a qualified report or a disclaimer of opinion. Special reports, including long-form reports and reports on compilation and review services, are covered in Chapter 21. The final chapter discusses management advisory services, tax services, and other types of services that are frequently provided by public accounting firms.

## Questions/Problems

For multiple-choice questions 1-1 through 1-6, indicate the letter of the single answer that *best* completes the statement or answers the question, and justify the choice that you have made.

**1-1.** An independent auditor's report expressing an unqualified opinion about a client's financial statements shows that

  a.  The company is in sound financial condition.
  b.  The company has a good system of internal control.
  c.  The company is well managed.
  d.  All of the above are true.
  e.  None of the above are true.

**1-2.** When compared with the auditor of fifty years ago, today's auditor places less relative emphasis upon

  a.  Confirmation.

  b.  Examination of documentary support.

  c.  Overall tests of ratios and trends.

  d.  Physical observation.

(Uniform CPA Examination)

**1-3.** Consistent application of GAAP

  a.  Is covered in the opinion paragraph of the auditor's report.

  b.  Would not be satisfied if there was a change in the expected life of a building.

  c.  Is important with respect to the effect of a change in the method of calculating depreciation.

  d.  All of the above are true.

  e.  Only (a) and (c) are true.

**1-4.** Generally accepted auditing standards

  a.  Are referred to in the opinion paragraph of the auditor's report. *NO*

  b.  Indicate what audit procedures are to be followed in any given situation. *NO*

  c.  Did not exist prior to the listing of ten standards by the Auditing Standards Board of the AICPA. *NO*

  d.  Relate primarily to quality of performance in auditing work. *yes*

**1-5.** Which of the following best describes why an investor would want an independent auditor's report on financial statements?

  a.  Any management fraud that exists would be detected by the independent auditor.

  b.  Important differences may exist between the interests of management in preparing the statements and the interests of the investor.

  c.  Any misstatement of the balance of an account would be corrected as a result of the independent auditor's work.

  d.  To determine whether the subject entity has an adequate system of internal control.

**1-6.** The reference to consistency in the standard short-form audit report

  a.  May be followed by an exception.

  b.  If not followed by an exception, indicates that this year's statements are comparable to those for any prior year. *only last year*

  c.  Indicates that the financial statements are comparable to those of other concerns in the same industry. *NO*

  d.  All of the above statements are true. *NO*

**1-7.** Why are users of financial statements likely to insist that the statements be accompanied by the opinion of an independent public accountant?

**1-8.** Distinguish between auditing standards and auditing procedures.

**1-9.** "The only statement of fact in the auditor's report is the statement that an examination was made in accordance with generally accepted auditing standards." Do you agree? Explain.

**1-10.** Why has consistency displaced conservatism as a primary consideration in the preparation of financial statements?

**1-11.** Feiler, the sole owner of a small hardware business, has been told that the business should have financial statements reported on by an independent CPA. Feiler, having some bookkeeping experience, has personally prepared the company's financial statements and does not understand why such statements should be examined by a CPA. Feiler discussed the matter with Farber, a CPA, and asked Farber to explain why an audit is considered important.

Required:

a. Describe the objectives of an independent audit.

b. Identify ten ways in which an independent audit may be beneficial to Feiler.

(Uniform CPA Examination)

**1-12.** The following two statements are representative of attitudes and opinions sometimes encountered by CPAs in their professional practices:

1. Today's audit consists of test checking. This is dangerous because test checking depends upon the auditor's judgment, which may be defective. An audit can be relied upon only if every transaction is verified.

2. An audit by a CPA is essentially negative and contributes to neither the gross national product nor the general well-being of society. The auditor does not create; he merely checks what someone else has done.

Required:

Evaluate each of the above statements and indicate

a. Areas of agreement with the statement, if any.

b. Areas of misconception, incompleteness, or fallacious reasoning included in the statement, if any.

(Uniform CPA Examination)

**1-13.** Present arguments *for* and *against* the proposal that "fairly" be deleted from the standard short-form audit report.

**1-14.** You have received a mail solicitation inviting you to contribute to Program Enlisting Ancillary Contributions to Equitably Nullify Onerous Wars (PEACE NOW). You are in favor of this organization's program and decide that you will make a contribution if you find no negative information in the organization's audited financial statements that you have requested. Suggest various facts or information that might appear in the audited financial statements that might cause you to decide not to contribute to PEACE NOW.

**1-15.** The suggestion has been made that the standard two-paragraph report on the auditor's examination be shortened to read as follows: "In our opinion the accompanying financial statements present fairly the financial position of X Company at December 31, 19  , and the results of operations and changes in financial position for the year then ended." Would you approve of such a change? Explain.

# Chapter 2

# THE AUDITING PROFESSION, ITS CODE OF PROFESSIONAL ETHICS, AND OTHER SELF-REGULATION

Chapter 1 pointed to the importance of generally accepted auditing standards in ensuring the quality of audit performance. The present chapter considers auditing as a professional activity and notes the influence of the American Institute of Certified Public Accountants, the professional association of practicing auditors, on the quality of auditing practice through the Code of Professional Ethics and in other ways, including the issuance of Statements on Auditing Standards by the Auditing Standards Board.

### Hallmarks of a Profession

Many groups proclaim themselves to be professional, but a body of practitioners providing services to the public does not acquire professional standing merely by self proclamation. Rather, recognition as a profession is a matter of public acceptance of those groups that have demonstrated that they merit such recognition. Although there is no single set of characteristics associated with public recognition of a profession, the following attributes tend to be common to groups generally recognized as having achieved professional standing:

1. Provision of a service in a field in which the public is untrained and hence unable to evaluate the quality of the service performed.
2. Evidence of the public interest in the provision of service of acceptable quality through laws restricting admission to practice to properly qualified persons.
3. Provision of a service that is essentially intellectual and that requires mastery of a substantial body of specialized knowledge by means of a formal educational process.
4. Presence of an underlying service motive that transcends the desire for monetary gain.
5. Recognition by practitioners that peer evaluation may be based on factors more important than financial success.
6. Existence of a strong voluntary organization dedicated to the advancement of the profession, with primary attention devoted to improvement of the services that the profession renders.
7. Active support of a code of ethical conduct by which the public may judge the professional stature of those in practice.

### Auditor-CPAs as Professionals

In general, public accountants providing auditing and other public accounting services such as tax assistance and management consultation possess all of the stated professional hallmarks. Recognition of these practitioners as professionals, however, exists primarily among persons who are involved in business and financial activities and who have occasion to rely on public accountants' services. Relatively limited contact with public accountants and their practice is the primary explanation for the fact that the public as a whole is less knowledgeable about the public accounting/auditing profession than about other professions such as medicine and law.

In almost all instances, independent auditors are certified public accountants, although many laws that require audits do not require that the auditor be a CPA. The public interest in public accounting practice is reflected in CPA laws in each of the fifty states and the District of Columbia that recognize competence to provide public accounting services by granting of the CPA certificate to persons who have demonstrated their qualifications.

The first state statute creating the CPA certificate was enacted in New York in 1896 and required passing an examination in accounting and related subjects. Other states enacted similar legislation in subsequent years. In 1916 what was then the American Institute of Accountants (now AICPA) formed a Board of Examiners to prepare examinations to be used to determine the qualification of applicants for Institute membership. This arrangement closely paralleled the practice developed in England by the Institute of Chartered Accountants, where after gaining membership through passing an examination, members were entitled to style themselves as "Chartered Accountants" or "CAs." Because state regulation of the professional designation in the U.S. was already well established, the American Institute offered the use of its membership examination to the states, with the understanding that any person who passed that examination as administered by a state would automatically be waived from being required to take the examination to qualify for membership in the Institute. This offer was gradually accepted by state boards of accountancy, and by the mid 1950s all states required a prospective CPA to pass the Uniform CPA Examination, which is prepared and graded under the direction of the Board of Examiners of the AICPA.

The development of a uniform national examination made it possible for CPAs to serve clients across state lines through reciprocity arrangements between states that enable a person certified in one state to be certified in another without retaking the CPA examination. The twice-yearly (May and November) examination as now constituted is administered over a two-and-a-half-day period totaling nineteen and one-half hours. A passing grade of seventy-five is required for each of the four parts of the examination: Auditing, Accounting Theory, Accounting Practice, and Business Law. However, all states offer "conditional credit" for passing one or two parts of the examination, with varying opportunities to pass the remaining part or parts without retaking the entire examination. In addition, most states require some combination of education and accounting experience to qualify for admission to the CPA examination or for issuance of the CPA certificate, with the typical requirement being a baccalaureate degree and one to three years of public accounting or other comparable work experience.

In 1969 the AICPA Committee on Education and Experience Requirements for CPAs recommended that at least five years of college study be required for the CPA certificate, and that for candidates meeting that standard, no qualifying experience should be required. At the time of this writing, only Colorado, Florida, Hawaii, and Utah have statutes requiring a minimum of a master's degree, but the Colorado requirement has been eliminated as a result of Sunset review. Some states have, however, waived their experience requirement for candidates who, in applying for the CPA certificate, present a master's degree and evidence of having completed certain prescribed accounting courses.

In terms of further regulation of public accounting as a matter of the public interest, all but a handful of states are now classed as "regulatory" states. In most of these states, current entrance into public accounting practice can be gained only by qualifying for the CPA certificate as a license to practice. But in such states noncertified accountants who were in public practice when the regulatory law was passed typically were entitled to licenses to practice public accounting and to use the title "Public Accountant" or "PA" so as not to exclude them from the means of livelihood that they had developed. The effect of such legislation is to create two classes of licensed practitioners, but the PA class gradually expires because no new PAs may be licensed in most cases. Eventually only persons in those states holding the CPA certificate will be licensed to practice.

Public accounting legislation in Canada corresponds generally with that in the United States, with the various provinces issuing the Chartered Accountant certificate that is the equivalent of the CPA certificate in the United States. By contrast the profession is administered quite differently in England, and, even though British accountants were much in evidence in the early days of the profession in America, the English system was not followed here. The government does not grant licenses in England; rather, the accountant gains recognition by achieving membership in one of the professional accounting associations, such as the Institute of Chartered Accountants in England and Wales. Institute membership requirements include passing a Foundation Examination and then Parts 1 and 2 of the Professional Examination, with the latter examinations usually taken near the end of a three- or four-year period of articled clerkship with an Institute member. The shorter articled period is for those who are university graduates.

Although many of the other hallmarks of a profession included in the earlier listing are relatively self-evident in public accounting practice, the matters of a strong voluntary organization dedicated to the advancement of the profession and a code of ethical conduct warrant further discussion.

### The American Institute of Certified Public Accountants

The AICPA has already been referred to in terms of its activities in establishing generally accepted accounting principles and generally accepted auditing standards. These activities date back to 1917 when the then American Institute of Accountants prepared a pamphlet published by the Federal Reserve Board entitled *Uniform Accounting*. The pamphlet was intended to make bankers and others aware of appropriate form and content for comparative financial statements and the nature of audits of such statements. A revised version of the Institute pamphlet was published by the Federal Reserve Board in 1929 with the more informative title *Verification of Financial Statements*.

From these early efforts to make financial statements and accounting more useful through the development of standards known as generally accepted accounting principles, there emerged in succession the Institute's Committee on Accounting Research and its Accounting Research Bulletins, the Accounting Principles Board and its pronouncements of Opinions, and now the separately constituted and independently financed Financial Accounting Standards Board, with the FASB originally having been proposed by the AICPA. All of these represent voluntary efforts by the professional organization to serve the public through improvements in financial reporting and the comparability and disclosures of financial statements.

In addition to these activities designed to improve financial reporting, the Institute sought to provide guidance for strengthening and improving auditing practice. The Institute pamphlets published by the Federal Reserve Board, setting forth current accepted practices in accounting and auditing, were succeeded on the technical auditing side by formation of the Committee on Auditing Procedure. The latter produced a series of fifty-four Statements on Auditing Procedure and developed the Statement of Generally Accepted Auditing Standards, which constitutes the conceptual framework for the quality aspects of examinations of financial statements. The committee's Statements on Auditing Procedure were codified in 1973 and issued as the first of a new series of Statements on Auditing Standards, with thirty-eight of these Statements having been issued to the date this is written. The Committee on Auditing Procedure was reorganized in 1973 and became the Auditing Standards Executive Committee, with a further name change in 1979 to Auditing Standards Board. The pronouncements of these bodies delineate the standards of auditing practice and state how the standards are to be implemented under specified circumstances and conditions.

As a further service to the profession, these accounting and auditing pronouncements are available in convenient reference form through an AICPA contract with Commerce Clearing House to publish the pronouncements in a codified loose-leaf service that is updated as new pronouncements are issued. The loose-leaf services are published under the title *AICPA Professional Standards*, with Volume 1 containing the following currently effective pronouncements in codified form:

Statements on Auditing Standards
Auditing Interpretations issued by the AICPA staff

Statements on Management Advisory Services
Statements on Responsibilities in Tax Practice
Statements on Standards for Accounting and Review Services

Volumes 3 and 4 contain the currently effective accounting pronouncements in codified form:

Accounting Research Bulletins
Opinions and Statements of the Accounting Principles Board
Accounting Interpretations issued by the AICPA
Statements and Interpretations of the Financial Accounting Standards Board
Statements of the International Accounting Standards Committee

The loose-leaf volumes are reprinted in paperbound form each July 1 for students and others who do not need the more expensive currently updated version. Each of the series of pronouncements is, of course, vital to maintaining uniform standards of accounting and auditing practice.

Other authoritative pronouncements of the AICPA that set forth guidelines for accounting and auditing standards in special situations are Statements of Position of the Accounting Standards Executive Committee, Industry Accounting Guides, and Industry Audit Guides. The accounting standards aspects of these pronouncements are being reviewed by the FASB and upon modification or acceptance by the FASB will achieve the same official status as other pronouncements of the FASB. In the meantime the FASB has stated that accounting matters treated in the guides are to be considered "preferable" when a company contemplates a change in accounting principle.

### Code of Professional Ethics

The last in the earlier list of hallmarks of a profession is the development and enforcement of a code of ethical conduct governing members of the profession. Such a code provides guidance to practitioners in various matters likely to arise in the course of conducting their practice, and provides clients and the public with a basis for judging a profession in terms of the behavioral standards that it has set for its members.

The word *ethical* is related to the Greek word meaning custom, and is closely related to the Latin word *moral*, also meaning custom. The idea of moral action incorporates the aspect of right and wrong in the development of custom, and it is in this sense that codes of professional ethics are intended to function. A code provides concepts and guidelines to which the practitioner is expected to adhere in conducting a practice on an ethical basis. The present AICPA code of professional ethics was adopted by vote of the Institute membership in 1973, after a complete rewriting of the code to state the concepts on a positive basis in contrast to the previous code's emphasis on specific inappropriate behavior.

The AICPA code is composed of the following four sections, all of which are incorporated in Volume 2 of *AICPA Professional Standards,* the loose-leaf service published by Commerce Clearing House.

1. Commentary on the ethical principles embodied in five broad concepts of professional ethics applicable to practice as a CPA
2. A statement of the rules of conduct
3. Interpretations of the rules of conduct issued by the AICPA Division of Professional Ethics
4. Rulings on the application of the rules of conduct in specific situations, also issued by the AICPA Division of Professional Ethics

The introductory section with its expository essays on the five major code topics and the related numbered rules of conduct are reproduced with the permission of the AICPA as an appendix at the close of this chapter.

Although the AICPA code constitutes what is considered to be ethical conduct for any CPA in public practice, the code's provisions are enforceable only with respect to AICPA members. Members not in public practice are bound only by Rules 102 and 501 of the Rules of Conduct (see appendix that follows this chapter). Furthermore, Rules 102 and 302 contain exceptions that relate to the performance of tax services. Penalties that may be assessed for violating the Rules of Conduct, after a hearing before the Ethics Division or the Trial Board of the Institute, include admonishment or the more severe actions of suspension or expulsion from membership in the AICPA. Further, of course, any violation that would result in damages to another party is subject to legal remedy through the civil courts.

The Institute code of ethics has also been widely adopted by the various state boards of accountancy and by the state societies of CPAs, the voluntary state organizations that parallel and complement the AICPA. Potential enforcement of the code is greatly strengthened with adoption by state boards of accountancy because they usually hold the power to suspend or revoke a CPA certificate that they have issued. As a consequence, violation of a state board rule can result in withdrawal of an accountant's right to practice as a CPA. Revocation of Institute membership or state board action based on ethical considerations is somewhat rare, the major exception being where such action is taken against members who have been convicted of a crime.

The introductory section of the code that sets forth the objectives and general principles of ethical conduct outlines the major topics and relationships addressed by the code, and presents a series of five essays on the following key aspects of the code (see the appendix to this chapter):

Independence, integrity, and objectivity
Professional competence and the observance of general and technical standards
Responsibilities to clients
Responsibilities to colleagues
Other responsibilities and practices

The specific rules of professional conduct that have been developed to guide the actions of those in professional practice are organized in relation to these same topics.

## The Primacy of Independence in Providing Auditing Services

Independence, addressed in Rule 101, is the first topic covered by the code, with that position suggesting its importance. The concern for independence is a unique aspect of the public accounting profession and is directly related to performance of the accreditation function in attesting to the fairness of financial statements. Since the only product of attestation is the credibility added to financial information by the audit report, it is essential that the auditor be independent and be so perceived by users of audited financial statements. No credibility can be added without an auditor's independence.

Normally a member of a profession is expected to be primarily concerned with a client's interests, with deference to the interests of another party carrying the potential of exposing the practitioner to breach-of-contract action by the client. In providing independent auditing services, however, the CPA must maintain a different position—one which involves being neither advocate nor adversary of the client. The independent attitude that the CPA maintains is expected to be one of unbiased impartiality with respect to the client. Rule 101 of the Rules of Conduct requires the CPA to be independent of the client in appearance, thus proscribing any financial or organizational relationship (such as stockholder, director, officer, or employee) and with financial independence being considered as compromised if there are even any unpaid fees for previously performed services when a new audit engagement begins. The requirement of Rule 102 for integrity and objectivity directly addresses the matter of independence, for any act suggesting that the CPA has been partial to the client's interests or point of view would indicate that the CPA had not acted independently.

Only so long as the public accountant maintains high standards of independence, objectivity, and integrity will audit reports continue to be useful to businesses, financial institutions, and investors. Without the aura of independence, objectivity, and integrity in the performance of auditing services, the auditor's attestation accrediting financial statements can be no more acceptable than representations and statements prepared by management.

There is also a collective aspect of independence with respect to CPAs and the public accounting profession as a whole. A practitioner is not, as a rule, known personally to third parties, such as stockholders who rely on auditors' reports, and such groups accept auditors' opinions principally on faith in CPAs as a group and faith in the public accounting profession. Thus the code of ethics with its exposition of ethical principles and rules of conduct is in part addressed to members of the public who rely on auditors' reports. Also, since public awareness that a single member of the profession has failed to maintain independence, integrity, and objectivity tends to lessen faith in independent audits in general, the profession as a whole has a strong interest in sustaining high standards of ethical conduct on the part of all of its members. Proscribed relationships to clients are especially to be avoided in this regard, for they involve an *appearance* of lack of independence, even though the auditor's report may in no way have been diminished by a lack of integrity and objectivity.

*Problems in Maintaining Independence.*   Extensive consideration is given in this and the preceding chapter to the subject of independence in audit engagements because independence is difficult to maintain. The auditor must remain independent of the business whose statements are being examined, and yet that business will normally have engaged the auditor and will pay the fee. Such a contractual relationship requires a delicate sense of balance with respect to differences that may arise during an audit engagement.

Should the auditor become carried away by a zeal for independence, the client may cooperate to the extent of making the auditor completely independent by severing the audit relationship and replacing the auditor. On the other hand, while there is a natural desire to want to maintain good client relations, moving too far in this direction may result in giving approval to statements that are misleading. Such a misstep can lead to lawsuits, a loss of reputation, and eventually a loss of other clients. Thus, it may readily be seen that the auditor finds independence much more difficult to maintain than does, for example, the internal revenue agent or the bank examiner, for neither of the latter need ever fear losing a client.

That maintaining the proper degree of independence is worth the effort is illustrated by the story of a newcomer to the profession who obtained his first big engagement as a result of losing out on another engagement when he refused to compromise his independence and integrity. The lost engagement resulted when a leading member of the city's financial community, who had an interest in the business the young auditor was examining, insisted that the statements be shown in a certain way. When the auditor refused to approve the statements in the desired form and could not induce the financier to change his mind, there was little choice but to terminate the engagement.

The auditor was certain this disagreement had created a powerful enemy, and he was understandably surprised when the financier contacted him not long afterward and asked him to examine another enterprise in which he had an interest. This time the circumstances were different, and to best protect his interests the financier was seeking an accountant whom he was certain could be relied upon to maintain his independence.

In a sense it appears that the independent auditor's difficulties arise from an attempt to serve two masters. The auditor naturally wants to maintain good relations with the client and at the same time must be certain that any report can be relied upon with complete confidence by third parties who are interested in the client's statements. Needless to say, concern for these third parties must always be foremost. Should this group lose confidence in the auditor's reports, loss of clients is likely to follow, for clients engage an independent auditor primarily to satisfy these third parties.

*Counteracting the Subversive Potential of the Client-Paid Fee.*   The concern for whether auditing services could be effectively provided for third parties when the auditor is selected and remunerated by the client was such that when the Securities Act of 1933 was being debated, Congress considered whether mandatory audits, to be fully satisfactory, would have to be performed by government-employed auditors. The selected alternative of clients contracting with independent professionals has, however, proven to be satisfactory, for there have been few problems related to lack of independence, and those who must secure audit services have benefited from freedom of choice and the incentives of competition. Although in recent years there has been some public and congressional criticism of the public accounting profession, financial statement accreditation by the public accounting profession has overall been favorably received, and auditor independence is not perceived as having presented any significant problems.

Nevertheless, steps have been taken to strengthen auditor independence and various proposals have been set forth for further change in that regard. An important change is that many publicly held companies have assigned responsibility for auditor selection and other significant audit engagement matters to an audit committee of the board of directors. Ideally the audit committee should be entirely composed of outside directors who have no other relationship with the company of which they are directors, for such an arrangement strengthens the auditor's position if there is disagreement with management about accounting or auditing matters. In the event of questionable management actions or management recalcitrance in accepting audit recommendations, the audit committee channel makes available a receptive ear if the auditor concludes that it is necessary to "blow the whistle."

Although there has been pressure on both the SEC and the AICPA to make it mandatory for audits of publicly held companies to be handled through such audit committees of outside directors, and although both bodies strongly favor such an arrangement, neither body has been willing to establish a requirement to that effect. The New York Stock Exchange has acted in that regard, however, and effective June 30, 1978, required all companies listed on that exchange to have an audit committee of independent directors, at least two of whom must be outside directors. The American Stock Exchange has also acted on this matter, but went only so far as to make a policy recommendation that audit committees be composed entirely of independent directors. Amex stated unwillingness to interfere with internal corporate affairs as the reason for limiting their position on audit committees to a policy recommendation.

The SEC has also recommended that audit committees nominate an auditor and that election of the auditor be by vote of the stockholders at the annual meeting of the corporation. Such election, although fairly common, seems to be largely perfunctory in publicly held companies, under the proxy system of stockholder voting.

Another recommendation has been for required rotation of the auditors of publicly held companies. This arrangement could be even more effective if coupled with a tenure provision that would provide for a fixed period of perhaps seven years during which the auditor could not be replaced except for demonstrably adequate cause. Such an arrangement would strengthen the auditor's position vis-à-vis the client and reduce the possibility for "shopping" when, because of a disagreement on an accounting matter, the client would like to find a more tractable auditor. A major objection to mandatory rotation is the start-up costs that would be incurred by a new auditor in gaining the necessary knowledge and understanding of the client's business and accounting and operating procedures. As a compromise alternative to auditor rotation, the SEC Practice Section of AICPA requires periodic rotation of the partner in charge of each SEC client engagement.

The commentary in this section should not be interpreted as an indication of an urgent need for reform. The fact that auditors have acted independently under the present arrangement, despite the potential for client influence, is evident from statistics reported in *The CPA Letter* of the AICPA for October 15, 1979. SEC-regulated companies are required to report on Form 8-K a change of auditors and whether prior to the change there was any disagreement with the auditors over accounting principles or auditing procedures. Analysis of the 8-K reports revealed 202 auditor changes involving disagreements in the years 1974 through 1978. The three most common types of disagreements involved questions of recoverability of the cost of certain assets, timing of expense recognition, and timing of revenue recognition. The 202 disagreement cases indicate that auditors do in fact act independently, and this independence is further supported by the rarity of cases in which auditors have been charged with not acting with independence, objectivity, and integrity. There is no indication in this study about whether the successor auditor took the same position on the disputed subject as the displaced auditor, but companies who now change auditors must report instances in which the successor auditor takes a different position.

### Competence and Observence of Technical Standards

The second sections of both the essays on ethical principles and the Rules of Conduct are directed to the quality of service provided by CPAs, with the intention of reminding practitioners and assuring clients about the importance of competent service and adherence to the technical standards of the profession. As with all questions of ethics the practitioner is responsible for the judgments that are made and thus must decide before accepting an engagement whether within the practitioner's firm there is sufficient knowledge and experience available to complete the engagement with professional competence. If the engagement is accepted, then in performing the requested service, the auditor must fully comply with all applicable auditing and accounting standards as reflected in pronouncements of the Auditing Standards Board, the Financial Accounting Standards Board, and all other authoritative sources. These requirements are specified in the following Rules of Conduct: Rule 201 that pertains to compliance with the general standards of auditing practice; Rule 202 that pertains to the technical standards that must be followed in examining financial statements, including the Statements on Auditing Standards issued by the Auditing Standards Board; and Rule 203 that specifies how an auditor is to proceed when the client's financial statements contain a departure from an accounting principle promulgated by the body designated by AICPA Council to establish such principles—at the present time, the Financial Accounting Standards Board.

Further indication of the concern that auditing services be of the highest quality is evident in Professional Standards at AU Sec. 161. That section states than an independent auditing firm, in order to comply with generally accepted auditing standards and the requirements of Rule 202 of the Rules of Conduct, is expected to establish quality control standards and procedures. Such standards and procedures should provide reasonable assurance of compliance with generally accepted auditing standards—in the conduct of individual audit engagements and in the conduct of a firm's practice as a whole. The elements of quality control are set forth in Statement on Quality Control Standards No. 1, "System of Quality Control for a CPA Firm," issued by the AICPA Quality Control Standards Committee and included in Professional Standards Vol. 2 at QC Sec. 10.

### Responsibilities to Clients

The practitioner's responsibility to clients to exercise due professional care is exceeded only by the practitioner's obligation to the public for independence, integrity, and objectivity. Responsibilities to clients include holding confidential all information not authorized by the client for release. This requirement of Rule 301 is essential in protecting a client's interests and ensuring that the client will not withhold information that might be vital to performing the requested services, merely in order to preserve the confidentiality of the information.

Rule 302 prohibiting contingent fees is primarily concerned with engagements to provide auditing services and is intended to bolster independence. Clearly an auditor might be tempted to compromise independence if payment of the audit fee were to be contingent on some event associated with the audited financial statements, such as the successful sale of a stock issue or obtaining a loan. It is thus important for all parties to be aware that such arrangements are prohibited.

### Responsibilities to Colleagues

Until 1979 two rules in this section addressed unprofessional actions that would constitute encroachment upon the practice of another practitioner. The shelter provided by those prohibitions was presumed to free the practitioner from the distraction of resisting encroachment and thus enable the practitioner to give undivided attention to retaining clients by rendering high quality services and to retaining employees by offering adequate compensation and opportunity for advancement. However, the Federal Trade Commission and the Department of Justice viewed these rules as restricting competition, and consequently Rule 401, prohibiting encroachment through direct solicitation of clients, and Rule 402, restricting offers of employment to an employee of another public accountant, have been withdrawn.

### Other Responsibilities and Practices

The final section of the code covers a variety of miscellaneous matters. Rule 501 on discreditable acts, based on the assumption that the public reputation of the profession is important to all members of the profession, specifically prohibits any act that would discredit the profession.

Committing fraud or a criminal act would be obvious examples of undesirable acts, and conviction for committing such an act has typically resulted in expulsion from the Institute and revocation of the person's CPA certificate.

Rule 502 prohibited all forms of advertising until it was amended by vote of the Institute membership in 1978. The basis for the rule had been that it is unseemly and unproductive for a professional to advertise, and that the public is best served if it seeks professional service on the basis of the reputation of the practitioner rather than on the effectiveness of the practitioner's advertising. The Department of Justice, however, with the urging of the FTC, had successfully challenged advertising restrictions of other professions, on the basis that such restrictions constituted restraint of trade and limitation of free speech. Given these forewarnings, the Institute membership voted to amend the prohibition of advertising to apply only to false, misleading, or deceptive advertising.

By Interpretation 502-4 relating to the advertising rule, the AICPA Ethics Division had proposed a significant relaxation of the Institute's long-standing opposition to any indication by a member of the Institute that the member is an expert or specialist in any specific area of practice such as estate and gift taxes or the design of computerized data processing systems. The proposal would have permitted self-designation as an expert or specialist through advertising or other forms of solicitation in a manner that is not false, misleading, or deceptive, provided that a member was prepared to substantiate the basis for any self-designation by presenting evidence of an appropriate combination of education and experience related to the specialty. The proposed interpretation has, however, since been withdrawn.

Rule 503 prohibits payment or receipt of commissions and is based on the principle that a CPA should be motivated by desire for excellence rather than material reward and should expect to be compensated entirely on the basis of the services rendered. Thus Rule 503 is intended to make clear that the CPA will not benefit financially from referring a client to another practitioner or recommending a particular service or piece of equipment if such referral is deemed to be desirable. Consequently the client can be reasonably assured that any referral or recommendation is in the client's best interests and that the CPA will not have been influenced by any possibility of personal gain.

Rule 504 on incompatible occupations likewise has a bearing on independence. It prohibits auditors from engaging in occupations, such as stockbroker or securities underwriter, that would involve a potential conflict of interest.

Rule 505, the final rule, places restrictions on firm names that might be construed as misleading or not customary. The rule also opens the way for a firm to practice as a professional corporation, a possibility that was prohibited prior to the initial adoption of this rule in 1969. The prohibition was based on the principle that a practitioner should not seek to limit liability for professional acts by practicing in the corporate form. Subsequently the corporate prohibition was removed, recognizing the attractiveness of the corporate form in the tax treatment of retirement benefit provisions and to limit the potential for inordinate losses from legal claims. Certain requirements were, however, imposed by Council of the AICPA, including a requirement that all shareholders and officers must be CPAs engaged in the practice of public accountancy and that all shareholders must be jointly and severally liable for the acts of the corporation unless adequate liability insurance is carried or capitalization is maintained that is deemed sufficient to offer adequate protection to the public. The AICPA Board of Directors recommended and Council approved in 1969 that liability insurance or capitalization in the amount of $50,000 per shareholder/officer and professional employee to a maximum of $2,000,000 would be deemed to offer adequate protection. The maximum amount would appear to be small for a large firm with publicly held clients, but only smaller firms have availed themselves of the corporate alternative. All large firms continue to practice as partnerships—partly because only that form of organization is completely acceptable in all fifty states.

### Other Professional Actions–The Commission on Auditors' Responsibilities

In 1974, recognizing various indications that a comprehensive re-examination of the professional performance of auditing services would be a timely activity, the AICPA Board of Directors created the Commission on Auditors' Responsibilities as an independent study group to "... develop conclusions and recommendations regarding the appropriate responsibilities of independent auditors. It should consider whether a gap may exist between what the public expects or needs and what auditors can and should reasonably expect to accomplish. If such a gap does exist, it needs to be explored to determine how the disparity can be resolved."[1]

Attorney Manuel F. Cohen, former chairman of the Securities and Exchange Commission, was named chairman of the commission, and other members were appointed from recognized positions in the spheres of business, public accounting, and education. The commission's activities were entirely funded by the AICPA. Chairman Cohen, who died unexpectedly shortly before completion of the commission's work, was

---

[1]*Report, Conclusions, Recommendations* (New York: The Commission on Auditors' Responsibilities, 1978), p. xi.

vital in directing the study by the commission and its staff, and the commission became popularly known as the Cohen Commission.

Creation of the commission represented recognition by the public accounting profession of its responsibility to serve the public. Commendable, too, was a desire to ascertain whether the needs of the public were being effectively addressed, so that any desirable changes might be undertaken. To that end, the commission was able to state in its final report that some of its tentative recommendations had already been adopted and others were under study by the AICPA. The commission's recommendations dealt with such matters as the reporting of significant uncertainties in financial presentations; clarification of the auditor's responsibility for the detection of fraud; the need for assurance on financial information and forecasts other than as embodied in annual financial presentations; the effectiveness of the auditor's report as a channel of communication; the education, training, and development of auditors; maintaining the independence of auditors; the process of establishing auditing standards; and self-regulation to maintain the quality of audit practice.

Among actions taken by the AICPA as indication of its responsiveness to the public interest and the provision of high quality service are

- Appointing public members to the AICPA Board of Directors
- Opening all deliberations by its standard-setting bodies to public participation
- Establishing a practice division within the Institute to regulate the two major classes of practice and giving rise to the following sections within the division:
  SEC Practice Section
  Private Companies Practice Section

In drawing up the bylaws for the SEC Practice Section, the Division for CPA Firms provided for a Public Oversight Board (POB) to monitor and evaluate the various activities of the SEC Practice Section. Members appointed to the POB included two former chairmen of the SEC and other highly regarded public servants and business executives. Although the initial members were appointed by the SEC Practice Section Executive Committee, the Board has since been made self-perpetuating with power to appoint and remove its members with the consultation and approval of the AICPA Board of Directors, thus giving the POB the maximum possible independence.

The POB met initially in March, 1978, and in its first year extensively reviewed the scope of management advisory services performed by member firms of the SEC Practice Section, primarily in relation to whether providing various services might tend to impair independence. In its conclusions the POB agreed with the action of the executive committee of the section in proscribing executive recruiting services for clients. But for other customarily performed services the POB felt that limitations should be predicated on a firm's own determination of whether providing a service might impair its independence in rendering an opinion on a client's financial statements. Factors influencing the POB's decision included: that management services are provided by a staff that is separate and distinct from the audit staff; that according to past indication, furnishing management advisory services to audit clients has not resulted in loss of independence; that increased disclosure has been required by the SEC in corporate annual reports pertaining to management consulting services provided by the client's auditor; and that the benefits of quality service provided by an auditing firm that is already fully informed about a client's operations is important to the client.

One of the POB's responsibilities is to monitor the regulatory and sanction activities of the section's peer review and executive committees. In this connection the POB gave close attention to the peer review process being developed within the SEC Practice Section. The Board approved plans that the triennial reviews be conducted by review teams appointed by the peer review committee of the SEC Practice Section, with the reviews to be in accordance with standards promulgated by the peer review committee. The POB also approved the option of engaging another SEC Practice firm to conduct the mandatory peer review but specified that such quality control reviews should be submitted to a quality control review panel that would issue its own report. The Private Companies Practice Section has also made mandatory, for its members, quality control reviews that had previously been voluntary. The specified reviews are similar to the reviews within the SEC Practice Section.

Both sections also specify a minimum amount of continuing professional education for professionals within the member firms. The SEC Practice Section requires mandatory rotation every five years of the partners responsible for the audits of SEC clients and specifies a scheduled amount of liability insurance to be carried by member firms.

To further instill public confidence in the quality of independent audit services, each practice section makes public the names of member firms, the firms' membership applications, and reports on the peer review of member firms' quality controls. A firm may be a member of both sections, and SEC Section quality control peer reviews are accepted as satisfying the Private Companies Practice Section peer review requirements.

### Continuing Professional Education

The large national public accounting firms, recognizing the continued updating and preparation for advancing responsibilities necessary to conduct an effective practice, instituted their own staff training and development programs many years ago, but smaller firms did not have the resources to conduct such programs. To enable smaller firms to realize the benefits of support activities such as professional development courses and seminars, preparation of manuals setting forth standardized procedures, and research and assistance on technical problems, a number of associations of independent firms have been established. Member firms retain their individual identity but combine to obtain the services that would be performed by the national office in larger firms.

The AICPA has also been active in developing an extensive portfolio of continuing professional development courses, seminars, and home study courses, primarily to assist smaller firms, although the materials are available to any member of the Institute. As further indication of AICPA concern for the quality of professional practice, the AICPA has proposed and supports a mandatory continuing professional education requirement of forty hours per year of study or attendance at courses and seminars—a requirement that has been adopted by most state boards of accountancy as a necessary qualification for continued licensing to practice as a CPA.

In addition to the activities cited above, extensive opportunities exist through professional organizations for sharing ideas and fostering new developments by way of committee activities, technical sessions at meetings, and the pages of professional journals. All of these activities contribute substantially to the advancement of the profession and the technical competence of its members.

### Summary

Effectively providing a professional service to the public entails a recognized group of qualified practitioners who are dedicated to providing service of the highest quality. For persons to be recognized as certified public accountants, state licensing boards require stated minimum amounts of education and experience and a passing grade on the national Uniform CPA Examination.

Through voluntary association in the AICPA and other professional organizations, qualified and licensed professionals assist each other in establishing and maintaining high standards of practice, backed by a code of ethics, all with the intended purpose of furthering the interests of the profession in providing the public with highest quality services.

The full scope of the AICPA Code of Professional Ethics is conveyed by the sections on ethical principles and the current rules of conduct, which are reproduced in the Appendix at the end of this chapter. For the more detailed interpretations and rulings that are also part of the code, the reader is referred to Volume 2 of *AICPA Professional Standards*, the loose-leaf service published by Commerce Clearing House.

## Appendix—Ethical Principles and Broad Concepts of Professional Ethics Applicable To Practice as a Certified Public Accountant[2]

### *Introduction*

A man should *be* upright; not be *kept* upright.

Marcus Aurelius

A distinguishing mark of a professional is his acceptance of responsibility to the public. All true professions have therefore deemed it essential to promulgate codes of ethics and to establish means for ensuring their observance.

The reliance of the public, the government and the business community on sound financial reporting and advice on business affairs, and the importance of these matters to the economic and social aspects of life impose particular obligations on certified public accountants.

Ordinarily those who depend upon a certified public accountant find it difficult to assess the quality of his services; they have a right to expect, however, that he is a person of competence and integrity. A man or woman who enters the profession of accountancy is assumed to accept an obligation to uphold its principles, to work for the increase of knowledge in the art and for the improvement of methods, and to abide by the profession's ethical and technical standards.

The ethical Code of the American Institute emphasizes the profession's responsibility to the public, a responsibility that has grown as the number of investors has grown, as the relationship between corporate managers and stockholders has become more impersonal and as government increasingly relies on accounting information.

The Code also stresses the CPA's responsibility to clients and colleagues, since his behavior in these relationships cannot fail to affect the responsibilities of the profession as a whole to the public.

The Institute's Rules of Conduct set forth minimum levels of acceptable conduct and are mandatory and enforceable. However, it is in the best interests of the profession that CPAs strive for conduct beyond that indicated merely by prohibitions. Ethical conduct, in the true sense, is more than merely abiding by the letter of explicit prohibitions. Rather it requires unswerving commitment to honorable behavior, even at the sacrifice of personal advantage.

The conduct toward which CPAs should strive is embodied in five broad concepts stated as affirmative Ethical Principles:

[2]Reproduced from the Code of Professional Ethics by permission of the American Institute of Certified Public Accountants, © 1981 by the American Institute of Certified Public Accountants, Inc.

*Independence, Integrity, and Objectivity.*  A certified public accountant should maintain his integrity and objectivity and, when engaged in the practice of public accounting, be independent of those he serves.

*General and Technical Standards.*  A certified public accountant should observe the profession's general and technical standards and strive continually to improve his competence and the quality of his services.

*Responsibilities to Clients.*  A certified public accountant should be fair and candid with his clients and serve them to the best of his ability, with professional concern for their best interests, consistent with his responsibilities to the public.

*Responsibilities to Colleagues.*  A certified public accountant should conduct himself in a manner which will promote cooperation and good relations among members of the profession.

*Other Responsibilities and Practices.*  A certified public accountant should conduct himself in a manner which will enhance the stature of the profession and its ability to serve the public.

The foregoing Ethical Principles are intended as broad guidelines as distinguished from enforceable Rules of Conduct. Even though they do not provide a basis for disciplinary action, they constitute the philosophical foundation upon which the Rules of Conduct are based.

The following discussion is intended to elaborate on each of the Ethical Principles and provide rationale for their support.

### Independence, Integrity, and Objectivity

*A certified public accountant should maintain his integrity and objectivity and, when engaged in the practice of public accounting, be independent of those he serves.*

The public expects a number of character traits in a certified public accountant but primarily integrity and objectivity and, in the practice of public accounting, independence.

Independence has always been a concept fundamental to the accounting profession, the cornerstone of its philosophical structure. For no matter how competent any CPA may be, his opinion on financial statements will be of little value to those who rely on him—whether they be clients or any of his unseen audience of credit grantors, investors, governmental agencies and the like—unless he maintains his independence.

Independence has traditionally been defined by the profession as the ability to act with integrity and objectivity.

Integrity is an element of character which is fundamental to reliance on the CPA. This quality may be difficult to judge, however, since a particular fault of omission or commission may be the result of honest error or a lack of integrity.

Objectivity refers to a CPA's ability to maintain an impartial attitude on all matters which come under his review. Since this attitude involves an individual's mental processes, the evaluation of objectivity must be based largely on actions and relationships viewed in the context of ascertainable circumstances.

While recognizing that the qualities of integrity and objectivity are not precisely measurable, the profession nevertheless constantly holds them up to members as an imperative. This is done essentially by education and by the Rules of Conduct which the profession adopts and enforces.

CPAs cannot practice their calling and participate in the world's affairs without being exposed to situations that involve the possibility of pressures upon their integrity and objectivity. To define and proscribe all such situations would be impracticable. To ignore the problem for that reason, however, and to set no limits at all would be irresponsible.

It follows that the concept of independence should not be interpreted so loosely as to permit relationships likely to impair the CPA's integrity or the impartiality of his judgment, nor so strictly as to inhibit the rendering of useful services when the likelihood of such impairment is relatively remote.

While it may be difficult for a CPA always to appear completely independent even in normal relationships with clients, pressures upon his integrity or objectivity are offset by powerful countervailing forces and restraints. These include the possibility of legal liability, professional discipline ranging up to revocation of the right to practice as a CPA, loss of reputation and, by no means least, the inculcated resistance of a disciplined professional to any infringement upon his basic integrity and objectivity. Accordingly, in deciding which types of relationships should be specifically prohibited, both the magnitude of the threat posed by a relationship and the force of countervailing pressures have to be weighed.

In establishing rules relating to independence, the profession uses the criterion of whether reasonable men, having knowledge of all the facts and taking into consideration normal strength of character and normal behavior under the circumstances, would conclude that a specified relationship between a CPA and a client poses an unacceptable threat to the CPA's integrity or objectivity.

When a CPA expresses an opinion on financial statements, not only the fact but also the appearance of integrity and objectivity is of particular importance. For this reason, the profession has adopted rules to prohibit the expression of such an opinion when relationships exist which might pose such a threat to integrity and objectivity as to exceed the strength of countervailing forces and restraints. These relationships fall into two general categories: (1) certain financial relationships with clients and (2) relationships in which a CPA is virtually part of management or an employee under management's control.

Although the appearance of independence is not required in the case of management advisory services and tax practice, a CPA is encouraged to avoid the proscribed relationships with clients regardless of the type of services being rendered. In any event, the CPA, in all types of engagements, should refuse to subordinate his professional judgment to others and should express his conclusions honestly and objectively.

The financial relationships proscribed when an opinion is expressed on financial statements make no reference to fees paid to a CPA by a client. Remuneration to providers of services is necessary for the continued provision of those services. Indeed, a principal reason for the development and persistence in the professions of the client-practitioner relationship and of remuneration by fee (as contrasted with an employer-employee relationship and remuneration by salary) is that these arrangements are seen as a safeguard of independence.

The preceding reference to an employer-employee relationship is pertinent to a question sometimes raised as to whether a CPA's objectivity in expressing an opinion on financial statements will be impaired by his being involved with his client in the decision-making process.

CPAs continually provide advice to their clients, and they expect that this advice will usually be followed. Decisions based on such advice may have a significant effect on a client's financial condition or operating results. This is the case not only in tax engagements and management advisory services but in the audit function as well.

If a CPA disagrees with a client on a significant matter during the course of an audit, the client has three choices—he can modify the financial statements (which is usually the case), he can accept a qualified report, or he can discharge the CPA. While the ultimate decision and the resulting financial statements clearly are those of the client, the CPA has obviously been a significant factor in the decision-making process. Indeed, no responsible user of financial statements would want it otherwise.

It must be noted that when a CPA expresses an opinion on financial statements, the judgments involved pertain to whether the results of operating decisions of the client are fairly presented in the statements and not on the underlying wisdom of such decisions. It is highly unlikely therefore that being a factor in the client's decision-making process would impair the CPA's objectivity in judging the fairness of presentation.

The more important question is whether a CPA would deliberately compromise his integrity by expressing an unqualified opinion on financial statements which were prepared in such a way as to cover up a poor business decision by the client and on which the CPA has rendered advice. The basic character traits of the CPA as well as the risks arising from such a compromise of integrity, including liability to third parties, disciplinary action, and loss of right to practice, should preclude such action.

Providing advice or recommendations which may or may not involve skills logically related to a client's information and control system, and which may affect the client's decision making, does not in itself indicate lack of independence. However, the CPA must be alert to the possibility that undue identification with the management of the client or involvement with a client's affairs to such a degree as to place him virtually in the position of being an employee, may impair the appearance of independence.

To sum up, CPAs cannot avoid external pressures on their integrity and objectivity in the course of their professional work, but they are expected to resist these pressures. They must, in fact, retain their integrity and objectivity in all phases of their practice and, when expressing opinions on financial statements, avoid involvement in situations that would impair the credibility of their independence in the minds of reasonable men familiar with the facts.

### General and Technical Standards

*A certified public accountant should observe the profession's general and technical standards and strive continually to improve his competence and the quality of his services.*

Since accounting information is of great importance to all segments of the public, all CPAs, whether in public practice, government service, private employment or academic pursuits, should perform their work at a high level of professionalism.

A CPA should maintain and seek always to improve his competence in all areas of accountancy in which he engages. Satisfaction of the requirements for the CPA certificate is evidence of basic competence at the time the certificate is granted, but it does not justify an assumption that this competence is maintained without continuing effort. Further, it does not necessarily justify undertaking complex engagements without additional study and experience.

A CPA should not render professional services without being aware of, and complying with, the applicable general or technical standards as interpreted by bodies designated by Council. Moreover, since published general and technical standards can never cover the whole field of accountancy, he must keep broadly informed.

Observance of the rule on general and technical standards calls for a determination by a CPA with respect to each engagement undertaken that there is a reasonable expectation it can be completed with the exercise of due professional care, with adequate planning and supervision and with the gathering of sufficient relevant data to afford a reasonable basis for conclusions and recommendations. If a CPA is unable to bring such professional competence to the engagement he should suggest, in fairness to his client and the public, the engagement of someone competent to perform the needed service, either independently or as an associate.

The standards referred to in the rules are elaborated and refined to meet changing conditions, and it is each CPA's responsibility to keep himself up to date in this respect.

### Responsibilities to Clients

*A certified public accountant should be fair and candid with his clients and serve them to the best of his ability, with professional concern for their best interests, consistent with his responsibilities to the public.*

As a professional person, the CPA should serve his clients with competence and with professional concern for their best interests. He must not permit his regard for a client's interest, however, to override his obligation to the public to maintain his independence, integrity, and objectivity. The discharge of this dual responsibility to both clients and the public requires a high degree of ethical perception and conduct.

It is fundamental that the CPA hold in strict confidence all information concerning a client's affairs which he acquires in the course of his engagement. This does not mean, however, that he should acquiesce in a client's unwillingness to make disclosures in financial reports which are necessary to fair presentation.

Exploitation of relations with a client for personal advantage is improper. For example, acceptance of a commission from any vendor for recommending his product or service to a client is prohibited.

A CPA should be frank and straightforward with clients. While tact and diplomacy are desirable, a client should never be left in doubt about the CPA's position on any issue of significance. No truly professional man will subordinate his own judgment or conceal or modify his honest opinion merely to please. This admonition applies to all services including those related to management and tax problems.

When accepting an engagement, a CPA should bear in mind that he may find it necessary to resign if conflict arises on an important question of principle. In cases of irreconcilable difference, he will have to judge whether the importance of the matter requires such an action. In weighing this question, he can feel assured that the practitioner who is independent, fair, and candid is the better respected for these qualities and will not lack opportunities for constructive service.

## Responsibilities to Colleagues

*A certified public accountant should conduct himself in a manner which will promote cooperation and good relations among members of the profession.*

The support of a profession by its members and their cooperation with one another are essential elements of professional character. The public confidence and respect which a CPA enjoys is largely the result of the cumulative accomplishments of all CPAs, past and present. It is, therefore, in the CPA's own interest, as well as that of the general public, to support the collective efforts of colleagues through professional societies and organizations and to deal with fellow practitioners in a manner which will not detract from their reputation and well-being.

Although the reluctance of a professional to give testimony that may be damaging to a colleague is understandable, the obligation of professional courtesy and fraternal consideration can never excuse lack of complete candor if the CPA is testifying as an expert witness in a judicial proceeding or properly constituted inquiry.

A CPA has the obligation to assist his fellows in complying with the Code of Professional Ethics and should also assist appropriate disciplinary authorities in enforcing the Code. To condone serious fault can be as bad as to commit it. It may be even worse, in fact, since some errors may result from ignorance rather than intent and, if let pass without action, will probably be repeated. In situations of this kind, the welfare of the public should be the guide to a member's action.

While the Code proscribes certain specific actions in the area of relationships with colleagues, it should be understood that these proscriptions do not define the limits of desirable intraprofessional conduct. Rather, such conduct encompasses the professional consideration and courtesies which each CPA would like to have fellow practitioners extend to him.

It is natural that a CPA will seek to develop his practice. However, in doing so he should not seek to displace another accountant in a client relationship by any means which will lessen the effectiveness of his technical performance or lessen his concern for the rights of third parties to reliable information. Further, he should not act in any way that reflects negatively on fellow practitioners.

A CPA may provide service to those who request it, even though they may be served by another practitioner in another area of service, or he may succeed another practitioner at a client's request. In such circumstances it is always desirable and required in some situations before accepting an engagement that the CPA who has been approached should advise the accountant already serving the client. Such action is indicated not only by considerations of professional courtesy but by good business judgment.

A client may sometimes request services requiring highly specialized knowledge. If the CPA lacks the expertise necessary to render such services, he should call upon a fellow practitioner for assistance or refer the entire engagement to another. Such assistance or referral brings to bear on the client's needs both the referring practitioner's knowledge of the client's affairs and the technical expertise of the specialist brought into the engagement. If both serve the client best in their own area of ability, all parties are well served as is the public.

### Other Responsibilities and Practices

*A certified public accountant should conduct himself in a manner which will enhance the stature of the profession and its ability to serve the public.*

In light of the importance of their function, CPAs and their firms should have a keen consciousness of the public interest and the needs of society. Thus, they should support efforts to achieve equality of opportunity for all, regardless of race, religious background, or sex, and should contribute to this goal by their own service relationships and employment practices.

The CPA is a beneficiary of the organization and character of his profession. Since he is seen as a representative of the profession by those who come in contact with him, he should behave honorably both in his personal and professional life and avoid any conduct that might erode public respect and confidence.

Solicitation to obtain clients through false, misleading, and deceptive statements or acts is prohibited under the Rules of Conduct because it will lessen the professional effectiveness and the independence toward clients which is essential to the best interests of the public.

Advertising which is false, misleading, and deceptive is also prohibited because such representations will mislead some of the public and thereby reduce or destroy the profession's usefulness to society. A CPA should seek to establish a reputation for competence and character through actions rather than words. There are many ways this can be done such as by making himself known through public service, by civic and political activities, and by joining associations and clubs. It is desirable for him to share his knowledge with interested groups by accepting requests to make speeches and write articles. Whatever publicity occurs as a natural by-product of such activities is entirely proper.

In this work, the CPA should be motivated more by desire for excellence in performance than for material reward. This does not mean that he need be indifferent about compensation. Indeed, a professional man who cannot maintain a respectable standard of living is unlikely to inspire confidence or to enjoy sufficient peace of mind to do his best work.

In determining fees, a CPA may assess the degree of responsibility assumed by undertaking an engagement as well as the time, manpower, and skills required to perform the service in conformity with the standards of the profession. He may also take into account the value of the service to the client, the customary charges of professional colleagues and other considerations. No single factor is necessarily controlling.

Clients have a right to know in advance what rates will be charged and approximately how much an engagement will cost. However, when professional judgments are involved, it is usually not possible to set a fair charge until an engagement has been completed. For this reason CPAs should state their fees for proposed engagements in the form of estimates which may be subject to change as the work progresses.

Other practices prohibited by the Rules of Conduct include using any firm designation or description which might be misleading, or practicing as a professional corporation or association which fails to comply with provisions established by Council to protect the public interest.

A member, while practicing public accounting, may not engage in a business or occupation which is incompatible therewith. While certain occupations are clearly incompatible with the practice of public accounting, the profession has never attempted to list them, for in most cases the individual circumstances indicate whether there is a problem. For example, there would be a problem of conflict of interest if a practicing CPA were to serve on a tax assessment board since he would be open to accusations of favoring his clients whether this was done or not. Moreover, they might, under some circumstances, create a conflict of interest in the CPA's independent relationship with his clients.

Paying a commission to outsiders is prohibited in order to eliminate the temptation to compensate anyone for referring a client. Receipt of a commission is proscribed since practitioners should look to the client, and not to others, for compensation for services rendered. The practice of paying a fee to a referring CPA irrespective of any service performed or responsibility assumed by him is proscribed because there is no justification for a CPA to share in a fee for accounting services where his sole contribution was to make a referral.

Over the years the vast majority of CPAs have endeavored to earn and maintain a reputation for competence, integrity, and objectivity. The success of these efforts has been largely responsible for the wide public acceptance of accounting as an honorable profession. This acceptance is a valuable asset which should never be taken for granted. Every CPA should constantly strive to see that it continues to be deserved.

### Rules of Conduct

*Rule 101—Independence.*   A member or a firm of which he is a partner or shareholder shall not express an opinion on financial statements of an enterprise unless he and his firm are independent with respect to such enterprise. Independence will be considered to be impaired if, for example:

A. During the period of his professional engagement, or at the time of expressing his opinion, he or his firm
   1. (a) Had or was committed to acquire any direct or material indirect financial interest in the enterprise; or
      (b) Was a trustee of any trust or executor or administrator of any estate if such trust or estate had or was committed to acquire any direct or material indirect financial interest in the enterprise; or
   2. Had any joint closely held business investment with the enterprise or any officer, director, or principal stockholder thereof which was material in relation to his or his firm's net worth; or
   3. Had any loan to or from the enterprise or any officer, director, or principal stockholder thereof. This latter proscription does not apply to the following loans from a financial institution when made under normal lending procedures, terms and requirements:
      (a) Loans obtained by a member or his firm which are not material in relation to the net worth of such borrower.
      (b) Home mortgages.
      (c) Other secured loans, except loans guaranteed by a member's firm which are otherwise unsecured.
B. During the period covered by the financial statements, during the period of the professional engagement, or at the time of expressing an opinion, he or his firm
   1. Was connected with the enterprise as a promoter, underwriter or voting trustee, a director or officer or in any capacity equivalent to that of a member of management or of an employee; or
   2. Was a trustee for any pension or profit-sharing trust of the enterprise.

The above examples are not intended to be all-inclusive.

*Rule 102—Integrity and Objectivity.* A member shall not knowingly misrepresent facts, and when engaged in the practice of public accounting, including the rendering of tax and management advisory services, shall not subordinate his judgment to others. In tax practice, a member may resolve doubt in favor of his client as long as there is reasonable support for his position.

*Rule 201—General Standards.* A member shall comply with the following general standards as interpreted by bodies designated by Council, and must justify any departures therefrom.

A. Professional competence. A member shall undertake only those engagements which he or his firm can reasonably expect to complete with professional competence.
B. Due professional care. A member shall exercise due professional care in the performance of an engagement.

C. Planning and supervision. A member shall adequately plan and supervise an engagement.
D. Sufficient relevant data. A member shall obtain sufficient relevant data to afford a reasonable basis for conclusions or recommendations in relation to an engagement.
E. Forecasts. A member shall not permit his name to be used in conjunction with any forecast of future transactions in a manner which may lead to the belief that the member vouches for the achievability of the forecast.

*Rule 202—Auditing Standards.* A member shall not permit his name to be associated with financial statements in such a manner as to imply that he is acting as an independent public accountant unless he has complied with the applicable generally accepted auditing standards promulgated by the Institute. Statements on Auditing Standards issued by the Institute's Auditing Standards Board are, for purposes of this rule, considered to be interpretations of the generally accepted auditing standards, and departures from such statements must be justified by those who do not follow them.

*Rule 203—Accounting Principles.* A member shall not express an opinion that financial statements are presented in conformity with generally accepted accounting principles if such statements contain any departure from an accounting principle promulgated by the body designated by Council to establish such principles which has a material effect on the statements taken as a whole, unless the member can demonstrate that due to unusual circumstances the financial statements would otherwise have been misleading. In such cases his report must describe the departure, the approximate effects thereof, if practicable, and the reasons why compliance with the principle would result in a misleading statement.

*Rule 204—Technical Standards.* A member shall comply with other technical standards promulgated by bodies designated by Council to establish such standards, and departures therefrom must be justified by those who do not follow them.

*Rule 301—Confidential Client Information.* A member shall not disclose any confidential information obtained in the course of a professional engagement except with the consent of the client.

The rule shall not be construed (a) to relieve a member of his obligation under Rules 202 and 203, (b) to affect in any way his compliance with a validly issued subpoena or summons enforceable by order of a court, (c) to prohibit review of a member's professional practices as a part of voluntary quality review under Institute authorization, or (d) to preclude a member from responding to any inquiry made by the ethics division or Trial Board of the Institute, by a duly constituted investigative or disciplinary body of a state CPA society, or under state statutes.

Members of the ethics division and Trial Board of the Institute and professional practice reviewers under Institute authorization shall not disclose any confidential client information which comes to their attention from members in disciplinary proceedings or otherwise in carrying out their official responsibilities. However, this prohibition shall not restrict the exchange of information with an aforementioned duly constituted investigative or disciplinary body.

*Rule 302—Contingent Fees.*　Professional services shall not be offered or rendered under an arrangement whereby no fee will be charged unless a specified finding or result is attained, or where the fee is otherwise contingent upon the findings or results of such services. However, a member's fees may vary depending, for example, on the complexity of the service rendered.

Fees are not regarded as being contingent if fixed by courts or other public authorities or, in tax matters, if determined based on the results of judicial proceedings or the findings of governmental agencies.

*Rule 501—Acts Discreditable.*　A member shall not commit an act discreditable to the profession.

*Rule 502—Advertising and Other Forms of Solicitation.*　A member shall not seek to obtain clients by advertising or other forms of solicitation in a manner that is false, misleading, or deceptive.

*Rule 503—Commission.*　A member shall not pay a commission to obtain a client, nor shall he accept a commission for a referral to a client of products or services of others. This rule shall not prohibit payments for the purchase of an accounting practice or retirement payments to individuals formerly engaged in the practice of public accounting or payments to their heirs or estates.

*Rule 504—Incompatible Occupations.*　A member who is engaged in the practice of public accounting shall not concurrently engage in any business or occupation which would create a conflict of interest in rendering professional services.

*Rule 505—Form of Practice and Name.*　A member may practice public accounting, whether as an owner or employee, only in the form of a proprietorship, a partnership, or a professional corporation whose characteristics conform to resolutions of Council.

A member shall not practice under a firm name which includes any fictitious name, indicates specialization, or is misleading as to the type of organization (proprietorship, partnership, or corporation). However, names of one or more past partners or shareholders may be included in the firm name of a successor partnership or corporation. Also, a partner surviving the death or withdrawal of all other partners may continue to practice under the partnership name for up to two years after becoming a sole practitioner.

A firm may not designate itself as "Members of the American Institute of Certified Public Accountants" unless all of its partners or shareholders are members of the Institute.


## Questions/Problems

For multiple-choice questions 2-1 through 2-5, indicate the letter of the single answer that *best* completes the statement or answers the question, and justify the choice that you have made.

**2-1.**   Smith, CPA, issued an "except for" opinion on the financial statements of Wald Company for the year ended December 31, 19X3. Wald has engaged another firm of CPAs to make a second audit. The local bank has knowledge of Smith's audit and has asked Smith to explain why the financial statements and his opinion have not been made available.

   a.   Smith cannot provide the bank with information about Wald under any circumstances.

   b.   If Wald consents, Smith may provide the bank with information concerning Wald.

   c.   If the other firm of CPAs consents, Smith may provide the bank with information concerning Wald.

   d.   The only way the bank can obtain information concerning Smith's audit is to obtain it by subpoena.

   (Uniform CPA Examination)

**2-2.**   Below are the names of four CPA firms and pertinent facts relating to each firm. Unless otherwise indicated, the individuals named are CPAs and partners, and there are no other partners. Which firm name and related facts indicates a violation of the AICPA Code of Professional Ethics?

   a.   Arthur, Barry, and Clark, CPAs (Clark died about five years ago; Arthur and Barry are continuing the firm).

   b.   Dave and Edwards, CPAs (The name of Fredricks, CPA, a third active partner, is omitted from the firm name).

   c.   Jones & Co., CPAs, P.C. (The firm is a professional corporation and has ten other stockholders who are all CPAs).

   d.   George and Howard, CPAs (Howard died three years ago; George is continuing the firm as a sole proprietorship).

   (Uniform CPA Examination)

**2-3.** A CPA's retention of client records as a means of enforcing payment of an overdue audit fee is an action that is

    a. Considered acceptable by the AICPA Code of Professional Ethics.

    b. Ill advised since it would impair the CPA's independence with respect to the client.

    c. Considered discreditable to the profession.

    d. A violation of generally accepted auditing standards.

(Uniform CPA Examination)

**2-4.** The Code of Professional Ethics discussed in this chapter and presented as an appendix to the chapter

    a. Is enforceable against any CPA in public practice.

    b. Does not bind, in Rule 101 on independence, a CPA who is the controller of a company.

    c. Prohibits a CPA who is providing tax services to a client from accepting an engagement on a contingent fee basis.

    d. Would prevent a firm from accepting an audit engagement from a company because a partner of the firm was controller of the company two years ago.

**2-5.** Rule 302 relating to contingent fees

    a. Further assures that an auditor will act independently.

    b. Has different implications for the CPA providing tax services than for the CPA providing audit services.

    c. Does not prohibit the auditor from determining an audit fee contingent upon the amount of time that is required for the audit.

    d. All of the above are true.

**2-6.** The text lists a number of attributes that tend to be common to groups recognized as having achieved professional standing. Select which of these attributes, and give your justification for believing that the attribute

    a. Is probably most significant in the general public's perception of public accounting as a professional activity.

    b. Is probably least significant in the general public's perception of public accounting as a professional activity.

**2-7.** Why is the public accounting profession as a whole desirous of inducing each member to maintain complete independence when examining financial statements for a client?

**2-8.** The Code of Professional Ethics of the American Institute of Certified Public Accountants (Rule 302) prohibits rendering professional service when the fee is contingent upon the findings or results of the service. Show how this rule relates to the independence of the public accountant.

2-9.    As a practical matter, does nomination of a company's auditor by the board of directors with a formal vote of approval by the stockholders give the stockholders an effective voice in the matter? Why? Propose some other approach to the problem.

2-10.   How can an auditor claim to be independent while fully subscribing to the right of the client to determine the form and content of the statements that the auditor is examining?

2-11.   Justify the fact that Rule 302 of the Code of Professional Ethics permits the accountant to accept an engagement on a contingent fee basis if the engagement pertains to representing the client in tax matters before a taxing authority.

2-12.   The attribute of independence has been traditionally associated with the CPA's function of auditing and expressing opinions on financial statements.

   a.   What is meant by "independence" as applied to the CPA's function of auditing and expressing opinions on financial statements? Discuss.

   b.   CPAs have imposed upon themselves certain rules of professional conduct that induce their members to remain independent and to strengthen public confidence in their independence. Which of the rules of professional conduct are concerned with the CPA's independence? Discuss.

   c.   The Wallydrag Company is indebted to a CPA for unpaid fees and has offered to issue to him unsecured interest-bearing notes. Would the CPA's acceptance of these notes have any bearing upon his independence in his relations with the Wallydrag Company? Discuss.

   d.   The Rocky Hill Corporation was formed on October 1, 19X1, and its fiscal year will end on September 30, 19X2. You audited the Corporation's opening balance sheet and rendered an unqualified opinion on it.

      A month after rendering your report you are offered the position of secretary of the Company because of the need for a complete set of officers and for convenience in signing various documents. You will have no financial interest in the Company through stock ownership or otherwise, will receive no salary, will not keep the books, and will not have any influence on its financial matters other than occasional advice on income tax matters and similar advice normally given a client by a CPA.

1. Assume that you accept the offer but plan to resign the position prior to conducting your annual audit, with the intention of again assuming the office after rendering an opinion on the statements. Can you render an independent opinion on the financial statements? Discuss.

2. Assume that you accept the offer on a temporary basis until the Corporation is underway and can employ a secretary. In any event you would permanently resign the position before conducting your annual audit. Can you render an independent opinion on the financial statements? Discuss.

(Uniform CPA Examination)

**2-13.** An auditor must not only appear to be independent; he must also be independent in fact.

Required:

a. Explain the concept of an "auditor's independence" as it applies to third party reliance upon financial statements.

b. 1. What determines whether or not an auditor is independent in fact?

   2. What determines whether or not an auditor appears to be independent?

c. Explain how an auditor may be independent in fact but not appear to be independent.

d. Would a CPA be considered independent for an examination of the financial statements of a

   1. Church for which he is serving as treasurer without compensation? Explain.

   2. Women's club for which his wife is serving as treasurer-bookkeeper if he is not to receive a fee for the examination? Explain.

(Uniform CPA Examination)

**2-14.** An auditor's report was appended to the financial statements of Worthmore, Inc. The statements consisted of a balance sheet as of November 30, 19X2, and statements of income and retained earnings for the year then ending. The first two paragraphs of the report contained the wording of the standard unqualified short-form report, and a third paragraph read as follows:

The wives of two partners of our firm owned a material investment in the outstanding common stock of Worthmore, Inc., on December 3, 19X2, in a transaction that did not result in a profit or a loss. This information is included in our report in order to comply with certain disclosure requirements of the Code of Professional Ethics of the American Institute of Certified Public Accountants.

Bell & Davis
Certified Public Accountants

Required:

a. Was the CPA firm of Bell & Davis independent with respect to the fiscal 19X2 examination of Worthmore, Inc.'s, financial statements? Explain.

b. Do you find Bell & Davis' auditor's report satisfactory? Explain.

c. Assume that no members of Bell & Davis or any members of their families held any financial interests in Worthmore, Inc., during 19X2. For each of the following cases, indicate if independence would be lacking on behalf of Bell & Davis, assuming that Worthmore, Inc., is a profit-seeking enterprise. In each case explain why independence would or would not be lacking.

    1. Two directors of Worthmore, Inc., became partners in the CPA firm of Bell & Davis on July 1, 19X2, resigning their directorships on that date.

    2. During 19X2 the former controller of Worthmore, now a Bell & Davis partner, was frequently called on for assistance by Worthmore. He made decisions for Worthmore's management regarding fixed asset acquisitions and the company's product marketing mix. In addition, he conducted a computer feasibility study for Worthmore.

(Uniform CPA Examination)

**2-15.** Gilbert and Bradley formed a corporation called Financial Services, Inc., each man taking 50 percent of the authorized common stock. Gilbert is a CPA and a member of the American Institute of CPAs. Bradley is a CPCU (Chartered Property Casualty Underwriter). The Corporation performs auditing and tax services under Gilbert's direction and insurance services under Bradley's supervision. The opening of the corporation's office was announced by a three-inch, two-column "card" in the local newspaper.

One of the corporation's first audit clients was the Grandtime Company. Grandtime had total assets of $600,000 and total liabilities of $270,000. In the course of his examination, Gilbert found that Grandtime's building with a book value of $240,000 was pledged as security for a ten-year-term note in the amount of $200,000. The client's statements did not mention that the building was pledged as security for the ten-year-term note. However, as the failure to disclose the lien did not affect either the value of the assets or the amount of the liabilities and his examination was satisfactory in all other respects, Gilbert rendered an unqualified opinion on Grandtime's financial statements. About two months after the date of his opinion, Gilbert learned that an insurance company was planning to loan Grandtime $150,000 in the form of a first-mortgage note on the building. Realizing that the insurance company was unaware of the existing lien on the building, Gilbert had Bradley notify the insurance company of the fact that Grandtime's building was pledged as security for the term note.

Shortly after the events described above, Gilbert was charged with a violation of professional ethics.

Required:
Identify and discuss the ethical implications of those acts by Gilbert that were in violation of the AICPA Code of Professional Ethics.

(Uniform CPA Examination)

# Chapter 3

# AUDITORS' LEGAL RESPONSIBILITIES AND OTHER EXTERNALLY IMPOSED REQUIREMENTS

The preceding chapter emphasized the self-regulating aspects of the public accounting profession accomplished through efforts of the American Institute of Certified Public Accountants, with the provision of auditing services as a focal point for those efforts. There are also, however, a variety of external influences affecting auditing practice, some of which were alluded to in the previous chapter, and these external influences are more extensively considered in this chapter. Consider first the salutary effect on auditing practice of the fact that legal claims can be levied against auditors if clients or third parties have suffered damages that can be attributed to deficient audit work.

### Responsibility to the Client under Common Law

The contract that provides for auditing services establishes a direct relationship between client and auditor. The contract should define the specific auditing services to be provided, but in addition it implies a responsibility to perform the services with due professional care—that is, without negligence. (This responsibility is also recognized in generally accepted auditing standards by the third general standard that specifies, "Due professional care is to be exercised in the performance of the examination and the preparation of the report.") If services are not of acceptable quality and the client suffers injury in the form of a financial loss as a consequence of the auditor's negligence, the client may sue on the basis of the tort that was committed in order that the client might be "made whole" through recovery of the damages suffered.

For example, assume the usual situation where an audit is contracted primarily for the benefit of third parties. Assume further that an employee had stolen assets from the client and concealed the defalcation by manipulating the accounting records. Even though the auditor failed to discover the defalcation because the auditor was negligent in performing the audit, the client would have no right of recovery from the auditor because the client's loss would not have been caused by the auditor. But such a right would exist if the employee subsequently disappeared, so that after discovery of the defalcation the client was unable to recover the loss from the employee. In that case it would be possible to argue that the client's loss was directly traceable to the auditor's negligence. Similarly if the employee remained on the job and continued to steal, the *subsequent* losses would be attributable to the auditor's negligence. To gain the right of recovery through court action, however, the client would have to prove that the auditor was in fact negligent, that the client suffered a loss, and that the loss resulted from the auditor's negligence.

Liability to a client for an auditor's negligence could occur under substantially different circumstances in the relatively rare situation where a client has engaged an auditor to examine the financial statements of some other concern. For example, assume that the client intends to purchase a going business, with the purchase price based at least in part on the assets and liabilities of the business and past operating results. If it later becomes known that the audited statements were actually incorrect or misleading, with a consequent unrecovered loss to the client for overpayment for the acquired business, and if the client is able to prove that the incurred loss resulted from the auditor's negligence, then the auditor would be liable in tort for the full amount of the damages that resulted from the auditor's negligence.

As another example, a major international accounting firm made settlement in a recent case involving a $350,000 claim filed by a church conference client. The client claimed a loss resulted because the accounting firm failed to notify the church conference trustees on a timely basis that the conference treasurer had funneled some $5 million of pension funds into loans of doubtful merit to companies set up by the treasurer and the treasurer's business friends.

### Responsibility to Third Parties

Because there can be no liability to a third party under a contract not involving the third party, the only liability to a third party would be for damages resulting from fraud—an actual intent by the auditor to deceive. This would be the case if an auditor issued an unqualified report on financial statements, knowing that the statements were incorrect or misleading. If a third party could prove 1) that the auditor knowingly attested to false or incorrect financial statements, and 2) that the loss suffered by the third party was a direct consequence of the auditor's fraudulent act, then the third party would be entitled to recover the consequent damages.

The courts have also held that gross negligence is tantamount to fraud, as, for example, in the extreme case where an auditor has issued a report on financial statements but made little or no effort to examine the statements and form an opinion about their fairness. Each of the above points was covered in the landmark decision, *Ultramares Corporation v. Touche* (255 N.Y. 170, 174 N.E. 441-1931). The accountants had supplied their client with thirty-two copies of their report, aware in a general way that these would be shown to banks and other creditors. In ruling that the accountants owed no duty to such third parties to perform their examination without negligence, the Court of Appeals stated in a decision written by Justice Cardozo:

> Our holding does not emancipate accountants from the consequences of fraud. It does not relieve them if their audit has been so negligent as to justify a finding that they had no genuine belief in its adequacy, for this again is fraud. It does no more than say that, if less than this is proved, if there has been neither reckless misstatement nor insincere profession of an opinion, but only honest blunder, the ensuing liability for negligence is one

that is bounded by the contract, and is to be enforced between the parties by whom the contract has been made. We doubt whether the average business man receiving a certificate without paying for it, and receiving it merely as one among a multitude of possible investors would look for anything more.

In an earlier decision Justice Cardozo had held in the case of *Glanzer v. Shepard* (233 N.Y. 236, 135 N.E. 275, 1922) that a public weigher of beans, engaged by the seller of the beans and directed to furnish the buyer with a copy of the statement of weight, was liable to the third party for negligence that resulted in certifying an incorrect weight. Liability was based on the assumption of a duty to weigh carefully for the benefit of those who it was known intended to rely on the stated weights—in other words, third parties who were *foreseen beneficiaries* of the audit contract. The situation in this case differs from *Ultramares,* where the specific recipients of the audited financial statements were unknown to the auditor except in a general way.

The class of protected third party beneficiaries was further extended, by an English case, to those who were *foreseeable* beneficiaries of the contract. In *Hedley Byrne and Co. Ltd. v. Heller and Partners, Ltd.* (A.C. 465, 1963) the House of Lords ruled, "[I]f in a sphere in which a person is so placed that others could reasonably rely upon his judgment or skill or upon his ability to make careful inquiry, a person takes it upon himself to give information or advice to be passed on to another person who, as he knows or should know, will place reliance upon it, then a duty of care will arise."

*Negligence and Errors in Judgment Distinguished.*    Crucial to the above cases and others that hinge on negligence as the cause of a loss is the question of what constitutes negligence. The term is perhaps best defined negatively in the auditing context as a failure to follow generally accepted auditing standards, but it should be noted that with the ever-present problems of judgment associated with all types of professional practice, an honest error in judgment would not constitute negligence. Negligence and errors in judgment are, however, separated by only a fine line and are contrasted in the following classical quotation from *Cooley on Torts:*

In all those employments where peculiar skill is requisite, if one offers his services, he is understood as holding himself out to the public as possessing the degree of skill commonly possessed by others in the same employment, and if his pretensions are unfounded, he commits a species of fraud upon every man who employs him in reliance on his public profession. But no man, whether skilled or unskilled, undertakes that the task he assumes shall be performed successfully, and without fault or error; he undertakes for good faith and integrity, but not for infallibility, and he is liable to his employer for negligence, bad faith or dishonesty, but not for losses consequent upon mere errors of judgment.[1]

*Responsibility for Failure To Detect Fraud in the Accounts or Financial Statements.* Clients and/or third parties may incur loss or damage if fraud is present in financial statements or the underlying accounting records and if the auditor fails to discover the fraud and take appropriate action. Two important questions arise from such situations: 1) Does the typical engagement to examine a concern's financial statements involve an auditor's responsibility for detecting fraud in the accounts? and 2) Should it be expected that fraud will be discovered if the auditor's examination is made in accordance with generally accepted auditing standards?

Professional Standards address these questions at AU Sec. 327.02-.03, using the terminology *errors and irregularities:*

> The term *errors* refers to unintentional mistakes in financial statements and includes mathematical or clerical mistakes in the underlying records and accounting data from which the financial statements were prepared, mistakes in the application of accounting principles, and oversight or misinterpretation of facts that existed at the time the financial statements were prepared.

> The term *irregularities* refers to intentional distortions of financial statements, such as deliberate misrepresentations by management, sometimes referred to as defalcations. Irregularities in financial statements may result from the misrepresentation or omission of the effects of events or transactions; manipulation, falsification, or alteration of records or documents; omission of significant information from records or documents; recording of transactions without substance; intentional misapplication of accounting principles; or misappropriation of assets for the benefit of management, employees, or third parties. Such acts may be accompanied by the use of false or misleading records or documents and may involve one or more individuals among management, employees, or third parties.

The auditor's responsibility in performing an independent examination of financial statements in accordance with generally accepted auditing standards, given the possibility that errors or irregularities may exist, is discussed in Professional Standards at AU Sec. 327.05-.06:

> The independent auditor's objective in making an examination of financial statements in accordance with generally accepted auditing standards is to form an opinion on whether the financial statements present fairly financial position, results of operations, and changes in financial position in conformity with generally accepted accounting principles consistently applied. Consequently, under generally accepted auditing standards the independent auditor has the responsibility within the inherent limitations of the auditing process . . . to plan his examination . . . to search for errors or irregularities

[1]Thomas A. Cooley, *Cooley on Torts,* 4th ed., rev. by D. Avery Haggard (Chicago: Callaghan, 1932), III, 335.

that would have a material effect on the financial statements, and to exercise due skill and care in the conduct of that examination. The auditor's search for material errors or irregularities ordinarily is accomplished by the performance of those auditing procedures that in his judgment are appropriate in the circumstances to form an opinion on the financial statements; extended auditing procedures are required if the auditor's examination indicates that material errors or irregularities may exist. . . . An independent auditor's standard report implicitly indicates his belief that the financial statements taken as a whole are not materially misstated as a result of errors or irregularities.

*Auditor Response to the Potential for Fraud.*   As has already been emphasized, the auditor has a fundamental obligation to conduct an examination in accordance with generally accepted auditing standards. Beyond this, AU Sec. 327.14 indicates what should be expected of an auditor if there is indication that errors or irregularities may exist:

If the independent auditor's examination causes him to believe that material errors or irregularities may exist, he should consider their implications and discuss the matter and the extent of any further investigation with an appropriate level of management that is at least one level above those involved. If after such discussions the auditor continues to believe that material errors or irregularities may exist, he should determine that the board of directors or its audit committee is aware of the circumstances. Also, he should attempt to obtain sufficient evidential matter to determine whether in fact material errors or irregularities exist and, if so, their effect. In this regard, the auditor may wish to consult with the client's legal counsel on matters concerning question of law. If practicable, the auditor should extend his auditing procedures in an effort to obtain such evidential matter. In some circumstances, however, it may be impracticable or impossible to obtain sufficient evidential matter to determine the existence, or related effect, of material errors or possible irregularities, or management may impose a limitation on the scope of the auditor's search for the evidential matter needed to reach a conclusion. When the auditor's examination indicates the presence of errors or possible irregularities, and the auditor remains uncertain about whether these errors or possible irregularities may materially affect the financial statements, he should qualify his opinion or disclaim an opinion on the financial statements and, depending on the circumstances, consider withdrawing from the engagement, indicating his reasons and findings in writing to the board of directors. In such circumstances, the auditor may wish to consult with his legal counsel.

Given the auditor's responsibility for detecting fraud, as set forth in professional standards, there remains the question, how should the auditor approach the typical examination? Three qualities are suggested as being particularly important: 1) Alertness, 2) Curiosity, and 3) Skepticism.

The auditor should be alert to the presence of conditions that might tempt a person to perpetrate fraud or that might facilitate committing and concealing a fraudulent act if a person has succumbed to temptation. The auditor should likewise be alert to any indication or suggestion that a material fraud may have occurred.

Along with being alert the auditor should have a strong sense of curiosity about how and why various aspects of a client's operations and financial results have come to be—especially if anything unusual is involved. Finally, there should always be a healthy skepticism concerning the evidence and explanations that come to the auditor's attention.

*Warning Signals That Fraud May Be Present.*   Alertness is especially pertinent when there are signals warning of a potential for fraud or that fraud may have occurred. To illustrate typical warning signals that should alert the auditor, the following categories of conditions that might be noted are suggested, and examples within each category are offered.

### Conditions conducive to perpetration of fraud:

Weaknesses in internal control (see Chapter 6).

Absence of an effective responsibility reporting system to highlight performance breakdowns. *check & control system in accounting system*

Lack of monitoring systems, such as internal audit (see Chapter 4), to assure that programmed controls are working.

Situations where management estimates have an important bearing on financial and operating results, such as warranty expense provisions or bad debt losses.

Tolerance of accounting errors and differences between physical assets and control records without effort to correct the underlying problems.

Existence of transactions with related parties or under conditions involving possible conflict of interest.

Managers or unsupervised employees who work unusual hours or take vacations piecemeal rather than in a block of time.

Transaction of business at widely dispersed distant locations.

Existence of purportedly inactive foreign subsidiaries.

### Conditions tending to induce the perpetration of fraud:

Management or employee compensation plans that are directly tied to reported performance.

Existence of financial or operating problems, such as negative cash flow, difficulty in meeting debt covenant or repayment requirements, sales or profits declining absolutely or in rate of growth.

Forecasts and other future expectations that have been publicly announced, thus creating pressure to meet those expectations.

Tax benefits or incentives that are available to the client.

Executives or employees who are known to have personal financial problems.

Conditions suggestive that fraud may have occurred:

*previous year* Abnormalities disclosed by the analytical review of financial and operating results, such as changes in profit margins, abnormal inventory shortages, or departure from past experience in inventory or receivables turnover.

Marked changes in "sensitive" expense accounts. *Travel – entertainment*

Large or otherwise abnormal year-end write-offs or adjustments of account balances.

Major new contracts that are entered into near the close of the fiscal year.

Evasive or unreasonable responses by management to audit inquiries.

Evidence of consistent management bias in choice of accounting methods or accounting estimates. *check all estimate accounts. (most)*

Inasmuch as there is always a possibility of errors, irregularities, or fraud, the auditor should be constantly alert to those possibilities. If an abnormality has occurred that materially affects the financial statements, an auditor's responsibility for detecting the distortion can be satisfied only by performing the audit examination with due professional care or, stated negatively, without negligence. The requirement of due professional care will be satisfied only if the examination is conducted in accordance with generally accepted auditing standards.

Nevertheless, there can be no guarantee that an examination conducted in accordance with generally accepted auditing standards will detect material fraud. Intent within the client's organization to deceive may produce records and other evidence that have every appearance of being valid and proper, thereby defying detection by normal auditing procedures applied with due care.

### Auditor Responsibilities under Common Law Summarized

The auditor owes to the client an obligation to perform the audit in accordance with generally accepted auditing standards, but that does not imply infallible judgment. An auditor who has acted negligently may be sued for breach of contract, with the client recovering all or part of the auditor's fee, or if a tort has been committed, the suit may be to recover damages incurred.

Similar protection against the tortious negligence of auditors has been extended by the courts to foreseen or foreseeable third party beneficiaries of an audit. Other third parties are protected only against fraud by the auditor in attesting to financial statements that are known by the auditor to be incorrect or misleading. Third parties are similarly protected against gross negligence, such as would be involved in attesting to financial statements when the auditor has made little or no attempt to conduct an examination that would provide a reasonable basis for the opinion expressed on the financial statements.

## Expanded Auditor Liability under the Federal Securities Acts

The Securities Acts have been characterized as disclosure statutes. As a direct result of disclosure problems that surfaced after the stock market debacle of 1929 and the ensuing depression, Congress legislated to help assure that investors would have available full and reliable information as a basis for their investment decisions.

*The Securities Act of 1933.* The 1933 Act required registering new security issues in excess of $500,000 (since changed to $1.5 million) that are sold across state lines and hence in interstate commerce. To accomplish registration, an issuer must file an S-1 or abbreviated S-7 or S-16 (proposed to be renumbered S-2 and S-3) registration statement including financial statements that have been certified by an independent public accountant or an independent certified public accountant. Acceptance of a registration statement by the SEC is granted on the basis of a review to determine that all material facts related to the proposed security issue and the issuer appear to have been disclosed. Only after such acceptance can the securities be sold. A prospectus containing the financial and other information shown in the registration statement must be furnished to any purchaser of the new securities before a purchase can be consummated.

Rule 242, adopted by the SEC in 1980, makes special provision for security issues by smaller businesses when the issues are essentially privately placed. A corporation may issue up to $2 million of securities in any 6-month period (subsequently proposed to be increased to $5 million and 12 months) without being subject to registration requirements, provided that persons or institutions purchase the securities in amounts of $100,000 or more. The presumption is that those purchasing in excess of the specified minimum amount will be sufficiently knowledgeable about investing and in a sufficiently strong bargaining position to demand any information, such as audited financial statements, deemed essential to making sound investment decisions. Lesser amounts of securities may be sold to a maximum number of "nonaccredited" purchasers, but the issuing company must then furnish certain specified information, including audited financial statements, to both classes of purchasers.

In connection with security issues that must be registered, the Act creates potential civil liability for any loss or damage incurred by a purchaser if there are materially false or inadequate representations in documents with which the various parties involved in the issue are associated. Associated parties would include the issuer, its directors, underwriters of the issue, and any signers of the registration statement as "experts," including auditors and lawyers. For auditors the effect of these civil liability provisions is to extend to purchasers of a new issue of registered securities the same protection that the common law extends to the auditor's client—in other words, protection against losses attributable to the auditor's negligence. But the act also greatly strengthens the position of purchasers in bringing action against the auditor since the purchaser has only to show that 1) a loss was incurred, with no necessity to show that the loss was caused by the auditor's negligence, and 2) the audited financial statements contained incorrect or misleading information. The burden of proof if the auditor is to avoid liability for purchaser's losses is then placed on the defendant auditor—to show that the audit was conducted without negligence or that the purchaser's loss was not attributable to any negligence that did occur.

The Securities Act of 1933 departed substantially from the common law on auditors' liability; these changes were the source of bewilderment and consternation to public accountants at that time. The situation prompted George O. May, one of the giants of the profession of that day, to remark:

> I cannot believe that a law is just or can long be maintained in effect which deliberately contemplates the possibility that a purchaser may recover from a person from whom he has not bought, in respect of a statement which at the time of his purchase he had not read, contained in a document which he did not then know to exist, a sum which is not measured by injury resulting from falsity in such statement.[2]

Yet, the 1933 Act has remained in effect, and the profession has accommodated itself to the strange new situation.

*The Securities Exchange Act of 1934.*   Whereas the 1933 act was concerned with information pertaining to the registration and sale of new security issues, the 1934 act related to providing continuing information for use by purchasers and sellers of registered securities traded through stock exchanges or the over-the-counter market. The basic information document that the SEC requires to be filed under the 1934 Act is the annual Form 10-K, the instructions for which are included in Regulation S-X. In addition to extensive disclosures of supplementary information required by Form 10-K, the following information must be included in Form 10-K and also in the registered company's annual report to stockholders:

> Audited financial statements, including audited balance sheets for two years and audited statements of income and changes in financial position for the most recent three years.

[2]As quoted in John L. Carey, *The Rise of the Accounting Profession* (New York: American Institute of Certified Public Accountants, 1969), I, 192.

Five-year summary of selected financial data for trend analysis.

Management's discussion and analysis of the registrant's operations and financial condition including liquidity, capital resources, and results of operations.

The preceding information can now be incorporated in Form 10-K by reference to the annual report, since the required information has been made common to both documents.

In addition to Form 10-K a registered company must file briefer quarterly information on Form 10-Q. No auditor association is required for the 10-Q information, but the SEC does encourage having the company's auditors review and report on the information (see Chapter 21), consistent with the proposed concept of "auditor of record." The thinking behind this concept is that all interim information that is to be made public would be *reviewed* by the company's auditor before it is released, thereby adding credibility to the information through having it associated with the auditor of record. However, only the annual financial statements or statements required in the registration of a security offering would actually be *audited.*

Section 18 of the 1934 act establishes auditor liability to both buyers and sellers of registered securities. In contrast to the 1933 act, however, an injured party must show reliance on the audited financial statements and must show that the security price was affected by false or misleading information included in such statements or by the omission of information from such statements. The act is also more charitable with respect to auditor defense, for the auditor is absolved of liability if it can be proved that the auditor ". . . acted in good faith and had no knowledge that such statement was false or misleading." (Section 18). A reasonable conclusion about the 1934 act is that it essentially follows the common law with respect to deceit actions and negligence. There were, however, some cases that had interpreted related SEC Rule 10b-5 as extending auditor liability to include losses attributable to auditor negligence, but the Supreme Court decision in *Ernst & Ernst v. Hochfelder* (425 U.S. 185, 1976) foreclosed that interpretation. As a result of that decision a Rule 10b-5 violation must involve intent to mislead or knowledge (*scienter*) that a statement was untrue or that a fact had been omitted.

### Professional Liability Insurance

Given that the law imposes financial obligation on auditors for failure to discharge adequately the responsibilities associated with their professional practice, it has long been customary to carry accountants' liability insurance. This serves as protection against claims resulting from inadvertent acts or losses resulting from departures from professional standards, as well as protection against the costs of legal defenses related to liability suits. Typically the insurance involves a deductible amount to be borne by the insured, and in the case of the large national and international firms, for which insurance of adequate amount is available only through Lloyd's of London, the deductible may be a million dollars or more.

Both the Securities Act of 1933 and the Securities Exchange Act of 1934 additionally subjected auditors and others to criminal penalties for fraudulent acts in connection with registered securities. Prominent cases involving criminal prosecution that resulted in penalties being assessed against auditors include Continental Vending (*United States v. Simon:* 425 F. 2d, 1969) and National Student Marketing (*United States v. Natelli:* F. 2d, 1975). Neither of these cases charged fraudulent intent from which the auditor might benefit; instead, the cases involved auditor acceptance in apparent good faith of treatments in the accounting records and financial statements that were later held to be not in conformity with generally accepted accounting principles. Continental Vending seems especially severe in this regard. The defendant auditors were found guilty relative to their decision about information to be disclosed concerning a particular transaction—a decision that involved an interpretation of auditing standards and accounting principles that was subsequently supported by reputable expert witnesses called on the defendants' behalf.

Premiums for malpractice insurance mounted rapidly in the late 1960s and early 1970s as a result of the surge of malpractice and tort liability suits that plagued most U.S. professions. It has been estimated that professional liability insurance premiums for the seventeen largest U.S. accounting firms are running in a range of $30 million to $40 million per year. The premiums to maintain such malpractice insurance have been likened to a socialization of the risks of professional practice, with auditors shifting the impact of risk to clients through higher fees, and clients passing the effect along to customers through higher charges for products and services.

Another aspect of the litigation explosion and the rise in legal activism has been to place auditors in a position similar to being guarantors of the accuracy of their clients' financial statements. Seemingly ignoring the judgment process that is inherent in professional practice, plaintiffs and their attorneys often proceed against auditors as if they were primarily responsible for financial statement representations and expected to be infallible in their judgment.

### Securities and Exchange Commission Actions Affecting Auditors

*Auditors' Independence.* The SEC has long been concerned with auditor independence, and the present wording of Rule 101 of the AICPA Rules of Conduct, dealing with independence (see Chapter 2), directly reflects that concern. Similarly the SEC has sought to strengthen auditor independence through the manner in which auditors are appointed, advocating nomination of the auditor by the audit committee of the client's board of directors and election of the auditor by vote of the stockholders. The SEC does not require that procedure, however, and as stated in Chapter 2, currently the only requirement for appointment by an audit committee is the New York Stock Exchange requirement.

The SEC has also sought to strengthen auditor independence by requiring publicity when a registered company changes auditors. The requirement is primarily directed to changes when there has been a disagreement between the auditor and the client on an accounting matter. Companies changing auditors must report the change to the SEC on Form 8-K, and also in the proxy statement sent to stockholders as a basis for absentee voting through a proxy when stockholders are unable to be present at annual or called stockholders meetings. In connection with an auditor change the company must report any disagreements with the displaced auditor that occurred in the two years prior to the change. Also, if transactions or events similar to those causing the reported disagreement occur during the year in which auditors were changed or in the following year, the transactions or events, if they have been accounted for on a different basis than they were before the change of auditors, must be disclosed; the effect of the different basis on the financial statements must also be shown. The intended effect of this requirement is to weaken the company's position relative to the independent auditor's in the case of a disagreement by adding a publicity "cost" to dismissing the auditor as a means of resolving the disagreement.

*Quality Control through Peer Reviews.*   As a result of SEC dissatisfaction in certain cases with what the SEC perceived to be the quality of audit work and the objectivity of decisions about controversial matters, the SEC censured several national accounting firms and required an independent review of their quality control procedures to determine whether the firms were in compliance with generally accepted auditing standards. Several years prior to the SEC action the AICPA had developed a voluntary peer review program oriented toward quality control. As an outgrowth of these activities and in recognition of SEC concerns about quality controls in auditing, the AICPA in 1974 issued Statement on Auditing Standards No. 4, "Quality Control Considerations for a Firm of Independent Auditors." That statement was superseded in 1979 by Statement on Auditing Standards No. 25, which refers to the authority of the new AICPA Quality Control Standards Committee with respect to quality control and states that a CPA firm should establish quality control procedures that provide adequate assurance of conformance with all aspects of generally accepted auditing standards (see Professional Standards AU Sec. 161). The elements of quality control enumerated in Statement No. 4 have in turn been incorporated in the first statement on quality control by the Quality Control Standards Committee, entitled *System of Quality Control for a CPA Firm* and incorporated in Professional Standards at QC Sec. 10. Matters covered include maintaining independence, assigning personnel to engagements, securing consultation on technical questions at appropriate levels within the firm, supervising audit engagements, maintaining programs for the professional development of firm personnel, considering the acceptance or continuance of clients, and maintaining a program of internal review to show whether established policies and procedures are being complied with.

More recently the AICPA responded to possible problems of substandard practice and of assuring adequate quality control measures by creating a Division for CPA Firms within the Institute to recognize differences in size and problems encountered by practice units ranging in size from individual practitioners or firms with relatively few partners to the huge national and international firms, such as the "Big Eight." As mentioned in the preceding chapter, the Division for CPA Firms has formed an SEC Practice Section and a Private Companies Practice Section, and a CPA firm may elect to join either or both sections on a voluntary basis. To retain membership, however, a firm must meet the various standards and requirements of the section, including a periodic peer review of the firm's quality controls.

*Reports on Clients' Internal Control.*   As a result of disclosures that many businesses had made illegal political contributions or questionable payments in order to secure contracts with foreign governments, the Foreign Corrupt Practices Act was passed in 1977. The Act made it illegal to arrange payments to foreign governments, officials, or political candidates for the purpose of exerting influence to obtain or retain business. Because these payments associated with corrupt practices were often concealed in the concern's accounting records, the Act amended the Securities Exchange Act of 1934 to require registered companies to keep books that fairly reflect all business transactions and to maintain internal control systems to assure execution of all transactions in accordance with management's authorization and to produce proper recording of all transactions.

Subsequently the SEC adopted a regulation that prohibited falsifying corporate books and records and making false, misleading, or incomplete statements to the concern's auditors. It also proposed a regulation requiring the management of a registered company to report on the adequacy of its internal control system, and for the concern's independent auditors to report on their agreement or disagreement with the management report on the adequacy of the concern's internal control system. The proposal has since been withdrawn, however, largely because of unfavorable reaction to the cost/benefit aspects of the requirement, but the SEC continues to encourage such reviews and reports. See Chapter 21 for a discussion of what is required for such a review and the standards of reporting on the review.

*Management Advisory Services.* The SEC has long maintained that providing nonaudit services to a client may have a pernicious effect on auditor independence, and some observers and financial statement users view management advisory services as potentially reducing audit independence. However, as stated in the preceding chapter, both the Commission on Auditors' Responsibilities and the Public Oversight Board of the SEC Practice Section of the AICPA concluded that an auditor's furnishing management advisory services to an audit client would be likely to have little if any negative effect on independence.

To inform financial statement users about the authorization of nonaudit services and the extent of such services, thus making it possible for users to assess the potential impact of providing such services on auditor independence, the SEC issued Accounting Series Release 250. This ASR requires a registered company to make proxy statement disclosure of nonaudit services and the percentage relationship of the fee for those services to the audit fee for each classification of such services exceeding 3 percent of the audit fee. The release also requires disclosure of whether the board of directors or audit committee has approved engaging the concern's auditor for such services.

In a related action Accounting Series Release 264 discusses specific factors that the SEC deems important for auditors, management, and audit committees to consider in deciding whether nonauditing services may threaten actual or perceived independence.

*Auditor Responsibility for Supplemental Financial Statement Disclosures.* In order to add credibility to quarterly and other interim operating information reported by registered companies, and to reduce year-end adjustments, some of which have affected previously reported quarterly data, the SEC requires footnote disclosure in annual reports to the SEC of quarterly sales, gross profit, net income, and earnings per share figures. Also, to provide statement users with some indication of inflation's effect on financial statements, the SEC required that certain larger registrants report information concerning the current replacement cost of inventories and depreciable assets and cost of sales and depreciation as computed on a replacement cost basis. When subsequently the FASB required larger companies to report supplementary replacement-cost and inflation-adjusted financial information, the SEC indicated that the FASB-required information would satisfy the requirements of Accounting Series Release 190.

Both quarterly operating information and replacement cost data are to be reported as supplementary information to audited financial statements, but the supplementary information may be labeled "unaudited." There is, however, certain auditor responsibility for the review of such unaudited data associated with financial statements, as set forth in Professional Standards at AU Sec. 720 and 730. AU Sec. 519 provides guidance to the auditor in reporting separately the results of a limited review of unaudited interim financial information, as further discussed in Chapter 21.

### Congressional Investigations of the Accounting Profession and Its Performance

In recent years two congressional committees have actively studied various facets of the public accounting profession and its performance. The committees were the Senate Subcommittee on Reports, Accounting, and Management, of the Committee on Governmental Affairs, under the chairmanship of the late Senator Lee Metcalf, usually referred to as the Metcalf Committee, and the House Subcommittee on Oversight and Investigations, of the Commerce Committee, under the chairmanship of then Representative John E. Moss, typically referred to as the Moss Committee. Both committees were engaged in extensive studies and investigations and conducted public hearings relating to the public accounting profession. The two committees considered substantially different matters, including the organization of the public accounting profession, the dominance of the Big Eight accounting firms, the independence of auditors, adherence to quality standards in independent audits, and the regulation of the accounting profession relative to practice before the SEC.

Although formation of the Commission on Auditors' Responsibilities (the Cohen Commission) preceded the investigations by the Senate and House subcommittees, the Cohen Commission addressed several matters that subsequently appeared as concerns of those committees, and the AICPA took various responsive actions even before the congressional committees' reports were issued. Of major importance among these actions were modulation of the Big Eight accounting firms' voices in the affairs of the AICPA and of the Financial Accounting Standards Board—in the latter case by reducing the disproportionate share of the FASB's financing that originated with the Big Eight firms.

The SEC Practice Section of the Institute's new Division for CPA Firms represented an effort to ward off direct government regulation of firms practicing before the SEC. Among the important responses of the SEC Practice Section, as mentioned in this and the preceding chapter, were creating a Public Oversight Board to monitor performance of member firms, instituting mandatory quality reviews of the firms, setting

a requirement for continuing professional development of all professional staff, requiring a "cold review" by another partner of all SEC
work, and instituting periodic rotation of the partners in charge of SEC
engagements.

The AICPA, in addition to forming the practice division, opened to
the public all committee proceedings involving the setting of technical
standards, placed public members on its board of directors, and made
changes in its procedures for disciplinary action against members for
substandard work.

### Stock Exchange Action Fostering Audit Committees of Independent Directors

As mentioned in the earlier discussion on independence, the New
York Stock Exchange initiated a requirement, effective June 30, 1978,
that all listed companies have an audit committee of independent directors, and the American Stock Exchange has recommended that listed
companies have an audit committee. Both the AICPA and the SEC have
recognized the contribution of an audit committee to auditor independence, but neither body has been willing to institute such a requirement.

**Table 3-1.** Auditors' Legal Liability Summarized*

| Legal Basis for Liability and Parties to Whom Liable | Liability for Stated Action | | |
| --- | --- | --- | --- |
| | Errors in Judgment | Negligence | Fraud (Including Gross Negligence) |
| Common Law | | | |
| Client | 0 | 1 | 1 |
| Foreseen or foreseeable third parties | 0 | 1 | 1 |
| Other third parties | 0 | 0 | 1 |
| SEC statutory law | | | |
| Securities Act of 1933 | | | |
| Purchasers of registered securities | 0 | 1 | 1 |
| Securities Exchange Act of 1934 | | | |
| Purchasers or sellers of registered securities | 0 | 0 | 1 |

0 = No liability
1 = Liable for damages resulting from stated action

*In all cases except those arising under the Securities Act of 1933, the plaintiff has the
burden of establishing 1) that the loss incurred resulted from relying on misleading financial
statements, and 2) that the auditor was negligent in failing to discover and correct the
misleading information.

### Summary

At the core of the concerns discussed in this chapter is the quality of
the professional practice of auditing. Both common law and statutory
law hold auditors responsible for the quality of audit work and impose

legal liability for the consequences of failing to meet professional standards. Although the standards are largely set by the profession itself, as discussed in Chapter 2, the courts have been an important factor in refining those standards and defining minimum acceptable levels of quality. Also important in this regard is the Securities and Exchange Commission, which has directed much of its effort toward improving standards of disclosure and standards of professional auditing practice.

The legal liability of auditors with respect to the variables that enter into determining such liability, as discussed in this chapter, are summarized in the matrix presented in Table 3-1.

## Questions/Problems

For multiple-choice questions 3-1 through 3-5, indicate the letter of the single answer that *best* completes the statement or answers the question, and justify the choice that you have made.

**3-1.** The following is *not* likely to be factor in the decision in a court case related to legal liability arising from the provision of audit services:
   a.  The reputation of the firm for quality audits.
   b.  Generally accepted auditing standards.
   c.  Whether the audited company is registered with the SEC.
   d.  Each of the above factors is likely to be related to the determination of legal liability.

**3-2.** An independent auditor has the responsibility to plan the audit examination to search for errors and irregularities that might have a material effect on the financial statements. Which of the following, if material, would be an *irregularity* as defined in Statements on Auditing Standards?
   a.  Misappropriation of an asset or groups of assets.
   b.  Clerical mistakes in the accounting data underlying the financial statements.
   c.  Mistakes in the application of accounting principles.
   d.  Misinterpretation of facts that existed when the financial statements were prepared.

(Uniform CPA Examination)

**3-3.** The ordinary examination of financial statements is *not* primarily designed to disclose defalcations and other irregularities, although their discovery may result. Normal audit procedures are more likely to detect a fraud arising from
   a.  Collusion on the part of several employees.
   b.  Failure to record cash receipts for services rendered.

    c.  Forgeries on company checks.

    d.  Theft of inventories.

(Uniform CPA Examination)

**3-4.** As generally conceived, the "audit committee" of a publicly held company should be made up of

    a.  Representatives of the major equity interests (bonds, preferred stock, common stock).

    b.  The audit partner, the chief financial officer, the legal counsel, and at least one outsider.

    c.  Representatives from the client's management, investors, suppliers, and customers.

    d.  Members of the board of directors who are not officers or employees.

(Uniform CPA Examination)

**3-5.** An independent auditor's liability arising out of the failure to detect errors or irregularities is likely to be different

    a.  With respect to a supplier from whom the client has purchased for the first time and a bank with which the client has a line of credit.

    b.  For errors and for an irregularity in which collusion is involved.

    c.  Depending on the materiality of the error or irregularity.

    d.  In each of the above instances.

**3-6.** Why is the Securities and Exchange Commission concerned with the independence of public accountants?

**3-7.** What responsibility does the Securities and Exchange Commission assume in connection with the financial statements of registered companies?

**3-8.** Explain how the auditor's failure to maintain independence may result in legal liability.

**3-9.** Under what circumstances may an auditor incur legal liability for failure to detect fraud?

**3-10.** How is the auditor's common law liability likely to differ in the case of ordinary negligence as compared with gross negligence or fraud?

**3-11.** Has the Securities Act of 1933 served in general to increase or decrease auditors' liability? Explain.

**3-12.** What is the apparent reason that the Securities and Exchange Commission would not recognize an accounting firm as independent for purposes of expressing an opinion on a client's financial statements, when members of the accounting firm staff had prepared the books of entry and the ledgers?

**3-13.** Jackson was a junior staff member of an accounting firm. He began the audit of the Bosco Corporation, which manufactured and sold expensive watches. In the middle of the audit he quit. The accounting firm hired another person to continue the audit of Bosco. Due to the changeover and the time pressure to finish the audit, the firm violated certain generally accepted auditing standards when they did not follow adequate procedures with respect to the physical inventory. Had the proper procedures been used during the examination, they would have discovered that watches worth more than $20,000 were missing. The employee who was stealing the watches was able to steal an additional $30,000 worth before the thefts were discovered six months after the completion of the audit.

Required:

Discuss the legal problems of the accounting firm as a result of the above facts.

(Uniform CPA Examination)

**3-14.** Explain what effect the fact that there are published lists of "warning signals" relative to the possible existence of fraud might have in a suit for damages against an independent auditor for failure to detect fraud.

**3-15.** With respect to "peer reviews" of accounting firms
   a.  Explain why the SEC has been interested in imposing or requiring such reviews.
   b.  What authority does the SEC have to impose such rules?

# Chapter 4

# INTRAORGANIZATIONAL AUDITING

---

**Internal Auditing**
    Discussion of Internal Auditing Standards
        Independence
        Professional Proficiency
        Scope of Work
        Performance of Audit Work
        Management of the Internal Auditing Department
    Types of Internal Audit Activity
    Management Orientation of Internal Auditing
    Summary of Internal Audit Objectives
**Legislative Government Auditing**
    Government Auditing Standards
**Independent, Internal, and Governmental Auditing Contrasted**
    Distinguishing Characteristics of Internal Auditing and Independent Auditing
    Selected Excerpts from Internal Audit Reports
    Examples of Internal Audit Projects
    Internal Auditing and the Smaller Business
**Appendix—Standards for the Professional Practice of Internal Auditing**

---

The ever-increasing scope of business operations generated by the Industrial Revolution, the development of nation-spanning railroads, and later the merger activities that created such supercorporations as General Motors and United States Steel Corporation brought forth management problems that were largely related to size. The need became apparent to devise ways of maintaining control over far-flung operations, detecting misappropriations of assets, and ascertaining the accuracy of accounting data on which management had to rely. A key solution to these problems was to institute auditing activities that were carried on *within* the organization.

First to appear in this context were the traveling auditors of railroads. Their function was to visit railroad ticket and freight agents to determine that all tickets, freight charges, and cash collections had been properly accounted for. Out of these activities has developed what is now known as internal auditing—a function performed within all sizable organizations, whether they are profit-seeking or not-for-profit, and whether they are privately organized or government-related. Within government, however, an additional type of auditing developed, which embodies some of the characteristics of both independent auditing and internal auditing. Described herein as legislative government auditing, these activities provide legislative bodies with investigative assistance to help facilitate their control over the government organizations that expend appropriated funds. The U.S. General Accounting Office (GAO) is the best known and most highly respected of all such audit organizations. Although today the GAO is exclusively engaged in auditing activities, it was originally formed, as its name suggests, to maintain accounting control over funds appropriated by the Congress.

The following discussion first considers internal auditing, and then legislative government auditing.

## Internal Auditing

The relatively recent origin and maturation of internal auditing is suggested by the fact that the first extensive treatise on the subject was published in 1941, and that year also marked the formation of a national organization of internal auditors—The Institute of Internal Auditors (IIA). In the intervening years the Institute has incorporated, has become international in scope (furthering the professional interests of some 25,000 members throughout the world), and has developed a professional examination program leading to the designation "Certified Internal Auditor."

In 1947 the IIA prepared and published a *Statement of Responsibilities of Internal Auditors,* subsequently revising the *Statement* in 1957 and again in 1971. The *Statement* defined internal auditing as ". . . an independent appraisal activity within an organization for the review of operations as a service to management. It is a managerial control which functiions by measuring and evaluating the effectiveness of other controls." Other portions of the *Statement* set forth the objectives and scope of internal auditing, the responsibility and authority associated with that activity, and the importance of independence in the effective functioning of internal auditing. Subsequently, the IIA recognized the desirability of a more comprehensive statement about internal auditing, which would address the criteria by which the activities of an internal auditing department should be evaluated, and in 1974 formed the Professional Standards and Responsibilities Committee to prepare a statement of internal auditing standards. The results of the committee's deliberations were published in 1978 in a booklet titled *Standards for the Professional Practice of Internal Auditing*.

The introduction to the standards booklet opens with the following definition of internal auditing, which constitutes the point of reference for the standards:

> Internal auditing is an independent appraisal function established within an organization to examine and evaluate its activities as a service to the organization. The objective of internal auditing is to assist members of the organization in the effective discharge of their responsibilities. To this end, internal auditing furnishes them with analyses, appraisals, recommendations, counsel, and information concerning the activities reviewed.

The general orientation and content of the standards are summarized below, but for a more complete understanding of the standards the reader is referred to the Appendix following this chapter, which includes a full listing of the standards along with many of the supplementary guidelines and explanatory comments that accompany the standards.

### Discussion of Internal Auditing Standards

Similarities and differences between internal auditing standards and the generally accepted standards for independent (external) auditors, as presented in Chapter 1, can be considered on the basis of the following information.

*Independence.* The critical matter of independence is especially important. Although common to the standards for both types of auditors, it must be accomplished in different ways for each. Independence of the internal auditor *within* the organization is best obtained by establishing a direct line of communication with the board of directors, customarily through its audit committee when such a committee exists. Fully independent responsibility for managing internal audit activity exists preferably at the level of first-line management, directly under the chief executive officer. Historically, however, direct line responsibility to the chief financial officer has been common—either to the vice-president of finance, if there is such a position, or to the controller, if that is the top financial position. The assumption is that the chief financial officer will have the technical capability to direct the internal audit activity, but independence is obviously strengthened if the director of internal auditing has complete freedom to operate under the aegis of the chief executive officer and has equal status with other members of first-line management. Preferably the organizational status, relationships, and functions of the internal auditing department should be set forth in a "charter" so that all members of the organization will be aware of the basic internal auditing functions and responsibilities.

Organizational independence helps in maintaining the independent mental attitude that is a key aspect of objectivity, for with independent organizational status internal auditors are insulated from pressure to subordinate their judgment to the immediate interests of others. It is also important that internal auditors not be expected to assume operating responsibilities, for then the benefits of an objective review will have been sacrificed. Operating responsibilities that have at times been assigned to internal auditors, on the basis of their independence and expertise, are the preparation of bank reconciliations and the design and implementation of accounting systems. Objectivity is not considered to be affected, however, if the internal auditor recommends standards of control for systems designs being developed or modified for other organizational units, and it is also appropriate for the internal auditor to review new or revised systems before they are implemented.

*Professional Proficiency.*   A wide scope of expertise should be represented within the internal audit staff, including, in addition to auditing and accounting, such disciplines as engineering, taxation, economics, finance, statistics, and electronic data processing. Also, the close interaction with management in all aspects of internal auditing makes essential an understanding of management principles and good business practice.

Because auditing involves constant review of others' work and possible criticism of their performance, skill in human relations and effective communication are important to the successful practice of internal auditing. The exercise of due professional care and the maintaining of competence through continuing education are likewise important.

*Scope of Work.*   Internal control (see Chapter 6) is a vital aspect of managing and controlling any operation. In the role of serving the organization, internal auditors give especially close attention to internal control, reviewing all controls for completeness and effectiveness, and making tests to ascertain that prescribed controls are functioning as intended. Preferably internal auditing should encompass the entire organization, and consequently the concern with controls should extend beyond internal accounting control to include administrative and operating controls as well.

*Performance of Audit Work.*   An internal auditor should fully understand the activity to be audited and then, after considering the scope and objectives of the planned audit, develop a program for accomplishing the audit. The program should comprehend the acquisition of sufficient, competent, relevant information to provide a sound basis for the audit findings and recommendations, which should be effectively communicated in a signed written report directed to the appropriate management official. The final step should be subsequent follow-up to ensure that appropriate action has been taken on reported audit findings.

*Management of the Internal Auditing Department.* Because internal auditing in a large organization may involve directing and supervising the activities of a hundred or more auditors, an effective organization is essential. There should be various levels of management and supervision with appropriate spans of control. All auditing activity should be carefully planned, and a program should be developed to provide assurance that appropriate quality standards are maintained. All of these activities should be implemented under the direction and control of the director of internal auditing.

### Types of Internal Audit Activity

Two basic types of internal audit activity are generally recognized today: financial auditing and operational auditing. Financial auditing is in a sense an expansion of the singular activity of the early traveling railroad auditors, which involved accounting for the revenue generated locally and the related cash and unused tickets. The financial audit activities of present day internal auditors are roughly comparable to audit activities of independent auditors. These activities include ascertaining the reliability and integrity of financial and operating information, evaluating the effectiveness of internal controls over the processing of that information, and verifying that the resources of the organization have been properly accounted for.

As internal auditing evolved, concern for internal controls broadened to include operating controls as well as financial controls and gave rise to the term *operational* (or *operations*) *auditing*. From this involvement with operating controls has emerged the emphasis that has become the focus of operational auditing: the economical and efficient use of resources and the accomplishment of organizational objectives and goals related to operations or programs.

### Management Orientation of Internal Auditing

Especially when engaged in operational auditing activities, the internal auditor becomes in a sense part of the management team, by taking a management approach in choosing operating areas to be reviewed and in evaluating the method of operation and the existing controls. The audit manual developed by the internal auditing division of one midwestern company emphasizes that operational audits are to be performed for management from a manager's point of view. The manual expands on that concept in these words:

> Auditing for management from a manager's point of view requires us to think like managers, to understand their concerns at various levels of the operation, and to identify our objectives with theirs. We must project ourselves into the position of the supervisor in charge of the operation and attempt to understand how management wishes to have the operation run.
>
> This does not mean that we are experts in all operations. Our field of qualification is controls, which are as broad and long as the Company itself. Controls of some type are established for every operation to ensure that management's objectives are met. They systematically detect and correct significant deviations from planned events. Controls operate on feedback of deviations which exceed acceptable performance standards. A few forms of control in our Company are organization, policies, systems, procedures, instructions, standards, committees, forecasts, budgets, schedules, records, charts of accounts, methods, devices, and reports.

Perhaps the finest testimonial to the success of operational audit activities occurs when management specifically requests internal audit assistance in resolving a problem that has arisen or in developing plans for operating changes. Such requests suggest that the internal auditors have attained the ultimate in acceptance of their services. Under such circumstances internal audit is providing an in-house consultation service in response to management-generated demand for such service, and providing such service can result in a request that the member of the internal audit staff who was involved be transferred into a position with direct management responsibility. Under such circumstances internal audit is effectively used as a training ground for line managers, with ultimate advantage to both the individual involved and the organization as a whole.

### Summary of Internal Audit Objectives

To bring the preceding broad-ranging discussion of internal auditing into sharper focus, the internal audit function should have organizational independence and should operate under a Charter that grants the right to carry out all activities necessary to accomplish the following objectives:

> –*Evaluation* of the performance of the various functional units within the organization, especially in terms of operating efficiency and the implementation of controls designed to achieve optimum results.
>
> –Ascertaining *compliance* with the organization's operating policies and procedures, and with the various controls that have been instituted.
>
> –*Verification* of the reliability and integrity of the operating and financial information on which management and others must rely in performing their

responsibilities. The existence of the organization's resources for which accountability is maintained should also be verified.

## Legislative Government Auditing

The present activities of the U.S. General Accounting Office originated with the passage of the Government Corporation Control Act of 1945 and the subsequent development of the Comprehensive Audit Program in 1949 by the Comptroller General in his capacity as GAO head. As an outgrowth of these activities, the Comptroller General instituted an interagency working group, composed of representatives of the GAO and federal executive departments and agencies, to develop a statement of government audit standards. The group was assisted by audit representatives of various state, county, and municipal governments and by representatives of a number of leading professional organizations. The working group produced a report that was published by the Comptroller General in 1972 under the title *Standards for Audit of Governmental Organizations, Programs, Activities and Functions.*

### Government Auditing Standards

The introduction to these standards contains the following statement about the basis for the standards:

> A fundamental tenet of a democratic society holds that governments and agencies entrusted with public resources and the authority for applying them have a responsibility to render a full accounting of their activities. This accountability is inherent in the governmental process and is not always specifically identified by legislative provision. This governmental accountability should identify not only the objects for which the public resources have been devoted but also the manner and effect of their application.

> This concept of accountability is woven into the basic premises supporting these standards. These standards provide for a scope of audit that includes not only financial and compliance auditing but also auditing for economy, efficiency, and achievement of desired results. Provision for such a scope of audit is not intended to imply that all audits are presently being conducted this way or that such an extensive scope is always desirable. However, an audit that would include provision for the interests of all potential users of government audits would ordinarily include provision for auditing all the above elements of the accountability of the responsible officials.

> Definitions of the three elements of such an audit follow.

> 1. *Financial and compliance*—determines (a) whether financial operations are properly conducted, (b) whether the financial reports of an audited entity are presented fairly, and (c) whether the entity has complied with applicable laws and regulations.

2. *Economy and efficiency*—determines whether the entity is managing or utilizing its resources (personnel, property, space, and so forth) in an economical and efficient manner and the causes of any inefficiencies or uneconomical practices, including inadequacies in management information systems, administrative procedures, or organizational structure.

3. *Program results*—determines whether the desired results or benefits are being achieved, whether the objectives established by the legislature or other authorizing body are being met, and whether the agency has considered alternatives which might yield desired results at a lower cost.

Following the above introductory statement is a summary of the standards, which is supplemented by detailed explanations of the various standards. The summary is here quoted in full, to indicate the orientation and scope of the standards. The reader will note the influence of the AICPA's *Generally Accepted Auditing Standards* but should especially consider the aspects of the governmental standards that are unique to that type of audit activity.

### General Standards

1. The full scope of an audit of a governmental program, function, activity, or organization should encompass:

 a. An examination of financial transactions, accounts, and reports, including an evaluation of compliance with applicable laws and regulations.
 b. A review of efficiency and economy in the use of resources.
 c. A review to determine whether desired results are effectively achieved.

In determining the scope for a particular audit, responsible officials should give consideration to the needs of the potential users of the results of that audit.

2. The auditors assigned to perform the audit must collectively possess adequate professional proficiency for the tasks required.

3. In all matters relating to the audit work, the audit organization and the individual auditors shall maintain an independent attitude.

4. Due professional care is to be used in conducting the audit and in preparing related reports.

### Examination and Evaluation Standards

1. Work is to be adequately planned.

2. Assistants are to be properly supervised.

3. A review is to be made of compliance with legal and regulatory requirements.

4. An evaluation is to be made of the system of internal control to assess the extent it can be relied upon to ensure accurate information, to ensure

compliance with laws and regulations, and to provide for efficient and effective operations.

5.   Sufficient, competent, and relevant evidence is to be obtained to afford a reasonable basis for the auditor's opinions, judgments, conclusions, and recommendations.

## Reporting Standards

1.   Written audit reports are to be submitted to the appropriate officials of the organizations requiring or arranging for the audits. Copies of the reports should be sent to other officials who may be responsible for taking action on audit findings and recommendations and to others responsible or authorized to receive such reports. Copies should also be made available for public inspection.

2.   Reports are to be issued on or before the dates specified by law, regulation, or other arrangement and, in any event, as promptly as possible so as to make the information available for timely use by management and by legislative officials.

3.   Each report shall:

   a.   Be as concise as possible but, at the same time, clear and complete enough to be understood by the users.
   b.   Present factual matter accurately, completely, and fairly.
   c.   Present findings and conclusions objectively and in language as clear and simple as the subject matter permits.
   d.   Include only factual information, findings, and conclusions that are adequately supported by enough evidence in the auditor's working papers to demonstrate or prove, when called upon, the bases for the matters reported and their correctness and reasonableness. Detailed supporting information should be included in the report to the extent necessary to make a convincing presentation.
   e.   Include, when possible, the auditor's recommendations for actions to effect improvements in problem areas noted in his audit and to otherwise make improvements in operations. Information on underlying causes of problems reported should be included to assist in implementing or devising corrective actions.
   f.   Place primary emphasis on improvement rather than on criticism of the past; critical comments should be presented in balanced perspective, recognizing any unusual difficulties or circumstances faced by the operating officials concerned.
   g.   Identify and explain issues and questions needing further study and consideration by the auditor or others.
   h.   Include recognition of noteworthy accomplishments, particularly when management improvements in one program or activity may be applicable elsewhere.
   i.   Include recognition of the views of responsible officials of the organization, program, function, or activity audited on the auditor's findings, conclusions, and recommendations. Except where the possibility of fraud or other compelling reason may require different treatment, the auditor's tentative findings and conclusions should be reviewed with such officials. When possible, without undue delay, their views

should be obtained in writing and objectively considered and presented in preparing the final report.

j.  Clearly explain the scope and objectives of the audit.

k.  State whether any significant pertinent information has been omitted because it is deemed privileged or confidential. The nature of such information should be described, and the law or other basis under which it is withheld should be stated.

4.  Each audit report containing financial reports shall:

a.  Contain an expression of the auditor's opinion on whether the information contained in the financial reports is presented fairly. If the auditor cannot express an opinion, the reasons therefore should be stated in the audit report.

b.  State whether the financial reports have been prepared in accordance with generally accepted or prescribed accounting principles applicable to the organization, program, function, or activity audited and on a consistent basis from one period to the next. Material changes in accounting policies and procedures and their effect on the financial reports are to be explained in the audit report.

c.  Contain appropriate supplementary information about the contents of the financial reports as may be necessary for full and informative disclosure about the financial operations of the organization, program, function, or activity audited. Violations of legal or other regulatory requirements, including instances of noncompliance, shall be explained in the audit report.

### Supplementary Standards for Computer-Based Systems

The above statement of standards was supplemented in 1979 by the pamphlet *Auditing Computer-Based Systems,* which addresses some special problems associated with audits that involve computer processing of data. The supplementary standards require that in these circumstances the auditor is expected to:

1.  Actively participate in reviewing the design and development of new data processing systems or applications, and significant modifications thereto, as a normal part of the audit function.

2.  Review general controls in data processing systems to determine that: (a) controls have been designed according to management directions and legal requirements, and (b) such controls are operating effectively to provide reliability of, and security over, the data being processed.

3.  Review application controls of installed data processing applications to assess their reliability in processing data in a timely, accurate, and complete manner.

## Independent, Internal, and Governmental Auditing Contrasted

All three types of audit activity have a fundamental concern for the fairness, completeness, and reliability of reported accounting information, although only independent and governmental auditors express an opinion on the accounting information. Governmental auditors have an additional concern that the underlying transactions being reported are in compliance with all laws and regulations applicable to the activities of the agency being audited.

All three sets of standards also recognize the importance of independence, proficiency, and due professional care in the performance of audit activity. Further, each of the three sets of standards refers to internal control, but only GAAS and the governmental standards refer to reliance on the system of internal control in expressing an opinion on reported financial information.

Evaluation of internal control is required in each instance, but only the internal and governmental standards are directly concerned with the effectiveness of internal control as an aspect of operations management. Internal and governmental standards are also concerned with efficiency and economy in the conduct of operations, as important variables affecting the results that have been achieved.

Finally, the governmental standards are unique in referring to an evaluation of the results achieved by the audited organization as an indication of the effectiveness of its programmed activities.

This chapter on intraorganizational audits concludes with an analysis of the major differences between internal and independent audits, excerpts from actual internal audit reports in order to provide a basis for further understanding the approach and the scope of operational audits performed by internal auditors, and some comments about internal auditing in smaller businesses.

### *Distinguishing Characteristics of Internal Auditing and Independent Auditing*

Although there is considerable similarity between internal auditing and independent auditing with respect to financial audits, even in this regard it is the differences that are most important to clearly understanding both types of activity. These differences are summarized as follows:

| Internal Auditing | Independent Auditing |
|---|---|
| Audit is performed by a company employee. | Audit is performed by a professional practitioner who is engaged as an independent contractor. |
| Primary concern is in serving the needs of the organization. | Primary concern is in fulfilling the needs of third parties for reliable financial data. |

## Internal Auditing

Internal audits have a direct influence on the scope of the independent audit.

Operations and internal control are reviewed primarily in order to develop improvements and induce compliance with established policies and procedures; not limited to financial matters.

Work is subdivided primarily according to operating functions and lines of management responsibility.

Auditor is directly concerned with the detection and prevention of fraud.

Auditor should be independent organizationally but ready to respond to the needs and desires of all elements of management.

Review of company activities is continuous.

## Independent Auditing

Independent audit is directly influenced by scope and quality of internal audit as a vital aspect of internal control.

Operations and internal control are reviewed primarily in order to determine scope of examination and reliability of financial data.

Work is subdivided primarily in relation to principal balance sheet and income statement accounts, grouped in relation to transactions common to both.

Auditor is incidentally concerned with the detection and prevention of fraud, except as financial statements may be materially affected.

Auditor should be independent of management both in fact and in mental attitude.

Examination of financial statements and supporting evidence is periodic—usually once a year.

## *Selected Excerpts from Internal Audit Reports*

The internal audit reports from which the following passages have been selected were prepared by internal auditors of Lockheed Aircraft Corporation. The company's extensive internal auditing department has been granted freedom to operate under the most advanced concepts of the internal auditor's functions and responsibilities, and the selections are intended to suggest how far afield from the area of accounting the internal auditor can profitably proceed in seeking to fulfill responsibility for service to the organization. The excerpts also illustrate the manner in which the examination focuses on the objectives of evaluation, compliance, and verification.

The first report deals with the activities of two sections of the company's inspection department.

### Purpose and Scope

We have made a review of the activities of the "A" and "B" Fabrication Inspection organizations in order to determine whether the functions and responsibilities assigned to those organizations were being performed in a satisfactory manner.

Our review was made to determine specifically:

1.  Whether the Company had provided procedures, in conformance with military requirements, which should ensure, if followed, satisfactory quality control over the parts and assemblies produced by the "A" and "B" Fabrication organizations;

2.  Whether inspection personnel had an adequate and consistent understanding of those procedures;

3.  Whether inspectors had been provided with adequate criteria for the acceptance of parts and assemblies;

4.  Whether inspections were adequate both as to timeliness and as to quality;

5.  Whether generally adequate corrective action had been taken to prevent the recurrence of defects discovered; and

6.  Whether the records of inspections maintained by the "A" and "B" Fabrication Inspection organizations were generally accurate and complete.

During the course of our examination, we (1) reviewed military specifications relating to quality control, (2) reviewed Company procedures relating to quality control, (3) interviewed and observed inspection personnel as to their understanding of those procedures, and (4) made tests of inspection records. Our review did not cover the use of sampling techniques by Inspection. We intend to examine this activity in connection with our review of the activities of the Inspection Technical Services Department.

### Opinions, Findings, and Suggestions

We were very much impressed with the progressive attitude displayed by Inspection management in such matters as the adoption of a new approach to fabrication inspection which involves the inspection of parts in process rather than only after completion (on its face, a definite improvement over the old method), the adoption and increasing emphasis on sampling techniques in parts inspection, and the practice of encouraging Production to assume a greater responsibility in the discovery of defective parts.

In our opinion, the functions and responsibilities assigned to the "A" and "B" Fabrication Inspection organizations were being performed in a generally satisfactory manner.

Among the comments on specific findings are those relating to the examination of Inspection Tags prepared by the first of the two inspection groups:

We found that Inspection Tags prepared and processed by "A" Fabrication Inspection were reasonably complete and accurate with the following exceptions:

1.  We noted a number of instances in which Inspection Tags bore manually written Inspection stamp numbers rather than the impression of the

originating inspector's stamp. Since the purpose of issuing stamps to inspectors is to ensure that only authorized personnel accept or withhold parts, we believe that Inspection should not process any Inspection Tags which do not carry the originating inspector's stamp. The applicable Inspection Directive clearly requires the use of the stamp.

We discussed this matter with the "A" Materials Review Coordinator and the Manager of the "A" Machined Parts and Sheet Metal Inspection Department and were informed that "A" Fabrication inspectors would be instructed to conform to the directive.

2. A comparison of 43 Inspection Tags with the Shop Orders against which the rejections had been made disclosed seven instances in which the Inspection Tag showed an incorrect Lot number and nine instances in which the Inspection Tag showed incorrect or incomplete Work Order charges. While errors in Lot numbers shown on Inspection Tags may not be overly significant, errors in Work Order charges shown on the Inspection Tags may result in incorrect accounting for rework and, possibly, replacement charges. Most of the Work Order inaccuracies which we noted involve instances in which not all of the Work Orders shown on the applicable Shop Order against which the rejection was made were noted on the Inspection Tag as required by the applicable Authorizing Directive.

We discussed this matter with responsible supervision and were informed that inspectors would be cautioned to improve the accuracy and completeness of Lot numbers and Work Orders shown on Inspection Tags.

The following report deals with an examination of certain controls maintained by the company's engineering department.

### Purpose and Scope

We have made an examination to determine whether it appears: (1) that the Engineering Branch management has provided adequate controls, which if operated effectively, would ensure, insofar as practicable, that production drawings, including Purchased Equipment drawings, Special Standards drawings, and related change documents will be accurate at the time of release to the Manufacturing organization; (2) that certain of these controls which we felt qualified to test were operating in a satisfactory manner; and (3) that the Engineering Branch management and the Project Engineering organization have provided an effective program designed to reduce engineering errors.

Specifically, our review of certain of the controls was directed toward determining: (1) whether engineering approval signatures as required by Engineering Management Memo 2030 and other applicable engineering procedures were being obtained on all production drawings and changes released by the Project Engineering organization; (2) whether all production drawings and change documents were being checked by the Project Checking Groups or other authorized personnel before being released by the Project Engineering organization; and (3) whether all significant errors noted and recorded by engineering checkers on check prints which they reviewed were being corrected prior to the release of the applicable production drawing or change document.

Our examination of the controls which have been provided was limited because we did not feel qualified to make tests of production drawings to determine whether the reviews made by project supervision and design specialists were adequate or whether the checking activity was being performed in a satisfactory manner.

During our examination, we: (1) reviewed the policies and procedures which pertained to the controls over the quality of engineering drawings and related change documents; (2) carried on discussions with personnel engaged in those control activities; (3) reviewed the error-study programs of the Project Engineering organization; and (4) made such observations and tests as we deemed necessary.

### Opinions, Findings, and Suggestions

We have discussed in the preceding paragraphs the direct measures which the Engineering Branch was taking at the time of our review in their program to reduce engineering errors. Previously we outlined other action taken which we classified as indirect.

We think that all of the error-reduction measures which we have discussed are very good but believe that the error-reduction program should go further. In that connection, it seems to us that the action taken thus far is directed more toward improving the means of detecting errors than on means for reducing the original commission of errors. We believe that if the original work performed by the design groups contained fewer errors this would tend to improve the quality of the checking work and, as a result, the drawings when released would contain fewer errors. We do not mean to imply that no effort has been taken to improve the quality of the original work for we have previously mentioned certain indirect action taken for that purpose. In addition, group engineers in each project informed us that drawings requiring correction as a result of the checking activity are reviewed in the design groups, and the persons responsible for the errors are required to make the necessary corrections. Such reviews serve a useful purpose of apprising design group personnel of the errors in drawings which they have released to the checking groups. Although this practice is commendable, we do not believe that such action alone is sufficient to bring about a strong and steady improvement in quality of original work performed by the design groups. We feel that there is a need for a program of continuous accumulation and reporting of statistical information by design group relating to the number of errors found as a result of the checking activity. It seems to us that this would bring about a greater emphasis on the quality of the work performed by individual design groups and also provide a factual, numerical basis for the Project Engineers to use in evaluating the performance of the Design Group Engineers. We discussed this with cognizant personnel and were informed that such a program was being formulated. In view of this action, we have nothing further to suggest.

## Examples of Internal Audit Projects

To further suggest the breadth of a comprehensive program of internal audit, a number of internal audit projects have been selected from the 3-year schedule of projects of the internal auditing department of Lockheed Aircraft Corporation. The complete schedule lists well over one hundred projects, which are grouped according to major departmental responsibilities: manufacturing, engineering, finance and accounting, marketing, and industrial relations. For example, under the Manufacturing Manager are grouped projects relating to manufacturing control, manufacturing engineering, material purchasing and handling, quality control, and production management. Nineteen separate projects concern manufacturing engineering, classified under the headings of tool engineering, process control, plant engineering, and project planning. The individual projects pertaining to tool engineering are

> Tool Inspection Department
> Project Tool Control Department
> Perishable Tools and Small Tool Repair Parts
> Standard Tool Cribs
> Tool Shop Load Forecasting
> Project Tool Design
> Manufacturing Standards

### Internal Auditing and the Smaller Business

The delegation of authority within an organization involves a need for some means of ascertaining how satisfactorily the associated responsibility has been discharged. A properly designed accounting system should capture and provide a basis for reporting on as many aspects of the performance of assigned responsibilities as possible, but some aspects of performance cannot be directly measured by accounting data. For example, how effectively work is organized and whether adequate controls have been instituted may not be readily apparent from a review of accounting outputs. Some form of direct review of the delegated activity may represent the only feasible means of evaluating the resulting performance. In small organizations, that review may be accomplished by the owner/manager, but as the organization grows and there is insufficient time available to the owner/manager for those review activities, responsibility for such reviews may be assigned to the organization's controller. As growth continues, the controller will likewise find a lack of time to make the desired reviews, and at that point the separate internal audit function is likely to be recognized, with further growth eventually resulting in the divorcing of the internal audit function from the control function and establishing it as an independent activity.

Of primary importance, review activity should be carried out, regardless of the size of the organization that is involved, and hence the question is not *whether* internal auditing should be done, but *who* should do it. In terms of the latter question, a manufacturing concern or one engaged in distribution is not likely to be able to justify a full-time position for internal auditing until there are in the neighborhood of 500 employees, but the threshold number would be considerably smaller for a financial institution because of the higher proportion of employees engaged in clerical activities.

The following examples are intended to suggest some internal audit activities that should be carried out regardless of the size of the organization. In smaller organizations the owner/manager would have to assume responsibility for the activity. Whenever there are cash collections, it is desirable to reduce the risk of loss from theft or burglary by endorsing customers' checks "For Deposit Only" as soon as they are received. This simple procedure is, however, one that is easily forgotten. Hence, the checks in the cash drawer should be examined from time to time to be certain that they have been properly endorsed.

A different but related problem would exist in the case of credit sales. A basic control would be that sales should be made only to customers for whom credit has been authorized. Also, every invoice that is written should be accounted for and verified as having been charged to accounts receivable. Credits to accounts receivable should be made only from the cash receipts record, except as the manager may approve allowances, returns, or the write-off of uncollectible accounts. To be assured that the controls are operative and all cash receipts have been properly accounted for, the owner or manager should, from time to time, leaf through the posted invoices to ascertain that sales are being made only to customers whose credit standing is good and that there are no missing numbers. The accuracy of the listing of the invoices for the daily sales record should be tested, and the record footed and the posting traced to the accounts receivable control. Control account postings for cash receipts should be balanced with bank deposits, and the control account reviewed for any credit entries that have not been approved. Also, periodically the owner or manager should balance customers' statements with the receivables control, place the statements in the mail, and then scrutinize the incoming mail for any correspondence from customers who have taken exception to the statements they have received.

These examples conclude the discussion of intraorganizational auditing, and in the next chapter the discussion returns to the consideration of audits by auditors who are external to the organization being audited. These auditors, as independent contractors, are not subject to control by clients, with the possible exception of their dependence on clients for the audit fee. The term *independent auditors* has been chosen in this text to stress that independent relationship, even though the term *external auditors* would be more consistent with the term *internal auditors*.

### Appendix—Standards for the Professional Practice of Internal Auditing[1]

(Each standard is followed by guidelines describing suitable means of achieving the standard, but only those guidelines that would be helpful

[1]Copyright 1978 by The Institute of Internal Auditors, Inc., Altamonte Springs, Florida. Reproduced by permission.

in gaining an initial understanding of internal auditing have been selected and included in the following excerpts. Dashed lines indicate guidelines that have been omitted.)

100 INDEPENDENCE—Internal auditors should be independent of the activities they audit.

.01 Internal auditors are independent when they can carry out their work freely and objectively. Independence permits internal auditors to render the impartial and unbiased judgments essential to the proper conduct of audits. It is achieved through organizational status and objectivity.

110 *Organizational Status*—The organizational status of the internal auditing department should be sufficient to permit the accomplishment of its audit responsibilities.

.01 Internal auditors should have the support of management and of the board of directors so that they can gain the cooperation of auditees and perform their work free from interference.

.1 The director of the internal auditing department should be responsible to an individual in the organization with sufficient authority to promote independence and to ensure broad audit coverage, adequate consideration of audit reports, and appropriate action on audit recommendations.

.2 The director should have direct communication with the board. Regular communication with the board helps assure independence and provides a means for the board and the director to keep each other informed on matters of mutual interest.

.3 Independence is enhanced when the board concurs in the appointment or removal of the director of the internal auditing department.

.4 The purpose, authority, and responsibility of the internal auditing department should be defined in a formal written document (charter). The director should seek approval of the charter by management as well as acceptance by the board. The charter should (a) establish the department's position within the organization; (b) authorize access to records, personnel, and physical properties relevant to the performance of audits; and (c) define the scope of internal auditing activities.

.5 The director of internal auditing should submit annually to management for approval and to the board for its information a summary of the department's audit work schedule, staffing plan, and financial budget. The director should also submit all significant interim changes for approval and information. Audit work schedules, staffing plans, and financial budgets should inform management and the board of the scope of internal auditing work and of any limitations placed on that scope.

.6 The director of internal auditing should submit activity reports to management and to the board annually or more frequently as necessary. Activity reports should highlight significant audit findings and recommendations and should inform management and the board of any significant deviations from approved audit work schedules, staffing plans, and financial budgets, and the reasons for them.

120 *Objectivity*—Internal auditors should be objective in performing audits.

.01 Objectivity is an independent mental attitude which internal auditors should maintain in performing audits. Internal auditors are not to subordinate their judgment on audit matters to that of others.

.02 Objectivity requires internal auditors to perform audits in such a manner that they have an honest belief in their work product and that no significant quality compromises are made. Internal auditors are not to be placed in situations in which they feel unable to make objective professional judgments.

.1 Staff assignments should be made so that potential and actual conflicts of interest and bias are avoided. The director should periodically obtain from the audit staff information concerning potential conflicts of interest and bias.

.2 Internal auditors should report to the director any situations in which a conflict of interest or bias is present or may reasonably be inferred. The director should then reassign such auditors.

.3 Staff assignments of internal auditors should be rotated periodically whenever it is practicable to do so.

.4 Internal auditors should not assume operating responsibilities. But if on occasion management directs internal auditors to perform nonaudit work, it should be understood that they are not functioning as internal auditors. Moreover, objectivity is presumed to be impaired when internal auditors audit any activity for which they had authority or responsibility. This impairment should be considered when reporting audit results.

.5 Persons transferred to or temporarily engaged by the internal auditing department should not be assigned to audit those activities they previously performed until a reasonable period of time has elapsed. Such assignments are presumed to impair objectivity and should be considered when supervising the audit work and reporting audit results.

.6 The results of internal auditing work should be reviewed before the related audit report is released to provide reasonable assurance that the work was performed objectively.

.03 The internal auditor's objectivity is not adversely affected when the auditor recommends standards of control for systems or reviews procedures before they are implemented. Designing, installing, and operating systems are not audit functions. Also, the drafting of procedures for systems is not an audit function. Performing such activities is presumed to impair audit objectivity.

200 PROFFESSIONAL PROFICIENCY—Internal audits should be performed with proficiency and due professional care.

210 *Staffing*—The internal auditing department should provide assurance that the technical proficiency and educational background of internal auditors are appropriate for the audits to be performed.

220 *Knowledge, Skills, and Disciplines*—The internal auditing department should possess or should obtain the knowledge, skills, and disciplines needed to carry out its audit responsibilities.

.01 The internal auditing staff should collectively possess the knowledge and skills essential to the practice of the profession within the organization. These attributes include proficiency in applying internal auditing standards, procedures, and techniques.

.02 The internal auditing department should have employees or use consultants who are qualified in such disciplines as accounting, economics, finance, statistics, electronic data processing, engineering, taxation, and law as needed to meet audit responsibilities. Each member of the department, however, need not be qualified in all of these disciplines.

230 *Supervision*—The internal auditing department should provide assurance that internal audits are properly supervised.

240 *Compliance with Standards of Conduct*—Internal auditors should comply with professional standards of conduct.

.01 The Code of Ethics of the Institute of Internal Auditors sets forth standards of conduct and provides a basis for enforcement among its members. The Code calls for high standards of honesty, objectivity, diligence, and loyalty to which internal auditors should conform.

250 *Knowledge, Skills, and Disciplines*—Internal Auditors should possess the knowledge, skills, and disciplines essential to the performance of internal audits.

.01 Each internal auditor should possess certain knowledge and skills as follows:

.1 Proficiency in applying internal auditing standards, procedures, and techniques is required in performing internal audits. Proficiency means the ability to apply knowledge to situations likely to be encountered and to deal with them without extensive recourse to technical research and assistance.

.2 Proficiency in accounting principles and techniques is required of auditors who work extensively with financial records and reports.

.3 An understanding of management principles is required to recognize and evaluate the materiality and significance of deviations from good business practice. An understanding means the ability to apply broad knowledge to situations likely to be encountered, to recognize significant deviations, and to be able to carry out the research necessary to arrive at reasonable solutions.

.4 An appreciation is required of the fundamentals of such subjects as accounting, economics, commercial law, taxation, finance, quantitative methods, and computerized information systems. An appreciation means the ability to recognize the existence of problems or potential problems and to determine the further research to be undertaken or the assistance to be obtained.

260 *Human Relations and Communications*—Internal auditors should be skilled in dealing with people and in communicating effectively.

270 *Continuing Education*—Internal auditors should maintain their technical competence through continuing education.

280 *Due Professional Care*—Internal auditors should exercise due professional care in performing internal audits.

300 SCOPE OF WORK—The scope of the internal audit should encompass the examination and evaluation of the adequacy and effectiveness of the organization's system of internal control and the quality of performance in carrying out assigned responsibilities.

.01 The scope of internal auditing work, as specified in this standard, encompasses what audit work should be performed. It is recognized, however, that management and the board of directors provide general direction as to the scope of work and the activities to be audited.

.02 The purpose of the review for adequacy of the system of internal control is to ascertain whether the system established provides reasonable assurance that the organization's objectives and goals will be met efficiently and economically.

.03 The purpose of the review for effectiveness of the system of internal control is to ascertain whether the system is functioning as intended.

.04   The purpose of the review for quality of performance is to ascertain whether the organization's objectives and goals have been achieved.

.05   The primary objectives of internal control are to ensure:

.1   The reliability and integrity of information

.2   Compliance with policies, plans, procedures, laws, and regulations

.3   The safeguarding of assets

.4   The economical and efficient use of resources

.5   The accomplishment of established objectives and goals for operations or programs

310 *Reliability and Integrity of Information*—Internal auditors should review the reliability and integrity of financial and operating information and the means used to identify, measure, classify, and report such information.

.01 Information systems provide data for decision making, control, and compliance with external requirements. Therefore, internal auditors should examine information systems and, as appropriate, ascertain whether:

.1   Financial and operating records and reports contain accurate, reliable, timely, complete, and useful information.

.2   Controls over record keeping and reporting are adequate and effective.

320 *Compliance with Policies, Plans, Procedures, Laws and Regulations*— Internal auditors should review the systems established to ensure compliance with those policies, plans, procedures, laws, and regulations which could have a significant impact on operations and reports, and should determine whether the organization is in compliance.

.01 Management is responsible for establishing the systems designed to ensure compliance with such requirements as policies, plans, procedures, and applicable laws and regulations. Internal auditors are responsible for determining whether the systems are adequate and effective and whether the activities audited are complying with the appropriate requirements.

330 *Safeguarding of Assets*—Internal auditors should review the means of

safeguarding assets and, as appropriate, verify the existence or such assets.

340 *Economical and Efficient Use of Resources*—Internal auditors should appraise the economy and efficiency with which resources are employed.

.01 Management is responsible for setting operating standards to measure an activity's economical and efficient use of resources. Internal auditors are responsible for determining whether:

.1 Operating standards have been established for measuring economy and efficiency.

.2 Established operating standards are understood and are being met.

.3 Deviations from operating standards are identified, analyzed, and communicated to those responsible for corrective action.

.4 Corrective action has been taken.

.02 Audits related to the economical and efficient use of resources should identify such conditions as:

.1 Underutilized facilities

.2 Nonproductive work

.3 Procedures which are not cost-justified

.4 Overstaffing or understaffing

350 *Accomplishment of Established Objectives and Goals for Operations or Programs*—Internal auditors should review operations or programs to ascertain whether results are consistent with established objectives and goals and whether the operations or programs are being carried out as planned.

.01 Management is responsible for establishing operating or program objectives and goals, developing and implementing control procedures, and accomplishing desired operating or program results. Internal auditors should ascertain whether such objectives and goals conform with those of the organization and whether they are being met.

.02 Internal auditors can provide assistance to managers who are developing objectives, goals, and systems by determining whether the underlying assumptions are appropriate; whether accurate, current, and relevant information is being used; and whether suitable controls have been incorporated into the operations or programs.

400 PERFORMANCE OF AUDIT WORK—Audit work should include planning the audit, examining and evaluating information, communicating results, and following up.

410 *Planning the Audit*—Internal auditors should plan each audit.

420 *Examining and Evaluating Information*—Internal auditors should collect, analyze, interpret, and document information to support audit results.

430 *Communicating Results*—Internal auditors should report the results of their audit work.

440 *Following Up*—Internal auditors should follow up to ascertain that appropriate action is taken on reported audit findings.

500 MANAGEMENT OF THE INTERNAL AUDITING DEPARTMENT—The director of internal auditing should properly manage the internal auditing department.

510 *Purpose, Authority, and Responsibility*—The director of internal auditing should have a statement of purpose, authority, and responsibility for the internal auditing department.

.01 The director of internal auditing is responsible for seeking the approval of management and the acceptance of the board of a formal written document (charter) for the internal auditing department.

520 *Planning*—The director of internal auditing should establish plans to carry out the responsibilities of the internal auditing department.

530 *Policies and Procedures*—The director of internal auditing should provide written policies and procedures to guide the audit staff.

540 *Personnel Management and Development*—The director of internal auditing should establish a program for selecting and developing the human resources of the internal auditing department.

550 *External Auditors*—The director of internal auditing should coordinate internal and external audit efforts.

560 *Quality Assurance*—The director of internal auditing should establish and maintain a quality assurance program to evaluate the operations of the internal auditing department.

.01 The purpose of this program is to provide reasonable assurance that audit work conforms with these Standards, the internal auditing department's charter, and other applicable standards. A quality assurance program should include the following elements:

.1   Supervision

.2   Internal reviews

.3   External reviews

.02 *Supervision* of the work of the internal auditors should be carried out continually to assure conformance with internal auditing standards, departmental policies, and audit programs.

.03 *Internal reviews* should be performed periodically by members of the internal auditing staff to appraise the quality of the audit work performed. These reviews should be performed in the same manner as any other internal audit.

.04 *External reviews* of the internal auditing department should be performed to appraise the quality of the department's operations. These reviews should be performed by qualified persons who are independent of the organization and who do not have either a real or an apparent conflict of interest. Such reviews should be conducted at least once every three years. On completion of the review, a formal, written report should be issued. The report should express an opinion as to the department's compliance with the *Standards for the Professional Practice of Internal Auditing* and, as appropriate, should include recommendations for improvement.

## Questions/Problems

For multiple-choice questions 4-1 through 4-5, indicate the letter of the single answer that *best* completes the statement or answers the question, and justify the choice that you have made.

**4-1.** The independent auditor should acquire an understanding of a client's internal audit function to determine whether the work of internal auditors will be a factor in determining the nature, timing, and extent of the independent auditor's procedures. The work performed by internal auditors might be such a factor when the internal auditor's work includes

a. Verification of the mathematical accuracy of invoices.
b. Review of administrative practices to improve efficiency and achieve management objectives.
c. Study and evaluation of internal accounting control.
d. Preparation of internal financial reports for management purposes.

(Uniform CPA Examination)

**4-2.** If the independent auditor decides that the work performed by internal auditors may have a bearing on the independent auditor's own procedures, the independent auditor should consider the objectivity of the internal auditors. One method of judging objectivity is to

a. Review the recommendations made in the reports of internal auditors.
b. Examine, on a test basis, documentary evidence of the work performed by internal auditors.
c. Inquire of management about the qualifications of the internal audit staff.
d. Consider the client's practices for hiring, training, and supervising the internal audit staff.

(Uniform CPA Examination)

**4-3.** In comparison to the external auditor, an internal auditor is more likely to be concerned with

a. Internal administrative control.
b. Cost accounting procedures.
c. Operational auditing.
d. Internal accounting control.

(Uniform CPA Examination)

**4-4.** Appropriate duties of an internal audit department would include

    a.  Reconciliation of bank accounts.

    b.  Designing a new accounting system.

    c.  Recommending changes in the accounting system.

    d.  All of the above activities would be appropriate for an internal audit department.

**4-5.** The Lockheed internal auditors' recommendation that the error-reduction program for engineering drawings should be expanded would have resulted from:

    a.  Operational auditing activities.

    b.  Compliance activities.

    c.  Verification activities.

    d.  None of the above.

**4-6.** Contrast generally accepted auditing standards and internal auditing standards, pointing out the major differences and stating what you believe accounts for those differences.

**4-7.** If a company is large enough to warrant having internal auditors, why will it usually be desirable to have an internal audit program rather than rely on the independent auditor for the necessary work?

**4-8.** "Internal auditors need not be concerned about the accuracy of company records if the company has an independent audit, since the independent auditors will make the necessary verification." Do you agree? Explain.

**4-9.** Give some examples of evaluation activities of the internal auditor that are not directly concerned with internal control.

**4-10.** What are the two major aspects of the internal auditor's independence?

**4-11.** Suggest some of the internal audit steps that should be performed from time to time by the manager of a small business that does not have an internal auditor.

**4-12.** Any one of several management officials may be selected to be responsible for the work of the internal auditor. List each official by title and explain why it would be good or bad to have the auditor report to that official.

**4-13.** How do operational audits differ from the more traditional internal auditing?

**4-14.** How should the concern of the internal auditor and the independent auditor differ with respect to a company's internal control in the areas of accounting controls and administrative controls?

**4-15.** Internal auditing is a staff function found in virtually every large corporation. The internal audit function is also performed in many smaller companies as a part-time activity of individuals who may or may not be called internal auditors. The differences between the audits by independent public accountants and the work of internal auditors are more basic than is generally recognized.

a. Briefly discuss the auditing work performed by the independent public accountant and the internal auditor with regard to:
   (1) Auditing objectives.
   (2) General nature of auditing work.
b. In conducting his audit, the independent public accountant must evaluate the work of the internal auditor. Discuss briefly the reason for this evaluation.
c. List the auditing procedures used by an independent public accountant in evaluating the work of the internal auditor.

(Uniform CPA Examination)

# Chapter 5

# ELEMENTS OF THE AUDIT PROCESS

We have noted that the objective of an independent audit is the accreditation of financial statements through the opinion reported by the auditor on the statements. We have also noted that the professional licensing that identifies qualified auditors by such titles as certified public accountant or chartered accountant significantly enhances the assurance conveyed by such auditors' reports.

This chapter is directed to the audit process that establishes the basis for reporting an opinion on a client's financial statements. Two separate but closely related activities are involved in this audit process:

1. Thoroughly evaluating the accounting system that converts into financial statements the data that pertain to events affecting the client.

This evaluation must consider internal controls that ensure the accuracy and completeness of the financial statements as well as conformity of the statements with generally accepted accounting principles, thereby communicating all essential financial and operating information to interested parties through the standardized language of accounting.

2. Sampling evidence in support of the assets, equities, revenues, and expenses reflected in the financial statements. This sampling of evidence is to provide further assurance to the auditor of the propriety, accuracy, and conformity with generally accepted accounting principles of the information generated by the client's accounting system and incorporated in the financial statements.

All audit activities must be carried out in accordance with generally accepted auditing standards, and the entire process must be closely controlled for quality to ensure the reliability of the resulting audit reports.

### System Flowchart Illustrating the Auditing Framework

The *system* flowchart presented in Figure 5-1 indicates the general framework of financial statement audits and provides an overall view of the audit process. The inputs and outputs of the audit are shown, as well as the relationship of the audit to the client's accounting system and the inputs and outputs of that system. Evidence of transactions and events affecting the client entity, which are inputs to the client's accounting system and are used by the auditor, are shown as well defined elements, as are the outputs of the accounting system and of the audit process. Less well defined, as suggested by the dotted boxes, are the generally accepted accounting principles that should be followed by the client in designing and operating the accounting system and the generally accepted auditing standards to be followed by the auditor in the various phases of the audit. Interpretation and judgment are vital in applying these broadly stated principles and standards to both the operation of the accounting system and the execution of the audit. Each of the ten auditing standards (Chapter 1) addresses a key aspect of the audit for which the auditor must judge that an appropriate level of quality has been maintained.

The varied means of satisfying the general standard pertaining to the auditor's technical training and proficiency are suggested by the amorphous form of that input. Personnel involved in the audit will include the partner of the accounting firm responsible for the audit engagement and such members of the firm's staff as may be assigned to participate in the engagement. Various levels of training and experience will be involved, with training and experience obtained in various ways. Included will be formal education, generally in business and accounting and leading to a baccalaureate degree or, increasingly in these days, to a master's

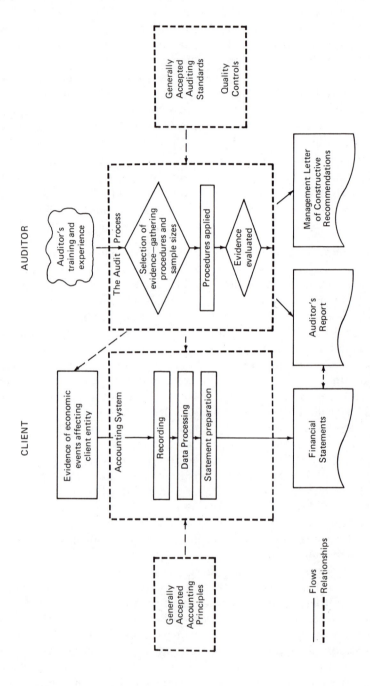

**Figure 5-1.** System Flowchart Indicating the Framework of Auditing

degree. Training and experience is also gained through supervised participation in a variety of audits, with increasing responsibility and decreasing supervision accompanying staff members' development. The third element of personnel preparation will be the continuing education and training that the individual staff members receive through seminars and courses presented by the accounting firm or various professional organizations.

The audit process uses these inputs through a variety of decisions involved in applying audit procedures and interpreting the results of those procedures, which the next section considers more fully. The outputs of the process are the client's audited statements—as modified if necessary according to the auditor's findings and recommendations and with the client's consent—and any constructive recommendations to be made to the client, which result from the auditor's extensive study and testing of the client's accounting and operating systems.

### Program Flowchart of the Audit Process

The audit process represented in the system flowchart is elaborated on in the *program* flowchart presented in Figure 5-2. The audit process may be viewed as research designed to test the hypothesis that the client's financial statements present fairly the financial position, results of operations, and changes in financial position of the client entity in conformity with generally accepted accounting principles that have been consistently applied. To ascertain whether the hypothesis can be accepted or must be rejected, the auditor prepares and executes an audit program to examine and evaluate two basically different types of evidence, as suggested earlier by the two types of audit activity involved in the independent audit:

- Indirect evidence in the form of the auditor's evaluation of the client's accounting system—specifically, how well internal controls ensure the accuracy and appropriateness of the data that are recorded and processed to generate the client's financial statements. (Indirect evidence is more fully discussed in Chapter 6.)
- Direct evidence to support the recorded transactions and resulting account balances as they appear in the entity's financial statements. (Direct evidence is more fully discussed in Chapter 7.)

A multitude of decisions must be made throughout the audit process—ranging from the ultimate decision of whether to accept the hypothesis that the client's financial statements are presented fairly in accordance with generally accepted accounting principles, to the lesser decisions, each of which may critically affect the final outcome of the auditor's opinion as expressed in the audit report. In making these deci-

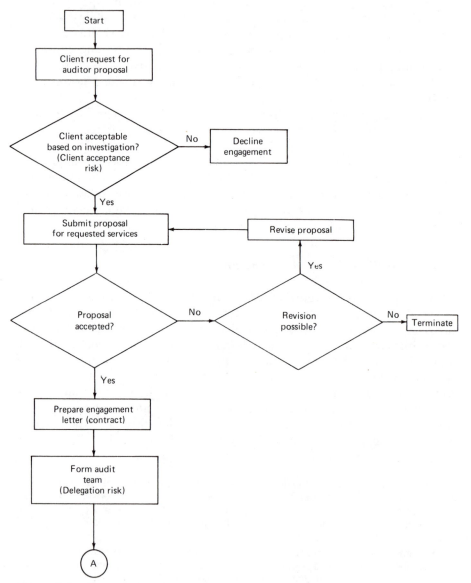

***Figure 5-2.*** Program Flowchart of Audit Process

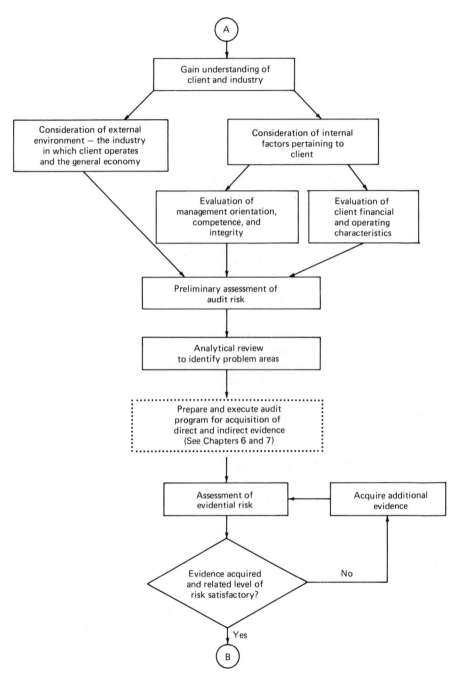

***Figure* 5-2.** Continued

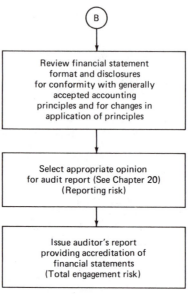

**Figure 5-2.** Continued

sions there is invariably a risk that the decision may be incorrect and the auditor will seek to keep this risk at a tolerable level. There is usually a trade-off whereby the risk can be reduced by incurring the cost of obtaining additional evidence or taking a different course of action. Audit experience gained from past participation in the decision process is indispensable in making decisions about risk and evaluating trade-offs.

### Risks and Decision Making in the Audit Process

The risks associated with the various activities and the related decisions involved in the typical audit are indicated in the program flow chart in Figure 5-2. Each of these risks involves the chance of a wrong decision, which could result in failing to detect a material error in the client's financial statements or issuing an audit report that is subsequently shown to be misleading. A wrong decision when a material misstatement is involved could result in debasement of the firm's reputation for quality audits and possible suit for damages by any party injured as a result of relying on the financial statements on the basis of the auditor's report. Examples of audit decisions with risk implications include whether to accept a new client, which staff members to assign to an engagement and which audit tasks to assign to each, what sample size is appropriate for an audit test, whether evidence that has been examined is adequate support for a recorded figure, whether an exception is present in the evidence, whether a problem should be resolved at the point of discovery or referred to a superior for discussion and resolution, plus many others. The complement of the risk to be assumed is the level of assurance desired, with greater assurance (less risk) normally obtainable only at an increased cost. Each of the types of risk shown in the program flow chart is briefly elaborated on, as follows:

*Client Acceptance Risk.* Prior to accepting an audit client, the auditor will wish to acquire as much information as possible about the client and the client's reputation. Potential clients of questionable standing in the business and financial community tend to be the ones involved in dubious practices and are most likely to have ulterior motives that may lead to attempts to "cook the books" or to prepare misleading financial statements. If nefarious activities are involved, there is always the possibility that the true facts can be successfully concealed from the auditor, only to come to light after the audited financial statements have been released and with consequent legal actions against the auditor by those who have suffered losses.

The fine line between propriety and impropriety must be recognized when investigating potential clients. It may not be obvious whether a tax return reflects a legitimate effort to minimize taxes or an attempt at tax evasion; whether complicated financial dealings are the result of capitalizing on high-risk leverage possibilities or represent an effort to conceal unfavorable circumstances through subterfuge and intent to mislead; or whether the client merely drives a hard bargain or is actually attempting to take advantage of others, and client acceptance risk is evident under these circumstances.

If the prospective client was previously served by another auditor, the successor should discuss with the predecessor any problems or disagreements that may have a bearing on the risk-related decision to accept the client. This consultation process is required by Professional Standards at AU Sec. 315, which states that the initiative in communicating with the predecessor auditor rests with the successor auditor, after obtaining permission from the client to make the necessary inquiries of the predecessor. In any case, however, more information is always better than less, and an auditor's practice is more likely to be free of awkward entanglements and troublesome legal problems if prospective clients are thoroughly investigated and carefully screened.

Even though investigation of a prospective client will rarely lead to a decision that the client acceptance risk is too great and the engagement should be declined, the investigation should be an essential first step in any prospective engagement. Assuming that a favorable decision has been reached, the auditor will prepare and submit to the prospective client a proposal or *engagement letter* (see Professional Standards AU Sec. 8002) identifying the type of service that is involved, such as audit, compilation or review (see Chapter 21), tax, or management advisory services. For audit services the letter should generally include reference to

The objective of an audit of financial statements.

The fact that management has primary responsibility for financial information.

The scope of the audit, including a statement that the audit is to be made in accordance with generally accepted auditing standards.

The form of the report or other communication of results of the engagement.

The fact that there is some unavoidable risk that a misstatement of the financial information may remain undiscovered as a consequence of testing and the inherent limitations of any internal control system.

The necessity of providing full access to records, documents, and other information requested in connection with the audit.

The amount of the fee or the basis on which the fee is to be determined.

Any of a variety of other matters that may pertain to the particular engagement, as discussed in Professional Standards at AU Sec. 8002.

Upon acceptance of the proposal or engagement letter as indicated by the signature of an appropriate officer of the client, that document becomes the contract governing the terms of the engagement and what is expected of each of the parties.

*Delegation Risk.*   Once a client has been accepted and the engagement letter has been prepared, setting forth the services to be performed, the audit team can be assembled. In general the team should include persons who are knowledgeable about SEC filings and regulations if the client is publicly held, and supervisory members of the team should be knowledgeable about the client industry and any accounting problems that are unique to the particular industry, as for example, manufacturing, land development, oil and gas exploration, financial institutions, or various types of retailing organizations.

A partner of the accounting firm will have ultimate responsibility for the work to be done, but most of the actual audit work will be performed by members of the firm's audit staff. Staff should be assigned to the engagement based on knowledge of the client industry and the general level of experience gained from past audits. Typically the more routine tasks will be assigned to staff who are less experienced in performing the work and in making the innumerable decisions likely to arise. The risk associated with delegating the tasks to be performed involves the staff member's skill in handling decisions—either to make any decision that is called for, or when the situation so requires, to refer the decision to someone at a higher level with added experience. Delegation risk involves balancing experience-related decision-making skill with the higher salary and client billing costs associated with greater skill and experience. The optimum choice should produce the minimum risk of a wrong decision, consistent with the penalties likely to be associated with a wrong decision, and the additional cost of a higher level of experience and decision skill.

*Preliminary Assessment of Audit Risk.* The central problem of auditing is assessing what is referred to as audit risk: the risk that there may be a material misstatement of the financial statements that is not detected by the audit process. Stated differently, it is the risk that the auditor may make a Type II error and accept the hypothesis that the financial statements are fairly presented in accordance with generally accepted accounting principles when in fact the hypothesis should be rejected. The Figure 5-2 program flow chart delineates factors that should enter into a preliminary assessment of this audit risk:

1. Knowledge of the client and the industry within which the client operates, including knowledge of problems that are peculiar to the client or to the industry and that may affect the client's financial statements.

2. Knowledge of the general environment within which the client operates, including the trend of the economy and prices, financial trends, the availability of labor and materials, and awareness of the impact that these various factors may be expected to have on the client's financial statements.

3. Evaluation of the orientation, competence, and integrity of the client's management. For example, is management mainly oriented to production, distribution, research, or finance, or does it take a balanced approach to all of the functions and is therefore likely to be coping with problems that develop in any of the areas? Is management primarily oriented toward service or toward profit? Does management tend to deal with problems as they arise on a day-to-day basis or does it successfully anticipate problems through an adequate planning horizon? Additionally there is the question of how competent management is in dealing with problems that are identified. Finally there is the basic question of the integrity of management. Integrity is especially difficult to assess, but any doubt about the integrity of management should be taken as a warning to exercise extreme caution—if indeed the auditor concludes that the engagement can continue rather than be terminated, for under those circumstances resignation from the engagement is likely to be the wiser course of action.

4. Evaluation of client financial and operating characteristics. The auditor should become aware of any financial or operating problems with which the client is confronted. The effect of any such problems must be unequivocally disclosed in the financial statements. The auditor should recognize and anticipate that the existence of these problems may induce the client to try to have the financial statements present a more favorable picture than actually exists. In extreme cases financial or operating problems may raise a question of whether the going concern assumption of accounting may continue to be satisfied, with a consequent problem of disclosing that possibility and the potential impact on the financial statements should bankruptcy occur.

*Evidential Risk.* The system flowchart of the auditing framework, Figure 5-1, indicated the integral role of decision making in the audit process. Chapters 6 and 7 more fully develop and explain what is involved in the audit process, but the essence of that core of activity is the acquisition and evaluation of evidence related to acceptance or rejection of the audit hypothesis. The first standard of field work requires the audit to be adequately planned, with decisions implicit in the planning, taking into account results of the preliminary audit risk assessment and any problems identified through the initial analytical review of the client's financial and operating results. This analytical review should identify such problems as reduced turnover of receivables or inventory, an abnormal gross margin rate for one or more months, marked year-to-year changes in the level of operations or operating results, and other indications of operating or financial aberrations.

The three basic audit variables—1) selection of audit procedures, 2) choice of the point in time at which the procedures are to be applied, and 3) the extent to which supporting evidence is to be sampled—involve decisions based on the preliminary assessment of audit risk and the results of the initial analytical review. Then the evidence acquired as a consequence of these planning decisions must be evaluated in terms of the adequacy of the evidence and the level of assurance desired (risk to be assumed). The program flowchart identifies this risk as the evidential risk and shows the result of a decision that the risk level is too high as a loop back to acquire additional evidence.

*Reporting Risk.* The final element of the overall risk associated with an audit engagement involves reviewing the client's financial statements in relation to the evidence that the auditor has accumulated to support the data contained in the statements. Specifically the auditor must be satisfied that the statements have been prepared in conformity with the consistent application of generally accepted accounting principles and that the classifications, captions, and supplementary notes to the statements give adequate disclosure of all financial and operating information likely to be important or useful to third parties who may use the financial statements. The reporting risk at this point relates to the question of whether the standard form of audit report is appropriate in the circumstances, or whether some modification of the report may be necessary, as is more fully discussed in Chapter 20.

### Total Engagement Risk

The total or ultimate risk associated with an audit engagement is a function of the individual risks assumed in connection with the various phases of the audit. This function may be expressed in the following form as a means of bringing together the various risks that have been discussed:

$$TER = f(ClAR, DelR, PAAR, EvR, RepR)$$

Where

$$
\begin{aligned}
TER\ &= \text{Total Engagement Risk} \\
ClAR\ &= \text{Client Acceptance Risk} \\
DelR\ &= \text{Delegation Risk} \\
PAAR\ &= \text{Preliminary Assessment of Audit Risk} \\
EvR\ &= \text{Evidential Risk} \\
RepR\ &= \text{Reporting Risk}
\end{aligned}
$$

## Accounting Firm Organization

Although there are many individual practitioners in the public accounting profession, most auditing is performed by accountants operating under a partnership arrangement or as a professional corporation. A multimember organization facilitates convenient interchange of ideas, provides the opportunity for specialization that makes it possible to provide more extensive services to clients with greater competence, and permits the development of an organization of sufficient size to handle audit engagements beyond the capacity of the individual practitioner. The need to be able to provide the necessary services for such super corporations as American Telephone and Telegraph company and General Motors has led to accounting firms that are national and international in scope, in contrast to professions in which organizations seldom extend beyond local partnerships.

The largest public accounting firms have hundreds of partners and thousands of employees serving their clients from scores of offices located throughout the world. Within these larger firms individuals normally specialize in such fields as auditing, management services, and tax services. The auditing staff is usually the largest and may reflect further specialization in accordance with the business activities of the firm's clients. Thus there may be specialists in the auditing of business organizations such as manufacturing concerns, banks, department stores, oil companies, and public utilities. In addition, some of the larger firms that serve mostly large clients have formed special groups to better serve their smaller clients on a more personal basis through staff who are generalists rather than specialists.

Management services encompass a broad range of consulting activities that are ideally subject to specialization, for included are such diverse areas as work simplification, production control, operations research, information systems, and electronic data processing. Likewise in the tax area, there may be specialists in corporate income taxes, estate and gift taxes, or tax shelters, to name a few. Further discussion of these services and limitations on the scope of such services is presented in Chapter 22.

### Overall Firm Management

The multioffice firm will have the overall management of the firm and certain support services centralized in a national or principal office. The equivalent of the chief executive officer will generally be referred to as the managing partner, although in many of the international firms there will be a board of directors or managing board, with the CEO chairing the board. Line authority will then lead jointly to a managing partner or director for each of the principal areas of service and to the partners in charge of the practice offices. In each practice office of sufficient size there will be a partner in charge of each of the service functions who reports directly to the partner in charge of the office. The national office director of a service function normally acts as a coordinator for that service function, with the partner in charge of the service function in each practice office then reporting indirectly to the national director of the service function as well as directly to the partner in charge of the office. The national director of the service function will assist in resolving problems that cannot readily be handled at the practice level, and will generally be assisted by a research and technical staff to research technical problems, propose firm policy on various matters, and prepare responses to exposure drafts on accounting and auditing standards.

An administrative partner in the principal office will have firmwide responsibility for the internal service functions such as accounting, secretarial and typing service, personnel records, and staff training and continuing education.

### Practice Office Organization

Each practice office usually operates as a relatively autonomous unit, but with general policy matters resolved at the national office level. The organization in the practice office will tend to parallel the national office organization. The organization is essentially the line type, with partners being the officers of the firm who can bind the firm to contracts and who are individually and collectively responsible for all work performed by the firm. The succeeding discussion primarily addresses the assignment of responsibilities within the auditing services area, but the same general plan is followed in the other service areas. There is, however, less routine work in the areas other than audit, so there will be proportionally fewer staff assistants in the other areas.

*Partner Level.* As was stated above, partners are the officers of the firm and are responsible for all work performed. Partners have varying shares in the partnership as set by the managing board, usually depending on the level of responsibility and experience. Each partner is responsible for contributing to the firm's capital, usually in proportion to the partnership share, and of course each partner shares in the profits of the firm in proportion to the partnership share.

An audit partner will generally (1) sign personally all reports or letters expressing the opinion of the firm, (2) pass judgment on any controversial issues concerning the scope of an examination or the application of generally accepted accounting principles, and (3) review the work of subordinates who are immediately under the partner's direction. In addition to these duties a partner is responsible for billing clients for services rendered and obtaining new clients. A partner will ordinarily be present at any important conferences with present or prospective clients.

*Manager or Supervisor Level.* A manager or supervisor assumes the lesser responsibilities of the partner and the more important ones of the senior accountant, thus taking over much of the work of planning and supervising audit engagements, reviewing work papers, making any necessary revisions of audit reports, and contacting the senior accountant or officials of the client as problems arise. The manager assumes full responsibility for making most decisions but must recognize those problems of sufficient importance to warrant being referred to a partner for final disposition.

*The Senior Accountant.* The senior accountant will generally be responsible for all details of the audit engagement, including preparation of the audit program, direction of the work in the field, and writing the audit report. The senior schedules the work of any assistants assigned to the engagement, supervises their performance of the work, reviews the working papers which they have prepared, undertakes personally the more difficult phases of the work, determines modifications to be made in the audit program as circumstances may warrant, and conducts most of the discussions with the client that arise during the course of the work. Most decisions pertaining to the engagement will be made by the senior accountant, but it is important that the senior recognize any matters that should more appropriately be resolved in consultation with the partner and/or manager of the engagement.

*Staff Assistants.* Much of the actual audit activity involving the examination of evidence is carried out by staff assistants, or "junior accountants" as they are sometimes called. Even though beginning assistants must be carefully instructed and supervised, they will be allowed to work more and more on their own as they demonstrate their ability to understand and carry out directions contained in the audit program. Other factors affecting the rate of progress are the ability to write clearly and proficiency in distinguishing minor problems and questions that should be handled personally from those matters which should be referred to the senior accountant for disposition.

There will be ample opportunity to judge an assistant's proficiency at putting thoughts on paper, for the assistant will find it necessary to describe in the working papers the work that has been done and the findings and conclusions reached. The importance of clear, forceful exposition in such cases stems from the fact that often the senior will evaluate the work done by the assistant almost entirely on the basis of the written comments in the working papers. Writing ability must also be demonstrated before an assistant can become a senior accountant, because the senior is expected to write the reports that are presented to the client. These reports must be extremely well written, since they are likely to be the principal means by which the client judges the work of the accounting firm.

Learning to distinguish questions and problems that should be taken up with the senior accountant from those that the assistant should be expected to resolve is important for the following reasons. Petty questions are bothersome to the senior accountant and tend to make it more difficult to complete the examination within the time estimate for the job. At the same time such questions show an undesirable lack of self-assurance and self-reliance. The opposite extreme is also to be avoided, however. The overconfident assistant is too likely to make decisions that ought to be referred to the senior accountant, thereby creating a risk that one of the decisions may turn out to be incorrect and result in negating all the careful work that has been done.

### Selection for Advancement

A senior accountant is usually permitted some choice of staff assistants to work on an engagement and will tend to select personnel who have demonstrated their ability to grasp and follow instructions, work quickly and accurately, and understand what is to be done, how it is to be done, and why it is being done. With the assistance of such persons the senior can expect to turn out a good audit well within the budgeted time. The result of this arrangement is a natural process of selection that quickly brings to the fore those with the proper ability and other necessary characteristics, and no member of the staff should ever assume that promotion to senior accountant did not occur because no one was aware of the staff member's talents.

Managers and partners in an accounting firm have equally close contact with the employees they supervise. Consequently promotion on the basis of clearly indicated merit is the rule, and a member of the staff can expect to advance just as quickly as there is evidence that the staff member is ready for additional responsibility. That such advancement is likely to be rapid and limited only by the individual's ability is indicated by the vigorous demand for personnel, resulting from the continued rapid expansion of the profession and the steady flow of staff members into responsible jobs in industry.

### Supervising the Audit

The first standard of field work states that "The work is to be adequately planned and assistants, if any, are to be properly supervised." Professional Standards at AU Sec. 311.09 goes on to state, "Supervision involves directing the efforts of assistants who are involved in accomplishing the objectives of the examination and determining whether those objectives were accomplished. Elements of supervision include instructing assistants, keeping informed of significant problems encountered, reviewing the work performed, and dealing with differences of opinion among firm personnel."

The following outline elaborates further on the comments on supervision found in Professional Standards:

A. Planning aspects of supervision include
    1. Determining what is to be done to satisfy the terms of the engagement and generally accepted auditing standards without exceeding the amount of work necessary to achieve satisfactory levels of assurance.
    2. Determining the amount of time that should be necessary to complete the specified tasks.
    3. Communicating the decisions on what is to be done and the expected time to complete the work through a written audit program and time budget.
    4. Assigning personnel to complete the specified tasks who have appropriate training and experience to effectively and efficiently complete the tasks.
B. Supervision includes determining that assistants understand
    1. The objectives of the engagement and of the specific tasks that they have been assigned to perform.
    2. How to perform the assigned tasks.
C. Effective supervision must have appropriate channels of communication that will
    1. Bring problems that have arisen to the attention of the supervisor so they can be resolved at that level.
    2. Assure consideration of the effect of all exceptions that have been noted.
    3. Include preparing written records of the work that has been done and of the conclusions reached.
D. There should be an established procedure for resolving differences of opinion that arise at the working level or at the various levels of supervision.
E. All completed work should be reviewed and accepted. Work that is rejected must be corrected or supplemented to make it acceptable.

### Concluding Comments; Quality Control

This chapter has described the general framework within which the audit process is carried out, the various risks that must be addressed in that process, and the typical accounting firm organization that has been developed to administer an accounting practice and to supervise the auditing segment of such a practice. An important consideration in auditing is adherence to high standards that will sustain and enhance the confidence of third-party users in audited financial statements. Essential to the attainment of such standards is a conscious effort to control quality through constant review of all activities.

Reviewing the work of subordinates has been noted to be important to effective supervision, and the need for conscious review extends to the topmost levels of accounting firm management. Review is also a salient feature of any system of quality control, with firm-wide review responsibility generally handled for the various offices of the firm by a review committee on a rotating basis and within each office on a sampling basis.

Quality control considerations for a firm of independent auditors were originally included in Professional Standards at AU Sec. 160, but in connection with the AICPA peer review programs and the increased emphasis on quality control, the material is now referenced in a separate section of Professional Standards at QC Sec. 10. Quality control considerations, which should be reviewed in connection with both intrafirm reviews and peer reviews, are stated to encompass the following:

Independence
Assigning personnel to engagements
Consultation in resolving accounting and auditing questions
Supervision
Hiring policies that ensure employing persons of integrity and possessing the necessary competence
Professional development through training and continuing education
Advancement of personnel to increased responsibility
Acceptance and continuation of clients
Inspection reviews to provide assurance that quality standards are maintained.

The next chapter considers the first phase of the audit process—the study and evaluation of a client's accounting system to provide indirect evidence of the likelihood that the accounting system and the internal controls of that system have produced financial statements that present fairly the client's financial position, results of operations, and changes in financial position, in conformity with generally accepted accounting principles.

## Questions/Problems

For multiple-choice questions 5-1 through 5-5, indicate the letter of the single answer that *best* completes the statement or answers the question, and justify the choice that you have made.

**5-1.** The *program* flow chart in the text for an audit engagement
   a. Stresses the inputs and outputs that are involved.
   b. Shows what audit procedures would be performed by the staff auditor(s) performing the engagement.
   c. Shows the relationship of generally accepted auditing standards to the auditor's opinion expressed on the client's financial statements.
   d. Illustrates that judgment is involved in making an audit.

**5-2.** A CPA establishes quality control policies and procedures for deciding whether to accept a new client or continue to perform services for a current client. The primary purpose for establishing such policies and procedures is
   a. To enable the auditor to attest to the integrity or reliability of a client.
   b. To comply with the quality control standards established by regulatory bodies.
   c. To minimize the likelihood of association with clients whose managements lack integrity.
   d. To lessen the exposure to litigation resulting from failure to detect irregularities in client financial statements.

   (Uniform CPA Examination)

**5-3.** An auditor is planning an audit engagement for a new client in a business that is unfamiliar to the auditor. Which of the following would be the most useful source of information for the auditor during the preliminary planning stage, when the auditor is trying to obtain a general understanding of audit problems that might be encountered?
   a. Client manuals of accounts and charts of accounts.
   b. AICPA Industry Audit Guides.
   c. Prior-year working papers of the predecessor auditor.
   d. Latest annual and interim financial statements issued by the client.

   (Uniform CPA Examination)

**5-4.** When a CPA is approached to perform an audit for the first time, the CPA should make inquiries of the predecessor auditor. This is a necessary procedure because the predecessor may be able to provide the successor with information that will assist the successor in determining

a.  Whether the predecessor's work should be utilized.
b.  Whether the company follows the policy of rotating its auditors.
c.  Whether in the predecessor's opinion internal control of the company has been satisfactory.
d.  Whether the engagement should be accepted.

(Uniform CPA Examination)

5-5.  The following would *not* be an aspect of the supervision of an audit engagement:
a.  Full knowledge of all aspects of generally accepted auditing standards.
b.  Evaluating client acceptance risk.
c.  Determining that there are adequate channels of communication for the audit staff.
d.  Ascertaining that members of the audit staff understand the objectives of the audit procedures that they are to perform.

5-6.  In late spring you are advised of a new assignment as in-charge accountant of your CPA firm's recurring annual audit of a major client, the Lancer Company. You are given the engagement letter for the audit covering the calendar year December 31, and a list of personnel assigned to this engagement. It is your responsibility to plan and supervise the field work for the engagement.

Required:

Discuss the necessary preparation and planning for the Lancer Company annual audit prior to beginning field work at the client's office. In your discussion include the sources you should consult, the type of information you should seek, the preliminary plans and preparation you should make for the field work and any actions you should take relative to the staff assigned to the engagement. Do not write an audit program.

(Uniform CPA Examination)

5-7.  What are the main functions normally performed by the partner of a public accounting firm?

5-8.  Jones, CPA, is approached by a prospective client who desires to engage Jones to perform an audit which in prior years was performed by another CPA.

Required:

Identify the procedures which Jones should follow in accepting the engagement.

(Uniform CPA Examination)

**5-9.** The first generally accepted auditing standard of field work requires, in part, that "the work is to be adequately planned." An effective tool that aids the auditor in adequately planning the work is an audit program.

Required:

What is an audit program, and what purposes does it serve?

(Uniform CPA Examination)

**5-10.** Johnson, Inc., a closely held company, wishes to engage Norr, CPA, to examine its annual financial statements. Johnson was generally pleased with the services provided by its prior CPA, Diggs, but thought the audit work performed was too detailed and interfered excessively with Johnson's normal office routines. Norr asked Johnson to inform Diggs of the decision to change auditors, but Johnson did not wish to do so.

Required:

a.  List and discuss the steps Norr should follow before accepting the engagement.

b.  What additional procedures should Norr perform on this first-time engagement over and beyond those Norr would perform on the Johnson engagement of the following year?

(Uniform CPA Examination)

**5-11.** Describe each of the two principal means by which the independent auditor acquires evidence on which to base the opinion to be expressed on the client's financial statements.

**5-12.** Discuss the relationship that exists between generally accepted accounting principles and generally accepted auditing standards.

**5-13.** Indicate the various points in the program flow chart in Chapter 5 at which decisions must be made and indicate at what level in the accounting firm organization each of the decisions is likely to be made.

**5-14.** Justify your conclusion whether direct evidence or indirect evidence is more important to the independent audit of financial statements.

**5-15.** What are the three basic audit variables that will be affected by the preliminary assessment of audit risk?

**5-16.** The auditor should obtain a level of knowledge of the entity's business, including events, transactions, and practices, that will enable the planning and performance of an examination in accordance with generally accepted auditing standards. Adhering to these standards enables the auditor's report to lend credibility to financial statements by providing the public with certain assurances.

Required:

a. How does knowledge of the entity's business help the auditor in the planning and performance of an examination in accordance with generally accepted auditing standards?

b. What assurances are provided to the public when the auditor states that the financial statements "present fairly . . . in conformity with generally accepted accounting principles applied on a consistent basis"?

(Uniform CPA Examination)

# Chapter 6

# THE SYSTEM-BASED AUDIT I

## Acquisition of Indirect Evidence through Evaluation of the Accounting System and Internal Control

---

---

The previous chapter directed attention to the accounting system as the means by which data relating to economic events affecting an entity are captured and processed to produce financial statements. If that processing system has been properly designed and operated, the financial statements it produces should accurately reflect the multifarious events that have affected the entity and should effectively communicate that information to interested parties.

Given that the purpose of an independent audit engagement is to assess the credibility of financial statements, it follows that the auditor will give critical attention to the accounting system that has produced those financial statements. To emphasize this point, this book refers to the audit as *system-based*. The initial phase of an audit involves a thorough study and evaluation of the accounting system and the various controls incorporated in the system in order to obtain indirect evidence that the financial statements present fairly the financial position and results of operations of the client entity in conformity with generally accepted accounting principles.

The discussion of this phase of the audit process begins with accounting systems—what they are, how they operate, and the controls that can be incorporated into them—so that the reader will understand

1. How an accounting system operates, and what documents and records are integral to the system.
2. What to look for in evaluating a system, and where the desired information is likely to be found.
3. How the conclusions reached after evaluating a system will affect the gathering of direct evidence to support the financial statements, as discussed in the next chapter.

### Accounting System Defined

An accounting system is the means by which data pertaining to the transactions and economic events affecting an entity are processed to produce operating and financial information needed by management to direct and control operations, and by stockholders, creditors, government agencies, and other third parties to use in their decision making relative to that entity. An accounting system encompasses the formal set of business forms and documents that reflect transactions or other economic events affecting the entity, and the procedures, records, and devices utilized to process data relating to the transactions and events for the purpose of producing financial statements and other needed operating and financial information. Information is thus the principal product of the accounting system, and the accounting system may be considered the core of the management information system (MIS) that produces needed feedback to management on all operating and financial aspects of an entity.

Sales and expense analyses, accounts receivable aging information, standard cost variances, and balance sheets and income statements would be examples of information produced by the accounting system. Information feedback that is equally important but is derived from segments of the MIS other than the system of accounts would include production and quality control reports, status reports on inventory quantities on hand or on order, volume of goods shipped, and analysis of salesmen's calls.

## The Management Information Cycle

Operations generate data that contain the image of those operations, and such data must be collected and summarized to develop that image, thereby producing the information needed by management. The processing of data is thus the essence of feedback systems, and these systems contain three basic elements:

Input     →     Processing     →     Outputs

(Data from events)   (Manual or by machine)   (Reports and Statements)

In a larger context, data processing is an element of the closed loop that constitutes the management cycle (see Figure 6-1).

In the design of an accounting system intended to satisfy the needs arising from the management cycle, the first consideration must be the end result desired: the feedback information needed by management to carry out its responsibilities for directing and controlling operations and for reporting to third parties.

### Outputs of the Accounting System

Financial statements, supporting details, and other analytical reports comprise the tangible outputs of an accounting system. A properly designed system will also provide intangible outputs or benefits, with the

**Figure 6-1.** The Management Information Cycle

most important of these being internal control over day-to-day operations, as discussed later in this chapter.

The reports and statements produced by the system must be designed to satisfy recipients' needs for feedback concerning the operations that are under those persons' direction and control. The concept of *responsibility reporting* for management reports is especially important in this regard. Each management official should receive reports that fully cover controllable expenses of all operations for which that person is responsible; a manager who is responsible for the activities of other managers should receive a report that summarizes the results achieved under each of those subordinate managers. The organization of the reports thus relates closely to the flow of responsibility apparent in a formal organization chart.

All reports should offer some means of evaluating reported results, such as a comparison with budgeted or standard amounts or with similar figures for the preceding month or the same month a year ago. The reports should also be accurate and timely, with reports available as soon after the close of the period being reported upon as possible. Stale information is of little value because it is received too late to institute corrective action. Stale or inaccurate information may also lead to the development of "bootleg records" as an informal, unauthorized attempt to obtain needed information more promptly or to detect errors, but with added cost for the duplicate records.

### Audit Trails within the Accounting System

An important aspect of the accounting system is the trail that transactions leave in the form of documents, records, and entries as they are processed through the system and condensed into financial statements.

This trail is often referred to as an *audit trail* because it makes it possible for the auditor to observe how a transaction moved through the accounting labyrinth and to obtain evidence to determine whether the resulting financial statements have been properly prepared. The audit trail is equally important to management in that it helps answer questions about the underlying details of the accounts and changes or variances reported by the accounting system. These questions might involve such matters as the cause of operating results that are out of line, questioned charges or credits to a customer's account, or the basis on which the amount of an employee's paycheck was determined.

### Classification of Accounts

Underlying any scheme of accounting reports is the set of detailed accounts in which the transactions and events affecting the business entity are recorded for summarization. A *classification of accounts* should list the accounts created within the accounting system, classified relative to the position of each account within the financial statement to which it is related. *Chart of accounts* is an alternative term for such a listing.

Included with the classification of accounts, or supplementary to it, should be a description of those items that are properly charged or credited to each account. This information makes the classification document particularly useful in determining into which account a given transaction should be entered. The accounts are generally numbered, so that the numbers may be used instead of account titles for machine processing and as a time-saving measure in recording transactions and in otherwise referring to the various accounts. Numbers are usually assigned on a *block* basis, so that the number indicates the section of the balance sheet or income statement to which an account applies.

Operating accounts should be organized with responsibility as the primary classification. For costs directly related to a particular product or product class, product categories would represent the secondary classification. All costs or expenses related to a particular product and/or responsibility would then be further classified according to the "object" or "nature" of the expense—materials, wages, supervisory salaries, supplies used, payroll taxes, and so on. Because only variable expenses are controllable, a further breakdown of expenses into variable and fixed categories may also be useful. In an account numbering scheme, position is the key to the classification of the costs and expenses, as for example:

$$A$$
$$XX\ YYY\ BZZ$$
$$C$$

where

$$X = \text{Department or responsibility}$$

$Y$ = Product classification
$A$ = Direct expense
$B$ = Indirect variable expense
$C$ = Indirect fixed expense
$Z$ = Object classification

Given such a classification and numbering scheme, costs and expenses can readily be compiled and reported as follows:

Responsibility, by product, by object—for expense control purposes.

Product costs, by responsibility and by object—for pricing decisions, for profitability retain-or-drop decisions, and for inventory valuation for accounting purposes.

Variable product costs—for use in a contribution margin approach to pricing when special circumstances may warrant.

Indirect expenses, by responsibility or cost center—for use in developing overhead rates to allocate overhead to products.

Thus it may be seen that a properly designed classification scheme should provide for a 4-dimensional analysis of costs and expenses, as suggested by Figure 6-2.

An important aspect of responsibility reporting is that any goods or

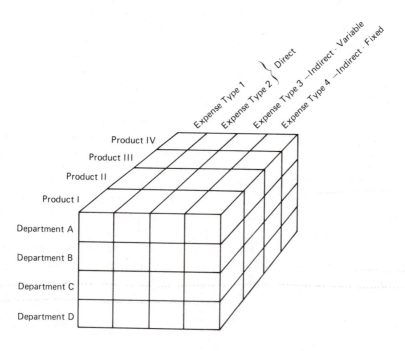

**Figure 6-2.** 4-Dimensional Analysis of Costs and Expenses

services for which the expense is related to usage, such as long distance telephone tolls or supplies, should be charged to the appropriate responsibility and object account. There are, of course, added accounting costs associated with maintaining the necessary usage records. These costs must be compared with the benefits expected to be derived from maintaining such records, to determine whether the cost is justified. The benefits in this regard are difficult to evaluate because they must be estimated, such as the benefit representing the control over usage that is obtained by making responsibility charges, in contrast to the "free good" situation that would otherwise prevail.

### Attributes of Effective Accounting Systems

In concluding this brief discussion of accounting systems, it is important to recognize that the following attributes are important to the effectiveness of the accounting system:

- Inputs and processing should be in conformity with generally accepted accounting principles to provide outputs that are also in conformity.
- Operating results should be reported in relation to the person with responsibility for those results at each level of management.
- Reports should include a basis for measuring progress against standards or planned goals.
- Fixed and variable costs and expenses should be reported as separate classifications for maximum value in making product pricing decisions and for control purposes.
- Highlighting of variances from standard or expectations is desirable in reporting, thereby facilitating management by exception.
- Communication is generally facilitated by aggregation and condensation, but no significant details should be lost or buried by such aggregation.
- Accuracy and precision are important but should be sought only within the constraints of cost/benefits analysis.
- Timeliness in the availability of information relative to management needs should be considered in cost/benefit analysis and in substituting estimates for more accurate data that may not be available soon enough.

These attributes of an effective accounting system are important to both independent and intraorganizational auditors. Independent auditors, of course, will be primarily interested in the conformity of outputs to generally accepted accounting principles, but, from a service to client standpoint, independent auditors should be alert for any shortcomings in internally reported information so that constructive suggestions can be provided in the supplementary letter to management. Internal auditors, given their primary mission of being of service to management, will have a direct interest and concern for the effectiveness of the accounting system and the information that is generated. Although internal auditors will focus on the effectiveness of information for internal use, they should also be cognizant of the conformity of information with generally accepted accounting principles.

## Internal Control

Elements of the management process include organizing, directing, and controlling, with the exercise of control representing the focal point of the present discussion. Because the control we are considering is accomplished internally within the system, it is referred to as internal control. Internal control is integral with an organization's accounting system and has a direct bearing on the accuracy and reliability of the outputs of that system.

The essence of control is regulating, in the sense of causing things to happen in accordance with a particular plan or objective. Examples range from a child's control of a pull toy to such relatively complex matters as piloting a jet airliner or controlling the operation of a nuclear power generating station. In controlling an organization, managers strive for the most effective and efficient techniques to control the various activities for which they are responsible, so as to attain such objectives as profit maximization, cost minimization, quality maintenance, and production quotas.

Steps in controlling organizational activities include

1. Organizing, planning, and making the decisions implicit in the development of a plan.
2. Authorizing action to implement plans that have been agreed upon.
3. Maintaining custody and control over usage of resources acquired in accordance with the plan.
4. Designing and operating an information system to accurately record, summarize, and report on all activities in order to provide necessary feedback on the results accomplished.
5. Taking such corrective action as may be prompted by feedback on past action and results.

### Administrative Control and Accounting Control Distinguished

Professional Standards at AU Sec. 320.27-.28 identifies two aspects of internal control, which are described as *administrative control* and *accounting control,* and are defined as follows:

Administrative control includes, but is not limited to, the plan of organization and the procedures and records that are concerned with the decision processes leading to management's authorization of transactions. Such authorization is a management function directly associated with the responsibility for achieving the objectives of the organization and is the starting point for establishing accounting control of transactions.

Accounting control comprises the plan of organization and the procedures and records that are concerned with the safeguarding of assets and the reliability of financial records and consequently are designed to provide reasonable assurance that:

a. Transactions are executed in accordance with management's general or specific authorization.

b. Transactions are recorded as necessary (1) to permit preparation of financial statements in conformity with generally accepted accounting principles or any other criteria applicable to such statements and (2) to maintain accountability for assets.

c. Access to assets is permitted only in accordance with management's authorization.

d. The recorded accountability for assets is compared with the existing assets at reasonable intervals and appropriate action is taken with respect to any differences.

The 5-step approach to controlling organizational activity previously presented varies somewhat from the AICPA statement, but both cover similar matters. Planning and the attendant decisions are preliminary aspects of administrative control, which the AICPA suggests is primarily concerned with the authorization of transactions (or other actions) and gives rise to the need for a means of ascertaining whether the authorized actions have been taken and what results were achieved. Thus the follow-up on authorizations is the point of interface between administrative control and accounting control, as shown by the program flowchart in Figure 6-3, which consolidates the steps in the management information cycle and the two aspects of internal control.

### Objectives of Internal Control Systems

As stated in the quotation from Professional Standards, internal accounting controls are concerned with safeguarding assets and with the reliability of financial records, and it is through addressing these concerns that the information needs of administrative control are satisfied. The basic objectives of the broader term *internal control* may be summarized as

1. *Controlling operations* through a system of authorizations and information feedback on the results achieved by those authorizations.

2. *Safeguarding assets* from loss through theft, waste, inefficiency, and misappropriation.

3. *Producing information* that is comprehensive, reliable, timely, and related to responsibility, so as to facilitate management control of operations.

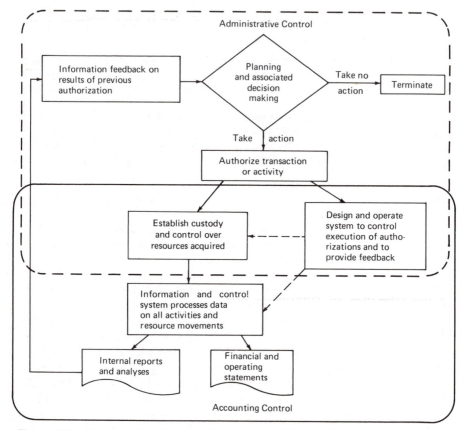

**Figure 6-3.** Program Flowchart of Information and Control System Showing Interfaces of Administrative and Accounting Controls

### Operations Subsystems as Study Units

To provide assurance that the objectives of internal control are achieved, various control features should be incorporated at critical points throughout the operations of an organization. However, because application of these control features will differ within the various functional segments of an organization, the systems material in later chapters of this text is organized around the major operating subsystems that will be found in any business enterprise or other organization engaged in economic activity. These subsystems represent the focal point of the systems-based audit, and the subsequent discussions of audit objectives and procedures in the "core" chapters of the text are likewise organized on the basis of these subsystems, which are as follows:

Sale of goods or services and collection of the amounts due from customers.

Acquisition of goods and services and recognition of the resulting liabilities.
Receipt, storage, and issuance or sale of inventories.
Cash receipts, disbursements, and control of cash balances.
Employment activities and processing of payroll transactions.
Acquisition, disposition, and depreciation of plant assets.
Capital acquisition and repayment. *notes – mort. debentures*

Although the various subsystems are relatively independent, it should be noted that interlocks tie the subsystems together, as in the cash payment for inventory purchases, the issuance of inventories for sale to customers, the collection of cash as a consequence of a sale, and the disbursement of cash for payroll or acquisition of plant assets.

### Operating Features To Achieve Internal Control

Generalized control features designed to provide assurance of achieving the objectives of controlling operations, safeguarding assets, and producing needed feedback information about the subsystems are set forth in this section. Along with the following descriptions of these control features, an example of how each control feature might be applied in the inventory subsystem area is presented in order to provide a reference point and to aid in understanding the control feature. The authorization aspect of administrative control is closely tied to operating control through the first and third control features.

*Documented Authorization.* All transactions should be authorized by management as a result of the management decision-making process, although authorization does not necessarily come directly from management. For instance, the computer preparation of a purchase order for an inventory item in a computerized system may in effect be "authorized" by the inventory control system designed by management that utilizes a computerized algorithm to relate order lead time, rate of use, and inventory quantity on hand to trigger the preparation of a purchase order.

Authorization should be documented to communicate unequivocal information on what action is to be taken and to provide evidence that the action was authorized. Thus the decision by production control that a given item of material is needed results in the preparation of a purchase request that authorizes the purchasing department to place a purchase order. The purchase order in turn authorizes a vendor to ship the desired material, the receiving department to accept the ordered materials, and the accounts payable department to initiate payment for the material.

*Record of Action Taken.* Management control implies that management must be able to determine that authorized actions have been taken. Thus evidence, in the form of a document or record, should be prepared for every action that is taken—as for example the purchase order copy that shows that an order was placed, or the receiving department notation on its copy of the purchase order showing the quantity received, which becomes an additional authorization input in payment for the purchase.

*Authorization/Record Comparison.*   Assurance should be obtained of the following three aspects of every transaction:

1.  The transaction was authorized.
2.  All authorizations resulted in action being taken.
3.  The action taken and the record of the action conform to each other and to the authorization.

To satisfy these three requirements, a specific control is necessary. Thus, production control should retain a control copy of the purchase request and compare the control copy with the copy of the purchase order that should be sent to production control. The comparison should be made to determine that a purchase order was prepared and that the description of the material, the quantity ordered, and the specified delivery date are correct. That a purchase transaction was properly authorized would be evidenced by the copy of the purchase order that should be sent to accounts payable to authorize payment for the purchase. Also, purchasing will want to know that every purchase order placed has been filled in accordance with the purchase order, and hence a "tickler file" copy of each purchase order should be held and filed according to requested delivery date. The receiving record should be routed through purchasing to indicate that the open purchase order can be removed from the tickler file, and the quantity and receiving date verified to show that the order was properly filled. A purchase order remaining open in the tickler file after the requested delivery date should generate an immediate inquiry to determine the status of the ordered item.

## Data Processing Activities

Following the completion of authorized actions and the preparation of records evidencing the transactions, data concerning the actions must be classified, recorded, and summarized to produce financial statements and all desired internal reports. The complete process, from authorization to financial statements, is pictured in Figure 6-4, which suggests the consolidation that occurs through summarizing information for feedback

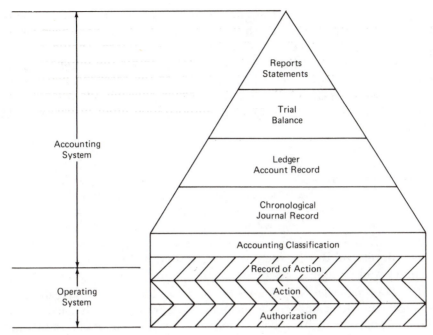

**Figure 6-4.** Diagram of Steps from Authorization of Actions to Preparation of Reports and Statements

to management and third parties in the form of reports and financial statements.

### Internal Accounting Control Objectives Applicable to Data Processing

In the accounting system segment of the internal control system, which relates to establishing accountability over assets as an element of safeguarding them and producing reliable, comprehensive feedback, the following processing control objectives are involved:

1. *Accounting activities are independent of operating responsibilities.* Organizational segregation of accounting and data processing from the functional responsibility for operations and custody of assets is necessary in order to have effective accountability control over operations and the custody and use of the assets of an entity.

2. *Only valid transactions are accepted for processing.* Any nonexistent or fictitious "transactions" should be screened out to avoid fraudulent efforts to extract assets or to conceal past extractions of assets. For example, the misappropriation of inventory items could be concealed by introducing a transaction that purports to transfer the items to another location or to show that they have been consumed internally.

3. *All transactions have been properly authorized.* Removal of inventory items for sale to a customer should be authorized by a shipping order generated in the sales order department.

4. *Every valid authorized transaction is entered in the accounting system.* The omission of an entry to record the shipment of inventory items could result in an overstated inventory balance and in failure to reorder the inventory item at the proper time, so that a stockout condition could result.

5. *The accounting entry correctly reflects the transaction.* Feedback information generated by the accounting system can be only as accurate as the entry of input into the accounting system, beginning with the accurate preparation of the document that evidences a transaction and extending to execution of computer input or entry in an accounting journal. An important control here is to prepare manually a totaled listing of each batch of items to be processed and compare that figure with a total developed during the initial processing of the input, to prove the accuracy and completeness of the input.

6. *The transaction is to be correctly classified.* The account classifications to which the debit and credit elements of a transaction are assigned to show the particular asset, equity, expense, or revenue accounts affected are directly related to the accuracy and usefulness of the representation of transactions in the feedback that is produced. The importance of correct classification is evident in a) the observance of generally accepted accounting principles in classifying transactions, and in b) the accounts that establish accountability over liquid assets that may be subject to theft, such as cash, receivables, and inventories. Computerized systems should include a "check digit" with every account number, including the account numbers that identify a customer, an inventory item, a vendor, or an employee. Computer programming then makes it possible for a computer algorithm to verify that the account number is correctly stated. The check digit will not prove, of course, that the classification (selection of the account number) was correct—only that the number chosen was correctly stated.

7. *Transaction data are to be correctly processed.* Processing accuracy is not a problem for computerized systems because the high accuracy of electronic processing and the various validity and redundancy checks that are built into the hardware make the equipment practically error free. Manual or machine-assisted manual systems, however, are subject to a variety of errors as a result of human mistakes. The system of double entry and the creation of control accounts over subsidiary ledgers are historically an important means of checking processing accuracy—although there are also other reasons for the development of these techniques. In machine-assisted systems there are various forms of proof, ranging from the simple old-and-new-balance proof to prove the old-

balance pick up and the amount posted, to more sophisticated proofs that can also prove that the correct account was selected. The manufacturers of "bookkeeping" (or "posting") machines can supply detailed information about the proof capabilities of their machines, some of which include the capability of electronically reading and magnetically recording encoded data such as account number and account balance.

### Processing Features To Achieve Accounting Control

Processing control to assure accuracy of accounting records can be achieved by incorporating the following processing control features.

*Matching of Authorization and Evidence of Action.* Documents evidencing action that has been taken represent inputs to the data processing that occurs within the accounting system. Authorization should be matched to the evidence of the action in order to establish that the action was authorized; thus, material should be accepted by the receiving department only if receiving has a copy of the purchase order, and another copy of the purchase order should be directed to accounts payable, to authorize payment of the vendor's invoice.

*Prenumbering of Documents.* Documents authorizing action or evidencing action that has occurred should be prenumbered to permit subsequent determination that every authorization and action has been accounted for. Thus, at the point that materials requisitions become input to the accounting system, every document number should be accounted for to reveal lost or mishandled requisitions. Failure to enter a requisition in the accounting records would result in an overstatement of inventory on hand and a subsequent failure to reorder the inventory item in time to prevent a stockout.

*Input Control Totals.* Traditional accounting systems and computerized applications of these systems are essentially what are referred to as batch processing systems, with a batch being all or portions of a day's transactions of a given type, such as sales, purchases, or inventory withdrawals. To prove accuracy of inputs in such systems it is always desirable to "double check" by having input totals determined by two independent operations in order to prove the accuracy and completeness of the data at the point of entry to the system. A classical example would be in accounting for sales on account. Customers' invoices can be prepared on a billing machine that accumulates a total of all invoices prepared. Then, as the accounting copies of the day's invoices are machine posted to customers' accounts, a byproduct of the posting operation is a listing of the invoices posted for the day, which becomes the sales journal. Comparing the billing machine total with the sales journal total for equality then proves that all of the invoices were correctly entered in the sales journal and posted to the customers' accounts.

A similar proof can be made of materials requisitions to be posted to inventory records. In a computerized batch system, however, the requisitions will show only quantities, because costs and extensions will be determined by the computer as an integral part of the processing operation. The control total for a batch of, say, fifty requisitions will in that case be based on the quantities requisitioned. The total itself is meaningless, but programming the computer to compare the predetermined total with a similar total of the batch quantities developed by the computer, as the card or tape input is processed to update the inventory records, will prove that the computer input was correctly prepared.

For so-called *on-line* systems each transaction is entered into the computer system at the time the transaction is effected. For example, customer orders are entered directly from a keyboard terminal, and if the item ordered is in stock, the computer prepares an invoice and updates the customers' receivable record, inventory records, and sales analysis records. In this situation it will be the operator's responsibility to check the visual record of the entry as it appears on the terminal cathode ray tube (CRT) screen to ascertain that the quantity entered agrees with the quantity on the source document (the customer's order). The operator will also enter the customer number and the item code identification for each item ordered, but the entry of this information is proved through using the check digit system referred to earlier.

*Control Account Totals for Detail Records.*   The classical system of maintaining a general ledger control account for, say, accounts payable as well as a detail ledger of the individual accounts payable similarly involves duplicate operations and a double check of the results. The monthly purchases journal total of material purchased is posted to the accounts payable control account, while the individual purchases are posted to the accounts payable ledger in which there is an account for each vendor. A trial balance listing of the accounts payable ledger at the end of the month should agree with the balance of the accounts payable control account—if all entries have been made and posted correctly. Similar control totals over detail records should be maintained in computer systems, but since all balances are updated daily and detail record totals can be readily obtained as a byproduct of each file processing run, the related totals and balances can, through proper programming, be compared at the end of every posting run by the computer itself.

*Trial Balance Proof of Debit/Credit Balances.*   The typical month-end trial balance proof of debit and credit balances in the general ledger is yet another version of the "do it twice to double check" proof that proves the accuracy of the entry and processing of the equal debit and credit aspects of each transaction.

### Monitoring Internal Control and the Accounting System

A final aspect of control is monitoring the control system to assure that the controls function as intended. Such monitoring should include both regular operating procedures and supplementary activities, as follows:

*Regular Comparison of Assets and Accountability Records.* Independent accountability control over assets is fully effective only if regular comparisons are made between the asset called for by the accountability records and the assets themselves, in order to establish that the assets have been fully accounted for. Examples include making cash counts to be balanced with cash account records, reconciling bank statements with bank account balances, verifying through written correspondence with customers that the records of amounts shown as receivable from them are correct, and comparing the physical quantities of inventory on hand with the related inventory records.

*Third-Party Proofs of Accounting Records.* Every time a document reflecting output of the accounting system reaches an independent party, there is an opportunity to detect processing errors that may have occurred despite the controls that have been instituted. For example, an error in computing an employee's pay is likely to be discovered and reported when the employee receives the erroneous paycheck—especially if the error results in underpayment of the amount due. Similarly, customers will audit sales invoices for errors before making payment and the same is generally true if monthly statements are sent showing the balances owed by customers. Each of those cases provides a valuable, additional check on the accuracy of the accounting records.

*Internal Audits.* Chapter 4 pointed out the importance of monitoring internal controls through the reviews and tests made by internal auditors. These programmed reviews represent a conscious effort by management to determine whether all feasible controls have been instituted and whether the controls are functioning effectively.

*Independent Audits.* As has been pointed out, and as is more fully discussed in the last portion of this chapter, independent auditors have a strong interest in a client's internal control. The reviews and tests made by independent auditors provide yet another form of monitoring internal control.

## Internal Control Implications of the Foreign Corrupt Practices Act

Congress in 1977 enacted the Foreign Corrupt Practices Act. As stated in Chapter 3, this Act relates primarily to prohibitions against payment of "gifts" to foreign governments, officials, agents, political parties, or political candidates, intended to exert unlawful influence in obtaining or retaining business. The internal control provisions of the Act require all domestic companies subject to SEC jurisdiction to keep books that fairly reflect all business transactions and to maintain systems of internal control in order to ensure execution of all transactions in accordance with management's authorization and to properly record all transactions. The internal control provisions are intended to charge company officials with responsibility for maintaining controls adequate to prevent illegal payments of questionable acts from occurring, as well as to prevent the concealment of such illegal payments in the accounting records.

## Internal Control and Independent Audits

Although our main concern is auditing, in this chapter's previous discussion the accounting system and internal control were introduced from the point of view of the management of operations. Management has been responsible for the genesis of accounting systems and internal control, and refinements and developments in those areas have been responses to management needs. Thus, to fully understand accounting systems and internal control, it is important that an auditor be aware of the reason for the existence of those systems and of control techniques that have been developed. With that background this discussion returns to the auditor's concern for the accounting system as the source of the information presented in the financial statements, and for internal control as an indicator of the validity and accuracy of that information. Together these matters constitute a source of indirect evidence that the financial statements present fairly financial position and results of operations. Internal control is of even greater concern to internal auditors, for they have direct interest in identifying and securing correction of weaknesses in internal control as an aspect of being of service to management.

An auditor must, of course, gain considerably more than a mere "understanding" of accounting systems and internal control if internal control is to become indirect evidence to support the opinion expressed on the financial statements. The internal control infused throughout the accounting system must be carefully evaluated to determine just how much the auditor can rely on the outputs of the accounting system. The extent of reliance warranted relates to the audit in the following three ways:

144

1.  The amount of reliance constitutes a fundamental basis for the auditor's opinion on the financial statements.

2.  The amount of reliance determines how much additional evidence the auditor will have to acquire in order to decide whether the hypothesis can be accepted that the financial statements present fairly financial position and results of operations. The acquisition of that direct evidence through what are termed substantive audit procedures is the subject of the next chapter. For the moment it should suffice to point out that reliance on internal control will affect those substantive procedures as follows:

   a.  Determining sample size for tests of supporting evidence to be examined.

   b.  Selecting a procedure from among alternative procedures to acquire direct evidence.

   c.  Deciding on the timing of the procedures, in terms of whether they are to be applied to more conclusive year-end data or whether they can be applied earlier in the audit to interim data. By applying the procedures to interim data, more even distribution of the audit work load can be achieved, but that can be done only if internal control can be relied upon to accurately update the interim balances to the end of the year.

3.  The results of the study and evaluation of internal control provide a secondary output of the audit process—the management letter that is customarily prepared as a vital "extra" audit service. The purpose of this document is to report to management any weaknesses in internal control or problem areas noted in the course of the auditor's study and evaluation of the accounting system and related internal controls. Professional Standards at AU Sec. 323.04 states, however, that any *material* weakness in internal control *must* be communicated to senior management and to the board of directors or its audit committee. A material weakness is defined at AU Sec. 320.68 as ". . . a condition in which the auditor believes the prescribed procedures or the degree of compliance with them does not provide reasonable assurance that errors or irregularities in amounts that would be material in the financial statements being audited would be prevented or detected within a timely period by employees in the normal course of performing their assigned functions."

Former AU Sec. 640 (now superseded by AU Sec. 642) raised a question about the usefulness of reports on internal control to present and prospective investors, creditors, customers, and other interested third parties. A difference in views is reported there, with some persons believing that a report on internal control would be useful to third parties in appraising management and management performance, whereas others believe that, since other areas of management performance likewise are not reported on, selecting only internal control for such reporting would result in distorted appraisals of management performance. The SEC has, however, encouraged registered companies to obtain such reports for the benefit of third parties, and reporting on internal control is discussed in Chapter 21.

### Determining Auditor Reliance on Internal Control

Having noted the various reasons for the auditor's concern for a client's system of internal control and having considered internal control from the standpoint of management objectives, let us next consider how the auditor proceeds to evaluate a client's internal control system to determine how much assurance can reasonably be obtained from it. Our immediate concern, however, is not quantification of that assurance, but rather it is to point out what should be done if a weakness or deficiency in internal control is noted that could affect the accuracy or fairness of a financial statement figure. The appropriate response is to extend the substantive tests of direct evidence relative to the questioned figure in order to compensate for the observed weakness or deficiency.

The evaluation of internal control involves the following steps:

*Study Each Subsystem.* Each of the client's subsystems should be studied to determine exactly what is done, the sequence of the work, who does the work, and who has ultimate responsibility for that work. The information obtained should be fully documented in the auditor's work papers by means of a narrative description or preferably by a flowchart as a "shorthand" representation of the subsystem. Such a flowchart should show the inputs to the system, what operations are performed, what decisions must be made, who performs each task, and intermediate and final forms of outputs of the subsystem in terms of documents and records. Careful study of a well prepared flowchart should make it easier to understand flows and relationships and to trace the origin and disposition of various documents—all of which are essential to understanding the system.

The necessary information can be obtained from any or all of such sources as

> Client procedure manuals, job descriptions, and flowcharts of the system.
> Inquiry of employees involved in the operation of the system.
> Examples of the forms, records, or other documents that are part of the system.
> A check of the auditor's understanding of the system by conducting what is generally referred to as a "walkthrough." In this procedure the auditor takes a transaction or event and "walks" it through every phase of the system to establish the accuracy of the narrative or flowchart that has been prepared and to be sure that the auditor fully understands what occurs within the

system. In instances in which the client has no documentation to which the auditor can refer, the basic gathering of information about the system must be obtained from the walkthrough.

Inquiry about changes in the system during the period being audited are important because any change occurring before or after the point in time that the auditor makes the study of the subsystem could change the results produced and affect the auditor's reliance on the system. Indications of change would be the introduction of new or revised forms, the issuance of updated portions of the client's procedures manual, and changes in the employees who are part of the system.

*Evaluate Each Subsystem.* Some form of standard checklist is used in almost all instances to guide or remind the auditor about the various features or aspects of internal control that should be present in a good system. These internal control features should provide reasonable control over operations through a system of authorizations and feedback; adequate safeguarding of assets; and comprehensive, reliable, and timely information outputs of the system. The checklist may be in the form of an internal control questionnaire that gives an extensive listing of internal control points for each subsystem, each question to be answered "Yes," "No," or "Not Applicable," and the questions so worded that "Yes" indicates a satisfactory condition and "No" an unsatisfactory condition. For example:

Are all disbursements properly authorized and supported by vendors' invoices, purchase orders, and receiving reports?

Are disbursement authorizations given by a person with no responsibility for purchasing or other operations?

In a slightly different approach, the checklist may contain for each subsystem a listing of the control features such as were given previously, with a provision for indicating whether each control feature is present in the system.

In addition to the information provided by questionnaires or checklists of internal control features, certain broad or overall aspects of achieving good internal control should receive attention. These are considered in the next section.

### Considerations in Evaluating Internal Control

Underlying any checklist used in evaluating internal control will be the following general considerations pertaining to the effectiveness of internal control:

*Independent accountability*  should be maintained through an organization plan that provides for segregation of responsibility for accounting records from any responsibility for operations or custody of assets.

*Regular comparisons*  should be made between accountability records and the assets being accounted for.

*Sound administrative practices*   related to an effective internal control system should include

1.  Written statements of management policies and objectives, including a code of conduct that establishes broad classes of actions that are required or prohibited on such matters as foreign payments, political contributions, grants and donations, gifts and entertainment, use of company assets, confidentiality of information, and conflicts of interest.

2.  Designation of a systems group that is charged with designing and modifying the accounting system and with incorporating all authorization and accounting controls that are feasible on a cost/benefit basis.

3.  Having in written and updated form such matters as organization charts, job descriptions, procedures manuals, and a chart of accounts, so as to avoid questions, attempts to shift responsibility for unsatisfactory performance, and inconsistent treatment of similar items.

4.  Use of budgets and standards to aid in planning and evaluating results through timely reported comparisons and variances.

5.  Written statements of accounting and internal control policies covering, for example, the minimum cost of capital items that are to be recorded as additions to plant rather than as current expenses, the minimum purchase order requiring competitive bids, and the period of time that various records are to be retained before they are destroyed.

*Competent personnel*  are essential to good internal control, for no system can be any better than the people who operate it. Prospective employees should be carefully screened to assure that only qualified people are employed, and performance should be evaluated in order to determine which employees should be retained and considered for advancement to more responsible positions. Training programs are an effective means of improving work quality and accelerating employee development, so as to increase the number of persons who are available to assume responsibility.

Thorough investigation of previous employment is important in selecting additional personnel to ascertain whether applicants left previous employment without prejudice. Blank periods in the employment record should be verified to avoid attempted coverup of unsatisfactory performance, fraudulent actions, or possibly incarceration for conviction of a criminal act.

*Fidelity bonds*  are an integral aspect of internal control, and employees entrusted with the custody of liquid assets should be bonded as an aspect of safeguarding assets. Although bonding may have some deterrent effect in preventing fraud or embezzlement, the safeguarding of assets is primarily achieved through insurance recoveries of losses caused by the fraudulent acts of employees.

*Constant monitoring* of internal control can be accomplished only through an effective review process that includes evaluating controls and testing to indicate whether there is compliance with prescribed procedures and controls. These evaluations and tests of compliance are customarily the responsibility of the internal audit staff, and the independent auditor should address the effectiveness of the internal audit function. If internal auditing is being accomplished in accordance with the standards for the professional practice of internal auditing presented in Chapter 4, there should be substantial assurance of the reliability of the information generated by the client's accounting system.

Possible consequences of management complacency and failure to maintain constant surveillance over internal control are suggested by Figure 6-5.

Our consideration of the independent auditor's reliance on internal control to indicate the validity and accuracy of accounting system outputs concludes with the question of whether indicated controls, as ascertained from the study and evaluation of internal control, are actually operating as intended. To answer this question the auditor utilizes the final step in examining internal control: performing tests of compliance of procedures actually in use with the procedures prescribed by the system of internal control.

### Compliance Testing of Internal Control

The auditor's objectives in compliance testing are perhaps best indicated by describing the types of tests that are normally made and the

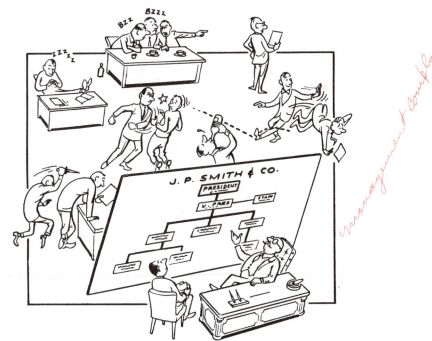

**Figure 6-5.** Internal "Control"

Source: *Systemation,* January 15, 1959, published by Systemation, Inc., Colorado Springs, Colo.

purpose of each test. However, compliance tests of a given internal control feature will not be necessary if the control feature is not to be relied on in determining the nature, timing, or extent of substantive tests of a particular type of transaction or the resulting account balances. The decision not to rely on internal control for a given type of transaction may be because

- The controls are not adequate to provide meaningful assurance that transactions have been properly processed and that the resulting account balances are reliable.
- The audit effort necessary to test compliance would exceed the reduction in substantive testing that would thereby be realized.

## Extent of Compliance Tests and Selection of Items

When transactions are to be examined for compliance testing, the extent of the sample and the selection of the transactions must be considered. Sample sizes may be determined subjectively or statistically, as discussed in Professional Standards at AU Sec. 320.62. In either case an auditor must decide how much confidence is sought from the test, as sample size will vary directly with the amount of confidence desired. (See Chapter 9 on sample selection and evaluation for a fuller discussion of this aspect of sampling.)

Another factor affecting the confidence to be derived from compliance testing and the consequent sample size is the independent auditor's initial confidence in the client's system of internal control. If internal control procedures are carefully laid out in procedures manuals; if operations are effectively organized with proper segregation of duties and optimal double checking of results; if employees are competent and adequately trained and supervised; and if the internal control system is effectively monitored by regular comparisons of assets and accountability records, by third-party proofs, and by a well-designed internal audit program that is staffed by competent, well-trained internal auditors, only a minimum of compliance testing should be necessary for the independent auditor to obtain the desired confidence in the effectiveness of a client's system of internal control. In fact, this writer believes that, given a comprehensive system of control and internal control monitoring, it should be defensible to reduce compliance testing to the absolute minimum of a sample of one of each type of transaction or control activity. The sample of one would actually be the walkthrough of a transaction discussed earlier, designed to ensure that the auditor has an accurate understanding of the prescribed system of internal control and has evidence that the system is in place with all of the stated controls operational. Despite the plausibility of the sample of one in the described circumstances, the reader should recognize that the sample of one is not a currently accepted practice, although at least one major public accounting firm uses a similar concept.

Because the financial statements reflect the results of transactions occurring throughout the year, compliance testing should likewise cover the entire period, with random selection of transactions being the preferred selection method. In most instances, however, an examination of financial statements for a fiscal year will begin well in advance of the end of the year. Beginning the audit early is desirable from the standpoint of spreading audit work more evenly throughout the year, but primarily to permit the earliest possible delivery of the audited financial statements after the fiscal year close.

In the so-called interim work, undertaken in preliminary stages of the audit before the year-end work can be commenced, the study and evaluation of internal control will be one of the earliest activities because the results of this work will have a direct bearing on the substantive tests of year-end balances. As a consequence of these circumstances, compliance tests conducted on a preliminary basis cannot possibly include internal control activities during the final portions of the year. Nevertheless, Professional Standards at AU Sec. 320.61 states that it may not be necessary to make tests throughout the period remaining after the date of the interim compliance testing. "Factors to be considered in this respect include (a) results of the test during the interim period, (b) responses to inquiries concerning the remaining period, (c) the length of the remaining period, (d) the nature and amount of the transactions or balances involved, (e) evidence of compliance within the remaining period that may be obtained from substantive tests performed by the independent auditor or from tests performed by internal auditors, and (f) other matters the auditor considers relevant in the circumstances."

### Nature of Compliance Tests

Under the caption "Nature of Tests of Compliance," Professional Standards at AU Sec. 320.57 states, "Accounting control requires not only that certain procedures be performed but that they be performed properly and independently. Tests of compliance, therefore, are concerned primarily with these questions: Were the necessary procedures performed, how were they performed, and by whom were they performed?" Various types of compliance tests or approaches to compliance testing are described and discussed in the following sections.

*Inspection Tests.* Authorization for an action to be taken and written communication of the authorization have been noted as being important to internal control. Likewise, if the authorization process includes ascertaining that certain supporting documents are present before an item such as a vendor's invoice is approved for payment, and that the invoice quantity, price, and terms are correctly stated, there should be evidence that these checking procedures have been completed in the form of a signature, initials, or an audit stamp. A compliance test to determine evidence that these aspects of the authorization process have been performed would involve inspecting documents for the required initials or other indication. Other examples of inspection tests would include seeing a bank reconciliation to establish that it had been prepared, or examining an adding machine tape as evidence that a required predetermined control total was prepared for a batch of documents before data entry to the computer.

*Reperformance Tests.* Even though there is indication that the above checking procedures were ostensibly performed, the auditor may wish to obtain evidence that the procedures were in fact performed and that they were performed correctly. Reperformance of the stated task by the auditor and obtaining the same result (for example, verifying the extension of quantity times unit price on an invoice) would provide the desired evidence.

*Inquiries and Observation.* Segregation of duties can be tested only by making inquiry, or by observing what tasks are performed by an employee or group or employees, and determining that no incompatible tasks or functions are involved. In some situations there may be no requirement for providing evidence that a task was completed, as for example when accounting for all sales invoice numbers before the invoices are entered in the sales journal. If there is no listing of invoice numbers with numbers crossed off to show that each number was accounted for, observation should at least indicate whether proper steps are being currently performed to account for the numbers. Inquiry can also be helpful, such as questioning whether the documents are received in numerical sequence, and if not, what proportion of the employee's time is spent placing the documents in that sequence prior to accounting for the numbers. Other meaningful inquiries would involve asking the employee what steps are taken if a number is missing, how frequently missing numbers are encountered, and what explanations have been obtained for why the numbers were missing.

### Auditor's Final Assessment of Internal Control

This completes our discussion of all but the final step in determining how much reliance the auditor can place on the internal control in a client's accounting system. To recap, the earlier stages are

Make preliminary identification of problem areas through analytical review

Obtain a description of procedures in each accounting subsystem

Evaluate each of the indicated internal controls for each subsystem for completeness

Perform compliance tests

The final assessment of internal control must be in terms of each of the subsystems, inasmuch as the assessment will directly affect the substantive testing of account balances produced by the subsystem. A major consideration is whether the internal controls of each subsystem appear to be effective in filtering out errors and irregularities that could affect the final operating and financial figures produced by the subsystem. Failure to perform the filtering effectively could result from a lack of certain control features in the system or from control features that are present in the system but not operating effectively to screen out errors. Any weakness or deficiency in internal control related to either the absence of a control or the failure of a control to function effectively must then be assessed in terms of the potential errors and irregularities that might flow through to the final accounting figures. The result of that assessment will determine the nature, extent, and timing of the auditor's substantive procedures, as discussed in the following chapter. The results of the assessment of internal control will also be the basis for the suggestions to be made to the client in the auditor's supplementary letter to management.

## Questions/Problems

For multiple-choice questions 6-1 through 6-5, indicate the letter of the single answer that *best* completes the statement or answers the question, and justify the choice that you have made.

**6-1.** The two phases of the auditor's study of internal accounting control are referred to as "review of the system" and "tests of compliance." In the tests of compliance phase the auditor attempts to

a. Obtain a reasonable degree of assurance that the client's system of controls is in use and is operating as planned.

b. Obtain sufficient, competent evidential matter to afford a reasonable basis for the auditor's opinion.

c. Obtain assurances that informative disclosures in the financial statements are reasonably adequate.

d. Obtain knowledge and understanding of the client's prescribed procedures and methods.

(Uniform CPA Examination)

**6-2.** The ultimate risk against which the auditor requires reasonable protection is a combination of two separate risks. The first of these is that material errors will occur in the accounting process by which the financial statements are developed, and the second is that

    a.  A company's system of internal control is not adequate to detect errors and irregularities.

    b.  Those errors that occur will not be detected in the auditor's examination.

    c.  Management may possess an attitude that lacks integrity.

    d.  Evidential matter is not competent enough for the auditor to form an opinion based on reasonable assurance.

          (Uniform CPA Examination)

**6-3.** Internal control is a function of management, and effective control is based upon the concept of charge and discharge of responsibility and duty. Which of the following is one of the overriding principles of internal control?

    a.  Responsibility for accounting and financial duties should be assigned to one responsible officer.

    b.  Responsibility for the performance of each duty must be fixed.

    c.  Responsibility for the accounting duties must be borne by the auditing committee of the company.

    d.  Responsibility for accounting activities and duties must be assigned only to employees who are bonded.

          (Uniform CPA Examination)

**6-4.** For effective responsibility reporting:

    a.  Costs and expenses should be grouped by "object" and then by responsibility under each object.

    b.  Costs and expenses should be grouped by responsibility, and then by "object" under each responsibility.

    c.  A standard cost system would be better than a job cost system.

    d.  Both (a) and (c) are true.

    e.  Both (b) and (c) are true.

**6-5.** A well-designed accounting system

    a.  Should involve an understanding of the information needs of management.

    b.  Should not sacrifice accuracy in order to gain timeliness.

    c.  Should involve cost of operating the system as the major design consideration.

    d.  All of the above are true.

**6-6.** Is exception reporting more important for product cost reporting or for responsibility reporting? Explain.

**6-7.** What are the management needs that a good system of internal control should fulfill?

**6-8.** Assume that you are preparing a chart of accounts for an appliance repair service. Customers bring small appliances to the shop for repair, but larger appliances are repaired in customers' houses. What reasons would lead you to recommend setting up separate revenue and expense accounts for outside service and in-shop service?

**6-9.** If responsibility accounting and reporting is to be followed for the item of factory supplies, what procedures and records must be utilized?

**6-10.** A construction company maintains a pool of heavy equipment that is used on construction jobs as needed, with the attendant depreciation expense charged to the job for which the equipment is used. What justification can you suggest for charging such depreciation on:

    a. A straight-line basis (time assigned to the job)?

    b. A units of use basis (actual operating time on the job)?

**6-11.** Why are budgets considered a form of internal control?

**6-12.** Internal control comprises the plan or organization and all of the coordinate methods and measures adopted within a business to safeguard its assets, check the accuracy and reliability of its accounting data, promote operational efficiency, and encourage adherence to prescribed managerial policies.

Required:

    a. What is the purpose of the auditor's study and evaluation of internal control?

    b. What are the objectives of a preliminary evaluation of internal control?

    c. How is the auditor's understanding of the system of internal control documented?

    d. What is the purpose of tests of compliance?

(Uniform CPA Examination)

**6-13.** Jordan Finance Company opened four personal loan offices in neighboring cities on January 2, 19X1. Small cash loans are made to borrowers who repay the principal with interest in monthly installments over a period not exceeding two years. Ralph Jordan, president of the Company, uses one of the offices as a central office and visits the other offices periodically for supervision and internal auditing purposes.

Mr. Jordan is concerned about the honesty of his employees. He came to your office in December, 19X1, and stated, "I want to engage you to install a system to prohibit employees from embezzling cash." He also stated, "Until I went into business for myself I worked for a nationwide loan company with 500 offices and I'm familiar with that company's system of accounting and internal control. I want to describe that system so you can install it for me because it will absolutely prevent fraud."

Required:

a. How would you advise Mr. Jordan on his request that you install the large company's system of accounting and internal control for his firm? Discuss.

b. How would you respond to the suggestion that the new system would prevent embezzlement? Discuss.

c. Assume that in addition to undertaking the systems engagement in 19X2, you agreed to examine Jordan Finance Company's financial statements for the year ended December 31, 19X1. No scope limitations were imposed.

1. How would you determine the scope necessary to satisfactorily complete your examination? Discuss.

2. Would you be responsible for the discovery of fraud in this examination? Discuss.

(Uniform CPA Examination)

6-14. You have been asked by the board of trustees of a local church to review its accounting procedures. As a part of this review you have prepared the following comments relating to the collections made at weekly services and record-keeping for members' pledges and contributions:

The church's board of trustees has delegated responsibility for financial management and audit of the financial records to the finance committee. This group prepares the annual budget and approves major disbursements but is not involved in collections or record-keeping. No audit has been considered necessary in recent years because the same trusted employee has kept church records and served as financial secretary for 15 years.

The collection at the weekly service is taken by a team of ushers. The head usher counts the collection in the church office following each service. He then places the collection and a notation of the amount counted in the church safe. Next morning the financial secretary opens the safe and recounts the collection. He withholds about $100 to meet cash expenditures during the coming week and deposits the remainder of the collection intact. In order to facilitate the deposit, members who contribute by check are asked to draw their checks to "cash."

At their request a few members are furnished prenumbered predated envelopes in which to insert their weekly contributions. The head usher removes the cash from the envelopes to be counted with the loose cash included in the collection and discards the envelopes. No record is maintained of issuance or return of the envelopes, and the envelope system is not encouraged.

Each member is asked to prepare a contribution pledge card annually. The pledge is regarded as a moral commitment by the member to contribute a stated weekly amount. Based upon the amounts shown on the pledge cards, the financial secretary furnishes a letter to requesting members to support the tax deductibility of their contributions.

Required:

Describe the weaknesses and recommend improvements in procedures for

a.  Collections made at weekly services.

b.  Record-keeping for members' pledges and contributions.

Organize your answer sheets as follows:

| Weakness | Recommended Improvement |
|---|---|
|  |  |

(Uniform CPA Examination)

**6-15.**  Western Meat Processing Company buys and processes livestock for sale to supermarkets. In connection with your examination of the Company's financial statements, you have prepared the following notes based on your review of procedures:

1.  Each livestock buyer submits a daily report of his purchases to the plant superintendent. This report shows the dates of purchase and expected delivery, the vendor and the number, weights and type of livestock purchased. As shipments are received, any available plant employee counts the number of each type received and places a check mark beside this quantity on the buyer's report. When all shipments listed on the report have been received, the report is returned to the buyer.

2.  Vendors' invoices, after a clerical check, are sent to the buyer for approval and returned to the accounting department. A disbursement voucher and a check for the approved amount are prepared in the accounting department. Checks are forwarded to the treasurer for his signature. The treasurer's office sends signed checks directly to the buyer for delivery to the vendor.

3.  Livestock carcasses are processed by lots. Each lot is assigned a number. At the end of each day a tally sheet reporting the lots processed, the number and type of animals in each lot, and the carcass weight is sent to the accounting department, where a perpetual inventory record of processed carcasses and their weights is maintained.

4.  Processed carcasses are stored in a refrigerated cooler located in a

small building adjacent to the employee parking lot. The cooler is locked when the plant is not open, and a Company guard is on duty when the employees report for work and leave at the end of their shifts. Super-market truck drivers wishing to pick up their orders have been instructed to contact someone in the plant if no one is in the cooler.

(5) Substantial quantities of byproducts are produced and stored, either in the cooler or elsewhere in the plant. Byproducts are initially accounted for as they are sold. At this time the sales manager prepares a two-part form; one copy serves as authorization to transfer the goods to the customer and the other becomes the basis for billing the customer.

Required:

For each of the numbered notes 1 to 5 above state:

a.   What the specific internal control objective(s) should be at the stage of the operating cycle described by the note.

b.   The control weaknesses in the present procedures, if any, and suggestions for improvement, if any.

(Uniform CPA Examination)

# Chapter 7

# THE SYSTEM-BASED AUDIT II

## Acquisition of Direct Evidence through Substantive Procedures

The preceding chapter considered how in a system-based audit the auditor gathers indirect evidence to determine whether or not the outputs of the accounting system are likely to be fairly stated, first by evaluating the internal control that has been incorporated in the accounting system and then by making compliance tests to determine whether the internal controls are functioning as intended. Although the evidence obtained through these audit procedures is circumstantial, it is highly useful and cost effective. It is the only practicable means of gaining reasonable assurance that the thousands, or hundreds of thousands, of transactions affecting the entity have been processed to produce statement outputs that reliably reflect the actual results.

Although evaluating internal accounting control is a practical necessity, it does not in itself provide a sufficient basis for an auditor's opinion on the financial statements. Further proof, in the form of direct evidence, is needed to bring to the desired level the auditor's assurance that the financial statements are fairly stated.

### Attaining Desired Assurance

The second standard of field work points to this need for further evidence as follows:

> There is to be a proper study and evaluation of the existing internal control as a basis for reliance thereon and for the determination of the resultant extent of the tests to which auditing procedures are to be restricted.

The auditing procedures to which the standard refers are known as *substantive* procedures, in that they relate to the underlying substance of account balances: the assets, liabilities, or owners' claims that are reflected by balance sheet accounts, or the summation of revenue and expense transactions presented by income statement accounts. The evidence gathered through these substantive procedures may thus be seen to be direct evidence, in contrast to the indirect evidence provided by the study and evaluation of internal control.

The reference in the standard to restricting these substantive procedures, based on the evaluation of internal control, derives from the fact that direct and indirect evidence are somewhat interchangeable; thus, the greater the assurance provided by internal control, the lesser will be the amount of assurance that must be obtained from substantive audit procedures.

The ultimate objective in auditing is to reach a desired overall level of assurance. Reaching the desired level of assurance involves qualitative judgmental decisions, as suggested by the terms *sufficient* and *competent* in the third standard of field work:

Sufficient competent evidential matter is to be obtained through inspection, observation, inquiries, and confirmations to afford a reasonable basis for an opinion regarding the financial statements under examination.

Aspects of auditing discussed in this chapter that relate to sufficiency decisions and levels of assurance are the nature and timing of substantive procedures, the use of sampling and the attendant problems of determining sample size, the competency of evidence that is examined, and cost/benefit considerations.

The level of assurance sought from the audit process to provide an adequate basis for the auditor's opinion is not readily quantifiable, but it would seem that it should be upwards of 90 percent, with 95 percent probably representing a reasonable norm. The proportion of that assurance derived from (1) indirect evidence in the form of reliance on the client's internal control system, and (2) direct evidence from substantive tests, is a function of the assurance provided by internal control in each subsystem of the client's accounting system.

Although the ultimate assurance sought relative to the accounts in each subsystem area will be about the same, the proportions obtained from direct evidence and indirect evidence will vary. Attaining the desired level of assurance with varying proportions of direct and indirect evidence is illustrated in Figure 7-1. The figure also shows that some risk will remain after the level of assurance to be attained has been chosen on the basis of cost/benefit analysis.

As the figure implies, the proportions of direct and indirect evidence are a function of the strength of internal control with respect to the financial statement figures under consideration. Thus, in the audit of a small concern with limited internal control, the bulk of the auditor's assurance would be obtained through substantive tests. The auditor must also consider the relative cost of acquiring the two forms of evidence. If,

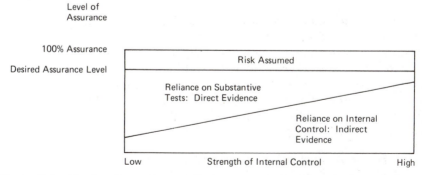

**Figure 7-1.** Varying Proportions of Reliance on Direct and Indirect Evidence in Reaching Desired Level of Assurance and Consequent Risk To Be Assumed.

for example, it would be more costly to perform the compliance tests to establish a basis for reliance on internal control than to extend the substantive tests to provide the desired assurance, then the auditing decision would be to operate at a point in the figure that would be to the left of what otherwise would be the case.

Note in Figure 7-1 the position of reliance on internal control as the underlying base for the desired level of assurance, with the substantive test of direct evidence added on top of the base. The figure also reflects the assertion in the second standard of field work that the evaluation of internal control determines the extent to which substantive tests may appropriately be restricted. Furthermore, the figure indicates that there is always some reliance on internal control, and at the other extreme, internal control cannot be the sole basis for assurance.

Of course, if there is no internal control, there can be no reliance; but if internal control is completely lacking, the auditor will probably have to conclude that no amount of substantive testing can reasonably be expected to compensate for the complete lack of internal control. There will be inadequate assurance that recorded asset outflows were actually related to benefits received or benefits to be received by the entity, or that liabilities or other asset outflows have been recorded for all benefits received by the entity. Under these circumstances the only feasible course of action is for the auditor to state that the records are unauditable and to disclaim any opinion on the financial statements.

At the other extreme, even with the most highly effective internal control possible, some confirming direct evidence should be obtained to produce reasonable assurance that there has not been an internal control failure, and that the accounts are fairly stated. Substantive audit procedures, even though minimal, should always be applied.

### Determining the Extent To Which Substantive Testing Can Be Restricted

In testing the audit hypothesis that the financial statements are fairly stated, the auditor is essentially concerned with 1) various means by which the client has sought to prevent errors from infiltrating the financial statements, and 2) various audit techniques that can be utilized to detect any material errors that may not have been screened out by the client's error prevention controls. However, there is always risk of reaching an incorrect conclusion because of the risk that a material error may have eluded detection at each of the following points:

1. Gaining a knowledge and understanding of the client to assess the likelihood that the financial statements may have been misstated intentionally or unintentionally.

2. Assessing the effectiveness of the system of internal control as it was designed to operate.

3. Performing compliance tests to determine whether designed internal controls are actually in place and operating as intended.

4. Performing substantive tests designed to detect any material errors that may have passed through the internal control filter, or irregularities that may have been introduced through override of internal control by management.

Taken together, control risk and substantive testing risk represent a joint risk and hence the product of the two risks. Thus, if the auditor concludes from the study and evaluation of internal control that the risk of an error passing through the internal control system without detection is a relatively high 20 percent, and if related substantive tests are so designed that there is as much as a 25 percent risk that the tests would not detect a material error or irregularity, the ultimate risk is 5 percent that a material error or irregularity occurring in the financial statements would not be detected. Inasmuch as the amount of reliance on the result of the audit process is the complement of the amount of risk, the assurance gained in these circumstances is the 95 percent assurance that might be judged reasonable in most instances.

The preceding analysis indicates the statistical rationale for determining the extent to which substantive procedures can be restricted, as expressed in the second standard of field work. The greater the adjudged effectiveness of internal control, the lower is the risk that the system of internal control will fail to detect a material error or irregularity, and consequently the greater is the risk that can be tolerated in substantive testing. Because risk and sample size are inversely related, this greater risk tolerance for the substantive testing permits restricting samples to a smaller size than would otherwise be justifiable.

### Consequences of Judgment Errors in Assessing Risk of Material Error in Financial Statements

In assessing the risk that a material error may exist in the financial statements on which the auditor intends to express an opinion, the auditor must balance the consequences of committing either a Type I or a Type II error. The outcomes of the risk assessment decision relative to the actual state of the financial statements are shown in the decision table in Figure 7-2. The auditor's decision is correct if no material error actually exists in the financial statements and the auditor concludes that audit procedures can properly be restricted, based on the study and evaluation of internal control and the results of analytical review in the preliminary assessment of audit risk. Conversely, the auditor's decision is also correct if a material error is present and the auditor decides to

| Auditor's Programming Decision Based on Assessment of Risk of Material Error | Actual State of Financial Statements: Material Error Present? | |
|---|---|---|
| | Yes | No |
| Expand procedures tests | Correct decision | Type I error Overauditing |
| Restrict procedures tests | • Type II error Underauditing | Correct decision |

**Figure 7-2.** Outcomes of Auditor's Assessment of Risk of Material Error Relative to Actual State of Financial Statements

expand (not to restrict) audit procedures in accordance with the second standard of field work.

The most serious error the auditor might make in this decision process would be not to expand audit procedures when a material error is actually present. The resulting Type II error, and an increased likelihood that the auditor will not detect the material error, may result in persons being misled by the financial statements and a malpractice charge if any party has suffered injury as a consequence of the material error. Although the negligence charge ought to be refutable if the auditor can show that there was a reasonable basis for deciding not to expand the audit tests, the costs of legal defense and the attendant unfavorable initial publicity make it highly desirable that there be no Type II errors.

To protect against Type II errors, it might seem that the auditor should take a defensive position and gain the added protection of expanded audit tests, but the consequence of that choice will be higher audit fees and possible loss of clients. However, increased defensiveness is a necessity at any time that the situation and observed conditions suggest a possible problem, such as if a client is experiencing financial or operating difficulties.

### Audit Procedures To Obtain Competent Evidential Matter

The third standard of field work refers to gaining access to evidential matter through the procedures of inspection, observation, inquiries, and confirmations. (The reader should note that, with the exception of confirmations, these procedures are also used in compliance testing.) We next consider each of these audit procedures, with inspection being the one that is more widely used.

*Inspection.* In seeking to prove that a given entry or record reflects an actual transaction that has been recorded in the correct account and in the correct amount, the auditor will generally look for evidence that the transaction was properly authorized—as for example a purchase order—as well as for evidence of the actual details of the transaction—such as a vendor's invoice showing quantity billed and unit price, and a receiving report showing the quantity actually received. By inspecting this supporting evidence, the auditor can verify that the transaction was correctly entered in the proper accounts. Inspection includes sighting physical assets as well as documentary evidence to support transaction entries or account balances, as in the instruction: "Inspect newly acquired assets in support of recorded additions to the plant asset account." Other verbs sometimes used to convey the same meaning as *inspect* include *examine, compare, sight, vouch,* and *agree,* as for example, "Compare (or vouch) the voucher register entry by reference to the supporting vendor's invoice," or "Agree the amount recorded in the voucher register with the supporting vendor's invoice."

*Observation.*   In contrast to inspection, which may involve after-the-fact investigation, observation will involve investigation while an act is actually being performed. One of the single most important audit procedures is inventory observation: observing the physical inventory counting so that the auditor can determine that actual counts were made and that prescribed procedures and controls have been carried out as intended. These controls would include counting by teams, with one of the persons being from the area where the inventory is stored, who would be familiar with the inventory items and the locations in which they are stored, and a second "independent" person from outside the area in which the inventory is stored, who accordingly would have no personal interest in manipulating the actual count of the items. Furthermore, although "count tags" are generally prepared to record the items counted, observation is necessary because subsequent inspection of the count tags in support of inventory amounts would not establish that the tags were based on actual floor counts of the stock. Instead, they could be fictitious records that were prepared in the office as purported support for inventory that did not exist.

*Confirmation.*   When the physical evidence of a situation is external to the client entity, when an intangible claim is represented rather than a tangible asset, inspection or observation may be impossible. In such cases the auditor should seek confirmation that the physical asset or intangible claim exists. Thus if inventory is stored in a public warehouse, the auditor may request through the client that the warehouse operator supply a written confirmation of the inventory quantities being held in storage. The most common use of the confirmation procedure, however, is in verifying the existence and amount of the major intangible asset on most balance sheets: accounts receivable. As with all confirmation requests, the request must originate with the client, who thereby authorizes the respondent to supply information to which only the client and respondent are privy.

*Inquiry.* Of the four procedures referred to in the third standard of field work as means of obtaining evidential matter, inquiry is perhaps the weakest in terms of the credibility of the evidence acquired. Inquiry is a means of eliciting information that is not otherwise available, but there may be no reasonable or practicable means of verifying the accuracy of the information provided. Thus, in terms of eliciting information not otherwise available, a segregation of incompatible duties to be performed by separate individuals leaves no audit trail of documentary evidence. Whether the control is operational can be satisfied only by inquiry. As another instance in which inquiry is the only feasible approach, consider that material requisitions are sorted into numerical order before being filed away for possible reference, and that a person has been made responsible for ascertaining that all requisitions in a batch are present before the batch is placed in storage. Although inspection of sample batches could be used to determine whether all of the requisitions are present in a batch, the time required to make the inspection probably would not be justified by the information acquired. Addressing an inquiry to the person with assigned responsibility for determining whether numbers are accounted for should provide some evidence, and other confirming evidence may be available. For instance, if losses of requisitions should occur frequently and the losses are not corrected, there are likely to be observable consequences, such as inventory shortages and stockouts, as well as understated costs or expenses. Furthermore, limitations of evidence acquired through inquiry can sometimes be partly overcome by requesting supplementary or confirming information in the response. The inquiry about accounting for requisition numbers could cover such related matters as what proportion of the employee's time is devoted to that task, how frequently exceptions are noted, what steps are taken when a number is missing, and what information has been disclosed through investigation of missing numbers.

*Analytical Review.* Not specifically mentioned by the third standard of field work as a procedure for obtaining evidence, analytical review was first recognized by that name in official literature in 1972, although the procedure itself was in fairly widespread use prior to that time. An extensive discussion of analytical review procedures was presented in Statement on Auditing Standards 23, which is referenced in Professional Standards at AU Sec. 318. The pronouncement classifies analytical review procedures as substantive tests of financial information, but states that the discussion of the procedures is intended only to offer guidance; no specific analytical review procedures are required by the pronouncement.

The premise underlying analytical review procedures is that relationships among data may reasonably be expected to remain stable unless there are conditions to cause a change in the relationships. For instance, the rate of gross margin in a retail business will tend to remain fairly constant, barring any change in the mix of sales with varying margins, or changes in market conditions affecting either the purchase price of goods or their selling price. If there is a marked change in the gross margin rate that can be fully explained by changes in sales mix or market conditions, then the auditor has confirming circumstantial evidence that the sales and cost of sales figures that determine the margin rate are fairly stated. Conversely, if there seem to be no known factors that account for the change, then the auditor should extend the examination of sales and cost of sales and also extend the examination of inventory as an element of cost of sales. It is this capacity to identify problem areas that may require more extensive examination and investigation that makes analytical review especially valuable early in the audit process, when the audit program is being developed, as was shown in Figure 5-2.

The relationships contemplated in analytical reviews may be simple month-to-month or year-to-year comparisons; or they may be more complex comparisons involving intrastatement relationships, such as the current ratio, or percent of variable expenses to sales; or interstatement relationships, such as the turnover of receivables or inventory. A more sophisticated approach to analytical review comparisons, which considers relationships over a longer period of time and recognizes trends that have affected the relationship, is the use of regression analysis. Some accounting firms have included regression analysis programs in their computer audit software package programs to facilitate the use of that analytical tool by their audit staff.

*Reperformance.* Another audit procedure not referred to in the third standard of field work is reperformance of a task to demonstrate whether it was correctly performed initially. Although reperformance is most commonly used as a form of compliance test, it is also useful in substantive testing, as in auditor recounts of physical inventory quantities to establish that the final inventory figures are based on inventory quantities that were correctly counted by client employees.

### Dual Purpose Tests

The compliance procedures discussed in the preceding chapter and the substantive procedures discussed in this chapter both represent a form of audit activity based on the underlying purpose of the activity: to provide evidence that account balances are fairly stated. The just-completed discussion of audit procedures involved classification of the procedures in terms of the nature of the evidence-gathering activity. With the exception of analytical review procedures, each of these types of procedures can be used to gather compliance evidence or substantive evidence. A single procedure may actually serve both purposes. For instance, confirmation of a receivable provides not only substantive evidence of the existence and amount of the receivable, but also evidence that the system of internal control is effective and is being complied with, when confirmation results show that the account balances are free of error. Similarly, the procedure of inquiry may be used in determining compliance with internal control, as suggested earlier, or in eliciting evidence related to substantive matters, such as the existence of liabilities that have not been recorded or the disposal of property that is still listed as an asset.

### Two Approaches to Substantive Tests: Inventory and Transaction

Substantive audit procedures can also be classified in terms of the approach that is involved in obtaining the substantive evidence. For balance sheet accounts representing the net effect of increases and decreases in underlying assets or equities, an *inventory* approach that involves the summation of the underlying evidence is most efficient and effective. However, for a plant asset account that may turn over once in several years, a *transaction* approach may be more efficient, assuming that the auditor established the correctness of the account balance at the close of the previous year. In that case, determining that all transactions involving changes in the account (additions and retirements) have been properly recorded is likely to involve less examination time than inspecting each of the underlying assets and the evidence of what each asset cost.

### Determining When Evidence Is Sufficient and Competent

This discussion now turns to the quantitative and qualitative aspects of evidence, which the third standard of field work refers to in terms of the evidence obtained being *sufficient* and *competent*. The question of how much evidence the auditor should obtain in support of each amount in the financial statements will be affected by the following factors:

1. The auditor's preliminary assessment of audit risk, based on knowledge about the client, about the industry in which the client operates, and about general economic conditions.

2. The confidence the auditor has been able to acquire over time in

the integrity of management and the reliability of information produced by the client's accounting system.

3. The relative risk associated with the particular financial statement item being examined. The relative risk that a particular item may be misstated, as contrasted to the general risk of misstatement that exists for all items in the financial statements, will be affected by a) any hint from analytical review that the item may not be properly stated, b) conclusions based on the study and evaluation of internal control pertaining to the item, c) the potential risk of misstatement that could result from the susceptibility of an asset, such as cash or certain inventory items, to theft or embezzlement, and d) the relative ease or difficulty of manipulating the accounting records to conceal any theft or embezzlement, or to intentionally misstate financial position and operating results.

4. The materiality of the item in question. Materiality involves the relative importance of an item when compared with such figures as net income, total assets, current assets, or current liabilities.

5. The competence of the evidence available in support of an item. The competence of evidence is more fully examined in a subsequent section of this chapter, but for the moment it should be recognized that if the competence of available evidence is limited, possibilities for overcoming the shortcoming may include examining additional amounts of the available evidential matter or examining other evidence that will corroborate the evidence in question. As an example, if inventory is priced on a standard cost basis, the pricing should be tested against the standards records. However, because the standard cost records are client-prepared and could be incorrectly stated, they should be corroborated by comparing them with actual materials invoices and labor tickets to determine the reasonableness of the standards.

6. The availability of collateral evidence. An especially powerful example of collateral evidence arises from the fact that net income can be determined not only as the excess of revenues over expenses, but also as the increase in net assets arising from operations over the stated period of time. Thus in a repeat audit, because the auditor will have verified assets and liabilities at both the beginning of the year (the audited balance sheet for the previous year) and at the end of the year, the change in net assets—after considering any changes in owners' equity resulting from capital transactions or asset distributions—will directly support net income as reported in the income statement. Such support for the net income figure indicates that revenues and expenses overall must be fairly stated, and hence the substantive testing of revenue and expense accounts is customarily less extensive than of asset and liability accounts.

### Variables Affecting Sufficiency of Evidence

As we have seen, internal control is a form of indirect evidence, with its sufficiency related to the strength of internal control present in the client's accounting system. The amount of direct evidence to be added to the indirect evidence then becomes a function of the reliance on internal control, as set forth in the second standard of field work. The variables available to the auditor for restricting the extent of tests are here treated in further detail.

*Trade-Off between Compliance and Substantive Tests.* The auditor must decide early in audit planning what the relative cost effectiveness is of making compliance tests—to determine the degree to which internal control may be relied upon—versus limiting or omitting the compliance tests and modifying the related substantive tests to achieve the desired level of assurance.

The succeeding discussion relates to the modification variables involved in substantive tests: their nature, timing, and extent.

*Nature of Tests.* In many instances there are alternative means by which evidence can be obtained, each procedure being of a different nature. For instance, the physical existence of a client's inventory can be established by observing the client's inventory-taking procedures; by inspecting some of the inventory items, including determination of the quantity of items on hand; or, in the case of inventories stored at a public warehouse, by requesting confirmation of the inventories from the warehouse operator. Similarly the amount of accounts payable can be established by examining vendor invoices in support of the recorded amounts, by requesting vendors to confirm the amount that is owed to them by the client, or by some combination of these or other procedures, including inquiry to determine what steps the client has taken to assure that all liabilities at the balance sheet date have been recorded. In selecting the particular tests to be performed, the auditor will seek to obtain an optimum result in terms of the efficacy of the alternative procedures and the cost of applying the procedures.

*Timing of Tests.* We have seen that internal control can be studied on a preliminary basis, leaving the auditor with the need to determine whether any changes in internal control occurred between the time of the preliminary study and the end of the year. An alternative is to wait until the end of the year to begin the study of internal control. Although waiting for the end of the year may be cost efficient, other factors must be considered. Clients frequently want the audited financial statements to be available soon after the end of the fiscal year, for the annual stockholders meeting or for other reasons, and doing preliminary work is helpful to an early delivery of the audit report. Also, although the use of a natural business year is gaining popularity, more businesses close their books at December 31 than at any other month end. As a consequence of that fact, coupled with the peak load for tax services to be rendered to individual taxpayers, most of whom file their returns on a calendar year basis, the public accounting profession experiences a heavy work load from January through April 15. Doing as much audit work as possible on a preliminary basis helps to spread that peak load.

If the client's system of internal control is good, some of the substantive procedures can also be performed on a preliminary basis. For instance, some companies make their annual physical inventory counts one or more months prior to the fiscal year closing. Such an arrangement makes it possible for the auditor to complete much of the substantive inventory testing at that time, provided that internal control can be relied on to properly reflect in the accounts all inventory transactions that occur between the count date and the end of the client's fiscal year. Based on such reliance and limited supplementary tests of the recording of transactions in the interim period, plus limited substantive tests of the year-end balance of the inventory account, the auditor should be able to gain adequate assurance that the inventory is fairly stated, with much of the work accomplished on an off-peak basis.

Timing is thus a variable affecting sufficiency. Evidence obtained at a preliminary date is not as conclusive as evidence directly related to the year-end financial statements; but the added cost of obtaining the desired sufficiency of evidence necessitated by the preliminary application of audit procedures can be expected to be more than offset by the benefits of reduced peak work loads and earlier completion of the audit.

*Extent of Samples.* Clearly the sufficiency of evidence is a function of the amount of evidence obtained, and amount is directly related to sample size. The question of determining sample size and the statistical interpretation of sampling results are extensively treated in Chapter 9, which deals with statistical sampling.

*Competence of Evidence: Fictitious Amounts vs. Omissions.* Inspecting evidence in support of a recorded amount or account balance should provide competent evidence that the amount is valid and has not been misstated; but that evidence will not be competent to reveal that an amount has been omitted from the population being verified. Omissions can be detected only by working from a reciprocal population in which the omitted amount is included. To demonstrate, assume that a listing of accounts receivable balances is to be verified by testing a sample of the listed balances against the accounts receivable subsidiary ledger from which the listing was purportedly prepared. Inspecting the subsidiary ledger account balances in support of the selected listings should provide competent evidence that the listed amounts are appropriately included and are not misstated. But the evidence provided *will not be competent to disclose an account that has been omitted* from the listing—either by oversight or in an attempt to conceal from the auditor the fact that the ac-

count is fictitious. The reciprocal population in this case is the accounts
receivable ledger, and the omitted account can be detected only by reversing the direction of the test and tracing amounts from the subsidiary
ledger to the listing of the accounts.

The design of the auditor's tests should include consideration of relative risk. If the auditor concludes that a risk of either fictitious *or* omitted amounts could be present, tests pertaining to the listed amounts
should be made in both directions, using a separate population for the
tests in each direction. The two possible conditions and the directionality
of tests to be made in recognition of those conditions may be summarized as follows:

*Testing to detect fictitious amounts (risk of overstatement):*

Record to be verified → supporting evidence

*Testing to detect omitted amounts (risk of understatement):*

Reciprocal population
of supporting evidence → Record to be verified

*Materiality.* Figures in the financial statements are more likely to be
important (material) to users of the statements if the figures are significant in amount or are of an especially critical nature, such as net income
or short-term liabilities. Those figures that are most material should be
supported by the greatest amount of reliable evidence. Materiality is
more fully discussed in the following chapter.

*Reliability of Evidence.* Reliability, the final factor to be considered relative to the sufficiency of evidence, varies in relation to the nature of the
evidence that is to be inspected. The following section classifies evidence
according to various characteristics that directly affect reliability.

### Reliability of Evidence Related to Classification by Nature

The most useful way to address the reliability of evidence is in terms
of the relative reliability of various classes or types of evidence. The classification system presented in the following discussion is directly related
to the focal point of the auditor's examination: the client's financial statements.

### Primary Evidence

The source of figures in a concern's financial statements is the general
ledger, which in turn receives its figures from the journals or books of
original entry that are maintained. These books of record constitute the

primary evidence in support of the financial statements. The auditor must, therefore, be certain that the statements agree with the ledger and must, in turn, be satisfied that the figures in the ledger originated from the various journals. The reliability of primary evidence will depend on the internal control present in the accounting system. The double-entry system itself, the balancing of subsidiary ledgers and control accounts, the cross-footing of journals, the use of control totals and equipment with built-in error-sensing devices, the division of responsibility for various phases of the work, and the work of the internal auditor all have a direct bearing on the reliability of records.

Once the auditor is satisfied that the statements agree with the primary evidence in the form of ledger and journals, the next step is to look to the propriety, validity, and accuracy of the ledger balances and the entries in the journals. The evidence pertaining to these matters (beyond the question of internal control) is considered to be supporting evidence, of which there are many types, varying greatly in reliability.

### Supporting Evidence

The amount of supporting evidence to be consulted by the auditor in corroboration of the books of record will vary inversely with the internal control that entered into the preparation of these records. The wide variation in the reliability of supporting evidence makes it important that each form of such evidence be carefully weighed to ascertain its true significance. The basic types of supporting evidence are discussed below in the approximate order of their reliability, commencing with the strongest forms.

*Physical Evidence.* Physical evidence is somewhat limited in that it exists only in support of the so-called tangible assets, such as inventory and plant equipment. Cash on hand is also included in the tangible classification for purposes of this discussion, despite the fact that in property taxation all forms of cash are usually treated as intangible assets.

Although it should be evident that actual examination of a given asset is the best possible evidence that the asset exists, all physical evidence is not equally reliable. Counting the cash on hand would appear to be adequate evidence of the correctness of the corresponding ledger balance, but the evidence is not fully conclusive if customers' checks are included in the total. Coin and currency may be quite safely accepted at their face, as counterfeiting is quite difficult and rather effectively discouraged; a check, however, is not only easily counterfeited but, even if authentic, may prove to be backed by insufficient funds. Consequently, a check should be further supported by evidence that the check was deposited and that the bank was able to collect the full amount. Even coins and currency may be questionable evidence under certain circumstances, as for instance if there are several separate cash funds maintained in separate locations. If the auditor does not take proper precautions, it is possible to be misled into believing that the full amount of cash called for by the ledger has been accounted for, when in fact the same coins and currency may have been counted several times at different locations!

The physical goods supporting an inventory figure may also prove to be less than perfect evidence, and the dollar valuation of the inventory units to arrive at amounts shown in the financial statements poses an additional problem. Flasks of "rare perfume" may actually be only cologne, or even less; and a storage area containing the exact number of television sets called for by the records may prove to be only a half-truth if the sets are defective, although carried at their full cost in the inventory. In a different vein, an independent diamond expert's written report on the weight and quality of a packet of stones may be better evidence than the auditor's own examination of the gems. By contrast, if a major portion of a client's inventory is stored in a public warehouse, the auditor may conclude that the warehouse should be visited to gain physical contact with the goods, even though a warehouse receipt for the goods is available for inspection and the auditor could also obtain a written statement from the warehouse confirming the quantity of goods in storage for the client.

*Documentary Evidence.*   The type of evidence most commonly consulted by the auditor is documentary evidence. Documents vary widely in terms of their reliability as evidence, however, and further classification of documentary evidence is necessary to provide a clue as to its reliability. One important basis of classification is whether it was prepared within the client's organization or by someone who is independent of the client.

*Externally Created Documents Sent Directly to the Auditor.*   If documents prepared by third parties are sent directly to the auditor, they ordinarily constitute evidence of a degree of reliability approaching that of physical evidence, or even exceeding the reliability of physical evidence, as in the case of the expert's report on the diamonds mentioned above. Such externally prepared documents lose part of their reliability if they pass through the client's organization before the auditor inspects them, as there is then a possibility that the documents may have been altered or that the documents are fictitious.

Extreme caution must be exercised whenever the auditor plans to rely on documentary evidence. This point may be illustrated by reference to the use of external evidence in verifying accounts receivable. The best indication of the validity of an account is to have the debtor confirm in writing to the auditor the amount that the debtor owes to the auditor's client. In requesting confirmation, the auditor not only asks that the reply be sent directly to the auditor, but a return envelope addressed to the auditor is enclosed to be used for the reply. In addition, the auditor should verify the address to which the confirmation request is to be mailed to ensure the authenticity of the reply. The possibility always exists that a fictitious account might be carried under the name of a well known and reputable firm, but with an incorrect address given. This address would be one to which the person responsible for creating the fictitious account would have access so that it would be possible to respond to the auditor's request with a fraudulent reply, indicating that the balance shown by the client's records was correct.

*Externally Created Documents in the Client's Posession.* The possibility that externally created documents that are in the client's possession may be fictitious or altered should not be taken to suggest that such documents are valueless as evidence. They are substantially more reliable than documents originating within the client's organization, and items such as bank statements and vendors' invoices constitute two of the most widely used forms of evidence.

Two considerations should always be kept in mind when the auditor uses such evidence. First, the document should be examined for an overall appearance of authenticity, and any alterations should be carefully investigated. It is the auditor's responsibility to determine whether an alteration is a correction made to rectify an unintentional error that occurred when the document was prepared, or whether the alteration was made at a later date for the purpose of misleading subsequent users of the document.

The second consideration in relying on evidence of the class under discussion is the relative ease with which a document may be counterfeited. A note receivable is likely to be extremely weak in this respect, because notes are commonly executed on forms available at any bank or stationery store, and the maker's signature is the only distinguishing feature. As the auditor is not a handwriting expert, nor expected to be one, a counterfeit note could be readily prepared and represented to the auditor as being authentic. The need for further supplementary evidence under such circumstances is obvious, and confirmation of the validity of the note by correspondence with the debtor is in order.

In contrast to the note receivable, a bond or stock certificate is quite commonly accepted on its face. Only a specialist can accomplish the intricate engraving of the certificate, and such specialists are ordinarily quite careful to accept business only from sources known to be authentic. Furthermore, the asset being verified and the certificate evidencing the asset gain additional reliability through regulation of the exchanges and brokers through which securities are traded, as well as the precautionary measures instituted by the exchanges themselves. About halfway between the note receivable and the engraved certificate in relative difficulty of counterfeiting and substitution is the vendor's invoice. Such a document would have to be specially printed, in contrast to the note form which can be purchased already printed, but the average printer in a large city would not be likely to be as careful about investigating a customer as would the engraver.

*Evidence Originating within the Client's Organization.* The auditor obtains a considerable proportion of the needed evidence from sources within the client's organization. Such evidence may be verbal, as is likely in connection with the response to an inquiry pertaining to internal control, but preferably and more frequently it will be documentary. In either case the evidence is likely to be less reliable than the classes of evidence previously discussed, for two reasons. First, the employees giving the information or preparing the documents are under the direct control of management, and therefore the evidence may not be fully acceptable in attempting to corroborate the representations of management. Second, if a defalcation has occurred, information given by employees or documents prepared by them may be falsified in an effort to conceal any manipulations relating to the defalcation.

*Internal Evidence Circulating outside the Business.* In spite of the limitations, however, in some instances evidence from internal sources may approach the reliability of externally created documents. For instance, a paid check bearing evidence of having passed through the bank is generally considered to be fairly conclusive evidence that a liability has been paid, that an expense has been incurred, or that the cost of a new asset has been properly shown in the records.

There are several reasons why a paid check may be considered as being highly reliable evidence. Because cash is the most liquid of assets, there will normally be relatively good internal control in the handling of cash, including its disbursement by check. This assurance of validity is further enhanced by the fact that a paid check has passed through the hands of persons outside the originating organization, presumably with no objection having been raised concerning the correctness of the check. Finally, the paid check gains in reliability because it can be tied in with the bank statement, which is externally created.

Only a few internally created documents are subject to any outside review, and none of them has as many protective features as does the paid check, particularly with respect to the limited availability of blank forms and the difficulty of making alterations. Other documents would include a copy of the purchase order returned with the vendor's acknowledgement, a copy of a bill of lading receipted by the carrier's agent, and a bank deposit slip showing a teller's stamp to indicate that the funds had been received.

*Internal Evidence Circulating Only within the Business.* Many internal forms and records, even though not receiving the additional validation accruing to documents that circulate outside the business, may still have a high degree of reliability, with internal control the determining factor. The internal control may be in the form of extensive review of the document by other employees after it is prepared, or segregation of duties so that the person preparing the document has no operating responsibility and therefore no reason for preparing a misleading document or giving misleading verbal information. A good illustration is a receiving report prepared in the receiving department. The report will be compared in the accounting department with the company copy of the purchase order for the material and with the vendor's invoice, reviewed again when the invoice is paid by the treasurer's office, and checked by the stock clerk to be sure that the quantity of goods shown on the receiving report has been delivered by the receiving department for placement into stock.

In contrast, an authorization created by the credit manager directing the bookkeeper to write off an uncollectible account is of limited value as evidence, because the bookkeeper would not be expected to make a critical review of the authorization. The situation is greatly changed, though, if the credit manager sends the authorization to a member of the controller's staff for approval, along with a copy of the customer's ledger sheet, a record of the collection action that has been taken, and any related correspondence. The controller's representative can act with full freedom because there is no direct line of responsibility between the controller and the credit manager. The controller's representative is not likely to approve the authorization unless it is valid, and there would be no reason to do otherwise, for there would be no opportunity to obtain company assets.

*Verbal Information and Written Certificates.* When the purpose in obtaining verbal information or written certificates from employees is to corroborate data obtained from other sources, the evidence may well be satisfactory. A repairman, traveling with a complete inventory of repair parts, may be requested to send the auditor a certificate listing the repair parts in his possession. Such a certificate is of little value as evidence that the repairman actually has the listed parts in his possession. But if the information in the certificate is desired to verify office records showing the amount of parts inventory charged out to the repairman, and the repairman is fully accountable for the value of those parts, the worth of the certificate as evidence would be considerably greater. To further illustrate the point, a verbal or written statement from the credit manager indicating the loss anticipated from uncollectible accounts receivable would hardly be a sound basis for determining the adequacy of the provision for bad-debt losses. But if the auditor had already aged the accounts receivable and arrived at an estimate of the possible loss, and the credit manager's estimate was in line with the auditor's estimate, the auditor should be entitled to additional confidence in both estimates.

To summarize briefly, the important factors affecting the reliability of internal evidence are (1) whether the documents have circulated through the hands of outside parties, (2) whether good internal control was involved in the preparation and use of documents, and (3) whether the evidence obtained must stand alone or serves to corroborate other evidence.

### Circumstantial Evidence

Those forms of evidence already presented represent direct evidence that may be consulted in the process of examining financial statements; but circumstantial evidence, which is a form of indirect evidence, is also quite important and useful. Circumstantial evidence involves circumstances from which a reasonable inference can be drawn about the existence of a given fact or the occurrence of a given event. More directly in the realm of auditing, it involves circumstances that support an inference as to the reasonableness or correctness of a given figure in a client's financial statements, or of the financial statements as a whole. Some of the forms of circumstantial evidence that the auditor commonly considers in the course of an examination include

1. The system of internal control.
2. The general orderliness and neatness of the client's records, storage areas, and production areas.
3. The qualifications and ability of the persons responsible for supervising and maintaining the accounting records.
4. The absence of any known or apparent reason to misstate figures in the financial statements.
5. The reasonableness of financial statement figures, as determined by analytical review, relative to general economic conditions, industry trends, and known changes within the client's own organization and operation.

Circumstantial evidence is perhaps most widely considered in examining the statements of large, quasi-public, industrial organizations and public utilities. The mass of detailed evidence existing in such concerns is so great that it makes extensive examination of the evidence economically unsound; and the strong circumstantial evidence available makes extensive reference to such detailed evidence relatively unnecessary. Perhaps the most important feature in an examination involving such organizations is the careful review of the extensive internal controls that are almost certain to be present, plus sufficient compliance tests to assure the auditor that the controls are operating effectively. Even the substantive tests of supporting evidence to the statement figures tend to be as much for the purpose of proving the internal control as for proving the figures themselves.

For small businesses, however, the situation is completely reversed. The centralization of authority and responsibility in one or two individuals may make even the strongest case of circumstantial evidence practically meaningless, and the auditor has no alternative but to compensate by making extensive reference to all the available forms of supporting evidence. Whether the business is large or small, however, the auditor must select evidence carefully, determine just how much evidence should be examined based on the circumstances, and evaluate the evidence judiciously in formulating an opinion concerning the financial statements in question.

### Summary

This chapter has added the superstructure of direct evidence, acquired through the application of substantive audit procedures, to the foundation of indirect evidence, acquired through the study and evaluation of the client's sytem of internal control. The totality of the direct and indirect evidence acquired constitutes the basis for the opinion to be expressed on a client's financial statements. The discussion of substantive procedures has covered the various types of procedures and has indicated how the procedures are adapted to given situations through varying the nature, timing, and extent of the procedures. Substantive procedures were also categorized according to whether the procedures represent a transaction or an inventory approach to the acquisition of direct evidence. Finally, various aspects of the sufficiency of evidence and the reliability of various types of evidence were presented and discussed.

The following chapter addresses the matter of how the results of audit activities and the direct and indirect evidence acquired are organized and brought together in the audit work paper files.

### Questions/Problems

For multiple-choice questions 7-1 through 7-6, indicate the letter of the single answer that *best* completes the statement or answers the question, and justify the choice that you have made.

**7-1.**   The size of an audit sample
   a.   Is directly related to obtaining "sufficient competent evidential matter."
   b.   Will be affected by the auditor's evaluation of the client's internal control.
   c.   Should not be directly proportional to the number of items in the population.
   d.   Each of the above is a true statement relative to audit samples.

**7-2.**   The most conclusive evidence that invoice No. 2468 charged to the account receivable from John Flush Plumbing Co. on December 28 has been paid would be:
   a.   A Jan. 15 credit posted to the J F P Account in the same amount as the invoice.
   b.   The bank deposit ticket for Jan. 15 showing an amount equal to the Jan. 15 payment posted to the J F P account.
   c.   The cash receipts book showing cash received from J F P in the amount of the invoice on Jan. 15.
   d.   The most conclusive evidence is not listed above.

**7-3.**   During the course of an audit, an auditor required additional research and consultation with others. This additional research and consultation is considered to be
   a.   An appropriate part of the professional conduct of the engagement.
   b.   A responsibility of the management, not the auditor.
   c.   A failure on the part of the CPA to comply with generally accepted auditing standards because of a lack of competence.
   d.   An unusual practice which indicates that the CPA should not have accepted the engagement.

   (Uniform CPA Examination)

**7-4.**   Which of the following types of documentary evidence should the auditor consider to be the most reliable?
   a.   A sales invoice issued by the client and supported by a delivery receipt from an outside trucker.
   b.   Confirmation of an account-payable balance mailed by and returned directly to the auditor.
   c.   A check issued by the company and bearing the payee's endorsement which is included with the bank statement mailed directly to the auditor.
   d.   A working paper prepared by the client's controller and reviewed by the client's treasurer.

   (Uniform CPA Examination)

7-5. Although the validity of evidential matter is dependent on the circumstances under which it is obtained, there are three general presumptions which have some usefulness. The situations given below indicate the relative reliability a CPA has placed on two types of evidence obtained in different situations. Which of these is an exception to one of the general presumptions?

   a. The CPA places more reliance on the balance in the scrap sales account at plant A where the CPA has made limited tests of transactions because of good internal control than at plant B where the CPA has made extensive tests of transactions because of poor internal control.

   b. The CPA places more reliance on the CPA's computation of interest payable on outstanding bonds than on the amount confirmed by the trustee.

   c. The CPA places more reliance on the report of an expert on an inventory of precious gems than on the CPA's physical observation of the gems.

   d. The CPA places more reliance on a schedule of insurance coverage obtained from the company's insurance agent than on one prepared by the internal audit staff.

(Uniform CPA Examination)

7-6. Audit programs are modified to suit the circumstances on particular engagements. A complete audit program for an engagement generally should be developed

   a. Prior to beginning the actual audit work.

   b. After the auditor has completed an evaluation of the existing internal accounting control.

   c. After reviewing the client's accounting records and procedures.

   d. When the audit engagement letter is prepared.

(Uniform CPA Examination)

7-7. Would circumstantial evidence in the form of a decrease in the percentage of purchase discounts earned relative to purchases be of more concern to the internal auditor or the independent auditor? Explain.

7-8. A cash credit posted to an account receivable subsequent to the balance sheet date would represent evidence that an actual receivable existed and that no loss would be incurred on the amount of the receivable that was collected. Would the evidence be equally conclusive as to the validity of the account (that is, that the receivable was not fraudulent) and as to its collectibility? Explain.

7-9. The balance sheet of the Jay Co. lists accounts receivable totaling

$100,000 and total assets of $1 million; the income statement shows a net income of $150,000. You estimate bad debt losses on the receivables to be $5,000. How much would you be willing to permit the company's provision for losses on bad debts to vary from your $5,000 estimate without considering the difference to be *material,* assuming that losses have been provided for on the same basis as in prior years? Give reasons for your answer.

**7-10.** List, in order of reliability, the various items of evidence that might be examined in support of each of the following:

   a.  A credit posted to a past-due account after the balance sheet date, showing the account was paid in full.

   b.  The material costs shown on a job cost card.

   c.  An account receivable on which no reply was received to the auditor's request that the customer confirm the balance of the account to the auditor.

**7-11.** Do tests of transactions generally play a more significant role in the examination of the balance sheet or in the examination of the income statement? Justify your answer.

**7-12.** During the course of an audit engagement an independent auditor gives serious consideration to the concepts of materiality. This concept of materiality is inherent in the work of the independent auditor and is important for planning, preparing, and modifying audit programs. The concept of materiality underlies the application of all the generally accepted auditing standards, particularly the standards of field work and reporting.

Required:

   a.  Briefly describe what is meant by the independent auditor's concept of materiality.

   b.  What are some common relationships and other considerations used by the auditor in judging materiality?

   c.  Identify how the planning and execution of an audit program might be affected by the independent auditor's concept of materiality.

(Uniform CPA Examination)

**7-13.** In his examination of financial statements, an auditor must judge the validity of the audit evidence he obtains.

Required:

Assume that you have evaluated internal control and found it satisfactory.

   a.  In the course of his examination, the auditor asks many questions of client officers and employees.

    1.  Describe the factors that the auditor should consider in evaluating oral evidence provided by client officers and employees.

    2.  Discuss the validity and limitations of oral evidence.

  b.  An auditor's examination may include computation of various balance-sheet and operating ratios for comparison to prior years and industry averages. Discuss the validity and limitations of ratio analysis.

  c.  In connection with his examination of the financial statements of a manufacturing company, an auditor is observing the physical inventory of finished goods, which consists of expensive, highly complex electronic equipment. Discuss the validity and limitations of the audit evidence provided by this procedure.

(Uniform CPA Examination)

**7-14.** You are the auditor of Star Manufacturing Company. You have obtained the following data:

A trial balance taken from the books of Star one month prior to year end follows:

|  | Dr. (Cr.) |  |
|---|---|---|
| Cash in bank *cut off statement – confirmation* | $ 87,000 | *yes* |
| Trade accounts receivable | 345,000 | *yes* |
| Notes receivable | 125,000 | *yes* |
| Inventories | 317,000 |  |
| Land | 66,000 | *no* |
| Buildings, net | 350,000 | *no* |
| Furniture, fixtures, and equipment, net | 325,000 | *no* |
| Trade accounts payable | (235,000) | *yes* |
| Mortgages payable | (400,000) | *yes* |
| Capital stock | (300,000) | *no* |
| Retained earnings | (510,000) | *no* |
| Sales | (3,130,000) | *yes if material* |
| Cost of sales | 2,300,000 |  |
| General and administrative expenses | 622,000 | *yes* |
| Legal and professional fees | 3,000 | *yes* |
| Interest expense | 35,000 | *yes* |

There are no inventories consigned either in or out.

All notes receivable are due from outsiders and held by Star.

Required:

Which accounts should be confirmed with outside sources? Briefly describe from whom they should be confirmed and the information which should be confirmed. Organize your answer in the following format.

| Account Name | From Whom Confirmed | Information To Be Confirmed |
| --- | --- | --- |
|  |  |  |

(Uniform CPA Examination)

**7-15.** Part a. In a properly planned examination of financial statements, the auditor coordinates his reviews of specific balance-sheet and income-statement accounts.

Required:

Why should the auditor coordinate his examinations of balance-sheet accounts and income-statement accounts? Discuss and illustrate by examples.

Part b. A properly designed audit program enables the auditor to determine conditions or establish relationships in more than one way.

Required:

Cite various procedures that the auditor employs that might lead to detection of each of the following two conditions:

1. Inadequate allowance for doubtful accounts receivable.
2. Unrecorded retirements of property, plant, and equipment.

(Uniform CPA Examination)

**7-16.** Evidential matter supporting the financial statements consists of the underlying accounting data and all corroborating information available to the auditor. In the course of an independent audit of financial statements, the auditor will perform detail tests of samples of transactions from various large-volume populations. The auditor may also audit various types of transactions by tracing a single transaction of each type through all stages of the accounting system.

Required:

a. What are the various audit objectives associated with a sample of transactions from a large-volume population?
b. What evidential matter would the auditor expect to gain from auditing various types of transactions by tracing a single transaction of each type through all stages of the accounting system?

(Uniform CPA Examination)

**7-17.** The third generally accepted auditing standard of field work requires that the auditor obtain sufficient competent evidential matter to afford a reasonable basis for an opinion regarding the financial statements under examination. In considering what constitutes sufficient competent evidential matter, a distinction should be made between underlying accounting data and all corroborating information available to the auditor.

Required:

a. Discuss the nature of evidential matter to be considered by the auditor in terms of the underlying accounting data, all corroborating information available to the auditor, and the methods by which the auditor tests or gathers competent evidential matter.

b. State the three general presumptions that can be made about the validity of evidential matter with respect to comparative assurance, persuasiveness, and reliability.

(Uniform CPA Examination)

**7-18.** Ratio analysis is often applied to test the reasonableness of the relationships among current financial data against those of prior financial data. Given prior financial relationships and a few key amounts, a CPA could prepare estimates of current financial data to test the reasonableness of data furnished by his client.

Argo Sales Corporation has in recent prior years maintained the following relationships among the data on its financial statements:

| | | |
|---|---|---|
| 1. | Gross profit rate on net sales | 40% |
| 2. | Net profit rate on net sales | 10% |
| 3. | Rate of selling expense to net sales | 20% |
| 4. | Accounts receivable turnover | 8 per year |
| 5. | Inventory turnover | 6 per year |
| 6. | Acid-test ratio | 2 to 1 |
| 7. | Current ratio | 3 to 1 |
| 8. | Quick-asset composition: 8% cash, 32% marketable securities, 60% accounts receivable | |
| 9. | Asset turnover | 2 per year |
| 10. | Ratio of total assets to intangible assets | 20 to 1 |
| 11. | Ratio of accumulated depreciation to cost of fixed assets | 1 to 3 |
| 12. | Ratio of accounts receivable to accounts payable | 1.5 to 1 |
| 13. | Ratio of working capital to stockholders' equity | 1 to 1.6 |
| 14. | Ratio of total debt to stockholders' equity | 1 to 2 |

The Corporation had a net income of $120,000 for the current year, which resulted in earnings of $5.20 per share of common stock. Additional information includes the following:

1. Capital stock authorized, issued eight years ago, and outstanding:
   Common, $10 per share par value, issued at 10% premimum
   Preferred, 6% nonparticipating, $100 per share par value, issued at a 10% premium

2. Market value per share of common at December 31: $78
3. Preferred dividends paid this year: $3,000
4. Times interest earned this year: 33
5. The amounts of the following were the same at December 31 as at the beginning of the year: inventory, accounts receivable, 5% bonds payable—due two years hence, and total stockholders' equity.
6. All purchases and sales were "on account."
   (a) Prepare in good form the condensed (1) balance sheet and (2) income statement for the year ending December 31, presenting the amounts you would expect to appear on Argo's financial statements (ignoring income taxes). Major captions appearing on Argo's balance sheet are: Current Assets, Fixed Assets, Intangible Assets, Current Liabilities, Long-term Liabilities, and Stockholders' Equity. In addition to the accounts divulged in the problem, you should include accounts for Prepaid Expenses, Accrued Expenses, and Administrative Expenses. Supporting computations should be in good form.
   (b) Compute the following for the current year (show your computations):
      (1) Rate of return on stockholders' equity
      (2) Price-earnings ratio for common stock
      (3) Dividends paid per share of common stock
      (4) Dividends paid per share of preferred stock
      (5) Yield on common stock

                                                    (Uniform CPA Examination)

# Chapter 8

# THE SYSTEM-BASED AUDIT III

## Documenting the Audit: Working Papers

The auditor's working papers are the vehicle for assembling the extensive and varied evidence that is gathered to support the auditor's opinion. The need for skill and care in working paper preparation is evident in the various purposes that they serve: (1) they assist directly in performing the audit; (2) they aid partners, managers, and seniors in reviewing and evaluating the work of those under their supervision; (3) they provide an historical record showing all the work that has been done to provide the basis for the auditor's report.

Working papers prepared by the auditor are the auditor's property, and they should be carefully preserved. They will be consulted, assuming that another audit is made for the following year, and often they prove useful in providing information to assist the client on problems arising at a later date. Should a charge of negligence ever be brought against the auditor, the auditor's working papers will constitute the principal evidence that the examination was made in accordance with generally accepted auditing standards. Both the preparer and the reviewer must be extremely careful that no holes are left in this defense.

### Content and Organization

Given the significance and function of audit working papers, it will be evident that they should contain documentation of every aspect of the audit process. There are two broad classes of documentation, each normally assembled in a separate working paper file. A *permanent file* will contain information that will be of value to each successive audit that is made. Information in the permanent file would include data concerning such matters as the corporate charter (or partnership agreement), long-term leases, bond indenture provisions, accounting policies and procedures, summaries of changes in the accounts for plant assets and accumulated depreciation, bad-debt experience, and product warranty expenses. In some instances flowcharts or narrative descriptions of the accounting system are held in the permanent file, but in others such information is brought forward each year to the current audit file.

The *current audit file* will contain the working papers pertaining to a specific engagement, for example:

Wilson Company
Audit, October 31, 19XX

The content and arrangement of the working papers in the current audit file is likely to be somewhat as follows:

1. Point sheet or agenda of work to be done, listing questions that have arisen in the course of the examination or as a result of the review of the working papers, and the comments giving the answers to the questions or the disposition of points that have been raised.
2. Audit program or work plan.
3. Internal control evaluation, including any questionnaires or checklists.
4. List of adjusting and reclassification entries.
5. The auditor's trial balance, or working balance sheet and income statement.
6. Lead schedules, or grouping sheets.
7. The detailed working papers, supporting schedules, and evidence obtained, including

   Analyses of accounts.

   Lists of transactions or item details selected for examination, with coded "tick marks" (see page 196) denoting the verification that has been performed.

   Memoranda describing audit activities carried out and reporting the conclusions about the client's figures and records derived from those audit activities, as for example after observing the client's physical inventory procedures.

Notes reporting the information obtained through inquiry or observation.

Replies to confirmation requests to banks, customers, suppliers, and other third parties.

Responses to inquiries addressed to the client's legal counsel, actuaries, or other consultants.

Letters setting forth representation by client officers concerning various accounting and financial matters (see Chapter 19).

### Identifying Information: Proper Headings

Each sheet of working paper should be complete in itself to preclude any question about what it is or where it belongs, should it become separated from the remainder of the working paper file. Most important in this respect is the heading, which should always contain three items of information: (1) name of the client; (2) title of the particular schedule, for example, "Analysis of Changes in Allowance for Doubtful Accounts"; and (3) the date of the statements being examined. If more than one sheet of paper is necessary to complete a given schedule or analysis, each sheet should contain not only the full 3-part heading but should also carry a notation that other pages are a part of the same schedule. Thus, the notation "1 of 2" indicates that the schedule is continued on a second page carrying the notation "2 of 2."

Each sheet of working paper should also contain the name or initials of the person who prepared the paper and the date on which the work was done. This information aids in fixing the responsibility for each phase of the work and makes it possible to contact the proper person if at any time there is any question about the schedule or the work that was done.

Occasionally members of the client's staff will assist the auditor by preparing certain schedules and analyses, which are then reviewed and tested by the auditor in the course of the examination. Such working papers should contain a notation that they have been prepared by the client (the initials "P.B.C." are often used for this purpose), as well as the initials of the auditor who performed the necessary verification. When working papers are reviewed by the senior accountant, manager, or partner, the reviewer should initial each sheet to indicate that the review has been made and to fix responsibility for such review.

### The Trial Balance

The key to any set of working papers is the trial balance, and the auditor will normally prepare the trial balance as soon as the client has made all year-end adjustments. The working-paper trial balance is prepared either directly from the ledger or from a trial balance that the client has prepared. In the latter case, as soon as the auditor's trial balance has been completed and the footings proved, each figure should be traced to the ledger for verification purposes, and the auditor should also ascertain that all ledger balances have been listed in the trial balance. An advantage of working from the client's trial balance is in knowing that the ledger is in balance.

If in preparing the audit trial balance the auditor discovers that the ledger is out of balance, no attempt should be made to locate the error unless the client specifically authorizes such action. Locating errors is a clerical job for which the client is not likely to be willing to pay professional fees. If the client does authorize the auditor to locate the error, the client should understand that such work will increase the audit fee beyond any estimate that may have been given previously.

Each trial balance page is likely to contain seven relatively standard column headings, as follows:

| Account Number and Title | Index | Final Balance Dec. 31, 19__ (Last Year) | Balance per Books Dec. 31, 19__ (This Year) | Adjustments and Reclassifications Dr.   Cr. | Final Balance Dec. 31, 19__ (This Year) |
|---|---|---|---|---|---|

The heading for the first column is self-explanatory, and the matter of indexing is discussed presently. The final figures from the previous audit are included for comparative and reference purposes, as well as to assure the proper starting figure when utilizing the transaction approach of verifying intervening transactions in order to establish the propriety of the closing balance of an account. The column for this year's balances should always include all revenue and expense balances, even if the client has already closed the balances of these accounts to the retained earnings account. The working papers must contain the full detail of the income statement, assuming that the auditor's opinion is to cover that statement as well as the balance sheet.

The figure used for the balance of the retained earnings account should be the balance at the beginning of the year, with dividends and the current year's earnings shown on succeeding lines. The sum of these three figures will then be the year-end balance of the account as it should appear in the balance sheet, and in this way the balance sheet and income statement will be fully tied together through the figure for net income. There should also be a schedule for the construction of the statement of changes in financial position, but of course this schedule is extracted from the trial balance columns. These points are illustrated in the trial balance for the audit of Machine Products Co. in the illustrative audit working papers that are available separately as a supplement to this text.

## Adjustments and Materiality

Unrecorded transactions, improperly recorded transactions, or incorrect account balances may necessitate recommendation to the client that adjusting (correcting) entries be made. Those adjustments accepted by the client should then be incorporated in the working papers. The auditor may only recommend that the adjustments be made, in view of the client's primary responsibility for the accounting records and the financial statements. In the event of the client's refusal to make a recommended entry, the auditor's recourse is through an opinion qualification concerning the financial statements if a material item is involved.

The matter of materiality was briefly mentioned earlier as a factor affecting the amount of evidence to be obtained, but further discussion is warranted at this point in relation to the materiality of adjustments to the financial statements. The adjustments may involve changes in statement amounts (quantitative adjustments) or additional disclosure of information (qualitative adjustments). The critical question concerning an adjustment is whether any decision by a user of the financial statements would likely be affected by whether or not the adjustment or additional disclosure had been made. Thus, the degree of importance to a statement user of a financial statement amount that would be affected by an adjustment, and the extent to which it would be affected, must be considered. Factors that will affect these aspects of materiality include the following:

1. Materiality is primarily a matter of relationship rather than absolute amount. Hence, the materiality of an improperly recorded credit sale is determined not on the basis of amount but on the basis of the percentage effect of the sale on sales, net income, and accounts receivable.

2. The threshold of materiality for a percentage relationship is determined in part by the point at which the effect of a difference would tend to become readily apparent. That point is generally in the range of 5 to 10 percent.

3. The threshold is affected by the relative importance of the figure to be changed. Thus, net income or total current assets would tend to be more important than sales or the amount of productive assets, and whereas 5 percent of net income might be material, 15 percent of productive assets might not be material.

4. The threshold is also affected by whether the base figure in question can be precisely determined (cash) rather than a figure that is the result of an approximation (depreciation).

5. For adjustments affecting net income when that figure is abnormally low, materiality may be more meaningfully assessed if expressed as a percentage of normal income. Thus, although an adjustment that is 15 percent of net income for the year might appear to be material, it might be considered immaterial if it is less than 5 percent of a normal amount of income.

6. An adjustment that would cause an existing trend in figures to be reversed or accelerated would be more material than an adjustment of a similar amount that would merely reinforce the trend.

7. If there are multiple adjustments to a figure and they are cumulative, the adjustments will be more material than if they tend to offset each other.
8. Quantitative or qualitative adjustments that involve "sensitive" matters, such as disbursements that could be held to be in violation of the Foreign Corrupt Practices Act or loans to officers or other transactions that are not at arm's length or that involve a conflict of interest, will tend to be more material than more normal items.

The foregoing analysis should suggest that materiality is not a matter for which there is a simple test or standard and that the materiality of a relationship cannot be resolved in terms of a specific percentage figure that will mark the separation of the material from the immaterial. A decision must be made in each situation, based on the pertinent aspects of a relationship as determined by the professional judgment of the auditor. A vital consideration in that decision is always the effect that an item might have on a third party using the financial statements. Would failure to insist on an adjustment or failure to disclose certain information be sufficient to cause a person to invest or not to invest in a company's securities; to induce a banker to make or deny a loan or to call an existing obligation; or to cause a customer or vendor to establish, discontinue, or resume relations? Seeking answers to such questions leads us inevitably to stress the presumed reactions of persons relying on the financial statements, and to the observation that materiality, like beauty, exists solely in the eye of the beholder.

### Adjusting Entries and Reversing Entries

Although some clients are quite willing to make any adjustments recommended by the auditor, it is well to consider human nature and the client's point of view in deciding whether or not a given adjustment or group of adjustments should be presented to the client. First, most people take considerable pride in their work and are likely to resent having their mistakes and shortcomings pointed out to them. Furthermore, by the time the auditor is ready to present recommended adjustments, the client will probably have closed the books for the year and have begun entering transactions for the following year, thus making it difficult for the client to record the adjustments in the records. Additional resistance is likely to arise if the client has already released preliminary financial figures to stockholders or creditors, making it awkward to have the audited statements show different figures. Finally, minor adjustments that do not materially affect the financial statements are likely to raise a question as to the auditor's sense of proportion and understanding and appreciation of the magnitude of the client's business—to say nothing of arousing a suspicion that the auditor's fee may be excessive as a result of the auditor's preoccupation with unimportant details. Given these circumstances, the auditor should seriously consider presenting adjustments to the client only if their effect, individually or in total, is such that the auditor would be forced to modify the opinion to be expressed on the financial statements if the client refused to accept the adjustments.

Any adjustments accepted by the client will, of course, be entered by the auditor in the proper columns on the work sheets. Most auditors also insist that the entries be recorded on the client's records to keep them in conformity with the financial statements, although if the books have been closed, entries affecting revenue or expense accounts can be posted to retained earnings.

To facilitate the client's recording of the entries, the auditor usually furnishes a list of the entries, along with any reversing entries to be made. A reversing entry will be necessary if the client has already recorded in the next accounting period a transaction that actually affects the fiscal year that the auditor is examining. For example, customers may have returned merchandise prior to the end of the year, but if the receiving department records of the returns were slow in reaching the accounting department, the entry for the returns might inadvertently be dated and posted to the records for the succeeding year. An adjustment to record the returns in the year under examination would result in duplicating the actual book entries to sales and accounts receivable, but by means of a reversing entry the effect of the original entry by the client would be cancelled.

### Reclassification Entries

Reclassification entries involve transfers of balances made within the auditor's working papers and hence within the financial statements as well. For example, the client may debit sales returns and allowances directly to the sales account, but if the total of these debits is to be shown separately on the statements, the auditor will transfer them to a separate line on the work papers by means of a reclassification entry. Another illustration would be the handling of credit balances in accounts receivable. If the auditor believes these are sufficiently material that they should be classified as a liability, the change can be accomplished by means of reclassification entry.

The entries for adjustments and reclassifications will normally be recorded initially on separate control sheets in the working papers, because only the adjustments will be presented to the client for entry in the accounting records. To further identify each type, adjustments may be numbered 1, 2, 3, and so forth, and reclassifications may be numbered 101, 102, 103, and so on. In addition to an entry number, each adjustment or reclassification should carry a description setting forth the reason for the entry and an indication of the working paper schedule from which the information for the entry was obtained. When the entry is posted to the auditor's working trial balance or lead schedule, the index number of the sheet to which the entry was posted should be noted alongside the appropriate figure on the adjusting entry page. The notation of the posting reference in this manner not only shows that the entry has been posted to the working papers, but also facilitates location of the sheet to which the entry was posted by anyone reviewing the working papers. The separate illustrative Machine Products Co. working papers may be consulted for examples of adjustments and reclassifications and how to handle them.

All adjusting or reclassification entries believed to be necessary should be listed on the control sheets, but the entries should not be posted to the trial balance until they have been reviewed and approved. When the working papers are subsequently reviewed, the reviewer may conclude that an entry is unnecessary because it is for some reason immaterial, incorrect, or improper. In such cases the reviewer should note the working papers accordingly, as for instance "Pass—not material," followed by initials to show who made the decision.

### Alternative Forms of the Trial Balance

In the sample headings for the trial balance given earlier, it should be noted that separate columns were not provided for debit and credit balances. This is because separate sheets are typically used for assets, equities (liabilities and the owners' investment), and income statement items. If a credit belongs on the asset page, as, for instance, the balance of the allowance for doubtful accounts, the amount will be shown in red, or circled, with similar treatment accorded any debit balances on the liability page. Revenues and expenses can be distinguished on the third page of the trial balance by separate grouping and by the description of each item.

In one form of the trial balance all accounts are listed on the appropriate trial balance page in the same sequence in which they appear in the ledger. The ledger sequence will, of course, usually correspond to the sequence in the statements. Remaining columns to the right of the "Final Balance" column can then be used to group similar items that will appear as one figure in the statements. Thus, the balances of three separate bank accounts and the petty cash fund can be listed in one column, and the total of this column can be shown in the balance sheet as "Cash." Combining related accounts on a statement greatly increases readability.

Under a second form of the trial balance related account balances are first listed on separate "lead schedules," or "grouping sheets," and the totals of the lead schedules are brought to the top trial balance pages. This method is sometimes referred to as the "working trial balance" method, or the "working balance sheet and income statement" method. Under this arrangement the top trial balance schedules, which summarize these totals, will be similar to the final form of the client's statements, and the statements to be presented in the auditor's report can be readily prepared from these schedules.

The advantage of the working trial balance arrangement is the ease with which the manager or principal in charge of the work can review the work papers. At the very front of the work paper file is a bird's-eye view of the statements, with all obscuring details removed and last year's figures available for comparison. Major problems are quickly spotted under such an arrangement. At the same time all supporting details are readily available in the lead schedules as the source of the figures on the top trial balance schedules.

The disadvantage of the working trial balance arrangement is the difficulty of transcribing ledger balances to the trial balance pages. Before a figure can be entered, the proper lead schedule must be located; and if the accounts in the ledger are not carefully arranged in statement order, considerable time can be lost turning from one lead schedule to another. And, of course, if the sheets do not balance, the process of locating the error by verifying each figure is equally cumbersome. Many auditors feel, however, that the advantages of the working balance sheet form of trial balance far outweigh the disadvantages. The separately published illustrative work papers for Machine Products Co. referred to in this text are based on the working trial balance alternative.

### Indexing

The auditor's trial balance should always show an index reference for each figure, to help any person using the working paper file to locate the work sheet schedule that supports any given figure. Each accounting firm ordinarily has a uniform plan of indexing, used on all working papers prepared by the staff. The advantage of a uniform plan is that any person connected with the firm can almost instantly locate any particular schedule in a file of work papers, regardless of who prepared the file.

Indexing systems vary greatly, and the system used in the illustrative working papers for this book is only one of many satisfactory systems. It was selected for use here partly because the author is familiar with this system, having worked with it for several years, but also because of its logical simplicity. The basic outline of the system is as follows:

| Trial Balance | Index |
|---|---|
| Assets | B/S-A |
| Liabilities and owners' equity | B/S-L |
| Income statement | I/S |

### Account

| Account | |
|---|---|
| Cash | A |
| Receivables and allowances for losses or discounts | B |
| Inventories | C |
| Prepaid expenses | L |
| Investments | N |
| Intangible assets | P |
| Plant and equipment and accumulated depreciation | U/V |
| Notes payable | AA |
| Accounts payable | BB |
| Accruals | CC |
| Accrued federal income taxes | FF |
| Deferred income | GG |
| Contingent liabilities | KK |
| Long-term liabilities | NN |
| Capital stock | SS |
| Retained earnings and other equity accounts | TT |
| Corporation minutes | XX |
| Sales and sales deductions | 10 |
| Cost of goods sold | 20 |
| Selling expense | 30 |
| General and administrative expense | 40 |
| Other income | 50 |
| Other expense | 60 |

The reader is encouraged to gain an understanding of this indexing system and of how working papers can be tied together through cross referencing, by studying the trial balance for the Machine Products Co. illustrative audit and relating the figures to the supporting working paper schedules for the specific balance sheet or income statement accounts.

### Tick Marks

The auditor makes frequent use in the work papers of a variety of symbols to indicate the work that has been done. These symbols are commonly referred to as *tick marks.* One of the tick marks that is used almost universally by auditors is as follows: И. Although there is a limitless variety, others likely to be used are √ ✗ ∅ **F.**

Since these tick marks have no special or uniform meaning in themselves, no tick mark should ever be used without giving an explanation of its meaning. On a bank reconciliation schedule, the legend explaining the marks used might appear somewhat as follows:

Ⅳ Traced to ledger balance.

√ Traced to bank statement.

∅ Paid check inspected.

**F** Footed and cross-footed.

The appropriate tick mark would then be placed next to any figures that had been verified as indicated by the legend.

### Documenting the Relationship of Internal Control Deficiencies to Substantive Tests

The relationship of the auditor's evaluation of internal control to the substantive auditing procedures to be performed has long been recognized, but the subject did not receive extensive treatment in the official literature until 1972 with the issuance of Statement on Auditing Procedure No. 54, "The Auditor's Study and Evaluation of Internal Control." This material is now incorporated in Professional Standards at AU Sec. 320 and includes a 23-page analysis plus two supplements (now superseded by SAS No. 39) that discuss the aspects of the relationship when statistical sampling is involved. Although the Sec. 320 material is quite complete, it does not address how the adaptation of substantive tests to the auditor's evaluation of internal control might be documented in the audit working papers—a matter that would seem to be important to the completeness of the working papers and to any legal defense involving the adequacy of the auditor's examination.

One accounting firm that has considered this problem has introduced what is referred to as a "bridging" technique. Each weakness in internal control, such as the omission or nonfunctioning of a control feature, is identified in the system flowchart or internal control checklist. Then, based on an analysis of how each such deficiency might affect the financial statements, the working papers must show how the deficiency gap has been "bridged" by a specific modification of the substantive testing program. For instance, if standard costs have not been revised near the end of the year to reflect inflation-caused increases in costs, then the material, labor, and overhead price variances should be analyzed to determine what portion of the variances may be attributable to actual cost increases, and that portion should be "spread back" to inventory and cost of sales. The internal control working papers relating to the standard cost system should flag the problem and reference the procedure in the audit program that compensates for the deficiency that has been noted.

Similarly if a client's inventory records are not handled on a perpetual basis, the working papers should demonstrate that inventory observation and test count procedures have been expanded to compensate for the resulting deficiency in the reliability of the client's inventory figures.

Some internal control deficiencies, however, might not require compensation, and those deficiencies should be so noted. As an example, production workers may have access to inventory materials, making it possible to remove items without an authorizing requisition. Any unauthorized removal would result in inventory shortages when the physical inventory is taken, and the deficiency should be reported in the auditor's management letter, but no actual audit program modification might be warranted, except to note the possible effect on inventory shortage figures.

### Confidential Treatment of Information Pertaining to the Client

In the course of making an examination the auditor should have unlimited access to information about the affairs of the client, and most of this information will find its way into the working papers. Much of the information may be of a type that the client ordinarily would not disclose to outsiders, including such matters as the amount of sales and gross margin for individual products, changes in product design and production, and the salaries of various officers and employees. Failure to keep such information confidential could easily be harmful to the client and be damaging to the reputation of the practitioner who violates a client's trust. Clients would hesitate to engage auditors if in so doing they would risk losing control over information that has been closely guarded from outsiders, and conversely, auditors would be hindered in making their examinations if clients attempted to withhold information in order to keep it confidential. The AICPA recognized the importance to present and prospective users of public accounting services, as well as the profession itself, of treating all information confidentially and, to assure others that confidences will not be breached, has incorporated the following into its Code of Professional Ethics as Rule 301: "A member shall not disclose any confidential information obtained in the course of a professional engagement except with the consent of the client."

Although the auditor is governed by the same professional considerations that apply to the attorney or the physician with respect to information received about the affairs of a client, communication between auditor and client is not privileged under the common law. Except in certain states where privilege is given by statute, the auditor, unlike the attorney or physician, may be required in court to produce working papers and to divulge any specifically requested information about a client to which the auditor might be privy.

### Control of Working Papers

The auditor should never leave working papers unattended in the client's office. At lunchtime and overnight the papers should be placed in a securely locked briefcase or in a sealed file drawer in order to keep any persons in the client's office from gaining unauthorized access to the papers. Such close control is necessary for two reasons. One is that persons in the client's employ might attempt to alter information recorded in the work papers for purposes of misleading the auditor or concealing some misdeed. Another reason is that the papers are likely to contain information that should not be made available to members of the client's organization, such as information concerning the scope of the examination or the method to be used in selecting items to be test-checked. Also, some of the information in the working papers, about the affairs of the client and salaries of various officers and employees, will be restricted by the client to a limited number of employees, and the auditor would be violating the confidential relationship with the client if such information should become available to unauthorized personnel.

### The Relationship of the Auditor and Staff to Client Officers and Employees

The image of auditors held by the many persons who have never had any actual contact with an auditor is relatively unflattering and likely to be related to the ferreting out of fraud. Actually the breadth of the auditor's work is reflected in a different type of personality. Partners and managers should be able to meet client executives on their own ground and be able to actively enter into discussions ranging from operating problems of the business to business conditions in general, and from state, national, and foreign affairs to the lighter concerns of the day. Cordiality, an easy manner, interest in a client's problems, and the ability to grasp questions and return helpful answers are as important to client relations as is the bedside manner of the physician.

Although contacts with client executives may well be on a social basis as well as a business basis, restraint is advisable, because the auditor must sometimes say "No" to the client, and independence can be difficult to maintain in the face of close friendship or personal indebtedness. At the staff level, contact with employees of the client should be limited to the confines of the client's office as much as possible. Fraternization with employees, particularly when it is solely an outgrowth of contacts in the client's office, is almost certain to present problems in the client's office, and again independence may suffer as a result.

Cordiality is another matter, however, and everything should be done to make the auditor's intrusion upon the daily routine of the client's office as courteous and painless as possible. Consideration for employees should include recognition that they have their regular work to perform and may not be able to drop everything to assist the auditor. Also, the auditor's tone of voice and manner should be such as to dispel the notion that the auditor considers every employee a potential thief or embezzler and that the auditor gains personal satisfaction from crucifying any napless employee whose inadvertent mistake may have been discovered. In part, the problem is merely one of courtesy, and minor aspects of the solution include having the auditor bring needed supplies, avoiding the use of the client's telephones, particularly for personal calls, and requesting permission to use client records or equipment—preferably only when not already in use.

### A Preview of Succeeding Chapters

Following the comprehensive treatment in this and the preceding chapters of the audit process and the approach of the system-based audit in acquiring direct and indirect evidence, attention is focused in the next chapter on the sampling aspects of auditing, including the use of statistical techniques. Chapter 10 addresses the reality that most sizable organizations today use computers extensively in processing accounting-related data and in a variety of other ways. The reader is introduced to various aspects of computer-based accounting records, and special attention is given to internal control techniques and problems associated with computerized systems. The chapter also discusses ways in which the computer can be used to assist in carrying out various audit procedures through specially developed audit software packages.

The following eight chapters represent the "core" of the book, dealing with the audit of the major subsystems, and information outputs of those accounting subsystems, as they tend to exist in businesses engaged in manufacturing or distribution activities. Each of the core chapters is organized around the objectives that are the focal point of an independent auditor's examination of financial statements. These objectives are listed below in the order in which they appear in the core chapters.

A. Evaluate internal control relative to the operating, data processing, and monitoring objectives of a satisfactory system of controls. The control techniques and features through which a client can attain those internal control objectives are presented in association with each objective.
B. Determine compliance with internal controls on which the auditor intends to rely.
C. Determine conformity of client's financial statements with disclosure and other requirements of financial accounting/reporting standards.
D. Perform substantive tests designed to satisfy these objectives related to the client's accounting records:
   1. Reasonableness of account balances.
   2. Synchronization of transactions and other events with the related records at the statement date and other critical test dates.
   3. Comprehensiveness of records (no transactions or amounts have been omitted).
   4. Accuracy of arithmetic or other clerical operations, including agreement of constituent details, such as subsidiary ledger balances, with control account or other totals.

5. Existence of underlying assets and liabilities.
6. Ownership of assets to which the client should have legal title.
7. Valuation of transactions and balances at cost, adjusted cost, or market, in conformity with generally accepted accounting principles.

Following these core chapters, Chapter 19 addresses some final matters necessary to wrap up the audit. Chapters 20 and 21 cover all aspects of reporting the audit findings, and the final chapter considers management advisory and other services commonly provided by public accounting firms.

## Questions/Problems

For multiple-choice questions 8-1 through 8-5, indicate the letter of the single answer that *best* completes the statement or answers the question, and justify the choice that you have made.

**8-1.** The independent auditor is likely to submit a *reversing entry* to be made by the client
 a. For some of the reclassification entries.
 b. For every adjusting entry.
 c. To correct the financial statements currently being examined.
 d. The main reason for submitting a reversing entry is not stated.

**8-2.** During the course of an audit engagement an auditor prepares and accumulates audit working papers. The primary purpose of the audit working papers is to
 a. Aid the auditor in adequately planning his work.
 b. Provide a point of reference for future audit engagements.
 c. Support the underlying concepts included in the preparation of the basic financial statements.
 d. Support the auditor's opinion.

(Uniform CPA Examination)

**8-3.** Audit working papers are used to record the results of the auditor's evidence-gathering procedures. When preparing working papers the auditor should remember that working papers should be
 a. Kept on the client's premises so that the client can have access to them for reference purposes.
 b. The primary support for the financial statements being examined.
 c. Considered as a part of the client's accounting records which is retained by the auditor.

    d.  Designed to meet the circumstances and the auditor's needs on each engagement.

(Uniform CPA Examination)

**8-4.** During an audit engagement pertinent data are compiled and included in the audit workpapers. The workpapers primarily are considered to be

    a.  A client-owned record of conclusions reached by the auditors who performed the engagement.

    b.  Evidence supporting financial statements.

    c.  Support for the auditor's representations as to compliance with generally accepted auditing standards.

    d.  A record to be used as a basis for the following year's engagement.

(Uniform CPA Examination)

**8-5.** Although the quantity, type, and content of working papers will vary with the circumstances, the working papers generally would include the

    a.  Copies of those client records examined by the auditor during the course of the engagement.

    b.  Evaluation of the efficiency and competence of the audit staff assistants by the partner responsible for the audit.

    c.  Auditor's comments concerning the efficiency and competence of client management personnel.

    d.  Auditing procedures followed, and the testing performed in obtaining evidential matter.

(Uniform CPA Examination)

**8-6.** Why is it essential that the auditor keep careful control over audit working papers?

**8-7.** What information should be included in the heading of each working paper schedule?

**8-8.** The bookkeeper of Sizzles and Burns Company follows the practice of charging supplies to a prepaid expense account when purchased. At the end of the year an inventory of supplies is taken and the appropriate adjustment made to the prepaid expense account. This adjustment has already been made for the fiscal year ended February 28. In the course of your audit review of the client's records you discover that during the year a $50 purchase of advertising supplies was incorrectly charged to "Office Supplies on Hand." What adjusting entry would you make in your working papers to correct this error? (Do not consider materiality.)

**8-9.** The preparation of working papers is an integral part of a CPA's examination of financial statements. On a recurring engagement a CPA reviews his audit programs and working papers from his prior examination while planning his current examination to determine their usefulness for the current engagement.

Required:

  a.  1.  What are the purposes or functions of audit working papers?

       2.  What records may be included in audit working papers?

  b.  What factors affect the CPA's judgment of the type and content of the working papers for a particular engagement?

  c.  To comply with generally accepted auditing standards a CPA includes certain evidence in his working papers, for example, "evidence that the engagement was planned and work of assistants was supervised and reviewed." What other evidence should a CPA include in audit working papers to comply with generally accepted auditing standards?

  d.  How can a CPA make the most effective use of the preceding year's audit programs in a recurring examination?

  e.  What advice should a CPA give a client about discontinuing the use of records needed in an examination and how should a CPA complete his examination when he finds that records reviewed by him in prior examinations have been discontinued by the client?

(Uniform CPA Examination)

**8-10.** An important part of every examination of financial statements is the preparation of audit working papers.

Required:

  a.  Discuss the relationship of audit working papers to each of the standards of field work.

  b.  You are instructing an inexperienced staffman on his first auditing assignment. He is to examine an account. An analysis of the account has been prepared by the client for inclusion in the audit working papers. Prepare a list of the comments, commentaries and notations that the staffman should make or have made on the account analysis to provide an adequate working paper as evidence of his examination. (Do not include a description of auditing procedures applicable to the account.)

(Uniform CPA Examination)

**8-11.** Comparison between the interoffice account of City Wholesale Hardware Co. with its surburban branch and the corresponding account carried on the latter's books shows the following discrepancies at the close of business, September 30, 19X1.

1. A charge of $870 (office furniture) on HO taken up by branch as $780.
2. A credit by HO for $300 (merchandise allowance) taken up by branch as $350.
3. HO charged branch $325 for interest on open account, which branch failed to take up in full; instead, branch sent to HO an incorrect adjusting memo, reducing the charge by $75, and set up a liability for the net amount.
4. A charge for labor by HO, $433, was taken up twice by branch.
5. A charge of $785 was made by HO for freight on merchandise, but entered by branch as $78.50.
6. Branch incorrectly sent HO a debit note for $293, representing its proportion of bill for truck repairs; HO did not record it.
7. HO received $475 from sale of truck which it erroneously credited to branch; branch did not charge HO therewith.
8. Branch accidentally received a copy of HO entry dated 10/10/X1 correcting No. 7 and entered a credit in favor of HO as of September 30, 19X1.

The balance of the account with the branch on the head office books showed $131,690 receivable from the branch at September 30, 19X1. The interoffice accounts were in balance at the beginning of the year.

a. Prepare a schedule showing your computation of the balance of the interoffice account on the branch books before adjustment on September 30, 19X1.
b. Prepare journal entries to adjust the branch books.
c. Prepare a reconciliation of the balances of the branch and home office accounts at September 30, 19X1, after making the adjustments in (b).

(Uniform CPA Examination)

**8-12.** Index the following related working paper schedules in accordance with the plan outlined in the text.

Inventory summary

Analysis of raw materials control account

Analysis of work in process control account

Test counts of raw materials

Summary of raw materials reduced to market

Pricing tests of raw materials

Number of days' supply on hand—major items of raw materials, current production

Number of days' supply on hand—major items of raw materials, replacement parts

**8-13.** From the following list of account balances supplied by your client, the Adams Co., prepare working balance sheet and profit and loss schedules, and any lead schedules that may be necessary. Do not head up money columns for other than the current year's balance.

| | |
|---|---:|
| Accounts payable | $45,328.14 |
| Accounts receivable-trade | 95,821.50 |
| Accumulated depreciation on plant and equipment | 4,871.30 |
| Accrued property taxes payable | 405.01 |
| Accrued salaries payable | 819.20 |
| Common stock | 80,000.00 |
| Cost of goods sold | 196,093.84 |
| Current provision for doubtful accounts | 1,005.90 |
| Depreciation expense | 1,421.15 |
| Dividends declared and paid | 12,000.00 |
| Due from officers and employees | 2,807.10 |
| Estimated loss on doubtful accounts | 2,190.18 |
| First National Bank-payroll account | 1,000.00 |
| First National Bank-regular account | 4,875.50 |
| Income taxes payable | 5,771.85 |
| Income taxes expense | 5,771.85 |
| Inventory-main warehouse | 85,914.20 |
| Inventory-branch warehouse | 23,109.45 |
| Inventory shortage | 1,390.58 |
| Last National Bank-special account | 2,019.80 |
| Merchandise in transit | 6,990.05 |
| Net sales | 287,194.52 |
| Officers' salaries | 15,120.30 |
| Office salaries | 20,201.58 |
| Office supplies expense | 721.37 |
| Petty cash fund | 250.00 |
| Plant and equipment | 12,304.10 |
| Prepaid expenses | 470.50 |
| Prepayments to suppliers | 7,120.18 |
| Reno Bank and Trust Co.-branch collections | 1,805.70 |
| Retained earnings-beginning of year | 86,208.26 |
| Selling expenses | 13,318.43 |
| Social Security taxes payable | 191.54 |
| Tax expense | 1,809.10 |
| Withholding taxes payable | 362.18 |

**8-14.** You have been engaged to examine the financial statements of Helen Corporation for the year 19X3. The bookkeeper who maintains the financial records has prepared all of the unaudited financial statements. The client has asked you to compute the correct income for the three years 19X1 through 19X3 and to prepare a corrected balance sheet as of December 31, 19X3.

In the course of your examination you discover the following:

1.  The Corporation includes sales taxes collected from customers in the Sales account. When sales tax collections for a month are remitted to the taxing authority on the 15th of the following month, the Sales Tax Expense account is charged. All sales are subject to a 3% sales tax. Total sales plus sales taxes for 19X1 through 19X3 were $495,430, $762,200 and $924,940, respectively. The totals of the Sales Tax Expense account for the three years were $12,300, $21,780 and $26,640.

2.  Furniture and fixtures were purchased on January 2, 19X1 for $12,000, but no portion of the cost has been charged to depreciation. The Corporation wishes to use the straight-line method for these assets, which have been estimated to have a life of ten years and no salvage value.

3.  In January 19X1 installation costs of $5,700 on new machinery were charged to Repairs Expense. Other costs of this machinery of $30,000 were correctly recorded and have been depreciated using the straight-line method with an estimated life of ten years and no salvage value. Current estimates are that the machinery has a life of twenty years, a salvage value of $4,200 and that the sum-of-the-years-digits depreciation method would be most appropriate.

4.  An account payable of $8,000 for merchandise purchased on December 23, 19X1, was recorded in January, 19X2. This merchandise was not included in inventory at December 31, 19X1.

5.  Merchandise having a cost of $6,550 was stored in a separate warehouse and was not included in the December 31, 19X2 inventory, and merchandise having a cost of $2,180 was included twice in the December 31, 19X3 inventory. The Corporation uses a periodic inventory method.

6.  The year-end salary accrual of $1,925 on December 31, 19X3, has not been recorded.

7.  A check for $1,895 from a customer to apply to his account was received on December 30, 19X1, but was not recorded until January 2, 19X2.

8.  Quarterly dividends of $2,500 have been declared near the end of each calendar quarter since the Corporation was organized. The bookkeeper has consistently followed the practice of recording all dividends at the date of payment, which is the 15th of the month following the month of declaration.

9.  At December 31, 19X1, sales catalogues advertising a special January, 19X2 white sale were on hand, but their cost of $1,360 was included in Advertising Expenses for 19X1.

10. At December 31, 19X3, there was an unexplained cash shortage of $48.

11. When the 500 shares of outstanding stock having a par value of $100 were initially issued on January 2, 19X1, the $55,000 cash received for them was credited to the Common Stock account.

12. The Corporation has used the direct writeoff method of accounting for bad debts. Accounts written off during each of the three years amount to $1,745, $2,200 and $5,625, respectively. The Corporation has decided that the allowance method would be more appropriate. The estimated balances for the Allowance for Doubtful Accounts at the end of each of the three years are: $6,100, $8,350 and $9,150.

13. On January 2, 19X2, $100,000 of 6% 20-year bonds were issued for $98,-000. The $2,000 discount was charged to Interest Expense. The bookkeeper records interest only on the interest payment dates of January 2 and July 1.

14. A pension plan adopted on January 2, 19X3, includes a provision for a pension fund to be administered by a trustee. The employees who joined

the Corporation in 19X1 and 19X2 were given credit for their past service. A payment of $25,000 for the full amount of these past service costs was paid into the fund immediately. A second payment of $15,000 was made into the fund near the end of 19X3. However, actuarial computations indicate that pension costs attributable to 19X3 employee services are $16,600. The only entries applicable to the pension fund made during 19X3 were debits to Pension Expense and credits to Cash. The Corporation wishes to make the maximum annual provision for pension cost in accordance with generally accepted accounting principles.

15. Property tax assessments of $15,600, $16,080 and $15,900 were made on January 1 of 19X1, 19X2, and 19X3, respectively. The assessments are billed each year following the assessment on July 1, the beginning of the fiscal year of the taxing authority, and taxes are payable in two equal installments on September 10 and December 10. The bookkeeper has always charged Property Tax Expense on the dates the cash payments are made. The Corporation wishes to charge the tax expense against revenue during the fiscal year of the taxing authority.

Required:

Prepare a working paper showing the computation of the effects of the errors upon income for 19X1, 19X2, and 19X3, and upon the balance sheet as of December 31, 19X3. The worksheet analysis should be presented in the same order as the facts are given with corresponding numbers, 1 through 15. (Formal journal entries or financial statements are not required.) Use the columnar headings given below for your working paper.

| | Income 19X1 | | Income 19X2 | | Income 19X3 | | Balance Sheet Corrections at December 31, 19X3 Amount | | |
|---|---|---|---|---|---|---|---|---|---|
| Explanation | Debit | Credit | Debit | Credit | Debit | Credit | Debit | Credit | Account |

(Uniform CPA Examination)

# Chapter 9

# SAMPLE SELECTION AND EVALUATION— JUDGMENTAL/STATISTICAL

When either compliance tests or substantive tests of a population involve inspection procedures, sampling is likely to be the cost efficient means of acquiring the desired audit evidence. The audit purpose of the sample will be to provide information about some characteristic of the population, with that characteristic generally involving either

- An attribute that each population item does or does not possess, such as whether a required authorization stamp is present or whether or not a given task has been performed correctly, or
- A variable associated with each population item, such as a quantity or a monetary value, with the variable typically being summed to obtain a total for the population.

Thus, audit sampling is customarily described in terms of whether it involves *attribute sampling* pertaining to some dichotomous characteristic or *variable sampling* pertaining to quantitative data.

Compliance tests generally involve attribute sampling, although it is possible to estimate the proportion of the population possessing or not possessing a particular attribute, by using a form of variable sampling. Substantive tests, on the other hand, typically are directed to a monetary amount and hence will usually involve variable sampling. However, in the approach to substantive testing that is commonly referred to as Dollar Unit Sampling, or DUS, the monetary result is obtained through error rate evaluation, which utilizes the attribute sampling approach of compliance testing.

### Sampling as a Source of Information

The object in sampling is to obtain information about a population characteristic that is of interest, without examining every item in the population. For example, in attribute sampling we might want to gain information about the probable maximum proportion of the items in the population that are defective in that they do not reflect the attribute of interest, such as a required approval or the presence of a supporting document such as a purchase order. In variable sampling, an approximation of the population total will be sought, and that total can either be an arithmetic or algebraic sum, such as the total dollar value of a client's inventory or the total dollar differences (plus or minus) between customers' ledger balances and the amounts reported by customers in their replies to confirmation requests.

With any type of sampling, the information obtained from the sample is likely to differ from the actual population characteristic, but it is possible, by setting the size of the sample to be examined, to control the *maximum amount* by which the sample information may differ from the true state or value of the population. It is also possible to control the *likelihood* that the sample information will differ from the true state or value of the population by more than the maximum difference that one is willing to tolerate. These two controllable factors are referred to as the *precision* of the estimate of the population characteristic derived from the sample and the *reliability* of that sample estimate (also referred to as the *confidence* in the estimate). The fact that the sample is likely to differ from the true state of the population is a consequence of the particular items that happen to be selected from the various items that constitute the population. The resulting variability of the sample information referred to as *sampling error* must be considered in designing the sample.

### The Sampling Parameters

Sampling involves making decisions about each of the following as a means of controlling sampling error:

1. Selection of items—determining which items are to be selected, or how the items are to be selected.
2. Size of the sample—how many items are to be selected.
3. Precision of the sample—how much the sample statistic may vary, as a result of sampling error, from the true value of the population parameter that is of interest.
4. Reliability of the sample statistic—the likelihood or confidence that the sample estimate of the population statistic will be within the precision limits set for the sample. The reliability or confidence level is expressed as a percentage, with the complement of that percentage representing the risk that, as a result of sampling error, the sample estimate may differ from the true population value by more than the precision limits that have been set for the sample.

Sample size is directly related to the precision and reliability desired for the sample. For example, assume that we are interested in estimating the maximum rate of error that has occurred in the client's costing of inventory requisitions. The larger the sample that is taken from the requisitions issued during the year, the more likely it will be that the error rate observed in the sample will approximate the error rate in the population as a whole. Although expressing an inference about the population in such general terms is of little value, a statistical approach to the problem can provide the desired guidance in determining sample size. Expressing the desired precision and reliability (confidence) in quantitative terms and using them in the proper algorithm will yield an appropriate sample size, as discussed later in this chapter. The following sections take a closer look at reliability and precision.

### Reliability/Confidence/Risk

Reliability or confidence is associated with the sampling distribution that can be expected from repeated samples of a given size taken from a given population. Repeated samples will yield different values for the population characteristic that is of interest, but the variability of these values will vary inversely with the size of the sample. Stated differently, the larger the sample, the greater the likelihood that the sample estimate will be representative of the true value of the population statistic.

Consider that an auditor seeks to arrive at an inference about a population statistic based on the value derived from a sample, but could be misled as a result of sampling error. A larger sample will be subject to less sampling error, and the auditor can have increased confidence in the conclusion that has been reached. To generalize, it can be said that as sample size is increased, reliability increases and risk (the complement of reliability) decreases.

### Precision

A closely related aspect of the reliability/confidence/risk problem is how large a potential difference the auditor will be willing to tolerate between the sample estimate of a population statistic and the actual statistic as calculated from the entire population—the precision of the sample estimate. A sample provides a point estimate of the population statistic, but the estimate is likely to deviate from the true value of the population statistic as a result of sampling error. Larger samples will be more representative of the population, and hence the sample estimate of the population statistic will deviate less from the actual population statistic as sample size is increased, resulting in greater precision at any given reliability level.

### Reliability, Precision, and Sample Size Interrelated

Although reliability and precision are aspects of every sample, the preceding discussion treated each of them individually, holding the other factor constant as the relationship of the one factor to sample size was examined. The direct relationship between reliability and precision becomes more evident if sample size is held constant and we consider what happens to, say, precision as the desired confidence level is varied. With a given sample size, if reliability is to be increased, the precision of the sample will decrease; that is, it will be necessary to tolerate a greater possible difference between the sample result and the true state of the population. Conversely, if greater precision is desired, there can be less reliability (less confidence) in the inference derived from a sample of given size.

In practice, of course, the auditor sets both the reliability (confidence level) and the precision that are desired, and then the sample size is determined that will produce the desired result. The sample size calculation for attribute sampling is based on the binomial distribution, but as a practical matter, sample size is usually determined from precalculated tables or by specifying the desired confidence and precision for computer calculation of sample size, using the statistical package of an audit software program.

For variables sampling, the calculations are less complex and can be readily performed by the auditor if a computer and the appropriate software are not available. As shall be noted later, however, there is yet another factor to be considered in determining sample size in the variables situation: the standard deviation of the population. Sample results will vary more widely with a higher standard deviation, and larger sample sizes are necessary to compensate for the greater variability in the population.

### Risk, Precision, and the Accept/Reject Decision

Let us now consider the possible outcomes of the sampling process and the resulting decision that a sampled population is either acceptable or not acceptable to the auditor, based on the reliability (risk) and precision that were set in determining the size of the sample to be taken. Sampling error may result in an erroneous decision to reject the population because it appears to lie outside the specified precision limit when the population in fact lies within the limit and should actually be accepted. In statistical terms this is referred to as a Type I error, and the associated risk of making a Type I error is termed the Alpha risk.

The converse of this situation is to erroneously accept the population because the sample results indicate that the population lies within the precision limit, when in fact the population lies outside the acceptable limit and should be rejected. This is known as a Type II error, and the associated risk of making such an error is termed the Beta risk.

In most audit situations the greatest concern is likely to be the Beta risk of a Type II error. That error could result from a compliance test that indicated that an internal control feature was working effectively when in fact it was not and hence ought not be relied upon in restricting a related substantive test of a financial statement figure. In substantive testing, a sample could indicate that the population was acceptable as being within the precision limit that was set based on materiality, when in fact the true population amount was actually outside the precision limit.

In either of the above situations the consequence could be expressing an opinion that the financial statements are fairly stated when actually those statements are in error by a material amount. If a party relied on the financial statements and suffered a loss because the statements were in error, a suit against the auditor for damages might result. As was stated in Chapter 3, however, an auditor should be able to defend against such a suit successfully if the auditor is able to demonstrate that no negligence was involved in reaching the opinion that the financial statements were fairly stated. To so demonstrate, the auditor would have to establish that the confidence level and precision used in determining the sample size were reasonable, that the sample results were correctly interpreted, and hence that the faulty opinion did not result from negligence. Rather, the erroneous decision to accept the population would be shown to have been the result of sampling error—the drawing from the population of a sample that was statistically unlikely to have been drawn.

The consequences of the opposite or Type I error are likely to be less serious. The Type I error of concluding that the population is unacceptable, when in fact it is acceptable, would simply result in the auditor or the client undertaking additional work to establish the actual acceptability of the population. It should be noted in passing, however, that both risks can be reduced, but only at the cost of taking a larger sample, which would be justified only if the cost/benefit relationship appeared to be favorable.

With the background information that has been presented and the introduction of various terms associated with statistical sampling, this discussion turns to the steps involved in sample design.

### Defining the Population

Because a sample is used to provide information about a population, it is important that the population be carefully identified. For example, in compliance testing of payroll procedures, there may be several distinct payrolls: productive workers paid on a piece rate basis, indirect hourly paid workers, and indirect salaried employees. Each of these types of payroll can be considered a separate population in view of the substantially different procedures involved. In a similar vein but in a different setting, a department store may have merchandise that is on the selling floor (floor stock), merchandise that is held in reserve near the sales floor to replenish the floor stocks (reserve stock), and merchandise that is too bulky to be stored near the sales floor and is held in a warehouse (warehouse stock). All three merchandise stocks will ordinarily be combined to present a single inventory figure on the balance sheet. However, because inventory-taking procedures involved are likely to be different, it is advantageous, for substantive testing of the inventory, to consider the inventory as consisting of three different populations, each to be sampled separately.

### Selecting Items for the Sample

The preferred method of selecting sample items in order to provide representativeness in the sample is to afford each item in the population an equal opportunity or probability of being selected. Technically termed probability selection, the method is commonly referred to as random selection.

*Random Selection.* The desired equal probability of selection may be achieved if the items in the population are serially numbered and a table of random numbers is used to select the items for the sample. For convenience in drawing the items from the population, it will usually be advantageous to rearrange the numbers obtained from the table into numerical sequence. This cumbersome 2-step process is greatly simplified by using a computer to do the work under the direction of the statistical program of a computer audit package. The auditor need only specify the number of items desired for the sample and the range of numbers from which the sample is to be drawn, and a random number generator will select the numbers to be drawn from the range of numbers in the population. The computer will then rearrange the numbers into numerical sequence and print out the list for the auditor in the most convenient form for use.

*Systematic (Interval) Selection.* A fairly good approximation of randomness can be obtained by using systematic or interval selection of items, and the method will ordinarily be much easier and quicker to apply than true random selection. The method involves the selection of every Nth item in a series, where the value of N is determined by dividing the total number of items in the population by the number of items to be included in the sample. Thus, in a sample of 100 to be selected from a population of 1,500 sales transactions, every fifteenth transaction would be selected. Statistically the method presents problems if the population itself is not random; but if the population is free of any periodicity, systematic selection is satisfactory, provided that a random start is used.

*Block Selection.* Although once fairly popular for some applications, as a consequence of the ease of selecting items for a sample, greater awareness of the representativeness problem as sampling became more scientific has practically eliminated the block selection method. If used, a block may include all transactions in a record for a period of time, or all items appearing within a chosen numeric or alphabetic range.

*Purposive Selection.* In its weakest form this method of selection is based on the auditor's perception of items that appear suspicious or questionable for any reason. Although this would appear to be an effective method of selection for audit purposes, research has shown that auditors differ considerably in the items that they select as satisfying whatever purpose they have in mind. As a consequence, the nonrepresentativeness of a sample so selected may involve the omission of critical items from the sample and lead to an incorrect conclusion.

If, however, the concept of selecting items on the basis of some underlying purpose is carefully formalized *and combined with random selection from those items not in the purposive sample,* the method may be quite useful. In this formalized approach purposive selection is, in effect, simply a variation of stratification, the selection method that is discussed next.

*Stratified Selection.*   A population may be stratified on any number of different bases, with items within each stratum subject to either 100 percent selection, or random selection if a stratum is to be sampled. As an example, the following strata and sample coverage might be specified in selecting accounts receivable to be confirmed through correspondence with customers:

> All account balances > $1,000
> All accounts < $1,000 and > $200 if
> > The account is more than two months delinquent or
> > The balance exceeds the authorized credit limit for the account, or
> > There has been no activity in the account during the past month
> A sample of $N$ items randomly selected from the remaining stratum

A slightly different approach that might be termed optimal dollar stratification is quite complex and involves numerous calculations to arrive at strata specification according to dollar amounts and the size of the sample to be drawn from each stratum. In essence, the method is an extension of simple stratification in which all items over a stated amount are included in the sample, and a specified number of items equal to or less than the stated amount are randomly selected. The dollar coverage obtained from the upper stratum has the effect of reducing the overall number of items to be sampled, and by increasing the number of separate strata to be sampled, the number of items to be sampled can be further reduced. A computer program is the only feasible means of determining optimal stratification, given the calculation problems associated with method.

*Cumulative Monetary Amount (CMA) Selection.*   This method of selection has been developed and is used primarily in connection with dollar unit sampling but can be used in other applications as well. The method may be viewed as a form of interval sampling that is applied to a variables interval (usually a monetary amount) rather than an item interval as in systematic selection. In applying the method, the number of items to be sampled is first determined (see DUS section later in this chapter), and dividing the dollar total of the population to be tested by this sample size produces the sampling interval. The dollar amounts of the population are then cumulated, and each item is selected for the sample that causes the cumulative total to exceed a multiple of the sampling interval. Thus the method identifies the particular dollars out of the population of dollars to be selected, but rather than only those particular dollars being selected for the sample, the items of which the particular dollars are a part become the sample.

The effect of CMA sampling is 1) to include all items in the sample that exceed the monetary sampling interval, and 2) to select smaller items with a probability of selection that is proportional to the monetary size of the items. The overall result is to approximate optimal stratification, as that method also relates the probability of selection to the size of an item.

A particular advantage of both of these selection methods is that they include all of the largest items, and these are the items that, if in error, will be of the greatest audit interest, for they will have the most significant effect on the total being tested.

To illustrate CMA sampling, assume that 100 individual accounts receivable are to be selected for confirmation from accounts receivable totaling $250,000. The sampling interval would be multiples of $2,500. The next step would be to add the accounts receivable on an adding machine, obtaining a subtotal after each addition. Any account that caused the subtotal to exceed $2,500 or some multiple thereof would be selected for confirmation. Although it might appear that considerable extra effort is required for this selection process, the reader should recognize that audit objectives for substantive procedures require proving that the sum of the individual items that comprise a total do in fact equal that total. Hence, the accounts must be footed (added) in any case, and the only extra step is to obtain a subtotal after each item and compare it with the appropriate multiple of the interval. If the records are computerized, the entire process is simplified, especially if an audit software package includes CMA sample selection.

### Determination of Sample Size: Attribute Sampling

As we have seen, the most common application of attribute sampling is in compliance testing, where the presence or absence of procedural errors is investigated. The problem must be addressed, however, not in terms of finding isolated errors, but rather whether errors (or omissions of required procedures) have occurred at a rate that is unacceptable to the auditor. Defining what would be an unacceptable error rate is particularly troublesome because most procedural errors will not directly affect the financial statements. As an example, incorrect costing of goods that have been sold will affect inventory and cost of goods sold at the time of making that entry under a perpetual inventory system, but the error will be corrected at the time the inventory account is adjusted to agree with the physical inventory.

A somewhat different problem arises if, say, an incorrect price is used in billing a customer and the customer is overcharged or undercharged.

If the customer's internal control procedures detect the error, the seller will be notified and the account will be adjusted. If the error is not detected by the customer and the customer pays the incorrect amount, the seller's financial statements will reflect a larger or smaller amount of assets and revenue than they actually should, but as a practical matter the statements show the amount of assets and revenue actually received, and are fairly stated in that respect.

The most reasonable approach under such circumstances is to consider how effective the client's system of internal control *should be* in preventing or screening out errors, and then set a maximum acceptable error rate that is somewhat in excess of the auditor's expectation. If a compliance testing sample indicates that the actual error rate in the population *could* be greater than what the auditor considered to be the maximum acceptable error rate, then the auditor would have to determine to what extent reliance on internal control should be limited in setting the nature, timing, and extent of related substantive audit procedures. Because there can be no definitive answer about what should be the maximum acceptable error rate in any given case, there is no alternative but to fall back on the notion that the answer must be determined in the light of the auditor's experience.

Let us proceed with an example in which the auditor is interested in the accuracy with which client employees have matched quantities shown on receiving reports for purchased materials with the quantities charged for on the suppliers' invoices. Assume that the auditor has determined that the maximum acceptable error rate for this matching process is 5 percent. We must next look at the amount of precision and the confidence level that the auditor seeks from the sample to be selected for the compliance test, as these will have a direct bearing on sample size.

*Precision.* On the basis of the 5 percent maximum acceptable error rate, it should be noted that a population with a 4.9 percent error rate would be acceptable, and a sample drawn from that population might actually reflect that 4.9 percent error rate. But such a sample result would not support a decision to accept the population even though the population is in fact acceptable, because a sample with a 4.9 percent error rate *could* have come from a population with a much higher error rate—or a much lower error rate for that matter.

Let us assume instead, however, that the sample covered 50 items and no errors were found in the sample. The reader will recognize that there would be a low likelihood of drawing such a sample from a population with 5 percent of the items in error, and hence it should be reasonable to accept the population as containing no more than 5 percent error when no errors appear in the sample. The *precision* of this decision is the difference between the error rate in the sample (zero in this case) and the stated maximum acceptable error rate.

We will next look at the related question of reliability, or confidence in the decision based on the sample result, and then see how these two factors can be used to determine sample size.

*Reliability.*    The reliability factor is related to the likelihood that a particular sample could have come from a given population. Thus a sample showing a 5 percent error rate would have about equal likelihood of coming from a population with an error rate in excess of 5 percent as from a population with less than a 5 percent error rate. Conversely, as in the example of a sample of 50 with no errors in the sample, it would be rather unlikely that the population would have an error rate of 5 percent or greater. That likelihood can be calculated using the binomial distribution, but the calculation is complex, and a set of tables offers a convenient alternative.

*Precision and Reliability Related to Sample Size.*    As noted earlier, precision and/or reliability are functions of sample size, with a larger sample offering greater precision or greater reliability, or some combination of the two. Turning that relationship around, if precision and reliability are specified, sample size can be determined, with the minimum sample that must be drawn to accept the population being one disclosing no errors.

Table 9-1, which is based on Poisson's distribution as an approximation of the binomial distribution, contains all the needed elements for attribute sampling, including evaluation of the sample result when one or more errors appear in the sample. Because the Poisson distribution is based on expected occurrences of an event within an infinite population, it may be noted that the only factors affecting the number of events expected to occur within various samples are the rate of occurrences within the population and the size of the sample. For any one sample from a given population, the number of occurrences appearing within the sample will thus be a matter of probability. The resulting probability function is derived in a unique manner for the Poisson distribution as an approximation of the binomial distribution. An especially important aspect of the Poisson distribution is that the probability of a given number of occurrences in a sample bears a linear relationship to the rate of occurrences within various populations for samples of a given size; and for any given number of occurrences in various samples, there is likewise a linear relationship between the size of the samples and the rate of occurrences within the populations from which they were drawn.

These linear relationships can be observed from Table 9-1 as follows:

For samples disclosing zero errors, the probability of such samples is an identical 92 percent for a sample of 25 drawn from a population with a 10 percent occurrence rate and a sample of 50 drawn from a population with a 5 percent occurrence rate; in other words, as sample size is doubled, the occurrence rate within the population is halved.

The relationship is identical for other frequencies of occurrence. For example, one occurrence or less, in a sample of 150, has an 80 percent probability of occurring when drawn from a population with a 2 percent occurrence rate, and the same 80 percent when sample size is doubled to 300 and the population occurrence rate is halved to 1 percent.

As a result of these linear relationships, the content of Table 9-1 can be rearranged and drastically reduced in size for audit usage as shown by Table 9-2.[1] The table converts the relationship of sample size and occurrence rate to factor values that represent the likely occurrences in the population for stated confidence (probability) levels. These factor values for number of occurrences are converted to an occurrence rate when the factors are divided by the sample size. Thus, of one error occurs in a sample of 150 and an 80 percent confidence level is sought, the factor value from Table 9-2 is 3.00. Dividing by sample size, $\frac{3.00}{150} = .02$, which is the maximum error rate that would be expected in the population at the 80 percent confidence level. This same result can be read from Table 9-1 for a sample of 150 disclosing one error.

Table 9-2 can also be used to determine the minimum sample size, given a desired confidence level and the maximum tolerable error rate for the population. The minimum sample would always presume zero errors in the sample. Therefore, if 95 percent confidence is sought that the error rate does not exceed 2 percent, the minimum sample (zero errors) would involve a factor value of 3.00 and a sample size of $\frac{3.00}{.02} = 150$. Once again, the same result can be obtained from Table 9-1.

### Attribute Sampling: An Example

To illustrate the use of Table 9-1, this discussion will continue with the earlier example in which 5 percent precision and a 90 percent confidence level are desired. The precision represents the spread between a zero error rate occurring in the sample and the maximum acceptable error rate of 5 percent for the population. The numbers in the 5 percent column represent the confidence levels for various sample sizes and various numbers of errors disclosed by the samples. The first number in the 5% column is 72, which the table refers to as the number of times in 100 that the auditor would be justified in concluding that the error rate in the population is less than 5 percent. The number 72 represents the confidence level (reliability), but since the confidence is only 72 percent, a larger sample is needed. The next larger sample of 50 can be seen to yield 92 percent confidence, and hence a sample of 50 would satisfy the auditor's requirements.

[1]For a more complete discussion of the derivation of the approach of Table 9-2, the reader is referred to Chapter 22 of Volume 1 *The External Audit* by Rodney J. Anderson, published in 1977 by Pittman Publishing Division of Copp Clark Limited, Toronto. The 2-volume work is one of the most comprehensive and authoritative treatises on auditing currently available.

**Table 9-1.** Implications of Accepting Data Based on the Number of Errors Disclosed by the Auditor's Sample*

| Sample Size | Number of Errors Disclosed | Number of Times in 100 That the Auditor Will Be Justified in Deciding That the Actual Error Rate Is Less Than: | | | | |
|---|---|---|---|---|---|---|
| | | .5% | 1% | 2% | 5% | 10% |
| 25 | 0 | 12 | 22 | 39 | 72 | 92 |
| 25 | 1 | 1 | 3 | 9 | 36 | 71 |
| 25 | 2 | 0 | 0 | 1 | 13 | 46 |
| 25 | 3 | | | 0 | 4 | 24 |
| 25 | 4 | | | | 1 | 11 |
| 25 | 5 | | | | 0 | 4 |
| 25 | 6 | | | | | 1 |
| 25 | 7 | | | | | 0 |
| 50 | 0 | 22 | 39 | 63 | 92 | 99 |
| 50 | 1 | 3 | 9 | 26 | 71 | 96 |
| 50 | 2 | 0 | 1 | 8 | 46 | 87 |
| 50 | 3 | | 0 | 2 | 24 | 73 |
| 50 | 4 | | | 0 | 11 | 56 |
| 50 | 5 | | | | 4 | 38 |
| 50 | 6 | | | | 1 | 24 |
| 50 | 7 | | | | 0 | 13 |
| 50 | 8 | | | | | 7 |
| 50 | 9 | | | | | 3 |
| 50 | 10 | | | | | 1 |
| 100 | 0 | 39 | 63 | 86 | 99 | 100 |
| 100 | 1 | 9 | 26 | 59 | 96 | 100 |
| 100 | 2 | 1 | 8 | 32 | 87 | 100 |
| 100 | 3 | 0 | 2 | 14 | 73 | 99 |
| 100 | 4 | | 0 | 5 | 56 | 97 |
| 100 | 5 | | | 2 | 38 | 93 |
| 100 | 6 | | | 0 | 24 | 87 |
| 100 | 7 | | | | 13 | 78 |
| 100 | 8 | | | | 7 | 67 |
| 100 | 9 | | | | 3 | 54 |
| 100 | 10 | | | | 1 | 42 |
| 150 | 0 | 53 | 78 | 95 | 100 | 100 |
| 150 | 1 | 17 | 44 | 80 | 100 | 100 |
| 150 | 2 | 4 | 19 | 58 | 98 | 100 |
| 150 | 3 | 1 | 7 | 35 | 94 | 100 |
| 150 | 4 | 0 | 2 | 18 | 87 | 100 |
| 150 | 5 | | 0 | 8 | 76 | 100 |
| 150 | 6 | | | 3 | 62 | 99 |
| 150 | 7 | | | 1 | 48 | 98 |
| 150 | 8 | | | 0 | 34 | 96 |
| 150 | 9 | | | | 22 | 93 |
| 150 | 10 | | | | 14 | 88 |
| 200 | 0 | 63 | 86 | 98 | 100 | 100 |
| 200 | 1 | 26 | 59 | 91 | 100 | 100 |
| 200 | 2 | 8 | 32 | 76 | 100 | 100 |
| 200 | 3 | 2 | 14 | 57 | 99 | 100 |
| 200 | 4 | 0 | 5 | 37 | 97 | 100 |
| 200 | 5 | | 2 | 21 | 93 | 100 |

*Table 9-1* (Continued)

| Sample Size | Number of Errors Dis-closed | .5% | 1% | 2% | 5% | 10% |
|---|---|---|---|---|---|---|
| | | **Number of Times in 100 That the Auditor Will Be Justified in Deciding That the Actual Error Rate Is Less Than:** | | | | |
| 200 | 6 | | 0 | 11 | 87 | 100 |
| 200 | 7 | | | 5 | 78 | 100 |
| 200 | 8 | | | 2 | 67 | 100 |
| 200 | 9 | | | 1 | 54 | 99 |
| 200 | 10 | | | 0 | 42 | 99 |
| 300 | 0 | 78 | 95 | 100 | 100 | 100 |
| 300 | 1 | 44 | 80 | 98 | 100 | 100 |
| 300 | 2 | 19 | 58 | 94 | 100 | 100 |
| 300 | 3 | 7 | 35 | 85 | 100 | 100 |
| 300 | 4 | 2 | 18 | 71 | 100 | 100 |
| 300 | 5 | 0 | 8 | 55 | 100 | 100 |
| 300 | 6 | | 3 | 39 | 99 | 100 |
| 300 | 7 | | 1 | 26 | 98 | 100 |
| 300 | 8 | | 0 | 15 | 96 | 100 |
| 300 | 9 | | | 8 | 93 | 100 |
| 300 | 10 | | | 4 | 88 | 100 |
| 300 | 11 | | | 2 | 81 | 100 |
| 300 | 12 | | | 1 | 73 | 100 |
| 300 | 13 | | | 0 | 64 | 100 |
| 300 | 14 | | | | 53 | 100 |
| 300 | 15 | | | | 43 | 100 |

*This table is developed from Poisson's distribution as follows:

$\bar{X}$ = average number of occurrences of a given event.

$T$ = number of times in 1,000 that $X$ or fewer occurrences can be expected in a sample under the conditions of $\bar{X}$.

Thus, if a sample of 100 is drawn from a series of data that has an average of 2 percent errors, $\bar{X}$ is 2, and the values for $X$ and $T$ are

$$
\begin{aligned}
0 &= 135 & 5 &= 983 \\
1 &= 406 & 6 &= 995 \\
2 &= 677 & 7 &= 999 \\
3 &= 857 & 8 &= 1,000 \\
4 &= 947
\end{aligned}
$$

In turn, when an average error of 2 percent is present, a sample of 100 will reveal one error or less 406 times in 1,000. The auditor may therefore conclude that the probability of finding more than one error is 594 (the complement of 406) and that, in accepting a sample of 100 showing one error as coming from a population that must have contained less than 2 percent errors, the probability of being correct is 59.4 percent.

The value indicated in the previous example is found on the line of this table showing sample size 100 and one error; under the 2 percent column, the figure 59 appears.

All probabilities less than $\frac{1}{2}$ are shown in the table as 0.

All probabilities greater than $99\frac{1}{2}$ are shown in the table as 100.

This table covers only the sample sizes and maximum allowable rates of error that are most likely to be needed. Values not shown can be derived by using a table of the Poisson distribution as described above.

Source: This table originally appeared as part of an article on statistical sampling by the author published in *The Journal of Accountancy*, January, 1954, and is reproduced here with permission.

**Table 9-2.** Factor Values for Evaluation of Attribute Samples as Derived from the Poisson Distribution

| Number of Occurrences in Sample | Factor Values for Confidence Levels | | | |
|---|---|---|---|---|
| | 80% | 90% | 95% | 99% |
| 0 | 1.61 | 2.31 | 3.00 | 4.61 |
| 1 | 3.00 | 3.89 | 4.75 | 6.64 |
| 2 | 4.28 | 5.33 | 6.30 | 8.41 |
| 3 | 5.52 | 6.69 | 7.76 | 10.05 |

$$\text{Maximum probable error rate} = \frac{\text{Factor value for desired confidence}}{\text{Sample size}}$$

$$\text{Minimum sample size*} = \frac{\text{Factor value for desired confidence}}{\text{Maximum tolerable error rate}}$$

*Minimum sample size assumes that no occurrences will appear in the sample. If occurrences appear in the sample, the sample can be evaluated for a revised maximum probable error rate, or alternatively an upward revised sample size must be calculated.

If the sample of 50 actually discloses one error, however, then there would be only 71 percent confidence, which would be unacceptable. But note that if the sample is extended and if errors continue to appear at the same rate, a sample of 100 with 2 errors would yield 87 percent confidence and a sample of 150 with 3 errors would yield 94 percent confidence—enough to warrant accepting the population. These relationships clearly indicate the greater information value of larger samples, as is also expressed in terms of greater precision or greater confidence.

In a similar fashion, the effect of changes in the precision desired on confidence or sample size can also be noted from the table.

Table 9-2, of course, will yield similar results, but sample size can be determined more precisely, and any size sample can be evaluated. Thus the sample of 50 from Table 9-1 to yield desired 90 percent confidence that the population error rate does not exceed 5 percent is actually excessive because it yields 92 percent confidence. The exact minimum sample size can be computed from Table 9-2 as 2.31 ÷ .05 = 46.2 or 47 to be conservative and round upward. Similarly if 3 errors have been disclosed by the sample, the minimum sample to accept the population with a 90 percent confidence level is 6.69 ÷ .05 = 133.8 or 134. If the sample of 150 determined from the first table is used and 3 errors appear, Table 9-2 indicates that at the 90 percent confidence level, the maximum error rate is less than 5 percent: 6.69 ÷ 150 = .0446.

### Adjustment for Population Size

Calculation of the Poisson distribution is based on populations of infinite size, and as a consequence the confidence levels shown will actually be higher when samples are drawn from finite populations. The larger the sample size in proportion to the population, the greater will be the information content of the sample. Thus the confidence levels as given in the table are slightly understated, and the smaller the population the greater will be the understatement. In other words the confidence levels given are conservative, or conversely, the sample sizes are larger than are actually necessary in sampling from a finite population.

If the population is relatively small, such that the sample exceeds 10 percent of the population, it may be considered advantageous to apply a finite correction factor to calculate the smaller sample size that will satisfy the auditor's requirements. The formula is

$$n' = \frac{n}{1 + \dfrac{n}{N}}$$

where

$n$ = sample size for infinite population
$n'$ = revised sample size for finite population
$N$ = population size

To illustrate, if the population size is 1,000 items and the indicated sample size is 100, the computation of the revised sample size would be

$$n' = \frac{100}{1 + \dfrac{100}{1000}} = 90.9 = 91$$

### Consideration of Alpha Risk

Although the emphasis in the preceding discussion has been on the reliability or confidence level when accepting a population, the complement of the confidence level is the Beta risk of a Type II error of accepting when the population should be rejected. It should be noted, however, that if the sample results indicate that the population cannot be accepted, nonacceptance is not the same as rejecting the population. For the previous illustration of a sample of 50 that disclosed one error when 5 percent precision was sought, the 71 percent confidence if the population is accepted represents a 71 percent Alpha risk if the population is rejected, for it is quite possible that the error rate in the population is actually less than 5 percent. But if the sample of 50 yields 4 errors, it is likely that the error rate is 5 percent or more, and there would be only 11 percent confidence in accepting the population as having less than a 5 percent error rate. In that case the Alpha risk of rejecting the population when it should be accepted is also a relatively low 11 percent, representing a fairly strong basis for a decision that the population should be rejected.

### A Further Comment about Beta Risk

If the auditor works with a uniform desired confidence level for compliance tests of, say, 90 percent and consequently a 10 percent Beta risk, it does not follow that 10 percent of the auditor's decisions to accept will be wrong. Such a result would follow only for populations that are at precisely the maximum acceptable error rate. In the vast majority of situations, if the system of internal control is functioning as intended, the actual error rate should be less than the maximum tolerable error rate, so that the true risk of an incorrect accept decison will be less than the risk inherent in the sample design. On the other hand, should the system of internal control be malfunctioning so that the actual error rate exceeds the maximum tolerable error rate, there will be an increased likelihood of detection of an error leading to a decision to reject the population, and the actual Beta risk will be less than the specified 10 percent.

### Estimation Sampling for Variables: Underlying Theory

Estimation sampling (or survey sampling or statistical estimation) is perhaps the most versatile statistical sampling technique available for use in auditing, for not only can variables such as dollar amounts be accommodated, but attributes can be estimated as well. Although the following discussion of the theory underlying estimation sampling is in terms of variables such as are the subject of substantive tests, the theory is equally applicable to attribute estimation.

The distribution of a population of individual values in relation to the arithmetic mean of the population constitutes the underlying basis for estimation sampling. It is known, for example, that 68.3 percent of the items in a normally distributed population will occur within ±1 standard deviation from the mean, 95.4 percent within ±2 standard deviations, and 99.7 percent within ±3 standard deviations. (The reader should recall that the standard deviation is computed by determining the deviation of each item in the population from the mean, squaring these deviations, summing the squared deviations, dividing this sum by the number of items in the population, and calculating the square root of the resulting quotient.)

A second important statistical concept involved in estimation sampling describes the results of taking repeated samples of a stated size and calculating the mean of the items in each sample. These sample means will tend to be normally distributed, with the mean of the sample means equal to the mean of the population. The standard deviation of the sample means (the standard error, in statistical parlance) and the behavior of the standard deviation of the sample means in relation to the size of the sample constitutes the focal point of estimation sampling. The larger the size of the repeated samples from which the sample means are computed, the smaller will be the standard deviation of the sample means. To indicate the extremes, if the sample size is 1, the standard deviation of the sample means will be equal to the standard deviation of the population. Conversely, if the sample size is equal to the population size, the standard deviation of the sample means will be 0, for the means of the samples will be identical to each other and to the mean of the population. The relationship of sample size and standard deviation of the sample means is pictured graphically in Figure 9-1.

A second factor affecting the standard deviation of the sample means is the standard deviation of the population, such that the greater the variability (magnitude of the standard deviation) of the population, the greater will be the variability of the sample means and hence the magnitude of the standard deviation of the sample means (the standard error). The relationship of the standard deviation of the sample means, sample size, and the standard deviation of the population is indicated by the equation

$$\text{Standard deviation of sample means} = \frac{\text{Standard deviation of population}}{\sqrt{\text{Sample size}}}$$

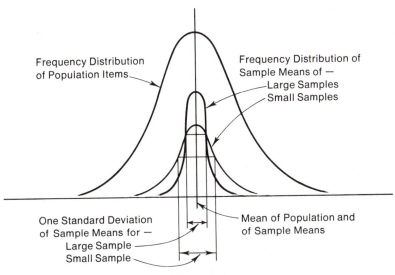

**Figure 9-1.**

This equation is based on an infinite population; the slight effect of the fact that the auditor works with finite populations is the finite correction factor that was discussed previously.

### Illustration of Estimation Sampling

Estimation sampling will be illustrated by showing how the total amount of accounts receivable can be estimated from a sample of the balances in an accounts receivable ledger. For instance, if we take a random sample of 100 accounts, total the account balances, and then determine the mean balance by dividing the total by 100, we might arrive at a mean of, say, $46.52 per account. Then, if by counting we determine that there are 1,400 accounts in the ledger, we would estimate total accounts receivable to be $65,128.00. However, we know that if we take a different random sample of 100 accounts, we will in all likelihood arrive at a different mean balance and thus a different estimate of the total receivables. How much the results of such samples of 100 might vary would depend on the variability of the population from which the samples are drawn. Also, of course, the variability of the sample results would represent an inverse relationship to the size of the sample.

Our immediate problem is to determine, for a given sample size from a stated population, how much the sample means might vary from the true mean of the population. Recall that the means of repeated samples of a given size from a stated population will tend to fall about the population mean in the pattern of a normal distribution, and the dispersion of these sample means about the true mean will be a function of the standard deviation of the population and the sample size. If for our population of accounts receivable balances we assume a standard deviation of $10.53, we can compute the standard deviation of the sample means to be $10.53/\sqrt{100}$, or $1.05. Given the behavior of normally distributed results, we can graph the means of repeated samples of 100 in the following manner, if we assume for the moment that the true mean of the population is the $46.52 calculated from our sample of 100 (Figure 9-2).

This graph can be interpreted as saying that given $46.52 to be the true mean of the population, about 68 percent of the means calculated from the sample of 100 would fall between $45.47 and $47.57; 95 percent of the sample means would fall between $44.42 and $48.62; and 99.7 percent of the sample means would fall between $43.37 and $49.67. From the known information, we can be certain that the shape of the curve is as shown, but the placement of the curve on the horizontal line depends on where the true mean of the population falls. In estimation sampling, we attempt to find out something about the true mean of the population, but we cannot spot the mean precisely on the horizontal line; we can only estimate a range within which we would expect the

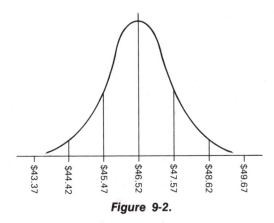

$43.37  $44.42  $45.47  $46.52  $47.57  $48.62  $49.67

*Figure 9-2.*

true mean to lie, with some stated confidence level for our estimate.

As stated above, assuming that the true mean is $46.52, we would expect 95 percent of the means of repeated samples of 100 to fall within 2 standard deviations, or a range from $44.42 to $48.62. But now let us drop the assumption that $46.52 is the true mean of the population and consider the usual situation where we have no information about the true mean. Our purpose in sampling is to estimate the mean of the population, but this estimate must of necessity be an interval estimate concerning a range of possible values. A correct point estimate of the true mean can be made only from a 100 percent sample.

What can we conclude from our sample of 100 with a mean of $46.52? With 95 percent confidence, we can say that it must have come from a population whose mean was no less than $44.42 and no greater than $48.62. This statement can be illustrated by Figure 9-3.

Thus we can see that it is not likely that the population mean is greater than $48.62 nor less than $44.42, for there is only a 2½ percent chance that we would obtain a sample mean of $46.52 or less from a population with a mean of $48.62, and only a 2½ percent chance of obtaining a sample mean of $48.52 or more from a population with a mean of $44.42. Combining these two statements, we can say with 95 percent confidence (5 percent risk of a sampling error) that the true mean of the population lies between $44.42 and $48.62, and thus we would estimate, with 95 percent confidence, a total population of $65,128.00 ± $2,940 [1,400 × $46.52 ± 1,400 × ($48.62 − $46.52 or $44.42 − $46.52)].

### Determining Sample Size in Estimation Sampling

In the preceding illustration of estimation sampling, we utilized an arbitrarily assumed sample of 100, but one of the main purposes of using statistical sampling techniques is to determine what size sample

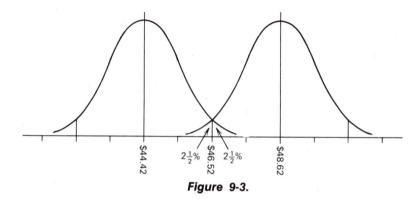

**Figure 9-3.**

must be taken. The two factors that must be specified in estimation sampling to calculate sample size are, of course, confidence level and precision, with confidence an expression of desired assurance that the true value of the population will lie within the range of the estimates based on the sample mean and with that range in turn determined by the precision desired in the estimation process.

The precision to be specified in estimation sampling is a matter of materiality. To approach this problem, let us assume that the general ledger accounts receivable control account for our 1,400 accounts receivable shows a balance of $67,241,89. Also, we shall assume that a difference of ± $5,000 from this balance would not materially affect the client's financial statements. This decision of materiality would be based on the importance of the maximum difference to be tolerated of $5,000 relative to such figures as the total accounts receivable, the total current assets, the current ratio, and the amount of net income. By saying that ± $5,000 would not be material, we must be willing to issue an unqualified opinion even if the true receivable balance might be as low as $62,241.89 or as high as $72,241.89.

We also know that presumably the mean account balance is $48.03 ($67,241.89/1,400), and that the standard deviation of the population is the previously stated $10.53.[2] Finally, because we have specified precision of ± $5,000 we know that we are seeking a sampling distribution of means centered on the indicated mean of $48.03 and extending to

[2]When working with computerized records and an audit software package, the computer will compute the standard deviation. If hard copy records are involved, an estimate of the standard deviation can be computed from the items in the sample. As an alternative to computation, the standard deviation can be estimated quite readily by randomly selecting 49 account balances, dividing the random listing of these 49 balances into seven groups of seven items, calculating the dollar range between the highest and lowest balance for each group, calculating the mean of these seven ranges, and dividing this mean by 2,704. (See Herbert Arkin, *Handbook of Sampling for Auditing and Accounting.* New York: McGraw-Hill Book Company, 1963, p. 108.)

points that with a likelihood of only 2½ percent could have come from a population whose mean is as low as $44.46 [($67,241.90 − $5,000) ÷ 1,400], or with a likelihood of 2½ percent from a population whose mean is as high as $51.60 [($67,241.89 + $5,000) ÷ 1,400]. These requirements may be graphed as shown in Figure 9-4.

This being the case, we are seeking a sample size in which the means of 95 percent of the samples, if drawn from a population with a mean of $48.03, would fall between $46.24 and $49.82, or $48.03 ± $1.79. Under those circumstances, as the graph shows, we can be relatively certain (95 percent confidence) that, even if we should draw a sample with a mean as low as $46.24, it did not come from a population with a mean less than $44.46; and if we should draw a sample with a mean as high as $49.82, that it did not come from a population with a mean greater than $51.60. We are thus saying that we desire a sampling distribution in which two standard deviations (which would include 95 percent of the sample means) would be $1.79, and hence one standard deviation would be $.895. At this point, sample size can be computed through use of the equation given previously, which can be rearranged to show:

$$\text{Sample size} = \frac{(\text{Standard deviation of population})^2}{(\text{Standard deviation of sample means})^2}$$

By inserting the values, we have:

$$\frac{(10.53)^2}{(.895)^2} = \frac{110.8809}{.801} = 138.4 = 139 \text{ (Rounding conservatively to the next higher number)}$$

We may then proceed to randomly select the desired sample of 139 account balances, and if the mean of the sample is no less than $46.24 and no greater than $49.82, we would have at least 95 percent confidence that the true value of the population is not less than $62,241.89, and not greater than $72,241.89. It may also be seen that if the true

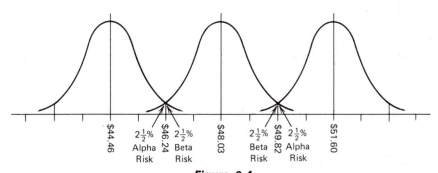

**Figure 9-4.**

value of the population is $67,241.89, as indicated by the accounts receivable control, we would not be likely to obtain a sample mean of less than $46.24 or more than $49.82. Stated in terms of risk, there is a 2-tailed Beta risk of 5 percent that the true value of the population could lie outside the range of $62,241.89 and $72,241.89. Similarly, there is a 2-tailed Alpha risk of obtaining sample means outside the range of $46.24 and $49.82 and rejecting a population for which the true value is within the acceptable range of $62,241.89 and $72,241.89.

The estimation technique just illustrated is technically referred to as mean-per-unit estimation (MPU) and was applied in what would be referred to as the hypothesis testing mode, where any actual difference between the total being tested and the details making up that total would increase the likelihood of not being able to accept the population. In using that approach, note that the details of the population are being proved against a total that is already known, and no further verification of the footing of the details is necessary.

If the items in the population are subject to audit correction, as in confirming accounts receivable, then other forms of statistical estimation will generally be more appropriate. These are known as difference estimation and ratio estimation. Difference estimation is illustrated in the next section, followed by a brief discussion of how ratio estimation differs from difference estimation.

### Illustration of Difference Estimation

The setting chosen to illustrate difference estimation is confirmation of accounts receivable on a positive basis; that is, where the customer is requested to reply to the confirmation request stating whether the indicated balance is correct or incorrect, and in the latter case stating what the correct amount should be. For nonresponses these requests may be excluded from the sample results, in which case the number of requests sent must be increased to allow for the nonresponses and an appropriate sample size for the responses that were received. This approach is questionable, however, in that theoretically the nonresponses should be considered to be a different population. As an alternative, only the number of confirmations needed to satisfy the sampling plan may be sent, and if there is no response after a second or third request, alternative procedures (see Chapter 11) can be applied to ascertain the correctness of the account balance.

The steps to be taken for difference estimation are as follows:

1. Prove the detail accounts receivable balances against the control account balance.
2. Compute sample size based on the precision and confidence desired, with precision based on the maximum tolerable error in the accounts (that is, the

total amount of error that would not be material). The standard deviation for the sample size calculation would be an estimate of the standard deviation of the population of differences and nondifferences expected from the confirmation responses.

3. Randomly select the accounts to be confirmed and send confirmation.
4. Compute the dollar amount of any differences in the balances, as reported in the replies or as determined by alternative audit procedures.
5. Compute the mean of the observed differences, assigning a zero difference to those accounts that are correct.
6. Compute the precision limits of the observed differences.
7. Evaluate the sample results.

These steps are illustrated using the receivables data that were the basis for the MPU example:

Establish that accounts receivable detail records are in agreement with the accounts receivable control.

Compute sample size based on the expected mean difference in the accounts, the expected standard deviation of the population of differences and nondifferences, and the desired confidence. Note that the maximum sample size would result from the worst possible assumption: differences equal to materiality are spread proportionally throughout the accounts. We will assume that past experience has shown that no more than 2 percent of the 1,400 accounts are likely to be in error, with a mean overstatement of these erroneous accounts of $25 or a total overstatement of $700 and a mean overstatement for the population of $.50 $\left(\dfrac{1,400 \times .02 \times \$25}{1,400}\right)$. Based on past experience, the standard deviation of the population of differences is estimated to be $15.

Defining a material difference as $5,000, the same as in the previous MPU illustration, the maximum allowable mean per account difference would be

$$\frac{\$5,000}{1,400} = \$3.57$$

We will estimate the mean per account difference of the entire population from the results of the confirmation requests sent to a sample group of customers, but of course the point estimate of differences calculated from our sample is likely to vary from the true mean per account difference of the 1,400 account population. We can control the extent of that variation through the size of the sample that is taken. Assuming that the true difference is the previously calculated estimate of $.50 overstatement per account, we would not want the sample estimate to exceed $3.57 per account, and hence the maximum variation we would wish to have occur in the sample would be $3.57 − $.50 = $3.07. If we seek 95 percent confidence from our sample, it would mean that we would want 95 percent of the point estimates of the mean per account differences to fall within a range of \$.50 ± \$3.07. That range would be roughly 2 standard deviations, and hence we desire the standard error of our estimate to be \$3.07/2 or \$1.535.

Substituting the values determined above in the equation for sample size we have

$$\text{Sample size} = \frac{(\text{SD of population})^2}{(\text{Standard error of the estimate})^2}$$

$$= \frac{(15)^2}{(1.535)^2}$$

$$= \frac{225}{2.356}$$

$$= 95.5 = 96$$

We can then proceed to randomly select 96 accounts to which positive confirmation requests are to be sent, and from the responses received plus the alternative verification from nonresponses, proceed to calculate our estimate of the maximum probable overstatement (or understatement) of the accounts receivable as follows.

1. Sum the difference disclosed by the confirmations, which we shall assume were as follows for 6 accounts reporting differences:

| Book Balance | Amount Confirmed | Books Overstated | Understated |
|---|---|---|---|
| \$128.51 | \$101.25 | \$ 27.26 | |
| 10.19 | 15.19 | | \$5.00 |
| 225.00 | 125.00 | 100.00 | |
| 38.20 | 36.00 | 2.20 | |
| 69.53 | 71.20 | | 1.67 |
| 87.15 | 78.15 | 9.00 | |
| | | $138.46 | $6.67 |
| | | 6.67 | |
| Net overstatement | | $131.79 | |

2. Compute the point estimate of the total differences for the entire population:

| | No. of Accounts | Amount |
|---|---|---|
| Net overstatement | 6 | \$131.79 |
| Correct accounts | 90 | 0.00 |
| Total | 96 | \$131.79 |

Sample estimate of mean per account
overstatement = $131.79/96 = $1.37

Estimated population overstatement
= 1,400 × $1.37 = $1,918

3.  Evaluate the sample results using a revised standard deviation for
    the population based on the sample and with a desired confidence
    of 95 percent that the total overstatement of the account does not
    exceed $5,000.

    Revised estimate of the standard deviation of the population of dif-
    ferences:

    | | Diff | (Diff)² |
    |---|---|---|
    | | 27.26 | 743 |
    | | (5.00) | 25 |
    | | 100.00 | 10,000 |
    | | 2.20 | 5 |
    | | (1.67) | 3 |
    | | 9.00 | 81 |
    | 90 correct amounts | 0 | 0 |
    | | | 10,857 |

$$SD = \sqrt{\frac{\Sigma(\text{Diff})^2 - n(\text{Mean Diff})^2}{n - 1}}$$

$$SD = \sqrt{\frac{10,857 - 96(1.37)^2}{95}}$$

$$= \quad \$10.60$$

Standard error of the estimate:

$$SE = \sqrt{\frac{(SD \text{ of population})^2}{\text{Sample Size} - 1}}$$

$$= \sqrt{\frac{(10.60)^2}{95}}$$

$$= \quad 1.09$$

Estimated maximum difference for 1,400 accounts based on 95 percent confidence or 2 standard errors of the estimate:

$$= 1.37 \times 1400 \pm (2 \times 1.09 \times 1400)$$
$$= 1918 \pm 3052$$
$$= 4970, - 1134$$

Reviewing the above results, we see that the sample disclosed a total overstatement of $131.79 for the 95 accounts or a mean overstatement of $1.37. This mean overstatement when applied to the entire population represented an estimated overstatement of $1,918. The precision of that estimate based on the specified 95 percent confidence is equal to approximately 2 standard errors of the sample estimate or $2 \times \$1.09 = \$2.18$, and multiplying that figure by the 1,400 accounts in the population yields an indicated precision of ± $3,052, with a 95 percent confidence level for that estimate. The estimated maximum overstatement of $1,1918 + $3,052 = $4,970 is just under the defined material difference of $5,000, and hence the receivables can be accepted with 95 percent confidence that the total is not materially in error.

Analysis of the details presented in the illustration reveals the following differences that occurred in the estimates based on the sample in contrast to the preliminary estimates used to calculate the sample size:

| | Preliminary Estimate | Sample Estimate |
|---|---|---|
| Average overstatement difference— | | |
| Per account | $.50 | $ 1.37 |
| For 1400 accounts | $700 | $1,918 |
| Standard deviation of differences | $15 | $10.60 |

Although the differences disclosed by the sample were greater than anticipated, the standard deviation of the differences was less than anticipated, and these factors offset each other so as to permit acceptance of the population in relation to the specified confidence and precision and the $5,000 definition of a material error.

### Some Comments on Fine Tuning

The difference estimation example and the mean-per-unit estimation example were both presented in terms of sampling from an infinite population, but because in each case a finite population was involved, a slightly smaller sample would suffice, as determined by applying the finite adjustment factor presented earlier. The reduction in sample size will be insignificant, however, in cases where the sample is less than ten percent of the population.

Also, both examples were based on a desired confidence of 95 percent, which was treated as being roughly 2 standard deviations of the sampling means (standard error of the estimate). Actually, 95 percent of the observations are calculated to fall within ± 1.96 standard errors, and 1.96 should be used instead of 2 in the various calculations. This so-called "Z" value for the various confidence levels likely to be sought in audit sampling is as follows:

$$50\% = .68$$
$$68\% = 1.00$$
$$80\% = 1.28$$
$$90\% = 1.65$$
$$95\% = 1.96$$
$$99\% = 2.58$$

An underlying assumption of the preceding discussion of sampling for variables estimation is that the variables being sampled are normally distributed and there is a relatively large number of errors in the population. If the number of errors is small and the errors are predominantly in one direction, the results of variables estimation are likely to be misleading. To overcome the problem, stratification of the population is necessary, and dollar unit sampling, which will be discussed shortly, offers an ideal solution. Before turning to DUS, however, this discussion will briefly consider ratio estimation, as a close companion to difference estimation.

### Ratio Estimation

Instead of working with differences, ratio estimation is based on the ratio of errors to originally stated amounts, but in all other respects the two approaches involve similar calculations and are subject to the limitations discussed above. Ratio estimation, however, is more efficient than difference estimation, as the standard deviation of the ratios will be proportionally smaller than the standard deviation of the differences.

### Dollar Unit Sampling with Cumulative Monetary Amount Selection

DUS is so named because each dollar (or other monetary denomination) unit in a population is considered to be a separate sampling unit. The sampling plan is always implemented with CMA selection, which provides assurance that the sample will be representative in terms of "average" dollars, and the transactions or accounts of which the individual dollars are a part will have a probability of selection that is proportional to their size. The resulting sample is evaluated in terms of the number of errors disclosed by the sample and the probable maximum error rate in the population, as determined by calculation or from a table such as Table 9-1 or 9-2. The probable maximum error rate (at a chosen confidence level) is then "priced" on some basis to determine the monetary precision that has been achieved.

Dollar unit sampling and evaluation are particularly advantageous in situations where a low error rate is expected, which it was noted are the situations in which difference and ratio estimation are least effective. This advantage is especially significant considering that effective internal control should preclude the existence of many errors in the populations being sampled. Another advantage is that CMA stratifies to include 100 percent sampling of all items that exceed the sampling interval, plus selection in proportion to size for lesser amounts. As a consequence, the auditor has maximum assurance that isolated material errors will be disclosed if material errors are present. DUS is equally appropriate and adaptable to attribute sampling for compliance tests, regardless of whether the focus is on procedural errors or on the monetary consequences of the procedural errors.

There is, however, considerable variation in the application of DUS depending on the nature of the monetary errors that might occur. Three possibilities exist:

One-direction errors, 100 percent misstatement
One-direction errors, fractional misstatement
Offsetting errors, fractional misstatement

Each possibility is briefly discussed here.

*One-Direction Errors, 100 Percent Misstatement.*    Typical of these single direction misstatements would be classification errors, such as classifying a receivable as current when it is actually past due, or capitalizing an expenditure when it should have been expensed. Because DUS is directed to the sampling of "average dollars," the maximum expected error rate in the population based on the number of errors disclosed by the sample can be applied directly to the population total. The resulting maximum expected dollar error is the precision of the sample and should be related to what the auditor considers would be a material difference.

*One-Direction Errors, Fractional Misstatement.*    Fractional misstatement of single-direction errors can occur in the classification examples given above if only a portion of the receivable is past due, or if the typical invoice associated with expenditures covers several items and only some of the items should be expensed. Another possibility would be in testing inventories to ascertain whether all items have been reduced to market when cost is less than market. Under these circumstances, if no errors are disclosed by the sample, we obviously have no information about errors in the population, but our minimum sample says that we can have some stated confidence that errors in the population do not exceed a stated rate. For zero sample errors the maximum error rate that may exist in the population will be greater than zero, and since we know nothing about those *possible* errors, we should conservatively estimate them to be 100 percent errors in order to evaluate the precision of our sample.

Assume that we have concluded that a one percent error rate is the maximum rate that we can accept without material distortion of the financial statements, and we seek 80 percent confidence in our decision. From Table 9-1 we can see that a sample of 150 will yield 78 percent confidence that the error rate does not exceed one percent, so we will need a slightly larger sample. Table 9-2 gives a factor value of 1.61 for 80 percent confidence and no sample errors, and dividing 1.61 by the one percent maximum acceptable error rate tells us that the minimum sample size should be 161. For a population of 161,000 dollars, we should sample 161 dollars or every 1,000th dollar. If our sample discloses no errors, we will have 80 percent confidence that the error rate does not exceed one percent. For those possible one percent errors, we should conservatively assume the worst situation possible—namely that they are 100 percent errors, and hence our sampling precision is $161,000 \times .01 = \$1,610$, the maximum error that we should expect to be present, with 80 percent confidence. Alternatively, using the factor value from Table 9-2 and the sampling interval, we obtain an identical result: $\$1,000 \times 1.61 = \$1,610$ maximum error.

But if our sample discloses one error, the maximum probable error rate at 80 percent confidence increases from one percent to 1.86 percent $(3.00 \div 161 = .0186)$. Further, if the error disclosed involves only a 60 percent overstatement (60 percent tainting in DUS parlance), we can assume that with the widening of our precision from 1.00 percent to 1.86 percent, the possible *additional* errors will be similar to the 60 percent error disclosed by our sample, and hence precision (maximum error) is now

$$
\begin{array}{ll}
(\$161,000)(.01) & = \$1,610 \\
(\$161,000)(.0086)(.60) & = \$\phantom{0}831 \\
& \phantom{=}\overline{\$2,441}
\end{array}
$$

or alternatively:

$$
\begin{array}{ll}
\$1,000 \times 1.61 & = \$1,610 \\
\$1,000\ (\$3.00 - 1.61)(.60) & = \$\phantom{0}834\ \text{(difference is due to rounding} \\
& \phantom{=}\overline{\$2,444}\ \text{in previous example)}
\end{array}
$$

If more than one error is disclosed, the above procedure should be extended to include the effect of the disclosure of the second error. It should be noted, however, that each succeeding error has a decreasing effect on the maximum error rate expected in the population, and the most conservative estimate of the maximum dollar error will be obtained if the error with the highest tainting percentage is introduced first in the above calculation, then the next highest, and so on.

*Understatement Errors.*   We must first face up to the prospect that when understatements occur, the understatement may exceed 100 percent and may in fact be infinite if an amount, such as a liability, is omitted from the population. The only way in which an audit test can attack omitted items is to apply the approach mentioned earlier of testing a reciprocal population. Thus in seeking unrecorded accounts payable at a balance sheet date of, say, June 30, the reciprocal population of disbursements after June 30 can be inspected for disbursements that liquidate liabilities that existed at June 30.

With respect to amounts that are included in the population but are understated, it may not be likely that the understatements will exceed 100 percent of the stated amount. If there is such a possibility, however, (a $100 amount is shown, but the correct amount is $300), the one-direction evaluation of tainting errors can be modified in the direction of conservatism by assuming that the likely tainting is more than 100 percent—say 200 percent, and then proceeding to evaluate the sample as discussed previously for fractional misstatements that are disclosed.

*Offsetting Errors; Fractional Misstatement.*   Although it might seem that a reasonable approach would be simply to offset the error taintings to obtain a most likely error rate for the net over- or understatement, the potentially larger of the two types of misstatement should be recognized as having a potentially greater effect. The simple offsetting approach and a preferred more conservative approach are illustrated and contrasted as follows, continuing with the same basic facts used in the previous illustration, but with the previous overstatement error (.60) and a smaller understatement error (.40) assumed to have been disclosed by the sample.

| | | | |
|---|---|---|---|
| Maximum possible overstatement— | | | |
| ($161,000) (.01) | = | $1,610 | |
| ($161,000) (.0086) (.60) | = | 831 | |
| Maximum overstatement— | | | $2,441 |
| Maximum possible understatement— | | | |
| ($161,000) (.01) | = | $1,610 | |
| ($161,000) (.0086) (.40) | = | 554 | |
| Maximum understatement | | | $2,164 |
| Maximum net overstatement | | | 277 |

Conservative net maximum overstatement—
Maximum possible overstatement, as above       $2,441
Less most likely understatement

$(\$161,000)\left(\dfrac{1}{161}\right)(.40)$      $=$      400

Net maximum overstatement      $2,041

Conservative net maximum understatement—
Maximum possible understatement, as above    $2,164
Less most likely overstatement

$(\$161,000)\left(\dfrac{1}{161}\right)(.60)$         600

Net maximum understatement      $1,564

## Relating Substantive Tests to the Evaluation of Internal Control and Compliance Tests

We have seen that an auditor's opinion that financial statements are fairly presented involves an implied assertion that no material errors are present in the statements. That implied assertion is based on the auditor's assumption that, subject to sampling risk, no material errors have gotten past the two filters on which the auditor has placed reliance:

- The client's system of internal control as subjected to compliance testing and evaluation by the auditor.
- The auditor's substantive tests.

This brings us to the question of how much risk the auditor will be willing to live with in designing substantive tests to provide, say, 95 percent assurance that the financial statements are free of material error. If the auditor concludes that the internal control system is 90 percent effective in filtering out material error existing in the unaudited financial statements, then substantive tests at as low as a 50 percent confidence level (50 percent risk) will yield the desired 95 percent confidence (5 percent risk: $.10 \times .5 = .05$). Although the 50 percent confidence level for the substantive tests seems low, it is statistically supportable based on the stated assumptions.

Some auditors contend, however, that a substantive test with only a 50 percent chance of detecting any material errors is hardly worth the effort in terms of the limited information that would be acquired, and argue that 80 percent confidence is as low as it seems reasonable to reduce confidence in any sampling situation. The 80 percent is, of course, strictly a judgment call—as are all risk specifications when sampling, including the observation that a 50 percent risk seems unreasonable.

### Concluding Observations

To conclude, it is important to recognize that statistical evaluation does not in any way change the auditor's approach to sampling. In the prestatistical sampling period, auditors were faced with the same problems of determining sample size and assessing the precision and confidence (risk) of their audit tests. These assessments were, of course, strictly intuitive. It was primarily the World War II advances in statistical quality control and the realization that these could be highly useful in auditing that focused attention on quantitative measures of precision and confidence and provided a means of answering the ageless question: How much sampling is enough? To answer that question effectively, the auditor should have a good understanding of the underlying theory of statistical sampling and of the various selection and evaluation techniques that can be used in compliance and substantive testing for attributes and variables. Acceptance sampling for attributes and statistical estimation are largely adaptations to auditing of applications developed for other uses, but DUS and CMA are essentially developments from within auditing practice. Pioneering work in this area was done by Kenneth W. Stringer of Deloitte, Haskins & Sells, as reported in the 1963 *Proceedings of the Business and Economics Statistics Section, American Statistical Association* in a paper titled "Practical Aspects of Statistical Sampling in Auditing." The definitive current work on DUS and CMA is *Dollar-Unit Sampling* by Donald Leslie, Albert Teitlebaum, and Rodney Anderson, published in 1979 by Copp Clark Pitman, Toronto.

### Questions/Problems

For multiple-choice questions 9-1 through 9-12, indicate the letter of the single answer that *best* completes the statement or answers the question, and justify the choice that you have made.

9-1. Which of the following is an advantage of systematic sampling over random number sampling?
   a. It provides a stronger basis for statistical conclusions.
   b. It enables the auditor to use the more efficient "sampling with replacement" tables.
   c. There may be correlation between the location of items in the population, the feature of sampling interest, and the sampling interval.
   d. It does not require establishment of correspondence between random numbers and items in the population.

(Uniform CPA Examination)

**9-2.** How should an auditor determine the precision required in establishing a statistical sampling plan?

   a. By the materiality of an allowable margin of error the auditor is willing to accept.
   b. By the amount of reliance the auditor will place on the results of the sample.
   c. By reliance on a table of random numbers.
   d. By the amount of risk the auditor is willing to take that material errors will occur in the accounting process.

   (Uniform CPA Examination)

**9-3.** What is the primary objective of using stratification as a sampling method in auditing?

   a. To increase the confidence level at which a decision will be reached from the results of the sample selected.
   b. To determine the occurrence rate for a given characteristic in the population being studied.
   c. To decrease the effect of variance in the total population.
   d. To determine the precision range of the sample selected.

   (Uniform CPA Examination)

**9-4.** Which of the following best describes the distinguishing feature of statistical sampling?

   a. It provides for measuring mathematically the degree of uncertainty that results from examining only a part of the data.
   b. It allows the auditor to have the same degree of confidence as with judgment sampling but with substantially less work.
   c. It allows the auditor to substitute sampling techniques for audit judgment.
   d. It provides for measuring the actual misstatements in financial statements in terms of reliability and precision.

   (Uniform CPA Examination)

**9-5.** A CPA examining inventory may appropriately apply sampling for attributes in order to estimate the

   a. Average price of inventory items.
   b. Percentage of slow-moving inventory items.
   c. Dollar value of inventory.
   d. Physical quantity of inventory items.

   (Uniform CPA Examination)

**9-6.** In estimation sampling for variables, which of the following must be known in order to estimate the appropriate sample size required to meet the auditor's needs in a given situation?

   a. The total amount of the population.

b.   The desired standard deviation.
c.   The desired confidence level.
d.   The estimated rate of error in the population.

(Uniform CPA Examination)

**9-7.**  The objective of precision in sampling for compliance testing of an internal control system is to

a.   Determine the probability of the auditor's conclusion based upon reliance factors.
b.   Determine that financial statements taken as a whole are not materially in error.
c.   Estimate the reliability of substantive tests.
d.   Estimate the range of procedural deviations in the population.

(Uniform CPA Examination)

**9-8.**  When using a statistical sampling plan, the auditor would probably require a smaller sample if the

a.   Population increases.
b.   Desired precision interval narrows.
c.   Desired reliability decreases.
d.   Expected error occurrence rate increases.

(Uniform CPA Examination)

**9-9.**  Jones, CPA, believes the industry-wide occurrence rate of client billing errors is 3% and has established a maximum acceptable occurrence rate of 5%. In the review of client invoices Jones should use

a.   Discovery sampling.
b.   Attribute sampling.
c.   Stratified sampling.
d.   Variable sampling.

(Uniform CPA Examination)

**9-10.**  An auditor selects a preliminary sample of 100 items out of a population of 1,000 items. The sample statistics generate an arithmetic mean of $60, a standard deviation of $6, and a standard error of the mean of $.60. If the sample was adequate for the auditor's purposes and the auditor's desired precision was plus or minus $1,000, the minimum acceptable dollar value of the population would be

a.   $61,000
b.   $60,000
c.   $59,000
d.   $58,800

(Uniform CPA Examination)

**9-11.** The major reason that the difference and ratio estimation methods would be expected to produce audit efficiency is that the

    a. Number of members of the populations of differences or ratios is smaller than the number of members of the population of book values.

    b. Beta risk may be completely ignored.

    c. Calculations required in using difference or ratio estimation are less arduous and fewer than those required when using direct estimation.

    d. Variability of the populations of differences or ratios is less than that of the populations of book values or audited values.

                              (Uniform CPA Examination)

**9-12.** Use of the ratio estimation sampling technique to estimate dollar amounts is inappropriate when

    a. The total book value is known and corresponds to the sum of all the individual book values.

    b. A book value for each sample item is unknown.

    c. There are some observed differences between audited values and book values.

    d. The audited values are nearly proportional to the book values.

                              (Uniform CPA Examination)

**9-13.** If a sample of 100 items reveals two errors, can the auditor reasonably conclude that roughly 2% of the items in the entire population are in error? Explain.

**9-14.** Since sampling always involves risk of a wrong conclusion, what is the advantage of using statistical sampling techniques?

**9-15.** In acceptance sampling the auditor may reach either of three decisions about the population after obtaining a sample. Explain.

**9-16.** In estimation sampling, what must be known (or calculated) about the population and what must be decided by the auditor in order to determine sample size and to estimate the value of the total population?

**9-17.** The table in this chapter for acceptance sampling shows that a sample of 100 items revealing no errors provides 86% confidence in accepting a population as not containing in excess of 2% errors. The table shows that the same sample results provide only 63% confidence in accepting the population as containing not more than 1% errors. If you were testing payroll rates against personnel department records, would the two alternatives for evaluating the sample of 100 items be equally acceptable? Explain.

**9-18.** In statistical sampling terms, how are smaller samples in testing account balances justified under conditions of good internal control?

**9-19.** The use of statistical sampling techniques in an examination of financial statements does not eliminate judgmental decisions.

Required:

a. Identify and explain four areas where judgment may be exercised by a CPA in planning a statistical sampling test.

b. Assume that a CPA's sample shows an unacceptable error rate. Describe the various actions that he may take based upon this finding.

c. A nonstratified sample of 80 accounts payable vouchers is to be selected from a population of 3,200. The vouchers are numbered consecutively from 1 to 3,200 and are listed, 40 to a page, in the voucher register. Describe four different techniques for selecting a random sample of vouchers for review.

(Uniform CPA Examination)

**9-20.** During the course of an audit engagement, a CPA attempts to obtain satisfaction that there are no material misstatements in the accounts receivable of a client. Statistical sampling is a tool that the auditor often uses to obtain representative evidence to achieve the desired satisfaction. On a particular engagement an auditor determined that a material misstatement in a population of accounts would be $35,000. To obtain satisfaction the auditor had to be 95% confident that the population of accounts was not in error by $35,000. The auditor decided to use unrestricted random sampling with replacement and took a preliminary random sample of 100 items (n) from a population of 1,000 items (N). The sample produced the following data:

Arithmetic mean of sample items ($\bar{x}$)     $4,000
Standard deviation of sample items (SD) $  200

The auditor also has available the following information:

Standard error of the mean $(SE) = SD \div \sqrt{n}$
Population precision $(P) = N \times R \times SE$

### Partial List of Reliability Coefficients

| If Reliability Coefficient (R) Is | Then Reliability Is |
|---|---|
| 1.70 | 91.086% |
| 1.75 | 91.988 |
| 1.80 | 92.814 |
| 1.85 | 93.568 |

**Partial List of Reliability Coefficients**

| If Reliability Coefficient (R) Is | Then Reliability Is |
|---|---|
| 1.90 | 94.256 |
| 1.95 | 94.882 |
| 1.96 | 95.000 |
| 2.00 | 95.450 |
| 2.05 | 95.964 |
| 2.10 | 96.428 |
| 2.15 | 96.844 |

Required:

a. Define the statistical terms "reliability" and "precision" as applied to auditing.

b. If all necessary audit work is performed on the preliminary sample items and no errors are detected,

    (1) What can the auditor say about the total amount of accounts receivable at the 95% reliability level?

    (2) At what confidence level can the auditor say that the population is not in error by $35,000?

c. Assume that the preliminary sample was sufficient,

    (1) Compute the auditor's estimate of the population total.

    (2) Indicate how the auditor should relate this estimate to the client's recorded amount.

(Uniform CPA Examination)

**9-21.** You desire to evaluate the reasonableness of the book value of the inventory of your client, Draper, Inc. You satisfied yourself earlier as to inventory quantities. During the examination of the pricing and extension of the inventory, the following data were gathered using appropriate unrestricted random sampling with replacement procedures.

- Total items in inventory (N)    12,700
- Total items in the sample (n)    400
- Total audited value of items in the sample    $38,400

- $\sum_{j=1}^{400} (x_j - \bar{x})^2$    312,816

- Formula for estimated population standard deviation

$$S_{x_j} = \sqrt{\frac{\sum_{j=1}^{j=n} (x_j - \bar{x})^2}{n-1}}$$

- Formula for estimated standard error of the mean

$$SE = \frac{S_{x_j}}{\sqrt{n}}$$

- Confidence level coefficient of the
  standard error of the mean at a 95%
  confidence (reliability) level                                    ±1.96

Required:

a. Based on the sample results, what is the estimate of the total value of the inventory? Show computations in good form where appropriate.

b. What statistical conclusion can be reached regarding the estimated total inventory value calculated in a. above at the confidence level of 95%? Present computations in good form where appropriate.

c. Independent of your answers to a. and b., assume that the book value of Draper's inventory is $1,700,000, and based on the sample results the estimated total value of the inventory is $1,690.00. The auditor desires a confidence (reliability) level of 95%. Discuss the audit and statistical considerations the auditor must evaluate before deciding whether the sampling results support acceptance of the book value as a fair presentation of Draper's inventory.

(Uniform CPA Examination)

9-22. Your client's physical inventory totals $100,000 and is made up of approximately 10,000 items that are relatively homogeneous in value. You conclude that you can accept the inventory extensions if you can be 95% confident that the true inventory figure is within $5,000 of the stated figure of $100,000. In testing the accuracy of inventory extensions, what sample size should be used in order to accept the inventory, assuming that no errors are found in the sample? (Use an acceptance sampling approach based on a test of attributes.)

9-23. Give your calculations in using an estimation sampling approach to question 9-22. The standard deviation of the population is calculated to be $1.00.

9-24. Levelland, Inc., a client of your firm for several years, uses a voucher system for processing all cash disbursements, which number about 500 each month. After carefully reviewing the company's internal controls, your firm decided to statistically sample the vouchers for eleven specific characteristics to test operating compliance of the voucher system against the client's representations as to the system's operation. Nine of these characteristics are noncritical; two are critical. The characteristics to be evaluated are listed on the worksheet on page 249.

Pertinent client representations about the system follow:

Purchase orders are issued for all goods and services except for recurring services such as utilities and taxes. The controller issues a check request for the latter authorizing payment. Receiving reports are prepared for all goods received. Department heads prepare a services-rendered report for services covered by purchase orders. (Services-rendered reports are subsequently considered receiving reports.)

Copies of purchase orders, receiving reports, check requests, and original invoices are forwarded to accounting. Invoices are assigned a consecutive voucher number immediately upon receipt by accounting. Each voucher is rubber-stamped to provide spaces for accounting personnel to initial when (a) agreeing invoice with purchase order or check request, (b) agreeing invoice with receiving report, and (c) verifying mathematical accuracy of the invoice.

In processing each voucher for payment, accounting personnel match each invoice with the related purchase order and receiving report or check request. Invoice extensions and footings are verified. Debit distribution is recorded on the face of each invoice.

Each voucher is recorded in the voucher register in numerical sequence after which a check is prepared. The voucher packets and checks are forwarded to the treasurer for signing and mailing the checks and canceling each voucher packet.

Canceled packets are returned to accounting. Payment is recorded in the voucher register, and packets are filed numerically.

Following are characteristics of the voucher population already determined by preliminary statistical testing. Assume that each characteristic is randomly distributed throughout the voucher population.

- Eighty percent of vouchers are for purchase orders; 20 percent are for check requests.
- The average number of lines per invoice is four.
- The average number of accounts debited per invoice is two.

Appropriate statistical sampling tables follow. For values not provided in the tables, use the next value in the table which will yield the most conservative result.

Required:

(a) Year one:

An unrestricted random sample of 300 vouchers is to be drawn for year one. Enter in column A of the worksheet the size of the resulting sample for each characteristic to be evaluated in the sample.

**Table 9-3.** Determination of Sample Size Percentage of Occurrences in Sample Reliability (Confidence Level): 95%

| Sample Size | Precision (Upper Limit) Percentage | | | | | |
|---|---|---|---|---|---|---|
| | 1 | 2 | 3 | 4 | 5 | 6 |
| 90 | | | | 0 | .8 | 1.2 |
| 120 | | | 0 | .8 | 1.2 | 1.7 |
| 160 | | 0 | .6 | 1.2 | 1.9 | 2.5 |
| 240 | | .4 | .8 | 1.7 | 2.5 | 3.3 |
| 340 | 0 | .6 | 1.2 | 2.1 | 2.9 | 3.5 |
| 460 | 0 | .9 | 1.5 | 2.4 | 3.3 | 3.9 |
| 1,000 | .4 | 1.2 | 2.0 | 2.9 | 3.8 | 4.7 |

**Table 9-4.** Probability in Percent of Including at Least One Occurrence in a Sample for Populations Between 5,000 and 10,000

| Sample Size | If the True Population Rate of Occurrence is: | | | | | |
|---|---|---|---|---|---|---|
| | .1% | .2% | .3% | .4% | .5% | .75% |
| | The Probability of Including at Least One Occurrence in the Sample is: | | | | | |
| 240 | 22 | 39 | 52 | 62 | 70 | 84 |
| 300 | 26 | 46 | 60 | 70 | 78 | 90 |
| 340 | 29 | 50 | 65 | 75 | 82 | 93 |
| 400 | 34 | 56 | 71 | 81 | 87 | 95 |
| 460 | 38 | 61 | 76 | 85 | 91 | 97 |
| 500 | 40 | 64 | 79 | 87 | 92 | 98 |
| 600 | 46 | 71 | 84 | 92 | 96 | 99 |
| 700 | 52 | 77 | 89 | 95 | 97 | 99+* |
| 800 | 57 | 81 | 92 | 96 | 98 | 99+ |
| 900 | 61 | 85 | 94 | 98 | 99 | 99+ |
| 1,000 | 65 | 88 | 96 | 99 | 99 | 99+ |

*Note: 99 + indicates a probability of 99.5% or greater.

**Table 9-5.** Evaluation of Results Number of Occurrences in Sample Reliability (Confidence Level): 95%

| Sample Size | Precision (Upper Limit) Percentage | | | | | |
|---|---|---|---|---|---|---|
| | 1 | 2 | 3 | 4 | 5 | 6 |
| 90 | | | | 0 | 1 | 1 |
| 120 | | | 0 | 1 | 2 | 2 |
| 160 | | 0 | 1 | 2 | 3 | 4 |
| 240 | | 1 | 2 | 4 | 6 | 8 |
| 340 | 0 | 2 | 4 | 7 | 10 | 12 |
| 460 | 0 | 4 | 7 | 11 | 15 | 18 |
| 1,000 | 4 | 12 | 20 | 29 | 38 | 47 |

**Table 9-6.** Levelland, Inc. Voucher Test Worksheet Years Ended December 31

| | Year 1 | Year 2 | | | | | | |
| | Column A | Column B | Column C | Column D | Column E | Column F | Column G | Column H |
| Characteristics | Sample Size | Estimated Error Rate | Specified Upper Precision Limit | Reliability (Confidence Level) | Required Sample Size | Assumed Sample Size | Number Errors of Found | Upper Precision Limit |
|---|---|---|---|---|---|---|---|---|
| **NONCRITICAL** | | | | | | | | |
| 1. Invoice in agreement with purchase order or check request. | | 1.1% | 3 | 95% | | 460 | 4 | |
| 2. Invoice in agreement with receiving report. | | .4% | 2 | 95% | | 340 | 2 | |
| 3. Invoice mathematically accurate. | | | | | | | | |
| a. Extensions | | 1.4% | 3 | 95% | | 1,000 | 22 | |
| b. Footings | | 1.0% | 3 | 95% | | 460 | 10 | |
| 4. Account distributions correct. | | .3% | 2 | 95% | | 340 | 2 | |
| 5. Voucher correctly entered in voucher register. | | .5% | 2 | 95% | | 340 | 1 | |
| 6. Evidence of Accounting Department checks. | | | | | | | | |
| a. Comparison of invoice with purchase order or check request. | | 2.0% | 4 | 95% | | 240 | 2 | |
| 5. Comparison of invoice with receiving report. | | 1.3% | 4 | 95% | | 160 | 2 | |
| c. Proving mathematical accuracy of invoice. | | 1.5% | 3 | 95% | | 340 | 10 | |
| **CRITICAL** | | | | | | | | |
| 7. Voucher and related documents canceled. | | At or near 0 | .75% | 95% | | 600 | 5 | |
| 8. Vendor and amount on invoice in agreement with payee and amount on check. | | At or near 0 | .4% | 95% | | 800 | 0 | |

(b)  Year two:
1.  Given the estimated error rates, specified upper precision limits, and required reliability (confidence level) in columns B, C, and D respectively, enter in Column E the required sample size to evaluate each characteristic.
2.  Disregarding your answers in column E and considering the assumed sample size and number of errors found in each sample as listed for each characteristic in columns F and G respectively, enter in column H the upper precision limit for each characteristic.
3.  On a separate sheet, identify each characteristic for which the sampling objective was not met and explain what steps the auditor might take to meet his sampling or auditing objectives.

(Uniform CPA Examination)

# Chapter 10

# AUDITS OF AUTOMATED DATA PROCESSING SYSTEMS

The first commercially available computer made its relatively un-heralded appearance in 1951 under the name Univac I. It required a true visionary to suspect even a hint of the literal explosion that was to follow in little more than a decade this seemingly insignificant event. Today, some four computer generations later, the principal computer manufacturer (IBM) has grown to the point where the market value of its outstanding capital stock exceeds that of any other private corporation. The outpouring of computers from a mere handful of companies has been matched by increased sophistication of not only the computers themselves, but also of those who design and program computer applications. Accompanying advances and developments have included the programming languages used to communicate with the computers and to instruct them in solving increasingly complex problems, the operating systems that control the execution of jobs under multiprogramming and time sharing, and the data management systems that perform standardized data handling functions.

Computers are available for lease or purchase and range from desk-type minicomputers to large-scale machines with functional performance measured in nanoseconds (billionths of a second) and on-line, random-access storage of billions of characters. Computer data processing service may be obtained from service centers providing complete service including programming, or from a "computer utility" operating on a time-sharing basis, with an input/output device located at the user's premises. The input/output device may be connected with the central computer through ordinary telephone lines and an acoustical coupler, with the user either providing the programming or using the on-line programs stored at the central processing location.

As a result of these developments, it may now be said that every large business and most medium-sized businesses are making at least some use of computers, and even the smallest businesses have access to computer power through computer service centers or their own minicomputers. Applications range from the automation of individual data processing tasks, such as payroll preparation or production scheduling, through the manipulation of involved mathematical models simulating production or marketing for a single company product or for an entire industry, and to the development of completely integrated management information systems (MIS) with the underlying data base management system (DBMS) on which an MIS is dependent.

Given these conditions, it is essential that all auditors have at least a general understanding of how computers function, how they are programmed, and the manner in which they are used in the automated processing of accounting-related data by means of what is commonly referred to as an EDP (electronic data processing) system. In developing this chapter, it has been assumed that the reader has some understanding of computer hardware and software, and consequently the discussion emphasizes the considerations in computer accounting applications and the vital aspects of internal control over EDP systems. The subsequent core chapters that relate to the audit of specific subsystem records also include reference to some of the special considerations when EDP systems are involved. The two basic approaches to computer processing of accounting data are introduced in the next section.

## Batch vs. On-Line Processing

Maintaining accounting records by computer is essentially a matter of file processing—sorting records of transactions into the appropriate file classifications and developing a cumulative file of the sorted records, usually with an accompanying updated dollar or other quantitative total for the file. The earliest accounting applications involved batch processing, and batch processing is still the most widely used approach to computerized records—primarily because of cost considerations. Less sophisticated, lower-cost hardware is involved, especially in terms of data storage and the cost per digit stored. The files and individual records included in the files are invariably identified by number because numbers are most readily handled by the computer binary logic.

The first operation in any computer processing system is converting data to machine-sensible form—usually the slowest, least accurate, and most costly aspect of the system because it involves human operation of a key-input device. The accuracy problem further adds to cost considerations in that some form of operator double-checking is essential when accuracy is critical. In some applications these problems are avoided by the use of optical scanning or the use of machine-sensible output from a previous process. Once data have been converted to machine-sensible form on punched cards, punched tape, magnetic tape, magnetic disk, or directly into operating storage, the transaction data for a batch system must be sorted into the same sequence in which the master file of, say, accounts receivable is maintained, because access to the file is possible only on a serial basis by passing the entire file through a tape drive to "read" the file. The sorted transactions are merged with the master file during this process to prepare a new updated master file. Separate programs and runs are needed to add or delete accounts, change addresses, credit terms, or credit limits, and to "post" sales transactions, cash receipts, returns and allowances, and the write-off of uncollectible accounts.

By contrast, on-line systems, which are so named because data files and programs are always "on line" to the main frame of the computer, necessitate bulk file storage that permits random access to file information. Magnetic disks are commonly used for this purpose. Real-time systems that accept data and produce output within time constraints necessary to direct or control operations are referred to as on-line, real-time (OLRT) systems. Airline reservation systems are one of the more widely known OLRT systems, with operators responding to customer inquiries about seat availability and booking space by reducing the inventory of available seats in accordance with the customer's request. Customer inquiries and orders for merchandise can be handled on a similar basis, but in most instances the real-time capability is not essential to those operations.

The key feature of on-line systems is that any stored data record can be accessed at any time, and hence transactions can be processed as they occur and without sorting in order to update master files. Data can be accepted from more than one source if the computer has multiprocessing capability, and various different applications programs are available for immediate use if there is multiprogramming capability. The stored data are the focal point of such systems, and data base management systems (DBMS) software for managing an entire data base takes care of assigning storage locations, access to data, and data updating. In less sophisticated on-line systems, however, maintenance of data files is handled through the particular applications programs that are involved.

### Effect of EDP on Audits and the Audit Trail

The introduction of EDP systems has affected audits in a number of ways. Internal control is generally improved to the extent that EDP personnel are less likely to be assigned both operating and accounting responsibilities, and the formalized procedures and discipline demanded by computers produce increased uniformity and consistency in the results that are obtained. In smaller installations, however, the consolidation of a variety of EDP functions among a limited number of personnel tends to weaken internal control and increase the opportunity to manipulate records for personal gain, because it is difficult to limit access to EDP records.

Automated data processing presents a further problem in its potential effect on the traditional audit trail. In manual systems with hard copy records it is relatively easy to trace a transaction through the records to the general ledger account that is ultimately affected, and conversely to gain access to supporting details for an amount that is included in the balance of an account. In an EDP system, however, much of the intermediate and final information that the auditor will need to work with will exist in the form of magnetic bits that can be interpreted only by the computer itself. That problem is mitigated in some batch systems by the preparation of printouts of all intermediate and final results, but such printouts are costly to prepare and are likely to be omitted unless they serve some specific operating need.

The situation is likely to be most serious in an on-line system, because in many instances transactions may be entered directly into the computer with no supporting document having been prepared. A typical example would be the direct entry of workers' start and stop times through the use of the computer's clock and machine-readable badges or ID cards. Key input by the worker can be used to add information about job number or number of pieces completed. In such cases the auditor may have to rely almost exclusively on controls that have been incorporated into the system and user review of system outputs for the accuracy of the outputs.

The ready access to information through remote terminals is an important feature of on-line systems, but an unwanted side effect of those systems is that information becomes more accessible to those who are not authorized to obtain the information and who may seek to manipulate information for their personal gain.

### Internal Control Considerations

Regardless of whether an audit involves manually kept records in hard copy form or computerized records in magnetic code, the auditor's first concern must be internal control over the system. Essentially all of the internal control objectives and features discussed in Chapter 6 are applicable to computerized systems, but a number of special internal control considerations that relate to automated systems will be discussed next. More extensive treatment of internal control and other aspects of EDP systems can be found in these publications:

> Statement on Auditing Standards No. 3, "The Effects of EDP on the Auditor's Study and Evaluation of Internal Control" (1974) is referenced in Professional Standards at AU Sec. 321
>
> AICPA Audit Guides: *The Auditor's Study and Evaluation of Internal Control* (1977), and *Audits of Service-Center-Produced Records* (1974)
>
> AICPA Computer Services Guidelines, *Management, Control and Audit of Advanced EDP Systems* (1976)
>
> Institute of Internal Auditors, *Systems Auditability and Control* (1977) and *Computer Control and Audit* (1976)

Computer processing systems controls are grouped into two principal categories: general controls that apply to all aspects of the system and applications controls that relate to the specific subsystems that have been computerized, such as billing, accounts receivable, and sales analysis, or inventory record keeping. General controls are discussed first.

### General Controls

Included in the general controls category are a) the organizational plan for the computer data processing function, b) documentation and implementation controls, c) hardware controls, and d) controls over access to equipment and to data files.

*Organizational Plan: Segregation of Functions.* Maximum internal control is achieved if various computer processing responsibilities are handled separately, and of course all persons associated with computer processing should be independent of any operating responsibility related to authorization or execution of transactions or custody of assets. The major groupings and subgroupings of computer processing responsibilities are as follows:

Applications systems
  Systems analysis and design
  Programming, including testing and debugging
Computer operations
  Design and programming of operating systems
  Machine operations
Data entry
  Control activities
  Key-input device operations
Card, tape, and disk pack library and storage

In smaller installations with fewer people involved, subdivisions of the various activities are likely to be combined, with some loss of internal control. Very small minicomputer installations may have only two people—the system manager/operator and a data entry clerk—with consequent further weakening of internal control.

Programming and data input tend to be the two most critical activities from an internal control standpoint. Programs can be modified to provide personal benefits, such as increasing the amount of a person's paycheck, or transferring employer funds to a person's receivable or deposit liability account. Other possibilities include causing program controls to be bypassed so that charges to a receivable account can be permitted to exceed authorized limits or causing a delinquent account to be shown as current when accounts are aged or delinquency notices are prepared. Similarly if a person can gain access to computer records and enter data, fictitious transactions can be introduced for personal gain, such as causing shipment of goods to be made to the perpetrator's address.

It might appear that people in computer operations would be in a particularly opportune position to make program changes or to introduce fictitious data, but those in operations programming are not likely to be familiar with applications programs, and machine operators are generally unskilled clerical employees who lack the knowledge of computers or programming to accomplish and conceal any fraudulent activities.

For batch systems with programs and data files stored off-line on magnetic tape, critical functions can be quite effectively isolated. Programmers should be permitted access to programs only with proper authorization to the tape librarian to release the program tapes to operations, and the changes to be made on the program tapes in operations likewise should be authorized. These controls tend to break down, however, with on-line systems that are accessed through remote terminals. Access to programs stored in memory can in some systems be limited to a specified terminal that can be closely controlled; constraints can be programmed into the operating system to limit acceptance of input from the special terminal to specified working hours, and special lock codes or passwords can be used. Unfortunately a clever programmer intent on accomplishing nefarious ends can probably find a means of circumventing such controls.

An additional approach to controlling unauthorized program changes is aimed not at prevention but at detection if an unauthorized change has been made. A well-controlled system should have a console printing device that is dedicated to preparing a log of each job run that shows the files and equipment used, the running time required, operator actions taken, and any error messages. Carefully reviewing such a log at the end of each day and checking the formal authorization for any operations involving changes to the program area of memory should disclose any unauthorized changes. Perhaps the greatest problem with this approach is the time/cost associated with the daily review of the log, because it contains so much detail.

*System Documentation, Review, and Testing.* To facilitate making program changes when necessary and to eliminate any "bugs" that may crop up in a program, complete documentation of every program is essential. Included in the run manual of such information should be flowcharts of the application, mapping of the data elements that comprise the various data records, a complete printout of the source program in compiler language, test data used in testing the program, and operator instructions concerning tapes to be mounted, switch settings, and restart procedures. Also included in the run manual should be complete records of all changes in the program together with indication that the changes have been reviewed and properly authorized.

Debugging and program testing are programmer responsibilities, but to effectuate the organizational controls mentioned previously, programmers should not be permitted direct access to the computer to do testing or to make program changes. As was stated, however, limiting access to a computer is problematical when systems are operated on line.

*Hardware Controls.* Controls that are built into computer equipment to ensure computer accuracy are referred to as hardware controls. These controls may function automatically, such as parity checks that can detect dropped or added bits, or they may be programmable, as in the case of comparisons of data from dual read heads or read-after-write heads. The program must indicate how many times data are to be backspaced and reread when errors are detected, and whether the computer is to be halted or other action taken after a specified number of re-peated failures.

Other programmable hardware controls include the file protect rings, which must be physically removed before it is possible to erase and write onto a tape file that contains live data. Also, *boundary protection* permits sections of the main core memory to be locked out to prevent accidental access to and alteration of the stored programs under which the com-puter is operating.

*Access and Environmental Controls.* Intentional physical assaults on computer equipment have occurred as computers have grown in impor-tance. As a consequence, the computer operations area must be made secure by physically limiting access to authorized persons. An entrance guard and visual inspection of badges, or a locking mechanism—that is either tumbler-actuated by a key or by magnetic sensing of proper cod-ing on a plastic pass card—may be used for access control.

Fire protection for the secured area is also a prime consideration. En-vironmental controls are yet another, but less critical, factor in that en-vironmental damage or the effect of the environment on processing activity will likely be more limited. Hardware and data storage media are, however, extremely sensitive to temperature, humidity, and dust, and these conditions must be adequately controlled.

Limiting physical access to the secured computer area to authorized operations personnel is only one part of the control program with re-spect to those who offer the greatest potential danger to the integrity of an automated data processing system: the computer programmers. Ref-erence has already been made to such controls as limiting access to spec-ified program and data files through a library system for off-line records, and by limiting access to on-line records to a designated termi-nal that emits a special identification code, plus a programmed require-ment to supply a required password. The printing of a log of all computer activity also serves as a means of detecting unauthorized activ-ity. A different aspect of protection, especially important with respect to data files, is replacing or reconstructing such files if accidental loss oc-curs. It is vital to maintain duplicate files and memory dumps, and to preserve daily input files and superseded master files for a sufficient period to permit reconstruction of updated master files through the ap-plication of the "grandfather-father-son" principle by rerunning previ-ous generations of input-and master-file tapes. Memory dumps, however, present a security problem in that through them access may be gained to otherwise restricted information.

### Application Controls

At this point the discussion shifts to controls that are job related—the controls that are incorporated within the specific computer applications that are developed to accomplish subsystem data processing. These controls are discussed relative to the three elements of all systems—inputs, processing, and outputs.

*Input Controls.* Processing results can be no more accurate than the data inputs to the processing equipment. This reality, coupled with the fact that most conversions of data into machine-sensible form are accomplished with human intervention and are, therefore, susceptible to error, points to the importance of accuracy controls over input. Verifying data transcribed onto punched cards is one form of control, with the verification handled on a blind basis by a key verifier that is operated much the same as the original encoding equipment. If data are transcribed directly onto magnetic tape or into computer storage files, verification may be made by operator comparison between the source document and a hard copy or video CRT display of what has been recorded in machine-sensible form.

Transaction amounts are the most important data element, with transcription accuracy best controlled by batching original documents and obtaining predetermined control totals of the amounts and record counts of the number of transactions or *hash totals* of identification numbers. Preferably control totals should be established by the department or persons authorized to originate transaction entry data, but if externally determined totals are not available, the totals should be developed by an independent control group within the data processing department. These totals can then be incorporated with the input data and the computer programmed to summarize the inputs as they are introduced and to compare that sum and the number of records processed with the predetermined totals, in order to detect the presence of any transcription errors or the loss of any record. Computer checks for missing numbers when records are numbered sequentially is yet another form of input control.

Account numbers or other identifying numeric codes that are repeatedly used should be verified automatically by a self-checking digit device on a key punch or by a programmed calculation by the computer. In one system, alternate digits of the account number are doubled, these doubled digits and the remaining digits are summed, and the low-order digit of this sum is compared with a precalculated check digit that is incorporated as an integral part of the identifying numeric code.

Other input controls include external identification of files and internal tape labels that are checked by computer as a new file is introduced, in order to determine whether the correct file is present. Trailer labels may contain a sum of balances or other variables in a file, and the computer can be programmed to sum the individual records as they are read into memory and to compare this sum with the total on the trailer label, in order to prove that all items are present in the file and have been correctly read from the input device.

The computer can compare account numbers and other identifying codes with a file of valid account numbers, or the numbers can be checked for the presence of the correct number of digits or of alphabetic characters at certain positions. An especially important aspect of such edit routines is the follow-up action that is taken once a record has been rejected. It is essential to the integrity of system output that rejected items be corrected and reintroduced into the system, for otherwise the affected account balances will be misstated and any decisions based on such reported information may be incorrect.

All departments originating transaction data should review and approve the data prior to release to data processing. Report totals and other output information should be reviewed by operations and/or by users to demonstrate whether processing activities were correctly performed. For instance, a computer listing of all changes made to any master file should be prepared in order to permit the department responsible for the file information to determine that all changes were correctly made.

*Processing Controls.* A first step in ensuring proper processing is to ascertain that a new or revised program is free of programming and logical errors. The debugging process, which is a programming responsibility, should include using test data that cover all conceivable conditions, which includes detecting errors and out-of-balance conditions and determining that computer processing results obtained under control of the program being tested agree with predetermined results computed manually.

Processing controls are of two types: hardware controls (which have already been discussed) and programmed controls. Programmed controls may be interpreted to include the label and total checks mentioned in the previous section, which are designed to detect incorrect operator keying of data, omission or loss of transactions, or inclusion of unauthorized transactions, as well as checks of account numbers against a file of authorized account numbers to ensure validity. Of other controls in this category, limit controls are perhaps most common, involving comparison of processing results with a programmed limit, such as $500 for payroll checks, before the computer is permitted to use a result for output or further processing. Another type of control is a crossfooting test to assure that the sum of, say, a series of classification totals equals the total of the amounts being distributed. Much different forms of programmed control are the printing of console messages for operator direction, and programmed tests to determine whether equipment and switch settings are correct.

*Output Controls.* Output should be distributed only to persons who need and use the reported data and who are authorized to receive it.

Control over access to information stored in data banks presents a problem when remote terminals are used to gain direct access to central master files. As mentioned, output from certain file segments may be restricted to specified terminals or to users who supply a special password. In a like manner, credit card transactions or debit card or automated bank teller transactions posted directly to central master files in the presaged "checkless society" may require the user to supply along with the card a special password or code number for the computer to check against the master file, in order to prove that the credit card holder is authorized to use it.

Before regular printed output is delivered to authorized recipients, it should be reviewed for obvious errors, reasonableness, and agreement with any predetermined control totals. Recipients should also review output for reasonableness and agreement with independently developed figures or approximations of the anticipated results. For instance, a cashier's cash count is a check on the cash balance determined by data processing; an employee generally will recognize any errors in the preparation of his or her paycheck; and physical inventory counts and comparisons with computer balances could reveal processing errors, although it woulld be difficult to differentiate such errors from physical inventory disappearance when reviewing reported differences.

### Monitoring of the Data Processing Function

Both data processing output users and internal auditors should actively monitor the data processing function. Users should participate in system design in order to be certain that their needs and specifications are made known and are satisfied if at all feasible, and internal audit involvement is highly desirable in order to ensure that adequate controls are incorporated as each application is developed. Users should also review the output they receive in order to be satisfied that the output is consistent with authorized inputs, and internal audit should make regular compliance tests to determine that all controls continue to operate. Thus both users and internal audit should be active in overseeing the effectiveness and accuracy of the activities related to computer processing.

### Evaluation and Compliance Testing of General Controls

As with all internal controls, the auditor must first determine from a preliminary review whether the controls pertaining to computer data processing appear to be adequate to permit reliance on them. If this preliminary review indicates, for example, that general controls are largely absent or inadequate, little reliance should be placed on the EDP system outputs, and consequently further review or testing of other aspects of EDP system controls would be unproductive. Instead, the auditor should proceed directly to substantive tests of the output, and of course there would be no basis for limiting or restricting these tests under the circumstances. In the more likely event that the preliminary review of the general controls indicates that there is a reasonable basis for reliance on the controls, the auditor should complete the review by obtaining more specific information about the controls and making compliance tests through inquiry, observation, and inspection, as related to the detailed aspects of the controls.

If the completed review and assessment of the general controls indicates that reliance can be placed on those controls, then the auditor should proceed in a similar fashion to complete the review and assessment of applications controls. The additional effort necessary to warrant placing reliance on the various applications controls should be expended, however, only when justified by the consequent reduction of effort in other aspects of the audit.

### Evaluation and Compliance Testing of Application Controls

If the review of general controls and the preliminary review of application controls indicate that there is a reasonable basis for reliance on any or all of the subsystem application controls, then the auditor will have to complete the review of those controls on which reliance tentatively is to be placed, including making appropriate compliance tests. For any given application, the run manual should be inspected for completeness—flowcharts, layout of data files, printout of the source program, full documentation of all changes to the program including indication that the changes were properly authorized, and complete operator instructions.

Compliance tests of input controls should include inspecting examples of predetermined batch control totals and of the subsequent computer output showing that all items of the batch have been correctly processed. Edit and other error listings should be reviewed to determine what disposition has been made of the errors. The integrity of a system is heavily dependent on tight control of rejected data. There must be assurance that each rejected item has been corrected and reentered into the system.

### Compliance Testing of Programmed Controls: Use of Test Data

Various edit and limit controls incorporated in application programs are especially important in ensuring data processing accuracy. The auditor must determine what controls have been specified for inclusion in a program and whether the controls are in place and functioning as intended. Examples in the processing of sales orders for invoicing and updating of accounts receivable would include

- Check digit verification of customer account number and item code number, or edit checks—against a master list of numbers or for the presence of alpha or numeric characters in certain positions.
- Verification of customer account status to sort out and print exception lists for orders from delinquent accounts or from accounts for which the order would cause the account to exceed the established credit limit.

Adequate documentation will enable the auditor to review the application program to ascertain what controls purportedly have been incorporated in the program, but that leaves the question of whether the program that is actually in use does in fact include the controls and whether the controls are operational. The most efficient solution to this problem for a batch-processing system will usually be to develop test data in the form of hypothetical transactions that include violations of each of the controls that are of interest to the auditor. The results of processing the valid and invalid test data against the accounts receivable file are first hand-calculated to determine what the various updated amounts and totals should be and what exceptions should appear in the report that is generated for the run. Then, immediately after the regular production program has been used for a processing run, the test data can be processed by the program against the updated master file. If the results of that run agree with the auditor's precalculated results, the auditor should be able to conclude that the program is processing the data and handling exceptions in accordance with the information contained in the run manual, consequently providing a basis for the auditor's final assessment of internal control for the application program in question.

It should be noted that the above test procedure would have no effect on the client's master file, and the "updated" master file incorporating the hypothetical test transactions can be erased and reused by the client. Testing an on-line system, however, involves the use of live records, with the result that the client's actual master file will be altered by the processing of the auditor's test data. The fictitious transactions must then be reversed in order to restore the master file to its original condition.

An alternative approach, to avoid the live records problem, is to process test data under regular program control into a separate independent master file that is comparable to the regular master file. This separate file, sometimes referred to as a *minicompany* file, is accessed by special identification of the test data, and the regular records are left untouched. The term "ITF" for "Integrated Test Facility" is also used to identify this special audit file and test approach.

## Records Maintained by a Service Center

The availability of cost-efficient minicomputers and a wide selection of software packages has led many smaller concerns to acquire their own computer rather than to turn to a service center to satisfy their data processing needs. Nevertheless, other concerns have concluded that service centers are advantageous as a means of avoiding the capital investment required for an in-house computer and the operating, maintenance, and capacity utilization problems that may be associated with computer ownership. Also, any monthly or seasonal peak activity periods can usually be handled much more expeditiously through a service center, as can a single job that requires more capacity than is available through the in-house machine.

For the independent auditor a client's use of a service center transfers the site of processing controls from the client's premises to the computer center. As a rule, the size of a service center, the number of personnel likely to be involved, and the importance of a reputation for fast, accurate service tend to result in good control over the processing activities. Also, service center personnel are not likely to have any client operating responsibilities, thus helping to ensure good internal control. But service center personnel will have as much or more opportunity to manipulate accounts and siphon away assets from a customer, and hence client-determined input totals should be balanced with output results, and all output should be carefully reviewed for errors or any indication of manipulation.

Depending on the significance of service-center processing to a client's financial statements and the advantages resulting from the trade-off between reliance on internal controls and making extended substantive tests, the auditor may conclude that controls at a service center should be as extensively reviewed as if the processing were done on the client's premises. Of particular interest under those circumstances, some larger service centers have engaged their own independent auditors to review and report on service center internal controls as a means of stressing the quality of their service and as an added service to their customers and their independent auditors. If a client auditor is satisfied with the reputation of the service center auditor and the adequacy of the review that has been made, no further review of service center controls should be necessary.

Nevertheless, some direct contact with service center processing may be necessary if the auditor decides to use the computer directly in making substantive tests of EDP output, as discussed in the next section.

## Substantive Tests of EDP Output

Although the various controls over computer processing are highly important in ensuring the accuracy and usefulness of system outputs, substantive tests of resulting financial statement figures are as important for these outputs as for the outputs of manual or other systems. Those substantive procedures that relate to reasonableness or gaining contact with underlying assets or liabilities will be unaffected by the fact that the accounting information is processed by computer, as for example conducting analytical review procedures or determining the existence of the assets or liabilities. Other substantive procedures, however, that involve reference to transaction detail or subsidiary records are dependent on gaining access to information that is held in machine-sensible form. On occasion, a straight printout of a balance file or transaction file will suffice for audit purposes, but in most instances it will be advantageous to utilize the computer to perform some processing steps in conjunction with preparing the printout.

Accounts receivable substantive procedures offer a prime example of potential for computer assistance to the auditor. In a single pass of a client's accounts receivable master file, depending on the content and format of the file, it may be possible to accomplish all of the following:

1. Sum all debit balances.
2. Sum all credit balances.
3. Age the open-item detail of debit balances according to month of sale.
4. Select the following accounts and prepare confirmation requests showing customer name and address and detail of all open items in the customer's record:
   a. All accounts ≥ $1,000.
   b. All delinquent accounts with balances ≥ $200 but < $1,000.
   c. A random sample of N accounts selected from accounts not classified as (a) or (b).
5. Prepare a list of any accounts for which the current balance exceeds the authorized credit limit.

*Audit Software Packages.*   A program would have to be written to accomplish the results just mentioned, and that would not be an inconsequential task. The solution to that problem has been the development of audit software packages by various accounting firms and others, the first of which was developed by Deloitte, Haskins & Sells and given the name "Auditape." Typically such audit packages require the preparation of specification sheets to accomplish three basic tasks:

1. A mapping of the data elements of the client's file from the respective positions of the client's record format into the data designations of the package program.
2. Determining the output that is desired and the format for the output.
3. Developing a logical means of extracting desired data from the client's files and manipulating the data to produce the desired output. The appropriate commands are then selected from the package list of commands and sequenced in accordance with the logical analysis of the problem. The commands are macroinstructions that the package program will cause to be executed in performing the specified task. Typical commands would include

CREATE from the client's file a work file that can be accessed using the auditor's data designations to specify the data for any of the following verbs:

SORT into any desired sequence.

SELECT data according to specified criteria.

SUM any designated data.

COMPARE related data from two different files, such as pay rates in a master file and a current payroll file.

CALCULATE any specified arithmetic function using the indicated operands.

PRINT any specified result or data items.

*Generalized Audit Programs.* A variation of the software package is the generalized program that is designed to accomplish relatively complicated and involved operations for a specialized client, such as a stock brokerage firm. Account statements to be confirmed with customers of a brokerage firm show both money and security balances; and margin account and short sales must be compared with funds on deposit and the market value of securities held to determine whether specified requirements have been satisfied. Using a generalized audit program is similar to using a software package in that a mapping is required from the client's EDP file format into the file structure of the auditor's program package, but the generalized program contains the complete program for all operations to be performed, so that no operations need be specified other than to select from certain alternatives available in the generalized program and to adapt to any minor differences that may be involved.

### Summary

An EDP system merely involves a different means of performing various accounting functions that otherwise would be accomplished less rapidly and less economically by methods that have not been automated and that are more likely to be subject to unauthorized deviations and processing errors. Thus, EDP systems involve the same internal control considerations as other types of systems. After gaining a general understanding of EDP operations, the auditor should make a preliminary investigation of general controls pertaining to the organization of the EDP function, including the segregation of various types of processing responsibility, documentation and implementation controls, hardware controls, and controls over access to equipment and data files. If this review indicates that the general controls are adequate to be relied on in assessing the effectiveness of applications controls, then compliance tests of the general controls must be made to provide indication that the general controls are functioning as intended.

Next, the same process must be followed in evaluating the applications controls over inputs, processing, and outputs. Then, based on the assessment of the effectiveness of those controls for each of the EDP applications, the auditor can determine the nature, timing, and extent of the substantive audit tests that are to be made. In carrying out compliance tests of processing controls, the auditor will usually find it advantageous to use the client's computer to process test data that will check the processing procedures and controls of the client's program. The client's computer will also have to be used in carrying out various substantive procedures on the client's data files, with audit software packages or generalized audit programs providing access to the data files and performing certain audit steps.

For any weaknesses in control or shortcomings noted in the client's EDP system, the auditor will wish to consider whether any or all of these should be reported to the client in a management letter, along with possible suggestions for correction or improvement.

## Questions/Problems

For multiple-choice questions 10-1 through 10-12, indicate the letter of the single answer that *best* completes the statement or answers the question, and justify the choice that you have made.

**10-1.** Which of the following client electronic data processing (EDP) systems generally can be audited without examining or directly testing the EDP computer programs of the system?

a. A system that performs relatively uncomplicated processes and produces detailed output.

b. A system that affects a number of essential master files and produces a limited output.

c. A system that updates a few essential master files and produces no printed output other than final balances.

d. A system that performs relatively complicated processing and produces very little detailed output.

(Uniform CPA Examination)

**10-2.** After a preliminary phase of the review of a client's EDP controls, an auditor may decide not to perform compliance tests related to the control procedures within the EDP portion of the client's internal control system. Which of the following would not be a valid reason for choosing to omit compliance tests?

a. The controls appear adequate.

b. The controls duplicate operative controls existing elsewhere in the system.

c.  There appear to be major weaknesses that would preclude reliance on the stated procedure.

d.  The time and dollar costs of testing exceed the time and dollar savings in substantive testing if the compliance tests show the controls to be operative.

(Uniform CPA Examination)

**10-3.**  Compliance testing of an advanced EDP system

a.  Can be performed using only actual transactions since testing of simulated transactions is of no consequence.

b.  Can be performed using actual transactions or simulated transactions.

c.  Is impractical since many procedures within the EDP activity leave no visible evidence of having been performed.

d.  Is inadvisable because it may distort the evidence in master files.

(Uniform CPA Examination)

**10-4.**  An auditor will use the EDP test data method in order to gain certain assurances with respect to the

a.  Input data.

b.  Machine capacity.

c.  Procedures contained within the program.

d.  Degree of keypunching accuracy.

(Uniform CPA Examination)

**10-5.**  If a control total were to be computed on each of the following data items, which would best be identified as a hash total for a payroll EDP application?

a.  Gross pay.

b.  Hours worked.

c.  Department number.

d.  Number of employees.

(Uniform CPA Examination)

**10-6.**  To replace the human element of error detection associated with manual processing, a well-designed automated system will introduce

a.  Dual circuitry.

b.  Programmed limits.

c.  Echo checks.

d.  Read after write.

(Uniform CPA Examination)

**10-7.**  Which of the following would lessen internal control in an electronic data processing system?

a. The computer librarian maintains custody of computer program instructions and detailed listings.
b. Computer operators have access to operator instructions and detailed program listings.
c. The control group is solely responsible for the distribution of all computer output.
d. Computer programmers write and debug programs which perform routines designed by the systems analyst.

(Uniform CPA Examination)

**10-8.** Accounting functions that are normally considered incompatible in a manual system are often combined in an electronic data processing system by using an electronic data processing program, or a series of programs. This necessitates an accounting control that prevents unapproved

a. Access to the magnetic tape library.
b. Revisions to existing computer programs.
c. Usage of computer program tapes
d. Testing of modified computer programs.

(Uniform CPA Examination)

**10-9.** Which of the following is an advantage of generalized computer audit packages?

a. They are all written in one identical computer language.
b. They can be used for audits of clients that use differing EDP equipment and file formats.
c. They have reduced the need for the auditor to study input controls for EDP-related procedures.
d. Their use can be substituted for a relatively large part of the required compliance testing.

(Uniform CPA Examination)

**10-10.** A primary advantage of using generalized audit packages in the audit of an advanced EDP system is that it enables the auditor to

a. Substantiate the accuracy of data through self-checking digits and hash totals.
b. Utilize the speed and accuracy of the computer.
c. Verify the performance of machine operations which leave visible evidence of occurrence.
d. Gather and store large quantities of supportive evidential matter in machine readable form.

(Uniform CPA Examination)

**10-11.** In a daily computer run to update checking account balances and print out basic details on any customer's account that was overdrawn, the overdrawn account of the computer program-mer was never printed. Which of the following control proce-dures would have been most effective in detecting this irregularity?

- a. Use of the test-deck approach by the auditor in testing the client's program and verification of the subsidiary file.
- b. Use of a running control total for the master file of check-ing account balances and comparison with the printout.
- c. A program check for valid customer code.
- d. Periodic recompiling of programs from documented source decks, and comparison with programs currently in use.

(Uniform CPA Examination)

**10-12.** Which of the following is necessary to audit balances in an on-line EDP system in an environment of destructive updating?

- a. Periodic dumping of transaction files.
- b. Year-end utilization of audit hooks.
- c. An integrated test facility.
- d. A well-documented audit trail.

(Uniform CPA Examination)

**10-13.** Computer data files involved in processing or updating are ac-cessed either serially or randomly. Give examples of the data storage media for each type of access and state what effect serial or random organization may have on the sequencing of trans-action files used to update the stored data file.

**10-14.** Why is it important to use test data in the debugging process?

**10-15.** Give several examples of the types of procedures that could be expected to be included in a generalized computer audit pro-gram package.

**10-16.** How would an auditor gain assurance that a client's data proc-essing control group has functioned effectively?

**10-17.** How would you satisfy yourself that the computer program used to process your test deck is the program regularly used by the client and agrees with the flow charts that you have re-viewed?

**10-18.** After determining that computer controls are valid, Hastings is reviewing the sales system of Rosco Corporation in order to de-termine how a computerized audit program may be used to as-sist in performing tests of Rosco's sales records.

Rosco sells crude oil from one central location. All orders are received by mail and indicate the preassigned customer identifi-cation number, desired quantity, proposed delivery date, method of payment, and shipping terms. Since price fluctuates daily, orders do not indicate a price. Price sheets are printed daily, and details are stored in a permanent disk file. The details of orders are also maintained in a permanent disk file.

Each morning the shipping clerk receives a computer printout which indicates details of customers' orders to be shipped that day. After the orders have been shipped, the shipping details are inputted in the computer, which simultaneously updates the sales journal, perpetual inventory records, accounts receivable, and sales accounts.

The details of all transactions, as well as daily updates, are maintained on discs which are available for use by Hastings in the performance of the audit.

Required:

a. How may a computerized audit program be used by Hastings to perform substantive tests of Rosco's sales records in their machine readable form? Do not discuss accounts receivable and inventory.

b. After having performed these tests with the assistance of the computer, what other auditing procedures should Hastings perform in order to complete the examination of Rosco's sales records?

(Uniform CPA Examination)

**10-19.** In the past, the records to be evaluated in an audit have been printed reports, listings, documents and written papers, all of which are visible output. However, in fully computerized systems which employ daily updating of transaction files, output and files are frequently in machine-readable forms such as cards, tapes, or disks. Thus, they often present the auditor with an opportunity to use the computer in performing an audit.

Required:

Discuss how the computer can be used to aid the auditor in examining accounts receivable in such a fully computerized system.

(Uniform CPA Examination)

**10-20.** George Beemster, CPA, is examining the financial statements of the Louisville Sales Corporation, which recently installed an off-line electronic computer. The following comments have been extracted from Mr. Beemster's notes on computer operations and the processing and control of shipping notices and customer invoices:

To minimize inconvenience Louisville converted without change its existing data processing system, which utilized tabulating equipment. The computer company supervised the conversion and has provided training to all computer department employees (except key punch operators) in systems design, operations and programming.

Each computer run is assigned to a specific employee, who is responsible for making program changes, running the program and answering questions. This procedure has the advantage of eliminating the need for records of computer operations because each employee is responsible for his own computer runs.

At least one computer department employee remains in the computer room during office hours, and only computer department employees have keys to the computer room.

System documentation consists of those materials furnished by the computer company—a set of record formats and program listings. These and the tape library are kept in a corner of the computer department.

The Company considered the desirability of programmed controls but decided to retain the manual controls from its existing system.

Company products are shipped directly from public warehouses which forward shipping notices to general accounting. There a billing clerk enters the price of the item and accounts for the numerical sequence of shipping notices from each warehouse. The billing clerk also prepares daily adding machine tapes ("control tapes") of the units shipped and the unit prices.

Shipping notices and control tapes are forwarded to the computer department for key punching and processing. Extensions are made on the computer. Output consists of invoices (in six copies) and a daily sales register. The daily sales register shows the aggregate totals of units shipped and unit prices which the computer operator compares to the control tapes.

All copies of the invoice are returned to the billing clerk. The clerk mails three copies to the customer, forwards one copy to the warehouse, maintains one copy in a numerical file, and retains one copy in an open invoice file that serves as a detail accounts receivable record.

Required:

Describe weaknesses in internal control over information and data flows and the procedures for processing shipping notices and customer invoices and recommend improvements in these controls and processing procedures. Organize your answer sheets as follows:

| Weakness | Recommended Improvement |
|---|---|
| | |

(Uniform CPA Examination)

**10-21.** The independent auditor must evaluate a client's system of internal control to determine the extent to which various auditing procedures must be employed. A client who uses a computer should provide the CPA with a flowchart of the information processing system so the CPA can evaluate the control features in the system. Shown in the following figure is a simplified flowchart, such as a client might provide. Unfortunately the client had only partially completed the flowchart when it was requested by you.

Required:

(a) Complete the flowchart shown in Figure 10-2.
(b) Describe what each item in the flowchart indicates. When complete, your description should provide an explanation of the processing of the data involved. Your description should be in the following order:
   (1) "Orders from Salesmen" to "Run No. 5."
   (2) "From Mailroom" to "Run No. 5."
   (3) "Run No. 5" through the remainder of the chart.
(c) Name each of the flowchart symbols shown in Figure 10-1 and describe what each represents.

(Uniform CPA Examination)

**10-22.** Roger Peters, CPA, has examined the financial statements of the Solt Manufacturing Company for several years and is making preliminary plans for the audit for the year ended June 30. During this examination Mr. Peters plans to use a set of gener-

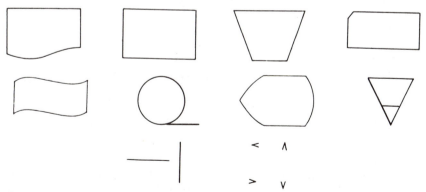

**Figure 10-1.** Flowchart symbols

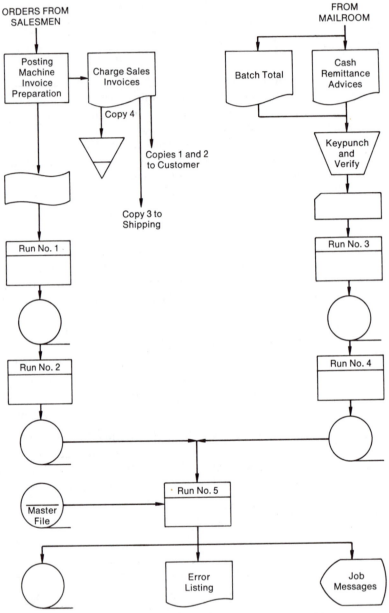

**Figure 10-2.** Flowchart to be Completed (Problem 10-21)

alized computer audit programs. Solt's EDP manager has agreed to prepare special tapes of data from Company records for the CPA's use with the generalized programs.

The following information is applicable to Mr. Peters' examination of Solt's accounts payable and related procedures:

### Master File—Vendor Name

| Vendor Code | Recd Type | Space | Blank | Vendor Name | Blank | Card Code 100 |
|---|---|---|---|---|---|---|

### Master File—Vendor Address

| Vendor Code | Recd Type | Space | Blank | Address—Line 1 | Address—Line 2 | Address—Line 3 | Blank | Card Code 120 |
|---|---|---|---|---|---|---|---|---|

### Transaction File—Expense Detail

| Vendor Code | Recd Type | Voucher Number | Blank | Batch | Voucher Number | Voucher Date | Vendor Code | Invoice Date | Due Date | Invoice Number | Purchase Order Number | Debit Account | Prd Type | Product Code | Blank | Amount | Quantity | Card Code 160 |
|---|---|---|---|---|---|---|---|---|---|---|---|---|---|---|---|---|---|---|

### Transaction File—Payment Detail

| Vendor Code | Recd Type | Voucher Number | Blank | Batch | Voucher Number | Voucher Date | Vendor Code | Invoice Date | Due Date | Invoice Number | Purchase Order Number | Check Number | Check Date | Blank | Amount | Blank | Card Code 170 |
|---|---|---|---|---|---|---|---|---|---|---|---|---|---|---|---|---|---|

**Figure 10-3.** Tape Formats, Problem 10-22

1. The formats of pertinent tapes are shown in Figure 10-3.
2. The following monthly runs are prepared:
   a. Cash disbursements by check number.
   b. Outstanding payables.
   c. Purchase journals arranged (1) by account charged and (2) by vendor.
3. Vouchers and supporting invoices, receiving reports, and purchase order copies are filed by vendor code. Purchase orders and checks are filed numerically.
4. Company records are maintained on magnetic tapes. All tapes are stored in a restricted area within the computer room. A grandfather-father-son policy is followed for retaining and safeguarding tape files.

Required:
(a) Explain the grandfather-father-son policy. Describe how files could be reconstructed when this policy is used.
(b) Discuss whether Company policies for retaining and safeguarding the tape files provide adequate protection against losses of data.
(c) Describe the controls that the CPA should maintain over:
   1. Preparing the special tape.
   2. Processing the special tape with the generalized programs.
(d) Prepare a schedule for the EDP manager, outlining the data that should be included on the special tape for the CPA's examination of accounts payable and related procedures. This schedule should show the
   1. Client tape from which the item should be extracted.
   2. Name of the item of data.

(Uniform CPA Examination)

# Chapter 11

# REVENUES AND RECEIVABLES

This and each of the seven succeeding core chapters discusses 1) the evaluation and compliance testing of internal control and 2) the audit objectives and substantive procedures relating to the particular operating subsystem that is the chapter's focal point. The revenues and receivables subsystem pertaining to the sale of goods and services and the collection of amounts due from customers has been chosen to introduce these core chapters primarily because of the reader's more likely personal familiarity with the documents and activities that are involved.

### Control Considerations

The revenue-producing activities of a concern engaged in manufacturing or distribution will represent the culmination of the cash cycle that begins with the disbursement of cash to liquidate liabilities incurred in acquiring raw materials or completed products and ends with the collection of the proceeds of product sales. Cash, as the most liquid and desirable of assets, must be tightly controlled to prevent and detect loss or theft, and that control must be sequentially transferred to the acquired inventories, to the receivables resulting from the sale of inventories, and back to the cash collected from those receivables. Hence, key points of control in the revenues and receivables subsystem should assure that inventory is released only on the basis of proper authorization, and that all authorized releases result in appropriate charges in the accounts receivable records. Such charges must be actively pursued to assure collection, and the cash that is collected must be fully accounted for and controlled. Accounting for sales must provide feedback of all information that is needed for operating and decision-making purposes by the sales department.

The essential activities associated with this subsystem are depicted in the stylized flowcharts presented in Figures 11-1 and 11-2, which are reproduced by permission from the AICPA booklet, *Internal Control*. In studying these flowcharts to gain an understanding of the activities, documents, and relationships that are involved, the reader should note the following comments that highlight or modify some aspects of the flowcharts, particularly if computer processing is involved.

### Comments on Illustrative Flowcharts of Sales/Receivables Procedures

1. The control tapes on invoices, remittance advices, and credit memos are shown as being entered directly in the general ledger accounts receivable control, but of course those amounts and details would first be entered in a journal or become the basis for preparing a journal voucher. For computer processing, the control tapes would become the

basis for proving the accuracy of data entry by including the control totals with the data to be entered for a programmed proof by the computer of the detailed amounts entered against the control total.

2. The aged trial balance should be prepared each month from the accounts receivable ledger and should be balanced against the accounts receivable control to prove the accuracy of the detailed receivables records. It is important that accuracy of the detail records be proved before statements are sent to customers, in order to ensure the correctness of the statements. The aging information is shown as being the basis for the sending of collection notices to customers, but the receivables should be reviewed for delinquencies more frequently than once a month—preferably daily or at least weekly. Prompt follow-up is important in terms of the time value of money as well as the increased likelihood of success in collecting the delinquent amounts. The main use of the aged trial balance should be to provide management with information about the status of accounts and the effectiveness of credit and collection policies.

3. The detailed receivables records must be maintained in a manner that will show when collection activity should be instituted and to permit preparation of the aged trial balance. An effective manual "bookless" system of open invoices develops this information by placing invoices in a receivables file under customer name and removing the invoices when payment is made. The open invoice approach is also useful in computer records, with an open item deleted from the computer file when payment is received. An alternative computer plan is to carry each account balance forward on an "aged" basis and apply payments first against the oldest balances, with all transaction detail for the month maintained in the file record, in order to permit preparation of monthly statements of customers' accounts showing all activity for the month and the aging of the ending account balance. If hand- or machine-posted hard copy records are maintained, entries for remittances received should be keyed to the related charges being paid, in order to show which items are unpaid as a basis for initiating collection action when the amounts become delinquent. Balance-forward records with complete detail for current month transactions are essential for retail credit, in order to provide customers with complete information about their accounts through monthly statements. Monthly statements also provide the basis for desirable third-party proof of account accuracy for internal control purposes.

4. The write-off authorizations for uncollectible accounts should be shown as going to the general ledger section for entry in those records, rather than to the internal auditor. The internal auditor should have no custody or responsibility relative to accounting records but should, of course, audit the various records, probably on a 100 percent basis for critical items such as write-offs of uncollectible accounts.

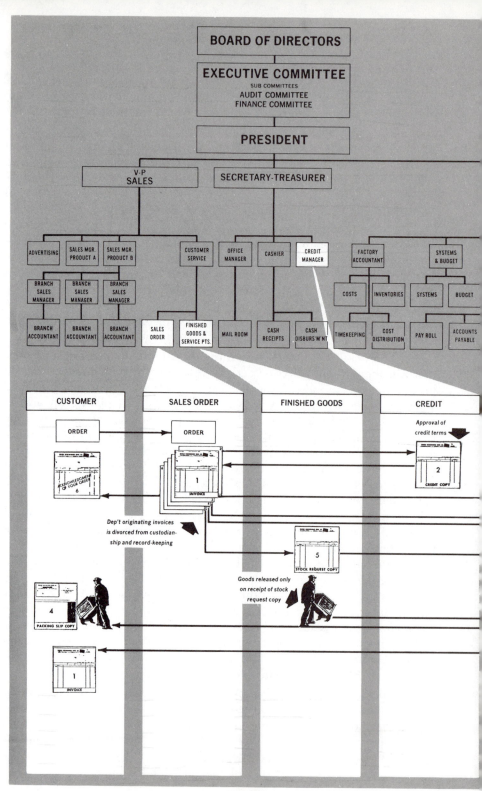

*Figure 11-1.*

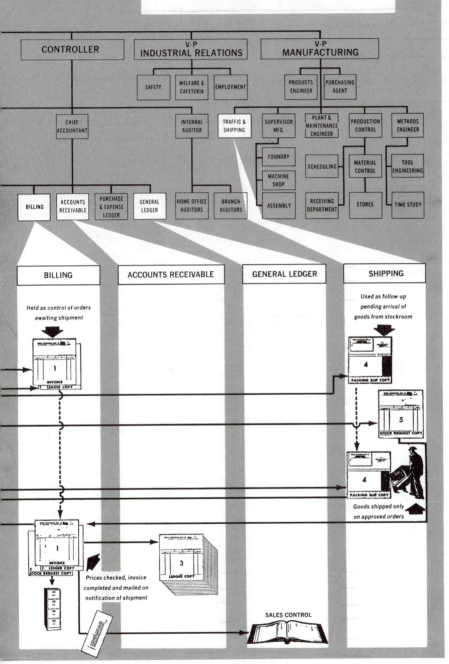

# SALES

PROCEDURAL FLOW CHART SHOWN IN RELATION
TO ORGANIZATION CHART TO PORTRAY
THE CONTROL OBTAINED THROUGH SEGREGATION
OF FUNCTIONAL RESPONSIBILITY

Source: AICPA *Internal Control*

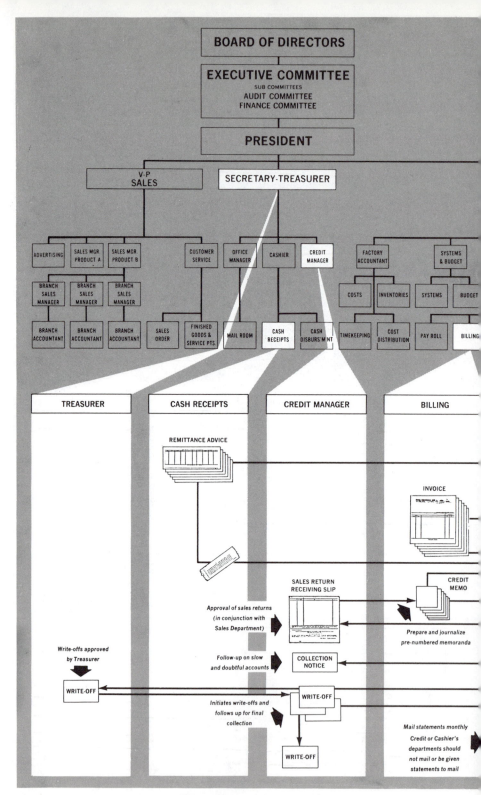

**Figure 11-2.**

# ACCOUNTS RECEIVABLE

PROCEDURAL FLOW CHART SHOWN IN RELATION
TO ORGANIZATION CHART TO PORTRAY
THE CONTROL OBTAINED THROUGH SEGREGATION
OF FUNCTIONAL RESPONSIBILITY

Source: AICPA *Internal Control*

283

The next section focuses on the internal control objectives and features that the auditor should consider in assessing the effectiveness of internal control over sales and receivables. Following each feature, the most likely type of compliance test for the feature is indicated in italics. The auditor's conclusions about the effectiveness of internal control in the subsystem area will directly affect the nature, timing, and extent of the substantive procedures to be applied to the various account balances that are the outputs of the subsystem. The objectives of these substantive procedures and comments about the application of the procedures constitute the final section of the chapter.

## Evaluation of Internal Control Objectives and Features

Internal controls are discussed under three main classifications of objectives. For each objective, features by which the objective can be accomplished are presented, with each feature followed by an indication of appropriate compliance tests given in italics.

### *Operating Objectives*

*All transactions are properly authorized.*

- Shipping orders are prepared only on the basis of written purchase orders from customers or orders reported by authorized order takers. *Inquiry, observation.*
- Orders from customers show validation for cash received by cashiers or show that extension of credit has been approved by the credit department. *Inspection.*
- Goods are removed from stock or services are performed only on the basis of properly authorized shipping orders or work orders. *Inquiry, observation. Inspection of authorizations for recorded sales or service revenue.*
- Goods leaving the premises are released only through the shipping department under proper authorization. *Inquiry, observation.*
- Security guards stationed at egress points prohibit removal of company property except with proper authorization. *Inquiry, observation.*
- Sales returns or allowances are properly authorized by sales department personnel, and returns are supported by receiving reports of returned goods. *Inquiry, observation, inspection.*

*All authorizations resulted in action being taken.*

- Customer orders are serially numbered or batched when received and subsequently accounted for in terms of shipping orders having been prepared. *Inquiry, observation.*
- Shipping orders are serially numbered and all numbers are accounted for when invoicing occurs, or

- The order department holds a copy of the shipping order in a tickler file, which is cleared when notification is received that goods have been shipped. *Inquiry, observation.*

*Access to assets is permitted only in accordance with management authorization.*

- Inventory is stored in a secure area properly protected from the elements, with access limited to authorized personnel. *Inquiry, observation.*

### Data Processing Objectives—Internal Accounting Control

*Accounting and computer operations are independent of all operating responsibilities.*

*Inquiry* and *observation* that maximum feasible segregation of these activities exists:

| Operating | Accounting/Data Processing |
|---|---|
| Selling | Billing |
| Sales order handling | Accounts receivable records |
| Credit | General ledger records |
| Shipping | Computer data entry |
| Collection follow-up | Computer operations |
| Cash handling | |
| Receiving | |

*Only valid transactions that were duly authorized are accepted for entry in the accounting records.*

- Invoices are prepared only on the basis of shipping orders showing that goods have been shipped. *Inspection.*
- Credits to accounts receivable originate only from cashier validations of cash received, properly approved credit memos for returns and allowances, or authorized write-offs of uncollectible accounts. *Inspection.*

*All transactions are entered in the accounting records.*

- All prenumbered shipping orders are accounted for when invoices are prepared. *Inquiry, observation.*
- All prenumbered invoices are accounted for at the point of entry in the accounting records or at the point of computer entry. *Inquiry, observation.*

*Accounting entries correctly reflect transaction amounts.*

- Variable information is verified when invoices are prepared or at the time of computer entry; identifying numbers should be verified through self-checking digits at the point of transcription to machine-sensible records or direct

computer entry. *Inquiry, observation, and–if price and quantity information is questionable and internal control is to be relied on–by reperformance.*
* Batch control totals are prepared for invoices, cash receipts, and other receivables credits and proved against amounts entered. *Inquiry, inspection.*

*Transactions are correctly classified for accounting entry.*

* A chart of accounts should set forth the appropriate items and transactions to be entered in each sales-related account, so that amounts will be recorded in conformity with generally accepted accounting principles (GAAP) for recognition of income and classification within the financial statements. *Inquiry, observation, inspection, reperformance.*
* Account classifications should be adequate to provide such information and reports to management as may be necessary or desirable. *Observation to indicate that adequate provision has been made to report information such as the following, with reporting on a responsibility basis whenever appropriate:*

A. Sales order handling: Daily reports
   1. Volume of orders received.
   2. Number of orders not completely processed at the end of the day.
   3. Order backlog, representing unfilled manufacturing orders or back orders for regularly stocked merchandise—number and amount of orders received, filled, and on hand at the end of the day.
   4. Sales lost because out of stock and no back order issued—number of orders and amount.
B. Sales order handling: Monthly reports
   1. Cost per order handled.
   2. Average number of orders not completely processed at the end of each day.
   3. Order backlog at end of month, net change since previous month and same month last year, and aging of the amount according to month shipment is expected to be made.
   4. Sales lost.
C. Shipping
   1. Numbers of orders shipped and total weight.
   2. Cost per order and per hundredweight of goods shipped.
D. Billing
   1. Number of invoices written and total number of line items.
   2. Cost per invoice and per line item.
E. Credit
   1. Number and amount of requests for credit: approved, rejected.
   2. Delinquency—aging of accounts, turnover, number of days' sales outstanding.
   3. Schedule of uncollectible accounts to be charged off, classified by reasons for noncollectibility.
   4. Amount of write-off for uncollectible accounts, current and past periods; percentage relationship to credit sales and accounts receivable.
   5. Ratio of credit sales to total sales.
   6. Collections on accounts receivable previously written off as uncollectible.
   7. Operating costs—amount and cost per unit of activity, such as credit applications received, sales orders, and delinquent accounts.

F. Accounts Receivable
   1. Number of entries posted and cost per entry.
   2. Differences between general and subledger controls and trial balance listings of detailed accounts receivable.
G. Sales Analysis
   1. Sales by department or major product lines, preferably compared with budget expectations and prior periods.
   2. Sales by territory, salesman, type of customer, and method of sale, further analyzed by department or product line.
   3. Sales returns and allowances, classified by cause, if available.
   4. Gross margin analysis of sales, in same classifications as for sales.
   5. External comparisons in terms of total industry sales and market potential.

## Recorded transactions are correctly processed.

- The following proofs should be utilized whenever appropriate *(Inquiry, observation, inspection, reperformance):*

  Updated subsidiary detail balances are regularly proved against running control totals.

  Periodic trial balances of general ledger accounts are prepared, in order to prove equality of debits and credits.

  Posting proofs are made of manually or machine-prepared records, to prove

  Correct pickup of previous balance.
  Correct posting of debit/credit amounts.
  Selection of correct account.

## Monitoring Objectives

*Regular comparison is made between accountability records of receivables and underlying assets; third-party proofs of accounting records.*

- Collection followup on delinquent accounts should establish validity of receivables records. *Inquiry, observation.*
- Monthly statements should be sent, especially on retail credit accounts. *Inquiry, observation.*
- Internal auditors should regularly confirm accounts receivable on a sampling basis. *Inquiry, inspection.*

## There is an effective internal audit function.

- Internal auditors should regularly review and evaluate internal controls, perform compliance tests, and if appropriate, make recommendations for improvement in the controls. *Inquiry, review of audit planning, inspection of working papers.*
- Internal auditors in retail organizations should consider the desirability of confirming receivable credits or cash refunds granted for returns and allow-

ances, in order to guard against employee fraud in this area. *Inquiry, observation.*

• The following operational audit activities, although not directly related to the reliability of accounting information, should be considered by the internal audit staff as an important service to management in the control of operations. The independent auditor may wish to review the operational audit activities of the internal audit staff, in order to provide an additional indication of the general effectiveness of management and efficiency of operations; any findings or recommendations resulting from such a review would appropriately be included in the independent auditor's management letter. *Inquiry* could pertain to such operational audit activities as

Review of customer order handling to ascertain that orders are filled promptly and accurately.

Review of sales promotion and advertising activities and company efforts to determine effectiveness of such activities.

Customer surveys to ascertain satisfaction with customer service and products ordered.

Review of new credit applications for completeness of investigation and soundness of resulting credit decisions in terms of approving poor credit risks or being overly conservative in rejecting marginal risks.

Review of collection procedures on delinquent receivables for adequacy and timeliness of follow-up activities.

Review of charged-off accounts for reasonableness of original credit approval and adequacy of efforts that were made to collect the accounts before being charged off.

Appraisal of internal reports for adequacy and timeliness; tests of accuracy of the reports against underlying data.

Determination that all potential sources of revenue have been adequately developed, including sales of scrap, waste, and vending machines located on company property.

Review of employee discount privileges to ascertain whether they are being abused.

### Supplementary Comments—Computer-Based Records

The following comments supplement and expand on some of the references in the internal control features to computer-based sales/receivables records. There is almost limitless potential for triggering action, such as follow-up on delinquent receivables, and obtaining reports and analyses, once data has been converted to machine-sensible form. Further, such action and reporting can be accomplished with near absolute processing accuracy and negligible marginal cost. Data conversion represents the critical aspect of computerized systems; the major direct costs and the greatest potential for error exist at that point.

In the sales-receivable area the usual system will require data converted to machine-readable form on only three variables: customer number, code number for each item ordered, and quantity of the item. All other information necessary to shipping, billing, and accounts receivable can be supplied from computer memory files, usually maintained on disks. This information would include such items as customer name and address; item description, weight, cost and selling price; special discounts; and credit terms. Converting customer order data to machine-readable form must be subject to tight control over the accuracy of this manual aspect of the operation, because the final outputs can be no more accurate than the original inputs. Customer number and item code number are easily controlled through use of self-checking digits. Quantity ordered obviously cannot be verified in the same way. The customary control for this variable is either key verification of a punched card record by "repeating" the original punching step, visual verification from a key-to-tape display unit to the source data, or the use of a predetermined hash total. The computer program can then perform all of the following operations, using the verified input data without further operator intervention:

1. Determine unit price and total billing amount for all items ordered.
2. Divert customer's order to an exception listing if there is an unpaid item that is past due or if the new order would raise the new account balance over the credit limit.
3. Check for stock availability of the order quantities.
4. Prepare backorder records for any items not in stock.
5. Deduct items to be shipped from the inventory balance on hand.
6. Develop total cost of items to be shipped for general ledger cost of sales entry.
7. Print shipping order, listing items in sequence by warehouse location.
8. Print customer invoice showing customer name, address, and credit terms, and for each item shipped the item code number, description, shipping weight, quantity, unit selling price, dollar extension, and dollar total for all listed items. The billing notice may be in punched card form, with the customer requested to return the card (or a stub from the card) with payment for the invoice. With this form of turnaround document, remittance information will be in machine-readable form, thus obviating costly key entry and verification of the remittance data.
9. Update customer accounts receivable record for the invoice total.
10. Store all necessary data for subsequent sales analyses.

## Substantive Audit Objectives and Procedures

The final and perhaps most crucial aspect of the typical audit is the acquisition of direct evidence through substantive audit procedures that are carefully tailored to the auditor's evaluation of related internal controls. These substantive procedures are discussed under the particular audit objectives to which they relate. The reader is encouraged to think through the audit situation in each of these core chapters, identifying the *questions to which the auditor must obtain answers* in order to be able to state that the particular accounts are presented fairly in the financial statements, in accordance with generally accepted accounting principles that have been consistently applied. The reader should then note the completeness of that analysis by comparing those questions with the audit objectives that are listed in the chapter, for the objectives represent questions that must be answered. The answers will be provided through using the audit procedures that will supply the desired information, and these should flow logically from careful consideration of the audit objectives. In essence, this text recommends a thoughtful, analytical approach to auditing rather than the torpid memorization of the stated objectives and a "laundry list" of the related audit procedures. Having already completed the discussion of the audit objectives pertaining to the evaluation and compliance testing of internal control—including the walk-through of representative transactions to gain a full understanding of how transactions are handled—the text now turns to the objectives and procedures relating to the substantive aspects of revenues and receivables.

### Conformity of Client's Financial Statements with Disclosure and Other Requirements of Financial Reporting Standards

The following standards are applicable to the reporting of revenues:

1. For enterprises whose securities are publicly traded, revenues and operating profit or loss are to be reported for major (10 percent or more of the total) industry segments and foreign operations or export sales. Revenues from major customers are to be similarly reported.
2. Nonoperating, nonrecurring revenue should be separately disclosed. For those rare items that qualify for treatment as extraordinary items, the items should be reported net of taxes.
3. Revenues may be reported net of returns and allowances unless the amounts offset might be significant to the statement user.

Reporting standards for receivables are predicated on the fact that trade receivables are generally described in terms such as "Accounts Receivable," "Accounts and Notes Receivable," or "Accounts Receivable Less Allowance for Uncollectible Accounts." If no further information is given, the statement reader should be warranted in making the following assumptions:

1. That all the receivables resulted from arm's-length transactions with third parties, and not from transactions with officers, employees, or subsidiary companies.
2. That only receivables resulting from normal trade transactions with customers are included.

3. That any potential losses have been provided for, and that therefore the full amount shown is expected to be realized in cash. (Notation should be made if a provision for doubtful accounts has been deducted from the gross receivables and only the net amount is shown in the balance sheet.)
4. That the amount of cash to be realized will be received within one year, or within one complete operating cycle if the cycle is longer than a year.
5. That the business has full ownership of the receivables, with no liens outstanding against them and no contingent liability for discounted receivables.
6. That no liabilities have been offset against the receivables.

Because statement readers are entitled by custom and good accounting practice to make the above assumptions, the auditor must determine that none of the assumptions has been violated. If investigation reveals that material amounts of receivables exist that cannot be properly classified with the trade accounts receivable, separate classification of those receivables in the balance sheet is essential. Some of the more common types of items that, if material, may have to be shown separately would include:

Installment receivables.
Receivables from officers or employees.
Receivables arising from sales or advances to nonconsolidated subsidiaries.
Receivables arising from transactions other than the sale of merchandise (for example, proceeds of the sale of plant assets, insurance claims, claims for tax refunds, or utility deposits).
Material credit balances in accounts receivable: these should be reclassified as current liabilities.

It is especially important that any receivables from officers of the client company be given full disclosure, in view of the fiduciary relationship that exists between the officers and the company. Disclosure is, however, like all other matters, subject to considerations of materiality, although it should be recognized that, for any given company, the dollar figure at which an item would become material will vary according to the item involved. Assuming total receivables from customers of $100,000, a $5,000 receivable from an insurance claim would probably not be sufficiently material to warrant separate disclosure, but a $5,000 loan to the president of the company would be an entirely different matter.

There are few procedures specifically designed to reveal the existence of receivables from other than customers, and as a consequence the auditor should be alert in performing each procedure relating to receivables or other accounts, in order that any facts bearing on the classification or presentation of receivables will be noted and given adequate consideration. If accounts receivable have been sold with recourse for uncollectible accounts, or if the accounts have been pledged to secure an indebtedness, the auditor must be certain that the statements contain full disclosure of the facts.

### Reasonableness of Account Balances

*Perform Analytical Review.*   Analytical review procedures provide evidence that the revenues/receivables accounts are fairly stated and hence represent part of the basis for the auditor's opinion. If the analytical review procedures reveal variations in the revenues or receivables accounts for which no rational explanation exists, then other substantive procedures must be extended in order for the auditor to become fully satisfied that the accounts are fairly stated or, conversely, that any material errors or improper changes in the accounts have been discovered and adjusted. Some types of review that can be made are suggested in the following paragraphs. Among possibilities especially to be watched for would be crediting of nonrecurring revenue to sales, and changes in classification or in the point in time at which revenues are considered to have been earned and realized. Illustrative working paper schedule 10 shows each of the major sales classifications analyzed by monthly totals in order to bring to light any unusual monthly variations in the sales figures. Improper crediting of a material amount of nonoperating, nonrecurring revenue to a sales account should, for example, be readily apparent from a review of monthly sales totals. On the other hand, variations may have been caused by actual operating events which, upon thorough investigation, fully account for the changes in operating results. Examples of such events would include strikes in the client's or suppliers' plants, vacations, delivery on a large contract, opening of a new branch, or introduction of a new product or new model.

Other comparisons evident on schedule 10 include the relationship of sales totals for the current year to those for the previous year, and on schedule 10-1 reference is made to industry trends. Justification for the substantial increase in sales of automated machines is stated in terms of known events occurring within the company. Sales returns and allowances are shown to be consistent with prior years by a comment on schedule 10-1, and comparative amounts are given on trial balance schedule I/S. Another important comparison is made on schedule 10 in terms of gross margin. Cost of sales amounts result from entirely different transactions and records and are usually handled by persons who have no responsibility for sales transactions. Consequently, a consistent year-to-year relationship between sales and cost of sales reinforces the credibility of each of the figures.

Similarly with respect to accounts receivable, schedule B-2 shows a comparable receivables turnover for the current and preceding years, and that the actual write-off of uncollectible accounts is consistent with the provision for such losses.

Yet another approach to the reasonableness of the accounting figures is to scan account entries for amounts that appear out of line with other entries in an account, and for irregular entries from other than the normal sources of entries to the account. Thus an entry to the sales or accounts receivable accounts from the cash disbursement record or the general journal would warrant careful investigation.

### Synchronization of Events and Records

The cutoff in recording sales transactions at the year end should result in sales transactions being recorded in the accounting period in which they occurred. Ordinarily, occurrence of a sale generates objective evidence that a sale has been consummated in the form of the receipt of cash or the creation of a legally enforceable receivable for a stated amount. Rendering of a service or legal transfer of title to goods or other property generally governs. Release of goods from the seller's plant in fulfillment of a valid sales contract may be accepted as sufficient objective evidence of a sale, however, even though the actual terms of the sale may defer transfer of legal title until the goods are delivered to the customer's premises or until they are paid for.

Proper cutoff in the recording of credit sales should result in the revenue being recorded in the period in which it was realized and in the receivable being recorded only if it represents a valid, legally enforceable claim against the purchaser. In most cases revenue is earned as a result of consummating a sales transaction, but under certain conditions the revenue may not be earned until a later date. Proper cutoff necessitates deferring the amounts not yet earned and reporting them as revenue only after goods have been delivered or services rendered. Magazine subscriptions paid in advance and sales amounts applicable to product service warranties are common examples of such deferred recognition of sales revenues. The credit portion of such a transaction represents a liability to the customer for goods or services and should be so presented in the balance sheet until the revenue has been earned.

The same considerations apply in relation to the cutoff of sales returns and allowances.

*Test Cutoff of Shipments.* The above discussion suggests that the auditor should be satisfied that revenue is recorded in the same period in which the shipment of goods occurred. Such satisfaction is gained by testing shipments made prior to the close of the year, as shown by shipping department records, and determining that the sales have been entered in the sales journal in the same period. Conversely, sales entered in the sales journal near the close of the year should be tested against shipping department records to ascertain that the goods were shipped in the same period. The auditor should consider any relative risk that sales might be either overstated or understated and think through the question of the direction of the test—that is, whether the test should be made primarily from sales records to shipping records or vice versa in each situation.

*Ascertain Existence of Recorded Receivables.*   Because evidence of a valid receivable at the balance sheet date indicates that the corresponding sales revenue has been realized, the audit of receivables helps to establish the propriety of the recorded sales, as well as the cutoff of sales transactions. The relationship of the examination of the balance sheet receivables figure to the examination of the income statement figure for sales is particularly significant when the auditing of receivables is accomplished as of the balance sheet date. Confirmation of receivables balances by correspondence with debtors should provide evidence of a clean cutoff, because the customer can be expected to take exception to amounts charged at the confirmation date for sales that were not consummated until a later date. The significance of receivables confirmation work with respect to the sales cutoff is substantially lessened under present-day practices of performing much of the audit work at a date prior to the balance sheet date, although unusual conditions noted at that time should alert the auditor for similar conditions at the balance sheet date. For example, receivables work is most helpful in revealing the practice of recording sales in instances where goods have been shipped on approval or on a consignment basis. Establishing the existence of the recorded receivables is discussed later in this chapter as a separate objective.

### Comprehensiveness of Records

The question of whether all revenues (and hence related cash or receivables) have been recorded is answered primarily through the following procedures related to two objectives that have already been covered.

*Evaluate Internal Control.*   It is in the client's primary interest that there be tight controls to assure that all revenues have been recorded, and this text has previously noted those controls. Goods should be released for shipment only when properly authorized, and the written authorizations should be accounted for to ascertain that the shipments have been invoiced and the invoices recorded. In view of client interest in the recording of all revenue, the auditor should be justified in relying primarily on internal control to prevent the omission of revenue from the accounting records. Also, as pointed out previously, the auditor will have only a secondary interest in unrecorded revenues that are a consequence of fraud, because, strictly interpreted, the client has realized no revenue and the financial statements are not misstated. Nevertheless, the auditor should be alert to any possibility of unrecorded revenue, in view of the client service aspects of information about such an occurrence.

*Test Cutoff of Shipments.* The cut-off tests discussed in the previous section can provide information about unrecorded revenues at the year end by working from evidence that goods have been shipped or a service rendered in order to determine whether related billing and recording have occurred.

### Arithmetic and Clerical Accuracy; Agreement of Details and Control Totals

Although it is the control account figure for receivables that appears in the financial statements, substantive audit procedures must of necessity be concerned with the detailed records of the individual receivables, making it essential that the auditor establish that the detail and control are in agreement.

*Prepare or Test Trial Balance of Subsidiary Ledger.* In most cases, assuming that internal control is satisfactory, the client will have prepared a trial balance of the receivables ledger and balanced the total with the general ledger control account. The auditor should compare the individual balances listed with the subsidiary ledger records and reference the total to the amount of accounts receivable shown in the audit work papers.

If internal control is satisfactory and there are a large number of individual accounts, the comparison of trial balance amounts with the subsidiary records can be limited to a test basis. Unless the accounts are fairly homogeneous, stratification would be in order, with all large balances included in the sample, plus a random sampling of smaller accounts. *Testing should be from the trial balance to the ledger sheets*, because the purpose of the test is to prove that all amounts shown on the trial balance are represented by actual accounts in the ledger. Another reason for making the test in this direction is that the relative risk of a possible misstatement of the receivables suggests that overstatement of the receivables is more likely than understatement. Manipulation to overstate the receivables could result from an attempt to better the apparent financial position of the concern through recording fictitious sales and receivables, or the overstatement could result from the abstraction of cash received from customers. In the latter case if a customer's account has been credited to avoid any implications that the account has become delinquent, the manipulator may have found it impossible to make a corresponding credit to the general ledger receivables control account. Under these circumstances it is likely that fictitious amounts would be inserted in the trial balance to present an appearance of balance between the detailed ledger and the control account. In order to detect such manipulations when the auditor is limiting to a test the comparison between the trial balance and the detailed ledger, it is essential that the auditor work from the trial balance to the ledger. The footing of the client's trial balance must also, of course, be proved in order to complete the verification process.

If the client records are computerized, the auditor should use an audit software package to sum the individual receivable records for balancing against the control. The same run should also be programmed to age the receivables (see the subsequent objective relating to valuation) and to select accounts for confirmation, printing either a list of the selected accounts or printing the confirmation requests directly.

For the converse situation when relatively few accounts and hardcopy records are involved, the auditor will usually include a complete aged trial balance in the working papers, verifying the correctness of the aging at the same time that the trial balance is verified or prepared.

Whenever the subsidiary ledger accounts fail to balance with the control account, the auditor should refer the matter to the client. Locating the difference is a clerical matter, and the auditor should not do the work unless specifically authorized to do so and the client understands that the audit fee will be increased accordingly. Should the receivables ledger be out of balance in a situation where internal control is weak, the auditor should be alert to the possibility that fraud may have occurred, particularly if the control account exceeds the total of the individual receivables.

It is important that the incidental aspects of trial balance procedures not be overlooked. The resulting intimate contact with the receivables is one of the principal means of disclosing the existence of accounts with officers or subsidiary companies, accounts arising from nontrade transactions, accounts maturing beyond the period of one year or the operating cycle (if longer than one year), accounts with credit balances, accounts that are secured, and accounts that have been pledged. In the latter case the lender may stamp the applicable ledger sheets, "This account pledged to _____ under loan agreement dated _____," in order to protect the security interest in the accounts.

### Existence of Receivables

The objectives and procedures relating to the substantiation of receivables and inventories underwent drastic change in the late 1930s. These changes and the events leading to them are discussed briefly here in order to give the reader a better understanding of generally accepted auditing standards as they exist today concerning receivables and inventories. Prior to 1939, independent examinations of financial statements seldom included procedures designed to enable the auditor to determine whether the receivables were valid obligations of existing concerns, and whether the inventories actually existed and were accurately counted as a basis for the final inventory figure. Although such procedures were occasionally performed, either at the suggestion of the auditor or at the request of the client, they were excluded from most examinations as being too costly and relatively unnecessary. Management usually certified the validity of the receivables and the accuracy of the inventory count, as well as the existence of the inventory, and this arrangement was generally understood and accepted by those who used audited financial statements.

In 1939, however, disclosures concerning the gigantic $20,000,000 McKesson and Robbins fraud provided dramatic evidence of the need to strengthen auditing standards with respect to receivables and inventories. The American Institute of Certified Public Accountants responded promptly and in September, 1939, adopted a report known as "Extensions of Auditing Procedure," which increased materially the auditor's responsibility concerning receivables and inventories. Despite the problems involved and the added expense to clients desiring an unqualified opinion on their financial statements, this report stated that henceforth an examination designed to permit the expression of an unqualified opinion must include correspondence with the client's debtors, in order to establish the validity of receivables, and must include observation and tests of the client's inventory taking in order to establish the existence and accuracy of the inventory. These added requirements are now understood to be part of generally accepted auditing standards and have provided a corresponding increase in the auditor's level of assurance concerning receivables and inventories. "Extensions of Auditing Procedure" became the first of a series of "Statements on Auditing Procedure," followed in 1973 by the successor series, "Statements on Auditing Standards."

*Confirmation Procedures.* The technique of ascertaining the existence of receivables through correspondence with the debtors is known as confirming, or circularizing, the accounts. Accounts may be confirmed on either a positive or a negative basis. For positive confirmation the customer is requested to reply, stating whether or not the amount shown as owing to the client is correct. For negative confirmation a reply is requested only if the amount shown is not correct. In either case the actual request should come from the client, because no relationship exists between the auditor and the debtor.

The positive confirmation request is usually in the form of a letter such as the one shown in Figure 11-3. A possible answer to the letter is included.

A negative confirmation request may also be made in letter form, but frequently it will be made in the form of a sticker or rubber stamp placed on a copy of the monthly statement if one is regularly sent to each customer. Such a request is usually made in this form:

---

Please notify our auditors at the address given below if this statement is not correct.

> Black and Decker, Certified Public Accountants
> 234 Main
> Kansas City, MO 64105

Should a discrepancy exist, any information you can furnish concerning the discrepancy will be greatly appreciated. Please use the enclosed business reply envelope in replying.

---

Confirmation requests should be mailed in envelopes bearing the auditor's return address, so that any that cannot be delivered will be returned to the auditor. The return envelope to be used by customers in replying should similarly bear the auditor's address.

The requests will usually be prepared by employees of the client, using a duplicated form and filling in name, address, and amount, if the confirmation is in letter form. The customer's name, address, and amount due on each request should be verified against the appropriate ledger sheet by the auditor to avoid errors, whether or not intentional. In addition, each request should be compared with the trial balance that the auditor has verified, in order to determine that no accounts have been omitted or shown with an incorrect balance. If the circularization is on a test basis, the work papers should show which accounts have been selected. Verification of the confirmations is, of course, irrelevant if the confirmation requests are computer-prepared from computerized records using the auditor's program package. Negative requests that are affixed to customer statements and the insertion of requests and return envelopes into mailing envelopes are most economically performed by client employees under the auditor's control and supervision. After the confirmation requests have been prepared and verified, if necessary, they must remain under the auditor's control until they are placed in a U.S. Postal Service depository. Failure to follow this precaution would give employees an opportunity to alter or remove confirmations pertaining to altered or fictitious accounts.

In examining commercial accounts in which account balances will include multiple charges, each of which has been separately invoiced, it may be more effective to select for confirmation individual unpaid invoices rather than seeking to confirm the entire account balance. Sam-

MACHINE PRODUCTS CO.
WICHITA, KANSAS 67202

December 12, 19__

Sampson and Co.
234 Erie Street
Chicago, Illinois 60602

Gentlemen:

In connection with the regular independent examination of our financial statements now being made by Black and Decker, Certified Public Accountants, please confirm to them the amount of your indebtedness to us at November 30, 19__. The amount of this indebtedness as shown by our records is indicated below in the space provided for your reply.

Please indicate whether the stated amount is correct. If a difference is reported, please give our auditors any information which might aid them in reconciling the difference.

Your reply should be made directly to Black and Decker, and a stamped, addressed envelope is enclosed for your convenience.

Very truly yours,

MACHINE PRODUCTS CO.

H. A. Onsgard

H. A. Onsgard,
Treasurer

Black and Decker:

The amount of $1,864.32 representing our indebtedness as shown by the records of Machine Products Co. at November 30, 19__ is correct with the following exceptions (if any): Our records show $1,265.29 The difference appears to be a payment which we made on November 28, 19—.

Signed Sampson + Co.
By D. A. Verbeck

***Figure 11-3.*** Confirmation Request Letter

ple sizes need not be appreciably larger under those circumstances, and customers will generally find it easier to establish the status of a particular invoice than to attempt to verify the entire balance of the account, given the likelihood of charges and payments that are in transit and the possible existence of disputed items. The confirmation response form should include a provision for the respondent to note the date of payment if the item has been paid. Payment information should aid the auditor in accounting for payments in transit and ascertaining that the customer's account has been properly credited. Cumulative monetary amount sampling would be especially applicable to the confirmation of selected invoices in terms of selecting larger items and evaluating the sample results.

The working papers should be noted to show all accounts on which replies have received to positive confirmation requests. The letters should be kept in the audit file, and a summary of the confirmation results should be prepared as illustrated in schedule B-1. Replies that show differences should be carefully investigated, and the explanation for any difference should be noted on the reply. Great care should be taken in investigating differences; each such difference is a potential clue to a defalcation or misstatement of the accounts until it is otherwise explained. Requests returned by the post office because they were undeliverable warrant particularly close attention.

Replies suggesting that a charge has been made but no goods purchased, that too much has been charged, or that credit has not been given for a payment that has been made signal danger, although investigation will usually show that an error was made in figuring an invoice, that a debit or credit was posted to the wrong account, or that the remittance was in transit. Any undue delay in entering the credit for a collection on account should suggest the possibility of *lapping*, a form of manipulation in which a remittance from customer A is appropriated, and then a later remittance from customer B is used to credit the account of A, a remittance from C is used to credit B, and so on.

If a client's internal control is especially good and reported differences are not material, the differences may be turned over to one of the client's employees for investigation, with a report to be made back to the auditor. The selected employee should obviously have no responsibility for receivables or the handling of cash, and a member of the internal auditing staff will usually represent the best possible choice.

The preceding comments concerning the confirmation of receivables should suggest the great value of the confirmation procedure. In addition to providing information about the effectiveness of the client's internal control, confirmation may reveal fictitious receivables and related fraud, errors or manipulation of the sales cutoff, consignment shipments charged as receivables, amounts which are in dispute, and freight allowances to be granted customers paying the freight on sales made of f.o.b. destination. Nevertheless, a reply to a positive confirmation request (or the absence of a reply to a negative request) does not necessarily constitute infallible evidence of an account's validity. The person signing the reply may not have ascertained all the facts before returning the request without exception, and there is always a possibility that an address has been used for a fictitious account at which a party to the fraud may obtain the letter and return it properly signed. Nonresponses also present a problem, but by sending an adequate number of requests, the auditor should have reasonable assurance that if misstated accounts could have a material effect on the financial statements, there will be at least one response that will signal the true condition of the accounts.

*Decisions Relating to Confirmation Procedures.* There are many points in the confirmation process where decisions must be made. These decisions should be made at the senior level or higher and must reflect generally accepted auditing standards. The first necessary decision will be whether to confirm all accounts or only part of the accounts on a test basis. If a test is considered adequate, the extent of the test must be determined, as well as the basis for selecting the accounts to be tested—obvious applications for statistical sampling. Also, the auditor must determine whether positive confirmations, negative confirmations, or both will be used, giving consideration to the greater assurance associated with a positive response and the uncertainty implications of no response to a negative request. These differences must be considered in relation to the added costs of positive requests associated with preparing the requests, postage for the replies, and investigating nonresponses.

Factors suggesting the need for extensive circularization, usually on a positive basis, would be weak internal control, indication that many amounts are in dispute, suspicion that fraud or numerous bookkeeping errors exist, or the existence of accounts with balances that are large relative to total receivables. On the other hand, if internal control is good and there is a large number of uniformly small accounts, negative confirmation of the accounts should be adequate. If there are a few large accounts along with a great number of small accounts, both positive and negative confirmations may be employed. The selection of larger accounts for confirmation gives the auditor a maximum amount of information for a minimum expenditure of time and provides relatively good assurance that the receivables are not materially misstated. The smaller accounts should not be ignored, however, for the auditor is also interested in the overall accuracy of the accounting. It should be noted that CMA selection will provide the desired combination of samples. It is also desirable that the selection of accounts to be confirmed include accounts that are seriously delinquent, accounts that exceed the assigned credit limits, accounts with certain classes of customers or from certain geographical areas or for certain types of products or services, recently opened accounts, accounts with recently increased activity, or accounts that are for other reasons unusual or questionable. Such selections will obviously be facilitated if the selection criteria can be programmed for computer application.

If internal control is weak because duties are inadequately segregated, it may also be desirable to confirm some of the accounts that have been written off as uncollectible. Although an asset is no longer in question, confirmation should reveal accounts for which collections have been misappropriated and then the accounts disposed of by fraudulently writing them off as uncollectible.

On occasion the client may request that certain accounts not be confirmed because of possible unfavorable customer reaction. The auditor should obtain a signed request listing the accounts that are not to be confirmed, and should be certain that the signer is a person of top-ranking authority rather than an employee who may be attempting to conceal a defalcation. The auditor must then decide whether the existence of these accounts can be established by alternative procedures and, in addition, must determine what effect, if any, honoring the request and substituting alternative procedures will have on the audit report. (See Chapter 20 for further discussion of exceptions and qualifications in the auditor's report.)

Confirmation results should be summarized for review by the manager or partner, in some fashion similar to the illustration on schedule B-1. When positive confirmation requests are used, the auditor must watch to see that replies are received covering an adequate percentage of the dollar amount of the accounts. Particular note should be made that replies are received on accounts that are exceptionally large or otherwise unusual. If the response is not adequate, second requests carrying an appropriate notation to that effect should be mailed. In some instances third requests, telephone calls, telegrams, or registered letters may be warranted.

*Alternative Procedures.* Occasionally no reply can be obtained on confirmation requests to certain major accounts. For instance, some companies and government agencies will not confirm balances as a matter of policy because their accounting records are so widespread that an undue amount of time would be required to answer the many requests that are received, and there would be no assurance that a reply would cover all open items. Confirmation of specific open charges, as mentioned earlier, is likely to be much more effective in these instances. If no reply can be secured from a major confirmation request, or if confirmation is not practicable or reasonable for some other reason, alternative procedures may be employed to determine the validity of the accounts.

Reference to evidence of subsequent payment of an account ordinarily constitutes indication of the account's existence. The best form of evidence is the customer's remittance advice that accompanied the payment. This document will have originated outside the client's organization, and will in addition specify the exact items being paid, so that there is no chance of accepting as evidence a remittance that actually pertains to a charge made after the confirmation date. Other forms of evidence relating to the payment of the account, arranged in descending order of reliability, would be the check sent by the customer, an authenticated bank deposit ticket listing a deposited check for the amount in question, entry of the remittance in the cash receipts book, and a credit posted to the customer's account. In a few special cases the auditor may control all incoming mail and inspect all remittances received after the balance sheet date, as evidence of the validity of the receivables at the balance sheet date. English accountants rely heavily on the subsequent payment of accounts receivable, and written confirmation of receivables is not required by their generally accepted auditing standards. The occurrence of the McKesson & Robbins fraud in the United States is largely responsible for the variation between the standards in England and the United States.

Should the customer be slow in paying an account for which confirmation has been requested but not received, the auditor may refer to other evidence indicating that the receivable exists. Such evidence would include the shipping department's notice of shipment, accompanied possibly by a receipted copy of the bill of lading, the customer's purchase order, and any correspondence referring to the shipment of the goods. It is also helpful to know that the customer indicated by the records is actually an existing business organization. Assurance of this fact can be obtained by referring to the Dun and Bradstreet Reference Book, a business or city directory, or a credit report if one is on file.

### Ownership of Receivables

Ordinarily there will be little or no question about the client's ownership or legal standing with respect to recorded receivables, inasmuch as they will have resulted from the sale of the client's products or services. The auditor should be alert, however, to any indication that accounts receivable have been factored, discounted, sold, or pledged as collateral, inasmuch as the effect of any such transactions must be properly reflected in the financial statements. Substantial blocks of cash receipts should be carefully reviewed to determine whether they represent the proceeds of any of the above types of transactions.

### Valuation of Receivables—Collectibility

The confirmation of a receivable does not provide any proof that the account will be collected. The customer's acknowledgment of indebtedness is no indication of ability to pay. Therefore, the auditor must employ other procedures in order to determine the collectibility of the receivables. The problem of collectibility relates primarily to the adequacy of the provision for doubtful accounts, because this provision should be sufficient to reduce receivables to an amount not in excess of the expected collections.

*Aging.* The best indication of the collectibility of a client's receivables can usually be gained by aging the accounts. As a general rule the longer an account has been unpaid, the less likely it is that the account will be paid. Open items comprising an account balance may be aged either according to the month of sale or according to whether the balance is current or past due, with separate columns to show how long the amounts are past due.

A choice must also be made as to whether accounts are to be aged on a first-in, first-out basis or on a specific-invoice basis. The difference between these two bases and the results obtained may be illustrated readily by the following simple example. The account that is shown is to be aged as of December 31.

| Date | Explanation | Debit | Credit | Balance |
|------|-------------|-------|--------|---------|
| Sept. 4 . . . . . . . . .Inv. #2418 | | $864.15 | | $ 864.15 |
| Sept. 7 . . . . . . . . .Inv. #2463 | | 152.97 | | 1,017.12 |
| Sept. 10 . . . . . . . .Cash | | | $864.15 | 152.97 |
| Nov. 26 . . . . . . . .Inv. #2738 | | 201.64 | | 354.61 |
| Dec. 2 . . . . . . . . .Inv. #2773 | | 286.51 | | 641.12 |
| Dec. 6 . . . . . . . . .Cash | | | 201.64 | 439.48 |

Aging this account by month of sale on a first-in, first-out basis, $286.51 would of course be classified as a December sale, leaving the remainder of the balance of $439.48 to be classified in some other month. The remainder is $152.97, and as it does not exceed the November sale of $201.64, the entire $152.97 would be classified "November." However, when payments are matched with charges on a specific-invoice basis, the balance is shown to be comprised of the December charge of $286.51 and the September invoice for $152.97. The period of time that has elapsed since the transaction occurred suggests considerable doubt that the amount will be collected. Thus aging the amount as "September" on a specific-invoice basis is much more realistic and informative than aging the amount as "November" under the first-in, first-out basis.

Although the preceding illustration would suggest that the specific-invoice basis should always be used, the alternative method is used quite frequently, primarily because it is easier to apply. The illustration does not indicate any particular difficulty in applying the specific-invoice basis, but relatively few entries are involved. When numerous transactions occur each month, the matching of debits and credits becomes rather a lengthy process unless the client has keyed debits and credits as remittances have been received.

Yet, if the individual receivable balances are small and relatively homogeneous, the quicker first-in, first-out method, even though less accurate and reliable, will produce a picture of the receivables sufficiently useful to permit a reasonable determination of the adequacy of the provision for doubtful accounts. As a general rule, however, large accounts that might have a substantial effect on the overall picture should be aged on a specific-invoice basis.

The entire balance of an installment account is usually aged according to the month in which the most recent installment payment was received. Alternatively, the balance may be aged according to the number of months that payments are in arrears.

Although the preceding comments might suggest that the auditor does the receivables aging, that should not ordinarily be the case, for desirable internal control features would include regular aging of receivables for management reporting of the results of credit and collection policies. When the client has done the necessary aging, the auditor will, of course, use the client information, subject to test verification by the auditor to establish the accuracy of the client aging. In testing the aging, the auditor should emphasize accounts aged as being current in order to be assured that the condition of the accounts is not worse than is indicated by the client's aging.

The comments on testing the client's aging would not apply if the receivables records are maintained by computer. There is no feasible way to test the client figures in that case, and the only solution is to obtain the aging from the computer records under the direction of the auditor's program.

*Interpreting Aging Results.* Once the auditor has the complete aging analysis, it must be used to determine whether the provision for doubtful accounts appears adequate. In some instances a schedule of estimated losses for each age group of an aging analysis may be developed from past experience. Such a schedule might appear as follows:

| Age Group | Estimated Percentage of Loss |
|---|---|
| Current | 0 |
| Past due | |
| 1 month | 10 |
| 2 months | 20 |
| 3 months | 30 |
| 4 months | 40 |
| 5 months | 50 |

Because differing conditions cause different results, no single schedule can be used for all clients, even if they are in the same field of business. Whenever a small number of accounts with large balances is present, individual consideration of each past-due amount is practically a necessity. Any useful information observed at the time the accounts are aged should be noted in a remarks column of the schedule. Notations of collections on past-due amounts received between the aging date and the time of the auditor's tests represent particularly useful information.

Later the senior accountant will review the past-due accounts with the credit manager and, using the remarks on the aging schedule and information furnished by the credit manager (verified by reference to credit reports, correspondence, or other data when necessary), prepare an estimate of possible losses from doubtful accounts. If this estimate materially exceeds the provision made in the records, the auditor should request that the client increase the recorded provision. If the client refuses to make the requested adjustment, the auditor will probably find it necessary to qualify the opinion to be rendered on the client's financial statements, indicating that the recorded provision for doubtful accounts is inadequate.

*Other Procedures Related to Collectibility.* The auditor should analyze all changes in the allowance account for uncollectibles, and the calculation of the current year's provision for losses should be reviewed. The dollar amount of the sales or receivables used as the base in this calculation should be verified, the percentage loss factor applied to the base should be unchanged from the previous year unless warranted by circumstances, and the product of the base times the rate should be verified. Past bad debt losses should be reviewed to determine whether the loss factor being used is adequate, based on past experience. The permanent files should be brought up to date each year to show the annual losses and provision for losses. Schedule B-2 is an example of the working paper analysis of the provision for losses to be included in the current audit file.

An intelligent appraisal of the adequacy of the current year's loss provision must be based in part on a knowledge of the client's credit and collection policies and of any changes that have occurred in these policies. The lengthening of credit terms, the reduction of minimum credit standards for accepting new accounts or increasing high credit limits, a change in collection procedures, or laxness in following up on delinquent accounts may all have repercussions on the client's bad debt losses. The auditor should be aware of these possibilities and, if necessary, recommend changes in the percentage loss factor used in providing for losses. Discussion with the credit manager and collection clerks and a review of a limited sample of new account applications that have been approved are means of securing internal information, and the auditor should always keep abreast of general economic conditions and developments.

Another important point that warrants careful attention is whether the posting of credits for returns or allowances may have been delayed either unintentionally or for the purpose of improving operating results and the current financial position. In addition to inquiry made of the proper persons about such a possibility, the auditor should review the returns and allowances posted in the period following the balance sheet date. An abnormal amount would indicate a possible carry-over from the year under review, and supporting papers covering individual returns and allowances should be examined on a test basis to determine whether the cutoff at the end of the year was made cleanly.

### Timing of the Audit Work

It should be possible to do much of the audit work on sales and receivables prior to the end of the client's fiscal year if internal control is satisfactory, although tests of the cutoff of sales, returns, and allowances must, of course, be deferred until after the end of the year. Trial balance work, confirmation, and aging would all be appropriately performed on a preliminary basis. If the results of this work are favorable, good internal control should give adequate assurance that similar conditions will exist at the balance sheet date. It is, nevertheless, advisable to seek further confirmation of such conclusions by testing intervening transactions and carefully reviewing year-end balances for unwarranted changes. If the year-end trial balance reveals the existence of large individual receivables balances, the auditor should determine that the balances are current and have not increased materially since the preliminary work was done. When substantial increases are noted, or when large new receivables appear on the trial balance, confirmation should be requested as of the balance sheet date to establish the validity of the balances.

In a first audit the auditor should review cutoffs and the adequacy of the allowance for doubtful accounts at the beginning of the year, inasmuch as these items directly affect the current year's income.

### Notes Receivable

Although most sales are completed on an open-account basis, in some fields trade acceptances are common, and installment sales of equipment are usually covered by notes. In addition, of course, financial institutions will require notes to be signed on loans or advances. The objectives and procedures presented in connection with the examination of accounts receivable are generally applicable to notes receivable as well, but certain additional procedures are necessary when notes receivable are present.

*Inspection of Notes Receivable.* Because a note may be negotiated to a third party without notice to the maker, confirmation of the recorded receivable with the maker of the note is not conclusive evidence that the payee of the note still has a valid asset. To be satisfied that notes receivable have not been sold, discounted, or pledged, the auditor should make a physical inspection of the notes. This inspection, or "count" of the notes, should include a comparison of the following information appearing on the notes with the client's note register, ledger sheets, or other record of the notes: name of payee, names of endorsers (if any), name of maker, principal amount of the note, date the note was made, maturity date, and interest rate (if any). The count should be made as of the close of business on the last day of the fiscal period, and control should be maintained over the notes until all other liquid assets, such as cash or securities, have been counted, in order to preclude conversion of any of the notes into cash and use of such cash to cover up any shortage that might exist. The form of working paper for the count of notes receivable is illustrated by schedule B-3.

Endorsements should be investigated at the time of the count inasmuch as they may be a clue to a temporary conversion of a note. The note might have been pledged or discounted, with the proceeds used to the personal advantage of some employee. Subsequent reacquisition of the note would, of course, be necessary to restore it to its proper place at the time of the auditor's count. Due dates should also be watched, because notes due more than one year after the balance sheet date may have to be placed in a noncurrent category.

Any notes owned by the client but not on hand at the time of the count should be confirmed with the present holders as well as with the maker. Notes not on hand should be out for a good reason, such as collection, or collateral for a loan. If for the latter reason, notation to that effect is required in the balance sheet.

To protect against unauthorized use or conversion of notes, the client should assign the responsibility for custody of notes receivable to a person who has no access to cash or to the accounting records.

*Notes Receivables Discounted.* Notes receivable records should be reviewed to determine whether credits to the notes receivable account represent actual collections or the proceeds of discounting. If notes have been discounted with recourse, the resulting contingent liability must be noted in the balance sheet. Furthermore, the auditor should obtain a written confirmation from the party who discounted such notes (ususally the client's bank) listing all unpaid notes still being held. In the case of banks such a listing will be obtained in connection with the use of the standard bank confirmation form (see schedule $\frac{A-2}{1}$), which requests the bank to provide complete information on any notes that it is holding that were discounted by the client. If any notes still held by the discounting party are past due, any expected loss and the endorser's liability should be reflected in the client's financial statements. All notes not yet paid, whether or not they have matured, should be confirmed directly with the maker, as there is always a possibility that the note that was discounted at the bank may be fictitious.

*Secured Notes.* If the notes are secured by collateral, the debtor should be asked to confirm the description and amount of collateral that was pledged. The collateral should be examined to ascertain that it has been properly accounted for and not merged with the client's assets or otherwise converted. Finally, the value of the collateral should be ascertained in order to determine whether the security is ample.

When the security given on a note is in the form of a mortgage, the mortgage should be examined or otherwise accounted for, and the auditor should ascertain that the mortgage has been recorded. In cases of savings and loan associations and commercial banks making regular real estate loans, there are many other documents that should be reviewed by the auditor, at least on a test basis. Such review will help to establish that the client's regular procedures and requirements are being followed, and will provide further evidence of the validity of the notes. The documents will include the loan application, appraiser's report and photographs of the property, attorney's title-search opinion or a title insurance policy, receipted tax bills or other evidence that property taxes have been paid, and an insurance policy or other evidence that the property is insured.

*Interest Income.* The client should follow the accrual basis of accounting for interest on notes receivable, and the auditor should determine that interest has been properly accrued at the balance sheet date. In addition, sufficient tests should be made to satisfy the auditor that all interest income earned during the year has been accounted for, as was done on schedule B-3.

## Questions/Problems

For multiple-choice questions 11-1 through 11-8, indicate the letter of the single answer that *best* completes the statement or answers the question, and justify the choice that you have made.

**11-1.** Which of the following is *not* a principal objective of the auditor in the examination of revenues?

   a. To verify cash deposited during the year.

   b. To study and evaluate internal control, with particular emphasis on the use of accrual accounting to record revenue.

   c. To verify that earned revenue has been recorded, and recorded revenue has been earned.

   d. To identify and interpret significant trends and variations in the amounts of various categories of revenue.

(Uniform CPA Examination)

**11-2.** For good internal control, the credit manager should be responsible to the

a. Sales manager
b. Customer-service manager
c. Controller
d. Treasurer

(Uniform CPA Examination)

**11-3.** An auditor is testing sales transactions. One step is to trace a sample of debit entries from the accounts receivable subsidiary ledger back to the supporting sales invoices. What would the auditor intend to establish by this step?

a. Sales invoices represent bona fide sales.
b. All sales have been recorded.
c. All sales invoices have been properly posted to customer accounts.
d. Debit entries in the accounts receivable subsidiary ledger are properly supported by sales invoices.

(Uniform CPA Examination)

**11-4.** In a *first audit* of a manufacturing concern the independent auditor should also test the *sales cutoff* at the *beginning* of the year because of the possible effect on the following in the financial statements for the audited year:

a. Inventory variance.
b. Accounts receivable.
c. Sales.
d. All of the above.

**11-5.** A sales clerk at Schackne Company correctly prepared a sales invoice for $5,200, but the invoice was entered as $2,500 in the sales journal and similarly posted to the general ledger and accounts-receivable ledger. The customer remitted only $2,500, the amount on his monthly statement. The most effective procedure for preventing this type of error is to

a. Use predetermined totals to control posting routines.
b. Have an independent check of sales-invoice serial numbers, prices, discounts, extensions, and footings.
c. Have the bookkeeper prepare monthly statements which are verified and mailed by a responsible person other than the bookkeeper.
d. Have a responsible person who is independent of the accounts-receivable department promptly investigate unauthorized remittance deductions made by customers or other matters in dispute.

(Uniform CPA Examination)

**11-6.** In which of the following instances of accounts receivable confirmation requests, returned to the auditor by the Postal Service with the notation shown, should the auditor be *least* concerned that a fraudulent account that does not exist may be involved?

    a. Moved, left no address.
    b. Addressee unknown.
    c. No such address.
    d. The existence of a valid receivable is questionable in each of these instances.

**11-7.** To determine that sales transactions have been recorded in the proper accounting period, the auditor performs a cutoff review. Which of the following *best* describes the overall approach used when performing a cutoff review?

    a. Ascertain that management has included in the representation letter a statement that transactions have been accounted for in the proper accounting period.
    b. Confirm year-end transactions with regular customers.
    c. Examine cash receipts in the subsequent period.
    d. Analyze transactions occurring within a few days before and after year end.

                              (Uniform CPA Examination)

**11-8.** In updating a computerized accounts receivable file, which one of the following would be used as a batch control to verify the accuracy of the posting of cash receipts as remittances?

    a. The sum of the cash deposits plus the discounts less the sales returns.
    b. The sum of the cash deposits.
    c. The sum of the cash deposits less the discounts taken by customers.
    d. The sum of the cash deposits plus the discounts taken by customers.

                              (Uniform CPA Examination)

**11-9.** What duties with respect to receivables should be handled separately under a good system of internal control?

**11-10.** Assume that you are engaged in an examination of financial statements for the year ended December 31, 19X1, and Congress has already legislated lower corporate income tax rates for 19X2. If your cutoff tests are to be made by selecting shipments from the shipping records and tracing the items to the sales register to determine whether sales were shipped and billed in the same period, would relative risk suggest that most of the shipments should be selected from the last few days of December, 19X1, or the first few days of January, 19X2? Explain.

**11-11.** Suggest various ways in which a branch manager of a retail chain store, who receives a bonus based on the store's profit, might attempt to inflate that profit. All accounting for the store is done locally under the manager's supervision.

**11-12.** (a) In connection with your receivables confirmation work for the December 31, 19X1 audit of Grey and Co., one request covering the balance of $629.51 is returned by the customer with the notation "We do not owe the above amount, since it was paid by our check dated December 30, 19X1." What would you do with this exception?

     (b) How would your answer be different if the customer said that the date of the check was December 20, 19X1?

**11-13.** As the independent auditor for the Jameson, Co., you have had employees of the credit department prepare negative accounts receivable confirmation requests, which you compared as to customer name and balance with the trial balance in your working papers before mailing the confirmation requests. No exceptions were noted from these procedures, and your audit report is subsequently issued in due course. Later, the client discovers that several sizable accounts receivable balances are entirely fictitious, apparently not discovered by you since a false address was typed on the related confirmation requests. The employee responsible for the fraud had merely collected the requests at this address and destroyed them, so you assumed that the accounts were correct. The loss on these accounts was sufficient to place Jameson Co. in bankruptcy, and you are being sued for damages by a creditor of Jameson who relied on your audit report in extending credit to the company.

Is it likely that the creditor will be able to recover damages from you? Why?

**11-14.** As you are selecting accounts receivable to be confirmed, the credit manager points out six accounts totaling $2,345.60 out of a total of $354,689.20 that you are asked not to confirm. The credit manager states that there has been a dispute in each case with voluminous correspondence as to whether the merchandise delivered met the customer's specifications, and that confirmation requests would not yield a useful reply and merely agitate the customers involved. How should such a request normally be handled, and how would you proceed in this instance?

**11-15.** No reply has been received on the second request for confirmation of the receivable balance from Sharp Cutlery Co., so you ask your assistant to use alternative procedures to establish the validity of the account and the collectibility of the balance. The assistant's working papers show that the December 31 balance of $2,356.19 was verified on the basis of the following cash credits that were posted to the account:

| | | |
|---|---|---|
| January 12 | ........................................ | $1,057.25 |
| 17 | ........................................ | 623.41 |
| 20 | ........................................ | 849.20 |

Explain why the verification is unsatisfactory, and what should have been done.

**11-16.** A partially completed charge sales systems flowchart follows. The flowchart depicts the charge sales activities of the Bottom Manufacturing Corporation.

A customer's purchase order is received and a 6-part sales order is prepared, therefrom. The six copies are initially distributed as follows:

Copy No. 1 - Billing copy—to billing department.
Copy No. 2 - Shipping copy—to shipping department.
Copy No. 3 - Credit copy—to credit department.
Copy No. 4 - Stock request copy—to credit department.
Copy No. 5 - Customer copy—to customer.
Copy No. 6 - Sales order copy—file in sales order department.

When each copy of the sales order reaches the applicable department or destination it calls for specific internal control procedures and related documents. Some of the procedures and related documents are indicated on the flowchart. Other procedures and documents are labeled letters (a) to (r).

Required:

List the procedures or the internal documents that are labeled letters (c) to (r) in the flowchart of Bottom Manufacturing Corporation's charge sales system.

Organize your answer as follows (note that an explanation of the letters a and b which appear in the flowchart are entered as examples):

| Flowchart Symbol Letter | Procedures or Internal Documents |
|---|---|
| a. | Prepare 6-part sales order. |
| b. | File by order number. |

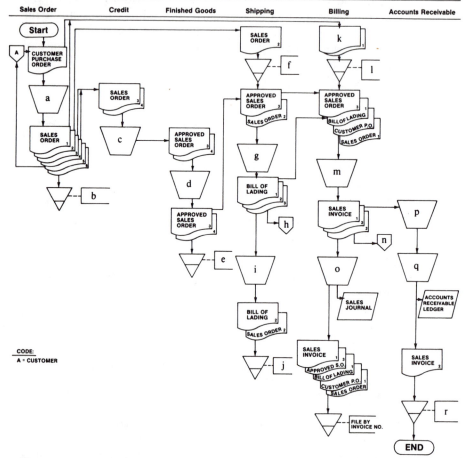

**Figure 11-4.** Bottom Manufacturing Corporation—Flowchart of Credit Sales Activities. (Uniform CPA Examination)

**11-17.** In your examination of the financial statements of the Kay Savings and Loan Association for year ended December 31, 19X1, you find a new account in the general ledger, Home Improvement Loans. You determine that these are unsecured loans not insured by any government agency, made on a discount basis to homeowners who are required to secure life insurance coverage provided by the Association under a group life insurance policy for the outstanding amount and duration of the loan. Borrowers are issued coupon books that require monthly installment payments; however, borrowers may prepay the outstanding balance of the loan at any time in accordance with the terms of their loan contract. This account constitutes a material amount of the total assets of the Association at December 31.

(a) Prepare an audit program for the examination of the new account, Home Improvement Loans.

(b) During your examination of the Home Improvement Loans account the vice-president in charge of the loan department hands you a list of 25 accounts with balances from $300 to $8,000, representing approximately 40% of the total account balance. He states that confirmation requests are not to be prepared for these 25 accounts under any circumstances because the borrowers have requested "no correspondence."

    (1) Would you comply with the vice-president's request? Discuss.

    (2) Assuming you complied with the vice-president's request and did not send confirmation requests to the "no correspondence" accounts, what effect, if any, would this compliance have upon your auditor's short-form report?

(Uniform CPA Examination)

**11-18.** Your client is the Quaker Valley Shopping Center, Inc., a shopping center with 30 store tenants. All leases with the store tenants provide for a fixed rent plus a percentage of sales, net of sales taxes, in excess of a fixed dollar amount computed on an annual basis. Each lease also provides that the landlord may engage a CPA to audit all records of the tenant for assurance that sales are being properly reported to the landlord.

You have been requested by your client to audit the records of the Bali Pearl Restaurant to determine that the sales, totaling $390,000 for the year ended December 31, 19X1, have been properly reported to the landlord. The Restaurant and the Shopping Center entered into a 5-year lease on January 1, 19X1. The Bali Pearl Restaurant offers only table service. No liquor is served. During meal times there are four or five waitresses in attendance who prepare handwritten prenumbered restaurant checks for the customers. Payment is made at a cash register, manned by the proprietor, as the customer leaves. All sales are for cash. The proprietor is also the bookkeeper. Complete files are kept of restaurant checks and cash register tapes. A daily sales book and general ledger are also maintained.

(a) List the auditing procedures that you would employ to verify the total annual sales of the Bali Pearl Restaurant. (Disregard vending machine sales and counter sales of chewing gum, candy, etc.)

(b)   Prepare the auditor's report that you would submit to the Quaker Valley Shopping Center, Inc. Assume that your examination of the records of the Bali Pearl Restaurant disclosed that sales were properly reported to the Shopping Center.

(Uniform CPA Examination)

**11-19.**   The Bryant Department Store has arrangements for customers to pay for purchases over $10.00 on a time-payment plan. The plan calls for a 10 percent down payment, a carrying charge of 10 percent on the balance after the down payment, and payments of $5.00 per month on balances up to $100.

An examination of financial statements for the store should include some form of aging analysis of the installment accounts, for purposes of evaluating the store's provision for doubtful accounts.

(a)   Suggest two different methods of aging such accounts.

(b)   Apply each of these methods to the following accounts, in an examination of balances at January 31.

(c)   Based on the results of your aging, which of the following two accounts would you judge to be the better risk from the standpoint of collectibility? Justify your answer.

J. K. Baker

| | | | | |
|---|---|---|---|---|
| May 10 | Clothing | 63.81 | | |
| | Carrying charge | 5.74 | | |
| | Down payment | | 6.38 | 63.17 |
| June 13 | Cash | | 5.00 | 58.17 |
| July 19 | Cash | | 5.00 | 53.17 |
| Dec. 30 | Cash | | 5.00 | 48.17 |
| Jan. 20 | Cash | | 5.00 | 43.17 |

A. S. Burton

| | | | | |
|---|---|---|---|---|
| June 20 | Sporting goods | 86.54 | | |
| | Carrying charge | 7.79 | | |
| | Down payment | | 8.65 | 85.68 |
| July 20 | Cash | | 5.00 | 80.68 |
| Aug. 20 | Cash | | 5.00 | 75.68 |
| Sept. 20 | Cash | | 5.00 | 70.68 |
| Oct. 20 | Cash | | 5.00 | 65.68 |
| Nov. 20 | Cash | | 5.00 | 60.68 |

**11-20.**   Following is the account of Creek and Brook, a customer of your client, whose financial statements you are examining as of November 30. In connection with this examination, you are asked on December 8 to do the following:

(a)  Age the account on a first-in, first-out basis.

(b)  Age the account on a specific-invoice basis.

(c)  Suggest possible explanations for past due amounts listed for (b).

**Creek and Brook**
Terms: 2/10, n/30

| | | | | | |
|---|---|---|---|---|---|
| July | 1 | Balance forward | | | $3,829.01 |
| | 5 | Inv. 813, | $1,406.18 | | 5,235.19 |
| | 15 | Cash | | $1,406.18 | 3,829.01 |
| | 23 | Inv. 841, | 621.75 | | 4,450.76 |
| | 31 | Inv. 860, | 416.01 · | | 4,866.77 |
| | | Cash | | 3,829.01 | 1,037.76 |
| Aug. | 13 | Inv. 874, | 534.51 | | 1,572.27 |
| | 17 | Inv. 880, | 108.94 | | 1,681.21 |
| | 20 | D.M. 21—Correct Inv. 841 | 25.16 | | 1,706.37 |
| | 23 | Cash | | 1,029.44 | 676.93 |
| | 25 | Inv. 892, | 321.65 | | 998.58 |
| | | Freight | 27.62 | | 1,026.20 |
| | 27 | Cash | | 108.94 | 917.26 |
| Sept. | 3 | Inv. 903, | 251.18 | | 1,168.44 |
| | 10 | Cash | | 534.51 | 633.93 |
| | 18 | Inv. 918, | 634.15 | | 1,268.08 |
| | 25 | Cash | | 349.27 | 918.81 |
| Oct. | 4 | Inv. 1,001, | 65.82 | | 984.63 |
| | 10 | Cash | | 225.94 | 758.69 |
| | 14 | Inv. 1,012, | 491.50 | | 1,250.19 |
| | 15 | C.M. 14 | | 25.24 | 1,224.95 |
| | 18 | Cash | | 592.05 | 632.90 |
| | 26 | Inv. 1,025, | 161.35 | | 794.25 |
| Nov. | 5 | Inv. 1,042, | 225.18 | | 1,019.43 |
| | 7 | Inv. 1,049, | 42.51 | | 1,061.94 |
| | 15 | Cash | | 500.00 | 561.94 |
| Dec. | 4 | Cash | | 200.00 | 361.94 |

**11-21.**  You are engaged in the annual examination of The Mountainview Corporation, a wholesale office supply business, for the year ended September 30. A review of internal control has revealed substantial weaknesses. You have been assigned to examine the accounts receivable. The following information is available at September 30:

1.  The general ledger accounts for accounts receivable and the allowance for doubtful accounts have debit balances of $780,430 and $470, respectively. The total of accounts receivable in the subsidiary ledger is $768,594.

2.  In preparing to confirm accounts receivable you find that the amounts vary greatly in size and decide upon a three-strata procedure. You will use (a) negative confirmation requests for accounts of less than $200; (b) positive confirmation requests, unrestricted random sampling and the technique of estimation sampling for variables for accounts

of $200 to $2,000; and (c) positive confirmation requests for all accounts of $2,000 or more.

3. Your review of accounts receivable and discussions with the client disclose that the following items are included in the accounts receivable (of both the control and the subsidiary ledgers):

(a) Accounts with credit balances total $1,746.

(b) Receivables from officers total $8,500.

(c) Advances to employees total $1,411.

(d) Accounts that are definitely uncollectible total $1,187.

4. Uncollectible accounts are estimated to be ½% of the year's net credit sales of $15,750,000.

5. The confirmations and analysis of the subsidiary ledger provide the following information:

(a) The 1,270 subsidiary ledger accounts with balances of less than $200 total $120,004. Twenty-seven confirmations show a net overstatement of $970. The client agrees that these errors were made.

(b) The 625 subsidiary ledger accounts with balances of $200 to $2,000 total $559,875. The following errors were reported in the replies received from the random sample of 50 positive confirmation requests (the appropriateness of a sample of 50 items was determined statistically based upon desired levels of precision and reliability and investigation established that the customers were correct):

| | Balance per Books | Correct Balance |
|---|---|---|
| Customer No. 714 | $ 847 | $ 827 |
| Customer No. 107 | 500 | 400 |
| Customer No. 101 | 1,900 | 2,100 |
| Customer No. 514 | 206 | 196 |
| Customer No. 909 | 1,400 | 1,250 |
| Customer No. 445 | 400 | —— |
| Customer No. 399 | 1,700 | 1,300 |
| Customer No. 184 | 557 | 597 |
| | $7,510 | $6,670 |

Subsidiary ledger balances of $37,280 were affirmed in the replies to all of the remaining 42 positive confirmation requests.

(c) The 28 accounts with balances of $2,000 and above comprise the remainder of the accounts receivable subsidiary ledger. Investigation established that errors existed in 5 of these accounts and that the net overstatement is $4,570.

Required:

(a) Prepare any journal entry (entries) required (1) to reclassify items which are not trade accounts receivable, (2) to write off uncollectible accounts, and (3) to adjust the allowance for doubtful accounts.

(b) Using the arithmetic mean of the sample as a basis, prepare a schedule computing an estimate of the dollar amount of the middle stratum of accounts receivable at September 30. (Do not compute the standard deviation.)

(c) Assuming that the net adjustment of accounts receivable computed in part "a" was $10,000 and that the estimate of the middle stratum in part "b" was $600,000, prepare a schedule computing an estimate of total trade accounts receivable at September 30.

(Uniform CPA Examination)

**11-22.** Your client, The Summer Comfort Corp., manufactures air conditioners in various sizes from ½ H.P. to 1½ H.P. The air conditioners are sold to distributors, who in turn sell to retail appliance dealers in their assigned areas. Distributors make the bulk of their purchases during the period from February through August. To induce distributors to buy in advance of the normal purchase period and thus reduce company inventories, which tend to build up under the company's policy of constant year-around production, discounts on list prices are given during certain months, as follows:

```
September  ...........................................10%
October    ........................................... 8
November   ........................................... 6
December   ........................................... 4
January    ........................................... 2
```

The company's fiscal year closes on August 31. In discussions with company officials, you learn that the larger volume of sales this year reduced overhead expenses when figured on a per-unit basis; variable costs per unit changed very little. In view of last year's very favorable sales trend, distributors ordered very heavily during the preseason period this year; but as the regular sales season progressed, it became evident that air conditioners were in oversupply, and sales by The Summer Comfort Corp. to its distributors dropped accordingly during that period. Sales of units by sizes and certain other information for the current year, as determined from analyses maintained by the company, were as follows:

| | No. of Units Sold | Total Sales | Distributor List Price | Cost of Sales |
|---|---|---|---|---|
| ½ H.P. | 815 | $ 80,096.53 | $ 99.60 | $ 54,533.28 |
| ¾ H.P. | 1,521 | 239,166.24 | 159.50 | 170,020.44 |
| 1 H.P. | 1,648 | 372,475.36 | 231.15 | 246,163.34 |
| 1½ H.P. | 1,120 | 330,287.48 | 299.75 | 214,905.60 |

The sales account for the current year appears as follows in the general ledger:

| Date | Description | Ref. | Dr. | Cr. | Balance |
|---|---|---|---|---|---|
| Sept. | | SR | | $ 18,718.42 | $ 18,718.42 |
| Oct. | | SR | | 47,835.96 | 66,554.38 |
| Nov. | | SR | | 78,201.39 | 144,755.77 |
| Dec. | | SR | | 99,831.56 | 244,587.33 |
| Jan. | | SR | | 122,293.66 | 366,880.99 |
| | | CR | | 1,416.90 | 368,297.89 |
| Feb. | | SR | | 176,785.06 | 545,082.95 |
| Mar. | | CD | | 586.39 | 545,669.34 |
| | | SR | | 259,978.03 | 805,647.37 |
| Apr. | | SR | | 103,991.21 | 909,638.58 |
| May | | SR | | 41,596.48 | 951,235.06 |
| June | | SR | | 31,197.36 | 982,432.42 |
| July | | SR | | 20,909.24 | 1,003,341.66 |
| Aug. | | SR | | 20,687.24 | 1,024,028.90 |

The following information relating to your examination for the current year is also obtained:

Examination of the cash receipts record for January reveals that the amount of $1,416.90 was received from the sale of an automatic drill press. The general journal also carries the following entry relating to the sale of the drill press:

Accumulated depreciation ...............$3,153.02
Loss on disposition of plant assets ........$2,116.38
  Machinery ...........................           $5,269.40

Examination of the purchase discount account has revealed that there is no entry for discounts taken in March.

The following information is abstracted from the audit working papers covering the previous year's examination of sales:

| | No. of Units Sold | Total Sales | Distributor List Price | Cost of Sales |
|---|---|---|---|---|
| ½ H.P. | 762 | $ 74,361.80 | $ 99.60 | $ 52,503.05 |
| ¾ H.P. | 1,428 | 225,966.72 | 159.50 | 164,371.01 |
| 1 H.P. | 1,560 | 293,539.60 | 191.75 | 239,940.11 |
| 1½ H.P. | 782 | 231,394.45 | 299.75 | 154,511.25 |

## Net Sales by Months

| | |
|---|---:|
| Sept. | $ 15,042.24 |
| Oct. | 30,753.02 |
| Nov. | 39,276.96 |
| Dec. | 56,157.69 |
| Jan. | 65,517.31 |
| Feb. | 116,995.22 |
| Mar. | 183,849.65 |
| Apr. | 91,924.87 |
| May | 83,568.48 |
| June | 58,497.65 |
| July | 41,784.33 |
| Aug. | 41,895.15 |
| | $825,262.57 |

Required:

Using the information just presented, prepare working papers covering your examination of sales and gross margin for the current year.

(Assume that internal control has aready been reviewed and showed no serious weaknesses.)

# Chapter 12

# PURCHASES, EXPENSES, AND ACCOUNTS PAYABLE

Raw materials or completed products are purchased and expenses are incurred for the purpose of generating revenue. Each expenditure associated with these purchases must be properly authorized and the resulting inventory or expense fully accounted for in order to be able to minimize these costs and expenses and hence maximize net income from operations. The discussion in this chapter is primarily related to purchases to acquire inventories, but similar considerations exist for the purchase of services and accountability for the resulting expense. Services will, however, be received at disparate locations representing the point of use, and acknowledgment of receipt of a service will originate from the location involved rather than from a central receiving area for all tangible acquisitions. Also, services do not involve subsequent accountability beyond the point of receipt or use, except to the extent that expenses should be charged or allocated to the product or service produced whenever feasible for inventory costing purposes and for pricing decisions in the sale of the product or service.

### Control Considerations

As stated, control must begin at the point of authorization for the purchase of items for inventory or of needed services. There must be evidence that the appropriate materials, goods, or services have been received and that the resulting charges are correct and are as authorized as necessary prerequisites to the authorization of disbursements to liquidate the resulting liabilities. Recognition of the liability for the purchase of goods and materials must also involve establishing accountability for the physical items received. The subsystem used to handle accounting and control over inventories and cost of sales is discussed in Chapter 13.

Typical activities associated with purchasing of goods and services and recognition of the related liabilities preparatory to payment are shown in Figure 12-1. The comments in the next section pertain to this flowchart.

### Comments on Illustrative Flowchart of Purchases/Payables Procedures

1. The flowchart indicates that purchases are initiated by the stores section of production control in the manufacturing division, but the only responsibility of the stores section should be custody of raw materials and finished goods. Purchase requisitions should be prepared by the material control section on the basis of production schedules for more costly materials and on the basis of inventory status reports for lower cost materials regularly carried in stock. The inventory records maintained under the factory accountant would be the source of the inventory status reports. In wholesale or retail organizations, buyers or department managers would make purchasing decisions based on similar inventory status reports. When inventory stocks are maintained on the

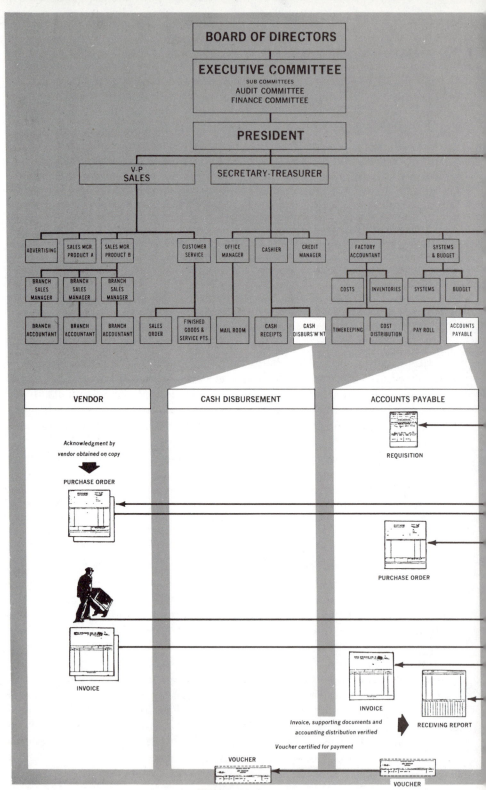

*Figure 12-1.*

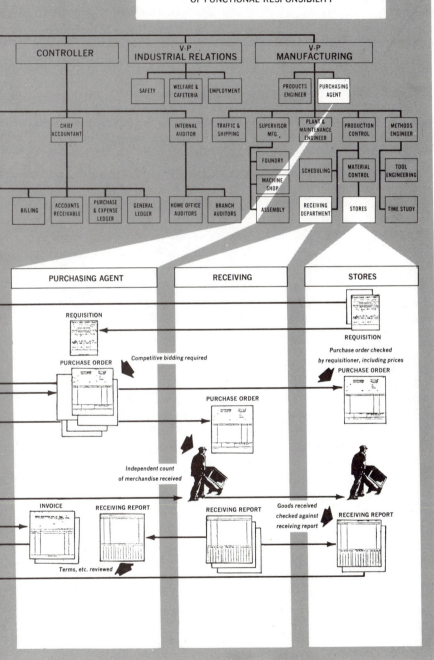

# PURCHASES

PROCEDURAL FLOW CHART SHOWN IN RELATION
TO ORGANIZATION CHART TO PORTRAY
THE CONTROL OBTAINED THROUGH SEGREGATION
OF FUNCTIONAL RESPONSIBILITY

CONTROLLER

V-P
INDUSTRIAL RELATIONS

V-P
MANUFACTURING

SAFETY
WELFARE &
CAFETERIA
EMPLOYMENT

PRODUCTS
ENGINEER
PURCHASING
AGENT

CHIEF
ACCOUNTANT

INTERNAL
AUDITOR
TRAFFIC &
SHIPPING
SUPERVISOR
MFG.
PLANT &
MAINTENANCE
ENGINEER
PRODUCTION
CONTROL
METHODS
ENGINEER

FOUNDRY
SCHEDULING
MATERIAL
CONTROL
TOOL
ENGINEERING

MACHINE
SHOP

BILLING
ACCOUNTS
RECEIVABLE
PURCHASE
& EXPENSE
LEDGER
GENERAL
LEDGER
HOME OFFICE
AUDITORS
BRANCH
AUDITORS
ASSEMBLY
RECEIVING
DEPARTMENT
STORES
TIME STUDY

PURCHASING AGENT

RECEIVING

STORES

REQUISITION

REQUISITION

PURCHASE ORDER

Competitive bidding required

Purchase order checked
by requisitioner, including prices

PURCHASE ORDER

PURCHASE ORDER

Independent count
of merchandise received

INVOICE
RECEIVING REPORT
RECEIVING REPORT
Goods received
checked against
receiving report
RECEIVING REPORT

Terms, etc. reviewed

Source: AICPA *Internal Control*

basis of past demand, an inventory model is used to determine the re-order point and the economic order quantity (EOQ). If record keeping is automated on a computer, the computer program will regularly make the reorder point and EOQ calculations and compare those results with the quantity on hand; if the quantity on hand is less than the reorder point, the computer program will prepare a complete purchase order including the vendor's name and address when there is a regular source of supply. If there is no regular source, the vendor information will be filled in by the purchasing department after bids have been obtained or price lists have been consulted.

2.   The department originating purchase requisitions will generally retain one copy in a tickler file, removing the copy from the file when the copy of the purchase order is received and verification is made that details of the purchase order are correct.

3.   One copy of the purchase order should be retained by the purchasing department in a tickler file arranged in serial number order. When acknowledgment is received from the vendor, the purchasing department copy of the order should be transferred to a tickler file arranged according to the date that delivery is to be made. Any orders remaining in the file after the scheduled delivery date would then become the basis for initiating follow-up action.

4.   The receiving department copy of the purchase order is the authorization for the goods to be received and to be inspected in order to determine whether the goods are as ordered. By not accepting goods for which no receiving authorization is on file, the business avoids costs of unpacking, repacking, and returning goods that have not been ordered. The receiving department copy of the purchase order should, however, have the quantity blocked out, thereby assuring that the receiving clerk will make an actual count of the goods. Because the purchase order contains all necessary identifying information, the receiving department copy usually becomes the receiving report upon entering the quantity received, thereby obviating writing the receiving information on a separate report form.

5.   As indicated, a copy of the receiving report form should accompany the goods in order to permit stores to verify that it has received all of the goods for which it will be held accountable.

6.   Accounts payable will assemble in a voucher packet its copy of the purchase order, the invoice that has been verified by purchasing, and the copy of the receiving report; verify the invoice for accuracy of price, shipping terms, extensions, and footing; indicate what accounts are to be charged for the purchase; and enter the purchase (or expense item) in the voucher register (purchases journal). If the system is computerized, the receiving reports and invoices will become inputs to the

computer, with the computer doing the required matching and developing the appropriate accounting entries.

7. Because the goods and the invoice will seldom arrive simultaneously, accounts payable should maintain a file of unmatched invoices and a file of unmatched receiving reports, removing an item from the file when the additional document is received.

8. If advance payments to vendors, partial shipments, and special discounts based on purchase volume are involved, it will usually be desirable that a detailed accounts payable ledger be maintained, with purchases recorded in the ledger when they are entered in the voucher register.

9. If payments are made according to the terms of each invoice, a voucher-check form is customarily prepared by accounts payable and held in a tickler file until the due date for the payment, at which time the voucher packet is forwarded to the cash disbursement unit for payment. The file of unpaid vouchers will constitute the vouchers (accounts) payable subsidiary record in that case.

10. At some point in the process, the audited voucher packet should be routed to the inventory records section for entry into the detailed perpetual inventory records. If the system is computerized, the inputs for the payables records will also provide the basis for computer updating of perpetual inventory records.

## Evaluation of Internal Control Objectives and Features

This section follows the pattern that was established in the preceding chapter on revenues and receivables, with related compliance tests shown in italics.

### Operating Objectives

*All transactions are properly authorized:*

- Purchase requisitions are initiated by material control or inventory records to authorize placing of purchase orders. *Inquiry, inspection.*
- Purchase orders are issued for all goods and services to be acquired. Telephoned orders should be confirmed by preparation of a written purchase order. Orders should be placed only after competitive bids are obtained when so required by company policy. *Inquiry, inspection.*
- One copy of the purchase order is used to authorize acceptance of incoming goods and materials. *Inquiry, observation.*
- Purchase returns are authorized by preparation of an accounts payable

debit memo and a shipping order for the goods to be returned. *Inquiry, observation.*

### All authorizations resulted in action being taken.

- One copy of the purchase requisition is held as a control copy, pending receipt of a copy of the purchase order to show that the order has been placed. *Inquiry, observation.*
- One copy of the purchase order is held as a control copy pending vendor acknowledgment of the order. Upon acknowledgment, the purchase order copy should be transferred to a tickler file according to promised delivery date, pending receipt of a copy of the receiving report to show that the items ordered have been received. *Inquiry, observation.*

### Access to assets is permitted only in accordance with management authorization.

- Materials and goods received are held in a secure area and released only on the basis of proper authorization in the form of a materials requisition, shipping order, or debit memo for goods to be returned. Goods purchased by a retail organization are usually transferred directly to the selling floor, but then the selling department should be responsible for security controls. *Inquiry, observation.*

## Data Processing Objectives—Internal Accounting Control

### Accounting and computer operations are independent of all operating responsibilities.

*Inquiry* and *observation* that maximum feasible segregation of these activities exists:

| Operating | Accounting/Data Processing |
|---|---|
| Materials control | Accounts payable records |
| Stores | General ledger records |
| Purchasing | Computer data entry |
| Receiving | Computer operations |

### Only valid transactions that have been duly authorized are accepted for entry in the accounting records.

- Prior to recording liabilities that are being recognized, a voucher packet should be prepared that includes the purchase order, receiving report, and vendor's invoice as authorization to recognize the liability. *Inspection.*

### All transactions are entered in the accounting records.

- Control copies of the purchase order and receiving report, plus a file of unmatched invoices (invoices received for which the receiving report has not yet been received) should ensure that all liabilities are entered in the records, although the recording of liabilities need not be closely controlled, because vendors can be expected to send notices on invoices for which payment is delinquent, as discussed in the previous chapter with respect to collection follow-up on accounts receivable. *Inquiry, observation.*

- Serial numbers of debit memos are accounted for to ensure that all adjustments and purchase returns are entered in the accounting records to reduce the recorded liability. *Inquiry, observation.*

### *Accounting entries correctly reflect transaction amounts.*

- The voucher that is prepared for a voucher packet should be verified by reference to the supporting documents before an accounting entry is made. *Inquiry, observation, inspection, reperformance of voucher audit activities.*
- Batch control totals or daily voucher register totals should be proved against amounts entered. *Inquiry, inspection.*

### *Transactions are correctly classified for accounting entry.*

- A chart of accounts should be used as the basis for designating the account coding of the debit distribution to be shown on the accounts payable voucher. *Inquiry, observation, inspection, reperformance.*
- Standard cost variances should be calculated and accounted for on the basis of the difference between invoice cost and standard cost. *Inquiry, inspection, reperformance.*
- Account classifications should be adequate to provide for appropriate responsibility reporting of expenses and accountability over assets received and should conform to GAAP. *Observation to indicate adequate responsibility reporting and asset accountability.*

### *Recorded transactions are correctly processed.*

- The following proofs should be utilized whenever appropriate (*Inquiry, observation, inspection, reperformance*):

    Updated subsidiary detail balances are regularly proved against running control totals.

    Periodic trial balances of general ledger accounts are prepared to prove equality of debits and credits.

    Posting proofs are made of manual or machine-prepared records to prove

    Correct pickup of previous balance.

    Correct posting of debit/credit amounts.

    Selection of correct account.

### *Monitoring Objectives*

*Regular comparison is made of liability records with underlying liabilities; third-party proofs of accounting records should be utilized.*

- Statements received from vendors (based on their accounts receivable records) should be reconciled with accounts/vouchers payable records. *Inquiry, inspection.*
- Managers of operations are held responsible for variances from budget or standard cost, and managers are thus prompted to review for accuracy reports of expenses for which they are responsible. *Inquiry, observation.*

*There is an effective internal audit function.*

- Internal auditors should regularly review and evaluate internal controls, perform compliance tests, and if appropriate, make recommendations for improvement in the controls. *Inquiry, review of audit planning, inspection of working papers.*
- Operational audit activities such as those in the following list should be considered by the internal audit staff as a service to management in controlling operations. *Inquiry* by the independent auditor about operational audit activities would be optional, but a management letter would appropriately include any findings or recommendations concerning operational audit coverage and general effectiveness of management and efficiency of operations with respect to such matters as

    Investigation of causes of excessive variances from budgeted expenses or standard costs.

    Adequacy of follow-up action on open items remaining in control files for purchase requisitions, purchase orders, receiving reports, and invoices.

    Establishment of reasonable policies in requiring competitive bids.

    Satisfaction of user departments with purchasing activities relative to materials costs and quality and vendor performance in terms of meeting delivery commitments.

    Cost/benefit review of internal control requirements relative to preaudit of vouchers payable for invoice accuracy and receipt of goods. (Companies frequently find that about 80 percent of the purchase orders placed account for only 20 percent of the dollar expenditures, and that the errors and discrepancies revealed through tight internal controls do not justify the cost of the controls over the large volume of smaller purchase orders.)

    Review to determine whether there is a need to report outstanding purchase orders or "open to buy" for a retail organization based on inventory planning and orders placed. When such reports are prepared, their accuracy should be subject to internal audit testing.

    Consideration of whether a report of purchase volume with major suppliers would represent useful management information and recommend that such information be developed and reported if it would be useful.

## Substantive Audit Objectives and Procedures

### Relative Risk Considerations

The reader should recall that internal control objectives for revenues and receivables involve protection against failure to record a receivable when a shipment of goods or provision of services has occurred. By contrast, internal control over payables is primarily concerned with preventing unauthorized expenditures and detecting liabilities that result from attempts to cause unauthorized disbursement of funds for personal gain or for an illegal purpose such as for political contributions or bribes.

The nature of the risks that should be considered in an independent audit also differ. For revenues and receivables the risk of overstatement is preeminent, resulting from the possibility that management might seek to present an improved appearance of operating results and/or financial position, or that receivables would be overstated as a result of an employee's fraudulent abstraction of customer remittances. With respect to purchases and liabilities, however, the opposite concern would prevail—namely, that the amounts might be understated. Such understatement could result from failing to record the liability for purchase transactions through oversight or as a result of a conscious attempt to produce an appearance of improved operating and financial results. To accommodate this risk that liabilities may exist but be unrecorded, the auditor should look to reciprocal populations that would contain evidence of the transactions that have occurred and trace such evidence to the accounting records, in order to determine whether any liabilities at the balance sheet date have not been recorded. Similar considerations and risks would exist for a privately held concern seeking additional financing, but the situation would be reversed if the likely objective would be to obtain the benefits of reduced income taxes. Under those circumstances client effort would be directed toward overstating expenses and liabilities, and the auditor should give special attention to that possibility in developing the audit program for substantive tests.

Although the audit objectives for substantive tests of purchases, expenses, and liabilities are identical to those introduced in the preceding chapter, the risk of omitted liabilities is addressed by giving special attention to the objective relating to the comprehensiveness of the accounting records. The following discussion considers those objectives and the related substantive audit procedures and tests.

### Conformity of Client's Financial Statements with Disclosure and Other Requirements of Financial Reporting Standards

The following standards are applicable to the reporting of expenses:

1. Significant costs and expenses should be listed as separate amounts in the interests of adequate disclosure. Cost of sales, depreciation and depletion, interest expense, and federal income taxes are items that are normally shown separately. When revenues are reported for business segments, related expenses should be similarly reported.

2. The amount of federal income taxes shown as an expense should

be based on transactions reflected in the income statement, except for minor recurring differences between book and taxable income. If the amount shown for federal income tax expense differs materially from the amount to be paid, as when income taxes are apportioned to expenses or incomes not appearing in the current income statement (tax allocation resulting from timing difference), or when there has been a carry forward or carry back of losses, the explanation for the difference should be given. The SEC also requires a reconciliation of the reported total tax expense and the tax expense computed at the statutory federal income tax rate.

3. Material nonoperating nonrecurring expenses and losses should be segregated from regular operating expenses. Gains or losses from discontinued operations should be reported net of tax following income from continuing operations. Prior period adjustments and related income taxes should be reported as adjustments of the opening balance of retained earnings, and the effect, if any, on income of the prior year should be disclosed. Those rare items qualifying for treatment as extraordinary items and the related taxes should be shown as the final item on the income statement before net income.

There are relatively few financial reporting considerations in presenting accounts payable in the balance sheet:

1. Only amounts owed to regular trade creditors are properly included as accounts payable. Liabilities arising from other types of transactions and material amounts owed to nonconsolidated affiliated companies should be shown separately.

2. Liabilities becoming due and payable within one year, or within one complete operating cycle if the cycle is longer than one year, should be classified as current liabilities.

3. Assets and liabilities should not be offset; hence, material amounts of accounts payable debit balances should be reclassified to the asset side of the statement.


### Reasonableness of Account Balances

*Perform Analytical Review.* Purchases will not appear as a separate item in the financial statements if inventory accounts are maintained on a perpetual basis under good internal accounting control. Of course, the purchases will be reflected in the inventory and cost of goods sold accounts, and the comprehensive analytical review procedures that are applicable to those accounts will indicate whether purchases have been stated fairly. Most important will be comparisons between current and previous years of inventory turnover and the percentage relationship of cost of sales to sales, or the complement of the latter figure, which would be the percentage of gross margin.

With respect to other expense items, perhaps the most important comparisons that the auditor should make are between the various costs and expenses for the current year and those for the preceding year. It is largely for this reason that final figures for the preceding year are included in the auditor's working trial balance. Figures should be compared in terms of absolute amounts, unit costs, and percentage relationships to sales whenever possible. Note that schedule I/S in the illustrative working papers, the top trial balance of the income statement accounts, is set up to permit two of these types of comparisons. Any substantial variations disclosed by such comparisons should be investigated, and the explanations should be noted in the auditor's working papers. Because variations may be the clue to classification errors or changes in classification, it is important that the auditor's investigations be thorough and that explanations not be accepted merely because they sound logical.

The monthly amounts charged to some of the more active expense accounts, such as cost of sales and payroll accounts, should be compared. Such a comparison is illustrated by schedule 20-1, which summarizes the monthly factory payroll distribution entries. Again, it is important that variations be investigated and explanations noted in the working papers.

When clients operate under a standard cost system, the system automatically compares material, labor, and overhead costs with standard amounts and reports the variations as separate figures. Schedule 20 illustrates the manner in which such variances may be treated in the operating accounts and shows how the major classes of variances can be subdivided to give management additional information. As with other variances, the auditor should investigate any amounts that appear out of line.

If clients prepare budgets, the auditor should compare actual and budgeted amounts. Such a comparison provides further evidence of the validity and consistency of the client's classification of expenses. Management officials should be thoroughly familiar with the causes for any budget variances, and the auditor should, therefore, discuss the variances with such officials. The auditor's general knowledge of the client's operations for the year should enable the auditor to ascertain whether the stated explanations of the budget variances are reasonable. The additional comprehension of operating figures which management gains through comparisons with budgeted amounts is a vital element of effective internal control.

The various explanations that the auditor gives in the working papers concerning variations that have been noted may often be valuable apart from their significance in substantiating reported costs and expenses. If the auditor prepares a long-form report for management, the explanations will provide the necessary information for the auditor's analysis of the results of operations, usually one of the most important sections of a long-form report.

The balance sheet amount of accounts payable will vary with the amount of recent purchasing activity and with the diligence exercised in cleaning up outstanding obligations at the end of the year. The auditor should consider these factors in deciding whether the accounts payable total reflects all amounts actually owed.

Another procedure by which the auditor may ascertain whether costs and expenses have been properly classified involves analyzing or scanning selected accounts. The accounts chosen should be those likely to be charged with items that are unusual or that occur only infrequently. Such items are, of course, more susceptible to classification errors. Typical examples of accounts that usually warrant the auditor's special attention would include miscellaneous expense, corporate expense, entertainment expense, royalty expense, charitable contributions, and legal and other professional fees. Other accounts that would tend to fall in the same category, but that are usually reviewed in connection with the examination of related balance sheet accounts, would include repairs and maintenance, interest expense, and losses on sales of securities or plant assets.

As illustrated by schedules 40-2 and 40-3, major items noted in analyzing or scanning the various accounts should be described, and the auditor's verification of the amounts should be noted. Typical verification procedures would include reference to authorization for the expenditures and examination of invoices or paid checks.

Manufacturing concerns are likely to find that factory overhead has been underapplied or overapplied to production, and if that situation exists, the auditor should give it close attention, especially if the amount is material. The occurrence of such a situation indicates that the overhead rate used during the year was not in line with the actual operating results. There may be some instances in which the auditor would feel justified in allowing the amount of underapplied or overapplied overhead to be taken directly to income, but such a treatment tends to distort net income. If distortion would result, the auditor should request that the client adjust the amount of overhead applied to agree with the actual experience for the year. As illustrated by adjusting journal entry number 2 in the illustrative working papers, the adjustment will affect inventory as well as cost of sales and will thus change the amount of net income for the year.

### Synchronization of Events and Records

The cutoff in recording expenses and the related liabilities at the end of the year is critical inasmuch as the expenses will affect net income and the liabilities will affect the current ratio. Given the relative risk discussed earlier that these items might be understated or omitted either intentionally or through oversight, the auditor should emphasize a search for unrecorded liabilities by thoroughly examining all reciprocal populations. In a first audit, synchronization must also be examined at the beginning of the year (the end of the preceding year) to detect any cutoff errors at that date inasmuch as such errors would also affect net income for the current year.

*Search for Unrecorded Liabilities; Examine Reciprocal Populations.* Because most liabilities arising from operating transactions will be payable within a relatively short period of time, entries in the voucher register and cash disbursements record following the close of the year will constitute the reciprocal population. In addition, the fact that liabilities may also be recorded through the general journal suggests the review of that record as well for the period subsequent to the balance sheet date.

The typical approach in the hindsight review of subsequent entries is to begin with voucher register entries in the following period, selecting all major amounts and a random sample of lesser amounts to provide maximum coverage as well as representativeness. Although emphasis should be on entries for the first two to four weeks of the following year, later entries should be scanned for large unusual items through the period until the completion of the audit field work. Supporting documents for the selected entries should then be examined to determine whether any liability existed at the balance sheet date. Locating the desired documents in the client's files tends to be a time-consuming clerical process, and hence the client should be encouraged to have a clerical employee locate the desired documents for the auditor. For any of these documents that indicate that a liability existed at the balance sheet date, including goods shipped f.o.b. shipping point prior to the end of the year, full details should be listed in the working papers, as was done on schedule BB-1.

Next, the cash disbursements record should be reviewed. All major disbursements should represent the payment of vouchers included in the year-end balance of accounts payable, or vouchers reviewed in connection with the examination of voucher register entries made after the balance sheet date. Investigation of any disbursements not previously covered in such examinations is likely to reveal an unrecorded liability.

The review of the general journal involves no special procedures, but each entry should be carefully studied for any hint that a year-end liability may be involved.

Unrecorded liabilities revealed by the above procedures should be analyzed carefully in terms of their materiality, since only material items need be referred to the client for adjustment. Some of the parameters of materiality are suggested by the following example, in which different degrees of materiality result even though the three items are of equal amount.

| Invoice Date | Date Goods or Services Received | Date Recorded in Records | Freight Terms | Description | Amount |
|---|---|---|---|---|---|
| 12/29 | 12/31 | 1/3 | F.O.B. shipping point | Materials | $500 |
| 12/28 | 1/3 | 1/3 | F.O.B. shipping point | Materials | $500 |
| 12/30 | 12/29 | 1/3 | —————— | Machinery repairs | $500 |

Based on invoice dates, all three items involve liabilities not recorded at December 31. Further investigation of the first item reveals that it was not included in the inventory cutoff reconciliation figure for unmatched receiving reports (although the materials were included when the physical inventory was counted), so that it has the effect of understating either purchases or, under the perpetual inventory method, the inventory variance. These errors would in turn cause an overstatement of income. The machinery repair item also understates an expense and overstates income. The second item represents a purchase of materials for which title is presumed to have passed at the balance sheet date,[1] and there is hence an unrecorded asset for merchandise in transit, but the item would not affect the income statement.

Differences in the materiality of each of the three items obviously are not related to the unrecorded liability, because all of the items are for the same amount and none of the amounts has been reflected in the records. Our attention must therefore be directed to the unrecorded debits for any indication that the items vary in materiality. The first and third items are more material for the following reasons:

1. They affect net income whereas the second item affects assets; net income is usually the most important figure on the financial statements.

2. The effect on net income of each of these items will be proportionally greater than the effect on total assets by the second item, because invariably the net income figure will be smaller than the figure for total assets.

3. Because the unrecorded liability for the second item is offset by an unrecorded current asset, items 1 and 3 will cause a greater distortion of the important current ratio.

The matter of materiality might be further refined by considering an unrecorded liability for the purchase of plant equipment costing $500. This item, because it does not affect net income, would be less material than items 1 and 3, but it would be more material than item 2 because of the greater distortion of the current ratio.

In most cases when unrecorded liabilities are found they will involve merchandise in transit, as the normal accounting routines do not pro-

---

[1]Based on the usually valid presumption that invoices are dated the day that materials are shipped. On occasion, however, customers may be granted delayed billing, in which case the date the goods were shipped or received will govern.

vide for recognition of such liabilities. As suggested by the preceding discussion, such unrecorded liabilities will have only a nominal effect on the financial statements unless relatively large amounts are involved. The result is that adjustment of the statements to reflect such items is often waived as not materially affecting the statements. Many a staff assistant, on being assigned for the first time to the search for unrecorded liabilities, has discovered thousands of dollars of unrecorded liabilities for merchandise in transit. But then the sense of accomplishment in having detected a misstatement of such a large amount in the client's figures may well be dissipated by the senior accountant's decision to pass any adjustment of the amount on the grounds of immateriality! Nevertheless, the working papers should contain a record of all unrecorded liabilities noted in the examination. Individual items may be immaterial, but the cumulative effect of a number of such items may well be another matter, and all of the information should be present so that the final decision on materiality can be made by the senior accountant, or perhaps even by the manager or partner. One accountant has said that he likes to have the information available, even on immaterial amounts, because the information can sometimes be used for "bargaining" purposes. That is, if there is another, more important adjustment that the client is reluctant to make, the client may be induced to make the one adjustment on the condition that the auditor will agree to waive the second adjustment.

If unrecorded liabilities affect net income, their relative materiality is partly offset by the effect of income taxes in the case of a corporation. A $10,000 understatement of expense would cause income to be overstated by only about $5,000. With corporate income tax rates at nearly 50 percent the decrease of $10,000 in income before taxes would be offset by about a $5,000 decrease in income taxes, leaving only a $5,000 decrease in net income after taxes. It might appear that the client would be anxious to make such an adjustment, and if so, the auditor should certainly oblige. On the other hand, unless tax rates change, the adjustment will merely cause a shift in taxes between two years, and the client may prefer not to reopen the accounting records for the adjustment if the auditor concludes that the effect is not material.

*Ascertain Existence of Recorded Payables.* As was true in the case of accounts receivable, audit procedures designed to determine the existence of the amount shown in the balance sheet may disclose errors or unrecorded transactions. (See the discussion under the *existence* objective.)

*Matching of Expenses and Revenues.* Expense debits resulting from the recognition of liabilities should represent either period expenses or the cost of benefits that have already been utilized in the revenue-producing process. The client's chart of accounts and voucher register entries during the year should be reviewed for compliance with the matching principle, and amounts properly recorded as prepaid expenses at the time the liability was recognized should be reviewed to determine whether the related benefits have been utilized at the balance sheet date, so that the amounts should be transferred to expense.

### Comprehensiveness of Records

*Evaluate Internal Control.* Although internal control over liabilities is primarily directed toward establishing the validity and propriety of liabilities before they are recorded and approved for payment, there should also be controls to ensure that all liabilities of an organization are recognized in the accounts. The documents prepared to show that goods or services have been received would be the major aspect of controls related to the recognition of liabilities. As mentioned, however, such controls over payables are not overly important because vendors can be expected to remind customers about liabilities if they are not paid when they become due.

*Search for Unrecorded Liabilities.* Again illustrating the dual aspects of various procedures, the search for unrecorded liabilities in testing the synchronization of events and the accounting records provides the auditor with an indication about the comprehensiveness of the accounting records and the existence of unrecorded liabilities.

### Arithmetic and Clerical Accuracy: Agreement of Details and Control Totals

*Prepare or Test Trial Balance of Subsidiary Ledger.* If a hard copy accounts payable ledger is maintained, the audit procedures with respect to the trial balance will be roughly comparable to those discussed under receivables, and the hard copy records make it possible for the auditor to carry out the trial balance work whenever convenient. Because understatement is the major concern in this case, however, if a sample is to be tested, the test should be from the ledger to the trial balance.

Timing of the tests becomes critical if the payables records are maintained on an open-item basis in the form of a file of unpaid vouchers or in magnetic form as part of an on-line system. Open-item files are subject to constant change as new payables are added and older ones are removed for payment. The only moment that the file will precisely reflect the accounts payable amount to be shown on the balance sheet will be at the close of business on the balance sheet date. To assist the auditor when computerized payables records are on line, a memory dump of the payables file at the close of business on the balance sheet should make it possible for the auditor to use the tape record of the payables at any time that is convenient to the auditor. The client's trial balance listing of the open items in an unpaid voucher file at the balance sheet date provides similar convenience if the client's records are manually maintained.

There still remains, however, the problem of inspecting the underlying documents in support of the file, or the listing of the amounts to prove the accuracy of the record. This procedure will become more time-consuming for every day that the procedure is delayed past the balance sheet date, because additional vouchers will have been removed from the file for payment. The vouchers removed for payment will have to be located either within the payment process, or in the paid voucher file if payment has been made—steps that are preferably carried out by the client's employees in the interest of minimizing the audit fee. Under these circumstances there will be no feasible way for the auditor to test from the voucher file to the listing in order to discover omitted items, but the audit steps related to searching for unrecorded liabilities should solve that problem.

Also to be considered relative to the trial balance testing are payables in process at the balance sheet date for which the necessary matching of related documents cannot be completed—vendor invoices received for which the goods have not yet arrived, and goods that have arrived but the invoice has not. If the client has instituted comprehensive closing procedures, the content of the file of unmatched invoices for goods shipped f.o.b. shipping point and all unmatched receiving reports should become the basis for an adjusting journal entry to record these additional liabilities. In that case these amounts will be part of the payables to be shown on the balance sheet, and the auditor should inspect these documents as well as the unpaid vouchers that had been processed in the normal fashion at the balance sheet date. The inclusion of unmatched receiving reports in the accounts payable total is illustrated in working paper schedule BB.

Any payables accounts with debit balances should be summed separately, and if the amount is material, the debit balances should be reclassified as a receivable. Furthermore, the reclassified amount should be subjected to normal audit procedures for receivables, including confirmation of the amounts shown on the client's records.

### Existence of Payables

Given the fact that if payables are misstated, they are more likely to be understated, an audit need give only limited consideration to the existence of those liabilities that have been recorded. The audit procedures applicable to the existence objective involve gaining contact with evidence of the liability, and the procedures also establish the correctness of the recorded amount and may indicate whether all liabilities have been recorded.

*Client Internal Controls.* Good internal control over the audit of liabilities prior to entry in the records and payment should provide substantial evidence of the existence of recorded liabilities. That evidence would be supplemented if the client receives monthly statements of account from major vendors and if the client reconciles those statements with the recorded liabilities. If compliance tests indicate that the prescribed procedures are in fact carried out, substantial assurance would be provided that liabilities have been properly recorded.

*Substantive Tests of Supporting Evidence.* Unlike accounts receivable, for which only limited external supporting evidence is generally available, vendor invoices and statements provide good externally created evidence in support of recorded accounts payable. In addition, if statements are available, they also supply evidence that all liabilities have been recorded. Inasmuch as relatively good evidence of liabilities should be available at the client's premises, confirmation of liabilities by correspondence with creditors is not a required audit procedure—an important contrast in the audit of payables as compared with the audit of receivables.

Nevertheless, if conditions are less favorable and internal control is weak, confirmation of accounts payable should be considered. The most expeditious approach to confirmation involves having the client request that statements of account be sent directly to the auditor, rather than requesting confirmation of a balance, because the added information available on the statement should facilitate accounting for reconciling items. Requesting that the statement be in open-item format should further simplify the reconciliation process. Statement requests should be mailed in advance of the date for which the statement is requested so that vendors with open-item files can extract the information on the only date that the files will reflect the requested information.

It should also be noted that confirmation of payables should help to disclose any unrecorded liabilities. To maximize the effectiveness of that aspect of the confirmation procedure, the requests should cover not only all accounts with large balances, but also any accounts with a large amount of activity during the year but with a zero or a small balance at the year end. These would be accounts that would be most likely to involve an understatement of the year-end balance on the client's records.

If the client is known to enter into forward purchase arrangements, the confirmation request to the vendor should also request the amount of unfilled purchase orders from the client held at the balance sheet date. If abnormal amounts of commitments exist, the information should be disclosed in the notes to the financial statements; and if firm prices have been agreed to, any declines in market prices below those prices should be recognized as a current loss under the lower of cost or market principle.

### Ownership of Payables

As a rule it can be safely assumed that the client is indeed the obligor for all liabilities that have been recorded; nevertheless, the possibility that the facts may be otherwise should not be overlooked, and all relevant information should be considered in determining whether accounts payable are fairly presented in the client's balance sheet.

### Valuation of Payables

Accounts payable will seldom involve valuation problems, although if any amounts are subject to interest charges, the accrued interest should be added to the liability account and shown as an expense of the period. If amounts are in dispute, a legal opinion should be obtained in order to determine what the amount of the liability is ultimately likely to be. Payables may be shown at gross or net of cash discounts, but the latter treatment is preferred.

### Timing of the Audit Work

The critical role of the cutoff in determining liability and expense amounts, and the fact that purchasing activity can be varied at the client's will, make it imperative that the substantive procedures related to payables be performed as of the client's balance sheet date. This situation represents another major difference between the examination of receivables and the examination of payables. As is true generally, however, the review and evaluation of internal control and analytical review procedures can be performed on a preliminary basis prior to the end of the year. With respect to purchases, these preliminary procedures plus the year-end procedures relating to synchronization of events and accounting records and the comprehensiveness of the records should provide an adequate basis for the auditor's opinion.

## Questions/Problems

For multiple-choice questions 12-1 through 12-7, indicate the letter of the single answer that *best* completes the statement or answers the question, and justify the choice that you have made.

**12-1.** To avoid potential errors and irregularities a well-designed system of internal accounting control in the accounts payable area should include a separation of which of the following functions?

a. Cash disbursements and invoice verification.

b. Invoice verification and merchandise ordering.

c. Physical handling of merchandise received and preparation of receiving reports.

d. Check signing and cancellation of payment documentation.

(Uniform CPA Examination)

**12-2.** Which of the following is an internal control procedure that would prevent a paid disbursement voucher from being presented for payment a second time?

a. Vouchers should be prepared by individuals who are responsible for signing disbursement checks.

b. Disbursement vouchers should be approved by at least two responsible management officials.

c. The date on a disbursement voucher should be within a few days of the date the voucher is presented for payment.

d. The official signing the check should compare the check with the voucher and should deface the voucher documents.

(Uniform CPA Examination)

**12-3.** To strengthen the system of internal accounting control over the purchase of merchandise, a company's receiving department should

a. Accept merchandise only if a purchase order or approval granted by the purchasing department is on hand.

b. Accept and count all merchandise received from the usual company vendors.

c. Rely on shipping documents for the preparation of receiving reports.

d. Be responsible for the physical handling of merchandise but *not* the preparation of receiving reports.

(Uniform CPA Examination)

**12-4.** A client's materials-purchasing cycle begins with requisitions from user departments and ends with the receipt of materials and recognition of a liability. An auditor's primary objective in reviewing this cycle is to

a. Evaluate the reliability of information generated as a result of the purchasing process.

b. Investigate the physical handing and recording of unusual acquisitions of materials.

    c. Consider the need to be on hand for the annual physical count if this system is *not* functioning properly.

    d. Ascertain that materials said to be ordered, received, and paid for are on hand.

(Uniform CPA Examination)

**12-5.** Which of the following would detect an understatement of a purchase discount?

    a. Verify footings and crossfootings of purchases and disbursement records.

    b. Compare purchase invoice terms with disbursement records and checks.

    c. Compare approved purchase orders with receiving reports.

    d. Verify the receipt of items ordered and invoiced.

(Uniform CPA Examination)

**12-6.** Only one of the following four statements, which compare confirmation of accounts payable with suppliers and confirmation of accounts receivable with debtors, is true. The true statement is that

    a. Confirmation of accounts payable with suppliers is a more widely accepted auditing procedure than is confirmation of accounts receivable with debtors.

    b. Statistical-sampling techniques are more widely accepted in the confirmation of accounts payable than in the confirmation of accounts receivable.

    c. As compared to the confirmation of accounts payable, the confirmation of accounts receivable will tend to emphasize accounts with zero balances at balance-sheet date.

    d. It is less likely that the confirmation request sent to the supplier will show the amount owed him than that the request sent to the debtor will show the amount due from him.

(Uniform CPA Examination)

**12-7.** Which of the following *best* explains why accounts payable confirmation procedures are *not* always used?

    a. Inclusion of accounts payable balances on the liability certificate completed by the client allows the auditor to refrain from using confirmation procedures.

    b. Accounts payable generally are insignificant and can be audited by utilizing analytic review procedures.

    c. The auditor may feel certain that the creditors will press for payment.

    d. Reliable externally generated evidence supporting accounts payable balances is generally available for audit inspection on the client's premises.

(Uniform CPA Examination)

**12-8.**   Why is the confirmation of accounts payable not required procedure?

**12-9.**   If receiving reports attached to invoices included in the accounts payable total show that the goods were received after the balance sheet date, what should the auditor do?

**12-10.**  What procedure will usually be most important in the auditor's search for unrecorded liabilities? Why?

**12-11.**  Compare the confirmation of accounts receivable with the confirmation of accounts payable under the following headings:
a.   Generally accepted auditing procedures. (Justify the differences revealed by your comparison).
b.   Form of confirmation requests. (You need not supply examples).
c.   Selection of accounts to be confirmed.

(Uniform CPA Examination)

**12-12.**  Mincin, CPA, is the auditor of the Raleigh Corporation. Mincin is considering the audit work to be performed in the accounts payable area for the current year's engagement.

The prior-year's working papers show that confirmation requests were mailed to 100 of Raleigh's 1,000 suppliers. The selected suppliers were based on Mincin's sample that was designed to select accounts with large dollar balances. A substantial number of hours were spent by Raleigh and Mincin resolving relatively minor differences between the confirmation replies and Raleigh's accounting records. Alternate audit procedures were used for those suppliers who did not respond to the confirmation requests.

Required:
a.   Identify the accounts payable audit objectives that Mincin must consider in determining the audit procedures to be followed.
b.   Identify situations when Mincin should use accounts payable confirmations and discuss whether Mincin is required to use them.
c.   Discuss why the use of large dollar balances as the basis for selecting accounts payable for confirmation might not be the most efficient approach and indicate what more efficient

procedures could be followed when selecting accounts payable for confirmation.

(Uniform CPA Examination)

**12-13.** On January 11 at the beginning of your annual audit of The Grover Manufacturing Company's financial statements for the year ended December 31, the Company president confides in you that an employee is living on a scale in excess of that which his salary would support.

The employee has been a buyer in the purchasing department for six years and has charge of purchasing all general materials and supplies. He is authorized to sign purchase orders for amounts up to $200. Purchase orders in excess of $200 require the countersignature of the general purchasing agent.

The president understands that the usual examination of financial statements is not designed, and cannot be relied upon, to disclose fraud or conflicts of interest, although their discovery may result. The president authorizes you, however, to expand your regular audit procedures and to apply additional audit procedures to determine whether there is any evidence that the buyer has been misappropriating Company funds or has been engaged in activities that involve a conflict of interests.

Required:
(a) List the audit procedures that you would apply to the Company records and documents in an attempt to:
  1. Discover evidence within the purchasing department of defalcations being committed by the buyer. Give the purpose of each audit procedure.
  2. Provide leads as to possible collusion between the buyer and suppliers. Give the purpose of each audit procedure.

(b) Assume that your investigation disclosed that some suppliers have been charging the Grover Manufacturing Company in excess of their usual prices and apparently have been making "kick-backs" to the buyer. The excess charges are material in amount.

What effect, if any, would the defalcation have upon (1) the financial statements that were prepared before the defalcation was uncovered and (2) your auditor's report? Discuss.

(Uniform CPA Examination)

**12-14.** Long, CPA, has been engaged to examine and report on the financial statements of Maylou Corporation. During the review phase of the study of Maylou's system of internal accounting control over purchases, Long was given the following document flowchart for purchases.

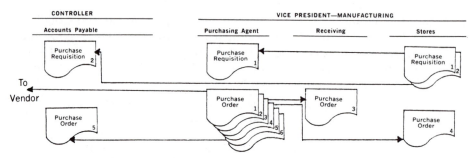

**Figure 12-2.** Maylou Corporation—Document Flowchart for Purchases

Required:

a. Identify the procedures, relating to purchase requisitions and purchase orders, that Long would expect to find if Maylou's system of internal accounting control over purchases is effective. For example, purchase orders are prepared only after giving proper consideration to the time to order, and quantity to order. *Do not comment on the effectiveness of the flow of documents as presented in the flowchart or on separation of duties.*

b. What are the factors to consider in determining—
   1. The time to order?
   2. The quantity to order?

(Uniform CPA Examination)

# Chapter 13

# COST OF SALES AND INVENTORIES

Labor
Overhead
Inventories Priced at Standard Cost
Pricing Verification of Work-in-Process Inventories
Pricing Verification Under the Retail Inventory Method
Ascertaining the Existence of Declines in Market Value
Determining Market Price
Testing Reductions of Inventory to Market Value

---

Inventories are maintained to ensure an uninterrupted production flow and to make possible prompt filling of customers' orders. In this capacity inventories function to compensate for differences in timing between ordering, production, and sale of goods as well as for seasonal differences in production and sales.

### Control Considerations

Control points over inventories include verification by the custodian of all quantities for which the custodian is to be charged in the accounting records, and proper authorization of items to be released from inventory and for which accountability is to be transferred to another organizational unit or charged as cost of sales. Regular physical inventory counts should be made and compared with the corresponding accountability records in order to ascertain the effectiveness with which custodianship responsibility has been discharged.

The activities associated with the subsystem for receiving and stocking raw materials, issuing them as needed for scheduled production, stocking the finished goods, and shipping the goods in response to customers' orders, as well as maintaining the essential inventory control and accounting records, are depicted in Figure 13-1. Because these activities are not depicted in flowcharts in the AICPA booklet *Internal Control*, a special flowchart has been prepared for this text, based on the technique and symbols used in the AICPA flowcharts.

### Comments on Illustrative Flowchart of Cost of Sales and Inventory Procedures

The amount of space required for the flowchart and the large number of activities depicted are indicative of the complexity of this subsystem. The combination of this complexity and the typically substantial number of different inventory items stocked present a major control problem for management and one of the most challenging and time-consuming aspects of an independent audit.

The system illustrated is based on standard costs inasmuch as standards produce much valuable management information about the efficiency of operations that would not otherwise be available. Standard costs are likewise used in the supplementary illustrative working papers for the audit of Machine Products Co. With standard costs it is unnecessary to include dollar amounts in the perpetual inventory records maintained in the stock ledger. Such dollar amounts must be included in actual cost systems in order to develop the cost information necessary to value all inventory movements for financial accounting purposes and to determine cost of sales.

The information about inventory quantities provided by the stock records is essential for making operating decisions about ordering materials and scheduling production and also in order to establish accountability for physical quantities. Accountability on a dollar basis is achieved through maintaining the general ledger inventory accounts on a perpetual basis by pricing all entries on the basis of standard cost. Both types of accountability are consummated through comparing physical inventory count quantities and values with the stock control and accounting records pertaining to inventories. Making physical inventory counts is a regular part of the accounting system, and internal controls are equally important to that activity as to the processing of inventory transactions.

All documents that authorize the movement of inventories are shown, and the reader should note how these documents then become the basis for entries to both the physical unit control records and general ledger accounting records.

The stock ledger records are sometimes maintained on a representational basis by using punched cards, with one card in the file for each stockkeeping unit in inventory. Pulling cards from the file equal to the number of units to be released from inventory results in a reduction of the unit control records, and the cards then become input for computer processing of the inventory movement for financial accounting purposes without the necessity of costly operator preparation of key inputs.

The discussion next turns to the internal control objectives and features pertaining to handling and recording inventory transactions as well as to physical inventory taking.

### Evaluation of Internal Control Objectives and Features

Continuing with the format of the preceding chapters, internal controls are discussed under the three main classifications of objectives relating to

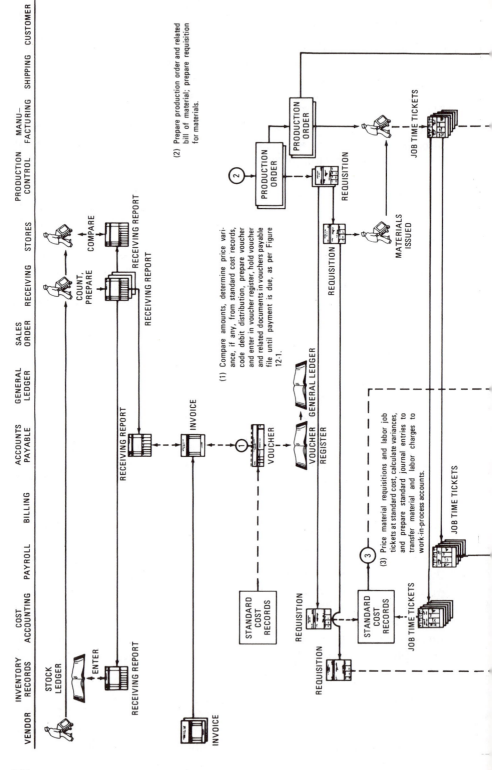

VENDOR    INVENTORY    COST        PAYROLL    BILLING    SALES    ACCOUNTS    GENERAL    GENERAL    SALES    RECEIVING    STORES    PRODUCTION    MANU-    SHIPPING    CUSTOMER
          RECORDS    ACCOUNTING                         ORDER    PAYABLE    LEDGER    LEDGER    ORDER                          CONTROL    FACTURING

(1) Compare amounts, determine price variance, if any, from standard cost records,
code debit distribution, prepare voucher
and enter in voucher register, hold voucher
and related documents in vouchers payable
file until payment is due, as per Figure
12-1.

(2) Prepare production order and related
bill of material; prepare requisition
for materials.

(3) Price material requisitions and labor job
tickets at standard cost, calculate variances,
and prepare standard journal entries to
transfer material and labor charges to
work-in-process accounts.

STOCK LEDGER
ENTER
RECEIVING REPORT
INVOICE
VOUCHER
STANDARD COST RECORDS
REQUISITION
STANDARD COST RECORDS
JOB TIME TICKETS

350

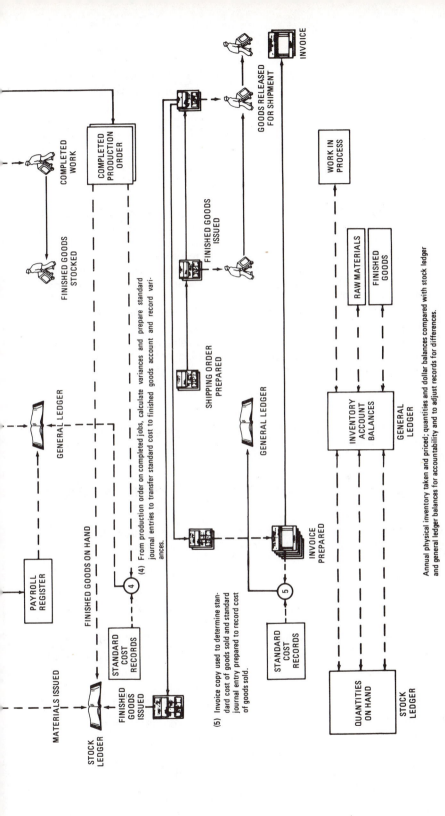

**Figure 13-1.** Flowchart for Inventories and Cost of Sales

Annual physical inventory taken and priced; quantities and dollar balances compared with stock ledger and general ledger balances for accountability and to adjust records for differences.

(4) From production order on completed jobs, calculate variances and prepare standard journal entries to transfer standard cost to finished goods account and record variances.

(5) Invoice copy used to determine standard cost of goods sold and standard journal entry prepared to record cost of goods sold.

351

operations, data processing, and monitoring of the controls, with each feature followed by an indication of appropriate compliance tests shown in italics.

### Operating Objectives

*All transactions are properly authorized.*

- Receiving of goods is authorized by a copy of the purchase order routed to the receiving department, as noted in the preceding chapter. *Inquiry, observation, inspection.*
- Raw materials are withdrawn from stores on the basis of material requisitions prepared from production orders, and accompanying bills of materials are prepared by the scheduling section of production control. *Inquiry, observation, inspection.*
- Completed production orders authorize the placing of finished goods in stock. *Inquiry, observation.*
- Finished goods are withdrawn from stock and released from the premises only on the basis of properly prepared shipping orders, as discussed in Chapter 11. *Inquiry, observation, inspection.*

*All authorizations resulted in action being taken.*

- Material requisitions and shipping orders are serially numbered, and all numbers are accounted for at the point of recording in the records. *Inquiry, observation.*

*Access to assets is permitted only in accordance with management authorization.*

- Raw materials and finished goods are stored in a secure area properly protected from the elements, with access limited to authorized personnel. *Inquiry, observation.*

### Data Processing Objectives—Internal Accounting Control

*Accounting and computer operation are independent of all operating responsibilities. Inquiry and observation* that maximum feasible segregation of these activities exists:

| Operating | Accounting/Data Processing |
|---|---|
| Receiving | Unit inventory records (stock ledger) |
| Storeskeeping | Cost accounting |
| Production control | Payroll |
| Manufacturing | General ledger records |

| Operating | Accounting/Data Processing |
|---|---|
| Shipping | Computer data entry |
| Physical inventory counts | Computer operations |
| | Pricing, extending, and footing physical inventory counts |
| | Adjusting inventory records for physical inventory differences |

A vital implication of the accounting/data processing activities listed above is that records be maintained of physical inventory quantities and that the inventory accounts in the general ledger be maintained on a perpetual basis in order to establish accountability for the inventories. Detailed records of inventory quantities are generally maintained for one or more of the following reasons:

1. To provide current information about quantities on hand as a basic input to the decision about when to reorder.
2. To provide historical information on inventory demand as an input to decision models on when to reorder (reorder point) and how much to reorder (EOQ).
3. To establish accountability for inventory quantities.
4. For systems using actual costs, to assemble information on quantities and related costs for the purpose of calculating the cost of items withdrawn from inventory as a necessary aspect of developing general ledger credits to perpetual inventory accounts.

In terms of the above reasons, the attendant records should be maintained only if justifiable on the basis that the benefits derived exceed the costs incurred. Reflecting this consideration, it will usually be advantageous to employ selective inventory controls, with maximum control limited to the bulk of the dollar value of goods handled that will often be concentrated in only some twenty percent of the inventory items. For low-value items, stock ledger records are dispensed with and no materials requisitions are prepared, workers merely withdrawing from stock stored in open areas those items needed for production. Cost transfers for low-value items are based on bills of materials and standard costs, and reordering is handled through periodic inspection of bins and storage areas to determine which items are running low. The *two-bin* system offers an alternative to periodic inspection, with a reorder point set on the basis of the usual considerations. That quantity of items is then placed in a reserve bin or in a package, and withdrawals are made from an alternate bin or the unpackaged stock. When the regular stock is exhausted and it is necessary to take items from the reserve bin or to use the packaged items, a traveling requisition stored with the reserve quantity is removed and sent to the purchasing department to initiate repurchase.

*Only valid transactions that were duly authorized are accepted for entry in the accounting records.*

- Material requisitions are prepared only on the basis of materials and quantities specified by production orders. *Inquiry, inspection.*
- Supplementary requisitions are issued and properly coded as a materials usage variance for additional materials needed to replace spoiled or rejected work. *Inquiry, inspection.*
- Finished goods are accepted for stock only on the basis of a completed production order and inspection reports showing the quantity of good production. *Inquiry, inspection.*
- Shipping orders and related invoices are the basis for entries for goods shipped. *Inquiry, inspection.*

*All transactions are entered in the accounting records.*

- Material requisitions and shipping orders are prenumbered, all numbers are accounted for at the point where the requisitions are entered in the accounting records, and the shipping orders become the basis for preparing invoices. *Inquiry, observation.*
- If inventory transfers or shipments of goods occur without appropriate accounting entries being made, the resulting inventory shortage or shinkage will emerge when physical inventory count results are compared with the accounting records. The accounting records should be adjusted accordingly. Consequently, it is important that physical inventory be regularly counted, either all at one time or on a staggered cycle basis, with critical or costly items being counted more frequently in order to achieve current accounting accuracy and to avoid stockouts or overstocks that may result from inaccurate records. *Inquiry, observation, inspection.*

*Accounting entries correctly reflect transaction amounts.*

- Variable information represented in accounting entries should be verified when the accounting entries are prepared to ensure accounting accuracy. Such verification is sometimes omitted for inventory movements because only internal accounts are affected and the effect of any errors will be corrected when physical inventory counts are made and the inventory accounts are adjusted to agree with the physical inventory figures. *Inquiry* and *observation* if such verification is incorporated in the system; reperformance is not necessary because errors will be corrected when the records are adjusted to agree with the physical inventory.
- Batch control totals are prepared, covering the quantities represented on material requisitions or shipping orders, and computer processing totals are developed and proved against the control totals. *Inquiry, inspection.*
- Comparing book records with physical inventory counts and making the necessary adjustments will correct any errors that may have occurred as a result of reduced or omitted controls. *Inquiry, observation, inspection.*

*Transactions are correctly classified for accounting entry.*

- Transfers between inventory accounts and to cost of sales should be in consonance with the physical movement of the inventory items. *Inquiry, observation, inspection.*

- Account classifications should be adequate to provide such accountability and responsibility reporting as may be necessary or desirable; cost of sales classifications should conform to sales classifications in order to permit determination of profit margins. *Observation.*
- Inventory differences, or variances, disclosed by physical inventory counts should be reported internally for control purposes but for external reporting are customarily and appropriately combined with the related cost of sales figures. *Inquiry, inspection.*

*Recorded transactions are correctly processed.*

- Accuracy of physical inventory counts is best ensured by making blind second counts, making a subsequent comparison of the first and second counts, and investigating and correcting any differences that occur. Also, inventory count tags or forms should be placed with the counted items so that an inspection will reveal whether all inventory items have been counted. These control features are evident in the inventory count tag shown in Figure 13-2. *Inquiry, observation, inspection.*
- Synchronization of entries in accounting records and related physical inventory movements is extremely important at those times when balances in detail records and general ledger controlling accounts are compared with each other and with physical inventory quantities. In addition to verification

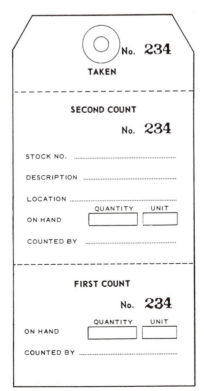

**Figure 13-2.** Inventory Count Tag

that all recent inventory movements have been fully reflected in the accounting records, consideration must be given to reconciling items likely to exist in the case of purchases, as represented by documents in the file of unmatched receiving reports. Also, if any purchase invoices have been recorded prior to receipt of the inventory items (the file of these items is sometimes referred to as the *prepaid invoice file*), the contents of this file must likewise be considered before comparing the records and the physical inventory to determine any shortage or overage that has occurred. *Inquiry, observation, inspection.*

- Detailed inventory records should be proved against related control account balances and the actual quantities on hand on a regular basis. However, inasmuch as entries transferring inventory costs affect only internal accounts, controls to achieve accounting accuracy are not usually considered to be justifiable on a cost/benefit basis. As a consequence, differences between the general ledger inventory records, the stock ledger records, and the physical quantities on hand tend to be commonplace, and management attention is generally directed toward keeping the differences within tolerable limits rather than toward eliiminating them entirely. *Inquiry, observation, inspection, reperformance.*

### Monitoring Objectives

*Regular comparison is made of the inventory records establishing accountability and the underlying physical inventory.*

- Inventory items should be counted at least once a year to ensure the accuracy of the records for management decision making and control purposes, although inconsequential items may be counted less frequently. The counting is often done at the close of business on the last day of the fiscal year and must be done on that basis if inventory records are maintained on a periodic basis. With perpetual inventory records, inventory may be counted prior to the close of the fiscal year, or occasionally after the end of the year. Choosing the earlier date may be a matter of convenience, in order to provide time to complete the pricing, extending, and footing of the inventory so that the information will be available by the close of the year and the year-end closing process will not be delayed.

  Another alternative is to use an inventory team to count the inventory on a continuous cycle basis and without shutting down production. However, in that case there is the added problem of controlling inventory movements to avoid double counting items both before they are moved and then in another location after they are moved, or of failing to count the items in either location. A particular advantage of the cycle basis is that it allows critical items to be placed on a shorter cycle, thereby reducing the likelihood that errors will result in stockouts or overstocking. *Inquiry, observation.*

- Internal auditors should oversee the inventory counting process in order to determine whether controls are functioning as intended and whether counting is being done accurately. *Inquiry, observation, inspection.*

### There is an effective internal audit function.

- Internal auditors should regularly review and evaluate internal controls, perform compliance tests, and when appropriate, make recommendations for improvement in the controls and the manner in which they are implemented. Controls relative to the taking of physical inventories are particularly important in this regard. *Inquiry, review of audit planning, inspection of working papers.*

- Abnormal amounts of inventory shortages should be investigated to ascertain whether preventable losses are occurring or whether the shortages are the result of unrecorded transactions or processing errors. *Inquiry, observation.*

- The following operational internal audit activities should be considered if the independent auditor decides to include management control of operations within the scope of the review of the internal audit function. *Inquiry* would be the principal basis for the review of these operational audit activities:

    Consideration of whether selective (ABC) inventory controls would be advantageous, and if selective controls have already been implemented, review of the appropriateness of the inventory control levels.

    Review of the method of reporting inventory shortages and the management actions taken when excessive shortages occur.

    Review of the inventory storage function from the standpoint of orderliness and accessibility of inventory items; efficient use of space; and protection against breakage, deterioration, damage from the elements, and unauthorized withdrawals.

    Review of the adequacy of stockroom controls and the preparation and handling of materials requisitions, especially those supplementary requisitions necessitated by spoiled work.

    Review of the methods for setting inventory reorder points and economic order quantities.

## Supplementary Comments–Computer-Based Records

If standard cost are used, inputs for all inventory transactions can be limited to the code number identification of items (including the use of a self-checking digit) and the quantity. For actual costs all receipts of inventory and inward transfers would also have to include monetary amounts at the point of computer input, but for issues and transfers out of inventory, unit costs would be determined by the computer and extended to obtain monetary amounts for the transactions.

Inventory requisitions would be prepared by the computer from materials lists associated with production orders, and shipping orders would be prepared in conjunction with the processing of customers' orders.

Open-item systems are an adaptation of the "tub file" system of manual record keeping and involve a separate record for each identifiable stock-keeping unit, whether it be an individual item or a case or other package containing a stated number of the individual items. The automated version based on punched-card data processing involves a one-to-one relationship between the units in stock and the punched cards in an open-item file. The open-item cards are "gang punched" from "master" cards—in sufficient number to provide one card for each unit of stock received—whenever inventory items are received. The cards will contain as a minimum the description of the item, its unit cost, and the selling price per unit. The completed cards are placed in the inventory file behind any other cards remaining in the file for the particular inventory item.

As orders are received, cards equal to the quantity of stock ordered are removed from the file. The cards are taken from the front of the section if Fifo costing is desired, or from the rear of the section if Lifo costing is to be used. A special card placed at the appropriate point in the file signals when the remaining quantity of an item on hand has reached the reorder point.

The selected cards, plus "header" cards for customer name and address, can then be processed to prepare an invoice for the sale. The computer accumulates and prints the total selling price from all identical cards when more than one unit of an item has been ordered and can, in the same processing run, accumulate the cost of the items that have been sold for the various inventory classifications for the general ledger cost of sales entry.

Most systems are operated on a *balance forward* basis that records all receipts and issues. In that case reorder point and EOQ for each inventory item can be regularly updated through computer programming, sometimes as often as after every inventory transaction, utilizing historical information that is retained primarily for that purpose. When the quantity on hand reaches the reorder point, typically the computer generates the appropriate purchase order or production order that is needed.

Regular checking of computer inventory balances on hand by physical count is important in ensuring the accuracy of the inventory records by eliminating any errors that have become imbedded in the inventory figures. Physical count quantities may be entered by operators as key input, or punched cards showing inventory description and location can be prepared in advance by the computer and the quantities counted can be entered by the count teams using a portable punching device or by mark sensing. Differences between computer balances and physical count quantities should be printed out by the computer and investigated before major differences are adjusted.

## Substantive Audit Objectives and Procedures

### Conformity of Client's Financial Statements with Disclosure and Other Requirements of Financial Reporting Standards

1.  Cost of sales should be reported on the same basis as sales figures, including reporting by segments when required, although for segment

reporting, cost of sales may be combined with other operating expenses and only the resulting operating profit or loss reported.

2.  Although inventory shortages, mark-down expense, standard cost variances, and losses from reduction of inventory to market value may be combined with the cost of sales figure in published statements (unless abnormal amounts are involved), all such figures, in view of their information value, should be presented separately in reports for internal use by management.

3.  For public companies having more than $1 billion in assets or $125 million of inventories and gross properties, supplementary information should be presented showing for the current year and in a five-year summary, the amount of inventories and cost of sales on both a current cost basis and a constant dollar basis, as required by FASB 33.

4.  The effect of any change in the method of accounting for inventories should be set forth in the financial statements, in accordance with the provisions in Professional Standards, AC Sec. 1051.

5.  Disclosure must be made if all or part of the inventories have been pledged to secure outstanding obligations or are subject to any other type of lien.

6.  Principal classes of inventory should be shown separately, generally in order of their liquidity, if significant in amount. In addition to the traditional 3-way separation between raw materials, work in process, and finished goods, other separations might include such items as goods out on consignment and merchandise in transit.

7.  Purchase commitments should be disclosed if they are material or out of line with past practice, and losses on firm purchase commitments should be provided for.

8.  Provisions for possible inventory price declines occurring after the balance sheet date should be made only by appropriations of retained income, and these reserves should not be deducted from inventory but shown as a portion of retained income.

As in the case of receivables, information pertaining to liens may exist in various places, such as in contracts for the purchase of inventory or in borrowing agreements, and the auditor must constantly be alert for any evidence that such liens exist.

### Reasonableness of Account Balances

*Perform Analytical Review.*   Cost of sales figures should bear a close relationship to sales on a continuing basis. Working paper schedule 10 shows cost of sales related to sales in terms of gross margin percentage, which is the complement of the cost of sales ratio. The percentage is computed for each of the three product lines as well as for the company as a whole, and the percentages for both the current and the preceding year are compared. Changes in the percentages should be investigated and accounted for.

For instance, a decrease in the rate of gross or net margin for the current year as compared with preceding years may be a danger signal. Investigation might show that selling prices had been declining in the latter part of the year—a situation that should suggest to the auditor that inventory pricing should be carefully scrutinized for any write-downs to market values that might be required. On the other hand, if the decreased margin percentage can be accounted for by rising material costs in the face of constant selling prices, the auditor will usually be justified in closing the investigation. But if the auditor discovers no change in the relationship of cost and selling prices, it will be necessary to look elsewhere for the cause of the decrease. The inventory cutoffs are probably the next area that would warrant investigation. Failure to adjust for merchandise charged to purchases but not received in time to be inventoried might prove to be the explanation. Another possibility would be an error in the cost of sales cutoff under the perpetual inventory plan. Goods may have been entered as cost of sales, although shipment and recording of the sale did not occur until the following period.

The cutoff of sales is still another area that might hold the answer to the decreased margin percentage. Further investigation of this cutoff might disclose that goods that had been shipped and reflected in cost of sales for the current period had not been taken into sales and receivables until the following period.

If neither price changes nor cutoff errors yield the explanation for the decreased rate of margin, the auditor should look to the client's physical inventory figures. Under the periodic inventory method an understatement of the inventory would result in an overstatement of cost of sales and an understatement of gross margin. The possibility that some merchandise had been overlooked or that an error had been made in counting, pricing, extending, or totaling the inventory would then have to be considered. If this possibility is raised before the auditor has completed work on the inventory, tests can be extended and slanted toward disclosure of a possible understatement under the concept of relative risk. If the perpetual inventory method is followed, errors in the physical inventory will affect net income through the inventory variation account.

Changes in the application of generally accepted accounting principles, such as from Fifo to Lifo inventory valuation, must also be considered as a possible cause of a change in the relationship of cost of sales to sales. It is important that the auditor become aware of any such modification in inventory costing because the lack of consistency must be disclosed in the financial statements.

An accounting error could similarly cause a change in the cost of sales percentage. If investigation discloses such an error, adjustment of the records will be necessary.

The analysis on schedule 10 shows an increase in margin, which is explained as being the result of an increase in the selling prices of automated machines associated with the generally increased demand for such machinery. Related inventory expenses, such as standard cost variances, inventory shortages, markdowns, and warehouse or stockroom expense, should also be reviewed in relation to the volume of inventory movement and in the light of any conditions known to exist. Schedule $\frac{C\text{-}1}{1}$ shows the relationship between the inventory shortage of raw materials and the amount of materials handled, and schedule C shows the changes of the three cost elements in work in process and finished goods. The auditor's permanent files on the engagement might well carry a chart or table summarizing such relationships over a period of years as a means of pointing up long-term trends. Inventory turnover is an especially useful figure for such a record.

Analysis and review of the relationship between two different figures is based on the assumption that each figure reinforces the other. If the figures are developed independently, as in the case of sales and cost of sales or other expenses, continuation of a reasonably constant relationship between the figures provides a basis for concluding that the figures have not been distorted. Additional independent figures are sometimes available in the form of physical volume of inventory and physical movement. If only a limited number of raw materials and finished products are involved, as in a steel mill, a coal mine, or a carbonated beverage plant, records of physical quantities purchased and sold are usually maintained. By converting these quantities into dollar amounts at average prices, the auditor has a further check on sales, purchases, cost of sales, and ending inventory.

As a final test of the records, major accounts should be scanned for any unusual entries, which should be investigated to determine whether the charges or credits are appropriate to the accounts in which they have been entered.

### Synchronization of Events and Records

Inventory cutoff errors will affect net income, either through the cost of sales figure or through the inventory variation between book and physical inventory. Although the cutoff of purchases has already been discussed, additional comments are included below so that the discussion at this point will be complete concerning all aspects of inventory cutoffs.

*Purchases Cutoff.* A faulty purchases cutoff may act to affect the financial statements in either of two ways. If goods have been received and included in the physical inventory but the purchase has not been recorded, net income and retained earnings will be overstated, and accounts payable will be understated. If goods for which the purchase has been recorded are not included in the physical inventory, net income will be understated, as will retained earnings and the inventory figure in the balance sheet. The overall effects will be the same under either the perpetual or the periodic inventory method, but details within the income statement will vary. A cutoff error under the periodic inventory method will misstate cost of sales through a misstatement of either purchases or ending inventory. Under the perpetual inventory method, errors affecting purchases or ending inventory will not affect the cost of goods sold figure, but will change the inventory variance figure. The simple examples shown in Table 13-1 illustrate the effect of cutoff errors.

The reader should note that the cost of sales figure in the perpetual inventory method differs from the cost of sales shown in the "correct" column of the example illustrating the periodic method. The difference is explained by the fact that the periodic method offers no opportunity to determine whether goods that were available for sale and not on hand at the end of the period were lost or were actually sold. Therefore, the figure that is labeled "cost of sales" is actually a combined figure for both cost of sales and cost of merchandise that has not been accounted for. The resulting figure is far less informative than the figures developed under the perpetual inventory method.

*Adjustments to Correct the Cutoff of Purchases.* Businesses seldom experience a clean cutoff of purchases in the normal course of operations at the year end. Instead, adjustments to both the book records and to the physical inventory are usually necessary to place the two on a common basis. The necessary adjustments may be readily determined if the accounting system reflects good internal control. In Chapter 12 mention was made of files for unmatched receiving reports and unmatched invoices, and earlier in this chapter mention was made of a file of prepaid invoices that have been recorded and paid before the goods have been received. The information provided by these files at the close of the year can be used in making needed adjustments to both book and physical inventory figures. Such use is illustrated below, based on the use of the perpetual inventory method:

|  | Accounts Payable | Inventory Per Books | Physical Inventory |
|---|---|---|---|
| Balance, December 31 | $15,000 | $32,000 | $30,000 |
| Add | | | |
| Unmatched receiving reports | 2,000 | 2,000 | |
| Prepaid invoices | | | 1,000 |
| | | $34,000 | $31,000 |

| | Accounts Payable | Inventory Per Books | Physical Inventory |
|---|---|---|---|
| Deduct | | | |
| Inventory shortage.......................... | | 3,000 | |
| Adjusted physical inventory, as above .... | | $31,000 | |
| Add | | | |
| Merchandise in transit (Unmatched invoices) | 4,000 | 4,000 | |
| Adjusted figures for statement purposes .. | $21,000 | $35,000 | |

Included in the merchandise in transit figure would be any invoices received after the balance sheet date if the invoices show that the merchandise had been shipped f.o.b. shipping point on or before the close of the year. If, however, the merchandise had been received and counted in the physical inventory, then the adjustment necessitated by the unmatched receiving reports would be the only adjustment necessary.

*Test Purchases Cutoff.* The procedures to test the purchase cutoff were fully described in the preceding chapter, in connection with procedures to search for unrecorded liabilities.

*Cost of Sales Cutoff.* As discussed in the chapter on sales and receivables, the sales cutoff will affect net income, and therefore the recording of sales and receivables must be made in accordance with the date on which goods have been shipped. There is, however, no significant problem with respect to the recording of the corresponding entry for cost of sales. If the goods in question are on hand at the balance sheet date, they will be included in the physical inventory and therefore appear on the financial statements as an asset. If the goods have left the premises, they will not be included in the physical inventory, and because the goods are therefore not accounted for as being on hand, their cost will appear as a charge against revenues. Under the periodic inventory method, goods no longer on hand will appear as cost of sales, and income will be correctly stated if the sale has been recorded.

When the general ledger inventory records are kept on a perpetual basis, cost of sales is determined independently and is not merely a difference figure representing the goods available for sale that were not accounted for in inventory at the end of the year. Under this method, costs are determined relative to each sale, and the inventory account is relieved of these costs. These costs are charged to cost of sales, and of course the entry for the cost figure should be made at the same time as the entry for the sale, even though the two entries are made independently. If a sale is recorded in one period but the cost of sales entry is not made until the following period, the result is obviously an understatement of cost of sales in the first period and an overstatement in the

**Table 13-1.**

## Periodic Method

| | Correct | $500 Purchase Recorded but Goods Not Included in Ending Inventory | $500 Included in Ending Inventory but Purchase Not Recorded |
|---|---|---|---|
| Sales | $15,000 | $15,000 | $15,000 |
| Cost of sales | | | |
| Beginning inventory | $ 3,000 | $ 3,000 | $ 3,000 |
| Purchases | 10,000 | 10,000 | 9,500 |
| Cost of goods available for sale | $13,000 | $13,000 | $12,500 |
| Ending inventory | 2,500 | 2,000 | 2,500 |
| Cost of sales | 10,500 | 11,000 | 10,000 |
| Gross margin | $ 4,500 | $ 4,000 | $ 5,000 |

## Perpetual Method

| | Correct | $500 Purchase Recorded but Goods Not Included in Ending Inventory | $500 Included in Ending Inventory but Purchase Not Recorded |
|---|---|---|---|
| Sales | $15,000 | $15,000 | $15,000 |
| Cost of sales and inventory variance | | | |
| Beginning inventory | $ 3,000 | $ 3,000 | $ 3,000 |
| Purchases | 10,000 | 10,000 | 9,500 |
| Cost of goods available for sale | $13,000 | $13,000 | $12,500 |
| Cost of sales (predetermined) | 10,200 | 10,200 | 10,200 |
| Gross margin | $ 4,800 | $ 4,800 | $ 4,800 |
| Book inventory, end of period | $ 2,800 | $ 2,800 | $ 2,300 |
| Physical inventory | 2,500 | 2,000 | 2,500 |
| Inventory variance | (300)* | (800)* | 200† |
| Net margin | $ 4,500 | $ 4,000 | $ 5,000 |

* Shortage.   † Overage.

following period. Although this shift will affect gross margin percentages for each of the two periods, there will be no effect on net income if a physical inventory is taken at the end of the first period. The goods that have been sold and delivered will still be in the book inventory but will not appear in the physical inventory. Because the physical inventory represents the true asset figure, the book inventory must be adjusted downward. This adjustment will give rise to a debit to the account "Inventory shortage," or "Inventory variance," which will offset the understatement of the cost of sales figure. If this shortage figure is deducted immediately below the gross margin figure on the income statement, the resulting net margin figure will be correct. In the following period the cutoff error will cause an opposite reaction: cost of sales will be overstated, gross margin will be understated, and the inventory variance will show an inventory overage which will offset the understatement of gross margin.

*Test Cost of Sales Cutoff.* As stated above, there is no cost of sales cutoff problem with respect to records kept under the periodic inventory plan. When perpetual inventory controlling accounts are maintained, the auditor should be satisfied that the outward movement of merchandise and the recording of both the sale and the cost of the sale occur in the same period. The audit technique is dependent upon the date of shipment, as shown by records prepared by the shipping department. This date should be compared with the date on which the transaction was included in the sales and cost of sales records. If either of the recording dates does not fall in the same fiscal period in which shipment was made, the need for a possible adjustment is indicated. If even a single cutoff error is noted, the auditor's tests should usually be expanded to determine whether other errors may have occurred. If the amounts disclosed by these tests are material, adjustment should be made. The reader should note, however, that a $1,000 error in sales cutoff will be relatively more material than a $1,000 error in the cost of sales cutoff. The explanation for this apparent enigma is that the sales cutoff will affect net income whereas the cost of sales error will not, because it will be offset by a compensating error in the inventory variance (assuming, of course, that the physical inventory count was made at the end of the year). This difference in materiality of the two types of cutoff errors also suggests that the auditor's tests of the cost of sales cutoff need not be as extensive as those of the sales cutoff.

*Cutoff Tests and Relative Risk.* Relative risk is an important consideration in planning cutoff tests. If there is any reason why a client might wish to understate or overstate income, the auditor should ordinarily expand cutoff tests and be particularly careful in reviewing those instances that would produce the desired result for the client. For instance, if it is known that a client plans to sell stock or bonds to raise additional capital, the auditor should recognize the possibility of a desire on the part of the client to overstate income in order to improve the market for the securities. Conversely, a scheduled decrease in income tax rates for the following year would suggest the desirability of shifting income to the low-tax year by understating income for the current year. To disclose a possible understatement of income the auditor should watch for goods shipped in the current year but billed in the following year, or goods received in the following year but recorded as a purchase in the current year. Overstatement of income would result if the preceding situations were reversed.

Although only purchases and sales have been referred to in the discussion of cutoff errors, the reader should recognize that similar cutoff problems are involved concerning purchase returns, or concerning transfer from raw materials to work in process and from work in process to finished goods, as well as in transfers from central warehouse inventories to branch inventories.

*Cutoff Tests When Inventory Counts Are at Other Than the Balance Sheet Date.* If inventory counting is done at a preliminary date or throughout the year, cutoff tests must be made at both the count date and at the balance sheet date.

### Comprehensiveness of Records

The question of whether all inventory and cost of sales transactions have been recorded can be answered primarily through the following procedures, which are discussed in relation to other objectives.

*Evaluate Internal Control.* Important controls related to the comprehensiveness of the accounting records would be the maintenance of files of unmatched invoices and unmatched receiving reports and the follow-up of items that have remained in these files for an inordinate length of time. With respect to inventory withdrawals, accounting for the serial numbers of prenumbered materials requisitions and shipping orders at the point where these documents become the basis for accounting entries should ensure the comprehensiveness of the accounting records.

Similar considerations exist with respect to taking the physical inventory. After count tags have been completed and placed with the inventory, a supervisor and/or an internal auditor should review the area to be sure that a count tag has been completed for every inventory item. Receiving and shipping areas should also be inspected in order to determine that any goods or materials held in those areas have been accounted for in terms of appropriate inventory instructions. As a final step related to comprehensiveness, the serial numbers of prenumbered inventory count tags should be accounted for when these tags become the basis for determining the total monetary value of inventory items.

*Test Cutoff of Purchases and Cost of Sales.* The cutoff tests discussed previously are equally important with respect to synchronization and the comprehensiveness of accounting records.

*Observation of Physical Inventory Taking.* In connection with the auditor's observation of the client's physical inventory taking procedures, as discussed subsequently under the existence objective, it is important to ascertain whether all inventory items have been counted and whether count tag serial numbers have been accounted for.

### Arithmetic and Clerical Accuracy; Agreement of Details and Control Totals

*Prepare or Test Trial Balance of Subsidiary Ledger.* If the client is accounting for the actual cost of inventories, the stock ledger or computer record file of inventory items will include balances in dollars as well as physical units. A trial balance of the dollar amounts should be prepared to be balanced with the related inventory control account. If the client has prepared such a trial balance (which should be the case if internal control is good), the auditor should test the trial balance amounts against the related amounts in the inventory records and prove the footing of the trial balance. If the records are computerized, an audit software package can be used to prove the detail balances against the control total.

In many cases, however, detail inventory records are maintained for quantities only, and when that is true, the tie-in of detail information and the control account balance must be accomplished on the basis of the listing that is prepared of the physical inventory count quantities. Under those circumstances the following procedures should be performed.

*Test Clerical Accuracy of Physical Inventory Sheets.* To compile dollar inventory totals, the quantities on count cards are typically transferred to inventory sheets, unit costs are entered and extended, and the extensions are summed to obtain the dollar total. The transcribing, pricing, extending, and footing of the total are all clerical activities that must be tested by reperforming the activities by either a staff auditor or by a paraprofessional (at less cost to the client) if such a person is available to carry out this subprofessional verification activity. The above comment assumes that unit cost information is available from a simple source, such as a standard cost listing. If determining unit costs involves anything that is more complicated, a staff auditor should carry out the required audit procedure inasmuch as the more complex objective of inventory valuation is involved, as discussed at a later point.

The testing of extensions and footings is frequently concentrated on larger items to obtain maximum coverage with a minimum of work, particularly if the risk of overstatement is present. Smaller items should also be included in the sample to ensure representativeness, however, and if the situation points to a more likely risk of understatement, the test should emphasize smaller amounts rather than the larger items. In addition to these reperformance tests, the auditor should scan the inventory sheets for reasonableness and consistency of extensions and footings with the elements that are the basis for the amounts shown.

### Existence of Inventories

As noted in the chapter on receivables, auditing standards relative to ascertaining the existence of receivables and inventories were drastically increased in 1939 as a result of the disclosure of the massive fraud involving these two assets in the McKesson and Robbins case. In order to gain satisfaction that inventories shown on the balance sheet actually exist, the auditor is required to gain direct contact with the principal inventory items represented in balance sheet figures. This contact is usually accomplished through observation and testing of the client's physical inventory-taking procedures, although as noted later, alternative procedures may be appropriate in some instances.

The following procedures and comments pertain to such inventory observation. If it is not possible to conduct the inventory observation required by generally accepted auditing standards because of a restriction imposed by the client, it will ordinarily be necessary to modify the auditor's report to disclose that fact and to state the effect on the auditor's opinion, as discussed in Chapter 20.

*Review Client's Planning for Inventory Counts.* It is essential that the auditor be appointed at a sufficiently early date to be able to review the client's plans for the physical inventory before counting begins. The review is a part of the internal control evaluation that will directly affect the auditor's inventory observation procedures, and the early review provides an opportunity to propose possible changes to improve the client's intended procedures. The first step in the planning process should be the client's designation of the person to be responsible for planning and supervising the taking of the physical inventory—generally the controller or some other person of sufficient rank and stature with a good knowledge of the company and its operations.

Written instructions should be prepared covering each separate job to be assigned to various employees, and steps should be taken to be certain that these instructions are fully understood and that each individual is impressed with the importance of carefully following the instructions. Counting of inventory items should normally not be done by the same employees who are responsible for custody of the inventory. If counting is done by teams of two employees, however, one member of each team may be an employee who is responsible for handling inventory items, for that person will be better informed as to the exact description and location of the items to be counted. Other considerations in planning and completing the physical count are the following:

1. The receiving and shipping departments should be cleared of all merchandise before counting is begun, and receiving reports and shipping documents prepared near the date of the inventory count should clearly show the date goods were received or shipped. These dates are extremely important in obtaining a good cutoff of transactions in the accounting department.

2. If all plant activity cannot be stopped during the inventory counting, provision must be made for items that are transferred from one location to another. The same item must not be counted in both locations, and of course care must be taken to see that an item that has been moved has not been omitted entirely from the counting process.

3. Inventory items should be stacked in neat piles, if at all possible, to facilitate accurate counting.

4. Consignment goods, obsolete or defective parts, or any other items not to be included in the inventory should be clearly marked.

5. Supervisors should be on hand to observe the counting process and to be certain that instructions are being followed. Each department should be inspected and cleared by a supervisor before the counting is considered to have been completed.

6. A "blind" second count is always the best assurance that counting has been accurately performed. The two counts should be compared by a third person, and differences should be cleared by an immediate recount.

7. Count tags or tickets should be prenumbered and all numbers accounted for as soon as the tickets are turned in, in order to ascertain that no tickets are omitted from the final inventory figures.

8. If detailed perpetual inventory records are maintained, the records should be adjusted to agree with the physical count. Major differences should be investigated before the physical count is accepted as being correct. There is always a possibility that the inventory was stored

in two locations, one of which was overlooked, that recent receipts or shipments have not been posted, or that items have not been properly identified.

9.    After the inventory counts have been prepared and checked as suggested above, the individual items can be priced and extended and inventory totals can be ascertained for comparison with the general ledger control and adjustment of that account.

*Observation of Physical Inventory Counts.*    As in all areas of the audit, the auditor, when warranted, relies heavily on the accounting figures and other representations of management. Consequently, it is important that the client's physical inventory instructions and the controls evident in those instructions be carried out exactly as planned. The audit problem is one of ascertaining compliance, and the auditor can resolve that problem only by being on hand to observe the inventory-taking activity. Such observation should satisfy the auditor on both the accuracy of the client's inventory figure and the existence of the inventory shown in the client's balance sheet.

The auditor's observation should encompass all internal control features represented in the client's inventory instructions, such as those discussed in the previous section on planning for the physical inventory, and special attention should be given to the adequacy and effectiveness of the supervision that is exercised over the inventory activities. Another important matter is the accounting for prenumbered tags to ensure that no used tags have been lost and the related inventory items omitted from the final inventory figures. Unused tags that are not properly accounted for and controlled by both the client and the auditor constitute a potentially serious audit risk. Some of the most extensive inventory frauds that have overstated inventory figures by millions of dollars have been accomplished by showing fictitious information on unused count tags and including the tags in arriving at the final inventory figure.

*Reasonableness of Inventory Quantities; Auditor Test Counts.*    The opinion to be expressed on the client's financial statements entails not only the existence of the inventories that are shown but also the fairness of the amount at which the inventories are stated. As the auditor tours areas in which inventory is stored, some items that have been counted should be reviewed on a general basis (sometimes referred to as making an "eye test") to determine whether the quantities shown by the count records appear reasonable. For other items actual counts should be made by the auditor to prove the accuracy of the client's counts. It will be best in making those tests if the auditor's counts can be compared immediately with the client's figures, as in cases where count tags are still present with the inventory items. By making the comparisons promptly, counting errors will become evident in sufficient time for the auditor to have the client take whatever steps are necessary to correct the counts, thus assuring the accuracy of remaining counts.

The auditor should prepare a record for the working papers showing the description, location, and quantity of every test count made. Such a record provides evidence in support of the auditor's opinion on the inventories, and is essential for an additional step that must be taken later: tracing the auditor's count figures into the final inventory records. This step is necessary to be sure that client count figures have not been either inadvertently or intentionally changed during the time when the client's remaining inventory steps are carried out, such as transcribing the inventory counts onto the final records or entering them for computer processing.

The auditor's count records will also become the basis for the working paper summary showing the extent of the auditor's inventory tests, as on schedule C-5 of the illustrative audit working papers. It will be evident that the auditor will obtain maximum dollar coverage with minimum audit work by concentrating on the high value items in the inventory, and will also gain maximum assurance that no errors are present in those items that hold the potential for the largest dollar errors. As further protection against material errors or fraudulent overstatement of inventories, the auditor should review the final inventory listings to be sure that all inventory items showing a large dollar value have been tested by the auditor. In this way the auditor can guard against the possibility that the items are fictitious or that count figures have been altered to increase the quantities shown.

*Special Considerations When Counts Are Made at Other Than the Balance Sheet Date.* As was stated earlier, cutoffs of both purchases and cost of sales must be made at both the count date and at the balance sheet date. For example, a purchase that has been received but not yet entered in the stock ledger would result in an apparent overage of the inventory item, and if the stock ledger record and the general ledger are adjusted to reflect that overage, the subsequent entry for the purchase will result in both records being overstated until the next inventory count is made. At that time an apparent shortage will be indicated, and only then will the adjustment to record that "shortage" correct the records.

Another problem associated with inventory count at dates other than the end of the fiscal year arises in the typical situation where inventory "shrinkage" occurs during the year. The difference in inventory disclosed by the physical inventory count will result in removing the accumulated loss from the records, but then additional losses will arise after the count date. If past experience indicates that these losses between the count date and the balance sheet date may be material, the estimated loss should be provided for in the accounts by reducing inventory and increasing the amount of the recorded shrinkage loss.

One additional step is essential when counting occurs throughout the year. The stock ledger should be reviewed to determine that every item was counted at least once during the year (or that a statistical sampling plan is in effect that makes an annual count of every item unnecessary, as discussed in Professional Standards at AU Sec. 311.11). The record should be adjusted for any indicated overage or shortage, with abnormal amounts pointing to the possibility that internal control has become ineffective.

*Alternative Procedures When Observation Is Not Possible.* At times the auditor may be unable to be present to observe the taking of the physical inventory, as for instance if the auditor is not engaged until after the close of the year. In such situations a vital link in the chain of verification procedures is missing, and the loss may be so important that the auditor will be unable to express an opinion on the fairness of the inventory figure. There is a possibility, however, that the auditor can be satisfied by alternative means. The auditor's approach under such circumstances will ordinarily be somewhat as follows. First the inventory plans and instructions should be reviewed as under normal circumstances. Then, from inquiry of the persons who supervised the inventory taking and did the actual counting, the auditor should attempt to determine whether a satisfactory inventory was taken. To corroborate the opinion formed from these inquiries, the auditor should inspect the actual physical inventory records, being careful to note the presence of the initials of persons who did the work, evidence that recounts were made when necessary, and any other indications of the validity and reliability of those records. Finally, the auditor should test the reliability of the physical inventory figures by tracing those figures to the perpetual inventory records to ascertain whether the perpetual records were adjusted when necessary. Also, the auditor should test supporting data for entries recording receipts and issues during the intervening period. Then, taking current balances based on these adjusted figures, the auditor should verify the current balances by making test counts of a substantial portion of the inventory items. Such tests should be much more extensive than the tests discussed in the previous section. The usual test counts are intended to provide a further basis for the auditor's conclusions based on the observation of the inventory taking; but when the auditor was not present at the inventory date, the tests must be adequate to substitute for the usual observation. As a final check on the conclusions reached in this manner, the auditor should make an especially careful investigation of inventory variances and variations in gross margin.

The above comments concerning alternative procedures are predicated on the existence of good internal control, including adequate perpetual inventory records. If these factors are not present, the auditor will ordinarily have no way to satisfactorily verify the balance sheet inventory figure at the later date and will be required to modify the opinion to be expressed on the financial statements. Depending on the materiality of inventories, it will be necessary either to exclude inventories from the opinion expressed, or more likely to disclaim an opinion on the financial statements as a whole. The disclaimer of opinion is likely to be the only acceptable alternative if inventories are significant in determining net income, as for manufacturing, wholesaling, or retailing concerns.

*Inventories Not in the Custody of the Client.* When inventories are stored in public warehouses, shipped on consignment, or held by the vendor for the client's convenience, the auditor should obtain written confirmation of those inventories directly from the the custodians, in addition to inspecting such available evidence as warehouse certificates. This requirement is a further reflection of the strengthening of auditing standards that occurred after the McKesson and Robbins fraud, with the requirement being stated in Professional Standards at AU Sec. 331.14-.15. That section states that if the amount of inventories in the hands of others is a significant proportion of the client's assets, then supplemental inquiries should be made to satisfy the auditor of the bona fides of the situation.

The extent of supplemental inquiries will vary according to the auditor's judgment as to each situation. In some cases reference to a directory of bonded public warehouses would be sufficient supplementary verification of the existence of warehouses confirming inventories in their custody. Further verification when a significant portion of the inventory is stored elsewhere would include audited financial statements as evidence that a warehouse has been properly bonded or that a consignee or vendor holding inventory for the client is solvent. An actual visit to the premises on which the inventories are stored offers maximum assurance that the situation has been properly represented to the auditor and is required in the extreme situation where the bulk of the inventories are stored away from the client's premises. In connection with such a visit the auditor should note that the client's inventory is properly segregated and identified. Test counts of some of the items would also be in order, although these recommendations would obviously be inapplicable if fungible goods are involved.

Even when such verification has been made, the auditor should still inspect warehouse receipts, because the absence of such receipts usually indicates that the inventory has been pledged as collateral. These inventories stored in the custody of others present special problems also for the auditors of those custodian organizations. The inventories will not be an asset of the custodian, but the auditor should ascertain whether the custodian's responsibility for goods held in the capacity of bailee has been effectively discharged by the maintenance of well controlled inventory records and that the quantities called for by the records are actually on hand.

### Valuation of Inventories at Lower of Cost or Market

The assignment of dollar values to the units of inventory determined by physical count is usually referred to as "pricing" the inventory. When an inventory is priced at the lower of cost or market, two distinct sets of prices are involved. The first figure to be determined will be the cost figure, and the auditor must be satisfied that cost figures have been derived by an acceptable method that has been consistently applied. If the client wishes to change the method of costing, say from first-in, first-out, to last-in, first-out, the ending inventory should be priced on both bases, and the client must disclose the difference between the two figures, representing the effect of the change, in a footnote to the statements. After the required cost figures have been determined, the substitution of market values must be considered if they are lower than cost.

In reference to the auditor's responsibility for inventory pricing, the auditor is primarily concerned with establishing the reasonableness of the client's representations as to the final inventory figure and the manner in which it was determined. Thus, as in all areas of the audit, the auditor's examination of inventory pricing will ordinarily be limited to a review of the client's methods, coupled with sufficient tests to assure the auditor that the methods represented by the client as being in use were actually used. Only when the auditor finds that there is insufficient basis for accepting the client's representations will it be necessary to undertake an extensive examination of inventory pricing.

*Cost.* The auditor's first step, as might be expected, will ordinarily be to ascertain what method of determining cost has been used, that is, Fifo, Lifo, average, standard, retail inventory method, or net selling price, and whether purchases are recorded at full invoice cost or net of cash discount. If the method used in costing the current inventory differs from that used in costing the previous inventory, that significant fact should be noted so that it will not be overlooked when the auditor's report is prepared. Next, the client's completed inventory sheets should be reviewed and items selected for the pricing test, as specified by the audit program. Full data on the items selected will usually be listed in the working papers, as illustrated in schedule C-5. Ordinarily an effort will be made to select times of high total value, thus giving maximum coverage with a minimum of items, but a representative group of items of lesser value should also be selected for examination. Depending on the internal control and the resulting reliability of the client's records, the stability of prices, the relative importance of the individual inventory items, and any other modifying factors, the pricing test may cover as little as 1 per cent of the total inventory value or as much as 90 percent.

To illustrate how the pricing verification of a test item selected as prescribed above might be handled, let us take a typical example and follow it through. Our client manufactures screw machine products and compiles costs on a job-order basis; inventories are accounted for on a Fifo basis. The following item has been recorded in the audit working papers for pricing verification after having been selected from the client's inventory sheets on a test basis:

| Stock Number | Description | Quantity | Unit | Cost | Extension |
|---|---|---|---|---|---|
| 418 | ¼" × 2" alloy studs | 13 | Gross | $2.66 | $ 34.58 |
| | | 50 | Gross | 2.58 | $129.00 |

The first step in the verification process should be to ascertain whether the cost shown agrees with the cost information recorded in the client's perpetual inventory record of finished goods. Reference to this record reveals that the most recent lot of these studs to be completed was produced under Job Order 3416 for 50 gross at a cost of $2.58 per gross. The preceding lot completed was J.O. 3351 for 100 gross at a cost of $2.66 per gross. This information establishes the correctness of the inventory pricing to this point but the cost figures must be further verified.

Because the two job lots represented in the ending inventory bear similar costs, and assuming that these costs are in line with the inventory record of costs on jobs completed earlier in the year, further verification of only one of the two jobs should be adequate. As job number 3416 was most recently completed and constitutes the bulk of the 63 gross on hand, selecting that job would be most logical.

The required records to complete this examination work may be "pulled" by the auditor, but if the client is willing to do the work, the audit fee will be thereby lessened. In retracing the client's costing process, the first record to be consulted would be the job cost sheet for J.O.3416, which appears in Figure 13-3.

The first point the auditor should note in reviewing the cost sheet is that the unit of count shown therein agrees with the unit of count on the inventory sheet. An inventory count shown as 63 each but priced at the cost per dozen or per gross will substantially overstate the final inventory value. On the other hand, an item counted in dozens or gross but priced at the cost for each item will have the opposite effect.

Each of the figures shown on the cost summary should be traced to supporting records in order to establish that final inventory cost figures have been derived from properly maintained factual records. Stated in

| JOB ORDER COST SHEET | | JOB ORDER NO. 3416 |
|---|---|---|

| STOCK NUMBER  418 | | COST SUMMARY | |
|---|---|---|---|
| DESCRIPTION  1/4" X 2" alloy studs | | MATERIAL | $70.32 |
| | | LABOR | 27.30 |
| | | OVERHEAD (115% X $27.30) | 31.39 |
| QUANTITY ORDERED  50 gross | DATE 12/14 | TOTAL | $129.01 |
| QUANTITY COMPLETED  50 gross | DATE 12/18 | UNIT COST PER  gross | 2.58 |

**MATERIAL**

| DATE | REQUISITION NO. | QUANTITY | DESCRIPTION | UNIT COST | TOTAL COST |
|---|---|---|---|---|---|
| 12/15 | 2953 | 120 | 10' x 1/4" alloy rods | $ .586 | $70.32 |
| | | | | | |
| | | | | | |
| | | | | | |
| | | | | | |
| | | | | | |
| | | | | | |
| | | | TOTAL MATERIAL | | |

**LABOR**

| DATE | CLOCK NUMBER | HOURS | RATE PER HR. | TOTAL | DATE | CLOCK NUMBER | HOURS | RATE PER HR. | TOTAL |
|---|---|---|---|---|---|---|---|---|---|
| 12/16 | 128 | 4 | $4.76 | $19.04 | | | | | |
| 12/17 | 128 | 1 | 4.76 | 4.76 | | | | | |
| 12/18 | 387 | 1 | 3.50 | 3.50 | | | | | |
| | | | | | | | | | |
| | | | | | | | | | |
| | | | | | | | | | |
| | | | | | | | | | |
| | | | | | | | | TOTAL LABOR | $27.30 |

*Figure 13-3.*

another way, the auditor's purpose is to ascertain that there is a complete set of connecting links beginning with payment for the goods or services used and ending with the final financial statement figure for inventory.

*Materials.* Requisition number 2953 may be inspected in support of the material cost, but because verification must go beyond the requisition, reference can be made directly to the perpetual inventory card, which should show the withdrawal of 120 10′ × ¼″ alloy rods. The following abstract of the perpetual inventory card shows that the withdrawal was correctly priced:

| Date | Req. or P.O. No. | Price | Received | Issued | Balance |
|------|------------------|-------|----------|--------|---------|
| 12/2 |  | $.574 |  |  | 50 |
| 12/5 | 604A | .586 | 300 |  | 350 |
| 12/8 | 2940 | .574 |  | 50 |  |
|  |  | .586 |  | 50 | 250 |
| 12/15 | 2953 | .586 |  | 120 | 130 |

Errors in pricing, particularly under first-in, first-out, can readily occur, however, and the auditor should be alert to such possibilities. For instance, in pricing and posting requisition 2940, the inventory clerk might easily overlook the fact that 50 units were still on hand at the old price of $.574. Had the entire issue of 100 been priced at the new figure of $.586, 50 of the units would have been overpriced $.012 each or a total of $.60. As a result, the raw material inventory would have been understated and the finished goods inventory overstated in the amount of $.60. Upon sale of the studs, net income resulting from the sale would be understated by the same amount. This error, in itself, would be insignificant, but as an indication that similar pricing errors might exist throughout the inventory, it would achieve greater importance. If other tests showed similar errors, the auditor would have to conclude that the client's inventory pricing method had not been properly applied. Because such a conclusion would invalidate the client's representations as to the pricing of inventory, the auditor would have to consider the probable overall effect of such errors on the final inventory figure. Should the auditor conclude that inventory and net income might be materially distorted, it would be necessary to request the client to recheck all inventory items for such errors and make an adjustment for the total amount disclosed. If the client declined to recheck and adjust the figures, the auditor would have to qualify the opinion to be rendered with respect to the inventory figure in the financial statements.

Returning to the verification of the inventory pricing of the 63 gross of studs in the finished goods inventory, the final step in the examination of material costs should be to verify the price of $.586 by consulting the vendor's invoice covering the purchase of materials recorded on December 5, which included the 120 rods used in producing the finished studs. A separate section of the perpetual inventory card, not shown above, would contain a record of the purchase orders placed, giving the name of the vendor. With this information the appropriate invoice can be located in the paid invoice file and the price verified against this externally created document.

The amount of work implied in verifying this one item should suggest the practical need for accepting the client's representations on inventory pricing, rather than making a complete verification of inventory pricing. The few tests actually made are then solely to establish the basis for the client's representations.

*Labor.* The cost sheet shows all the details necessary to permit verification of the labor cost charged to the job. Assuming that the payroll week ends on December 18, the individual time cards supporting both labor charges should be filed with the time cards for that week. The cards should show that each worker worked on job 3416 for the number of hours shown on the cost sheet. To complete the verification, cards showing rate per hour authorized for each of the two workers can be inspected in the payroll department. Proof of the extension of the hours and rate verified, as suggested above, can then be made.

*Overhead.* The overhead of $31.39 allocated to the production of the lot of 50 gross of studs represents the application of the plant overhead rate of 115 percent to the labor cost of producing the studs. The auditor should, of course, verify this calculation. But more important is the examination of the manner in which the 115 percent rate was computed. In most instances the rate is set at the beginning of the year, based on past experience. The auditor should determine the reasonableness of such an estimate by relating total labor cost for the year to total factory overhead cost for the year, noting that no change has been made in the classification and treatment of the various factory overhead items. In most instances the actual burden rate so calculated will differ slightly from the predetermined rate used during the year. Inventory pricing of the individual items is seldom corrected for this difference. Instead, if the difference is not large, the corresponding over- or underapplied overhead expense is merely treated as an income statement item of the current year. If the overhead variance is too significant to permit such a treatment, distortion of the financial statements can be avoided if the variance is "spread back" by a pro rata allocation to inventory and cost of sales, as illustrated on schedule C-7. It is not proper, however, to use this treatment if the variance represents idle capacity, for such "costs" should not be included in inventory.

*Inventories Priced at Standard Cost.* Many businesses keep their records on a standard cost basis to obtain added operating information and to simplify the accounting process. Some minor variations in audit procedure are necessitated by such records, but no major problems should result. The auditor's first concern when standard costs are used will ordinarily be to ascertain the methods used by the client in establishing the standards, and then to review these findings in relation to the variances from standard produced by the year's operations. If the variances are not excessive and bear a reasonable relationship to previous experience, the auditor can be fairly certain that operations have progressed smoothly and that the standards reflect current prices and production techniques. A few tests of the records should bear out this conclusion.

Excessive variances point to an opposite conclusion. Large price variances indicate that the standards do not reflect current prices, and large use variances suggest production changes that have not been embodied in the standards being used. Because production changes are ordinarily made to increase efficiency, usage variances will tend to be credit balances. To obtain a fairly stated inventory figure, large variances should be apportioned between inventory and cost of sales and treated as corrections of these figures in the financial statements. Usage variances resulting from inefficiency in the plant would be an exception to the above recommendation. Such variances reflect actual losses and should be taken to the income statement as period expenses. Any variances that are not excessive may be treated as income statement items, regardless of cause, as net income will not be materially affected. Although each variance should be separately reported in internal reports to facilitate control, variances are commonly lumped with cost of sales in published financial statements.

Apart from the question of how to treat variances from standard, the auditor's problem is simply one of testing final inventory prices against the client's book of standard prices and rates, and testing a representative group of entries in which actual costs are converted to standard. The purpose of testing these entries is to show whether the standards being used are current and to ascertain whether variances are being correctly recorded.

*Pricing Verification of Work-in-Process Inventories.* Work-in-process inventories present no problem if the client is using a standard cost system. While observing the physical inventory count, the auditor should note that count tickets accurately list the parts or materials that are represented in each lot of work-in-process items selected for test. Because additional parts or materials may have to be added before the product is complete, failure to specify what items have already been added to the lot might result in the assumption that all necessary parts or materials were present, with inventory overstated as a result. Similarly, each operation that has been completed should be listed on the count ticket so that the final inventory figure will include only the cost of those operations.

When job costs are used, the materials that have been issued to each job can be ascertained much as was suggested above under standard cost procedure. The cost of labor that has been added to a job must, however, be accepted largely on the basis of the labor cost shown on the job cost summary, subject to review of the year-end cutoff of these charges.

The overall reasonableness of the cost shown for each job in process can be tested by reviewing the total costs on the jobs when they are finally completed. If total costs are in line with costs on similar jobs completed at prior times, the presumption should be warranted that costs charged against uncompleted jobs at the balance sheet date are fairly stated.

*Pricing Verification Under the Retail Inventory Method.* The pricing of inventories maintained under the retail method begins at the time that the client takes the physical inventory, and the auditor's inventory observation should include observation and test verification of the recording of retail prices on the inventory tags or sheets. The source of such figures for inventory purposes is, of course, price tags or other price marking of the merchandise on hand. The records of cost and selling price maintained for each department should also be tested in order to calculate the ratio of cost to selling price that is used to reduce the retail value of the inventory to its approximate cost. Proper handling of markups and markdowns is essential to correct inventory valuation, and entries for these amounts should be tested.

*Ascertaining the Existence of Declines in Market Value.* The problem of detecting decreased market values is one of the best illustrations of the fact that a competent audit must go beyond the confines of the client's accounting department. Determining the existence of unrecorded obsolescence is an example. Certain industries operate under conditions of constant style or model changes, and knowledge that such a situation exists should place the auditor on guard in watching for market declines. In other cases change occurs gradually, but the auditor should always watch for products that have been dropped from the client's line of merchandise or are beginning to move slowly. Careful review of perpetual inventory records will usually reveal such instances. Further investigation is warranted whenever the inventory quantity of an item becomes excessive in relation to recent withdrawals or sales. If such conditions become widespread in the client's business, they will also be evident in reduced inventory turnover calculated on an overall basis. Constant or increasing inventory figures in the face of declining sales are almost a sure sign that an inventory problem exists.

The auditor must also be alert to evidence of obsolescence or physical deterioration during the observation of the physical inventory count. Crushed boxes, broken pieces, scratched or oxidized metal surfaces, and dusty items stored in inaccessible locations are all signs that a write-down to market value may be in order.

Direct observation of existing conditions should always be supplemented by discussion with any employees or officials who should be acquainted with the condition of the inventory. These would include the supervisor of the stockroom, the purchasing and sales managers, the treasurer, and even the president.

Most of the officials just mentioned should also be able to supplement the auditor's knowledge of current market prices of both purchased materials and the concern's finished product. General conclusions about price levels must, however, be confirmed by test comparisons between current prices and those in effect six months or a year before.

*Determining Market Price.* If the auditor's inquiry and observation have shown that the reduction of inventory items to market value is a problem, the auditor's next step is to determine whether the client has properly computed and used the reductions to market value. The total inventory should be figured both at cost and at the lower of cost or market. By computing both totals, the client can separate the effect of inventory write-downs from the inventory variance resulting from other causes. Such information gives the client better control and enables the auditor to obtain a clear picture of what has actually occurred.

In general, inventories are priced at replacement cost if that is lower than the original cost, but there are two exceptions. If decreasing sales prices for a product are not accompanied by corresponding price decreases in the market in which the product or raw materials for its manufacture were purchased, inventory should be valued at net realizable value if that is lower than cost or replacement cost—the so-called "ceiling" for inventory valuation.

Occasionally replacement costs may fall while sales prices remain constant or fall at a slower rate. Under such circumstances use of replacement cost results in the recognition of a loss in one period and the production of an abnormally large profit in the following period when the sale occurs. To avoid such shifting of profits between periods, inventory should not be reduced to a price lower than net realizable value less the normal margin of profit: the so-called "floor" for the inventory valuation. Both exceptions to the replacement cost rule represent abnormal situations that are not likely to occur, but the possibility must always be considered.

*Testing Reductions of Inventory to Market Value.* The auditor must, of course, ascertain that market prices used to value inventory below its original cost have been properly determined by the client. The auditor's first step should be to determine current replacement cost for those items selected for test. (The test should include some items that the client has continued to carry at original cost.) Information on current replacement cost may be obtained from many possible sources, although ordinarily only one best source will be used in connection with any single item.

For materials traded on organized commodity exchanges, market quotations at the close of business on the balance sheet date are obviously the best indication of current replacement costs. For other materials, current price lists issued by principal suppliers should be consulted if available. When price lists are not available, the cost of the latest purchase of the inventory item may be used if the elapsed time from the date of purchase to the balance sheet date is not too great, and if price changes during the intervening period would tend to be insignificant. In the absence of a recent purchase and any other information, written requests to one or more vendors for current price quotations may be in order. Ordinarily the auditor need not be concerned about net realizable value and normal profit margins, but these figures must be verified on a test basis if abnormal price movements have occurred.

Proper handling of markdowns under the retail inventory method will automatically reduce inventory to the lower of cost or market. Merchandise should be reviewed to ascertain that all price changes have been noted on the price tags, and markdowns taken subsequent to the balance sheet date should be reviewed for price changes that may actually apply to the year being examined. Sale advertisements appearing after the balance sheet date should be reviewed in relation to the pricing of the merchandise at the balance sheet date.

The considerations pertaining to the use of market price in valuing inventory apply also to firm purchase commitments not protected by firm sales contracts. Losses on such commitments should be recognized just as if the goods were actually on hand. The account credited when such losses are recognized may be classified as a current liability. As has been previously stated, the total amount of purchase commitments should be disclosed by a balance sheet footnote if the commitments are abnormal.

## Questions/Problems

For multiple-choice questions 13-1 through 13-7, indicate the letter of the single answer that *best* completes the statement or answers the question, and justify the choice that you have made.

**13-1.** Failure to account for material requisition numbers
   a. Could result in an out-of-stock condition.
   b. Could result in an overstock condition.
   c. Could result in an overstatement of material costs charged to work in process.
   d. Each of the above could result.

**13-2.** The inventory reorder point

a. Represents the minimum amount of inventory that should be on hand at any one time.
b. Will be lower if there is an increase in "lead" time.
c. Will be higher if there is an increase in demand.
d. None of the above is correct.

**13-3.** Purchase cutoff procedures should be designed to test that merchandise is included in the inventory of the client company, if the company
a. Has paid for the merchandise.
b. Has physical possession of the merchandise.
c. Holds legal title to the merchandise.
d. Holds the shipping documents for the merchandise issued in the company's name.

(Uniform CPA Examination)

**13-4.** When an auditor tests a client's cost accounting system, the auditor's test are *primarily* designed to determine that
a. Quantities on hand have been computed based on acceptable cost accounting techniques that reasonably approximate actual quantities on hand.
b. Physical inventories are in substantial agreement with book inventories.
c. The system is in accordance with generally accepted accounting principles and is functioning as planned.
d. Costs have been properly assigned to finished goods, work-in-progress, and cost of goods sold.

(Uniform CPA Examination)

**13-5.** A CPA observes his client's physical-inventory count on December 31, 19X1. There are eight inventory-taking teams, and a tag system is used. The CPA's observation normally may be expected to result in detection of which of the following inventory errors:
a. The inventory-takers forget to count all of the items in one room of the warehouse.
b. An error is made in the count of one inventory item.
c. Some of the items included in the inventory had been received on consignment.
d. The inventory omits items on consignment to wholesalers.

(Uniform CPA Examination)

**13-6.** The physical count of inventory of a retailer was higher than shown by the perpetual records. Which of the following could explain the difference?
a. Inventory items had been counted but the tags placed on

the items had *not* been taken off the items and added to the inventory accumulation sheets.

b. Credit memos for several items returned by customers had *not* been prepared.

c. *No* journal entry had been made on the retailer's books for several items returned to its suppliers.

d. An item purchased "FOB shipping point" had *not* arrived at the date of the inventory count and had *not* been reflected in the perpetual records.

(Uniform CPA Examination)

**13-7.** The carrying value of inventory will most likely be required to be reduced when

a. Selling prices are steady but replacement costs are falling.

b. Selling prices are falling but replacement costs are steady.

c. Technological developments have lowered prices in the industry.

d. Each of the above would be equally likely to require that inventory carrying value be reduced.

**13-8.** Why do business concerns typically have better internal control over cash and receivables than over inventories?

**13-9.** The Brandywine Company normally uses about 200,000 gallons of spirits per year as one of the basic ingredients in the product it manufactures, ordering the spirits on a 10-day delivery basis. At December 31, the company had outstanding a firm purchase committment for 50,000 gallons of spirits at a price of $1.00 per gallon. The company follows generally accepted accounting principles in pricing its inventories.

(a) Assuming that the market price for spirits at December 31 is $1.10 per gallon, how should the purchase commitment be shown in the financial statements (if at all)? Justify your answer.

(b) How would your answer to part (a) be changed (if at all) if the market price were $.90 instead of $1.10 at the balance sheet date? Justify your answer.

(c) If the conditions under (b) prevailed, give the journal entry to record the purchase of the 50,000 gallons in the following year.

**13-10.** For each of the following situations, indicate whether the stated facts would *overstate, understate,* or have *no effect* on net income for the year ended December 31. The client is on a perpetual inventory system; the physical inventory was taken at the close of business on December 31, and the book inventory was adjusted to agree with the physical inventory without taking the following items into consideration:

(a) There was a file of unmatched receiving reports at December 31.

(b) The client accounts for purchase discounts using the method that shows "purchase discounts lost." The ending inventory was costed by using the prices shown on vendor invoices.

(c) No cost of sales entry was made for goods sold, shipped, and billed to a customer on December 31.

(d) Vendor invoices were on hand at December 31, but had not been recorded because the goods had not been received. The invoice terms were all f.o.b. shipping point.

(e) At the close of the preceding year goods had been received, but the entries to record the purchases were not made until the current year.

**13-11.** You are engaged in your first examination of a client's financial statements for the year ended December 31, 19X1. The client has already made the necessary book entries to record the physical inventory at the end of the year. In the course of your test of cutoffs at the beginning and end of the year, you discover that

1. Invoices totaling $5,653.95 were entered in the voucher register in January, 19X1, but the goods were received in December, 19X0. The client did not consider these items in recording the physical inventory.

2. Sales of $10,243.50, which cost $7,519.80, were made in December, 19X1, and the goods shipped then, but the related book entries were not made until January, 19X2. No consideration was given to this fact in recording the physical inventory.

Give the adjusting entries that should be made in your working papers under the assumption that

(a) The general ledger inventory is maintained on a *perpetual* basis.

(b) The general ledger inventory is maintained on a *periodic* basis.

**13-12.** Your client's fiscal year closes on December 31, but the physical inventory was taken at November 30, and the general ledger perpetual inventory account was adjusted downward at that date to bring it into agreement with the physical inventory amount. The client did not give any consideration at either November 30 or December 31 to unmatched receiving reports in the accounts payable department files. The total amounts were

November 30                    $3,269.20
December 31                     3,892.15

Give the adjusting entries, if any, that you would make in your working papers.

13-13.   In an annual audit at December 31, 19X1 you find the following near the closing date:

   (1)   Merchandise costing $1,822 was received on January 3, 19X2 and the related purchase invoice recorded January 5. The invoice showed the shipment was made on December 29, 19X1, *f.o.b. destination*.

   (2)   Merchandise costing $625 was received on December 28, 19X1 and the invoice was not recorded. You located it in the hands of the purchasing agent; it was marked *on consignment*.

   (3)   A packing case containing product costing $816 was standing in the shipping room when the physical inventory was taken. It was not included in the inventory because it was marked *hold for shipping instructions*. Your investigation revealed that the customer's order was dated December 18, 19X1 but that the case was shipped and the customer billed on January 10, 19X2. The product was a stock item of your client.

   (4)   Merchandise received on January 6, 19X2 costing $720 was entered in the purchase register on January 7, 19X2. The invoice showed shipment was made f.o.b. supplier's warehouse on December 31, 19X1. Since it was not on hand at December 31, it was not included in inventory.

   (5)   A special machine, fabricated to order for a customer, was finished and in the shipping room on December 31, 19X1. The customer was billed on that date and the machine excluded from inventory although it was shipped on January 4, 19X2.

*Assume that each of the amounts is material.*

   (a)   State whether the merchandise should be included in the client's inventory.

   (b)   Give your reason for your decision on each item in (a) above.

(Uniform CPA Examination)

13-14.   You have been engaged by the management of Alden, Inc., to review its internal control over the purchase, receipt, storage, and issue of raw materials. You have prepared the following comments which describe Alden's procedures.

—Raw materials, which consist mainly of high–cost electronic components, are kept in a locked storeroom. Storeroom personnel include a supervisor and four clerks. All are well trained, competent, and adequately bonded. Raw materials are removed from the storeroom only upon written or oral authorization of one of the production foremen.

–There are no perpetual–inventory records; hence, the storeroom clerks do not keep records of goods received or issued. To compensate for the lack of perpetual records, a physical–inventory count is taken monthly by the storeroom clerks who are well supervised. Appropriate procedures are followed in making the inventory count.

–After the physical count, the storeroom supervisor matches quantities counted against a predetermined reorder level. If the count for a given part is below the reorder level, the supervisor enters the part number on a materials–requisition list and sends this list to the accounts–payable clerk. The accounts–payable clerk prepares a purchase order for a predetermined reorder quantity for each part and mails the purchase order to the vendor from whom the part was last purchased.

–When ordered materials arrive at Alden, they are received by the storeroom clerks. The clerks count the merchandise and agree the counts to the shipper's bill of lading. All vendors' bills of lading are initialed, dated, and filed in the storeroom to serve as receiving reports.

Required:

Describe the weaknesses in internal control and recommend improvements of Alden's procedures for the purchase, receipt, storage, and issue of raw materials. Organize your answer sheet as follows:

| Weaknesses | Recommended Improvements |
| --- | --- |
| | |

(Uniform CPA Examination)

**13-15.** You are making an examination of the statements of the Modern Department Store at December 31. The following figures are presented to you at the time you commence your examination:

```
Book Inventory January 1:
    Cost  ....................................... $110,406.19
    Selling  ....................................  154,305.91
Transactions for the Year:
    Purchases
        Cost  ....................................  421,401.40
        Selling  .................................  604,367.18
```

| Sales | 586,565.94 |
|---|---|
| Mark-ups (selling) | 1,052.03 |
| Mark-downs (selling) | 7,831.20 |
| Physical inventory December 31 (selling) | 162,325.87 |

In the course of your examination, you discover the following:

1. Markdowns totaling $1,256.00 were shown on price tags, but not recorded on the books.
2. Merchandise with a sales value of $786.00 was out of the store on demonstration at the inventory date, and not included in the physical inventory.
3. The purchases figure includes invoices for merchandise costing $3,624.98, but the merchandise had not been received. The invoices were dated December.
4. Merchandise with a sales value of $2,152.00 was counted in the inventory, but the invoices had not been received or recorded at December 31.
5. Invoices totaling $10,325.72 were on hand for merchandise shipped to your client in December, but the invoices were not recorded and the merchandise had not been received at December 31.
6. Merchandise totaling $2,376.52 was on hand and included in the inventory, but had already been sold and the sale was recorded in December.
7. All electric light bulbs are stocked on a consignment basis. The inventory of light bulbs totaled $1,271.90, and was included in the physical inventory.

Required:

1. Computations to arrive at the book inventory figure at cost and at selling price before considering items 1 to 7 above.
2. The inventory figure which should appear in your client's balance sheet, after considering items 1 to 7. (All goods are purchased f.o.b. shipping point).
3. The income statement for the store through net margin on sales, in form ready for typing.
4. A statement as to how the auditor would likely have uncovered the information in items 1 to 7 above.

**13-16.** The cost-of-goods-sold section of the income statement prepared by your client, Biltwell Bird Cage Co., for the year ended December 31, appears as follows:

| Inventory, January 1 | $ 3,215.80 |
|---|---|
| Purchases | 21,172.15 |
| Cost of goods available for sale | $24,387.95 |
| Inventory, December 31 | 4,321.80 |
| Cost of goods sold | $20,066.15 |

Although the books have been closed, your working paper trial balance is prepared showing all accounts with activity during the year. This is the first year your firm has made an examination. The January 1 and December 31 inventories appearing above were determined by physical count of the goods on hand on those dates, and no reconciling items were considered. All purchases are f.o.b. shipping point.

In the course of your examination of the inventory cutoff, both at the beginning and end of the year, you discover the following facts:

### Beginning of the year

1. Invoices totaling $364.15 were entered in the voucher register in January, but the goods were received during December.
2. December invoices totaling $796.16 were entered in the voucher register in December, but goods were not received until January.

### End of the Year

3. Sales of $564.20 (cost, $423.10) were made on account on December 31 and the goods delivered at that time, but all entries relating to the sales were made on January 2.
4. Invoices totaling $591.40 were entered in the voucher register in January, but the goods were received in December.
5. December invoices totaling $421.10 were entered in the voucher register in December, but the goods were not received until January.
6. Invoices totaling $1,215.40 were entered in the voucher register in January, and the goods were received in January, but the invoices were dated December.

Required:
(a) The adjusting entries to be made in your work papers, assuming the Company is on a periodic inventory basis.
(b) The adjusting entries to be made in your work papers, assuming the Company maintains the inventory control account on a perpetual basis. The book inventory figure at December 31 was $4,321.80, and the physical inventory agreed with that figure.
(c) Corrected cost-of-goods-sold schedules under the assumptions in (a) and (b) above.

**13-17.** The Paris Company manufactures and sells four products, the inventories of which are priced at cost or market, whichever is lower. A normal profit margin rate of 30% is usually maintained on each of the four products.
The following information was compiled as of December 31.

| Product | Original Cost | Cost to Replace | Estimated Cost to Dispose | "Normal" Selling Price* | Expected Selling Price |
|---------|---------------|-----------------|---------------------------|-------------------------|------------------------|
| A | $35.00 | $42.00 | $15.00 | $70.00 | $ 80.00 |
| B | 47.50 | 45.00 | 20.50 | 95.00 | 95.00 |
| C | 17.50 | 15.00 | 5.00 | 35.00 | 30.00 |
| D | 45.00 | 46.00 | 26.00 | 90.00 | 100.00 |

* "Normal" selling price = original cost ÷ (100%—the normal 50% gross margin rate).

Required:

(a) Why are expected selling prices important in the application of the lower-of-cost-or-market rule?

(b) Prepare a schedule containing unit values (including "floor" and "ceiling") for determining the lower of cost or market on an individual product basis. The last column of the schedule should contain for each product the unit value for the purpose of inventory valuation resulting from the application of the lower-of-cost-or-market rule.

(c) What effects, if any, do the expected selling prices have on the valuation of products A, B, C, and D by the lower-of-cost-or-market rule?

(Uniform CPA Examination)

**13-18.** The following figures are from work papers testing inventory pricing for a December 31 examination. The inventory is priced on a first-in, first-out basis.

| | Per Inventory | | | Per Invoices Examined by Auditor | | |
|------|----------|--------|---------|--------------|----------|--------|
| Item | Quantity | Price | Total | Invoice Date | Quantity | Price |
| A ..... | 150 | $1.40 | $210.00 | 12/15 | 300 | $1.50 |
| B ..... | 2,000 | .28 | 560.00 | 12/20 | 500 | .28 |
| C .... | 104 | .75 | 78.00 | 5/17 | 300 | .75 |
| D .... | 2,980 | .25 | 745.00 | 2/5 | 3,000 | .25 |

State whether you would question the inventory price used by the client, the auditor's verification, or both, under the following circumstances (give reasons):

(a) Material prices have been rising steadily.

(b) Material prices have been declining but sales prices have remained steady.

(c) Material prices and sales prices have been declining.

**13-19.** Your client has already adjusted the general ledger perpetual inventory account to agree with the physical inventory; the client's fiscal year ends December 31. In reviewing cost of sales entries for January, you discover an item costing $1,500 that was actually shipped and billed in December. Give the adjusting entry and reversing entry (if any) you would recommend under each of the following assumptions:

(a) The physical inventory was taken on November 30.
(b) The physical inventory was taken on December 31.

(Assume that the client's books have not yet been closed).

**13-20.** Your client takes a physical inventory on November 30, adjusts the perpetual inventory control account for any shortage, and then uses the December 31 balance of the inventory account in its financial statements for the year. It is thus necessary for you to make cutoff tests at both November 30 and December 31. In connection with the two purchases listed below covered by such cutoff tests, no adjustment had been made by the client.

| Amount | Invoice Date | Invoice Terms F.O.B. | Date Goods Received | Date Invoice Entered in Voucher Register |
|---|---|---|---|---|
| $241.61 | 11/28 | Shipping Point | 12/3 | 11/29 |
| 163.95 | 12/27 | Destination | 12/30 | 1/2 |

Give the adjusting entries (if any) that you would make in your working papers, disregarding the question of materiality.

**13-21.** Ace Corporation does not conduct a complete annual physical count of purchased parts and supplies in its principal warehouse but uses statistical sampling instead to estimate the year-end inventory. Ace maintains a perpetual inventory record of parts and supplies and believes that statistical sampling is highly effective in determining inventory values and is sufficiently reliable to make a physical count of each item of inventory unnecessary.

Required:
(a) Identify the audit procedures that should be used by the independent auditor that change or are in addition to normal required audit procedures when a client utilizes statistical sampling to determine inventory value and does not conduct a 100 percent annual physical count of inventory items.
(b) List at least ten normal audit procedures that should be performed *to verify physical quantities* whenever a client conducts a periodic physical count of all or part of its inventory.

(Uniform CPA Examination)

**13-22.** In connection with his examination of the financial statements of Knutson Products Co., an assembler of home appliances, for the year ended May 31, 19X1, Ray Abel, CPA, is reviewing with Knutson's controller the plans for a physical inventory at the Company warehouse on May 31, 19X1. Note: In answering the two parts of this question do not discuss procedures for the physical inventory of work in process, inventory pricing or other audit steps not directly related to the physical inventory taking.

Part a.   Finished appliances, unassembled parts and supplies are stored in the warehouse, which is attached to Knutson's assembly plant. The plant will operate during the count. On May 30 the warehouse will deliver to the plant the estimated quantities of unassembled parts and supplies required for May 31 production, but there may be emergency requisitions on May 31. During the count the warehouse will continue to receive parts and supplies and to ship finished appliances. However, appliances completed on May 31 will be held in the plant until after the physical inventory.

Required:

What procedures should the Company establish to insure that the inventory count includes all items that should be included and that nothing is counted twice?

Part b.   Warehouse employees will join with accounting department employees in counting the inventory. The inventory-takers will use a tag system.

Required:

What instructions should the Company give to the inventory takers?

(Uniform CPA Examination)

13-23.   An auditor is conducting an examination of the financial statements of a wholesale cosmetics distributor with an inventory consisting of thousands of individual items. The distributor keeps its inventory in its own distribution center and in two public warehouses. An inventory computer file is maintained on a computer disk, and at the end of each business day the file is updated. Each record of the inventory file contains the following data:

Item number
Location of item
Description of item
Quantity on hand
Cost per item
Date of last purchase

Date of last sale
Quantity sold during year

The auditor is planning to observe the distributor's physical count of inventories as of a given date. The auditor will have available a computer tape of the data on the inventory file on the date of the physical count and a general purpose computer software package.

Required:

The auditor is planning to perform basic inventory auditing procedures. Identify the basic inventory auditing procedures and describe how the use of the general purpose software package and the tape of the inventory file data might be helpful to the auditor in performing such auditing procedures.

Organize your answer as follows:

| Basic inventory auditing procedure | How general purpose computer software package and tape of the inventory file data might be helpful |
|---|---|
| 1. *Observe the physical count, making and recording test counts where applicable.* | *Determining which items are to be test counted by selecting a random sample of a representative number of items from the inventory file as of the date of the physical count.* |

(Uniform CPA Examination)

**13-24.** The complete audit program for the verification of the raw materials inventory of the Madison Manufacturing Co. is given below. In addition, certain data are given pertaining to company figures and audit work that has already been completed.

Using the information given, you are to prepare the final work sheet covering the verification of inventory, showing the results of your examination of inventory items not yet verified, and including the totals carried forward from work sheets previously completed. If no further information is given concerning any point in the audit program, assume the work was completed and no exceptions were found.

Also, prepare a summary showing the extent and results of all inventory work performed.

1. Observe taking of physical inventory by client on December 31, noting that all procedures covered by client's printed instructions are followed.

2. Make independent counts of about 2 percent of the inventory items, and record in our work papers for tracing to the final inventory sheets. Select items of substantial value.

3. Select 25 material requisitions and 25 purchase transactions from the last 3 days of current period and the first 3 days of following period, for examination of cutoff on raw materials.

4. Verify pricing, which is on an average cost basis, on all items counted by us and on all other items with a value of $500 or more; in addition select two other items from each page of the client's inventory. Verify by examining average cost shown by perpetual inventory records, and noting cost per unit on most recent purchase. For every third item selected for price test, examine the vendor's invoice in support of the most recent purchase. If most recent purchase is below previous average cost, investigate reason for difference, and make note in our papers if it appears the item should be priced at market rather than cost.

5. Discuss price situation generally with purchasing manager as to raw materials and with sales manager as to finished product, to ascertain whether any general write-down of inventory costs may be necessary.

6. Maintain a careful watch for obsolete or unusable parts.

7. Check clerical accuracy by verifying extensions and footings of every third inventory sheet. Scan other sheets for extension or footing errors.

8. Prepare entry to adjust book inventory to agree with physical inventory. Ignore errors disclosed by our examination unless they are material.

Information concerning work done or to be done:

Items selected for pricing test from last three pages of the inventory:

| Part No. | Quantity | | Cost | Total |
|----------|----------|------|------|-------|
| 2204 .............. | 162 | | $4.39 | $ 711.18 |
| 2210 .............. | 1,864 | | .13 | 242.32 |
| 2213a .............. | 415 | | 1.19 | 493.85 |
| 2213b .............. | 764 | | 1.13 | 863.32 |
| 2220 .............. | 13 | doz. | 2.34 | 30.42 |
| 2234 .............. | 265 | | 3.82 | $1,012.30 |
| 2241 .............. | 549 | | .98 | 538.02 |
| 2246 .............. | 175 | | 2.14 | 374.50 |
| 2249 .............. | 318 | | 1.83 | 581.94 |
| 2264 .............. | 65 | | .39 | 25.35 |
| 2277 .............. | 204 | | .81 | 165.24 |

(Above part numbers counted during physical inventory: 2213b, 2234.)

Average costs on above items as shown by perpetual inventory records (costs are per unit of one unless otherwise indicated):

| | | | | |
|---|---|---|---|---|
| 2204 | . . . . . . . . . . . . . $4.39 | | 2241 | . . . . . . . . . . . . $ .98 |
| 2210 | . . . . . . . . . . . . . .13 | | 2246 | . . . . . . . . . . . . 2.14 |
| 2213a | . . . . . . . . . . . . 1.19 | | 2249 | . . . . . . . . . . . . 1.83 |
| 2213b | . . . . . . . . . . . . 1.13 | | 2264 | . . . . . . . . . . . . .39 |
| 2220 | . . . . . . . . . . . . . 2.34 | | 2277 | . . . . . . . . . . . . .81 |
| 2234 | . . . . . . . . . . . . 3.82 | | | |

Data from vendor's invoices covering items to be traced thereto:

| Part No. | Voucher No. | Date | Quantity | Price |
|---|---|---|---|---|
| 2213a . . . . . . . | 14891 | 12/13 | 300 | $1.19 |
| 2234 . . . . . . . . . . | 14906 | 12/15 | 500 | 3.84 |
| 2249 . . . . . . . . . . | 12246 | 9/17 | 1,000[a] | 1.80 |

[a]These items bought at a special close-out price—regular price from new supplier will be $1.95.

Total of worksheets covering remainder of inventory:

| | No. of Items | Dollar Value |
|---|---|---|
| Items selected for price test . . . . . . . . . | 118 | $ 41,964.92 |
| Items tested to vendors' invoices . . . . . | 39 | 14,251.83 |
| Items test counted included in above figures . . . . . . . . . . . . . . . . . . . . . . . . . . . | 33 | 18,249.51 |
| Differences disclosed— | | |
| Inventory overstated . . . . . . . . . . . . . . | | 1,321.15 |
| Inventory understated . . . . . . . . . . . . . | | 926.57 |

| Other data— | | |
|---|---|---|
| Raw materials inventory | **Last Year** | **This Year** |
| Per books . . . . . . . . . . . . . . . . . . . . | $ 67,964.84 | $ 87,465.19 |
| Per physical | | |
| Dollar value . . . . . . . . . . . . . . . . . . . . | 60,364.29 | 78,216.45 |
| No. of items . . . . . . . . . . . . . . . . . . | 1,529 | 1,603 |
| Raw materials used . . . . . . . . . . . . . . | $694,205.46 | $851,319.82 |
| Results of test of clerical accuracy | | |
| Total dollar value of pages verified . . . . . . . . . . . . . . . . . . | | $ 24,816.92 |
| Errors disclosed by above test— | | |
| Inventory overstated . . . . . . . . . . . . . . . . . . . . . . . . . . . . . . | | 433.41 |
| Inventory understated . . . . . . . . . . . . . . . . . . . . . . . . . . . . | | 926.53 |
| Errors disclosed by scanning— | | |
| Inventory overstated . . . . . . . . . . . . . . . . . . . . . . . . . . . . . | | 521.19 |

**13-25.** John Conrey was the managing member of the 3-partner firm that had been formed to develop and produce a new high efficiency heat pump. The idea for the new approach to heat pump design was the brain child of Don Tyler, who was a tinkerer and inventor of sorts. He was responsible for overseeing development and production of the new unit.

Bob Cash handled financial matters for the firm, which was operating under the name of Heat/Cool Plus. Cash had personally supplied much of the capital to launch Heat/Cool, he had general administrative responsibility for accounting and other office functions, and he was currently engaged in seeking additional financing from Venture Capital, an SBIC located in the city in which Heat/Cool was operating. In connection with the financing negotiations, Heat/Cool was in the process of incorporating and had engaged Anders & Young, CPAs, to examine Heat/Cool's financial statements.

This was the first audit for Heat/Cool and was to cover the firm's financial statements for the year ending April 30. John Birch was the senior accountant responsible for the engagement, and he was assisted in the examination at various times by staff accountants Charlene Jones and Paul Roberts. Arrangements for the engagement were completed early in April, so that the April 30 physical inventory taking could be observed, and Birch began planning the engagement immediately.

In familiarizing himself with Heat/Cool's operations, Birch learned that the firm had been in operation for about two years, with most of the first year spent in developing the heat pump unit and preparing for production. Production of the first lot of 100 units was commenced that year and completed by May 10. Several additional lots of 100 were completed during the current year, and to satisfy the increasing demand, lot size for production orders was raised to 250.

Ten distributors were currently handling sales of the units. In order to gain distribution, the initial distributors handled the units on a consignment basis, and that arrangement was still in effect, although the latest distributors who were signed up were required to purchase their stock on n/15 terms. The distribution arrangements and the increasing production volume had presented cash flow problems for Heat/Cool, and Cash had borrowed heavily from the Friendly National Bank to finance operations. It was planned that the major part of the loans from Friendly National would be repaid from the proceeds of the sale of common stock to Venture Capital.

Cash was primarily responsible for the development of Heat/Cool's accounting system. Unit records were maintained for all production parts and materials but were not tied in with the financial records. "Standard" costs were developed on the basis of the experience with the first two production lots, but were being revised to reflect rising prices, and the current April 30 inventory was to be priced based on the new standard costs.

Material costs were transferred to a work-in-process account at standard as materials were issued for a production order and memorandum records were maintained for the costs on each production lot. Labor costs were charged to the work-in-process ledger account and accumulated in the memorandum production lot cost records. At the completion of a production lot, the standard cost of material, labor, and overhead was charged to a finished goods account, with credits to work in process for material and labor and to "Applied Overhead" for the overhead costs. The overhead amounts for the current year, based on the relationship of overhead cost to direct labor cost for the first year, were to be revised to reflect current experience for use in inventory pricing at the end of the year.

The physical inventory count was to be taken at the close of business on April 30. Counting of raw materials was to be commenced on April 30 as soon as materials received that day had been checked in and placed in stock. A 2-part prenumbered tag was to be used for the count, which was to be made by storeroom and shop personnel. Individuals counted the various items and recorded the counts on tags along with necessary identifying information, location, and so forth, attaching the tag to the materials when completed.

The plant superintendent and the general foreman divided the responsibility for checking various plant areas to ensure that all items had been tagged, reviewing the information recorded on the tags, and removing the count portion of the tags.

Work-in-process inventory for the production order being worked on was to be based on the standard costs of the materials and labor charged to the production order and recorded in the memorandum record of the costs accumulated against the production order, plus the related overhead expense.

No finished units were expected to be on hand, as demand was running high and units were shipped as soon as they were completed. There were, however, a number of previously sold units expected to be on hand, as there was a continuing problem with the switchover valve assembly, and a number of units had been returned to Heat/Cool for reworking in an effort to remedy that problem.

Required:
Considering the circumstances detailed above, state why Birch

should be especially alert in conducting this audit. Suggest changes that he might wish to request the company to make prior to taking inventory on April 30, and list potential problem areas that should be identified and closely watched in connection with the inventory and other related segments of the examination.

# Chapter 14

# CASH: RECEIPTS, DISBURSEMENTS, BALANCES

**Appendix—Supplementary Cash Audit Procedures**
The Techniques of Defalcation
Kiting
Lapping
Detection of Fraud and the Four-Column Bank Reconciliation
  Balances
  Receipts and Deposits
  Disbursements

---

Cash handling and the control of cash balances tend to be critical in designing financial operating and accounting systems and developing adequate internal controls for those systems. The problem is accentuated by the attractiveness of cash with its power to command economic goods of all types, its portability in terms of the relationship of bulk to value, and its accessibility through orders to pay and transfer authorizations even though it has been deposited with a financial institution.

It is important that the auditor give close attention to cash, and extensive audit scrutiny is further warranted by the fact that cash is essentially the "eye of the needle," with practically all business transactions involving the receipt or disbursement of cash at some point in time.

### Control Considerations

Control over cash should be exercised at the earliest possible point— that is, when cash proceeds flow into the entity, whether from accounts receivable collections, cash sales, dispositions of assets, or direct borrowing. Cash accountability established at that point should then be discharged only on the basis of disbursements that have been duly authorized. Cash balances for which custodians are accountable that are either on hand or in a bank account should be verified regularly on an independent basis by cash count or bank account reconciliation.

Essential features of systems to control and handle cash receipts and cash disbursements are shown in the AICPA flowcharts presented in Figures 14-1 and 14-2. The following comments pertain to these flowcharts.

### Comments on Illustrative Flowcharts of Cash Handling Procedures

1.  Cash receipts are shown as originating from both cash sales and from collections on accounts receivable.

2.    The handling of cash receipts and disbursements are responsibilities within the treasury function and hence are under the treasurer's direction, but other operating personnel may also be involved, as in the cash of retail sales clerks, or mail room employees who report to an administrative officer.

3.    The functions shown as being carried out by the home office auditors would clearly result in maximum internal control, inasmuch as the auditors have no conflicting operating or accounting responsibilities. However, reading cash register totals by using a control key, receiving duplicate deposit slips directly from the bank, and reconciling bank statements are accounting-related activities. As was noted in the earlier discussion of internal auditing, assigning such activities to the internal audit function has the effect of limiting internal audit independence and effectiveness and further leaves such accounting activities without an effective review.

4.    Mail room employees need not prepare a list of mail receipts if accompanying remittance advices are compared with check amounts and then separated, with checks going to the cashier for preparation of a deposit slip and deposit of the funds in the bank. The cash receipts record can then be prepared as an accounting function from the remittance advices, or as a byproduct of posting to the accounts receivable records. The duplicate deposit slips from the bank should be received by an accounting clerk with no other cash responsibilities and compared with the cash receipts record of cash collections based on remittance advices, plus the daily cash register totals. A special key is required to print out the cash register totals, but for electronic registers that are the source of computer input, the totals are obtained as a computer output.

5.    When a check is signed, the related voucher and supporting documents should be marked "paid" to preclude their being resubmitted for payment. These documents should then be filed in the accounts payable section, with the file usually arranged chronologically by vendor to facilitate "audit trail" reference in response to inquiries from vendors about whether certain items have been paid.

6.    Typically checks are not signed manually, but by the use of a signature plate in a check signing machine. Control over check signatures is maintained through custody of the signature plate (or plates when two signatures are required), the use of a key to operate the equipment, and a nonresettabe counter that keeps track of the number of checks signed. The counter total should be compared with the previous reading plus the number of checks shown on the transmittal tape accompanying each batch of checks and supporting documents submitted for payment.

7.    All major disbursements should be by check in order to realize maximum control over authorized disbursements, to obtain assurance that there will be a record in the form of a paid check for all cash

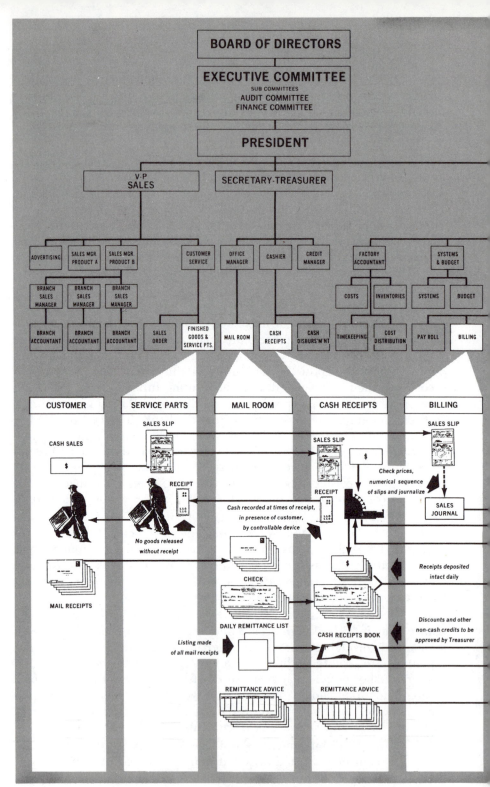

**Figure 14-1.**

# CASH RECEIPTS

PROCEDURAL FLOW CHART SHOWN IN RELATION
TO ORGANIZATION CHART TO PORTRAY
THE CONTROL OBTAINED THROUGH SEGREGATION
OF FUNCTIONAL RESPONSIBILITY

CONTROLLER | V-P INDUSTRIAL RELATIONS | V-P MANUFACTURING

SAFETY | WELFARE & CAFETERIA | EMPLOYMENT | PRODUCTS ENGINEER | PURCHASING AGENT

CHIEF ACCOUNTANT | INTERNAL AUDITOR | TRAFFIC & SHIPPING | SUPERVISOR MFG. | PLANT & MAINTENANCE ENGINEER | PRODUCTION CONTROL | METHODS ENGINEER

FOUNDRY | SCHEDULING | MATERIAL CONTROL | TOOL ENGINEERING

MACHINE SHOP

ACCOUNTS PAYABLE | ACCOUNTS RECEIVABLE | PURCHASE & EXPENSE LEDGER | GENERAL LEDGER | HOME OFFICE AUDITORS | BRANCH AUDITORS | ASSEMBLY | RECEIVING DEPARTMENT | STORES | TIME STUDY

## ACCOUNTS RECEIVABLE | GENERAL LEDGER | AUDITORS | BANK

*Charges from Billing should offset credits from Cashier*

**CASH SALES CLEARING ACCOUNT**

*Auditors keep register key and check totals*

DEPOSIT SLIP

*Detail entries must prove to control*

**ACCOUNTS RECEIVABLE CONTROL**

DEPOSIT SLIP

*Receive duplicate deposit slips directly from bank*

DAILY REMITTANCE LIST

REMITTANCE ADVICE

Source: AICPA *Internal Control*

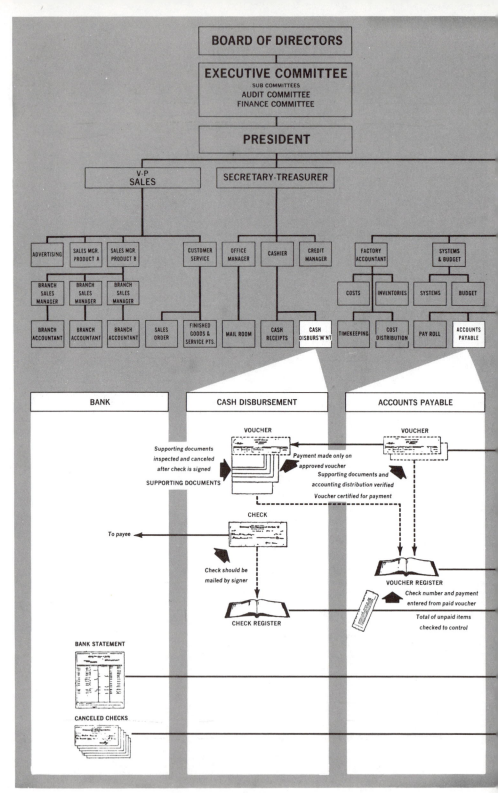

*Figure 14-2.*

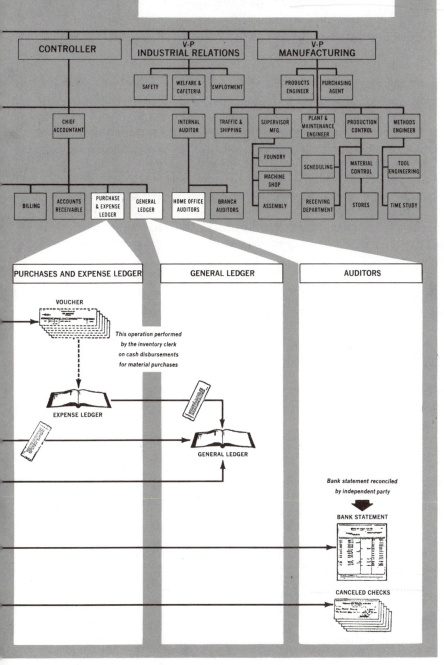

# CASH DISBURSEMENTS

PROCEDURAL FLOW CHART SHOWN IN RELATION
TO ORGANIZATION CHART TO PORTRAY
THE CONTROL OBTAINED THROUGH SEGREGATION
OF FUNCTIONAL RESPONSIBILITY

CONTROLLER

V-P INDUSTRIAL RELATIONS

V-P MANUFACTURING

SAFETY | WELFARE & CAFETERIA | EMPLOYMENT

PRODUCTS ENGINEER | PURCHASING AGENT

CHIEF ACCOUNTANT

INTERNAL AUDITOR | TRAFFIC & SHIPPING | SUPERVISOR MFG. | PLANT & MAINTENANCE ENGINEER | PRODUCTION CONTROL | METHODS ENGINEER

FOUNDRY

SCHEDULING | MATERIAL CONTROL | TOOL ENGINEERING

MACHINE SHOP

BILLING | ACCOUNTS RECEIVABLE | PURCHASE & EXPENSE LEDGER | GENERAL LEDGER | HOME OFFICE AUDITORS | BRANCH AUDITORS | ASSEMBLY | RECEIVING DEPARTMENT | STORES | TIME STUDY

## PURCHASES AND EXPENSE LEDGER

VOUCHER

*This operation performed
by the inventory clerk
on cash disbursements
for material purchases*

EXPENSE LEDGER

## GENERAL LEDGER

GENERAL LEDGER

## AUDITORS

*Bank statement reconciled
by independent party*

BANK STATEMENT

CANCELED CHECKS

Source: AICPA *Internal Control*

405

disbursed, and to minimize the risk of loss by holding cash only in the form of bank deposits.

8. Minor disbursements are most economically and efficiently handled through a petty cash fund. The disbursements may be in cash form or by check drawn on a special account, with all disbursements being verified against appropriate supporting documents at the time that reimbursement of the petty cash fund is requested, rather than prior to the disbursement as for most items.

9. Another variation in disbursement procedure is the use of purchase-order drafts for amounts up to some established limit, such as $1,000. For this system a purchase order is accompanied by a check payable to the vendor and signed by an authorized purchasing representative. The vendor, after shipping the ordered goods, completes the "invoice" portion of the check, completes the check for the amount that is due (but not to exceed the limit printed on the check), and deposits the check. For further protection, the reverse side of the check can be preprinted, "For deposit only to the account of the payee." A postaudit of each transaction after the purchase-order draft has been paid can then cover verification of price, extension, and receipt of the specified quantity of material.

## Evaluation of Internal Control Objectives and Features

Internal control objectives and the features through which the objectives can be accomplished with respect to cash transactions and balances are discussed in terms of the three main classifications of objectives that have been previously used. Procedures used to test compliance with each feature are also shown.

### Operating Objectives

*All transactions are properly authorized.*

- Cash sales are made only by authorized persons, and the amount of cash received is recorded through a registering device. *Inquiry, observation.*
- Credits to accounts receivable for collections received are made only on the basis of remittance advices or other documents evidencing the receipt of cash. *Inquiry, inspection.*
- Checks for disbursements are signed only by the treasurer or other persons who have been duly authorized to sign checks. *Inquiry, inspection.*
- Check requisitions or checks prepared by accounts payable and presented for signature are in payment of duly authorized transactions, as evidenced by supporting documents such as check requisitions bearing an authorized signature, or purchase orders, invoices, and receiving reports. These docu-

ments should be marked "Paid" or otherwise cancelled at the time of payment, to prevent their reuse. *Inquiry, observation, inspection.*

- Petty cash disbursements are limited to specifically authorized transactions and are made only on the basis of approved requests or presentation of documents evidencing a past disbursement of an authorized type. *Inquiry, inspection.*
- All checks that have been outstanding in excess of a stated period of time, such as one year, should be restored to the cash account and a liability recorded; subsequent clearing of the check or a request for a new check should be subjected to appropriate investigation. *Inquiry, inspection.*

*All authorizations resulted in action being taken.*

- Control totals of cash received are balanced against general and subsidiary ledger records of related credits to sales, accounts receivable, or other accounts as appropriate. *Inquiry, observation, inspection.*
- Controls to ensure that authorized disbursements have been made are generally unnecessary; rather, those parties expecting to receive payment are relied upon to initiate follow-up if the payment is not received. *Inquiry.*
- Checks in excess of a stated amount that have been outstanding for more than a stated period of time should be investigated by contacting the payee to ascertain why the check has not cleared through banking channels. *Inquiry.*

*Access to assets is permitted only in accordance with management authorization.*

- All cash except necessary change and petty cash funds is deposited in authorized bank accounts, so that withdrawals are limited to checks carrying authorized signatures or to authorized transfers of funds. *Inquiry, observation.*
- Change funds and the proceeds of cash sales are held in locked drawers, cash registers, or areas to which access is limited, such as for teller areas of a bank. *Inquiry, observation.*
- For maximum control, disbursements should not be made from cash receipts; all cash receipts should be deposited intact. *Inquiry, inspection.*

### Data Processing Objectives—Internal Accounting Control

*Accounting and operating responsibilities should be segregated or subjected to appropriate controls when segregation is not possible.*

- Accounting personnel should not have custody or access to cash funds. *Inquiry, observation.*
- Personnel who handle cash or execute cash transactions should have no accounting responsibilities or any other operating responsibilities. *Inquiry, observation.*
- When cash sales are involved, there is an unavoidable combination of handling merchandise, cash, and originating accounting records that calls for

maximum controls through registering each transaction and monitoring transactions as closely as is feasible. *Inquiry, observation.*

- Persons who open mail containing cash receipts should have no other operating or accounting responsibilities. Accountability for cash received should be established by preparing a list of all receipts or separating the cash and related remittance advices and transmitting them to cashiers and accounting personnel, as appropriate. Accountability control over those who open mail containing collections should be established through the accounts receivable records. *Inquiry, observation.*

*Only valid transactions that were duly authorized are accepted for entry in the accounting records.*

- Cash disbursements journal or check record entries should be prepared by cash disbursement personnel, or by accounting personnel from check copies. Cash entries should be balanced against prelists of authorized disbursements prepared in accounts payable. *Inquiry, observation.*
- There should be no problem with respect to unauthorized entries for cash receipts, given that the converse problem is most likely, as addressed by the next objective.

*All transactions are entered in the accounting records.*

- The principal problem here is that all cash receipts have resulted in accounting entries. Control should be established through the previouslly mentioned mail room listing of cash receipts or the reading of cash registers by accounting personnel using a required authorization key. *Inquiry, observation.*
- Check numbers should be accounted for to ascertain that there is an entry for every check. Checks that have been voided should be retained as evidence that the checks have not been used. *Inquiry, inspection.*

*Accounting entries correctly reflect transaction amounts.*

- Book entry totals should be proved against related batch totals, such as deposit tickets, cash register totals, or lists of vouchers to be paid. *Inquiry, observation, inspection.*

*Transactions are correctly classified for accounting entry.*

- If all cash disbursements clear through accounts payable, classification of charges will be accomplished when the liability is recorded. Debits associated with the subsequent cash disbursement will then be to the control account for accounts or vouchers payable. *Inquiry, inspection.*
- Credits resulting from cash sales should be classified according to the product or department that is involved, or to a liability account if revenue is collected in advance of the delivery of the product or service. *Inquiry, observation, inspection.*
- Credits resulting from collections of receivables should be classified according to any separate receivables controls that are maintained. *Inquiry.*
- For effective cash management and projection of future cash flows, as well

as for monitoring accounting results, information such as the following should be reported daily and possibly on a month-to-date or quarter-to-date basis. Budgeted amounts relating to any of the figures should be included to aid in evaluating results.

*Recorded transactions are correctly processed.*

|  | Accounts Receivable | Accounts Payable | Cash |
|---|---|---|---|
| Balance Yesterday | $10,221.18 | $7,421.90 | $5,019.23 |
| Today's —Charge sales | 1,823.51 |  |  |
| —Invoices registered |  | 1,118.20 |  |
|  | $12,044.69 | $8,540.10 |  |
| —Accounts receivable collections | 1,625.73 |  | 1,625.73 |
|  |  |  | $6,644.96 |
| —Accounts payable paid |  | 1,720.80 | 1,720.80 |
| Balance today | $10,418.96 | $6,819.30 | $4,924.16 |

- Monthly trial balances of general and subsidiary ledger accounts and proof totals of items processed that are balanced against predetermined control totals should provide assurance that transactions have been correctly processed. *Inquiry, observation, inspection.*

## Monitoring Objectives

*Regular comparison is made of accountability records with underlying assets; third-party proofs of accounting records.*

- Accounting personnel should regularly reconcile bank statements with the organization's cash records. *Inquiry, inspection.*
- Tellers' cash funds, change funds, and petty cash funds should be counted on a surprise basis, and as frequently as is warranted by the cash amounts involved. Such counts are often made by internal auditors, but a preferable arrangement is to have other employees make such counts so that the counting can be subjected to internal audit review. *Inquiry, observation, inspection.*
- Cash sale transactions in which sales personnel handle cash and create accounting records should be subjected to customer monitoring through cash register display of recorded amounts and issuance of printed receipts or carbon copies of sales checks. *Inquiry, observation.*
- The fact that sales are exchange transactions makes it possible to monitor the recording of sales transactions through control over the delivery of goods or services. Cash receipts from sales of gasoline or other liquids can be controlled through meters on dispensing devices, and perpetual inventory records that are relieved on the basis of authorized sales transactions will reveal the existence of unrecorded sales transactions through inventory shortages. *Inquiry, observation, inspection.*
- Third-party monitoring of accounts receivable collections should be ob-

tained through sending statements to customers and through collection follow-up activities. *Inquiry, observation, inspection.*

- Correct preparation of disbursement checks will presumably be monitored by the payees of the checks. No compliance testing should be necessary, nor would it be possible.

*There is an effective internal audit function.*

- Internal auditors should regularly review and evaluate internal controls relating to cash, perform compliance tests, and if appropriate, make recommendations for improvement in the controls. *Inquiry, review of audit planning, inspection of working papers.*
- Internal auditors should occasionally make surprise cash counts and audit bank reconciliations by proving the correctness and propriety of all amounts shown on bank reconciliations. *Inquiry, inspection of working papers.*
- Operational audit activities representing an important service to management in the control of operations, although not related to the reliability of accounting information, may be reviewed by the independent auditor to provide additional indication of the general effectiveness of management and efficiency of operations. Findings or recommendations resulting from such independent audit review appropriately would be included in the independent auditor's management letter. *Inquiry* concerning internal audit activities could extend to such aspects of cash management and security of cash amounts as

    Using bank "lock box" arrangements to handle cash received from accounts receivable on a regional basis to accelerate the availability of cash collections.

    Deferring all cash disbursements to the latest possible date, while realizing all cash discounts that are justifiable relative to the opportunity cost of paying by the discount date.

    Maintaining all bank account balances as shown by bank records at specified minimums (such as compensating balances), with arrangements on disbursement accounts for wire transfer of funds to the accounts to cover checks presented for payment each day. (It should be noted that for accounts maintained on this basis, the company's record of the cash balance will show an overdraft at any time that outstanding checks exceed the minimum balance to be maintained at the bank.)

    Placing all surplus cash, including amounts realized from the above cash management practices, in interest-bearing investments of appropriate term.

    Evaluating all bank services relative to the cost of the services—especially with respect to the rate of interest charged on borrowed funds.

    Ensuring adequate security in the form of vaults, working areas with limited access, and lockable cash drawers should be provided for all cash that is held on the premises.

## Supplementary Comments—Computer-Based Records

Accounts receivable billings accompanied by a turnaround document in machine-readable form represent the principal means of eliminating key-entry of data pertaining to receivables collections. Cash sales recording can be automated by the use of a "wand" or other scanning device to read uniform product codes that are printed on package labels or tags. Computer memory is accessed on the basis of the machine-sensed code number to supply product description and price, to update inventory records, and to supply cash register printed output of details as a basis for completing the sale transaction.

Disbursement checks should be imprinted with account number in magnetic ink character recognition (MICR) code representation for automated bank processing of checks. Check amounts are then typically printed by the bank in MICR form as a part of the proof activities by the first bank to handle the checks. To permit automated preparation of outstanding check lists from computer-maintained records of checks issued, machine-readable checks can be issued in punched card form or as paper checks with check number and amount of the check printed in a type font that can be read by an optical scanning device. The computer input obtained from the machine-readable checks is then used to match the cleared checks against the file of checks issued, with the output of this operation being a listing of checks that are still outstanding.

The most recent development in computerized processing of cash receipts and disbursements involves what is known as the *automated clearing house* (ACH). A forerunner of this system has been the submission of annual employee earnings statements (the W-2 form) to the Internal Revenue Service in magnetic tape form rather than as hard copy output, thus obviating the need for the IRS to reconvert data for further computer processing at the IRS. (The economical advantage of this arrangement is suggested by the fact that for a considerable period of time the IRS has had sufficient budgetary resources to match only the W-2 information submitted in magnetic tape form with the corresponding earnings data on employees' income tax returns.)

The other most widespread use of electronic records as the means of transferring information and funds has been the direct deposit of payroll funds to employees' bank accounts by way of computer tape. The ACH system operates on the same basis of submitting orders on magnetic tape to make payments to other parties through their accounts maintained at banks located within the clearing house area. Principal advantages of paying accounts through an ACH system include eliminating the cost of preparing, signing, and mailing checks, as well as of processing checks that have cleared the bank in order to reconcile bank and book balances. An associated disadvantage is loss of the use of funds that would be available during the float period while checks are clearing through the banking system. On the other hand, those receiving payments through an ACH receive immediate credit of the payments to their accounts and thus have earlier availability of the deposited funds.

## Substantive Audit Objectives and Procedures

As for the subsystems previously covered, the discussion of audit objectives and substantive procedures pertaining to cash balances and transactions begins with considering the disclosure and other requirements of financial reporting standards.

### Conformity of Client's Statements with Disclosure and Other Requirements of Financial Reporting Standards

Ordinarily all cash will be shown on the balance sheet as one figure, described simply as "Cash" or "Cash on hand and in banks." Only in rare cases will the amount of cash on hand be of sufficient importance to warrant being shown as a separate figure. Similarly, little is added to the usefulness of a statemment by breaking down the cash in banks figure among the various banks. The amount of cash shown, however, must be "free" and available immediately for general business purposes. This requirement indicates that any of the following items that are material in amount must be shown separately from the cash figure, either as another form of current asset, under a noncurrent classification, or disclosed parenthetically:

1. Amounts represented by certificates of deposit or savings deposits. Even though savings deposits can usualy be withdrawn on demand, the bank retains the right to require a stated number of days' notice before paying out the funds.
2. Funds for plant expansion, sinking funds, or any other funds that are to be used for nonworking capital purposes. The mere fact that the fund is held by the company rather than by a trustee is unimportant; the intended use to be made of the fund is the governing factor.
3. Minimum or "compensating" bank balances that must be maintained in accordance with bank loan agreements. The restricted amount may be shown parenthetically or by footnote.
4. Foreign balances that are not to be used in connection with foreign operations and that cannot be readily converted into domestic currency because of exchange restrictions.
5. Expense advances to employees for travel or other purposes. These advances are not available for general purposes and are essentially prepaid expenses.
6. Deposits of any form, such as deposits on contracts, deposits with utilities, or escrow deposits.

Custom with respect to the presentation of bank overdrafts has undergone considerable change. At one time standard practice required that any overdraft be shown as a liability. Current practice is more realistic and recognizes that if bank balances are readily transferable, overdrafts may be netted against balances in other banks, and only net overdrafts need be shown as a liability. A minimum balance to be maintained in connection with a loan or other agreement with a bank would not be readily transferable, and therefore an overdraft should not be offset against such an amount.

### Reasonableness of Account Balances

*Perform Analytical Review.* Unlike the other areas that have been discussed, cash is unlikely to bear a consistent relationship to other accounts other than as a consequence of management intent to minimize the amount of this nonproductive asset in accordance with a cash management program. From a service standpoint, however, the auditor should give careful attention to a client's cash situation, for there may be opportunities to point out ways of improving cash flow, obtaining a return on temporary excess cash balances, or borrowing on more advantageous terms to meet current cash needs.

*Scan Cash Account Entries.* Although not done from the standpoint of ascertaining reasonableness, the study of cash operations should include a scanning of cash account entries for any abnormal amounts or unusual sources, such as the general journal. Such entries or amounts may be a clue to some form of cash manipulation or of an unusual transaction that should be carefully reviewed for propriety and to determine whether the transaction was appropriately recorded from an accounting standpoint.

### Synchronization of Events and Records

The cutoff of cash transactions is important with respect to proper statement of the cash figure, as well as other balance sheet or income statement figures. Furthermore, attempts at "window dressing" (explained later) are likely to involve the cash balance.

*Cutoff of Cash Receipts.* The auditor must be satisfied that the cash receipts records have not been held open to include cash collections received after the balance sheet date. This point is particularly important if cash sales are involved, because income will be affected. If all cash collections pertain to accounts receivable, the financial picture is changed only slightly by improperly moving receivables into cash. Holding open the cash receipts book under these circumstances may, however, be merely a prelude to holding open the cash disbursements book as well, which has a more significant effect on financial position.

There are two conclusive procedures that the auditor can apply to determine whether the cutoff of cash receipts has been properly handled. If the auditor is at the client's premises at the close of business on the last day of the fiscal year or at the beginning of the following day, a count of all undeposited cash receipts will establish the proper cutoff of cash. Based on that count, the auditor will know how much cash was actually received up to the close of business, and any attempt by the client to include in the records cash received after that point will be immediately apparent to the auditor. Should the auditor wish to avoid making a time-consuming cash count, an alternative is to retain control of the undeposited receipts until they reach the bank. Control can be established by sealing the cash in an envelope or pouch, which can then be locked in the client's safe until the bank deposit is ready to be made. With such precautions no additional cash subsequently received can be added to the deposit without the auditor's knowledge, and the bank's entry for the deposit on the bank statement will establish the amount of cash that was held by the client at the close of the year.

It will seldom be feasible, however, for the auditor to be present at each client's office on the balance sheet date. Nor will the auditor's presence be necessary in most instances. Instead, the auditor can usually make satisfactory verification of the cutoff of cash receipts through a careful examination of deposits in transit listed on the client's year-end bank reconciliation. All such deposits in transit, if valid and including only cash received up to the close of the fiscal year, should be credited by the bank on the next business day following the close of the client's fiscal year. A deposit not reaching the bank on this time schedule carries a strong presumption that cash received subsequent to the balance sheet date has been included.

Other evidence that ought to suggest the possibility that the cash cutoff is not as it should be would include exceptionally heavy cash receipts or sales recorded at the end of the fiscal year, light cash receipts or sales recorded for the early days of the following year, and an unusually low accounts receivable balance at the year end.

*Cutoff of Cash Disbursements.* The auditor must be particularly careful to watch for any evidence that the cash disbursements record has been held open. The resulting simultaneous reduction of cash and accounts payable will improve the current ratio—an understandable objective if financial condition and credit standing are weak or if a bond indenture specifies a minimum current ratio that has not been maintained. Should the client be unable to reduce liabilities at the balance sheet date because sufficient cash was not available, the auditor should realize that the required cash can be "generated" by holding open the cash receipts book.

Evidence that the cash disbursements record has been held open is less conclusive than is evidence concerning the cutoff of cash receipts.

For instance, substantial disbursements at the year end coupled with limited disbursements during the first part of the following period would not necessarily mean that the cash disbursements record had been held open. Many businesses make a special effort at the end of the year to reduce their liabilities. If the cash is available, and if the checks are placed in the mail before the year end, the resulting improved financial picture is entirely proper. The auditor's problem, of course, is to be satisfied that the checks were actually in the mail and therefore beyond the client's control by the close of the year. If the auditor can be satisfied on this point, the large number of outstanding checks on the bank reconciliation and the abnormally low amounts of payables need cause no concern.

If the auditor is at the client's office at the close of the year, the serial number of the last check that has been written should be noted and inquiry should be made to determine that this and all previous checks have been placed in the mail. Any additional checks that the client might then wish to show as disbursements of the expiring fiscal year would be readily detected by the auditor, and it would be apparent if the checks had been written and mailed after the close of the year.

As the auditor will seldom be on hand at the end of the year, some other means of verifying the cutoff of cash disbursements must obviously be employed. The necessary evidence can usually be obtained by examining the checks paid by the bank during the first part of the month following the close of the year. For those checks that were outstanding at the end of the year, the auditor should note the lapse of time from the date of each check to the date the check was charged against the client's account, as indicated by the bank's cancellation placed on the check when it is paid. If this time period is longer than should be warranted for the check to reach the payee, be deposited, and be returned to the client's bank, the auditor should suspect that the check may have been mailed after the close of the year. If it develops that this check is but one of a block of outstanding checks that did not clear the bank within a reasonable period of time, the evidence of what apparently occurred would be quite conclusive. When the evidence is placed before the client, it should bring forth full admission from the client as to what was done, and the client should be expected to consent to correct the records so that they will reflect the true financial picture. Any tendency by the client to deny what has apparently happened should be regarded by the auditor with considerable suspicion and should cause the auditor to question the client's integrity.

*Window Dressing.* Although window dressing does not necessarily misrepresent a client's financial position at the balance sheet date, the effect is misleading and therefore undesirable. Holding the cash books open is a method of window dressing that does actually misrepresent the facts.

A form of window dressing that strictly speaking does not misrepresent the facts results if an officer who has borrowed funds from a corporation repays the loan shortly before the balance sheet date and then is readvanced those funds after the close of the year. Careful review of cash transactions and entries in accounts with officers occurring near the balance sheet date should reveal any window dressing that may have been attempted.

### Comprehensiveness of Records

The possibility of unrecorded cash collections is the only problem with cash from a comprehensiveness standpoint, in that once cash has been made a matter of record, any reductions in cash balances must be accounted for. Auditor investigation of the comprehensiveness of cash records is primarily in term of controls over transactions involving cash receipts.

*Evaluate Internal Control.*  We have already considered the matter of control over the two major types of transactions that involve cash receipts: collections on receivables and cash sales. Such controls constitute the only feasible means by which the auditor can be assured of the comprehensiveness of records of cash receipts from these sources. Spasmodic receipts from nonoperating sources, such as sales of scrap material, sales of machinery and equipment, and income from investments, should be similarly controlled through requiring authorizations and establishing independent accountability through accounting accruals for any income such as interest that is to be received on a regularly anticipated basis.

*Test Cash Cutoffs.*  As in other instances previously discussed, cutoff tests at the year end should reveal any transactions that are unrecorded in the current period as a result of being recorded in the following period.

### Arithmetic and Clerical Accuracy: Agreement of Details and Control Totals

Because all cash held by a bank or held in a cash fund is generally recorded in a single account, there will be no supporting details to be proved for arithmetic or clerical accuracy.

### Existence of Cash

*Counts of Cash on Hand.*  Petty cash funds, change funds, and undeposited receipts generally comprise all or most of the cash on hand. If the amounts are material, the auditor should plan to count the cash at the close of the year. Otherwise, imprest funds to be counted can be counted at any time that is convenient for the auditor, with the added advantage that some element of surprise is injected into the count. If the client's internal auditor has made surprise cash counts during the year and fund amounts are nominal, review of the internal auditor's working papers may be substituted for cash counts by the independent auditor. If undeposited receipts are not material, they need not be counted, because they can be verified through reference to the record of their prompt deposit on the bank statement for the following period. If the deposit was delayed in reaching the bank, the auditor should carefully investigate the possibility that the cash receipts book was held open or that the cashier included subsequent receipts in the deposit to cover up a shortage.

If cash is to be counted, the auditor must be certain that all cash and any assets that are readily negotiable or easily pledged are counted simultaneously or kept under the auditor's control until all counting is completed. By exercising this precaution, the auditor can be assured that funds that have already been counted are not used to make up a shortage in another fund still to be counted. If good internal control has been violated by permitting a fund custodian to handle other funds not under company control (such as flower or party funds), these other funds should also be counted and balanced with available records. Otherwise these funds could be used to offset a shortage in the company funds.

For the auditor's protection all funds or negotiable instruments should be counted in the presence of the custodian of the assets. If the auditor fails to exercise this precaution and the fund is revealed to be short of the required amount, the auditor will have little defense to the custodian's possible assertion that, "It was all there when I gave it to you." As further protection, the auditor should have the custodian sign a receipt stating that the count was made in the custodian's presence and the funds returned intact at the completion of the count. Schedule A-1 contains an example of such a receipt obtained in connection with the count of a petty cash fund.

Some accounting firms go to the extreme of not permitting audit staff to handle any of the client's funds. Instead, the custodian is requested to count the fund under the surveillance of the auditor. A variation of this arrangement is useful when substantial amounts of cash are on hand, as in the case of a large department store. The store's internal auditors or other employees not connected with the cashier's department can be requested to count the cash under the independent auditor's supervision. Because a considerable measure of internal control is evident in such an arrangement, a limited number of accountants from the independent auditing firm can supervise and observe the counting being done by a large number of store employees.

*Coins and Currency.* Regardless of how the actual counting of cash is to be handled, some agreement must be reached in advance on what shall be done concerning bundled currency and wrapped coins. Because the coins constitute an insignificant portion of the fund, the rolls of coins can usually be accepted for listing on the count sheet without opening and counting any of the rolls. If desired, a few of the rolls can be broken open and counted as a test, or the paper wrappers can be scratched open to verify that the rolls contain coins and not pieces of lead pipe of the appropriate size and weight. The auditor should, of course, note whether the diameter and length of the rolls correspond with what would be expected for the following standard contents:

| Denomination | Number of Coins | Value of Roll |
|---|---|---|
| Dollars | 20 | $20.00 |
| Halves | 20 | 10.00 |
| Quarters | 40 | 10.00 |
| Dimes | 50 | 5.00 |
| Nickels | 40 | 2.00 |
| Pennies | 50 | .50 |

Bundled currency presents more of a problem because of its greater value. If only a few bundles are involved, the auditor should probably open and count each bundle. If there are quite a few bundles, as in the case of a bank, and if internal control is adequate, the bundles may be test-counted. For smaller-denomination bills only 5 or 10 percent of the bundles may be counted, but for bills of large denomination 50 percent or more of the bundles should probably be counted.

As is shown on schedule A-1, the auditor's work sheet should list the quantity and total value of each denomination of coin and currency. Loose items should be listed separately from the wrapped or bundled items. Listing each quantity and its total value reduces the possibility of error in figuring total values for the various denominations and assists in locating counting errors if the auditor's count does not balance with the accounting records.

*Checks.* Customers' checks or checks cashed as an accommodation are almost certain to be encountered in making a cash count. If only a few checks are on hand, the auditor may list the checks on the worksheet, as is shown on schedule A-1. An adding-machine-tape listing of the checks will usually suffice if the checks are numerous. In some instances, when many checks are present, the auditor may not even total the checks. If they are part of the day's business to be deposited the next day and have been handled under good internal control, the auditor may simply permit the client's employees to prepare the regular deposit. The deposit should then be kept under the auditor's control during the count of other funds and until the deposit reaches the bank. Because the bank must prove the deposit anyway, the auditor merely asks the bank to notify the auditor whether the actual deposit agreed with the amount shown by the client on the deposit ticket.

If the auditor plans to count the checks on hand, each check should be carefully examined in an effort to substantiate its validity and collectibility. Points to be observed would include

1. Date: a postdated check cannot be classified as cash, and a check bearing an old date suggests that the check is possibly being held because it is uncollectible.
2. Payee: checks should be made payable to the client, except in those instances where authorization exists to accept checks payable to others as an accommodation.
3. Endorsement: checks not payable to the client should bear the endorsement of the original payee and that of the person who transferred the check to the client, if that person was not the payee. Second endorsements may suggest the possibility that the first endorsement has been forged.
   As a protective measure, all checks should be endorsed by the client, "For deposit only."
4. Maker: checks that have been signed by an employee or officer should always be carefully investigated to determine whether the checks are valid and properly included in the fund being counted.

The best test of validity is depositing the checks to determine whether they can be collected. The checks should be controlled by the auditor until they reach the bank, to prevent other checks from being substituted for any checks that are not valid or collectible. The bank should be requested to notify the auditor if any of the checks are not collected, or at the very least the auditor should inspect the bank statement for the following period to see if any uncollectible checks have been charged back against the client's account.

*Undeposited Receipts.* The auditor should ascertain that all cash on hand representing receipts from customers has been recorded in the appropriate record. If all or part of the receipts are not recorded, the unrecorded receipts that have been included in the counted cash would serve to cover up any shortage that existed. Furthermore, the receipts should be recorded *before* the auditor makes the count, so that the auditor can compare individual items in order to determine whether lapping has occurred. (See Appendix at the end of this chapter for more information about lapping.)

*Petty Cash Funds.* If petty cash funds are counted at other than the balance sheet date, part of the funds will likely have been disbursed, and receipted petty cash vouchers or other supporting data will be present in their place. This condition should not hold true at the balance sheet date. Any disbursements occurring before that time should be reimbursed in order to reflect the expenses in the proper period and to have the fund in cash form, thus permitting the entire balance to be classified as cash. If such reimbursement has not been made, technically the auditor should prepare an adjusting entry in order to have the statements reflect the actual conditions. As a practical matter, however, the amounts will usually not be material, and the adjustment can be waived as was done on schedule A-1.

Any disbursement vouchers that are on hand at the time of the petty cash count should be listed in the auditor's working papers. The date, recipient, purpose, and amount of each disbursement should be shown, although if a large number of disbursements has been made, an adding-machine-tape listing will usually suffice. Each voucher or invoice should be reviewed to determine that it bears a current date, has been approved or receipted as required, has not been cancelled, and is in accordance with the authorization for the operation of the fund. In addition, some auditors request a responsible official to review the list and sign a statement indicating that each item represents a valid and appropriate disbursement. This procedure is evident on schedule A-1.

*Confirmation and Reconciliation of Cash in Bank.* The auditor's first consideration in verifying cash in bank is to ascertain the actual balance on deposit. Even though this balance can be determined by referring to the bank statement, standard practice requires that independent confirmation of the bank balance be obtained directly from the bank. To facilitate obtaining such confirmation, plus important information on other relationships between the client and the bank, the Standard Bank Confirmation Inquiry form should be used. This form, a copy of which is shown as Schedule $\frac{A\text{-}2}{1}$, has been approved by the AICPA and the Bank Administration Institute. The printed form consists of an original and a duplicate copy. The request for the specified information must be signed by one of the client's officers whose signature is on file at the bank. A bank should not release confidential information about a customer's affairs without proper authorization, and the duplicate copy is retained by the bank to prove that it had such authorization.

The automation of bank records has made it desirable to list all accounts and give account numbers to aid the bank in looking up the necessary information; but if the client's internal control is weak and the possibility of fraud exists, it may be preferable to omit this information, as there will then be less likelihood that the bank will overlook any accounts carried for the client but not shown by the client's records. In addition to the data on bank balances the confirmation request also covers the following points, which are of vital importance to other phases of the audit examination: any direct liability of the client to the bank on loans, acceptances, or other types of paper; any contingent liability for discounted notes or as guarantor for others; and any other direct or contingent liability, any open letters of credit, and any collateral held by the bank. The bank should, of course, date and sign the form before it is returned to the author.

The verification of cash in bank is far from completed when the auditor has secured confirmation of the balance on deposit. Invariably the client's balance for the bank account will reflect transactions not yet recorded by the bank. These reconciling items, which must account for the difference between the client's balance and the bank's balance, must be carefully verified before the auditor can be satisfied that the amount of cash in bank specified by the client's records has been adequately accounted for.

When internal control is adequate, the client will have prepared a bank reconciliation, based on the bank statement for the last month of the client's fiscal year and setting forth the various reconciling items. The auditor should obtain this reconciliation and prove that the reconciliation is mathematically correct. The validity and accuracy of the reconciling items must also be verified. The most obvious approach to this problem would appear to be reperformance of the process employed by the client in constructing the reconciliation. Actually, however, this is neither the most efficient nor the most conclusive solution. *The most effective approach is to review subsequent events to determine whether incomplete transactions have been completed as would be expected, and to ascertain whether any incomplete transactions at the balance sheet date have been omitted from the reconciliation.*

*Bank Cutoff Statement.* The principal source of information that the auditor uses in proving reconciling items is the bank cutoff statement. This is simply a bank statement covering a specified number of days following the close of the client's fiscal year. For very large businesses with considerable check activity, a five- to ten-day period may be adequate, but for smaller businesses with less internal control the statement may cover two weeks or even a full month. The request to the bank for the cutoff statement must be signed by the client and should direct the bank to deliver to the auditor the bank statement and accompanying paid checks for the specified period. The possibility that a member of the client's organization might alter the statement or tamper with the accompanying checks makes it most desirable that the statement be delivered by the bank directly to the auditor. Should circumstances make such delivery impossible, the auditor should be particularly careful to scrutinize the bank statement for alterations and *determine that all debits on the statement are properly supported by paid checks or bank debit advices.* This step is known as "proving" the bank statement. As a guard against the substitution of spurious checks or bank advices, each document should be inspected to ascertain that the date of payment perforated or stamped by the bank falls within the period covered by the bank statement.

When internal control is adequate, procedures based on the cutoff statement should be sufficient to prove the validity of the client's reconciliation and thus substantiate the cash balance. These procedures are discussed in the following three sections. If internal control is weak, additional procedures as described in the Appendix to this chapter should be considered.

*Deposits in Transit.* In verifying deposits in transit, the auditor should realize that *a shortage of cash in bank can be concealed by an overstatement of deposits in transit.* The verification procedures that are ordinarily followed should detect any possible overstatement if the procedures are properly applied. These procedures follow:

1. Trace the deposit-in-transit figure to the client's cash records to determine that the figure agrees with the amount of cash shown as received on the last business day. If more than one day's receipts are involved, thorough investigation of the situation should be made.
2. Compare the deposit-in-transit figure with the count of cash on hand, if such a count was made by the auditor at the close of the year. Cross-reference the two schedules.
3. Trace the deposit-in-transit figure to the cutoff bank statement. The date of the bank entry for the deposit should be noted in the working papers, as was done on schedule A-2. Any deposit that does not reach the bank by the next business day should be investigated. Possible causes of such a delay might include holding open the cash receipts record and using subsequent collections to make up a shortage.
4. Ascertain that all checks deposited were collected by noting whether the cutoff statement shows any debit memos for checks charged back against the client's account.

*Outstanding Checks.* The most troublesome and potentially dangerous item on the bank reconciliation is outstanding checks. The greatest danger is not, as the neophyte often assumes, that a check may have been included that is not actually outstanding, but that *a check that is outstanding may have been omitted or shown at less than the actual amount.* In terms of relative risk, the most likely possibility is that the ledger figure for cash may exceed the cash on deposit as a result of a defalcation. Any attempt to conceal the resulting shortage of cash through manipulation of the figure for outstanding checks on the bank reconciliation must of necessity involve an *understatement* of that figure or the *omission* of a check that is actually outstanding. If this point is not clear, the reader should work out a simple illustration to prove that concealment of a cash shortage by means of manipulating outstanding checks must involve an understatement of the outstanding checks.

The incorrect listing of a check on the bank reconciliation can be readily detected in several ways, as will be shown presently, but ascertaining that an outstanding check has been omitted is far more difficult. Because the omitted check is not known to the auditor, there is no specific point at which to begin investigation. An omitted check may have been written months, or even years, before the beginning of the auditor's investigation. A review of all checks written since the previous audit would be required to discover the existence of an outstanding check that has been purposely omitted from the bank reconciliation. The magnitude of such an undertaking should be evident when it is realized that many businesses write thousands of checks every month. Furthermore, the results of such an investigation would not necessarily be fully conclusive. In view of such problems and limitations, the auditor can hardly be expected to state that the cash figure is correct. It should be possible, however, to determine with reasonable assurance whether the figure is fairly stated, which is adequate for the needs of most third parties who refer to and rely on financial statements. The auditor's opinion that cash is fairly stated should be taken to mean that no pronounced misstatement has occurred that would be likely to affect a reader's decisions based on the company's financial position.

The usual audit procedures employed in the search for significant amounts of outstanding checks that may have been omitted from the bank reconciliation are listed here. When internal control is weak or fraud is suspected, certain additional procedures may be employed. These are included among the more detailed procedures that are used in conjunction with the proof of cash and are discussed in the Appendix to this chapter. The following procedures represent a typical approach to the verification of outstanding checks under conditions of reasonably good internal control:

1. While the checks returned with the bank cutoff statement are still in order according to the dates on which they were paid by the bank, examine the checks for predating; that is, for a bank endorsement that predates the date of the check. A check evidencing such predating should suggest the possibility that kiting has occurred, or perhaps that a bill had to be paid but the check was not recorded until after the end of the year in order to avoid showing an overdraft on the books. (See the discussion of kiting in the Appendix to this chapter.)

2. Sort the paid checks into serial-number order, or have an employee of the client do so under the auditor's supervision.

3. Ascertain from the cash disbursement records the number of the last check recorded during the fiscal year under examination.

4. Review checks bearing a higher serial number to be certain they are all dated for the following year. If any of these checks are payable to

cash, officers, or banks, investigate the checks to ascertain that they are proper, have not been issued as a part of window dressing, and do not relate to the fiscal year under examination. Large checks for round amounts should receive particularly close scrutiny.

5.   Perform the following procedures with respect to checks bearing a date or serial number showing that they were written before the close of the client's fiscal year:

a.   Trace each check to the copy of the client's list of outstanding checks in the audit working papers. Be sure that each check is listed and that the correct amount is shown. *This is the single most effective procedure for disclosing omissions or inaccuracies resulting in an understatement of outstanding checks*. The procedure is based on the presumption that the payee of a check will normally cash or deposit the check as quickly as possible, and that as a result most checks outstanding at the balance sheet date are likely to clear the bank within a relatively short period of time after the balance sheet date. This presumption should hold true especially for large checks, which might materially misstate the cash figure if not properly included on the bank reconciliation.

b.   Note on the list of outstanding checks those checks that have been paid by showing the date on which each check was paid by the bank, as was done on schedule A-2. A review of these dates should indicate whether the cash disbursements record may have been held open.

c.   Trace the checks, on a test basis, to the cash disbursements record to ascertain their agreement with that record as to date, number, payee, and amount.

6.   Review the list of outstanding checks for any checks that did not clear the bank during the period covered by the cutoff statement. Trace the amounts shown for these checks to the cash disbursements records to determine that the correct amounts have been listed as outstanding. If any of these checks are large in amount, also examine supporting data such as invoices to further evidence the correctness of the amount. In addition, discuss these large checks with the client to find out why they have not cleared. In some cases correspondence with the payee, in order to obtain further information, may be warranted. The need for such precaution stems from the possibility that the payee may be holding the check because the amount is in dispute. If so, there may be an additional liability that should be reflected on the client's records.

7.   Prove the footing of the list of outstanding checks.

8.   If there is a potential for fraud as a result of a deficiency in internal control, review the list of outstanding checks in the working papers for the previous year's examination for checks that had not cleared the bank by the close of the examination. If these checks do not appear as outstanding at the close of the current year, they should be located in the client's files of checks paid during the current year. Inspect the

checks, on a test basis if they are numerous, comparing the amounts with those shown by the outstanding-check list, and noting that endorsements are proper and that no second endorsements are given. These checks should be accounted for because old outstanding checks are least likely to be presented for payment and therefore are the ones most likely to be dropped from the list of outstanding checks in order to conceal the theft of cash. Many companies, after checks have been outstanding a specified length of time, attempt to contact the payees and induce them to deposit the checks or to request duplicates if the originals have been lost. If such efforts are unsuccessful, the checks are then written back on the books and taken up as income or as a liability. This procedure reflects much better internal control than does permitting the checks to remain listed as outstanding.

*Other Reconciling Items.* If reconciling items other than deposits in transit or outstanding checks appear on the bank reconciliation, the auditor should determine that the items are valid and have been properly shown. If an item first appears on the client's records, the auditor should ascertain that the item is recorded in the same amount by the bank in the following month or that the client's records are corrected in the following period. For instance, if the client properly prepared a check drawn on Bank A, but recorded the check as a withdrawal against Bank B, reconciling items for the same amount should appear on the bank reconciliations for both banks. When the check is finally paid, the auditor should examine both the check and the original entry to verify the facts and should note that a correcting entry has been made in the following period.

Many reconciling items will first be recorded on the bank's records. If the bank has improperly charged a check to the client's account, the error will be discovered when the client prepares the bank reconciliation. The bank will then issue an advice of correction in the following month. The auditor should note the original entry and that the proper correction appears in the bank statement for the following month, supported by the bank's correction advice. Service charges are another type of reconciling item that first appears on the bank's records. The auditor should inspect the bank's charge ticket and then determine that the charge is recorded by the client in the following period. Technically, the adjustment should be reflected in the period under examination, but when the amount is not material the auditor should waive the adjustment for practical reasons.

*Timing.* In the examination of cash, as well as in most other phases of an audit, part of the work can be performed in advance of the balance sheet date if internal control is satisfactory. The review of internal control is perhaps the most obvious procedure that can be handled readily on a preliminary basis. Imprest cash funds can also be counted beforehand, assuming that the amounts are not material.

Bank reconciliations for the principal bank accounts can also be verified on a preliminary basis. In addition to following all year-end procedures as described previously, the auditor should make any counts of cash, notes receivable, investments, and any other negotiable assets at the date of the preliminary bank reconciliation. The purpose of such simultaneous verification is, of course, to prevent the transfer of funds from one asset to another to conceal a shortage.

Even though a complete examination of cash in bank has been performed at an earlier date, certain additional procedures will be necessary at the balance sheet date. Entries to the cash accounts during the period from the date of the preliminary verification work to the year end should be reviewed for propriety and reasonableness and traced to source records if added verification is desired. The auditor should also determine that a proper cutoff of cash receipts and cash disbursements was made at the end of the year. The client's bank reconciliations at the balance sheet date should be reviewed and compared with the preliminary reconciliations. Bank confirmations for the balance sheet date should be obtained and the bank balance figure compared with the corresponding figure on the client's bank reconciliation. The book balance figure on the reconciliation should be compared with the corresponding figure in the grouping sheet in the auditor's working papers.

### Ownership of Cash

There should be no problem with ownership inasmuch as cash in the client's possession or on deposit in the client's bank accounts can be presumed to be the client's. That will be true even if the cash is held in a fiduciary capacity, as in the case of a deposit or an advance payment, but of course a liability must be shown for the associated obligation.

A bank requirement that a compensating balance be maintained does not affect the ownership of the cash on deposit. It does, however, constitute a restriction on the availability of the cash to meet operating needs, and the restriction should be disclosed in the financial statements. The AICPA has developed a form letter that should be used to confirm with the bank the compensating balance that is required and to obtain information on any other restrictions that may exist.

### Valuation of Cash

Cash denominated in a foreign currency must be converted to the monetary unit where the client is domiciled, but no other valuation problems should be involved with cash.

## Appendix—Supplementary Cash Audit Procedures

The attractiveness of cash to the embezzler (embezzlement involves the theft of funds with which a person has been entrusted) suggests the desirability of supplementary audit procedures when internal control weaknesses present tempting opportunity to those whose moral fiber is flawed and who are faced with a pressing need for cash. Critical deficiencies would exist if a person handles cash collections or signs checks and also has record-keeping responsibilities, and the situation is further aggravated if the same person also prepares bank reconciliations.

Under these circumstances the auditor should consider whether to undertake certain supplementary cash procedures. The decision is complicated by the fact that the normal audit procedures already discussed should be adequate to detect any material overstatement of cash or diversion of collections on receivables, and the major remaining problem is likely to involve unrecorded income. Not only is the existence of such unrecorded income difficult to ascertain, but there is aso the question of whether the financial statements are misstated if the unreported income is not shown. Once again it must be recognized that the financial statements are the representations of management, and it is a management responsibility to control all sources of income to prevent any loss resulting from failure to account for all income of the organization.

Given these factors, it is unclear whether the auditor should undertake supplementary cash audit procedures—particularly because they will reveal a defalcation only if the accounting records have been altered or if the abstracted funds have at some point flowed through a cash fund or a bank account. Of course if, after discussion with your client, supplementary procedures are authorized, it will be clear that the client expects to bear the added cost. In some cases, however, the auditor may feel that the situation is such that the supplementary procedures should be undertaken without advance authorization, in order to provide additional assurance to the client that funds have been properly accounted for. The auditor may also feel that the procedures should be utilized to avoid the possibility of client dissatisfaction. Even though the auditor's engagement letter has stated that the examination is not designed to detect frauds that do not have a material effect on the financial statements, it is at best awkward to have a fraud come to light after the audit has been completed.

If the auditor is to undertake supplementary procedures aimed at the detection of fraud, it is important to be aware of the more common methods by which funds can be abstracted and the shortage concealed. Such awareness should point to the places in which the auditor should look for possible fraud and to the evidence that might exist that would indicate that fraud had occurred. Most of the more common ways in which funds can be abstracted and the resulting shortage concealed are discussed next.

## The Techniques of Defalcation

Cash receipts can be abstracted and the resulting shortage concealed by any of the following means:

A. Withholding all or part of the proceeds of a cash sale and either recording no amount on the cash register or sales check or recording less than was actually collected.
B. Withholding cash collected from customers on accounts receivable, recording the collection, and concealing the resulting cash shortage by
   1. Underfooting the cash receipts column in the cash book and overfooting the sales discount column by a similar amount.
   2. Recording discounts on collections when the full invoice amount was actually remitted because the discount period had expired, or overstating the amount of discount taken.
   3. Overstating cash disbursements. (See the material below on cash disbursements.)
   4. Manipulating the bank reconciliation by
      a. Overstating deposits in transit.
      b. Understating outstanding checks.
      c. Falsifying additions or subtractions on the reconciliation.
   5. Kiting. (See the discussion below.)
C. Withholding cash collected from customers on accounts receivable, making no book record of the collection at the time. The customer can be prevented from learning that proper credit for the payment has not be received by
   1. Withholding any statements or credit follow-ups that would normally be sent.
   2. Lapping. (See the discussion below.)
   3. Subsequently placing a fictitious credit to the customer's account indicating
      a. The account was written off as a bad debt.
      b. A merchandise return or allowance was granted.
      c. The account was paid. The records can be kept in balance by making an offsetting debit to a fictitious account receivable or by crediting the general ledger controlling account for receivables and debiting some general ledger account other than cash. As an alternative, no offsetting debit entry need be made and the trial balance of accounts receivable can be manipulated to conceal the lack of agreement with the accounts receivable control.
D. Recording sales on account at less than the correct amount but billing customer for the full amount. The difference can then be withheld when the account is paid.

Cash in petty cash funds and cash in bank can be obtained and the shortage concealed by the following means:

A. Removing cash from the petty cash fund and either allowing the fund to remain short or
   1. Raising vouchers being submitted to the general cashier for reimbursement of the petty cash fund.

2. Writing fictitious vouchers, forging approvals.

3. Changing dates on vouchers which have previously been reimbursed and submitting them for a second reimbursement.

B. Preparing checks payable to self and forging the signatures or using blank checks that have been signed in advance. The paid checks are then destroyed when they are returned by the bank, and cash is credited to relieve the ledger account of the misappropriated funds by

1. Overfooting cash disbursements and underfooting purchase discounts. If expenses are debited through the cash disbursements record, balance can also be maintained by overfooting expense totals.

2. Raising the entry for another check and also raising the amount of the check after it has been paid by the bank.

C. Preparing checks payable to others, forging the endorsements, and cashing the checks or depositing them in a special bank account opened for that purpose. Authorized signatures can be obtained on the checks by

1. Submitting fictitious invoices and other supporting data.

2. Submitting invoices that have previously been paid. (The fraudulent check can be destroyed after it has been paid, and the original check substituted in its place, after changing the date and the number of the check.)

D. Overpaying a vendor's invoice and appropriating the vendor's refund check.

E. "Padding" the payroll by continuing to prepare checks for employees who have been terminated or by adding fictitious employees to the payroll. Endorsements can be forged on the checks when they are cashed.

## Kiting  inter-bank business

The manipulation involved in kiting is one that employs the "float" period (the time that it takes for a check to clear the bank on which it is drawn) to conceal a cash shortage within the business, or to prevent an actual overdraft from being detected by the bank that is involved. When kiting is used to conceal a shortage of cash in bank, its detection will reveal that a defalcation has occurred, as well as the fact that the client's financial position is overstated. The manner in which this form of manipulation is accomplished is shown by the following example. A company located in Kansas City has a sales branch in New York. All collections in New York are deposited in a special bank account there. Only the treasurer of the company, who is located in Kansas City, is authorized to sign checks transferring funds from the New York account to the regular account in Kansas City. Just before the end of the year the two bank accounts appear as follows (ignoring reconciling items):

|  | Kansas City | New York |
|---|---|---|
| Balance per bank | $15,000 | $10,000 |
| Balance per books | 20,000 | 10,000 |

The Kansas City bank account is short $5,000, representing collections that the cashier has withheld. To conceal the shortage, the cashier draws a transfer check on December 31 to transfer $5,000 from New York to Kansas City. The treasurer signs the check because the check appears to be a regular check drawn in the normal course of business. The cashier then deposits the check in the Kansas City bank but enters the check in the company records for January. The check will thus appear as a deposit on the Kansas City bank statement on December 31, but because of transit time will not appear as a withdrawal on the New York bank statement until several days later. The result is that at December 31 the Kansas City bank would show $20,000, the amount called for by the books, the New York bank would still show the $10,000 called for by the books for that account, and no shortage would appear to exist. The shortage will reappear, of course, as soon as the transfer check is paid by the New York bank.

The auditor's best course of action in seeking to detect the existence of kiting is to prepare a schedule of all interbank transfers made during the last few days of the current year and the first few days of the following year. The transfer check in the above example would be shown on a schedule of interbank transfers in this manner:

| Check No. | Kansas City Bank | New York Bank | Date Withdrawn Per Books | Date Withdrawn Per Bank | Date Deposited Per Books | Date Deposited Per Bank |
|-----------|------------------|---------------|--------------------------|-------------------------|--------------------------|-------------------------|
| 4297 | $5,000 | $5,000 | 1/2 | 1/3 | 1/2 | 12/31 |

This schedule shows at a glance that something is amiss.

Other means of detecting kiting can be used either in lieu of or to supplement the analysis of interbank transfers. In the case just discussed, a comparison of deposits recorded by the bank with deposits shown on the books for the last few days of the year would show a bank deposit for which there would be no corresponding book entry. (If such a discrepancy is not the result of kiting, an alternative possibility is that an employee is replacing money that was "borrowed" from the bank account at an earlier date.) Another procedure to detect kiting is to examine all checks paid by each bank during the first few days following the close of the year. Checks dated before the close of the year should agree with corresponding entries in the cash disbursements record and should be listed as outstanding on the bank reconciliation. The check in question, bearing a date of December 31, would appear in neither place.

It might seem that the preceding method of detection would break down if the check were simply dated "January 2." Such a possibility is unlikely because the bank should refuse to accept such a check for deposit on December 31, although it is quite possible that the bank teller would not notice the postdating of the check. If the check *did* pass the bank, the auditor can still uncover the irregularity. Banks always endorse customers' checks by stamping both the bank name and the date of the transaction on the back of each check. Thus the auditor has only to take the checks paid by the New York bank during the first few days of January and compare the date on the face of each check with the date of the earliest bank endorsement appearing on the reverse side. Any bank endorsement that predates the date of the check is a danger signal.

An additional form of kiting, used to "pad" a concern's cash position and operating results, involves recording a transfer check as an income item, offset by a disbursement entry that is deferred until the following fiscal period.

In some instances the float period is used, not to conceal a book shortage, but as a means of concealing an overdraft from the bank, and in effect using the bank's credit without authorization and without payment of interest. For instance, a company may have two bank accounts in widely separated places, each account having a balance of $1,000. The company must pay a $5,000 debt, and does so by drawing a check on Bank A. To prevent the bank from dishonoring the check for lack of sufficient funds, a check for $4,000 is drawn on Bank B and deposited in Bank A. This check will in turn overdraw the account in Bank B, so a check for $4,000 is drawn on Bank A and deposited in Bank B to cover the original transfer check drawn on Bank B. The process must be repeated constantly until sufficient funds can be deposited to permit all checks to be covered. Although this might seem to be a rather unlikely course of action, a case is reported in which a California corporation obtained $100 million from its banks in this manner, writing checks for as much as $29 million!

## Lapping

Lapping is another form of embezzlement in which the embezzler must "keep running to keep even." As stated in the chapter on receivables, lapping of collections on accounts receivable can be detected by confirming account balances with customers. Lapping may also be disclosed by a careful examination of the cash records if customers pay by check, and provided they do not pay in round amounts as in the case of installment accounts. When each check received is for a different amount, the check received from A and appropriated by an employee will not be covered exactly by the check received from B a day or two later. Thus the entry in the cash receipts record crediting A for the check received from B will not agree with the amount of the check. The difference can be made up by depositing additional cash if B's check is smaller, or by making an additional credit to some other account if B's check is larger than the credit which must be made to A's account.

Although the total of the day's collections, shown by the cash receipts record, and the total of the deposit ticket, showing the amount of cash deposited, will agree when lapping has occurred, the individual amounts listed on the deposit ticket will not agree with the individual amounts shown by the cash receipts book. An item-for-item comparison of these two records will therefore show whether lapping has occurred. As there is a possibility that a duplicate deposit ticket in the client's possession may have been altered to conceal an irregularity, a copy of any deposit ticket to be used by the auditor should first be sent to the bank with a request that the bank compare the ticket with its copy. If the two copies agree, the bank will "authenticate" the deposit ticket with a stamp showing that it agrees with the copy in the bank's records.

A word of caution is warranted about placing too much reliance on bank deposit tickets, even if they have been authenticated by the bank. Most banks prove each customer's deposit in total only, as a part of their "proof" operation. Thus it is quite possible that a deposit ticket could show details that differed from the actual checks deposited, and the discrepancy would be discovered by the bank only if the deposit did not prove, necessitating a comparison of the bank's listing with the depositor's listing. Consequently, there is a possibility that an employee who is familiar with both auditing procedures and banking procedures might contrive to destroy the effectiveness of the detailed comparison of an authenticated deposit ticket with the cash receipts record.

### Detection of Fraud and the Four-Column Bank Reconciliation

The reader should be able to devise procedures that will reveal most of the forms of fraud that have been discussed. Some of these procedures will be performed in connection with the examination of accounts other than cash. The procedures relating specifically to the detailed examination of cash receipts and cash disbursements are usually performed in conjunction with the preparation of a 4-column bank reconciliation, an operation that is sometimes referred to as a "proof of cash." A simple example of this type of reconciliation is given below, and a more complete example appears on Schedule A-3.

| | Balance November 30 | December Deposits | December Withdrawals | Balance December 31 |
|---|---|---|---|---|
| Transactions per bank | $2,800 | $1,500 | $1,800 | $2,500 |
| Deposits in transit | | | | |
| November 30 ....... | 300 | 300 | | |
| December 31 ...... | | 250 | | 250 |
| Outstanding checks | | | | |
| Checks written prior | | | | |
| to December 1 .... | 1,100 | | 900 | 200 |
| Checks written in | | | | |
| December ........ | | | 700 | 700 |
| Transactions per books | | | | |
| .................... | $2,000 | $1,450 | $1,600 | $1,850 |

The reconciliation is usually prepared covering a period of one month, although a longer period can be used. The reader should note that reconcilement is effected between bank and book figures at the beginning and close of the period, as well as for receipts and disbursements during the period. If the reconciliation is made for the last month of the year, it obviates the need for separate verification of the year-end reconciliation. Use of the form in connection with a detailed examination of cash for a given period has these advantages:

1. All balances, transactions, and reconciling items are logically arranged for review.
2. The figures in the reconciliation become the starting point for the specific verification procedures.
3. The source and disposition are shown for every reconciling item, and any differences between bank and book figures are forced out into the open.

In preparing the reconciliation, the figures for the two balance columns are obtained from reconciliations prepared by the client. The figure for total deposits per bank may appear on the bank statement, or it can be readily determined by preparing an adding-machine tape of the deposits shown on the bank statement. The figure for withdrawals per bank can then be inserted by "plugging" the difference to complete the line for transactions per bank. The figures for transactions per books should be obtained from the general ledger account for the particular bank account being examined. Reconciling items originating or clearing through the columns for deposits and withdrawals can then be inserted as called for by changes in the reconciling items at the beginning and end of the period. For example, of the $1,100 in checks outstanding at November 30, only $200 remain outstanding at December 31. Therefore, $900 in checks must have been paid by the bank in December, and because these checks were entered in the books prior to December, the amount becomes a reconciling item in the column for withdrawals. To show that the amount is to be deducted from withdrawals per bank in order to reconcile to withdrawals per books, the amount is not encircled.

With the completion of the reconciliation form, the more important process of verifying the figures can begin. Each figure should be keyed to a description in the working papers of the actual verification work that has been performed. The following are typical verification procedures:

*Balances*

1. Trace bank balances to the bank statement for the period involved. Also, carefully examine the bank statement for erasures or alterations. Request confirmation of the bank balances as an added precaution.

2. Verify book balances against the balances shown in the general ledger.

3. Prove the footing of all four columns of the reconciliation.

### Receipts and Deposits

1. Prepare an adding-machine tape, listing each deposit per bank. Note thereon the date each deposit was recorded by the bank and the date the cash was recorded on company records. Investigate any deposits not reaching the bank by the next business day.

2. Subtract from the total of the above tape the deposit in transit at the beginning of the period, and add the deposit in transit at the end of the period. The new total should agree with the recorded deposits per book, unless other reconciling items are present.

3. Obtain authenticated duplicate deposit tickets for one or more days' deposits, including the deposit at the close of the period, as a test for lapping. Compare each deposit ticket, item for item, with the recorded cash receipts items.

4. Prove the footings of all columns of the cash receipts book for one or more days.

5. Trace the recorded cash receipts for the days selected under item 4 to documents supporting the individual entries. Such documents may include customers' remittance advices, carbon copies of cash receipts forms, cash register tapes showing totals for the day, cash register reconciliation forms showing resulting cash overages or shortages, and adding-machine tapes totaling sales checks issued for the day. In the last instance the sales checks should be re-added to prove the validity of the client's tape, and all sales check numbers should be accounted for, beginning with the last number of the previous day and ending with the first number of the following day.

6. Verify sales discounts taken by customers during the period under review. Calculate the amount of the discount to which the customer is entitled, and by reference to the original sales invoice or the debit entry in the customer's account, determine that payment was made within the discount period.

### Disbursements

1. Ascertain that all checks paid by the bank during the period are present.

    a. Prepare an adding-machine tape of the checks, and balance the total with the figure for bank withdrawals in the bank reconciliation form. This proof of disbursements per bank, coupled with certain other procedures stated below, obviates the need to prove the footing of the client's cash disbursements record. In preparing the tape of the checks, a subtotal should be taken after listing the last of the checks dated prior to the period being examined. This subtotal will be the source of the figure for checks outstanding at the beginning of the period but paid during the period (the figure of $900 in the reconciliation presented earlier).

b. Inspect the payment date perforated into each check or stamped on its face to determine that the check was actually paid during the period under examination.

2. Trace to the list of checks outstanding at the beginning of the period each check that was issued prior to the period and was paid during the period. Ascertain that each of these checks is listed correctly and that none has been omitted from the list of outstanding checks. Place a tick mark alongside each amount so verified on the list of outstanding checks.

3. Verify against the cash disbursement record the amount of each outstanding check not shown as paid in the preceding step, and trace the amount to a copy of the client's list of checks outstanding at the close of the period. Every outstanding check not paid during the period *must* be shown as outstanding at the end of the period.

4. Compare each check paid during the period with its cashbook entry as to date, number, payee, and amount, and determine that the check bears an authorized signature, that the check is properly endorsed, and that any second endorsements, particularly by an officer or employee, can be reasonably explained. For each check written and paid during the period being examined, place a small tick mark alongside the appropriate entry in the cash disbursements record.

5. Trace the amount of each cash disbursement entry not tick-marked as a result of the previous step to the list of checks outstanding at the close of the period, noting that each unpaid check is listed correctly and that none has been omitted. (These five procedures will establish the validity of the client's list of outstanding checks at the close of the period.)

6. Prove the footing of the list of outstanding checks at the close of the period, and ascertain that the total agrees with the corresponding figure in the bank reconciliation form.

7. Account for all check numbers, commencing with the last check issued at the close of the previous period and ending with the first check issued at the beginning of the following period. Inspect all voided checks, making certain that the checks have been multilated to prevent their use. Any check numbers not represented by paid or voided checks *must* be listed as outstanding at the close of the period.

8. Determine (usually on a test basis) the validity of the disbursements listed in the cash disbursements record during the period by examining invoices, receiving reports, payroll records, or other supporting documents.

a. The vendor's name and the amount of each invoice should agree with the corresponding entry, and the invoice should be addressed to the client.

b. Each invoice should be noted for any evidence that it may have been paid previously; hence an invoice bearing an old date should always be regarded with suspicion. As an indication of good internal control, each invoice should carry a notation showing the date it paid, and that date should agree with the date on the check.

c. Invoices should bear evidence that required approvals were given.

d. Any disbursements to officers, employees, or banks should receive particularly close scrutiny.

e. Reimbursements to petty cash funds should be reviewed in detail; supporting vouchers should be totaled and inspected for propriety and necessary approvals.

f. Interbank transfers should be scheduled in the manner recommended earlier.

    If the procedures that have just been discussed are thoroughly understood and carefully applied, they should be adequate to disclose most efforts designed to conceal the embezzlement or theft of cash. The principal exceptions would be cash that is withheld at the time a sale is made, with no recording of the sale or recording at a reduced amount, and kickbacks by suppliers representing billings to the company in excess of the correct amounts. The cash-sales problem points up the undesirability of having one person in control of all phases of a transaction. The kickback from the supplier illustrates the problem of collusion and suggests that owners and managers should review all operating figures carefully for any hint of excessive expense or decreasing margin on sales. Furthermore, they should be wary of any relationships between employees and suppliers or customers that would suggest possible conflict of interest.

    Generally speaking, the detailed audit of a client's cash transactions should give the auditor reasonable assurance that (a) cash receipts have been fully accounted for, (b) cash disbursements have been made only for authorized and valid purposes, and (c) cash balances are intact.

## Questions/Problems   *correct answers*

For multiple-choice questions 14-1 through 14-8, indicate the letter of the single answer that *best* completes the statement or answers the question, and justify the choice that you have made.

**14-1.** As an in-charge auditor you are reviewing a write-up of internal-control weaknesses in cash receipt and disbursement procedures. Which one of the following weaknesses, standing alone, should cause you the *least* concern?

    a. Checks are signed by only one person.

    b. Signed checks are distributed by the controller to approved payees.

    c. Treasurer fails to establish bona fides of names and addresses of check payees.

    d. Cash disbursements are made directly out of cash receipts.

(Uniform CPA Examination)

**14-2.** An internal management tool that aids in the control of the financial management function is a cash budget. The principal aim of a cash budget is to

    a. Insure that sufficient funds are available at all times to satisfy maturing liabilities.

    b. Measure adherence to company budgetary procedures.

    c. Prevent the posting of cash receipts and disbursements to incorrect accounts.

    d. Assure that the accounting for cash receipts and disbursements is consistent from year to year.

(Uniform CPA Examination)

**14-3.** An effective internal accounting control measure that protects against the preparation of improper or inaccurate disbursements would be to require that all checks be

    a. Signed by an officer after necessary supporting evidence has been examined.

    b. Reviewed by the treasurer before mailing.

    c. Sequentially numbered and accounted for by internal auditors.

    d. Perforated or otherwise effectively cancelled when they are returned with the bank statement.

(Uniform CPA Examination)

**14-4.** A bank "lock box" arrangement *Not applicable here!*

    a. Would be used to keep marketable securities in a safe place.

    b. Would be likely to exist with several banks if a company sells to customers throughout the United States.

    c. Results in a weakening of internal control.

    d. Is not related to the time-value of money.

**14-5.** Which of the following internal accounting control procedures would be effective in preventing duplicate payment of vendors' invoices?

    a. The invoices should be cancelled by rubber stamping, perforation, or other means *prior* to submitting the payment voucher for approval.

    b. Voucher forms should be prenumbered, and all numbers should be accounted for.

    c. Paid checks should be sent by the bank to persons other than the cashier or accounting department personnel.

    d. Properly authorized and approved vouchers with appropriate uncancelled documentation should be presented to the person authorized to sign checks.

**14-6.** The theft of cash from an employer's bank account can be concealed by

a. Including a fictitious outstanding check on the bank reconciliation.

b. Overfooting the cash column of the cash receipts book.

c. Recording a fictitious disbursement for the purchase of inventory.

d. Any of the above methods.

**14-7.** The Jackson Company records checks as being issued on the day they are written; however, the checks are often held a number of days before being released. The audit procedure which is *least* likely to reveal this method of incorrect cash-disbursements cutoff is to

a. Examine checks returned with cutoff bank statement for unreasonable time lag between date recorded in cash-disbursements book and date clearing bank.

b. Reconcile vendors' invoices with accounts payable per books.

c. Reconcile bank statement at year end.

d. Reconcile exceptions to account-payable confirmations.

(Uniform CPA Examination)

**14-8.** Kiting is a technique that might be used to conceal a cash shortage. The auditor can *best* detect kiting by performing which of the following procedures?

a. Examining the details of deposits made to all bank accounts several days subsequent to the balance sheet date.

b. Comparing cash receipts records with the details on authenticated bank deposit slips for dates subsequent to the balance sheet date.

c. Examining paid checks returned with bank statements subsequent to the balance sheet date.

d. Comparing year-end balances per the standard bank confirmation forms with the like balances on the client's bank reconciliations.

(Uniform CPA Examination)

**14-9.** What steps should a concern take to prevent "duplicate payment" of invoices?

**14-10.** How does the auditor verify deposits in transit and outstanding checks on a year-end bank reconciliation?

**14-11.** Discuss briefly what you regard as the more important deficiencies in the system of internal control in the following situation, and in addition include what you consider to be a proper remedy for each deficiency:

The cashier of the Easy Company intercepted customer A's check payable to the company in the amount of $500 and deposited it in a bank account that was part of the company petty cash fund, of which he was custodian. He then drew a $500 check on the petty cash fund bank account payable to himself, signed it and cashed it. At the end of the month while processing the monthly statements to customers, he was able to change the statement to customer A so as to show that A had received credit for the $500 check that had been intercepted. Ten days later he made an entry in the cash received book that purported to record receipt of a remittance of $500 from customer A, thus restoring A's account to its proper balance, but overstating cash in bank. He covered the overstatement by omitting two checks, the aggregate amount of which was $500, from the list of outstanding checks in the bank reconcilement.

(Uniform CPA Examination)

**14-12.** An auditor, in making a cash count at December 31, discovered that the cashier had not yet balanced records or made up the daily deposit. Cash on hand included both currency and checks. No other cash or negotiable instruments were held by the company. The auditor recorded the count of the cash, totaling $15,-394.72, and released the cash to the cashier.

The cashier's fund was $5,000, and the auditor subsequently noted a bank deposit dated January 2 on the January bank statement in the amount of $10,394.72, whereupon it was concluded that satisfactory verification of all cash on hand had been made.

    (a) What opportunities were open to the cashier as a result of the manner in which the auditor made the examination?

    (b) What should the auditor have done?

**14-13.** Given below are five interbank cash transfers that occurred near the end of your client's fiscal year:

| | Bank A *Bank sending* | | Bank B *Bank depositing* | |
| | Disbursing Date | | Deposit Date | |
| Check No. | Per Bank | Per Books | Per Bank | Per Books |
|---|---|---|---|---|
| (c) 1234 | 12/31 | 12/30 | 12/31 | 12/30 |
| 1245 | 1/2 | 12/30 | 12/31 | 12/31 |
| (a) 1256 | 1/3 | 12/31 | 1/2 | 1/2 |
| (b) 1267 | 1/3 | 12/31 | 1/2 | 12/31 |
| (d) (e) 1278 | 1/2 | 1/2 | 12/31 | 1/2 |

*not recorded until next year*

Which of these cash transfer checks

(a) indicates an error in cash cutoff at December 31?
(b) would appear as a deposit in transit on the December 31 bank reconciliation?
(c) would not appear as outstanding on the December 31 bank reconciliation?
(d) suggests that kiting may have occurred?

(Uniform CPA Examination-adapted)

**14-14.** What procedures in connection with verifying the 4-column bank reconciliation will reveal the fact that a check charged on the bank statement for the period under examination has been abstracted from the accompanying file of paid checks?

**14-15.** Preparing checks, recording disbursements, and reconciling the bank account are all handled by J. M. Carter of the Cordo Company. Carter notes that a check for $100 has been outstanding for more than one year and probably will not be cashed. He therefore takes a check from the back of the checkbook and writes it payable to himself for $100, forges the treasurer's signature, cashes the check, and attempts to conceal the disbursement by omitting the original check from the list of outstanding checks on subsequent reconciliations and destroying the fraudulent check after it has been paid by the bank.

(a) What is the principal internal control weakness that should be corrected?
(b) What audit procedures would disclose the manipulation?

**14-16.** You are auditing the Alaska Branch of Far Distributing Co. This branch has substantial annual sales, which are billed and collected locally. As a part of your audit you find that the procedures for handling cash receipts are as follows:

Cash collections on over-the-counter sales and C.O.D. sales are received from the customer or delivery service by the cashier. Upon receipt of cash the cashier stamps the sales ticket "paid" and files a copy for future reference. The only record of C.O.D. sales is a copy of the sales ticket, which is given to the cashier to hold until the cash is received from the delivery service.

Mail is opened by the secretary to the credit manager and remittances are given to the credit manager for review. The credit manager then places the remittances in a tray on the cashier's desk. At the daily deposit cutoff time, the cashier delivers the checks and cash on hand to the assistant credit manager, who prepares remittance lists and makes up the bank deposit, which is then taken to the bank. The assistant credit manager also posts remittances to the accounts receivable ledger cards and verifies the cash discount allowable.

You ascertain that the credit manager obtains approval from the executive office of Far Distributing Co., located in Chicago, to write off uncollectible accounts. You also ascertain that the credit manager has retained as of the end of the fiscal year some remittances that were received on various days during the last month.

(a) Describe the irregularities that might occur under the procedures now in effect for handling cash collections and remittances.

(b) Give procedures that you would recommend to strengthen internal control over cash collections and remittances.

(Uniform CPA Examination)

**14-17.** The town of Commuter Park operates a private parking lot near the railroad station for the benefit of town residents. The guard on duty issues annual prenumbered parking stickers to residents who submit an application form and show evidence of residency. The sticker is affixed to the auto and allows the resident to park anywhere in the lot for twelve (12) hours if four quarters are placed in the parking meter. Applications are maintained in the guard office at the lot. The guard checks to see that only residents are using the lot and that no resident has parked without paying the required meter fee.

Once a week the guard on duty, who has a master key for all meters, takes the coins from the meters and places them in a locked steel box. The guard delivers the box to the town storage building where it is opened, and the coins are manually counted by a storage department clerk who records the total cash counted on a "Weekly Cash Report." This report is sent to the town accounting department. The storage department clerk puts the cash in a safe and on the following day the cash is picked up by the town's treasurer who manually recounts the cash, prepares the bank deposit slip, and delivers the deposit to the bank. The deposit slip, authenticated by the bank teller, is sent to the accounting department where it is filed with the "Weekly Cash Report."

Required:

Describe weaknesses in the existing system and recommend one or more improvements for each of the weaknesses to strengthen the internal control over the parking lot cash receipts.

Organize your answer sheet as follows:

| Weakness | Recommended Improvement(s) |
| --- | --- |
| | |

(Uniform CPA Examination)

**14-18.** The Art Appreciation Society operates a museum for the benefit and enjoyment of the community. During hours when the museum is open to the public, two clerks who are positioned at the entrance collect a five dollar admission fee from each nonmember patron. Members of the Art Appreciation Society are permitted to enter free of charge upon presentation of their membership cards.

At the end of each day one of the clerks delivers the proceeds to the treasurer. The treasurer counts the cash in the presence of the clerk and places it in a safe. Each Friday afternoon the treasurer and one of the clerks deliver all cash held in the safe to the bank, and receive an authenticated deposit slip which provides the basis for the weekly entry in the cash receipts journal.

The board of directors of the Art Appreciation Society has identified a need to improve their system of internal control over cash admission fees. The board has determined that the cost of installing turnstiles or sales booths or otherwise altering the physical layout of the museum will greatly exceed any benefits that may be derived. However, the board has agreed that the sale of admission tickets must be an integral part of its improvement efforts.

Smith has been asked by the board of directors or the Art Appreciation Society to review the internal control over cash admission fees and provide suggestions for improvement.

Required:

Indicate weaknesses in the existing system of internal control over cash admission fees, which Smith should identify, and recommend one improvement for each of the weaknesses identified.

Organize the answer as indicated in the following illustrative example:

| Weakness | Recommendation |
| --- | --- |
| 1. There is no basis for establishing the documentation of the number of paying patrons. | 1. Prenumbered admission tickets should be issued upon payment of the admission fee. |

(Uniform CPA Examination)

**14-19.** Toyco, a retail toy chain, honors two bank credit cards and makes daily deposits of credit card sales in two credit card bank accounts (Bank A and Bank B). Each day Toyco batches its credit card sales slips, bank deposit slips, and authorized sales return documents, and keypunches cards for processing by its electronic data processing department. Each week detailed computer printouts of the general ledger credit card cash accounts are prepared. Credit card banks have been instructed to make an automatic weekly transfer of cash to Toyco's general bank account. The credit card banks charge back deposits that include sales to holders of stolen or expired cards.

The auditor conducting the examination of the 19X1 Toyco financial statements has obtained the following copies of the detailed general ledger cash account printouts, a summary of the bank statements and the manually prepared bank reconciliations, all for the week ended December 31, 19X1.

Required:

Based on a review of the December 31, 19X1, bank reconciliations and the related information available in the printouts and the summary of bank statements, describe what action(s) the auditor should take to obtain audit satisfaction *for each item* on the bank reconciliations.

**Table 14-1.** Toyco—Detailed General Ledger Credit Card Cash Account Printouts for the Week Ended December 31, 19X1

|  | Bank A<br>Dr. or (Cr.) | Bank B<br>Dr. or (Cr.) |
|---|---|---|
| Beginning Balance |  |  |
| —December 24, 19X1 | $12,100 | $ 4,200 |
| Deposits |  |  |
| —December 27, 19X1 | 2,500 | 5,000 |
| —December 28, 19X1 | 3,000 | 7,000 |
| —December 29, 19X1 | 0 | 5,400 |
| —December 30, 19X1 | 1,900 | 4,000 |
| —December 31, 19X1 | 2,200 | 6,000 |
| Cash Transfer |  |  |
| —December 27, 19X1 | (10,700) | 0 |
| Chargebacks |  |  |
| —Expired cards | (300) | ( 1,600) |
| Invalid deposits (physically deposited in wrong account) | ( 1,400) | ( 1,000) |
| Redeposit of invalid deposits | 1,000 | 1,400 |
| Sales returns for week ending December 31, 19X1 | (600) | ( 1,200) |
| Ending Balance |  |  |
| —December 31, 19X1 | $ 9,700 | $29,200 |

**Table 14-2.** Toyco—Summary of the Bank Statements for the Week Ended December 31, 19X1

| | Bank A | Bank B |
|---|---|---|
| | (Charges) or Credits | |
| Beginning Balance | | |
| —December 24, 19X1 | $10,000 | $ 0 |
| Deposits dated | | |
| —December 24, 19X1 | 2,100 | 4,200 |
| —December 27, 19X1 | 2,500 | 5,000 |
| —December 28, 19X1 | 3,000 | 7,000 |
| —December 29, 19X1 | 2,000 | 5,500 |
| —December 30, 19X1 | 1,900 | 4,000 |
| Cash transfers to general bank account | | |
| —December 27, 19X1 | (10,700) | 0 |
| —December 31, 19X1 | 0 | (22,600) |
| Chargebacks | | |
| —Stolen cards | (100) | 0 |
| —Expired cards | (300) | ( 1,600) |
| Invalid deposits | ( 1,400) | ( 1,000) |
| Bank service charges | 0 | (500) |
| Bank charge (unexplained) | (400) | 0 |
| Ending Balance | | |
| —December 31, 19X1 | $ 8,600 | $ 0 |

**Table 14-3.** Toyco—Bank Reconciliations for the Week Ended December 31, 19X1

| Code No. | | Bank A | Bank B |
|---|---|---|---|
| | | Add or (Deduct) | |
| 1. | Balance per bank statement —December 31, 19X1 | $8,600 | $ 0 |
| 2. | Deposits in transit —December 31, 19X1 | 2,200 | 6,000 |
| 3. | Redeposit of invalid deposits— (physically deposited in wrong account) | 1,000 | 1,400 |
| 4. | Difference in deposits of December 29, 19X1 | (2,000) | (100) |
| 5. | Unexplained bank charge | 400 | 0 |
| 6. | Bank cash transfer not yet recorded | 0 | 22,600 |
| 7. | Bank service charges | 0 | 500 |
| 8. | Chargebacks not recorded —Stolen cards | 100 | 0 |
| 9. | Sales returns recorded but not reported to the bank | (600) | (1,200) |
| 10. | Balance per general ledger —December 31, 19X1 | $9,700 | $29,200 |

Assume that all amounts are material and all computations are accurate.

Organize your answer sheet as follows using the appropriate code number *for each item* on the bank reconciliations:

| Code No. | Action(s) to be taken by the auditor to obtain audit satisfaction |
|---|---|
| 1. | |

(Uniform CPA Examination)

**14-20.** In connection with your audit of the ABC Co. at December 31, you received from a company employee a bank reconciliation that shows:

| | |
|---|---|
| Balance per bank | $15,267 |
| Deposits in transit | 18,928 |
| | $34,195 |
| Checks outstanding | 21,378 |
| Balance per books | $12,817 |

As part of your verification you obtain the bank statement and cancelled checks from the bank on January 15. Checks issued from January 1 to January 15 per the books were $11,241. Checks returned by the bank on January 15 amounted to $29,-219. Of the checks outstanding December 31, $4,800 were not returned by the bank with the January 15 statement, and of those issued per the books in January, $3,600 were not returned.

(a) Prepare a schedule showing the above data in proper form.

(b) Suggest four possible explanations for the condition existing here, and state what your action would be in each case, including any necessary journal entry.

(Uniform CPA Examination)

**14-21.** The total cash disbursements for the month of April as shown by the bank statement received by the X Co. were $25,219.85. Given the following information, not all of which is applicable to the problem, compute the total cash disbursements for April that would be shown in the cash account of the X Co., and prepare a reconciliation between the total disbursements per bank and per books.

1. Checks outstanding at March 31 totaled $568.19.
2. Checks outstanding at April 30 totaled $915.89.

3. In March, an X Co. check for $129.75 was charged by the bank as $192.75. The bank corrected this mistake by issuing a credit memo in April, entered as a deposit.

4. A check of the Z Co. in the amount of $78.90 was erroneously charged by the bank against X Company's account in April.

5. A check for $45.87 issued by X Co. in January has never cleared the bank and has been presumed lost. A stop payment order was issued to the bank and the X Co. wrote off the check by entering it in red in its check register for April.

6. An X Company check for $157.25 was certified by the bank in March and paid by the bank in April.

**14-22.** You are the in-charge accountant examining the financial statements of the Gutzler Company for the year ended December 31. During late October, you, with the help of Gutzler's controller, completed an internal control questionnaire and prepared the appropriate memorandums describing Gutzler's accounting procedures. Your comments relative to cash receipts are as follows.

All cash receipts are sent directly to the accounts-receivable clerk with no processing by the mail department. The accounts-receivable clerk keeps the cash-receipts journal; prepares the bank-deposit slip in duplicate; posts from the deposit slip to the subsidiary accounts-receivable ledger; and mails the deposit to the bank.

The controller receives the validated deposit slips directly (unopened) from the bank. He also receives the monthly bank statement directly (unopened) from the bank and promptly reconciles it.

At the end of each month the accounts-receivable clerk notifies the general-ledger clerk by journal voucher of the monthly totals of the cash-receipts journal for posting to the general ledger.

Each month, with regard to the general-ledger cash account, the general-ledger clerk makes an entry to record the total debits to cash from the cash-receipts journal. In addition, the general-ledger clerk on occasion makes debit entries in the general-ledger cash account from sources other than the cash-receipts journal, that is, funds borrowed from the bank.

Certain standard auditing procedures that are listed below have already been performed by you in the audit of cash receipts. The extent to which these procedures were performed is *not* relevant to the question.

- Total and cross-total all columns in the cash-receipts journal.
- Trace postings from the cash-receipts journal to the general ledger.

- Examine remittance advices and related correspondence to support entries in the cash-receipts journal.

## Required:

Considering Gutzler's internal control over cash receipts and standard auditing procedures already performed, list all other auditing procedures and reasons therefor which should be performed to obtain sufficient audit evidence regarding cash receipts. *Do not discuss the procedures for cash disbursements and cash balances. Also do not discuss the extent to which any of the procedures are to be performed. Assume adequate controls exist to assure that all sales transactions are recorded.* Organize your answer sheet as follows:

| Other Audit Procedures | Reason for Other Audit Procedures |
| --- | --- |
|  |  |

(Uniform CPA Examination)

14-23. The following information was obtained in an audit of the cash account of Tuck Company as of December 31. Assume that the CPA has satisfied himself as to the validity of the cash book, the bank statements, and the returned checks, except as noted.

1. The bookkeeper's bank reconciliation at November 30:

| | | |
| --- | --- | --- |
| Balance per bank statement | | $ 19,400 |
| Add deposit in transit | | 1,100 |
| Total | | 20,500 |
| Less outstanding checks | | |
| #2540 | $140 | |
| 1501 | 750 | |
| 1503 | 480 | |
| 1504 | 480 | |
| 1505 | 30 | 2,300 |
| Balance per books | | $ 18,200 |

2. A summary of the bank statement for December:

| | |
| --- | --- |
| Balance brought forward | $ 19,400 |
| Deposits | 148,700 |
| | 168,100 |
| Charges | 132,500 |
| Balance, December 31 | $ 35,600 |

3. A summary of the cash book for December before adjustments:

| | | | |
|---|---|---|---|
| Balance brought forward | .................. | | $ 18,200 |
| Receipts | .............................. | | 149,690 |
| | | | 167,890 |
| Disbursements | ........................ | | 124,885 |
| Balance, December 31 | .................. | | $ 43,005 |

4. Incuded with the cancelled checks returned with the December bank statement were the following:

| Number | Date of Check | Amount of Check | |
|---|---|---|---|
| #1501 | November 28 | $ 75 | This check was in payment of an invoice for $750 and was recorded in the cash book as $750. |
| #1503 | November 28 | $580 | This check was in payment of an invoice for $580 and was recorded in the cash book at $580. |
| #1523 | December 5 | $150 | Examination of this check revealed that it was unsigned. A discussion with the client disclosed that it had been mailed inadvertently before it was signed. The check was endorsed and deposited by the payee and processed by the bank even though it was a legal nullity. The check was recorded in the cash disbursements. |
| #1528 | December 12 | $800 | This check replaced #1504 that was returned by the payee because it was multilated. Check #1504 was not cancelled on the books. |
| — | December 19 | $200 | This was a counter check drawn at the bank by the president of the Company as a cash advance for travel expense. The president overlooked informing the bookkeeper about the check. |
| — | December 20 | $300 | The drawer of this check was the Tucker Company. |
| #1535 | December 20 | $350 | This check had been labeled NSF and returned to the payee because the bank had erroneously believed that the check was drawn by the Luck Company. Subsequently the payee was advised to redeposit the check. |
| #1575 | January 5 | $10,000 | This check was given to the payee on December 30 as a postdated check with the understanding that it would not be deposited |

until January 5. The check was not recorded on the books in December.

5. The Tuck Company discounted its own 60-day note for $9,000 with the bank on December 1. The discount rate was 6%. The bookkeeper recorded the proceeds as a cash receipt at the face value of the note.

6. The bookkeeper records customers' dishonored checks as a reduction of cash receipts. When the dishonored checks are redeposited, they are recorded as a regular cash receipt. Two NSF checks for $180 and $220 were returned by the bank during December. The $180 check was redeposited, but the $220 check was still on hand at December 31.

   Cancellations of Tuck Company checks are recorded by a reduction of cash disbursements.

7. December bank charges were $20. In addition a $10 service charge was made in December for the collection of a foreign draft in November. These charges were not recorded on the books.

8. Check #2540, listed in the November outstanding checks, was drawn two years ago. Since the payee cannot be located, the president of Tuck Company agreed to the CPA's suggestion that the check be written back into the accounts by a journal entry.

9. Outstanding checks at December 31 totaled $4,000 excluding checks #2540 and #1504.

10. The cutoff bank statement disclosed that the bank had recorded a deposit of $2,400 on January 2. The bookkeeper had recorded this deposit on the books on December 31 and then mailed the deposit to the bank.

    Prepare a 4-column reconciliation (sometimes called "proof of cash") of the cash receipts and cash disbursements recorded on the bank statement and on the company's books for the month of December. The reconciliation should agree with the cash figure that will appear in the company's financial statements.

    (Uniform CPA Examination)

14-24. Glatfelt Rural Electric Power Cooperative issues books of sight drafts to the foremen of its ten field crews. The foremen use the drafts to pay the expenses of the field crews when they are on line duty requiring overnight stays.

The drafts are prenumbered and, as is clearly printed on the drafts, are limited to expenditures of $300 or less. The foremen prepare the drafts in duplicate and send the duplicates, accompanied by expense reports substantiating the drafts, to the general office.

The draft duplicates are accumulated at the general office and a voucher is prepared when there are two or three draft duplicates on hand. The voucher is the authority for issuing a company check for deposit in an imprest fund of $5,000 maintained at a local bank to meet the drafts as they are presented for payment. The Cooperative maintains a separate general ledger account for the imprest fund.

The audit of the voucher register and cash disbursements disclosed the following information pertaining to sight drafts and the reimbursement of the imprest fund:

1. Voucher #10524 dated 12/31, paid by check #10524 dated 12/31, for the following drafts:

| Draft # | Date | Crew # | Explanation | Amount |
|---------|------|--------|-------------|--------|
| 6001 | 12/24 | 3 | Expenses, 12/22—24 | $160 |
| 2372 | 12/28 | 6 | Expenses, 12/26—28 | 310 |
| 5304 | 12/30 | 7 | Cash advance to foreman | 260 |
| | | | Voucher total | $730 |

2. Voucher #10531 dated 12/31, paid by check #10531 dated 1/3, for the following drafts:

| Draft # | Date | Crew # | Explanation | Amount |
|---------|------|--------|-------------|--------|
| 4060 | 12/29 | 1 | Expenses, 12/27—29 | $150 |
| 1816 | 1/3 | 4 | Expenses, 1/1—3 | 560 |
| | | | Voucher total | $710 |

3. Voucher #23 dated 1/8, paid by check #23 dated 1/8, for the following drafts:

| Draft # | Date | Crew # | Explanation | Amount |
|---------|------|--------|-------------|--------|
| 1000 | 12/31 | 9 | Expenses, 12/28—31 | $270 |
| 2918 | 1/3 | 10 | Expenses, 12/28—31 | 190 |
| 4061 | 1/7 | 1 | Expenses, 1/4—6 | 210 |
| | | | Voucher total | $670 |

4. All the above vouchers were charged to Travel Expense.
5. Examination of the imprest fund's bank statement for December, the January cutoff bank statement, and accompanying drafts presented for payment disclosed the following information:

    a.  Reimbursement check #10524 was not credited on the December bank statement.

    b.  The bank honored draft #2372 at the established maximum authorized amount.

    c.  Original drafts drawn by foremen but not presented to the client's bank for payment by 12/31 totaled $1,600. This total included all December drafts itemized above except #4060 and #2372, which were deducted by the bank in December.

    d.  December bank service charges listed on the December bank statement but not recorded by the client amounted to $80.

    e.  The balance per the bank statement at December 31 was $5,650.

(a)  Prepare the auditor's adjusting journal entry to correct the books at December 31. (The books have not been closed.) A supporting working paper analyzing the required adjustments should be prepared in good form.

(b)  Prepare a reconciliation of the balance per bank statement and the financial statement figure for the imprest cash account. The first figure in your reconciliation should be the balance per bank statement.

(Uniform CPA Examination)

# Chapter 15

# PAYROLL COSTS AND LIABILITIES

Despite the effect of automation on production processes, labor remains a major element of manufacturing cost, and labor is, of course, the single most important cost in the rapidly growing service field. Given the magnitude of these costs, it is essential that they be closely controlled through a variety of reports and analyses, and these information requirements coupled with the many repetitive calculations for large numbers of employees have made the payroll area a prime candidate for computerization. Payrolls thus tended to be the first application of computers in the data processing field as it became apparent that computers could be utilized for applications other than the extensive "number crunching" associated with research, design, and other problems that could be solved mathematically.

### Control Considerations

Payroll controls should be instituted at the point where employment and termination occur, plus at the point where determination is made of the amount of wages or salary to be paid to bona fide employees on the basis of authenticated records of time worked or units of output produced. To complete the control picture, payroll costs should be accounted for and reported on a responsibility basis.

With these introductory background comments, let us consider the flow chart of payroll procedures in Figure 15-1.

### Comments on Illustrative Flowchart of Payroll Procedures

1. The number of different functional activities involved in payroll processing greatly limits the opportunity to perpetrate fraud—provided, of course, that the organization is of sufficient size to make feasible the subdivision of payroll activities among so many different departments or persons.

2. The two basic inputs to the payroll system are workers' attendance time as recorded on clock cards (the basis for determining compensation earned), and job time (the basis for the cost distribution of payroll charges). These independent time records should be balanced for each employee as a timekeeping function prior to any further processing and balanced again at the end of the accounting process through the payroll clearing account. The clearing account is debited for the total wages earned and credited for the total charges distributed to the various detailed cost and expense accounts. The account should have a zero balance after both entries are posted.

3. The payroll bank account is handled on an imprest basis, with the check transferring funds to the payroll account and the credits to the various liability accounts prepared by accounts payable on the basis of the payroll register prepared by the payroll department.

4. The employees' paychecks are prepared by the payroll department, as are earnings statements (not shown) that must accompany the checks to report the amount earned and the various deductions taken in arriving at the amount of net pay for which each employee's check is drawn. The checks are then signed in the cash disbursements unit and should be delivered to a paymaster for distribution to the employees. Both the cash disbursements unit and the paymaster are part of the treasurer's organization.

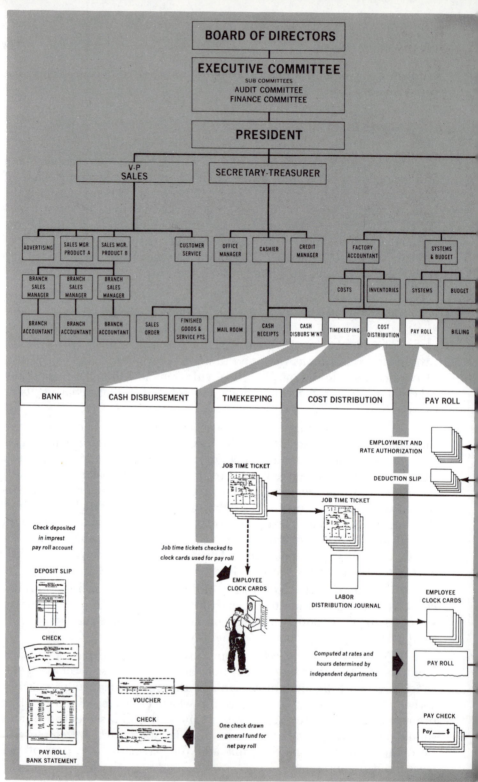

**Figure 15-1.**

# PAY ROLL

PROCEDURAL FLOW CHART SHOWN IN RELATION
TO ORGANIZATION CHART TO PORTRAY
THE CONTROL OBTAINED THROUGH SEGREGATION
OF FUNCTIONAL RESPONSIBILITY

Source: AICPA *Internal Control*

5. The information on gross earnings and deductions developed by the payroll department, which appears on the payroll and on the employee's earnings statement, must also be maintained on a cumulative record for each employee. This cumulative record is necessary to determine whether employees' year-to-date earnings have reached the taxable limit for FICA taxes (social security). The cumulative record also provides information for the quarterly and annual earnings reports that must be furnished to the federal and state government, as well as for the annual W-2 employee's earnings statement showing total earnings and total tax deductions.

### Computer Processing of Payrolls

Various degrees of computerization of payroll processing are possible, with the following comments pertaining to a relatively advanced on-line, real-time system. Inputs originate from worker-actuated terminals that accept and read employee ID numbers from plastic identification cards. The terminals also have keyboard input to accept job numbers or account numbers that identify the particular work activity in which the employee is engaged and which become the basis for the distribution of payroll charges. At the beginning of the day the employee "clocks in," using the ID card and keying in the job number or activity account number pertaining to the work to which the employee has been assigned, and depresses the "start" key. These steps cause the computer to open two files—one for the employee's overall time and the other for the job or account number. The time at which the input took place is recorded in each of the two files. If the employee changes jobs during the day, the same terminal operations are performed, causing the computer to close the first job record, calculate and record the elapsed time for that job, and open a record for the new activity in which the employee is engaged. At the close of the day the employee inserts the ID card and depresses the "stop" key, which closes both the record for the day and the record for the last job that was opened and computes the elapsed time for both the day and the last job.

At the end of the payroll period the computer summarizes each employee's total time for the period and the total time that the employee worked on the various jobs or types of activity during the period. The summarized information is then processed against the payroll master file that contains complete information about each employee, including name and address, social security number, department to which assigned, rate of pay, exemptions for withholding tax purposes, authorized deductions, and year-to-date totals for gross earnings and deductions for FICA tax, federal and state withholding tax, and any other items for which cumulative data are required. Outputs of this run would include a check and earnings statement for each employee, the payroll register, and the total charges to each job or expense activity. Also as a part of this run the master file year-to-date totals would be updated.

This concludes these introductory comments about the processing of payroll records. The preceding discussion should serve as a basis for the discussion that follows on evaluation of internal controls and substantive audit objectives and procedures.

## Evaluation of Internal Control Objectives and Features

### Operating Objectives

*All transactions are properly authorized.*

- Employees are added to the payroll at a stated rate of pay only upon authorization from the employment or personnel department and after required investigation of the employee's references and past employment history. *Inquiry, inspection.*
- A time card prepared for each employee and stamped with start and stop times for the day constitutes the authorization to pay an employee for the indicated hours. A time recorder should preferably be used to record start and stop times to ensure an accurate record. The recorder should be located at a convenient point of ingress and egress. The recorder should be operated under the surveillance of a security guard, who should limit entry to the premises to authorized persons and observe any infraction of a rule that should subject an employee to possible discharge for stamping the card of any other employee. In this way an employee is precluded from stamping another employee's card to generate compensation for an employee who is not present and working. Comparable control exists over computer inputs of time data through the necessity of using an ID card to record the time information. *Inquiry, observation, inspection.*
- The transfer of funds to the payroll imprest account is authorized by the payroll register prepared by the payroll department, showing the details of each employee's earnings and deductions. *Inquiry, inspection.*
- The final paycheck for a terminating employee is issued only after an exit interview and authorization of the check by the personnel department. *Inquiry, observation.*
- Overtime and any other pay supplements, such as to bring a piecework employee up to a guaranteed earnings rate, should be authorized in writing and carry an authorized signature. *Inquiry, inspection.*
- Officers' salaries should be authorized by the board of directors. *Inspection* procedures should include abstracting information about salary authorizations from the minutes of the board of directors and verifying that the total amount of officers' salaries for the year is in agreement with such authorization, as illustrated on working paper schedule 40-1.

*All authorizations resulted in action being taken.*

- Authorizations for the final checks to terminating employees should be prenumbered and accounted for by the payroll department in order to ascertain that all terminated employees are removed from the payroll. *Inquiry, observation.*

*Access to assets is permitted only in accordance with management authorization.*

- Entry to the plant premises or other areas to which access should be limited should be controlled by security guards and the use of identification badges. *Inquiry, observation.*
- Access to payroll funds is best controlled through the use of an imprest bank account to which funds are transferred only on the basis of payroll totals and from which funds are disbursed only through properly authorized paychecks. *Inquiry, inspection.*
- Control over the disbursement of payroll funds should be completed by releasing the checks to a paymaster or other designated person who is responsible to the treasurer. In distributing checks to employees, the paymaster should require positive identification of each employee before a check is released to the employee. Such identification is vital in preventing "padding" by placing fictitious persons on the payroll or by retaining terminated employees and using fraudulent time records to cause checks to be prepared for such persons. Protection against padding is accomplished by making it impossible for persons who might seek to undertake padding to obtain the checks that would have been prepared and signed. *Inquiry, observation.*
- Unclaimed checks for absent employees should be controlled by a duplicate listing of such checks prepared by the paymaster. The checks and one copy of the listing should be turned over to a cashier, who should hold the checks until they are claimed. An absent employee upon returning to work should obtain a form signed by the personnel department or the employee's supervisor, evidencing that the employee was absent and authorizing delivery of the check upon presentation of the form and proper identification. Periodic audit of the list should be made by determining that the check is still being held or that it has been replaced by the authorization form. *Inquiry, observation.*

### Data Processing Objectives–Internal Accounting Control

*Accounting and computer operations are independent of all operating responsibilities.*

*Inquiry* and *observation* that maximum feasible segregation of these activities exists:

| Operating | Accounting/Data Processing |
|---|---|
| Personnel | Timekeeping |
| Plant supervision | Payroll records |
| Security guards | Detail cost records |
| Cash disbursement | General ledger |
| Paymaster | Computer data entry |
| | Computer operations |

*Only valid transactions that were duly authorized are accepted for entry in the accounting records.*

- A new employee is issued an identification badge or card only after adequate investigation by the personnel department and acceptance of the prospective employee by the supervisor to whom the employee will be responsible. *Inquiry.*
- A new employee is added to the payroll at a stated rate of pay only on the basis of an authorization from the personnel department. *Inquiry.*
- Time worked is accepted by the payroll department only on the basis of time clock indication on a time card issued by the payroll department, or is accepted by computer on the basis of an entry through the use of an ID card. *Inquiry, inspection.*

*All transactions are entered in the accounting records.*

- Balancing of attendance clock time and job time by timekeeping, and of payroll and expense distribution amounts through the payroll clearing account, provide verification that all time worked was processed for payment. *Inquiry, inspection.*
- If time is not reported for any employee carried on the payroll, an absence report should be prepared and then reviewed by the employee's supervisor. *Inquiry.*
- Prenumbered termination notices should be accounted for by the payroll department to provide assurance that all terminated employees are removed from the payroll. *Inquiry, observation.*

*Transactions are correctly classified for accounting entry.*

- A responsibility reporting system and review by supervisors of the payroll costs with which they have been charged should provide adequate assurance that job time has been correctly reported and classified. *Inquiry.*
- Employees should be provided with complete information and instructions about account and job. numbers to which their time is to be charged. *Inquiry.*

*Recorded transactions are correctly processed.*

- The previously mentioned proofs of attendance time and job time, the review of responsibility-oriented reports, and periodic general ledger trial balances provide assurance that recorded transactions have been correctly processed. *Inquiry, observation, inspection.*

### Monitoring Objectives

*Regular comparison of accountability records of payroll amounts with underlying activity; third-party proofs of accounting records.*

- Employee verification of check and earnings statement amounts for gross earnings, deductions, and net pay provide an important monitoring of payroll amounts. *Inquiry, observation* (that earnings statements are furnished).
- Holding management accountable for results reported on a responsibility basis provides additional assurance that the recorded amounts are correct. *Inquiry, observation.*

*There is an effective internal audit function.*

- Internal auditors should regularly review and evaluate internal controls and perform compliance tests, including occasional payoffs (or observations thereof) with positive employee identification required (see subsequent discussion of the payoff process as a substantive audit procedure.) *Inquiry, observation, inspection* of internal audit working papers.
- A variety of operational audit activities should be considered by the internal audit staff as an important service to management in the control of operations. Independent auditor review of these operational audit activities provides additional indication of the general effectiveness of management. *Inquiry* concerning operational audit activities such as the following:

  Review of the process for setting standards and budgeting payroll costs.

  Analysis of variances from budgeted or standard costs.

  Study of effectiveness of plant security system, including control over persons entering company premises and use of time cards and time clocks.

  Study of safety and general working conditions in the plant.

  Consideration of whether management has taken adequate steps to assure maximum effectiveness and economy of manufacturing methods, evaluation of new machine tools and production processes, efficiency of plant layout, reduction of scrap and waste, adequacy of quality control, and other matters related to labor productivity and efficiency.

  Review of efforts to reduce absenteeism and vandalism, and to deal with alcohol and drug abuse by employees.

  Review of compliance with wages, hours, safety, and health laws and regulations.

## Substantive Audit Objectives and Procedures

Although payrolls will usually represent a major element of a client's operating expense, the independent auditor's examination of the expense and related accrued liability is likely to require only a small proportion of the total audit effort. Among the factors that tend to account for this disparity are the following:

1. Close attention by management to payroll methods, expense control fostered by an awareness of the importance of labor costs, consequent close attention to responsibility reporting, standard and budgeted costs, and other means of controlling labor costs.

2. The high volume of individual repetitive payroll transactions in large concerns makes possible substantial economy through specialization of accounting tasks within distinct organizational units, and the resulting subdivision of activities produces good internal control.

3. The monitoring of payroll amounts by employees, management, and the government through various payroll taxes and related reports tend to ensure accurate records.

4. Year-end liabilities related to payrolls tend to be of limited materiality relative to the amount of payroll expense for the year and to other assets and liabilities. As a consequence, audit effort is directed primarily to payroll expense, and the strong internal controls make it possible to limit the amount of substantive testing that is necessary.

5. Year-end cutoffs and liability amounts can be readily substantiated in most instances through review of client procedures and analytical review of statement amounts.

The objectives and procedures related to payroll expense and liabilities are considered next.

### Conformity of Client's Financial Statements with Disclosure and Other Requirements of Financial Reporting Standards

Fringe benefits that involve an obligation to be liquidated in the future, such as vacation pay or pension fund contributions, must be provided for and shown as a liability.

Direct and indirect labor costs should be accounted for in inventory, but standard cost variances and most other wages are accounted for as period charges.

For internal purposes, reporting on a responsibility basis is highly desirable.

### Reasonableness of Account Balances

*Perform Analytical Review.* Year-to-year comparisons of dollar amounts or of relationships are most useful in ascertaining the reasonableness of payroll-related amounts. Increases or decreases in absolute amounts should be related to changes in the level of activity, changes in wage rates, or other known factors that would account for a change in the reported amount. Changes in labor costs per unit or in relation to dollar sales should be studied carefully. In the illustrative work papers, schedule C analyzes the changes in labor and other elements that comprise the various inventory balances, in order to highlight any significant changes in the relationships of these figures. Schedule 20 compares the amount of labor, labor standard cost variances, and other elements in cost of sales for the current and preceding year.

Month-to-month comparisons are similarly useful, for they will show when any material changes occurred, including changes in classifying items for reporting purposes. Schedule 20-1 illustrates such a comparison and shows how significant changes were accounted for.

Payroll taxes should bear a reasonable relationship to payroll expense, and Schedule CC-2 shows how entries in various payroll tax accounts may be summarized, supported by examination of tax returns and paid checks, and then related to total payroll expense.

Accrued wages at the end of the year should represent the proportion of the total payroll cost for the last payroll period at the end of the year that the number of working days in the period prior to the end of the year bears to the total number of working days in the period.

### Synchronization of Events and Records

*Test Cutoff of Payroll Transactions.* Many companies determine the actual hours worked to the end of the year in the last payroll period of the year and extend these for each employee by the employee's wage rate to obtain the total accrued payroll. That method also can be used to develop the expense distribution for the debit portion of the accrual entry. If that technique has been used to obtain the accrual entry, the auditor should review the client's calculations and the supporting figures, but tests of supporting evidence should not be necessary unless the auditor has reason to question the client's figures. Instead, the auditor should be justified in relying on the overall test of the payroll accrual described as a reasonableness test in the previous section.

### Comprehensiveness of Records

The extensive monitoring of payroll records by employees when they receive their paychecks and earnings statements and the tie-in of payroll amounts with related payroll taxes should provide adequate assurance of the comprehensiveness of the payroll records. Familiarity with tax laws and regulations is, however, essential in order to determine whether all such taxes have been correctly provided for.

### Arithmetic and Clerical Accuracy; Agreement of Details and Control Totals

Once again the relatively immaterial balance sheet amounts associated with payroll and the typically good internal control should make it unnecessary to perform tests of arithmetic and clerical accuracy—other than those involved in compliance testing. Although cumulative employee earnings records could be balanced against total wages and total tax and other deductions for the year, the time and effort necessary to perform that procedure would seldom be justifiable.

### Existence of Payroll Liabilities

The existence of liabilities is not ordinarily an audit problem inasmuch as inclusion of a nonexistent liability would unfavorably affect net income and financial position. Nevertheless, it will be desirable to trace all payroll liabilities to subsequent disbursements and to review tax returns involved in the remittance of tax amounts due.

The auditor should be satisfied, however, of the existence of employees who are being paid—in other words, that the payroll has not been padded. Padding should be difficult to accomplish in a well-controlled system, and even in poorly controlled systems amounts stolen through padding are not likely to be material in relation to the financial statements. Nevertheless, to protect the client's interests, the independent auditor should ascertain that the internal auditor observes a payoff from time to time. If there is no internal auditor and internal control is weak, the independent auditor should consider whether to observe a payoff as a means of protecting the client's interests and avoiding the awkwardness of a subsequent disclosure that padding had occurred but was not detected by the audit.

In observing a payoff, the auditor should assume control of the payroll register and payroll checks on an unannounced basis, making certain that checks are present for every employee listed on the register. Positive identification should be made of each employee receiving a check, and no employee should receive more than one check. Unclaimed checks should be listed, and the auditor should be notified before any of these checks are released.

### Ownership of Payroll Liabilities

The comments in the preceding section are equally applicable to the question of ownership, which is essentially related only to asset amounts.

### Valuation of Payroll Liabilities

Valuation in this case is essentially a matter of computing the amounts owed, with the exception of defined benefit pension plans. For such plans various actuarial assumptions must be considered in determining the annual contribution to be made to the pension fund. That determination should be made by a recognized actuary, but the auditor should review the actuary's work for reasonableness.

## Questions/Problems

For multiple-choice questions 15-1 through 15-5, indicate the letter of the single answer that *best* completes the statement or answers the question, and justify the choice that you have made.

**15-1.** It would be appropriate for the payroll accounting department to be responsible for which of the following functions?
   a. Approval of employee time records.
   b. Maintenance of records of employment, discharges, and pay increases.
   c. Preparation of periodic governmental reports as to employees' earnings and withholding taxes.
   d. Temporary retention of unclaimed employee paychecks.

(Uniform CPA Examination)

**15-2.** Which of the following procedures would normally be performed by the auditor when making tests of payroll transactions?
   a. Interview employees selected in a statistical sample of payroll transactions.
   b. Trace number of hours worked as shown on payroll to time cards and time reports signed by the foreman.
   c. Confirm amounts withheld from employees' salaries with proper governmental authorities.
   d. Examine signatures on paid salary checks.

(Uniform CPA Examination)

**15-3.** One of the auditor's objectives in observing the actual distribution of payroll checks is to determine that every name on the payroll is that of a bona fide employee. The payroll observation is an auditing procedure that is generally performed for which of the following reasons?
   a. The professional standards that are generally accepted require the auditor to perform the payroll observation.
   b. The various phases of payroll work are *not* sufficiently segregated to afford effective internal accounting control.
   c. The independent auditor uses personal judgment and decides to observe the payroll distribution on a particular audit.
   d. The standards that are generally accepted by the profession are interpreted to mean that payroll observation is expected on an audit unless circumstances dictate otherwise.

(Uniform CPA Examination)

**15-4.** Which of the following is the *best* way for an auditor to determine that every name on a company's payroll is that of a bona fide employee presently on the job?

    a. Examine personnel records for accuracy and completeness.

    b. Examine employees' names listed on payroll tax returns for agreement with payroll accounting records.

    c. Make a surprise observation of the company's regular distribution of paychecks.

    d. Visit the working areas and confirm with employees their badge or identification numbers.

(Uniform CPA Examination)

**15-5.** An auditor decides that it is important and necessary to observe a client's distribution of payroll checks on a particular audit. The client organization is so large that the auditor *cannot* conveniently observe the distribution of the entire payroll. In these circumstances, which of the following is *most* acceptable to the auditor?

    a. Observation should be limited to one or more selected departments.

    b. Observation should be made for all departments regardless of the inconvenience.

    c. Observation should be eliminated and other alternative auditing procedures should be utilized to obtain satisfaction.

    d. Observation should be limited to those departments where employees are readily available.

(Uniform CPA Examination)

**15-6.** Most businesses must pay time-and-one-half for work in excess of 40 hours during a work week. Under what circumstances should method (a) be used in computing payrolls? Method (b)?

    (a)   40 hrs $\times$ \$10.00 = \$400

           4 hrs $\times$ \$15.00 = $\underline{\$\ 60}$

                            $\underline{\$460}$

    (b)   44 hrs $\times$ \$10.00 = \$440

           4 hrs $\times$ \$ 5.00 = $\underline{\$\ 20}$

                            $\underline{\$460}$

**15-7.** Explain why the paymaster should not be permitted to hold unclaimed wages until the employee calls for them, but rather should list the unclaimed wages and turn them over to someone else for distribution to the employee.

**15-8.** What are the principal reasons for maintaining an earnings record for each employee?

**15-9.** How should wage rates be verified in connection with a test of factory payroll?

**15-10.** What should the auditor do about unclaimed pay checks after observing a payroll payoff?

**15-11.** What audit procedures would disclose that the payroll was padded by retaining on the payroll employees who had resigned?

*observation of payroll payment*

**15-12.** Your client's bookkeeper has discovered that most employees do not reconcile total withholding tax shown on their W-2 forms with the amounts withheld during the year. Accordingly, the bookkeeper would understate the amount of withholding tax posted to various employees' cumulative earnings records and increase the tax posted to the bookkeeper's own summary record by the same amount. Following the end of the year the bookkeeper would claim a refund for the excess withholding tax shown on the W-2 form. Should the customary examination of financial statements disclose the manipulation? Explain. What procedures would disclose the manipulation?

**15-13.** In connection with his examination of the financial statements of the Olympia Manufacturing Company, a CPA is reviewing procedures for accumulating direct labor hours. He learns that all production is by job order and that all employees are paid hourly wages, with time-and-one-half for overtime hours.

Olympia's direct labor hour input process for payroll and job-cost determination is summarized in the flowchart that follows.

Steps A and C are performed in timekeeping, step B in the factory operating departments, step D in payroll audit and control, step E in data preparation (keypunch), and step F in computer operations.

Required:

For each input processing step A through F:

(a) List the possible errors or discrepancies that may occur.

(b) Cite the corresponding control procedure that should be in effect for each error or discrepancy.

*Note:* Your discussion of Olympia's procedures should be limited to the input process for direct labor hours, as shown in steps A through F in the flowchart. *Do not discuss* personnel procedures for hiring, promotion, termination, and pay rate authorization. *In step F do not discuss* equipment, computer program, and general computer operational controls.

Organize your answer for each input-processing step as follows:

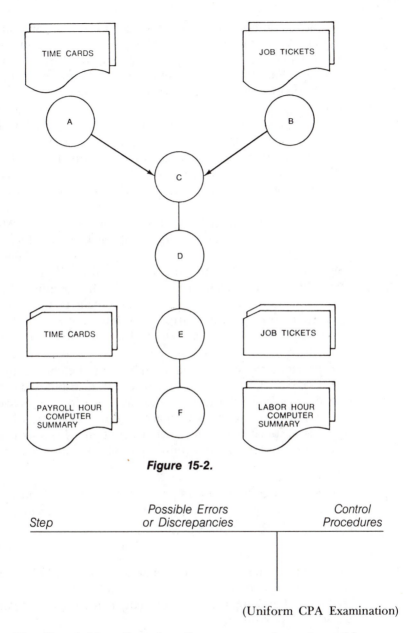

**Figure 15-2.**

| Step | Possible Errors or Discrepancies | Control Procedures |
|------|----------------------------------|--------------------|
|      |                                  |                    |

(Uniform CPA Examination)

**15-14.** The Kowal Manufacturing Company employs about fifty production workers and has the following payroll procedures

The factory foreman interviews applicants and on the basis of the interview either hires or rejects the applicants. When the applicant is hired, he prepares a W-4 form (Employees' Withholding Exemption Certificate) and gives it to the foreman. The foreman writes the hourly rate of pay for the new employee in the corner of the W-4 form and then gives the form to a payroll clerk as notice that the worker has been employed. The foreman verbally advises the payroll department of rate adjustments.

A supply of blank timecards is kept in a box near the entrance to the factory. Each worker takes a timecard on Monday morning, fills in his name, and notes in pencil on the timecard his daily arrival and departure times. At the end of the week the workers drop the timecards in a box near the door to the factory.

The completed timecards are taken from the box on Monday morning by a payroll clerk. Two payroll clerks divide the cards alphabetically between them, one taking the A to L section of the payroll and the other taking the M to Z section. Each clerk is fully responsible for her section of the payroll. She computes the gross pay, deductions and net pay, posts the details to the employees' earnings records, and prepares and numbers the payroll checks. Employees are automatically removed from the payroll when they fail to turn in a timecard.

The payroll checks are manually signed by the chief accountant and given to the foreman. The foreman distributes the checks to the workers in the factory and arranges for the delivery of the checks to the workers who are absent. The payroll bank account is reconciled by the chief accountant who also prepares the various quarterly and annual payroll tax reports.

Required:

List your suggestions for improving the Kowal Manufacturing Company's system of internal control for the factory hiring practices *and* payroll procedures.

(Uniform CPA Examination)

**15-15.** You are auditing the financial statements of the Soo Company for the year ended December 31, 19X1. Following are transcripts of the Company's general ledger accounts for salary expense and payroll taxes.

| Date | Explanation | Fol | Debit | Credit | Balance |
|------|-------------|-----|-------|--------|---------|
| 12/31/X1 | Weekly payrolls (Total of 12 monthly summary entries) | CD | $44,470 | | $44,470 |

**Payroll Taxes Expense**

| Date | Explanation | Fol | Debit | Credit | Balance |
|------|-------------|-----|-------|--------|---------|
| 1/10/X1 | Quarterly remittance | CD | $4,100 | | $ 4,100 |
| 4/20/X1 | Quarterly remittance | CD | 3,801 | | 7,901 |
| 7/14/X1 | Quarterly remittance | CD | 3,327 | | 11,228 |
| 10/18/X1 | Quarterly remittance | CD | 3,320 | | 14,548 |

**Payroll Taxes Withheld**

| Date | Explanation | Fol | Debit | Credit | Balance |
|------|-------------|-----|-------|--------|---------|
| 1/1/X1 | Balance forward | | | $3,200 | $3,200 |

**Employer Payroll Taxes Payable**

| Date | Explanation | Fol | Debit | Credit | Balance |
|------|-------------|-----|-------|--------|---------|
| 1/1/X1 | Balance forward | | | $900 | $900 |

The following additional information is available:

1. Copies of the quarterly tax returns are not available because the typist did not understand that the returns were to be typed in duplicate. The pencil drafts of the tax returns were discarded.
2. Your audit of the payroll records revealed that the payroll clerk properly computed the payroll tax deductions and the amounts of quarterly remittances. You are able to develop the following summary:

| Quarter | Gross Salaries | Payroll Taxes Withheld F.I.C.A. | Income | Net Salaries |
|---------|----------------|----------------------------------|--------|--------------|
| First | $13,600 | $425 | $2,600 | $10,575 |
| Second | 12,000 | 375 | 2,280 | 9,345 |
| Third | 12,800 | 325 | 2,400 | 10,075 |
| Fourth | 18,700 | 225 | 4,000 | 14,475 |

3. The Soo Company did not make monthly deposits of taxes withheld. You determine that the following remittances were made with respect to 19X1 payrolls:

| | 4/20/X1 | 7/14/X1 | 10/18/X1 | 1/12/X2 |
|---|---------|---------|----------|---------|
| F.I.C.A. (6¼%) | $ 850 | $ 750 | $ 650 | $ 450 |
| Income Tax | 2,600 | 2,280 | 2,400 | 4,000 |
| State Unemployment Insurance (2.7%) | 351 | 297 | 270 | 162 |
| Total | $3,801 | $3,327 | $3,320 | $4,612 |

4. The effective Federal Unemployment Tax rate for 19X1 is .8%. The laws of the state in which Soo Company does

business do not provide for employee contributions for state unemployment insurance.

Required:

(a) Prepare a worksheet to determine the correct balances at December 31, 19X1 for the general ledger accounts, Salary Expense, Payroll Taxes Expense, Payroll Taxes Withheld, Employer Payroll Taxes Payable. (Disregard accrued salaries at year end.)

(b) Prepare the adjusting journal entry to correct the accounts at December 31, 19X1.

(Uniform CPA Examination)

**15-16.** James, who was engaged to examine the financial statements of Talbert Corporation, is about to audit payroll. Talbert uses a computer service center to process weekly payroll as follows:

Each Monday Talbert's payroll clerk inserts data in appropriate spaces on the preprinted service center prepared input form, and sends it to the service center via messenger. The service center extracts new permanent data from the input form and updates master files. The weekly payroll data are then processed. The weekly payroll register and payroll checks are printed and delivered by messenger to Talbert on Thursday.

Part of the sample selected for audit by James includes the following input form and payroll register:

**Table 15-1.** Talbert Corporation Payroll Input—Week Ending Friday, Nov. 23, 19X1

| | —Employee Data—Permanent File— | | | —Current Week's Payroll Data— | | | | |
| | | **W-4** | **Hourly** | **Hours** | | **Special Deductions** | | |
| *Name* | *Social Security* | *Information* | *Rate* | *Reg* | *OT* | *Bonds* | *Union* | *Other* |
| A. Bell | 999-99-9991 | M-1 | 10.00 | 35 | 5 | 18.75 | | |
| B. Carr | 999-99-9992 | M-2 | 10.00 | 35 | 4 | | | |
| C. Dawn | 999-99-9993 | S-1 | 10.00 | 35 | 6 | 18.75 | 4.00 | |
| D. Ellis | 999-99-9994 | S-1 | 10.00 | 35 | 2 | | 4.00 | 50.00 |
| E. Frank | 999-99-9995 | M-4 | 10.00 | 35 | 1 | | 4.00 | |
| F. Gillis | 999-99-9996 | M-4 | 10.00 | 35 | | | 4.00 | |
| G. Hugh | 999-99-9997 | M-1 | 7.00 | 35 | 2 | 18.75 | 4.00 | |
| H. Jones | 999-99-9998 | M-2 | 7.00 | 35 | | | 4.00 | 25.00 |
| J. King | 999-99-9999 | S-1 | 7.00 | 35 | 4 | | 4.00 | |
| *New Employee* | | | | | | | | |
| J. Smith | 999-99-9990 | M-3 | 7.00 | 35 | | | | |

**Table 15-2.** Talbert Corporation Payroll Register—Nov. 23, 19X1

| Employee | Social Security | Hours Reg | Hours OT | Payroll Regular | Payroll OT | Gross Payroll | Taxes Withheld FICA | Taxes Withheld Fed | Taxes Withheld State | Other Withheld | Net Pay | Check No. |
|---|---|---|---|---|---|---|---|---|---|---|---|---|
| A. Bell | 999-99-9991 | 35 | 5 | 350.00 | 75.00 | 425.00 | 26.05 | 76.00 | 27.40 | 18.75 | 276.80 | 1499 |
| B. Carr | 999-99-9992 | 35 | 4 | 350.00 | 60.00 | 410.00 | 25.13 | 65.00 | 23.60 | | 296.27 | 1500 |
| C. Dawn | 999-99-9993 | 35 | 6 | 350.00 | 90.00 | 440.00 | 26.97 | 100.90 | 28.60 | 22.75 | 260.78 | 1501 |
| D. Ellis | 999-99-9994 | 35 | 2 | 350.00 | 30.00 | 380.00 | 23.29 | 80.50 | 21.70 | 54.00 | 200.51 | 1502 |
| F. Frank | 999-99-9995 | 35 | 1 | 350.00 | 15.00 | 365.00 | 22.37 | 43.50 | 15.90 | 4.00 | 279.23 | 1503 |
| F. Gillis | 999-99-9996 | 35 | | 350.00 | | 350.00 | 21.46 | 41.40 | 15.00 | 4.00 | 268.14 | 1504 |
| G. Hugh | 999-99-9997 | 35 | 2 | 245.00 | 21.00 | 266.00 | 16.31 | 34.80 | 10.90 | 22.75 | 181.24 | 1505 |
| H. Jones | 999-99-9998 | 35 | | 245.00 | | 245.00 | 15.02 | 26.40 | 8.70 | 29.00 | 165.88 | 1506 |
| J. King | 999-99-9999 | 35 | 4 | 245.00 | 42.00 | 287.00 | 17.59 | 49.40 | 12.20 | 4.00 | 203.81 | 1507 |
| J. Smith | 999-99-9990 | 35 | | 245.00 | | 245.00 | 15.02 | 23.00 | 7.80 | | 199.18 | 1508 |
| Totals | | 350 | 24 | 3,080.00 | 333.00 | 3,413.00 | 209.21 | 540.90 | 171.80 | 159.25 | 2,331.84 | |

Required:

(a) Describe how James should verify the information in the payroll input form shown above.

(b) Describe (but do *not* perform) the procedures that James should follow in the examination of the November 23, 19X1 payroll register shown above.

(Uniform CPA Examination)

**15-17.** A CPA's audit working papers contain a narrative description of a *segment* of the Croyden Factory, Inc., payroll system and an accompanying flowchart (Figure 15-3) as follows:

The internal control system with respect to the personnel department is well functioning and is *not* included in the accompanying flowchart.

At the beginning of each work week payroll clerk No. 1 reviews the payroll department files to determine the employment status of factory employees and then prepares timecards and distributes them as each individual arrives at work. This payroll clerk, who is also responsible for custody of the signature stamp machine, verifies the identity of each payee before delivering signed checks to the foreman.

At the end of each work week the foreman distributes payroll checks for the preceding work week. Concurrent with this activity, the foreman reviews the current week's employee timecards, notes the regular and overtime hours worked on a summary form, and initials the aforementioned timecards. The foreman then delivers all timecards and unclaimed payroll checks to payroll clerk No. 2.

Required:

(a) Based upon the narrative and accompanying flowchart, what are the weaknesses in the system of internal control?

(b) Based upon the narrative and accompanying flowchart, what inquiries should be made with respect to clarifying the existence of *possible additional weaknesses* in the system of internal control?

Note: Do not discuss the internal control system of the personnel department.

(Uniform CPA Examination)

**15-18.** You are reviewing audit work papers containing a narrative description of the Tenney Corporation's factory payroll system. A portion of that narrative is as follows:

Factory employees punch time clock cards each day when entering or leaving the shop. At the end of each week the timekeep-

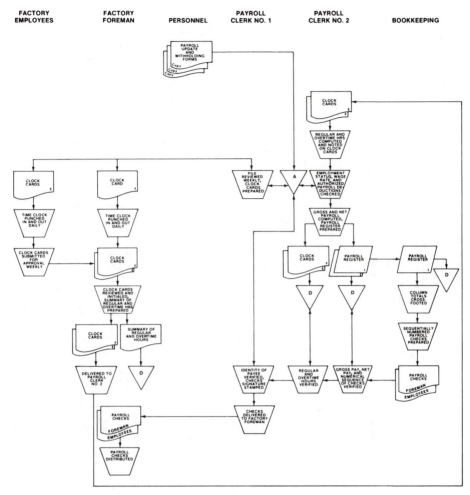

| FACTORY EMPLOYEES | FACTORY FOREMAN | PERSONNEL | PAYROLL CLERK NO. 1 | PAYROLL CLERK NO. 2 | BOOKKEEPING |
|---|---|---|---|---|---|

**Figure 15-3.** Croyden Inc., Factory Payroll System

ing department collects the timecards and prepares duplicate batch-control slips by department showing total hours and number of employees. The timecards and original batch-control slips are sent to the payroll accounting section. The second copies of the batch-control slips are filed by date.

In the payroll accounting section payroll transaction cards are keypunched from the information on the timecards, and a batch total card for each batch is keypunched from the batch-control slip. The timecards and batch-control slips are then filed by batch for possible reference. The payroll transaction cards and batch total card are sent to data processing where they are

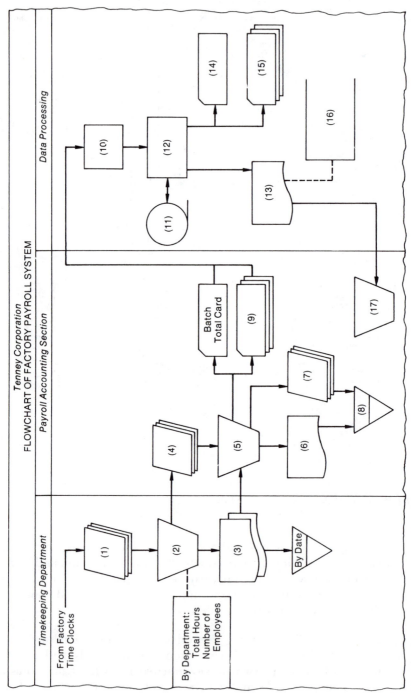

**Figure 15-4.** Flowchart for Problem 15-18

474

sorted by employee number within batch. Each batch is edited by a computer program that checks the validity of employee number against a master employee tape file, and the total hours and number of employees against the batch total card. A detail printout by batch and employee number is produced, which indicates batches that do not balance and invalid employee numbers. This printout is returned to payroll accounting to resolve all differences.

In searching for documentation, you found a flowchart of the payroll system that included all appropriate symbols (American National Standards Institute, Inc.) but was only partially labeled. The portion of this flowchart described by the above narrative appears on page 474.

Required:

(a) Number your answer 1 through 17. Next to the corresponding number of your answer, supply the appropriate labeling (document name, process description, or file order) applicable to each numbered symbol on the flowchart.

(b) Flowcharts are one of the aids an auditor may use to determine and evaluate a client's internal control system. List advantages of using flowcharts in this context.

(Uniform CPA Examination)

# Chapter 16

# DEPRECIATION
# AND PLANT ASSETS

The importance of capital goods in the highly developed economies of the Western world suggests that depreciation expense and plant asset accounting would represent major problems to both the company accountant and the independent auditor. The magnitude of the problem is lessened, however, by the following factors:

1. As implied by the term "fixed assets," the turnover is much slower than the turnover of current assets, and the assets remain in the business for a longer time period.
2. There are relatively few transactions to deal with inasmuch as the typical unit of property and equipment involves a comparatively large dollar amount.
3. Accounting errors will have a less material effect on the financial statements than errors involving current assets, and third parties will not be directly affected by the errors. Consequently, controls to prevent or eliminate errors are not as important as for current asset items.
4. Security measures to prevent loss are not as critical as for current assets because the physical size and limited usefulness of most plant assets minimize the likelihood of theft.

### Control Considerations

The factors listed tend to reduce the importance of internal control over plant assets and transactions involving those items and to simplify the independent auditor's examination of plant asset accounts. For large concerns with substantial activity and investment in plant assets, control should begin at the point where proposals for new acquisitions or major modifications of existing facilities are first considered. Different levels of approval are customarily required, depending on the amount of the proposed expenditure, with major items often being required to clear through a capital-budgeting committee that might include such persons as the plant superintendent, the chief engineer, and the controller. Proposals for complete facilities involve policy considerations and are likely to require approval at the board of directors level.

Regardless of the requested amount, a proposal should be supported by cost estimates, savings or other returns expected, and any other justification for the expenditure that will permit a ranking of proposals as a means of allocating available funds to the most productive uses. Return on investment, payout period, and cost of capital are all important in arriving at optimal decisions.

Once authorization has been granted, monthly progress reports comparing budgeted and actual expenditures should be prepared and reviewed, in order to control these expenditures. As individual plant asset units are acquired, plant ledger records should be prepared to establish accountability for the physical assets and to provide a basis for subsequent accounting for depreciation, repairs, and retirements.

Each of the points included above is represented in the next section on internal control objectives and features.

# Evaluation of Internal Control Objectives and Features

## Operating Objectives

*All transactions are properly authorized.*

- Expenditures for plant assets should be processed through regular accounts payable procedures, with budgetary authorization and contractual agreements replacing purchase orders as formal authorization for expenditures. *Inquiry, inspection.*
- Dispositions of plant assets should be authorized at an appropriate level through work orders to dismantle and remove equipment and to authorize release from a controlled shipping area. *Inquiry, observation, inspection.*

*All authorizations resulted in action being taken.*

- No formal procedures to assure that action is taken are necessary, in that there will be relatively few transactions and the person or department responsible for initiating authorization requests or effectuating acquisition of purchase items will develop an informal system of surveillance over each authorization until all action has been completed.

*Access to assets is permitted only in accordance with management authorization.*

- Plant assets should be subject to access controls to prevent unauthorized use. Automotive vehicles and computers warrant special controls to prevent unauthorized use. *Inquiry, observation.*

## Data Processing Objectives–Internal Accounting Control

*Accounting and computer operations are independent of all operating responsibilities.*

*Inquiry* and *observation* that maximum feasible segregation of these activities exists:

| Operating | Accounting/Data Processing |
|---|---|
| Authorization of expenditures | Plant ledger records |
| Disbursement of funds | General ledger records |
| Installation, repair, and maintenance | Computer processing |
| Productive use of equipment | |
| Access controls | |

*Only valid transactions that were duly authorized are accepted for entry in the accounting records.*

- Given the nature of fixed assets, no special procedures beyond control over related cash transactions are necessary to control entries to accounts and records associated with plant assets.

*All transactions are entered in the accounting records.*

- Disbursements for acquisitions are assured of entry in the accounting records as a result of accountability over cash or other assets given up in the acquisition process.
- Dispositions of plant assets should be accomplished through preparation of work orders to authorize removals. The work orders should be prenumbered and the numbers accounted for at the time that the work orders become the basis for entry in plant and general ledger records to record dispositions. Cash proceeds or trade-in allowances associated with dispositions should be recorded as a receivable in conjunction with the entry to record the disposition. *Inquiry, observation, inspection.*

*Accounting entries correctly reflect transaction amounts.*

- Normal controls over recording of liabilities and dispositions of plant assets should provide adequate control over accuracy of recording transactions. The double entry system and balancing of plant ledger records against controlling account totals provide further assurance of accuracy. *Inquiry.*

*Transactions are correctly classified for accounting entry.*

- A chart of accounts should set forth the types of items to be charged to the various plant asset accounts to reflect similar types of assets and life expectancies and also to maintain proper distinction between expenditures that should be capitalized and those that carry no future benefit and therefore should be expensed. To facilitate this process and to minimize record keeping for capitalized items, it is desirable to establish a minimum amount that is to be capitalized, with lesser items expensed despite the future benefits to be obtained. The cutoff amount should be set at a figure that will reasonably preclude material distortion of operating results as a result of this expedient. *Inquiry, observation, inspection.*
- Depreciation methods and policies should be established that are appropriate to the concern's situation, involving such matters as
  Depreciation method (straight line, double declining balance, units of production)
  Group v. unit depreciation
  Life expectancy for various types of assets
  Allocation of depreciation to various operating units and responsibility areas
  Determination of amount of depreciation to be charged in year of acquisition and year of disposition.

*Recorded transactions are correctly processed.*

- Regular trial balances of general ledger accounts should be prepared to prove equality of debits and credits; detailed plant ledger records should be balanced periodically against related controlling accounts. *Inquiry, inspection.*

## Monitoring Objectives

*Regular comparison is made of plant asset accountability records with underlying assets; third-party proofs of accounting records.*

- There is no opportunity for third-party proofs of plant assets, but periodically a physical inventory of these assets should be taken and compared with the records. Such inventories are customarily taken on a cycle basis, with a three-to-five-year cycle generally considered adequate in view of the limited turnover and negligible effect on the financial statements of such discrepancies as may occur. To facilitate such cycle inventories, each physical item and its corresponding plant ledger record should be identified with a serial number, and the ledger records should be grouped according to areas of the plant in which the assets are located and according to the person who is charged with responsibility for the assets. *Inquiry, observation, inspection.*

*There is an effective internal audit function.*

- Internal auditors should regularly review and evaluate internal controls, including plant asset inventory procedures; perform compliance tests; and when necessary, make recommendations for improvement in the controls. *Inquiry, review of audit planning, inspection of working papers.*
- The following operational audit activities suggest possibilities for being of service to management in the control of operations.

  Review of procedures for expenditure proposals and the related evaluation process.

  Review of competitive bid procedures for authorized expenditures for plant assets.

  Post audit of proposals for plant expenditures to evaluate accuracy of estimates of cost and return on investment or other anticipated benefits; investigation of significant overruns of expenditures relative to authorized amounts.

  Analysis of performance, reliability, and operating and repair costs for those types of equipment where alternative choices exist, as for example automobiles and trucks, heating and air conditioning equipment, and pollution control devices such as dust collectors and liquid effluent filtration and treatment equipment.

  Review of accounting for cash proceeds or trade-in allowances in connection with disposition of assets, including whether maximum realization was obtained.

  Review of maintenance procedures for effectiveness and indication that equipment may be under- or over-maintained.

  Consideration of whether maximum tax advantages have been obtained relative to depreciation policies and special credits that are available.

### Supplementary Comments—Computer-Based Records

Although plant asset records are readily adaptable to computerization, the costs of programming for this application are likely to exceed the benefits unless there are large numbers of records, as in the case of a public utility or a very large manufacturing concern.

## Substantive Audit Objectives and Procedures

The limited turnover of plant assets and the large dollar amount of most of these items reduces the amount of auditing that must be done as compared with current assets. These factors also make it advantageous to utilize a transaction approach to the examination rather than the inventory approach that is more efficient for current assets with their higher turnover. We consider first the objective of conformity with GAAP.

### Conformity of Client's Financial Statements with Disclosure and Other Requirements of Financial Reporting Standards

Plant assets should be carried at cost less accumulated depreciation, with depreciation charges determined by an accepted method that systematically allocates depreciation to the accounting periods that benefit from the use of the assets. Changes in the method of accounting that would materially affect comparability of financial statements must be reported in accordance with financial reporting standards for a change in accounting principle. Both cost and the accumulated depreciation for major classes of assets should be shown in the balance sheet, and the amount of depreciation charged for the period should be disclosed in the income statement or in the notes to the financial statements. Further, for companies with more than $1 billion in assets or $125 million of inventories and gross investment in plant assets, Financial Accounting Standards Board Statement No. 33, "Financial Reporting and Changing Prices," requires that supplementary figures be given for depreciation adjusted for the effect of general inflation and for the effect of changes in specific prices of assets (depreciation based on current costs). Statement 33 also requires that the current cost of all property, plant, and equipment net of accumulated depreciation also be shown, together with the increase in the current cost of these assets for the year and the related increase in the inflation-adjusted cost of the assets.

Major classes of plant assets should be separately reported for information purposes. Liens on plant assets, resulting from mortgages or other forms of security interest, must be disclosed in the financial statements to show that the assets will not be available to general creditors in the event of liquidation of the business. Disclosure should also be made if there are material amounts of fully depreciated assets still in use or material amounts of assets still subject to depreciation that are not currently in productive use.

### Reasonableness of Account Balances

*Perform Analytical Review.* Annual depreciation charges should bear a reasonable relationship to the cost of the various classes of assets involved and the expected life of the assets. The Internal Revenue Service maximum rates that have been established represent a relatively liberal approach that maximizes depreciation charges as an investment incentive. These rates ordinarily should not be used for accounting purposes unless they represent reasonable expectations for the actual life of the assets involved.

Changes in depreciation expense on a year-to-year basis should be analyzed to determine whether they are reasonable in relation to known additions or retirements of plant assets. Changes in depreciation expense, resulting from a change in rate, should be investigated to determine that there is reasonable justification for the change in rate, and the results should be reported as discussed earlier.

Turnover of plant assets in relation to sales should be reviewed, and the auditor should be satisfied that changes in turnover rates are consistent with known changes in sales volume or acquisitions or dispositions of plant assets.

### Synchronization of Events and Records

*Test cutoffs.* The cutoff of purchases of plant assets should be adequately tested by the test of the cutoff of accounts payable and the review of subsequent entries to record or liquidate liabilities. The cutoff on dispositions of assets is discussed in the subsequent sections on the transaction approach to determining the existence of plant assets. Depreciation on plant asset acquisitions or dispositions during the current year should be calculated in accordance with the client's policy concerning the calculation of depreciation in the year that additions or dispositions occur. The auditor should test the determination of depreciation amounts to ascertain that the stated policy has been applied as intended.

For any plant assets that are being constructed by the client, all related charges should be capitalized, including interest on borrowed funds, and these amounts should be reported as construction in progress until the project is completed and placed into productive use, at which time depreciation charges should commence.

### Comprehensiveness of Records

Controls over the acquisition, depreciation, and disposition of plant assets; the examination of transactions involving cash; and tests of cutoffs should provide sufficient evidence of the comprehensiveness of the accounting records relative to plant assets, and no further audit activity should be necessary, except as noted later with respect to possible unrecorded retirements.

### Arithmetic and Clerical Accuracy; Agreement of Details and Control Totals

Audit tests of depreciation in connection with ascertaining reasonableness and the tests of cutoffs should provide sufficient evidence of clerical accuracy in determining depreciation amounts. If the client maintains a plant ledger and a general ledger controlling account, the detail records should be balanced against the control at least once a year. Because the auditor will generally follow the transaction approach in substantiating plant asset amounts, it should not be necessary to test the client's trial balance of the plant ledger, but the auditor should at least inspect the most recent trial balance and determine that the total does in fact agree with the control account. If the plant ledger also shows the accumulated depreciation for each asset, the client should balance a listing of those figures against the general ledger account for accumulated depreciation.

All major retirements or dispositions of plant assets and a small sample of lesser ones should be listed on a worksheet such as schedule U-3. The cost of assets retired should be substantiated by reference to detailed plant ledger records, or, in the absence of such records, by reference to the entry for the original purchase in the general records. The accumulated depreciation should likewise be traced to the plant ledger, but in addition it should be independently verified by the auditor, based on the original cost, period of use, and established rate of depreciation. Trade-in allowances received should be proven against the purchase documents for the new asset acquired. Substantial proceeds from sales of usable assets should be traced to the record of cash receipts. Proceeds of sales of scrap from junked machinery are not usually considered in figuring the gain or loss on disposition, but are merely recorded as other income. The total amount of gain or loss on disposition, reflecting the net effect of original cost, accumulated depreciation, and proceeds of sale, should be cross-referenced to the appropriate income or expense account, as was done on U-3. Gains or losses that are material should be disclosed separately in the income statement.

### Existence of Plant Assets

Adequately monitored plant asset records will demonstrate the existence of plant assets through the client's periodic physical inventory of plant assets, and the inventory procedures should be reviewed by the auditor. The resulting general indication of the existence of the plant assets should be further supported by a test review of the plant ledger records to determine that the records selected for the test carry notations that the assets were on hand at the time of the most recent inventory taking. However, in most instances the auditor will place primary reliance on the transaction approach and related procedures to establish the existence of the client's plant assets.

In the most likely situation involving a repeat audit, the existence of the various plant assets called for by the opening balance of the plant asset accounts is accepted on the basis of the previous year's examination. Given that reference point and the slow turnover of these assets, the auditor can gain assurance of the existence of the assets represented by the year-end balance by testing the existence of additions to the accounts during the year and ascertaining that all retirements that occurred were recorded. The first step in this process is to schedule major additions to the asset accounts.

*Schedule Major Additions.* The auditor, or preferably client employees, should analyze charges to asset and accumulated depreciation accounts and schedule them on a worksheet similar to schedule U-1. Each major expenditure should be listed with adequate identifying and explanatory information. A few smaller charges should also be listed individually to provide a representative sample, but most of the smaller items can be grouped in a single balancing figure, as in U-1. As in other situations, the auditor's intent should be to cover the major part of the dollar total while examining only a minimum number of individual items.

*Test Validity of Scheduled Additions.* The various documents supporting the items listed or described above should then be pulled from the files by the auditor, or preferably by one of the client's employees. Included will be disbursement vouchers with supporting invoices and receiving reports, and journal vouchers. The journal vouchers will usually be supported by work orders, which may in turn have underlying data in the form of invoices, material requisitions, and labor tickets. Reference should also be made to the initial approval of major expenditures by the appropriate authority, such as a capital expenditures committee or the board of directors.

If construction work has been done by independent contractors, architects' certificates should be available showing percentage completion and stating that the work has been satisfactory. Such certificates should be available in support of both progress and final payments.

The supporting data should be compared with the listed amounts on the auditor's worksheet and the worksheet figures tick-marked to show that the amounts are correct. The auditor should also review the supporting data for proper approvals and indication of receipt of materials at this time. If there is any question about the actual amount disbursed in any given case, the paid check is further evidence of the amount involved.

The supporting data should be noted for any indication that only part of a total amount due may have been paid. For example, a construction contract may entitle the purchaser to withhold a stated percentage of each progress payment until the job has been completed and accepted. Such amounts should be capitalized and recorded as a liability.

In accordance with generally accepted accounting principles, only expenditures that will benefit future years should be capitalized. When the auditor reviews the data supporting additions to plant asset accounts, note should be made whether generally accepted accounting principles were adhered to in treating the amounts as asset additions, including interest on borrowed funds during construction. Tick-marks should be used to indicate that such a review was made and that tick-marked items have been properly capitalized.

Amounts capitalized should be recorded net of any cash discounts allowed for prompt payment, and net of any actual or imputed interest on installment purchases. The investment credit reducing the liability for federal income taxes may also be shown as a deduction from the related asset, under the theory that the credit is a form of "discount" designed to encourage plant expenditures. Transportation and installation costs are properly included in the total amount capitalized. If assets have been constructed by the client, all material and labor costs are properly included in the amount to be capitalized. There is no set rule as to the proper treatment of overhead charges on such jobs. Certainly any overhead expenses directly attributable to a given project should be capitalized. If normal overhead items also benefit the project, regular overhead can be added to the total construction cost at the normal rate. Any properly capitalized expenditures relating to leased property should be carefully noted, inasmuch as they should be classified as leasehold improvements on the balance sheet, rather than being included with the client's regular plant asset classifications.

As an expedient, purchases of small tools can be charged directly to expense if net income is not distorted by such treatment. Some companies, however, follow the more elaborate method of treating small tools on a perpetual inventory basis.

Capital leases that in substance represent installment purchases of the property should be recorded at the discounted amount of future payments specified for the lease.

*Maintenance and Repairs.* The procedures described above should be adequate to assure the auditor that the total additions to plant assets have been correctly stated and reflect transactions that were properly capitalized. But to be satisfied that proper distinction has been maintained between capital and revenue charges, the auditor must also consider the expense accounts that contain charges related to plant assets. These will usually be the repair and maintenance accounts.

The data supporting entries to these accounts should be tested, but tests need not be as extensive as the tests of capitalized amounts. The reduced need for testing is justified largely by the fact that the individual charges will tend to be relatively small, and the test of a few carefully selected items should suffice, particularly if the client has good internal control. If a properly qualified person in the accounting department "codes" each expenditure to show the account to which it should be charged, the results of those decisions can be accepted, provided that items tested show judgement to have been sound.

Among the items to be selected should be any large or otherwise unusual amounts detected in the course of the auditor's overall review of the repair expense accounts. If the auditor detects any material variations in repair expenses from year to year or from month to month, the causes for those variations should be sought out by inquiry and by tests of unusual items that appear to have increased the total amount. The auditor should also scan the detailed record of charges for the year, seeking any items that appear unusual or out of line. (See schedule U-2.)

In setting the scope of tests pertaining to the classification of capital and revenue charges, the auditor may well be guided by the relative risk factor. In a year of poor earnings, or in a year when a high earnings figure might help ensure the success of additional financing, the auditor should concentrate (although not exclusively) on the review of charges to the asset accounts to detect any attempt to inflate earnings by capitalizing charges that should be expensed. Conversely, in a year when high earnings might make the negotiation of a reasonable labor contract more difficult, or in a year when income tax reductions have been announced to be effective in the following year, the auditor might well broaden the examination of expense charges on the theory that the client might endeavor to conceal part of the income for the year by overstating such charges.

Always, of course, income tax considerations point to the desirability of expensing items if there is any question about whether they should be expensed or capitalized, but some clients may be prone to expense also some items that clearly should be capitalized, and the auditor should constantly be alert to that possibility.

*Establish Existence of Scheduled Additions.*   Each item listed on the schedule of additions to plant assets should be physically inspected by the auditor, note being made that the item inspected bears a reasonable relationship to the recorded description and cost. The schedule of additions should show that such inspection has been made, as on schedule U-1.

*Establish Existence on an Overall Basis.*   In a general way the auditor should be satisfied that the physical facilities observed in the "get-acquainted" tour of the plant bear a reasonable relationship to the balances carried in the ledger, the main concern being to detect any obvious overstatement of plant assets. Branch plants of considerable size will usually be visited every year, and all regular procedures carried out. For smaller units, such as branch sales offices or retail stores of a large chain, rotating visits over a two- to ten-year period are common. New units, or those having major capital additions, should be visited during the year, if at all possible, to establish the existence of tangible assets in support of book figures. For those branches that are not visited in any one year, sales and expense reports and active bank accounts present useful evidence of the continued existence of assets at those locations.

*Small Tools.* If small tools are carried as an asset, the account balance will be either an approximate figure that is never changed, or it will be based on an inventory of the tools on hand. In the first instance the auditor need only be satisfied that small tools do exist in the plant and that the figure used is reasonable. If an inventory is taken, the same procedures employed in the substantiation of merchandise inventory should be followed, except on a more limited basis.

*Remotely Located Equipment.* Unlike manufacturing companies, whose plant assets are usually clustered at one or more locations, some concerns will have plant assets distributed over a wide area. Examples of companies with operations of this type would include public utilities, motor carriers, construction contractors, and juke box and vending machine operators.

The internal control in most public utility concerns is usually adequate to permit the auditor to accept the existence of the plant assets and additions thereto without inspection of the assets, except for such major items as generating or pumping stations. For other items the review of additions and retirements through test inspection of closely controlled work orders, plus the existence of carefully maintained detailed plant records, should give the auditor adequate assurance of the existence of the client's plant assets. Further assurance can be gained by relating revenues and sales statistics to the total plant investment and comparing the resulting figures with those for previous years.

Because motor carriers' principal productive assets are their trucks, and most of these will be on the road, the auditor may be faced with a difficult problem in attempting to become satisfied about the existence of the major portion of such companies' equipment, which will be a significant item on the balance sheet. Important evidence of the existence of these assets should, however, be present in the office in the form of certificates of title, license registration receipts, and insurance policies containing detailed listings of the insured equipment. Detailed records showing gasoline and oil consumption and repair expenses would also support the existence of the equipment called for by the general records.

In the case of construction contractors it will usually be desirable for the auditor to visit several locations at which work is in progress to be satisfied by inspection that the specified equipment is actually present. Internal control will seldom be adequate to assure the auditor of the existence of the assets called for by the general records without at least some test inspections of the equipment.

Vending machine operations present a particularly difficult problem of asset verification. Internal records showing the amount of inventory placed in each machine and the resulting periodic collections of cash receipts should be of some help, particularly if the cash receipts figures can be tied in with daily deposits. In addition, it would be well for the auditor to make further tests by accompanying several route service people and noting not only the existence of the machines listed for the route, but also the inventory stored in the machines and the cash collected.

*Returnable Containers.* Certain companies, such as beverage and chemical concerns, often have a substantial investment in returnable containers. The existence of containers on hand can be readily verified, but those containers "with the trade" present a considerable problem. Although the asset account may correctly show all containers shipped to customers, there is no assurance that all of the containers will be returned. Those that customers have lost, broken, or appropriated for other uses can no longer be shown as an asset and must be written off the books.

To estimate how many containers held by customers are likely to be returned, statistics are developed by occasional tests. A cutoff date is selected, and a record maintained of all containers returned after that date that were shipped on or before that date. This record will then show the number of containers with the trade at that date, and the records can be adjusted for those containers that were not returned.

The figure for containers with the trade is directly related to the volume of business being done and is usually stated as representing X number of days' sales prior to the cutoff date. This figure for the number of days' sales represented in the inventory of containers with the trade varies but slightly from year to year, and consequently an inventory of containers with the trade can be estimated at any time by determining the amount sold in the specified number of days preceding the date for which the figure is desired. Trade associations in industries where this problem is prevalent frequently develop average statistics, thus obviating the need for many companies ever to make such a test.

For the auditor whose client owns returnable containers, the audit procedures to be followed are quite simple. The maximum asset value for containers must not exceed the cost of containers on hand plus those estimated to be with the trade, determined as suggested above. Each of these figures should be independently tested or calculated by the auditor. The auditor should note that accumulated depreciation on containers lost has been removed from the accounts and that any liability for deposits on containers has been adjusted to correspond with the number of containers estimated to be with the trade and to be returned. The net effect of the cost, accumulated depreciation, and deposits pertaining to containers lost will then be the net gain or loss to be recognized on such containers.

*Initial Audits.* If the current auditor has not examined the client's accounts previously but the accounts have been examined by another auditor, the new auditor can take considerable assurance from the situation if the predecessor took no exception to the plant asset figures. The successor auditor should request permission to review the predecessor's plant asset working papers. If the successor is satisfied on the basis of this review with the predecessor's work, only limited tests of transactions affecting plant assets in prior years need be made to establish that the opening balances of the plant accounts can be accepted. If there has been no predecessor auditor, or if the successor auditor has no confidence in the predecessor's work, the examination of transactions in prior years must be much more extensive.

The examination of prior transactions is simplified and reduced if the client maintains a plant ledger that has recently been adjusted to agree with an inventory of plant assets. The first steps would be, of course, to establish the authenticity of a trial balance of the ledger and to determine that the assets listed were shown to be on hand by the physical inventory. Next, some of the major assets and a representative proportion of the less costly items should be selected for examination. Expenditures should be substantiated in much the same manner as in a repeat audit, and the accumulated depreciation should be verified. Then, as a supplement to these procedures, the auditor should review all past debits and credits to the various general ledger accounts. Any entries that appear to be unusual in any way should be investigated. Particularly important would be any entries suggesting an appraisal write-up or a major adjustment to past depreciation. All relatively large amounts should be investigated, including entries for the retirement of assets. If any major purchases of assets are disclosed that were not covered in the tests based on the plant ledger, these purchases should be verified and carefully studied. Depreciation charges for preceding years should be related to those for the current year, and material year-to-year variations should be investigated.

*Procedures When No Plant Ledger Is Maintained.* The absence of a plant ledger suggests that internal control is likely to be limited and must be compensated for by more extensive testing. Furthermore, the auditor will be forced to be less selective in testing because there is no ledger record showing which assets are still in use. Plant additions will have to be selected at random from the general ledger record. Because many assets acquired years previously may still be in use, additions in the early years will have to be tested almost as extensively as those in later years, even though many of the acquisitions selected may already have been retired. Entries for retirements will have to be given considerably more attention than when there is a plant ledger. The double check on retirements afforded by the plant ledger and a physical inventory will be missing and must be compensated for by additional audit work. If major amounts of unrecorded retirements exist, the situation must be corrected to avoid misstatement of asset and depreciation figures, as well as to record any losses associated with the retirements.

*Ascertain That All Retirements Have Been Recorded.*   In the transaction approach, special attention must be paid to the possibility that assets have been retired or disposed of but no entry made to remove the items, for the failure to record the retirement would allow nonexistent assets to remain on the books and be reported in the financial statements. Obviously, internal control over outward movement of plant assets and the reflection of such movements in the accounting records are quite important to the auditor. If the accounting entries are overlooked at the time of disposition, monitoring as an alternative control should generate the necessary accounting entry as a result of the absence of the item when the next physical inventory of plant assets is taken.

The auditor must, however, consider the possibility that dispositions have occurred without appropriate accounting recognition of the event. To test for the existence of unrecorded retirements, the auditor should turn to a reciprocal population where evidence exists of the transaction disposing of the assets. Among the possibilities for gaining access to the reciprocal population are the following:

1. Question management and supervisory personnel in the factory about retirements that they know have occurred.
2. Investigate major plant additions to ascertain whether they represent additional facilities or replace old assets that have been retired. Note especially on purchase invoices for new assets any indication that a trade-in allowance has been granted.
3. Review miscellaneous income accounts for possible proceeds of sales of machines that have been scrapped or junked. (Because there is seldom satisfactory control over such proceeds, the auditor should also attempt to determine that the proceeds of known dispositions of plant assets have been accounted for.)
4. Investigate the possibility that major changes in plant layout or in the type of design of the product being produced may have resulted in the retirement of some plant assets.
5. Review work orders, tracing any indicated retirements to the records to confirm that they have been recorded.

6. Review plant ledger records on a test basis to ascertain that all items not noted as being on hand at the time of the last physical inventory have been removed from the accounts.

7. If insurance coverage on buildings or contents has been reduced, investigate the possibility that part of the plant assets may have been sold or otherwise disposed of.

## Ownership of Plant Assets

*Examine Evidence of Ownership.* The absence of rental payments when a business is using productive assets is an indication that the assets are owned by the business. Further evidence should be available, however, and should be examined by the auditor. For real property there should be a deed that has been duly recorded, an abstract of title, and an attorney's title opinion or a title guarantee policy. Although these are highly technical legal documents, the auditor should at least note that each shows the client to be the legal owner of the property. If there is a question concerning the client's title to any property, or if there is a possibility that a lien may exist against the property, there is no acceptable substitute for an attorney's opinion on the matter.

Readily accessible evidence that can be examined to show acquisition and ownership of specific items of property other than real estate would include contracts, invoices, and paid checks. Tax bills present further evidence of ownership. The bills should be addressed to the client, and the description and location of the property as shown on the bills should agree with the property carried as an asset by the client. Insurance carried on property is also an indication of ownership. Insurance policies should be inspected by the auditor in order to determine that they relate to the assets in question.

*Liens.* Most property liens will be disclosed through the examination of liabilities, but the auditor should also be alert for evidence of the existence of liens during other phases of the audit. For instance, a purchase contract examined to establish ownership of an asset may prove to be a conditional sales contract with part of the balance still unpaid. The examination of insurance policies may also disclose the existence of a lien. Sometimes such policies must be deposited with the mortgagee to show that any security is adequately protected. Thus the absence of any insurance policies should always suggest the possible existence of a lien. The fact that a policy is on hand and not deposited with someone else is not, however, sufficient basis for concluding that no mortgage lien exists. Careful study of the policy may reveal an endorsement assigning the proceeds of any claims to a mortgagee.

Paid tax bills are sometimes presented to a mortgagee as evidence that taxes have been paid, and the absence of such bills carries much the same significance as missing insurance policies. The paid tax bills should also be examined as evidence that no liens have resulted from unpaid taxes.

### Valuation of Plant Assets

The various aspects of the valuation of plant assets have all been covered previously under other objectives but are summarized at this point to consolidate the information under the valuation objective. The principal elements are the recording of additions at cost, including interest on borrowed funds during construction, proper accounting for repairs and maintenance, including extraordinary repairs, removal of related cost and accumulated depreciation from the accounts when assets are retired, and the recording of depreciation to allocate asset costs to the periods in which the benefits of ownership and use are realized. Supplementary information must also be provided for certain larger companies with respect to adjustments for the effects of inflation and to reflect current costs of similar assets or productive capacity.

### Questions/Problems

For multiple-choice questions 16-1 through 16-5, indicate the letter of the single answer that *best* completes the statement or answers the question, and justify the choice that you have made.

**16-1.** Which of the following is an internal accounting control weakness related to factory equipment?

    a. A policy exists requiring all purchases of factory equipment to be made by the department in need of the equipment.

    b. Checks issued in payment of purchases of equipment are not signed by the controller.

    c. Factory equipment replacements are generally made when estimated useful lives, as indicated in depreciation schedules, have expired.

    d. Proceeds from sales of fully depreciated equipment are credited to other income.

                              (Uniform CPA Examination)

**16-2.** Which of the following *best* describes the independent auditor's approach to obtaining satisfaction concerning depreciation expense in the income statement?

    a. Verify the mathematical accuracy of the amounts charged to income as a result of depreciation expense.

    b. Determine the method for computing depreciation expense

and ascertain that it is in accordance with generally accepted accounting principles.

c. Reconcile the amount of depreciation expense to those amounts credited to accumulated depreciation accounts.

d. Establish the basis for depreciable assets and verify the depreciation expense.

(Uniform CPA Examination)

**16-3.** Which of the following audit procedures would be *least* likely to lead the auditor to find unrecorded fixed asset disposals?

a. Examination of insurance policies.

b. Review of repairs and maintenance expense.

c. Review of property tax files.

d. Scanning of invoices for fixed asset additions.

(Uniform CPA Examination)

**16-4.** In connection with his review of plant additions, the CPA ordinarily would take exception to the capitalization of the cost of the

a. Major reconditioning of a recently acquired secondhand lift truck.

b. Machine operator's wages during a period of testing and adjusting new machinery.

c. Room partitions installed at the request of a new long-term lessee in the client's office building.

d. Maintenance of an unused standby plant.

(Uniform CPA Examination)

**16-5.** Which of the following explanations might satisfy an auditor who discovers significant debits to an accumulated depreciation account?

a. Extraordinary repairs have lengthened the life of an asset.

b. Prior years' depreciation charges were erroneously understated.

c. A reserve for possible loss on retirement has been recorded.

d. An asset has been recorded at its fair value.

(Uniform CPA Examination)

**16-6.** What are the functions of a detailed plant ledger?

**16-7.** How can information on the amount of accumulated depreciation be useful to the user of financial statements?

**16-8.** How does the usual examination of property, plant, and equipment differ from the examination of current assets?

**16-9.** How does the auditor proceed in substantiating additions to plant assets?

**16-10.**  What procedures can the auditor employ to discover retirements that have not been recorded?

**16-11.**  What are the principal differences in an independent auditor's examination of plant assets in contrast to the examination of cash?

**16-12.**  Your client recorded (among others) the following entries for the current year:

| | | |
|---|---:|---:|
| Depreciation expense | $100,000 | |
|     Accumulated depreciation | | $100,000 |
|     (Straight line depreciation | | |
|     for the year) | | |
| Retained earnings | 10,000 | |
| Accumulated depreciation | 70,000 | |
|     Machinery | | 80,000 |
|     (To record the loss on | | |
|     disposition of machinery) | | |
| Cash | 6,000 | |
|     Miscellaneous income | | 6,000 |
|     (To record cash received from | | |
|     disposition of $80,000 of machinery) | | |
| Income Tax Expense | 65,000 | |
|     Liability for income taxes | | 65,000 |
|     (To record federal income tax | | |
|     liability for the year): | | |
|       Net income (before depreciation | | |
|       but including miscellaneous income) | | $300,000 |
|       Accelerated depreciation | | 160,000 |
|       Net income | | $140,000 |
|       Loss on disposition of assets | | 10,000 |
|       Net income subject to tax | | $130,000 |
|       Income tax at 50% current rate | | $ 65,000 |

Required:

Adjusting journal entries to correct any errors evident in the above information and to bring the records into conformity with generally accepted accounting principles.

**16-13.**  In connection with the annual examination of Johnson Corp., a manufacturer of janitorial supplies, you have been assigned to audit the fixed assets. The company maintains a detailed property ledger for all fixed assets. You prepared an audit program for the balances of property, plant, and equipment but have yet to prepare one for accumulated depreciation and depreciation expense.

Required:

Prepare a separate comprehensive audit program for the accumulated depreciation and depreciation expense accounts.

(Uniform CPA Examination)

**16-14.** You have been engaged to audit the December 31 financial statements of the Smith Equipment Corporation, which was formed several years ago and sells or leases construction equipment such as bulldozers, road scrapers, and dirt movers, to contractors. The Corporation at year end has 50 pieces of equipment leased to 30 contractors who are using the equipment at various locations throughout the state.

The Smith Equipment Corporation is identified as the owner of the leased equipment by a small metal tag attached to each machine. The tag is fastened by screws so that it can be removed if the machine is sold. During the audit, you find that the contractors often buy the equipment that they have been leasing, but the identification tag is not always removed from the machine.

The Corporation's principal asset is the equipment leased to the contractors. While there is no plant ledger, each machine is accounted for by a file card that gives its description, cost, contractor-lessee, and rental payment records. The Corporation's system of internal control is weak.

You were engaged upon the recommendation of the president of the local bank. The Smith Equipment Corporation, which had never had an audit, had applied to the bank for a sizeable loan; the bank president had requested an audited balance sheet.

You barely know John Smith, the principal stockholder and president of the Smith Equipment Corporation; he has a reputation for expensive personal tastes and for shrewd business dealings, some of which have bordered on being unethical. Nevertheless, Mr. Smith enjoys a strong personal allegiance from his contractor-lessees, whose favor he has curried by personal gifts and loans. The lessees look upon Mr. Smith as a personal friend for whom they would do almost anything. Often they overlook the fact that they are dealing with the Corporation and make their checks payable to Mr. Smith, who endorses them over to the Corporation.

(a) List the audit procedures that you would employ in the examination of the asset account representing the equipment leased to the contractors.

(b) Although your audit procedures, including those you described in answering part (a), did not uncover any discrepancies, you have been unable to dismiss your feeling that

Mr. Smith and some of the contractor-lessees may have collaborated to deceive you. Under this condition, discuss what action, if any, you would take and the effect of your feeling upon your auditor's opinion. (Assume that you would not withdraw from the engagement.)

(Uniform CPA Examination)

**16-15.** In connection with a first examination of the Soda Pop Company as of December 31, you have obtained the following information:

**Balances, December 31**

| | |
|---|---:|
| Bottles | $3,122.51 |
| Cases | 3,617.00 |
| Accumulated depreciation—cases | 1,827.82 |
| Deposits | 3,931.75 |
| Sales, December | 4,187.20 |
| Sales, year to date | 88,629.18 |
| Depreciation on cases | 904.25 |

A physical inventory of cases and bottles on hand at December 31 was as follows:

| | |
|---|---:|
| Cases | 1,923 |
| Bottles | 46,152 |

Cases are to be depreciated at the rate of 25 percent per year, with depreciation charged for one-half year for cases purchased during the year, and one-half year for cases lost or destroyed during the year. Cases costing $419 were purchased during the year.

Deposits are charged as follows:

| | |
|---|---:|
| Case | $0.27 |
| Bottles (24 per case @ $0.02 per bottle) | 0.48 |
| Total deposit, full case | $0.75 |

Average costs:

| | |
|---|---:|
| Bottles | $1.75 per 100 |
| Cases | 0.50 each |

Selling price of Pop—$0.80 per case

Through the trade association for the carbonated beverage industry you are able to ascertain that companies, on the average, find the inventory of containers with the trade at any one time that will be returned for deposit refund amounts to about 21 days' sales (based on 24 business days per month). Prepare a work sheet for your examination of the above accounts, showing any adjusting entries you would recommend.

**16-16.** In prior years your client, Noches, Inc., a manufacturing company, has used an accelerated depreciation method for its depreciable assets for both federal income taxes and financial reporting. At the beginning of 19X1 the Corporation changed to the straight-line method for financial reporting. As a result, depreciation expense for the year was $200,000 less for financial reporting than for income tax reporting, an amount which you consider to be material. The Corporation did not use interperiod income tax allocation in 19X1. Taxable income for 19X1 was $600,000. Assume that the income tax rate was 48% and ignore the tax surcharge and state and local income taxes.

Required:

(a) Financial statement presentation:
   1. Describe the effects of the accounting change of Noches' 19X1 balance sheet, income statement and funds statement. Cite specific amounts in your answer.
   2. Explain what disclosure of the accounting change should be made in Noches' 19X1 financial statements.

(b) Auditor's report:
   1. Assuming that the financial statement disclosure is considered to be adequately informative, discuss the effects that the change in depreciation methods should have on the auditor's report.
   2. Assuming that the financial statement disclosure of the change in depreciation methods is not considered to be adequately informative, discuss the effects on the auditor's report.
   3. Discuss whether the auditor's report should indicate approval of the change in depreciation methods.
   4. Discuss the effects on the auditor's report of the failure to use interperiod income tax allocation.

(Uniform CPA Examination)

**16-17.** Rivers, CPA, is the auditor for a manufacturing company with a balance sheet that includes the caption "Property, Plant and Equipment." Rivers has been asked by the company's management if audit adjustments or reclassifications are required for the following material items that have been included or excluded from "Property, Plant & Equipment."

1. A tract of land was acquired during the year. The land is the future site of the client's new headquarters, which will be constructed in the following year. Commissions were paid to the real estate agent

used to acquire the land, and expenditures were made to relocate the previous owner's equipment. These commissions and expenditures were expensed and are excluded from "Property, Plant & Equipment."

2. Clearing costs were incurred to make the land ready for construction. These costs were included in "Property, Plant and Equipment."

3. During the land clearing process, timber and gravel were recovered and sold. The proceeds from the sale were recorded as other income and are excluded from "Property, Plant & Equipment."

4. A group of machines was purchased under a royalty agreement that provides royalty payments based on units of production from the machines. The cost of the machines, freight costs, unloading charges, and royalty payments were capitalized and are included in "Property, Plant and Equipment."

Required:

(a) Describe the general characteristics of assets, such as land, buildings, improvements, machinery, equipment, fixtures, that should normally be classified as "Property, Plant & Equipment," and identify audit objectives (how an auditor can obtain audit satisfaction) in connection with the examination of "Property, Plant & Equipment." Do not discuss specific audit procedures.

(b) Indicate whether each of the above items numbered 1 to 4 requires one or more audit adjustments or reclassifications, and explain why such adjustments or reclassifications are required or not required.

Organize your answer as follows:

| Item Number | Is Audit Adjustment or Reclassification Required? Yes or No | Reasons Why Audit Adjustment or Reclassification is Required or Not Required |
|---|---|---|
| | | |

(Uniform CPA Examination)

**16-18.** In connection with a recurring examination of the financial statements of the Louis Manufacturing Company for the year ended December 31, 19X1, you have been assigned the audit of the Manufacturing Equipment, Manufacturing Equipment—Accumulated Depreciation and Repairs to Manufacturing Equipment accounts. Your review of Louis's policies and procedures has disclosed the following pertinent information:

1. The Manufacturing Equipment account includes the net invoice price plus related freight and installation costs for all of the equipment in Louis' manufacturing plant.

2. The Manufacturing Equipment and Accumulated Depreciation accounts are supported by a subsidiary ledger which shows the cost and accumulated depreciation for each piece of equipment.

3. An annual budget for capital expenditures of $1,000 or more is prepared by the budget committee and approved by the board of directors. Capital expenditures over $1,000, which are not included in this budget, must be approved by the board of directors, and variations of 20% or more must be explained to the board. Approval by the supervisor of production is required for capital expenditures under $1,000.

4. Company employees handle installation, removal, repair, and rebuilding of the machinery. Work orders are prepared for these activities and are subject to the same budgetary control as other expenditures. Work orders are not required for external expenditures.

Required:

(a) Cite the major objectives of your audit of the Manufacturing Equipment, Manufacturing Equipment—Accumulated Depreciation and Repairs of Manufacturing Equipment accounts. Do not include in this listing the auditing procedures designed to accomplish these objectives.

(b) Prepare the portion of your audit program applicable to the review of 1969 additions to the Manufacturing Equipment account.

(Uniform CPA Examination)

# Chapter 17

# MISCELLANEOUS EXPENSES, LOSSES, REVENUES, ASSETS, AND LIABILITIES

---

---

This omnibus chapter covers all financial statement items that have not been covered in the preceding chapters, except the permanent or long-term debt and equity financing items that are covered in the following chapter. Because the miscellaneous items that are the subject of this chapter typically involve only infrequent transactions, controls are generally less extensive than for regularly recurring transactions of high daily frequency. Certain basic controls should however, always be present—particularly original authorization of the transactions and then the authorization of cash disbursements associated with acquisition of an asset or liquidation of a liability. In addition, if a liquid asset is acquired, there should be proper custody and accounting control over the asset.

## Evaluation of Internal Control Objectives and Features

### Operating Objectives

*All transactions are properly authorized.*

- All acquisitions of assets or services should be authorized at an appropriate level of management, for example:
  Temporary or longer-term investment of funds—treasurer and/or an investment committee of officers or directors.

Purchase of office supplies and postage stamps—office manager (factory supplies should be subject to controls and procedures similar to those for inventories of productive materials).

Rental of space or equipment—management official primarily responsible for custody and use of the facilities.

Insurance—treasurer.

Travel or other advances—office manager.

Deposits that guarantee payment for services such as transportation or utilities—treasurer.

*Inquiry* and *inspection* to determine that controls are in place and functioning.

- All transactions involving the borrowing of funds should be authorized by the treasurer and/or any special committee designated to authorize the creation of indebtedness. *Inquiry, inspection.*

- All disbursements to liquidate liabilities resulting from the acquisition of assets or services or to liquidate liabilities arising from borrowing transactions should be approved by the person responsible for acquiring and/or using the asset or service or incurring any financial obligation for borrowed funds; authorization of the treasurer for the actual disbursement should be contingent upon the aforementioned authorization. *Inquiry, inspection.*

## All authorizations resulted in action being taken.

- No formal controls to ensure that action is taken should be necessary inasmuch as the transactions involved would be irregular in occurrence and of sufficient importance that the person responsible for authorizing a transaction can be expected to follow through to be sure that action has been taken. *Inquiry.*

## Access to assets is permitted only in accordance with management authorization.

- Investments in negotiable instruments are preferably placed in safekeeping with a bank or trust company or held in a safe deposit box for which it is specified that two authorized persons must sign the entrance request form to gain access to the box. *Inquiry, observation.*

- If movement of negotiable instruments in and out of custody is so frequent as to require more convenient controlled access, the instruments should be held in a safe or vault that offers adequate fire and burglary protection and is subject to dual control that requires two keys or two dial combinations to be opened. *Inquiry, observation.*

- Postage stamps should be held under lock and key, and use should be limited to company business. Maximum control over postage is obtained through use of a postage meter, and the meter also facilitates charging the various departments for the postage that has been used.

- Telephone toll calls or use of Wide Area Telephone Service (WATS) lines are preferably controlled by having such calls placed through an operator or automatic recording equipment to limit calls to authorized persons and to obtain a record of the origin and destination of each call for expense allocation purposes. *Inquiry, observation, inspection.*

### Data Processing Objectives—Internal Accounting Control

*Accounting and computer operations are independent of all operating responsibilities.*

*Inquiry* and *observation* that maximum feasible segregation of these activities exists:

| Operating | Accounting/Data Processing |
|---|---|
| Treasurer | General ledger |
| Investment committee | Travel advances and reimbursements |
| Vault control | Investment records |
| Office manager | Insurance records |
| Mail clerks | Computer data entry |
| Telephone operators | Computer operations |
| Cash disbursements | |

*Only valid transactions that were duly authorized are accepted for entry in the accounting records.*

- Cash disbursements should be supported by disbursement authorizations and evidence of the receipt of goods or services. *Inquiry, inspection.*
- Borrowing of funds should be supported by authorization documents that should be the basis for recording the resulting liabilities and receipt of funds. *Inquiry, inspection.*

*All transactions are entered in the accounting records.*

- Authorization documents for borrowing of funds should be numerically controlled to ensure that the resulting liabilities and receipt of funds are properly recorded. *Inquiry, observation, inspection.*
- The recording of disbursements should be controlled in connection with procedures related to the handling of cash transactions. *Inquiry, observation, inspection.*
- Interest revenue and income from other investments should be accrued and recorded by standard monthly journal entries in order to establish accounting control over the associated asset inflows. *Inquiry, inspection.*

*Accounting entries correctly reflect transaction amounts.*

- Because the transactions encompassed by this chapter occur infrequently and irregularly, no special controls over the correct recording of transactions are feasible.

*Transactions are correctly classified for accounting entry.*

- Authorizations for disbursements should indicate the accounts to be charged in connection with the disbursements, with expenses to be accounted for by responsibility and by object of the expenditure as outlined by a chart of accounts. *Inquiry, inspection.*

- When whole life insurance policies are carried on company executives, the cash surrender value of such policies should be accounted for as an investment asset. *Inquiry, inspection.*

*Recorded transactions are correctly processed.*

- The following proofs should be utilized whenever appropriate (*Inquiry, observation, inspection, reperformance*):

    Balances in subsidiary ledgers maintained for investments, advances to employees, insurance policies, notes payable, or other assets or liabilities should be proved regularly against related control account balances.

    Periodic general ledger trial balances should be prepared to prove the equality of debits and credits.

## Monitoring Objectives

*Regular comparison is made of accountability records with underlying assets; third-party proofs of accounting records.*

- Certificates or other documents evidencing investments should be subject to periodic count by internal auditors and balanced against the related records. *Inquiry, inspection.*
- Advances to employees and officers should be verified against the amounts reported in connection with claims filed for reimbursement. *Inquiry, inspection.*
- From time to time internal auditors should obtain written confirmation of advances shown as outstanding. *Inquiry, inspection.*

*There is an effective internal audit function.*

- Internal auditors should regularly review and evaluate internal controls, perform compliance tests, and when appropriate, make recommendations for improvement in the controls. *Inquiry, review of audit planning, inspection of working papers.*
- As stated above, internal auditors should make periodic counts of certificates or other documents evidencing investments and prove those items against the related records controlling the items. *Inquiry, inspection.*
- Cash surrender value of life insurance policies on members of the organization, as shown in the accounting records, should be verified annually by correspondence with the insurance company, and the insurance company should also be requested to indicate whether any loans are outstanding against cash surrender value in order that the internal auditor may verify that the loans are properly recorded in the accounting records. *Inquiry, inspection.*
- The following operational audit activities, although not directly related to the reliability of accounting information, should be considered by the internal audit staff as an important service to management in the control of opera-

tions. The independent auditor may wish to review the operational audit activities of the internal audit staff to provide an additional indication of the general effectiveness of management and efficiency of operations; any findings or recommendations resulting from such a review would appropriately be included in the independent auditor's management letter. *Inquiry* could pertain to such operational audit activities as

Review of insurance coverage to ascertain that it is consistent with known risks to which the organization is subject.

Review of investment of idle funds to ascertain that such funds have been invested promptly and at maximum return consistent with an acceptable level of risk.

Review of mail and telephone communication expenses and of the management policies relating to usage of these media to ascertain that these services are effectively utilized at minimum cost.

Review of leasing activities to ascertain whether adequate procedures have been instituted to obtain favorable terms and whether purchase alternatives and options have been given appropriate consideration.

Review of financial planning to ascertain that needs for funds have been adequately anticipated and that alternative sources of funds have been considered in order to minimize borrowing costs.

## Substantive Audit Objectives and Procedures

The various assets and liabilities that are discussed in this chapter are for the most part subjected to substantive audit procedures that involve either the inventory or the transaction approach or some combination of the two, as the situation and audit efficiency may dictate. Similarly, in the examination of the revenue and expense accounts that are related to these assets and liabilities, the substantive procedures that are typically applied are directly affected by whether the inventory or the transaction approach was utilized in the examination of the corresponding asset or liability account. As each audit objective is addressed in the following pages, the particular assets, liabilities, revenues, or expenses that are most effectively substantiated in relation to that objective are indicated.

### *Conformity of Client's Financial Statements with Disclosure and Other Requirements of Financial Accounting Standards*

The following considerations are applicable to all financial statement presentations:

1. Appropriate classification
    Balance sheet
        Current
        Noncurrent
            (Deferred taxes should be classified on the same basis as the asset or liability to which they are related.)

Income statement
    Continuing operations
        Regular recurring items (These may be further distinguished as operating or financing)
        Nonrecurring items
    Discontinued operations
    Taxes on income (optionally including investment credit)
    Extraordinary items (net of related income taxes)

2. Material amounts of assets and liabilities should not be offset.
3. Customary disclosures—
    Measurement basis for assets and liabilities
    Restrictions of any kind
    Liens
    Contingent assets or liabilities
    Material commitments
    Terms pertaining to debt or equity
4. Disclosure of material changes in accounting principles or changes of estimates; effect on comparability.
5. Subsequent events having a material effect on the entity and its operations or finances of subsequent periods, but not affecting statement amounts for the period in which the subsequent events should be disclosed.
6. Disclosure of significant accounting policies.
7. Reporting of earnings per share.
8. SEC reporting requires that reconciliations be presented to account for differences between income tax expense as reported and the taxes to be paid (including the effect of deferred taxes) and also to account for the difference between the statutory income tax rate and the effective tax rate indicated by reported amounts.

### Reasonableness of Account Balances

*Perform Analytical Review.* For all items for which regular accruals or amortization are involved, year-to-year comparisons should show a high degree of stability. Any marked changes in amount should be investigated to ascertain whether acquisitions or dispositions have occurred or whether there has been a change in estimate or the manner in which the item is being accounted for. All such changes should, of course, be properly accounted for or disclosed.

### Synchronization of Events and Records

The examination of all acquisitions and dispositions, plus cutoff tests in connection with cash and accounts payable, should be adequate to reveal whether changes in asset or liability amounts have been recorded in the proper period. Audit review of balance sheet amounts, as in the case of prepaid insurance or the provision for future warranty costs, plus review of the accruals or amortizations associated with such items as patents or copyrights, investments, notes payable, and taxes should indicate whether expenses and revenues have been recorded in the periods in which the related benefits have been received or the revenue earned.

### Comprehensiveness of Records

Internal controls over the inflows and outflows of assets, particularly cash, should provide reasonable assurance that assets or liabilities associated with inflows or outflows of working capital are properly incorporated in the accounting records. Additionally, however, through the auditor's understanding of the client and knowledge about the industry in which the client is operating, plus knowledge of tax laws, the auditor should be competent to ascertain whether all likely assets, liabilities, revenues, and expenses of the client have been reflected in the accounting records and financial statements.

*Search for Unrecorded Liabilities.*   As a consequence of the possibility that liabilities have arisen that the client has not recorded, either intentionally or through oversight, special effort and consideration should be directed to that eventuality inasmuch as material amounts could be involved that would significantly affect the client's financial position and results of operations. A wide variety of procedures may be employed in seeking out liabilities that have not been recorded, several of which have previously been mentioned in connection with other accounts—particularly cash and accounts payable.

The procedures most commonly employed in the auditor's search for unrecorded liabilities, including those that have been earlier introduced, are described, but the compilation should not be taken to be exhaustive. Unrecorded liabilities may also be disclosed through procedures that are not directly related to this objective. For example, investigation of a large check that was outstanding at the end of the year and that did not clear with the cutoff bank statement may reveal that the check has not been deposited because there is a dispute about the amount of the liability that the check purportedly was drawn to liquidate. Endorsing and depositing the check may be subject to a legal interpretation that the entire liability has been discharged. Little can specifically be done to discover such eventualities, and the only recourse available to the auditor is constant alertness plus an innate sense of curiosity and inquisitiveness that may reveal the true state of affairs.

In a first audit the following procedures are equally applicable to unrecorded liabilities *at the beginning* of the year—not in terms of any effect of the liabilities on financial position at that date, but rather for the possible effect of the items on income for the year being examined.

*Review of Subsequent Transactions.* All liabilities will eventually be reflected in the records, either through payment or by transfer of other assets. This fact, combined with the usual auditing situation that involves procedures that must be carried out following the close of the client's fiscal year, makes it possible for the auditor to capitalize on the advantages of hindsight in the quest for information about unrecorded liabilities. The review of a reciprocal population in the form of following-year entries in the voucher register and cash disbursement record has already been discussed relative to disclosure of unrecorded accounts payable. Other records that should be consulted for leads on unrecorded liabilities would be the general journal and minutes of directors' meetings.

*Confirmations.* The Standard Bank Confirmation form (see $\frac{A\text{-}2}{1}$) should be sent to all banks with which the client has done business during the year. The replies will list any direct or contingent liabilities to those banks, and an opportunity therefore exists to detect any liabilities not recorded in the client's records. A similar opportunity exists for disclosing unrecorded liabilities through confirmation of accounts payable or by analysis of vendors' statements. Although the requests for confirmation or a statement of the account are sent primarily to vendors with whom there is a large year-end balance, the auditor should review purchasing activity for the year and send requests to any vendors with whom a substantial volume of business was done, especially if there is no year-end balance.

*Consignment Sales.* The review of subsequent transactions may reveal a payment to a consignor for goods sold prior to the end of the year. The auditor should seek to make the necessary adjustment if the liability is material and was not recorded. The auditor should also examine the inventory record of consigned goods for the purpose of noting whether any goods have been sold but no liability recorded.

*Information from Client's Attorney.* Most businesses of medium size or above retain counsel to handle legal matters that may arise. The attorney should be requested to inform the auditor, in writing, of any lawsuits or claims pending against the client. The attorney should also be requested to state an opinion of the likelihood of an unfavorable outcome and to provide an estimate of the amount of the potential loss or the likely range of such loss. The request to the attorney should also list all unasserted claims of which the client has knowledge, and the attorney should be requested to state whether the list is complete. Finally, the attorney should be requested to provide information about any other liabilities of an unusual nature of which the attorney is aware, and about the amount of any fees or reimbursable expenses that may be owed by the client.

If the client does not engage an attorney on a retainer basis, a clue to the possible existence of pending legal matters may be gained from an analysis of any expense accounts to which legal fees may be charged. The payment of any such fees should be a signal for the auditor to investigate the situation to determine whether any liability exists or may be likely to result.

*Client's Representations.*    Until liabilities are made a matter of record, information about them may be solely within the knowledge of officers of the organization. Because those officers are primarily responsible for the information in the financial statements, it is both proper and customary to ask the officers for any information about possible unrecorded liabilities. Any liabilities known to them but which through oversight had not been recorded should be brought to light in this manner. The reader should not assume, however, that a statement from the officers relieves the auditor of any responsibility for discovering unrecorded liabilities. There is always a possibility that information may be intentionally withheld or unintentionally overlooked, so the auditor must still make all the usual tests, thus indicating the reliability and accuracy of the representations made by the client's officers.

To avoid any possibility of error or misunderstanding, the representations should be made in writing. A possible form for such a representation is given here. Note the list of contingent liabilities, which is included to assist the officers in recalling any such liabilities that might exist.

### Client's Liabilities Representation

Date _____

To (name of auditor):

To the best of our knowledge all known or ascertainable direct liabilities of the company at (date) have been recorded in the accounts at that date, with the exception of minor items which are carried forward from month to month in ordinary operations.

The company had no material contingent liabilities that were not provided for in the accounts at (date), except as set forth below:

|  | *Amount if Determinable* |
|---|---|
| *Kind of Contingent Liability* | |
| Upon customers' or other notes that were discounted, sold, or otherwise transferred | |
| Upon drafts negotiated | |
| For Federal or state income taxes | |
| For accommodation endorsements | |
| For guarantees of notes or securities of other issuers | |
| For guarantees of company products or services | |
| Under repurchase agreements | |
| Upon leases | |
| Under contracts or purchase agreements | |
| Under profit sharing arrangements | |

| Kind of Contingent Liability | Amount if Determinable |
|---|---|

Under pending lawsuits
For all other contingent liabilities of any nature

The company has entered into purchase commitments that approximated
$_____ at (date), which have arisen in the ordinary course of operations
and contain no unusual amounts.

(Signed)

_____

(President or other principal officer)

_____

(Treasurer or chief financial officer)

_____

(Controller or chief accounting officer)

*Revenue Agents' Reports.* The auditor should always ascertain whether
an agent of the Internal Revenue Service has examined and closed any
income tax returns during the period since the auditor was last in the
client's office. If any returns have been examined, the agent's report
should be reviewed to see whether additional taxes have been assessed.

*Interest Expense.* Interest expense and the amount of interest-bearing
obligations outstanding during the year should be reconciled. There is
always a possibility that interest is being paid on an unrecorded note, the
proceeds of which have been appropriated by some officer or employee.

*Notes, Bonds, Warehouse Receipts.* If serially numbered notes, bonds, or
warehouse receipts are issued by the client, all serial numbers should be
accounted for in order to detect any instruments that have been issued
but not recorded. When notes or bonds are shown by the records to
have been liquidated, the paid documents should be inspected by the
auditor. The absence of the cancelled document evidencing the original
liability would suggest that the recorded payment may have been for
some other purpose and that the original obligation is still outstanding.
In cases where there may be any question, the paid check can be examined as further evidence of what actually happened to any payments
made.

*Review of Cash Receipts Record.* The auditor should review cash receipts for the audit period for any large receipts. Such receipts should
be traced into the accounts to verify that the corresponding credit has
been properly recorded, regardless of whether the cash represents the
proceeds of a note or loan or the result of some other form of transaction.

*Receiving Records.* All merchandise received prior to the balance sheet
date should either be paid for or reflected in the total for accounts pay-

able. Only in special cases will it be necessary to make a special review of the receiving records, however, because the verification of the inventory cutoff and the review of subsequent transactions should reveal any significant amounts of materials that have been received but not recorded as a liability.

*Review of Directors' and Stockholders' Minutes.*   Minutes of directors' and stockholders' meetings may contain authorizations to borrow money, declaration of a cash dividend that is unpaid at the end of the year, reference to contracts that may obligate the company, or mention of claims or lawsuits pending against the company. As a consequence, such minutes should be carefully read and pertinent information abstracted in the working papers to permit subsequent comparison with ledger entries concerning the actions taken and any resulting liabilities. (See schedule XX.)

*Review of Operations.*   The client's operations should be studied for any types of transactions that might involve liabilities not recorded at the balance sheet date. As an obvious illustration, any company with a weekly payroll is certain to have a liability at the end of the year for accrued wages. Other liabilities whose existence should become apparent with a thorough understanding of the client's operations would include container deposits, accrued royalties, accrued interest payable, service guarantees, accrued commissions, consignment accounts payable, and reimbursement for expenditures made by officers or employees.

*Expense Comparisons.*   A month-to-month comparison of expenses that revealed reduced expenses in the final month of the year might suggest that there is a liability for unpaid expenses.

*Knowledge of Tax Laws.*   Even though the auditor cannot be an expert in all possible taxes to which the client might be subject, the auditor should at least be familiar with the principal types of taxes and should note that all such taxes have been paid or accrued. Among the more common taxes are city, state, and federal income taxes, gross earnings taxes, payroll taxes, excise taxes, sales taxes, stock transfer taxes, and franchise taxes.

*Review of Company Contracts.*   All major contracts entered into by the client should be reviewed by the auditor for any direct or contingent liabilities that may have been created. Labor contracts, especially, should be reviewed, because they may contain provisions obligating the client for insurance benefits, sick leave, pension payments, or vacation pay based on the number of months worked in a given period with payment to be made even if an employee leaves the company. Lease agreements must be reviewed to determine whether an operating or a capital lease is involved and whether any resulting liability has been recorded.

*Workmen's Compensation Insurance.* Compensation insurance is usually handled by making an advance deposit based on estimated payrolls, with either a refund or additional payment being made later based on actual payrolls. When the policy year terminates on or shortly after the balance sheet date, there is always a possibility that actual payrolls have exceeded the original estimate and that an additional premium may be due.

### Arithmetic and Clerical Accuracy; Agreement of Details and Control Totals

Internal accounting controls, including the proof of equality of debits and credits, should provide adequate assurance of recording accuracy without the need for substantive audit procedures, except in those instances where detailed records are maintained in support of controlling account balances. Examples would include subsidiary records of investment assets such as capital stocks or bonds, a register of insurance policies, and a register of commercial paper or other notes payable that are outstanding. In these instances the auditor should prove the client's trial balance listing on the details by footing the listing and tracing all or at least a sample of the items listed to the detailed records. The auditor should prepare such a trial balance if the client's internal controls are deficient in that respect.

### Existence of Assets and Liabilities

As a general rule, there should be some form of documentary evidence available within the client's organization to support most assets and liabilities. In addition, the existence of highly liquid assets, and assets or liabilities such as installment notes that are subject to change as a result of transactions involving outside parties, should be substantiated by some form of direct communication—usually a request to confirm the amount involved. For some of the more common assets and liabilities, evidence that should be available to support the existence of the items is indicated below.

*Investments in Bonds and Capital Stocks.* The certificates evidencing such investments should be held under adequate protection. Auditor access to the certificates should be available only through appropriate authorization, and a client representative should be present for the entire time that is necessary for the auditor to count (inspect) the securities and prepare a working paper record of the certificates that have been counted.

Should the certificates pertain to investments in so-called "private" companies (companies whose securities are not publicly held or widely traded), confirmation of the investment should generally be obtained from the investee company, and audited financial statements or other evidence of the existence of the company should be obtained. Certificates held in safekeeping, out for transfer, or pledged as collateral should be confirmed with the holders, and any related lien must be disclosed in the financial statements.

*Cash Surrender Value of Life Insurance.*   When "whole" or "ordinary" life insurance policies are carried on the management or partners of an organization, the cash surrender value that increases annually is an investment asset of the organization that owns the policies. To warrant continuing to carry this asset, the auditor should confirm that the policy is still in effect, is owned by the client, and that any use of the cash surrender value as a basis for borrowing from the insurance company has been properly recorded by the client. The annual increase in the cash surrender value reduces insurance expense below the amount of premiums paid.

*Prepaid Insurance.*   Any insurance premiums that have been paid that represent the cost of future protection are properly carried as an asset and may be classed as a current asset on the basis of being immaterial, even though the premium may have been paid in advance for more than one year. The existence of the asset should be established by inspection of insurance policies and determining that the portion of the premium that is unearned and is carried as an asset has been properly computed.

As a constructive service to management, the auditor should find it useful to review the client's insurance coverage from the standpoint of whether the various risks normally insured against are adequately covered.

*Prepaid Taxes.*   Property taxes are typically paid in advance of the period in which the tax revenues will be utilized by the taxing body. Although as a matter of convenience and simplicity most tax payments are expensed when paid, if the client chooses to treat prepayments as an asset in accordance with generally accepted accounting principles, the existence of the asset should be established by relating the payment made to the statement assessing the tax; and if the payment has not been receipted on the tax statement, by examining the paid check that was issued to remit the amount assessed. The portion properly treated as prepaid should then be calculated.

*Expense Advances and Deposits.*   The existence of these amounts should be tested in accordance with their materiality by confirmation from the person or organization holding the advance. Alternatively, an expense advance can be substantiated by examining the succeeding expense report that is filed and noting that the amount of advance deducted from the expense claim agrees with the amount shown in the records at the balance sheet date.

*Prepaid Commissions.*   These are similar to expense advances, and their existence can similarly be established by confirmation or by reference to the subsequent transaction that reports the earning of the amount that was advanced.

*Postage.*   The existence of postage on hand is readily determined if the client has capitalized on the internal control potential of postage meters, for reading of the "descending" dial of the meter at the balance sheet date will establish the amount properly carried as an asset. If the postage is in the form of stamps and material amounts are involved, the client should arrange for persons other than the custodians to count the stamps on hand at the balance sheet date, with the auditor observing the count.

*Plant Rearrangement Costs.*   If substantial expenditures for plant rearrangement have been capitalized, the auditor should substantiate the asset through a transaction approach that is similar to that for the plant asset accounts. The amounts capitalized should be substantiated and the existence of future benefits established, with amortization taking place on a systematic basis over the period in which the future benefits are expected to be received.

*Leaseholds.*   Amounts paid to obtain an operating lease or payment in advance of rent due for a final period of a lease may be classified as a deferred charge or as an intangible asset. The transaction approach should be used to establish the existence and amount of the asset.

*Other Intangible Assets.*   The cost of acquired patents, copyrights, franchises, or goodwill is properly carried as an intangible asset with existence established by the transaction approach. The auditor should determine whether the diminution of anticipated future benefits represented by the unamortized balance of the intangible have been reduced, thereby requiring a write-off of some portion of the remaining balance of the asset account.

*Notes Payable.*   As mentioned previously, unrecorded liabilities, rather than the existence of those liabilities that have been recorded, represent the greater audit risk. Nevertheless, the existence of recorded liabilities should be established, generally in conjunction with establishing the amount of the liability. Notes payable should be confirmed with the holders of the notes, with the confirmation also covering the terms of the note and any collateral that has been pledged to secure the loan. The information on collateral is necessary in order that the auditor may ascertain the existence of the assets that have been pledged and also that the resulting lien is disclosed in the financial statements. If interest on the notes is to be paid currently rather than at maturity, the confirmation should also elicit information on the date to which interest has been paid. All unpaid interest should be accrued and reported as a liability in the balance sheet.

The amount of interest expense recorded for the year should be related to the terms of the notes and the average balance outstanding during the year, in order to provide evidence that both the liability and the expense are appropriately stated.

*Consignment Accounts Payable.* This liability cannot be verified with the consignor because the amount must be determined by the consignee. The auditor should, however, confirm with the consignor the amount of goods for which the consignee is accountable, and then determine that either the goods are still on hand or the appropriate liability has been recorded for the goods that have been sold.

*Revenue Received in Advance.* For prepaid subscription income, prepaid rent income, and other similar items, the client's calculation of the liability at the balance sheet date for revenue that is applicable to future periods should be reviewed to determine the existence and amount of the liability and also the amount properly reported as having been earned during the year.

*Liability under Product Warranties.* Sales contracts should be reviewed for any expressed or implied warranties, and past experience or engineering estimates used to estimate the future liability arising from current sales as well as the amount to be charged against current income.

*Liability Arising from Capital Leases.* When analysis of a lease agreement indicates that a capital lease is involved, the present value of the future lease payments must be recorded, and the auditor should review the computation of this liability amount, thereby providing evidence of the existence of the liability and its valuation.

*Pension Plan Liability and Expense.* Current and past service costs must be reported as expense in accordance with existing financial accounting standards. Any difference between the expense provision and the amount funded for the year must be reported as accrued or prepaid pension cost, with the underlying computations reviewed by the auditor. The auditor should also review the required disclosures in relation to defined benefit plans, including the present value of accumulated plan benefits and the net assets available to provide those benefits.

*Income Taxes Payable.*   Given that income taxes are usually the major taxes payable by a successful corporation, it is important that the auditor be knowledgeable about the highly complicated federal, state, and local income tax laws in order to determine whether an adequate provision has been made for the client's income tax expense and liability. In some instances the auditor will be engaged to prepare the client's tax returns; but even if that is not the case because there is adequate tax competence within the client's organization, the auditor must be sufficiently knowledgeable about income tax laws and regulations to be able to review the client's income tax accrual. As this review is being made, the auditor should be alert to any opportunities to effect tax savings, for such recommendations are one of the finest stimulants to good client relationships.

In addition to the review of the income tax accrual, the auditor should examine paid checks for the payments that have been recorded against the total liability, to provide evidence that the remaining liability is the amount actually due. In a first audit the auditor should also review all previous tax returns for years that are still open to ascertain whether there may have been an underpayment of taxes with a corresponding liability for the additional taxes, interest, and penalties that may still be due.

State income taxes are further complicated by the fact that taxes may be assessed by states other than where a corporation is domiciled but in which business is being conducted.

*Claims Subject to Litigation.*   As indicated in the previous discussion of the comprehensiveness objective, the existence of claims that have been asserted against the client as well as any potential claims that are as yet unasserted should be ascertained through correspondence with the client's attorney. Based on the attorney's response concerning the likelihood of an unfavorable outcome of any pending litigation and an estimate or range of the loss that might be incurred, the auditor will have to decide which of the following alternatives is appropriate:

1.  Recognition of the loss in the financial statements by a provision for the estimated liability.
2.  Footnote disclosure of the contingency along with any indication of the amount of the claim that has been asserted.
3.  Omission of any reference to the potential liability on the basis that the contingency is highly remote or is immaterial.

*Commitments.*   The existence of future commitments that are sufficiently material to require disclosure should be ascertained from the review of contracts for purchase or lease of materials or equipment, licensing agreements, employment contracts, profit-sharing agreements, pension plans, and similar items.

*Other Contingencies.*   The existence of contingent liabilities arising from discounted notes or accounts receivable, accommodation endorsements, open letters of credit, and other contingencies that are subject to footnote disclosure should be ascertainable from the review of transactions likely to involve such contingencies and from the standard bank confirmation form.

### Ownership of Assets and Liabilities

The ownership of the various assets encompassed by this chapter will generally be indicated by the possession of the assets or of documents of ownership such as stock or bond certificates. In other cases contracts will indicate where title or other incidents of ownership may rest, and pursuit of the objective of existence may likewise provide indication of ownership.

As further evidence of ownership, registered securities should bear the name of the client (or the client's nominee) as the registered owner. Ownership of bearer securities can usually be further verified by reference to the certificate numbers listed in the transmittal advice supplied when the certificates are delivered, or to the certificate numbers in the audit work papers for the previous year for purchases made in a prior year. Numbers that do not correspond with these records would indicate that the securities may have been sold during the year without authorization and the proceeds converted for personal use, with the securities temporarily replaced at the time of count by repurchase or the borrowing of like securities.

Liens against any assets indicated by the absence of the pledged asset or reference to the lien in a purchase or loan agreement must, of course, be disclosed in the financial statements. Evidence of the existence of liabilities should also be examined for indication that the client is the party named as obligor.

### Valuation of Assets and Liabilities

The auditor must be satisfied that assets and liabilities have been recorded at cost as determined from initial transaction amounts and reflecting present value if appropriate. These initial amounts must then be adjusted for the utilization of benefits associated with asset amounts, and for the discharge of liability amounts through payment of cash or provision of goods or services. Assets or liabilities for which there is an associated interest factor should be carried at their present value.

The valuation of each of these miscellaneous assets or liabilities and all investment income should be accounted for in accordance with generally accepted accounting principles. Market value of investments should likewise be recorded or disclosed as required by GAAP.

The auditor should determine that the proceeds from the sale of any investment or other assets have been properly accounted for. The proceeds of sale must be allocated between the carrying value of the asset as adjusted to the date of sale, any accrued interest or other income received as a part of the sale proceeds, and any gain or loss on the sale transaction.

Working papers should detail all balances and transactions related to investment accounts and should indicate what verification has been performed in support of those amounts. A common arrangement of the work sheet for investments follows, with the listed items used as column headings across the page and a separate line devoted to each security held. Each line should foot across the page, and totals that relate to financial statement amounts should be cross-referenced to the corresponding figures in the working paper balance.

1. Description of security (name of issuer, type of security, maturity and rate)

Balance at beginning of year

2. Face amount or number of shares
3. Cost or book value

Purchases

4. Date
5. Face amount or number of shares
6. Cost

Sales (Deductions)

7. Date
8. Face amount or number of shares
9. Cost or book value
10. Net proceeds (memo only)
11. Gain or loss (memo only)
12. Amortization of premium or discount

Balance at end of year

13. Face amount or number of shares
14. Cost or book value
15. Market value

Interest or dividend income

16. Interest accrued at the beginning of the year
17. Interest or dividend income earned during the year

18. Interest or dividends received during the year
19. Interest accrued at the end of the year

The valuation of each of the miscellaneous assets or liabilities will directly affect a related expense or revenue account. The auditor should associate changes in balance sheet amounts with the amount recorded for the corresponding expense or revenue in order to establish that the expense or revenue has been correctly valued.

No further discussion of auditor verification of the valuation of these miscellaneous assets, liabilities, expenses, and revenues is included at this point inasmuch as the substantive audit procedures pertaining to valuation of these items and the calculation of amounts were essentially covered in connection with the discussion of existence under that objective.

## Questions/Problems

For multiple-choice questions 17-1 through 17-5, indicate the letter of the single answer that *best* completes the statement or answers the question, and justify the choice that you have made.

**17-1.** A company holds bearer bonds as a short-term investment. Custody of these bonds and submission of coupons for interest payments normally is the responsibility of the
  a. Treasury function.
  b. Legal counsel.
  c. General-accounting function.
  d. Internal-audit function.

(Uniform CPA Examination)

**17-2.** In order to avoid the misappropriation of company-owned marketable securities, which of the following is the best course of action that can be taken by the management of a company with a large portfolio of marketable securities?
  a. Require that one trustworthy and bonded employee be responsible for access to the safekeeping area, where securities are kept.
  b. Require that employees who enter and leave the safekeeping area sign and record in a log the exact reason for their access.
  c. Require that employees involved in the safekeeping function maintain a subsidiary control ledger for securities on a current basis.
  d. Require that the safekeeping function for securities be assigned to a bank that will act as a custodial agent.

(Uniform CPA Examination)

**17-3.** The financial management of a company should take steps to see that company investment securities are protected. Which of the following is *not* a step that is designed to protect investment securities?

    a. Custody of securities should be assigned to persons who have the accounting responsibility for securities.

    b. Securities should be properly controlled physically in order to prevent any unauthorized usage.

    c. Access to securities should be vested in more than one person.

    d. Securities should be registered in the name of the owner.

(Uniform CPA Examination)

**17-4.** In connection with a review of the prepaid insurance account, which of the following procedures would generally *not* be performed by the auditor?

    a. Recompute the portion of the premium that expired during the year.

    b. Prepare excerpts of insurance policies for audit working papers.

    c. Confirm premium rates with an independent insurance broker.

    d. Examine support for premium payments.

(Uniform CPA Examination)

**17-5.** The auditor can best verify a client's bond sinking fund transactions and year-end balance by

    a. Recomputation of interest expense, interest payable, and amortization of bond discount or premium.

    b. Confirmation with individual holders of retired bonds.

    c. Confirmation with the bond trustee.

    d. Examination and count of the bonds retired during the year.

(Uniform CPA Examination)

**17-6.** A note payable owed by your client is not due until two years after the current balance sheet date, but in the course of your review of subsequent disbursements you discover that the note has been paid off prematurely. Should the note be classified in the balance sheet as a current liability or as a long-term liability? Why?

**17-7.** Does the fact that certain securities are in the client's possession necessarily prove that the securities are owned by the client? Explain.

**17-8.** List six different prepaid expenses or deferred charges, and for each indicate from what documents you would obtain evidence as to:

(a) The amount of the original disbursement.

(b) The period over which the amount should be written off.

**17-9.** Your client has acquired a piece of property subject to an existing mortgage (the mortgage was not assumed) and, since the client is not legally obligated by the mortgage, proposes to deduct the mortgage from the cost of the property in the financial statements. Would this treatment affect your opinion as expressed in your short-form audit report? Explain.

**17-10.** The Hymine Manufacturing Company, Inc., which has been doing business for ten years, has engaged you to examine its financial statements. The Company has never before engaged the services of a CPA. Its Federal income tax returns have been prepared by the Company's chief accountant.

(a) In an initial engagement, the CPA usually applies the auditing procedure of reviewing the client's Federal income tax returns for prior years. What are the general purposes or objectives of this auditing procedure? (In this part do not list specific items of information available from this source.)

(b) An objective of the review of prior years' income tax returns is to obtain specific items of information pertaining to the client's accounting and income tax practices. List these specific items and explain each item's relevance to the CPA's examination. (For example, prior years' income tax returns would be reviewed for any net operating loss carryover that would be applied to any income tax liability for the year under examination.)

(Uniform CPA Examination)

**17-11.** You have been making annual audits of the XYZ Sales Company. During the past few years the company's earnings have shown a slight but steady decline.

At the beginning of this year's audit, you obtain company-prepared financial statements that show a significant increase in earnings for this year over the prior three years. The company is engaged in a wholesaling operation and resells to retailers the products purchased from various manufacturers. There have been no unit price changes in either purchases or sales. The method of operation remains the same, so the increased efficiency does not account for the increase in income. The company's other sources of revenue remain the same. In short, the business has been run on the same basis as in the past. In addition, you are aware that management is anxious to present a favorable statement of income, since it is facing a struggle for control with a group of stockholders who charge that income may be overstated by understating expired costs and expenses or liabilities, or overstating assets.

The company is on a Fifo inventory basis. A physical inventory was taken at the year end. A tag system was used and all tags were accounted for.

Required:

Draw a line down the middle of a lined sheet(s) of paper.

(a)  To the left of the line, state the ways that expired costs and expenses or liabilities may have been understated, or assets overstated.

(b)  To the right of the line, for each item mentioned in part (a), outline in a few words the audit steps that would reveal each understatement or overstatement.

(Uniform CPA Examination)

**17-12.**  You are to make an examination of the bond investment account of the Sanders Company in connection with an examination of the financial statements as of December 31, 1983. This is the first time such an examination has been made. Your working papers should include provisions for analyzing all 1983 transactions, including those affecting the income statement.

Transcripts of the accounts and a summary of pertinent information on brokers' advices of purchase or sale are given below.

### INVESTMENT ACCOUNT

| 1983 | | Debit | Credit | Balance |
|---|---|---|---|---|
| Jan 1 | Balance .................. | | | 30,200.00 |
| | 10M Underhill Co. ......... | | | |
| | ($10,800) .................. | | | |
| | 20M Carlyle, Inc. .......... | | | |
| | ($19,400.00) .............. | | | |
| Feb. 15 | 20M Arthur Corp. .......... | 20,650.00 | | 50,850.00 |
| Sept. 1 | Carlyle, Inc. .............. | | $9,850.00 | 41,000.00 |

### INTEREST INCOME

| 1983 | | | | |
|---|---|---|---|---|
| Feb. 3 | Carlyle, Inc. .............. | | 600.00 | 600.00 |
| June 5 | Underhill Co. .............. | | 500.00 | 1,100.00 |
| July 2 | Arthur Corp. .............. | | 600.00 | 1,700.00 |
| Aug. 4 | Carlyle, Inc. .............. | | 600.00 | 2,300.00 |
| Dec. 3 | Underhill Co. .............. | | 500.00 | 2,800.00 |

| Date | Quantity | Description | Price | Interest | Amount |
|------|----------|-------------|-------|----------|--------|
| **Purchases** | | | | | |
| 11/30/81 | 10M | Underhill Co. 10's J&D, June 84/89 | $103 | $500.00 | $10,800.00 |
| 2/1/82 | 20M | Carlyle, Inc. 6's F&A, Feb. 1987 | 97 | . . . . . . | 19,400.00 |
| 2/15/83 | 20M | Arthur Corp. 6's J&J, July 1986 | 102 1/2 | 150.00 | 20,650.00 |
| *Sales* | | | | | |
| 9/1/83 | 10M | Carlyle, Inc. 6's F&A, Feb. 1987 | 98 | 50.00 | 9,850.00 |

Required:

(a)  Set up a worksheet to analyze the year's transactions, beginning with a corrected balance at 1/1/83, and showing all 1983 entries as they should appear. Use the following column headings:

A.  Investment account
    1. Balance 1/1/83
       (a)  Face
       (b)  Premium or (discount)
    2. Purchases
       (a)  Face
       (b)  Premium or (discount)
    3. Sales
       (a)  Face
       (b)  Premium or (discount)    ⎫ ⎧ The total of these three
       (c)  Profit or (loss)          ⎬ ⎨ columns will be the net
            (memo only)               ⎭ ⎩ cash proceeds of the
                                           sale.
    4. Amortization
    5. Balance 12/31/83
       (a)  Face
       (b)  Premium or (discount)
B.  Accrued interest receivable
    1. Accrued at 1/1/83
    2. Accrued during 1983 (The total of this column plus or minus the total Amortization column above is the interest income for the year.)
    3. Received during 1983 (Show the accrued interest purchased on the Arthur Corp. bonds as a negative figure in this column.)
    4. Accrued at 12/31/83

(b)  Prepare adjusting entries to correct the books at December 31, 1983, to agree with your worksheet, assuming the books have not been closed. Explanations for each entry should show clearly how the amounts were determined. Correct income of prior years through retained earnings.

**17-13.** You have been engaged to examine the financial statements of the Elliott Company for the year ended December 31, 19X3. You performed a similar examination as of December 31, 19X2. Following is the trial balance for the company as of December 31, 19X3.

| | Dr. (Cr.) |
|---|---|
| Cash | $ 128,000 |
| Interest receivable | 47,450 |
| Dividends receivable | 1,750 |
| 12% secured note receivable | 730,000 |
| Investments at cost: | |
|    Bowen common stock | 322,000 |
| Investments at equity: | |
|    Woods common stock | 284,000 |
| Land | 185,000 |
| Accounts payable | (31,000) |
| Interest payable | (6,500) |
| 8% secured note payable to bank | (275,000) |
| Common stock | (480,000) |
| Paid-in capital in excess of par | (800,000) |
| Retained earnings | (100,500) |
| Dividend revenue | (3,750) |
| Interest revenue | (47,450) |
| Equity in earnings of investments | |
|    carried at equity | (40,000) |
| Interest expense | 26,000 |
| General and administrative expense | 60,000 |

You have obtained the following data concerning certain accounts:

The 12% note receivable is due from Tysinger Corporation and is secured by a first mortgage on land sold to Tysinger by Elliott on December 21, 19X3. The note was to have paid in 20 equal quarterly payments beginning March 31, 19X3, plus interest. Tysinger, however, is in very poor financial condition and has not made any principal or interest payments to date.

The Bowen common stock was purchased on September 21, 19X3, for cash in the market where it is actively traded. It is used as security for the note payable and held by the bank. Elliott's investment in Bowen represents approximately 1% of the total outstanding shares of Bowen.

Elliott's investment in Woods represents 40% of the outstanding common stock which is actively traded. Woods is audited by another CPA and has a December 31 year end.

Elliott neither purchased nor sold any stock investments during the year other than noted above.

Required:

For the following account balances, discuss (1) the types of evidential matter you should obtain and (2) the audit procedures you should perform during your examination.

(a) 12% secured note receivable.

(b) Bowen common stock.

(c) Woods common stock.

(d) Dividend revenue.

(Uniform CPA Examination)

**17-14.** In connection with his examination of the financial statements of Belasco Chemicals, Inc., Kenneth Mack, CPA, is considering the necessity of inspecting marketable securities on the balance-sheet date, May 31, 19X3, or at some other date. The marketable securities held by Belasco include negotiable bearer bonds, which are kept in a safe in the treasurer's office, and miscellaneous stocks and bonds kept in a safe deposit box at The Merchants Bank. Both the negotiable bearer bonds and the miscellaneous stocks and bonds are material to proper presentation of Belasco's position.

Required:

(a) What are the factors that Mr. Mack should consider in determining the necessity for inspecting these securities on May 31, 19X3, as opposed to other dates?

(b) Assume that Mr. Mack plans to send a member of his staff to Belasco's offices and The Merchants Bank on May 31, 19X3, to make the security inspection. What instructions should he give to his staff member as to the conduct of the inspection and the evidence to be included in the audit working papers? (Note: Do not discuss the valuation of securities; the income from securities; or the examination of information contained in the books and records of the Company.)

(c) Assume that Mr. Mack finds it impracticable to send a member of his staff to Belasco's offices and The Merchants Bank on May 31, 19X3. What alternative procedures may he employ to assure himself that the Company had physical possession of its marketable securities on May 31, 19X3, if the securities are inspected (1) May 28, 19X3? (2) June 5, 19X3?

(Uniform CPA Examination)

**17-15.** You are engaged in the audit of the financial statements of the Sandy Core Company for the year ended December 31, 19X1. Sandy Core Company sells lumber and building supplies at wholesale and retail; it has total assets of $1,000,000 and a stockholders' equity of $500,000.

The Company's records show an investment of $100,000 for 100 shares of common stock of one of its customers, the Home Building Corporation. You learn that Home Building Corporation is closely held and that its capital stock, consisting of 1,000 shares of issued and outstanding common stock, has no published or quoted market value.

Examination of your client's cash disbursements record reveals an entry of a check for $100,000 drawn on January 23, 19X1 to Mr. Felix Wolfe, who is said to be the former holder of the 100 shares of stock. Mr. Wolfe is president of the Sandy Core Company. Sandy Core Company has no other investments.

(a)  List the auditing procedures you would employ in connection with the $100,000 investment of your client in the capital stock of the Home Building Corporation.

(b)  Discuss the presentation of the investment on the balance sheet, including its valuation.

                                        (Uniform CPA Examination)

**17-16.**  The Moss Company manufactures household appliances that are sold through independent franchised retail dealers. The electric motors in the appliances are guaranteed for five years from the date of sale of the appliances to the consumer. Under the guaranty defective motors are replaced by the dealers without charge.

Inventories of replacement motors are kept in the dealers' stores and are carried at cost in The Moss Company's records. When the dealer replaces a defective motor, he notifies the factory and returns the defective motor to the factory for reconditioning. After the defective motor is received by the factory, the dealer's account is credited with an agreed fee for the replacement service.

When the appliance is brought to the dealer after the guaranty period has elapsed, the dealer charges the owner for installing the new motor. The dealer notifies the factory of the installation and returns the replaced motor for reconditioning. The motor installed is then charged to the dealer's account at a price in excess of its inventory value. In this instance, to encourage the return of replaced motors, the dealer's account is credited with a nominal value for the returned motor.

Dealers submit quarterly inventory reports of the motors on hand. The reports are later verified by factory salesmen. Dealers are billed for inventory shortages determined by comparison of the dealers' inventory reports and the factory's perpetual records of the dealers' inventories. The dealers order additional motors as they need them. One motor is used for all appliances in a given year, but the motors are changed in basic design each model year.

The Moss Company has established an account, Estimated Liability for Product Guaranties, in connection with the guaranties. An amount representing the estimated guaranty cost prorated per sales unit is credited to the Estimated Liability account for each appliance sold, and the debit is charged to a Provision account. The Estimated Liability account is debited for the service fees credited to the dealers' accounts and for the inventory cost of the motors installed under the guaranties.

The engineering department keeps statistical records of the number of units of each model sold in each year and the replacements that were made. The effect of improvements in design and construction is under continuous study by the engineering department, and the estimated guaranty cost per unit is adjusted annually on the basis of experience and improvements in design. Experience shows that, for a given motor model, the number of guaranties made good varies widely from year to year during the guaranty period, but the total number of guaranties to be made good can be reliably predicted.

Required:

(a)  Prepare an audit program to satisfy yourself as to the propriety of transactions recorded in the Estimated Liability for Product Guaranties account for the year ended December 31, 19XX.

(b)  Prepare the worksheet format that would be used to test the adequacy of the balance in the Estimated Liability for Product Guaranties account. The worksheet column headings should describe clearly the data to be inserted in the columns.

(Uniform CPA Examination)

**17-17.**  The Lewis Company, a manufacturer of heavy machinery, grants a 4-year warranty on its products. The Estimated Liability for Product Warranty account shows the following transactions for the year:

| | |
|---|---|
| Opening balance | $45,000 |
| Provision | 20,000 |
| | 65,000 |
| Cost of servicing claims | 12,000 |
| Ending balance | $53,000 |

A review of unsettled claims and the Company's experience indicate that the required balance at the end of the year is $80,000 and that claims have averaged 1½% of net sales per year.

The balance in Accrued Federal Income Taxes is $27,000, which adequately covers any additional liability for prior years' income taxes and includes a $25,000 provision for the current year. For income tax purposes only the cost of servicing claims may be deducted as an expense.

The following additional information is available from the Company's records at the end of the current year:

| | |
|---|---:|
| Gross sales | $2,040,000 |
| Sales returns and allowances | 40,000 |
| Cost of goods sold | 1,350,000 |
| Selling and administrative expense | 600,000 |
| Net income per books before income taxes | 50,000 |

Prepare the necessary adjusting journal entries, giving effect to the proper accounting treatment of product warranty and Federal income taxes. Support each entry with clearly detailed computations. The books have not been closed. The Company has not allocated income taxes in the past. Assume a rate of 50% for income tax calculations.

(Uniform CPA Examination)

**17-18.** Prepare a work sheet covering your examination of the account "Miscellaneous Administrative Expense," in connection with your year-end examination of Pratt Products Co. The general ledger account appears as follows:

**Miscellaneous Administrative Expense**

| Date | Description | Reference | Dr. | Cr. | Balance |
|---|---|---|---|---|---|
| Jan. 31 | | VR | $1,000.00 | | $1,000.00 |
| | | J-3 | 7.86 | | 1,007.86 |
| Feb. 28 | | VR | 20.00 | | 1,027.86 |
| | | J-8 | 8.15 | | 1,036.01 |
| Mar. 31 | | VR | 2,015.00 | | 3,051.01 |
| | | J-15 | 7.29 | | 3,058.30 |
| Apr. 30 | | VR | 1,636.28 | | 4,694.58 |
| | | J-23 | 9.05 | | 4,703.63 |
| May 31 | | VR | 250.00 | | 4,953.63 |
| | | J-29 | 7.36 | | 4,960.99 |
| June 30 | | VR | | $17.64 | 4,943.35 |
| July 31 | | VR | 1,020.00 | | 5,963.35 |
| | | J-32 | 8.17 | | 5,971.52 |
| Aug. 31 | | VR | 15.00 | | 5,986.52 |
| | | J-36 | 7.63 | | 5,994.15 |

| | | | |
|---|---|---|---|
| Sept. 30 | VR | 20.00 | 6,014.15 |
| | J-40 | 7.02 | 6,021.17 |
| Oct. 31 | VR | 2,481.39 | 8,502.56 |
| | J-43 | 7.82 | 8,510.38 |
| Nov. 30 | VR | 318.81 | 8,824.19 |
| | J-47 | 8.20 | 8,832.39 |
| Dec. 31 | VR | 569.95 | 9,402.34 |
| | J-50 | 8.92 | 9,411.26 |

Reference to journal voucher J-23 reveals that the amount of $9.05 represents bank service charges for the month of March. Other journal entries are presumed also to be for bank charges. Your year-end bank reconciliation shows that service charges for December were $9.45.

The voucher register contains a miscellaneous column that is analyzed at the end of the month and recapped to show the charges to the various accounts that are affected. Analysis of the individual entries reveals the following breakdown of the monthly charges to Miscellaneous Administrative Expense:

January
  Barton and Barrister .......................... $1,000.00

February
  R. B. Holden, Cashier ......................... $    20.00

March
  American Red Cross .......................... $   100.00
  Bright & Early ................................ 1,900.00
  R. B. Holden, Cashier ........................ 15.00
  $2,015.00

April
  R. B. Holden, Cashier ........................ $   110.00
  Barton and Barrister .......................... 1,000.00
  Proxy, Inc. ................................... 476.28
  Damon Runyon Cancer Fund ................. 50.00
  $1,636.28

May
  R. B. Holden, Cashier ......................... $  250.00

June
  R. B. Holden, Cashier ......................... $    17.64 Cr.

July
  R. B. Holden, Cashier ......................... $    20.00
  Barton and Barrister .......................... 1,000.00
  $1,020.00

August
  R. B. Holden, Cashier ......................... $    15.00

September
    R. B. Holden, Cashier . . . . . . . . . . . . . . . . . . . . . . .   $    20.00

October
    Barton and Barrister . . . . . . . . . . . . . . . . . . . . . . .   $2,456.39
    R. B. Holden Cashier . . . . . . . . . . . . . . . . . . . . . . .      25.00
                                             $2,481.39

November
    United Fund Drive . . . . . . . . . . . . . . . . . . . . . . .   $  250.00
    R. B. Holden, Cashier . . . . . . . . . . . . . . . . . . . . . . .      63.81
                                             $  313.81

December
    R. B. Holden, Cashier . . . . . . . . . . . . . . . . . . . . . . .   $    20.00
    Bonn's Department Store . . . . . . . . . . . . . . . . . . . .     234.95
    R. B. Holden, Cashier . . . . . . . . . . . . . . . . . . . . . . .     315.00
                                             $  569.95

The following information is obtained by examination of supporting records and discussion with various company officials.

The custodian of the office petty cash fund, R. B. Holden, submits a voucher the first of every month claiming reimbursement for disbursements made during the preceding month. The voucher for December disbursements is always made before the end of the month, however, in order to reflect December transactions in the proper year.

All postage used in the general office is purchased with petty cash funds, and represents the only petty cash disbursement affecting Miscellaneous Administrative Expense, except as follows:

(a)  The May voucher for petty cash disbursements made in April included an advance of $225 to P. D. Holcomb, President, to cover expenses of a trip to visit the company's East Coast warehouse. The actual expenses were $187.36 and the balance of the advance was returned to Holden the following month.

(b)  Several office employees worked overtime during October to prepare a special report, and were reimbursed from the petty cash fund for the cost of their suppers and cab fares to their homes, in the total amount of $43.81.

(c)  P. D. Holcomb received an advance of $300 in December for expenses relating to a trip to attend a trade association meeting to be held from January 3 to January 6.

Minutes of the Board of Directors contain the following actions:

| Meeting Date | Action |
|---|---|
| 11/14 | Reappointed the firm of Bright & Early to make the annual examination of the company's financial statements. |
| 12/15 | Authorized retaining Barton and Barrister for legal services for another year, retainer fee of $4,000 to be paid quarterly, in advance, beginning in January. |
| 1/15 | Authorized contribution to American Red Cross, $100.00. |
| 3/15 | Authorized mailing to stockholders of annual report for previous year, together with notice of annual stockholders meeting and proxy form for stockholders unable to attend the meeting. |
| | Authorized engagement of Proxy, Inc., to solicit return of stockholders' proxies, for fee of $300 plus out-of-pocket expenses. |
| 4/15 | Authorized contribution to Damon Runyon Cancer Fund $50. |
| 11/15 | Authorized contribution to United Fund Drive, $250. |

The statement from Bonn's Department Store contains the description "Purchases by A. C. Powers." On questioning Mr. Powers, the office manager, you learn that this is a bill covering the purchase of Christmas gifts for office employees.

The statement from Barton and Barrister attached to the voucher entered in October reads as follows:

| | |
|---|---|
| Retainer Fee | $1,000.00 |
| Legal and out-of-pocket expenses relating to defense of patient infringement suit | 1,456.39 |
| | $2,456.39 |

Your working papers should explain all unusual items and should show any adjustments or reclassifications you would recommend. Show all possible adjustments, regardless of materiality. In addition, prepare a list of points concerning items about which you would want further information, or which you would want to bring to the attention of the senior accountant.

# Chapter 18

# LONG-TERM DEBT AND OWNERS' EQUITY

Although from a legal standpoint long-term notes and bonds are grossly different from capital stock and retained earnings, they are from a finance and accounting point of view quite similar in many ways. It is for reason of these similarities that all long-term sources of capital are covered in this final core chapter dealing with internal control considerations and audit objectives and substantive procedures.

## Control Considerations

Authority to obtain funds by obligating the entity or issuing capital stock should be tightly controlled by limiting that authority to the treasurer or to specific persons responsible to the treasurer. Amounts in excess of some stated figure should preferably be authorized by the board of directors as well. Immediately upon receipt of the funds, control should be transferred to accountability for the proceeds of the financing activity.

## Evaluation of Internal Control Objectives and Procedures

### Operating Objectives

*All transactions are properly authorized.*

- Issuance of long-term notes, bonds, or capital stock will occur infrequently but be material in amount. Given these circumstances, the treasurer should carefully consider the nature and duration of long-term capital needs, market conditions, internally generated funds, and the company's financial structure in developing proposals for future financing. The final decision and authorization to proceed with the necessary legal, underwriting, and SEC registration requirements (if applicable) should come from the board of directors, with accompanying approval from the stockholders for such matters as new classes of capital stock or increases in the number of authorized shares. *Inquiry, inspection.*
- Dividends must be authorized by the board of directors, after consideration is given to management recommendations, which should take into account retention of earnings to support future capital needs, whether the dividend should be in cash or stock, the availability of cash for cash dividends, and the likely effect of existing or contemplated dividend policy on the market price of the company's stock. *Inquiry, inspection.*
- Authorization to call bonds prior to their maturity date or to reacquire shares of the company's own capital stock should ordinarily come from the board of directors, based on the recommendation of the treasurer. *Inquiry, inspection.*
- Payment of interest when due or of obligations at their maturity should require no authorization other than that of the treasurer for the required disbursement of the funds. *Inquiry, inspection.*

*All authorizations resulted in action being taken.*

- As a result of the infrequency of transactions and the materiality of the amounts involved, no special controls or procedures should be necessary to ensure that authorizations resulted in action.

## Data Processing Objectives—Internal Accounting Control

*Accounting and computer operations are independent of all operating responsibilities.*

*Inquiry* and *observation* that maximum feasible segregation of these activities exists:

| Operating | Accounting/Data Processing |
|---|---|
| Recommendation of financial policies | General ledger records |
| Handling of receipt and disbursement of funds, including payments of interest and dividends and redemptions of principal | Trustee's records of holders of registered bonds for payments of interest and principal at maturity |
| Issuance of certificates by bond trustee | Records of holders of notes issued by the company and the amount of those notes |
| Issuance of stock certificates (often handled by an external transfer agent) | Stockholders' ledger record of shares held by each stockholder |
| Approval of all stock certificates issued by an independent registrar if stock is listed on a stock exchange | Preparation of dividend checks and interest checks for notes |
| Arrangements for annual stockholders' meeting, including preparation of proxy statement and tabulation of ballots | Preparation of SEC 8-K and 10-K reports and quarterly and annual reports to stockholders |

*Only valid transactions that were duly authorized are accepted for entry in the accounting records.*

- Records of receipt or disbursement of funds should originate in the treasurer's department. *Inquiry, observation.*
- When the client maintains stockholder records, evidence of transfers of ownership should originate in the corporate secretary's department. *Inquiry, observation.*

*All transactions are entered in the accounting records.*

- Notes and stock certificates issued by the company should be prenumbered, and these numbers should be accounted for as they are reported to the accounting department on documents evidencing transactions. *Inquiry, observation.*

*Accounting entries correctly reflect transaction amounts.*

- Given the materiality of amounts likely to be involved and the infrequency of financing transactions, no special controls should be necessary to ensure that entries correctly reflect transaction amounts.

### Transactions are correctly classified for accounting entry.

- All entries should be made in conformity with generally accepted accounting principles—a result that should be relatively assured given the materiality and infrequency of transactions and the close involvement of management in these transactions. *Inquiry, inspection.*

### Recorded transactions are correctly processed.

- The general ledger trial balance and trial balances of detail records, such as a stockholders' ledger or a record of notes payable that are in agreement with the related control accounts, provide the main assurance that recorded transactions are correctly processed. *Inquiry, inspection.*

## Monitoring Objectives

### Regular comparison is made of accountability records with underlying items; third-party proofs of accounting records.

- Interest and dividend payments and the mailing of proxies to stockholders constitute the main basis for contact with these parties to provide evidence that the detail and general ledger record pertaining to their relationship to the company are correct. *Inquiry, observation.*

### There is an effective internal audit function.

- Internal auditors should regularly review and evaluate internal controls, perform compliance tests, and when the situation warrants, make recommendations for improvement or correction. *Inquiry, review of audit planning, inspection of working papers.*
- If the company acts for itself in issuing notes or stock certificates and handles transfers of stock ownership, the internal auditor should occasionally make surprise counts of unissued notes or stock certificates and account for redemptions of notes by examining the paid notes and account for stock transfers by examining the cancelled stock certificates that have been surrendered. *Inquiry, inspection of working papers.*
- The following operational audit activities, although not directly related to accounting information or controls, should be considered by the internal audit staff as a service to management in its control of operations.

  Review of financing activities to ascertain that feasible alternatives were adequately considered in arriving at ultimate financial decisions.

  Review of stock transfer operations if these are handled internally, to ascertain that adequate controls are in effect over the issuance of stock certificates, and that stock transfers are handled on an expeditious basis.

  Review of the decision process relating to dividend declarations, to determine that consideration has been given to all aspects of the recommendations presented to the board of directors.

Consideration of the adequacy of the operating and financial information that is regularly reported to the board of directors.

Review of procedures in the preparation and publication of the concern's annual report to stockholders and consideration of the form and content of that document relative to the likely or perceived needs of the stockholders as a group.

## Substantive Audit Objectives and Procedures

In this section considerations relating to any of the sources of long-term financing are discussed as each of the audit objectives is covered.

### *Conformity of Client's Financial Statements with Disclosure and Other Requirements of Financial Reporting Standards*

The following standards are applicable in the reporting of long-term sources of capital:

1. Maturity dates, call provisions, subordination provisions, interest rates, security interests representing liens on assets, sinking fund requirements, convertibility provisions, and other pertinent information applicable to long-term debt should be disclosed either parenthetically or in notes to the financial statements.
2. Unamortized bond premium or discount is to be reported in conjunction with the outstanding bonds.
3. Capital leases must be reported at the present value of future lease payments, supplemented by information concerning lease expiration dates and annual payments to be made.
4. Minimum rentals due on operating leases should be disclosed in the aggregate and by year for each of the five succeeding years, plus indication of the basis for any contingent lease payments.
5. Current maturities of long-term obligations should be reported as current liabilities unless repayment is not to be made from working capital assets.
6. Commitments under unconditional obligations not reported directly in the balance sheet must be disclosed for each of the next five years and in the aggregate.
7. Different classes of capital stock should be reported separately, along with information about preference or convertibility provisions. Par or stated value and number of shares authorized, issued, in the treasury, and outstanding should be reported for each class of stock.
8. Full information about any changes in capital stock accounts during the year should be reported, as should information about outstanding stock options or warrants.
9. All changes in retained earnings during the period reported on should be disclosed, including net income, cash or stock dividends, corrections of

prior-year income, and appropriations and restorations of amounts to retained earnings reserves.

10. Any reservations of retained earnings should be disclosed, and the only permissible charges against reserves should be to restore unneeded amounts to retained earnings.

11. Earnings per share amounts, based on outstanding shares and on a fully diluted basis before and after the amounts per share of any extraordinary items, must be reported for publicly held companies.

12. When a deficit has been eliminated by a reduction in contributed capital through a quasireorganization, any retained earnings arising after the reorganization should be dated for a period of five to ten years.

### Reasonableness of Account Balances

*Perform Analytical Review.* The low turnover of accounts associated with long-term financing results in maximum reliance being placed on the analysis of transactions affecting the accounts, so that little can be gained from analytical review. One exception to this statement is that the amount of interest expense on notes or bonds should be related to the effective rate of interest on the obligations at the time of issue.

### Synchronization of Events and Records

The materiality of transaction amounts affecting long-term sources of capital should generally result in adequate attention to the transactions to ensure that the transactions will be correctly recorded in the proper period.

### Comprehensiveness of Records

The materiality of transaction amounts, plus controls over cash inflows and outflows, should ensure the recording of long-term capital transactions in most instances. One possibility to be watched, however, would be the liability for a cash dividend declared prior to the balance sheet date and to be paid following the balance sheet date.

### Arithmetic and Clerical Accuracy; Agreement for Details and Control Totals

Double entry accounting provides the principal assurance that the infrequent long-term capital transactions are correctly recorded, except when detail records are maintained for notes or capital stock that has been issued.

*Prepare or Verify Trial Balance of Subsidiary Ledger Records.* If numerous long-term notes are issued, or if a company handles stock-transfer transactions internally, detail records should be maintained showing the amount or number of shares held by each creditor or stockholder. Regular trial balances of these records should be proven against the related control account, and the trial balance at the balance sheet date should be verified by the auditor by tracing (on a test basis if a large number of detail accounts is involved) listed items to the subsidiary records and footing the trial balance.

### Existence of Long-Term Debt and Owners' Equity Amounts

The existence of the investment interests of these providers of capital to the client is established primarily through the examination of transactions affecting the related accounts.

*Bonds Payable.* In connection with the issuance of bonds and the verification of entries to record the transactions, the auditor should thoroughly study the trust indenture under which the bonds were issued for the terms of the issue and the manifold provisions relating to the bonds. All pertinent facts should be summarized and placed in the permanent file for the client. The following list suggests some of the more important matters that should be ascertainable from the indenture, with many of these having a direct bearing on the financial statements.

1. Descriptive title of the issue.
2. Maximum amount of bonds authorized.
3. Interest rate and dates.
4. Maturity date.
5. Date and price, if bonds may be called before maturity.
6. Name of trustee and registrar.
7. Possible restrictions on use of bond proceeds.
8. Assets pledged as security.
9. Any special obligations concerning pledged assets, such as carrying a minimum amount of insurance and making necessary repairs.
10. Restrictions on payment of dividends during the period the bonds are outstanding. (Such provisions usually state that only income above a certain amount each year shall be available for the payment of dividends. A requirement may also be made that dividends can be paid only if working capital or the current ratio exceeds a certain figure.)
11. Convertibility provisions. (Such provisions will necessitate reserving shares of unissued stock to accommodate bondholders who may exercise the convertibility privilege.)
12. Provisions for repayment. (Some stated or calculated amount may be required to be paid into a sinking fund or used to retire bonds purchased on the open market.)

13. Name of trustee to whom sinking fund payments are to be made.
14. Restrictions on additional borrowing while the bonds are outstanding.

*Contributed Capital* In a similar fashion a corporation's charter and articles of incorporation (or the partnership agreement for that form of organization) should be examined to ascertain that the organization has been duly constituted and so that all significant information can be noted and considered relative to the verification and presentation of owners' equity accounts in the financial statements. The charter will include such information as the classes of stock that have been authorized, the number of shares authorized, the par value of the stock or the fact that the stock has no par value, and any special privileges or rights of the various classes of stock. Entries associated with the issuance, retirement, or conversion of capital stock or acquisition as treasury shares should be reviewed to ascertain that they have been properly recorded in relation to generally accepted accounting principles and that associated inflows or outflows of assets have been properly accounted for. Most such transactions will require the approval of the board of directors, and the auditor's analysis of the transactions should be cross-referenced to the authorization noted in the abstract of the minutes of board of directors' meetings.

If the corporation directly handles the issuance of stock certificates, the stock certificate book should be examined and all certificate stubs to which the original or surrendered certificate is not attached should be noted and the number of shares shown as issued should be totalled and balanced with the general ledger record of the number of shares issued. Shares that have been reacquired as treasury stock should be counted, and the related transactions should be examined to determine whether acquisitions or dispositions during the audit period have been properly recorded.

*Retained Earnings.* The existence of the amount shown as retained earnings is in effect proved through an inventory approach, for retained earnings is simply the residual after deducting liabilities and capital stock from total assets. The amount of each of these other balance sheet items should, of course, have been substantiated through the audit procedures applied in examining each of the items, thus also establishing the appropriateness of the retained earnings figure.

As a double check of retained earnings, however, a transaction approach should also be used. In a repeat audit, the opening balance of retained earnings will be the audited balance at the close of the previous year. Using this figure as the starting point, as on schedule TT, all current year entries affecting retained earnings should be detailed. These may include

Adjustments to the opening balance representing corrections of prior year income. (Note, however, if comparative statements are to be presented for prior years, any such income statements should be restated for the applicable correction amounts, with any remaining amount of correction treated as an adjustment to the opening retained earnings of the earliest year.) Any such adjustment should be cross-referenced to the schedule on which the amount and propriety of such adjustment have been determined.

Net income for the year cross-referenced to the schedule I/S, the working trial balance for the income statement.

Dividends, cash or stock, declared during the year cross-referenced to the abstract of the board of directors minutes at which the action was taken, as shown on schedule XX. Verification should be made that the dividend amount is equal to the per share amount of declaration multiplied by the number of shares outstanding at the declaration date. The amount of retained earnings capitalized per share of stock in connection with a stock dividend that is likely to be considered by recipients to be a distribution of current earnings because it is less than 20 or 25 percent of the outstanding shares should be capitalized at an amount equal to the fair value of the additional shares issued.

Changes in the amount of retained earnings appropriated to reserves during the year, cross-referenced to directors' action in establishing such reserves or restoring them to retained earnings.

In an initial audit the appropriateness of the opening balance of retained earnings for the audit year should be established by reviewing a predecessor auditor's working papers or, in the absence of a prior audit, by analyzing all entries to the account since the inception of the business to determine that only net income amounts, deductions authorized by the board of directors for dividends, or other amounts that are in accordance with generally accepted accounting principles, are reflected in retained earnings.

In addition to these activities directed to establishing the appropriateness of the balance of the retained earnings account, attention must be directed to any restrictions on the distribution of retained earnings that may have arisen, such as for

Arrearages of cumulative preferred dividends
Restrictions arising out of bond trust indentures
Restrictions imposed by state law, resulting from the purchase of shares for the treasury

*Confirmations from Third Parties.* The existence of certain liabilities and capital contributions of owners should be verified by written communication with third parties, as follows:

Long-term notes: remaining principal balance, interest rates, maturity date, and assets pledged to secure payment confirmed with holders of such notes.

Bonds payable: amount of bonds outstanding confirmed with the trustee for the bond issue.

Capital stock shares: if an independent registrar and/or transfer agent has been engaged, confirm details of each class of stock, including par value or no-par value status, preferences, convertibility features, and number of shares authorized, issued, and outstanding.

## Ownership; Observation of Legal Requirements

There should be no ownership questions associated with liabilities or owners' equity, but the auditor should ascertain whether legal requirements applicable to these third party relationships have been met and whether the rights of various parties have been respected, including any resulting limitations or restrictions on client activities. The auditor must gain satisfaction about such matters as the following; must become aware of any related restrictions or limitations through careful reading of contract terms, trust indentures, articles of incorporation, and minutes of board of directors' meetings; and should also be aware of legal provisions or government regulations that may impinge on the organization and its actions. Should the auditor be in doubt about any of these matters it is important that the opinion of the client's attorney be sought.

1. Has the business been legally incorporated?
2. Have provisions of the corporate charter been adhered to concerning such matters as the type of activity the company is entitled to engage in and the classes of stock and number of shares that the company is authorized to issue?
3. Have any state stock transfer taxes been paid and the tax stamps properly handled?
4. Can unissued stock be sold at a discount?
5. Is the corporation permitted to reacquire or retire outstanding stock?
6. Have any legal or contractual restrictions on the payment of dividends been observed? These might result from the acquisition of treasury stock, bond indenture agreements, or cumulative preferred dividends in arrears.
7. Have any restrictions on the use of retained earnings for the payment of dividends been disclosed in the balance sheet?
8. Has all contributed capital been separately accounted for and retained intact for the protection of creditors, unless distributions are permitted by state law?
9. Should any common stock shares be reserved for convertibility provisions or stock options or warrants, and have the restrictions been disclosed?

## Valuation of Long-Term Debt and Owners' Equity

All account entries should be made in accordance with generally accepted accounting principles, with special consideration given to the following:

Amortization of bond premium or discount, preferably in accordance with the effective interest method.

Capital lenses capitalized at the present value of future lease payments.

Capital stock at par or stated value, with amounts in excess of par or stated value treated as additional amounts of paid-in-capital.

Treasury stock acquisitions recorded at cost or par or stated value; gains or losses on treasury stock transactions to be recorded as elements of paid-in capital, except for losses in excess of previous gains, which should be charged to retained earnings.

Inasmuch as the transaction approach is utilized for each of the accounts with which we are concerned in this chapter, each recorded transaction should be analyzed to determine that it corresponds with amounts in the underlying documents pertaining to the transaction and that the transaction has been recorded in accordance with GAAP.

### Audit of Partnerships and Sole Proprietorships

One of the most important points that the auditor should watch for in the audit of an unincorporated business is the proper separation of business and personal transactions. Such transactions must be properly handled if the true income of the business is to be determined. Personal expenses paid from business funds should be charged against the owner's equity rather than as an expense of the business. Conversely, business expenses paid from personal funds must be brought into the business records. Tax considerations tend to foster the payment of personal expenses from business funds, particularly in the case of social activities that may have some limited business connection. Borderline cases are usually decided in favor of the treatment that will result in the lowest tax, with the additional advantage of pleasing the client. Excessively liberal treatment of such items may, however, work to the disadvantage of both the auditor and the client. The auditor's independence may be questioned, and the client's tax return is likely to be subjected to a more critical review if it becomes apparent that the client has taken excessive expense deductions.

In the examination of a partnership the auditor should be satisfied that the provisions of the partnership agreement have been carried out as they pertain to the distribution of net income and the maintenance of partners' capital and drawing accounts. Points likely to be covered in the agreement would include the basis of distributing profits, including any provisions for salaries or interest; maximum drawings permitted during the year; minimum capital balances to be maintained; additional capital to be contributed; and the treatment of loans by the partnership to or from the partners.

The financial statements of an unincorporated business should point out that no provision for income taxes has been made because such taxes are assessed against and are a liability of the owner(s) and not the business.

## Questions/Problems

For multiple-choice questions 18-1 through 18-6, indicate the letter of the single answer that *best* completes the statement or answers the question, and justify the choice that you have made.

18-1. Where *no* independent stock transfer agents are employed and the corporation issues its own stocks and maintains stock records, cancelled stock certificates should

    a. Be defaced to prevent reissuance and attached to their corresponding stubs.

    b. *Not* be defaced, but segregated from other stock certificates and retained in a cancelled certificates file.

    c. Be destroyed to prevent fraudulent reissuance.

    d. Be defaced and sent to the secretary of state.

                               (Uniform CPA Examination)

18-2. Many of the Granada Corporation's convertible bondholders have converted their bonds into stock during the year under examination. The independent auditor should review the Granada Corporation's statement of changes in financial position to ascertain that it shows

    a. Only financial resources used to reduce convertible debt.

    b. Only financial resources provided by issuance of stock.

    c. Financial resources provided by the issuance of stock and used to reduce convertible debt.

    d. Nothing relating to the conversion because it does not affect net working capital.

                               (Uniform CPA Examination)

18-3. If a company employs a capital stock registrar and/or transfer agent, the registrar or agent, or both, should be requested to confirm directly to the auditor the number of shares of each class of stock

    a. Surrendered and canceled during the year.

    b. Authorized at the balance sheet date.

    c. Issued and outstanding at the balance sheet date.

    d. Authorized, issued, and outstanding during the year.

                               (Uniform CPA Examination)

18-4. When a company has treasury stock certificates on hand, a year-end count of the certificates by the auditor is

a. Required when the company classifies treasury stock with other assets.

b. Not required if treasury stock is a deduction from stockholders' equity.

c. Required when the company had treasury stock transactions during the year.

d. Always required.

(Uniform CPA Examination)

**18-5.** An audit program for the examination of the retained earnings account should include a step that requires verification of the

a. Gain or loss resulting from disposition of treasury shares.

b. Market value used to charge retained earnings to account for a two-for-one stock split.

c. Authorization for both cash and stock dividends.

d. Approval of the adjustment to the beginning balance as a result of a write-down of an account receivable.

(Uniform CPA Examination)

**18-6.** The auditor is concerned with establishing that dividends are paid to stockholders of the client corporation owning stock as of the

a. Issue date.

b. Declaration date.

c. Record date.

d. Payment date.

(Uniform CPA Examination)

**18-7.** What auditing procedures should be undertaken by an independent auditor in connection with outstanding bonds that have been reacquired on the open market and retired?

**18-8.** What information should be included in the balance sheet concerning capital stock?

**18-9.** How should the creation and disposition of general purpose contingency reserves be handled? Why?

**18-10.** What supporting records should be examined in relation to the balance sheet amount for capital stock when the client maintains the stock records?

**18-11.** For what points should the auditor watch to ascertain whether transactions affecting the stockholders' equity have been in accordance with legal requirements and the rights of various groups?

**18-12.** What problem is often faced in the audit of unincorporated businesses?

**18-13.** In the course of your December 31, 19X5 audit of a client's machinery account, you discover that the following machine was sold for $10,000 cash on December 20, 19X5.

| | |
|---|---:|
| Cost January 1, 19X1 . . . . . . . . . . . . . . . . . . . . . . | $100,000 |
| Straight-line depreciation on 10-year estimated life recorded to December 31, 19X5 . . . . . . . | 50,000 |

Federal income taxes on recorded income for 19X5 have already been recorded at the prevailing 50% rate, but capital gains and losses are subject to a 25% rate. The only entry made for the sale of the machine on December 20, 19X5 was as follows:

| | |
|---|---:|
| Cash . . . . . . . . . . . . . . . . . . . . . . . . . . . . . . . . . . . . . . . . . | $10,000 |
| Machinery . . . . . . . . . . . . . . . . . . . . . . . . . . . . . . . . . . | $10,000 |

Give the adjusting entry or entries to correct the accounts in the auditor's working papers.

**18-14.** Your client's records indicate that a gain was realized during the year you are examining, as a result of the sale of treasury shares that were purchased earlier in the same year.

(a) What audit procedures would you employ in satisfying yourself that the gain was properly recorded?

(b) How should the gain be shown in the financial statements?

**18-15.** List the various circumstances that might result in a restriction of the availability of retained earnings for dividend distributions. For each, state how the auditor would ascertain that such a restriction existed.

**18-16.** You were engaged to examine the financial statements of Ronlyn Corporation for the year ended June 30, 19X1.

On May 1, 19X1, the Corporation borrowed $500,000 from Second National Bank to finance plant expansion. The long-term note agreement provided for the annual payment of principal and interest over five years. The existing plant was pledged as security for the loan.

Due to unexpected difficulties in acquiring the building site, the plant expansion had not begun at June 30, 19X1. To make use of the borrowed funds, management decided to invest in stocks and bonds, and on May 16, 19X1, the $500,000 was invested in securities.

Required:

(a) What are the audit objectives in the examination of long-term debt?

(b) Prepare an audit program for the examination of the long-term note agreement between Ronlyn and Second National Bank.

(c) How could you verify the security position of Ronlyn at June 30, 19X1?

(d) In your audit of investments, how would you
   1. Verify the dividend or interest income recorded?
   2. Determine market value?
   3. Establish the authority for security purchases?

(Uniform CPA Examination)

**18-17.** Superior Products, Inc. for the first time is including a 5-year summary of earnings and dividends per share in its 19X5 annual report to stockholders. At January 1, 19X1, the Corporation had issued 7,000 shares of 4 percent cumulative, nonparticipating, $100 par value preferred stock and 40,000 shares of $10 par value common stock of which 108 shares of preferred and 4,000 shares of common stock were held in the treasury.

Dividends were declared and paid semiannually on the last day of June and December. Cash dividends paid per share of common stock and net income for each year were:

|                          | 19X1      | 19X2       | 19X3     | 19X4      | 19X5      |
|--------------------------|-----------|------------|----------|-----------|-----------|
| Net income (loss) ....   | $126,568  | $(11,812)  | $47,148  | $115,824  | $193,210  |
| Dividend on Common:      |           |            |          |           |           |
| June 30 ...........      | .40       | .11        | .10      | .40       | .60       |
| December 31 ......       | .48       | .11        | .30      | .40       | .40       |

In addition, a 10 percent stock dividend was declared and distributed on all common stock (including treasury shares) on April 1, 19X3, and common was split 5 for 1 on October 1, 19X5. The Corporation has met a sinking-fund requirement to purchase and retire 140 shares of its preferred stock on October 1 of each year, beginning in 19X4, using any available treasury stock. On July 1, 19X2, the Corporation purchased 400 shares of its common stock and placed them in the treasury and on April 1, 19X4, issued 5,000 shares of common stock to officers, using treasury stock to the extent available.

Required:

(a) Prepare a schedule showing the computation of preferred stock dividends paid semiannually and annually for the five years. Use the following columnar headings:

|      |                     | Number of Shares | | Dividends Paid | |
|------|---------------------|-----------------------|-------------|--------------|----------|
| Year | Half<br>(1st or 2nd) | Purchased<br>and Retired | Outstanding | Semiannually | Annually |

(b) Prepare a schedule that shows for each of the five years the cash dividends paid to common stockholders and the average number of shares of common stock outstanding after adjustment for the stock dividend and split. Use the following format:

| Dividend Date | Shares of Common Stock In Treasury | Outstanding | Dividends Paid Per Share | Total | Common Stock Adjusted for: 10% Stock Dividend | 5 for 1 Stock Split |
|---|---|---|---|---|---|---|
| 6/30/X1 | | | | | | |
| 12/31/X1 | | | | | | |
| | | Total for year | | | | |
| | | Average for year | | | | |

(Continue this format for remaining 4 years)

(c) Prepare a 5-year financial summary presenting for each year:
1. Net income and dividends paid, and
2. Earnings and dividends per share for common stock.

(Uniform CPA Examination)

**18-18.** (a) The board of directors of Tabac, Inc., not a closely held corporation, declared an "ordinary stock dividend" equal to 5 percent of the corporation's outstanding common stock, to be issued to common stockholders of record as of April 15. The corporation's treasury stock was to be used for this purpose to the extent available. The market value of the common stock just prior to the declaration was $64 per share and remained at substantially that figure for more than a month after the issuance of the dividend shares.

The corporation's equity accounts at the dates of declaration and record included the following balances:

| | |
|---|---|
| Preferred stock, $5 cumulative (no par), authorized 25,000 shares; in treasury 130 shares; outstanding 10,402 shares | $1,053,200 |
| Common stock (par $50), authorized 50,000 shares; in treasury 880 shares; outstanding 27,780 shares | 1,433,000 |
| Paid in surplus—amounts contributed in excess of par value of common shares | 251,464 |
| Retained earnings | 963,425 |
| Treasury stock, $5 cumulative preferred (at cost) | 14,922 |
| Treasury stock, common (at cost) | 40,920 |

At the time of declaration the board directed that retained earnings in the amount of the aggregate par value of the dividend shares be transferred to the appropriate permanent capital accounts.

You are to

(1) Prepare an entry that will record the net effect of the board's actions.

(2) Generally accepted accounting principles involve certain recommendations for the consideration of boards of directors in situations similar to that outlined in this problem. Discuss the Tabac board's action relating to the retained earnings transfer in the light of these recommendations. Include in your discussion the gist of the recommendations that pertain to the retained earnings transfer, the reasons advanced for the recommendations, and the propriety of the board's transfer at par value.

(3) Assuming that the entry in (1) had not been made and that the board had followed generally accepted accounting principles, prepare an entry that will give effect to the issuance of the dividend stock in accordance therewith.

(b) Assume the same facts as set forth in *a*, except that the dividend declaration equalled 40 percent (instead of 5 percent) of the outstanding common shares and had resulted in a substantial reduction in the market value of the common shares of Tabac, Inc.

What is recommended in such a case? Does the board's transfer of retained earnings on a par value basis conflict with or conform to these recommendations? *Explain.*

(Uniform CPA Examination)

**18-19.** The following schedule sets forth the short-term debt, long-term debt, and stockholders' equity of Darren Company as of December 31, 19X4. The president of Darren has requested that you assist the controller in preparing figures for earnings per share computations.

Short-term debt:
| | |
|---|---:|
| Notes payable—banks | $ 4,000,000 |
| Current portion of long-term debt | 10,000,000 |
| Total short-term debt | $ 14,000,000 |

Long-term debt:
| | |
|---|---:|
| 4% convertible debentures due April 15, 19Y6 | $ 30,000,000 |
| Other long-term debt less current portions | 20,000,000 |
| Total long-term debt | 50,000,000 |

Stockholders' equity:
  $4.00 cumulative, convertible preferred stock; par value
    $20 per share; authorized 2,000,000 shares; issued

| | |
|---|---:|
| and outstanding 1,200,000 shares; liquidation preference $30 per share aggregating $36,000,000 ....... | 24,000,000 |
| Common stock; par value $1 per share; authorized 20,000,000 shares; issued 7,500,000 shares including 600,000 shares held in treasury .............. | 7,500,000 |
| Additional paid-in capital ......................... | 4,200,000 |
| Retained earnings ................................ | 76,500,000 |
| Total ......................................... | 112,200,000 |
| Less cost of 600,000 shares of common stock held in treasury (acquired prior to 19X4) ............ | 900,000 |
| Total stockholders' equity ........................ | 111,300,000 |
| Total long-term debt and stockholders' equity ....... | $161,300,000 |

*Explanation of Short-Term Debt, Long-Term Debt,
and Stockholders' Equity Including Transactions
During the Year Ended December 31, 19X4*

- The "Other long-term debt" and the related amounts due within one year are amounts due on unsecured promissory notes that require payments each year to maturity. The interest rates on these borrowings range from 6 percent to 7 percent. At the time that these monies were borrowed, the bank prime interest rate was 7 percent.
- The 4 percent convertible debentures were issued at their face value of $30,000,000 in 19X6 when the bank prime interest rate was 5 percent. The debentures are due in 19X6 and until then are convertible into the common stock of Darren at the rate of 25 shares for each $1,000 debenture.
- The $4.00 cumulative, convertible preferred stock was issued in 19X3. The stock had a market value of $75 at the time of issuance when the bank prime interest rate was 9 percent. On July 1, 19X4, and on October 1, 19X4, holders of the preferred stock converted 80,000 and 20,000 preferred shares, respectively, into common stock. Each share of preferred stock is convertible into 1.2 shares of common stock.
- On April 1, 19X4, Darren acquired the assets and business of Brett Industries by the issuance of 800,000 shares of Darren common stock in a transaction appropriately accounted for as a purchase.
- On October 1, 19X3, the company granted options to its officers and selected employees to purchase 100,000 shares of Darren's common stock at a price of $33 per share. The options are *not* exercisable until 19X6.

*Additional information:*

- The average and ending market prices during 19X4 of Darren common stock were as follows:

|  | Average Market Price | Ending Market Price |
|---|---|---|
| First Quarter | $31 | $29 |
| Second Quarter | 33 | 32 |
| Third Quarter | 35 | 33 |
| Fourth Quarter | 37 | 34 |
| Average for the year | 34 | — |
| December 31, 19X4 | — | 34 |

- Dividends on the preferred stock have been paid through December 31, 19X4. Dividends paid on the common stock were $0.50 per share for each quarter.
- The net income of Darren Company for the year ended December 31, 19X4, was $8,600,000. There were **no** extraordinary items. The provision for income taxes was computed at a rate of 48 percent.

Required:

a. Prepare a schedule which shows the adjusted number of shares for 19X4 to compute:
  1. Primary earnings per share.
  2. Fully diluted earnings per share.
b. Prepare a schedule which shows the adjusted net income for 19X4 to compute:
  1. Primary earnings per share.
  2. Fully diluted earnings per share.
  *Do not compute earnings per share.*

(Uniform CPA Examination)

# Chapter 19

# CAPPING THE AUDIT FIELD WORK

---

---

In its discussion of systems-based audits this text has considered each of the basic operating/accounting subsystems to be found in the typical industrial concern organized to generate profit. The objective of such discussion has been to show how evidence can be acquired in support of each type of revenue, expense, asset, liability, and owner's equity likely to be present in the financial statements of such an organization, in

551

order to express an opinion that the financial statements do (do not) present fairly the financial and operating results of the organization, in conformity with the consistent application of generally accepted accounting principles.

There are, however, certain general audit matters that must be covered in an examination before the field work will be complete and the audit fully wrapped up:

> Test general ledger entries
> Read and abstract minutes of directors' and stockholders' meetings
> Review the client's Statement of Changes in Financial Position or assist the client in preparing the statement.
> Consider the possibility of related party transactions, conflicts of interest, or irregularities
> Apply procedures to discover subsequent events affecting the financial statements being audited
> Obtain a representation letter from management of the client
> Submit adjusting and reversing entries to be recorded by the client
> Obtain signed copy of financial statements in final form
> Review and give final acceptance to field work and all other aspects of the engagement
> Conduct overall review of audit practice for quality control

### Test of General Ledger Entries

Selecting one month and tracing all figures shown in such source records as journals, journal vouchers, and work sheets, to the corresponding entries in the general ledger is a vestige of early audits that largely emphasized bookkeeping accuracy. Nevertheless, especially in the audit of smaller clients with limited internal controls, a final test of bookkeeping accuracy is desirable to provide evidence that all entries in the general ledger have in fact originated from journals or other source records that the auditor has encountered in the study of the client's system and the evaluation of internal controls.

A reasonable test would be to select one month of the year and trace all figures in source records to the corresponding entries in the general ledger, reviewing each entry in a general way to determine that it appears proper and reasonable and tick-marking the entry in the ledger. After all source records have been covered by the above test, and without having relinquished control over the records, the auditor should review each general ledger account to be certain that all entries for the test month have been tick-marked. In this way the auditor can be satisfied that all ledger entries for the test month were valid and originated from appropriate sources. Any entries not ticked should be investigated, as they may indicate that unauthorized entries have been made to the ledger—possibly to cover a defalcation, to conceal an out-of-balance condition, or to manipulate the records to show a more favorable financial or operating picture.

### Abstract of Minutes of Directors' and Stockholders' Meetings

At numerous points in the preceding chapters reference was made to matters that would be found in the minutes of meetings of the board of directors or stockholders. Included were such items as authorization of plant expenditures, approval of contracts with other companies or individuals, authorization of loans or sale of capital stock, declaration of dividends, appointments of officers, and designation of compensation to officers. The importance of the actions and matters considered at stockholders' and directors' meetings suggests the need for the auditor to be fully informed about those matters in order to be in a position to express an unqualified opinion on a client's financial statements.

To gain the required information, the auditor should obtain a photo copy of the minutes or request permission to read the minutes, making an abstract of all matters that have a bearing on the financial statements. Those matters should then be cross-referenced to the working paper schedules that are affected, as was done on schedule XX. In a first audit for the client the auditor should read all minutes since the inception of the business, although fewer items from a prior year will be abstracted in the working papers than in the case of minutes for the current year. Matters of only momentary importance, such as the authorization of officers' salaries or short-term loans, would be ignored; however, actions authorizing new bank accounts and designating persons empowered to sign checks on those accounts, declaring dividends, authorizing the sale of stock or bonds, revaluing assets, or adjusting any account balances are examples of items that should be noted.

Having full knowledge of such matters is so important to the auditor that if the client declines to permit examination of the minute books, the auditor must conclude that it is not possible to obtain sufficient information to warrant expressing a favorable opinion on the client's financial statements. A client might seek to deny the auditor access to the minute books on the basis of the confidential nature of actions recorded in the minutes. The fact that those matters are of sufficient importance to warrant confidentiality suggests that the auditor should know about the actions in order to consider their possible effect on the financial statements, and the client should have no fear that the auditor will commit a breach of confidence. The auditor's professional practice is contingent, among other things, upon an avowal to treat confidentially all information concerning a client's affairs, and the code of professional ethics by which the auditor is governed further evidences that fact (Rule 301).

To stress the importance of making the minutes of all meetings available, many auditors ask the secretary of the client corporation to prepare a letter addressed to the auditor listing all meetings of the board of directors and stockholders held since the auditor's previous examination. In that letter the corporate secretary should also be asked to state that the full and complete record of those meetings has been presented to the auditor for inspection. This minute letter should be filed with the auditor's abstract of the minutes as evidence of the client's actions. The auditor is then protected if subsequent events should reveal that the audited statements were incorrect or misleading, and that the sole evidence of the true facts was contained in the minutes of a directors' or stockholders' meeting that were not presented to the auditor for scrutiny.

### Statement of Changes in Financial Position

Almost all of the discussion of the auditor's examination has related to the general ledger accounts that appear in the basic financial statements: balance sheet and income statement. The auditor's opinion, however, also encompasses the statement of changes in financial position, and obviously the examination must extend to that statement as well. Since the statement is essentially a recapitulation of the operating, financing, and investment activities of the reporting entity, audited balance sheets at the beginning and end of the period, reflecting the results of those activities, constitute the basis for the statement, and no specific added auditing activities are required with respect to the base figures.

There must be, however, a review of the transactions that affect the changes in the balance sheet accounts inasmuch as the statement of changes must report the flow of *all financial resources*. Of obvious importance under these circumstances would be nonworking capital accounts that include the effect of transactions that increase or decrease those accounts—acquisitions and retirements of plant assets, for example. The flows may be accounted for in terms of changes in working capital or changes in cash. Although most statements are prepared on a working capital basis, the author's preference is for cash flows inasmuch as cash is the key element in financing activities and of primary interest to creditors and investors. The expressed preference, however, is for the approach that reports cash flows related to each major balance sheet account, rather than the approach that adjusts net income for changes in working capital items and reports the relatively less useful figure, "cash flow from operations." The preferred cash approach has the effect of moving changes in working capital accounts from the secondary position of a supporting schedule into the statement proper and discloses them in terms of the result of the management of such resources as receivables, inventories, and payables. The changes in these accounts generate or absorb scarce cash resources just as surely as changes in nonworking capital accounts.

Working paper schedule F/P illustrates the development of the figures for the statement of changes. The working capital basis was used for this illustration in recognition of the predominance of this flow medium in published financial statements.

### Related-Party Transactions, Conflicts of Interest, Irregularities

At all times during an examination the auditor should be alert to the possibility of sham transactions with related parties, indications of conflict of interest in transactions with related parties, indications of conflict of interest in contracts that have been negotiated, or of records of transactions that involve outright fraud. Previous reference has been made to these possibilities, but the matter is raised again at this point because in an audit much of the detail substantive work will be done by relatively inexperienced staff assistants who may not recognize certain clues that point to the existence of acts such as these. Consequently, during the final review process it is desirable that these possibilities be given further consideration by the senior or manager in charge of the engagement. Special attention should be given to any material transactions during the year, to substantial sales to new customers, and to any unusual transactions occurring near the year end.

An obvious example of a related-party transaction would be a sale to a subsidiary company, necessitating the elimination of the sale and cost of sales amounts and any profit on the transaction if the goods have not yet been sold to a third party in an arm's-length transaction. An auditor should immediately recognize the need for proper adjustments and eliminations as soon as the existence of such a transaction becomes apparent. But a similar problem requiring comparable action would be much less obvious if the related party is not a subsidiary of the client, but rather a company in which a controlling interest is held by the same person or group that holds the controlling interest in the client. The profession has moved to delineate the problems associated with related-party transactions in SAS No. 6 (Professional Standards AU Sec. 335). The statement suggests procedures for determining the existence of related parties, identifying transactions with related parties, examining those transactions, and judging whether disclosure of specific related-party transactions is adequate. SAS No. 6 also alerts the auditor to a variety of motivating conditions under which related-party transactions may be effected that are outside the ordinary course of business and hence require especially imaginative investigation.

Conflict-of-interest situations are somewhat similar to the related-party matter except that the client-related party will not have a controlling interest in the client, but will be an officer of the client, who is in a position to directly affect client decisions and who can personally benefit from those decisions through profits realized from another concern doing business with the client company. Conflict-of-interest situations should be of direct concern to any business, and many businesses actively review those possibilities as an aspect of good internal control. For the auditor one recourse to either related-party or conflict-of-interest possibilities is through the representation letter requested from the client; such letters are discussed later in this chapter, and the reader should note especially item 13 in the representation letter on page 559.

Past revelations of substantial illegal or improper payments by U.S. corporations, both here and abroad, have resulted in passage of the Foreign Corrupt Practices Act. Violations of the provisions of this act requiring adequate internal controls over accounting records and prohibiting foreign payments related to influencing a foreign government can give rise to substantial financial penalties. Consequently, the auditor should be alert to possible violations of provisions of the act from the standpoint of disclosure of the penalties or other financial effects of such violations.

### Subsequent Events Affecting Financial Statements Being Audited

The auditor's report specifically states that it pertains to a balance sheet for a given date and the related income statement and statement of changes in financial position for a period ending on the balance sheet date. Nevertheless, the auditor is held responsible for disclosing events occurring after the balance sheet date that have an important bearing on the financial statements. The period of responsibility for such disclosure ordinarily extends to the date of the auditor's report. AU Sec. 560 of Professional Standards fully develops this problem of events subsequent to the financial statements.

*Types of Events.*   Two types of events that may occur after the balance sheet date should receive the auditor's attention. The first of these types has already been referred to in the preceding chapters dealing with the examination of statement figures and *requires adjustment of the financial statements* if a material amount is involved. Included are events that provide evidence of conditions that existed at the balance sheet date or that relate to estimates inherent in the preparation of financial statements, such as the subsequent collection of a large account receivable that had appeared doubtful of collection at the balance sheet date, the initiation of bankruptcy proceedings against a customer with a large receivable balance on the client's books, the payment of a major liability that existed but had not been apparent at the balance sheet date, and events covered by the usual cutoff tests. The auditor's regular examination procedures should be designed to reveal all such subsequent events, and the auditor is expected to make full use of the information.

The second type of event that might occur subsequent to the balance sheet date involves conditions that did not exist at the balance sheet date and therefore *would not require adjustment* of the statements, although *future statements would be affected*. Nevertheless, the events should be disclosed by footnote in the current statements, in view of the significance these events might have to a person attempting to reach a decision based on the financial statements. Examples would be the subsequent sale of a large bond issue with restrictive covenants; merger with another company; disposal of a large portion of the client's productive assets; or serious losses resulting from fire, flood, or other casualty.

*Responsibility for Disclosure.* When events of either type occur, the primary responsibility for making any needed adjustment or disclosure in the financial statements rests with management. The auditor should, however, extend certain audit procedures to cover the period between the balance sheet date and the date of the auditor's report, because there exists an obligation to make independent verification of the adequacy of the representations and disclosures made by management. If the auditor discovers events and concludes that the events require disclosure, and if the client refuses to make such disclosure, the auditor must take recourse in the content of the audit report by disclosing the events and qualifying the reported opinion concerning the financial statements.

*Audit Procedures.* Audit procedures to be used by the auditor in reviewing events occurring subsequent to the balance sheet date would include the following:

1. Examination of data to ensure that proper cutoffs have been made.
2. Review of cutoff bank statements for evidence of returned checks.
3. Review of accounts receivable collections.
4. Review of cash receipts book for proceeds of loans or significant sales of inventory or plant assets.
5. Review of general journal for material entries.
6. Review of any subsequent interim financial statements that the client has prepared.
7. Review of minutes of directors' or stockholders' meetings.
8. Inquiry of management concerning events that may have occurred. (See comments below on letters of representation concerning such inquiry.)

As suggested earlier, the auditor's responsibility for disclosure of subsequent events extends to the date of the report in most instances, and the report date should therefore correspond with the date the auditor's work in the client's office was completed. If the report cannot be issued until a much later date and the auditor wishes to have the report date correspond with the actual issuance of the report, a statement should be included that the report is based on field work completed at an earlier date.

*Events Occurring after Completion of Field Work.* In connection with reports incorporated in registration statements filed in accordance with the Securities Act of 1933, the auditor is charged with responsibility for disclosing the effect of any events requiring either adjustment of the financial statements or disclosure through footnotes *until the registration statement becomes effective*—in other words, until the Securities and Exchange Commission has indicated its acceptance of the registration statement and the new securities can thus be offered for sale. The consequence of this requirement is to extend the auditor's responsibility for procedures pertaining to subsequent events beyond the date of the report and up to the effective date of the registration statement.

The above requirements are partially applicable to nonSEC reports as well, in that any events that affect the financial statements and that come to the auditor's attention after the date of the report (the date that field work was completed) but before the report is issued, should be reflected in the statements through adjustment or through footnote disclosure, whichever is appropriate, before the auditor's report is issued. In those circumstances the auditor may use "dual dating" of the report ("February 22, 19__, except for Note XY to the financial statements as to which the date is March 10, 19__"), or the report may be dated as of the latter date. In that case, however, the auditor's responsibility for subsequent events is extended to the date of the report.

AU Sec. 561 of Professional Standards concerns a somewhat different type of "subsequent" problem. If subsequent to the issuance of a report the auditor becomes aware of facts that existed prior to the date of the report and that would have affected the financial statements being reported on had such facts been known, the auditor should consider whether action should be taken to prevent future reliance on the report. If it is believed that persons may be currently relying on the financial statements who would be likely to attach importance to the newly discovered information, the auditor should advise the client to make appropriate disclosure of the newly discovered information and of its impact on the financial statements to any persons likely to be relying on the financial statements. If the client refuses to make such disclosure, the auditor should notify each member of the board of directors of such refusal and further state that in the absence of disclosure by the client steps will be taken to notify regulatory agencies and persons known to be relying on such report that the report should no longer be relied upon.

### Letter of Client Representations

Professional Standards at AU Sec. 333 require the independent auditor to obtain certain written representations from management in an examination that is to be made in accordance with generally accepted auditing standards. In the course of an examination management makes many representations through the recording of transactions, through the preparation of financial statements, and in response to specific inquiries by the auditor. Those representations are part of the evidential matter of the audit and supplement the other audit procedures necessary to form an opinion on the financial statements.

Written representations are desirable to confirm oral representations, to indicate whether the representations continue to be appropriate, and to reduce the possibility of misunderstanding about the representations. They also complement other auditing procedures, as in the case of the auditor's investigation of related party transactions, with a representation that management has no knowledge of any such transactions that have not been disclosed. Furthermore, the representations may provide the only means of access to information that may be solely within the ken of management, such as an intent to discontinue a line of business or to commit liquid funds to a specific project. Required supplementary disclosures such as unaudited replacement cost information should also be supported by written representations about the basis on which the information was prepared.

It is important to recognize that these representations in no way reduce the auditor's responsibility separately to discover or verify the matters referred to in such representations. An example of the possible form for a letter of representation to be submitted to the indicated members of management for their completion and signature is provided here.

#### Representation Letter

January 29, 19X4

Black and Decker
Certified Public Accountants
Kansas City, Missouri 64105

This letter is furnished in connection with your examination of our financial statements for the year ended December 31, 19X4. The purpose of the letter is to give you our assurance that to the best of our knowledge and belief the company's accounts and financial statements have been maintained and prepared in such a manner as to properly present the financial position and results of operations of this company. In this connection we make the following representations, which we understand have been or will be reviewed or checked by your representatives within the normal scope of your examination of our accounts:

1. The company has satisfactory title to all assets; and all mortgages, security interests, or other liens outstanding against the assets have been recorded in the accounts.

2. Cash balances are subject to no restrictions on use or withdrawal other than compensating balance requirements that have been confirmed to you by our bank.

3. Raw materials, work in process, finished goods, and supplies have been physically inventoried at October 31, 19X4, and the accounts were adjusted to agree with the physical inventory.

4. All inventories were priced at the lower of cost or market, and adequate provision was made for obsolete or otherwise unsalable items.

5. The carrying value of all property, plant, and equipment that was retired, abandoned, sold, or otherwise disposed of at December 31, 19X4, has been removed from the accounts.

6. The depreciation provided during the year and the amount of accumulated depreciation at December 31, 19X4, were adequate to cover the amortization of the cost of property, plant, and equipment over the life expectancy of those assets.

7. The company had no unrecorded or contingent assets of material amount at December 31, 19X4.

8. To the best of our knowledge all known or ascertainable direct liabilities of the company at December 31, 19X4, have been recorded in the accounts at that date, with the exception of minor items that are carried forward from month to month in ordinary operations.

9. The company had no material contingent liabilities that were not provided for in the accounts at December 31, 19X4, except as set forth below:

| *Kind of Contingent Liability* | *Amount if Determinable* |
| --- | --- |
| Upon customers' or other notes that were discounted, sold, or otherwise transferred | |
| Upon drafts negotiated | |
| For federal or state income taxes | |
| For accommodation endorsements | |
| For guarantees of notes or securities of other issuers | |
| For guarantees of company products or service | |
| Upon leases | |
| Under repurchase agreements | |
| Under contracts or purchase agreements | |
| Under profit-sharing arrangements | |
| Under pending lawsuits | |
| For all other contingent liabilities of any nature | |

10. The company has entered into purchase commitments that approximated $350,000 at December 31, 19X4, which have arisen in the normal course of operations and contain no unusual amounts.

11. Amounts due from directors, officers, or stockholders have been identified as such in the accounts.

12. The company has no shares of its capital stock reserved for officers and employees, options, warrants, conversions, or other requirements.

13. All transactions reflected in the accounting records have resulted from negotiations conducted at arm's length, and there has been no participation by management in outside concerns involved in significant purchase and sale transactions.

14. No events have occurred and no facts have been discovered since the balance sheet date that would make the financial statements materially inaccurate or misleading.

_____

President (or executive officer)

_____

Treasurer (or chief financial officer)

_____

Controller (or chief accounting officer)

All accounts are stated in conformity with generally accepted accounting principles, which have been applied on a basis consistent with that of the preceding year.

_____

Controller (or chief accounting officer)

### List of Adjusting and Reversing Entries To Be Recorded by the Client

Often the auditor's examination will reveal adjustments to be made to the client's records. The auditor should prepare a copy of the adjustments shown in the working papers, for approval and acceptance by the client (reflecting the fact that the financial statements are the client's representations) and for the client's use in making the necessary adjusting entries in the accounting records. If any of the entries relate to transactions already recorded by the client in the *following period*, the auditor may also find it desirable to give the client a list of reversing entries to be made. The auditor should maintain the recommended distinction in the working papers between adjusting entries and reclassification entries, and only the adjusting entries should be given to the client.

In England the auditor is required to state that the financial statements in the audit report agree with the client's books, and thus the client must make all adjusting entries that the auditor has made in the audit working papers. Although no such requirement exists in the United States, the auditor will usually be well advised to follow the requirement as nearly as possible. One difficulty often stands in the way, however: the client will usually have closed the books for the year before the auditor's examination has been completed. Under those circumstances, adjustments affecting income or expense can be made to the retained earnings account.

The auditor will generally find it advantageous to verify the posting of the adjustments after they have been made. If the adjustments have not been made, or if they have been made incorrectly, the audit for the following year will be complicated accordingly.

### Signed Copy of Client's Financial Statements

Although the practice is not universal, it will usually be advantageous for the auditor to obtain a signed copy of the client's financial statements in their final form. The principal officer of the client and the chief accounting or financial officer should sign the statements, with a notation that they are the final statements for the year. If the client does not prepare financial statements but relies on the auditor to do so, a copy of the statements prepared by the auditor should be reviewed by the appropriate officers and signed by them to indicate their acceptance of the statements.

There are two reasons for obtaining signed financial statements. One is to stress that the client has primary responsibility for the statements. The second is to forestall any complaint by the client that the statements in the auditor's report do not agree with those the client has prepared. In view of the second reason the importance should be noted of presenting to the client the list of adjusting entries as recommended in the preceding section. If the statements to be signed by the client have been prepared by the auditor and differ from statements that the client has prepared, a reconciliation of the figures in the two statements should be helpful to the client in connection with giving the requested acceptance and signature.

### Review and Final Acceptance of Field Work

As an audit engagement draws to a close, those with supervisory responsibility must be satisfied that all persons involved in the audit gained sufficient understanding of the client, the client's industry, and the client's accounting system and internal controls, to have been able to complete the audit satisfactorily and thereby to have acquired sufficient evidence to support the opinion to be expressed on the client's financial statements. All audit activity and the working papers reflecting the results of that activity should be reviewed toward that end.

At the first level of review responsibility the senior staff member supervising the engagement should review in detail everything connected with each phase of the engagement. In reviewing a given segment of the examination, the senior should note that each audit program step has been "signed off" by the person who did the work, so that nothing has been omitted. Then the related working papers should be reviewed to determine that

1. A full understanding of the client's accounting system and internal controls was obtained.
2. Adequate compliance tests were made of those controls on which reliance was to be placed.
3. Significant weaknesses or deficiencies were noted for inclusion in the letter of recommendations prepared for management—the "management letter"; that any weaknesses determined to be material were reported to the board of directors; and that substantive audit procedures were appropriately modified to compensate for all weaknesses.
4. Appropriate analytical review procedures were applied and all variations or exceptions were adequately investigated and cleared, and the final results are consistent with known client developments as well as with industry and general economic conditions.
5. All open items, points for further investigation, and questions raised in the working papers have been satisfactorily cleared.
6. If required by firm policy and practice, the person performing each work segment has prepared a memo stating the conclusions reached and that the conclusions justify the opinion to be expressed on the financial statements.
7. The financial statements fairly reflect the client's financial and operating results, and all necessary disclosures have been made.
8. All necessary representations were obtained, and a signed copy of the final financial statements is included in the working papers.
9. Any appropriate suggestions have been made for changes in the following year's audit.

As the review of each working paper schedule is completed, the reviewer's initials should be recorded thereon to evidence the review and acceptance of the schedule.

The manager and partner should also review the working papers, although in much less detail than would be the case for the audit senior, and in less detail for the engagement partner than for the engagement manager. Especially important at these higher levels of responsibility would be a careful reading of the final financial statements for reasonableness, clarity, and completeness. Depending on the situation, marked changes from the prior year financial statements might be traced to supporting working papers to be sure that analytical review procedures addressed these changes adequately and the resulting investigation supported the figures shown in the financial statements. These final reviews would also extend to any checklists that the senior auditor would be expected to complete, thus providing assurance that all of the steps called for by the checklists had been completed.

Reviews of the working papers would tend to be limited to such matters as the list of open points to determine what kinds of problems or loose ends were present and to determine how these matters were resolved and that all of the points had been cleared. Attention would also be profitably directed to adjusting and reclassification entries to ascertain what kinds of problems had arisen and to be sure that the entries to correct the records and financial statements were appropriate. Knowledge of the client from past engagements would suggest likely problem areas, and some detailed study of the working papers relating to these areas would provide indication whether adequate evidence was acquired to support the auditor's opinion that the related information was fairly stated in the financial statements.

For SEC clients some accounting firms also require what may be referred to as a "cold review." This review would be by a partner who is extensively involved with SEC work and who preferably has some experience with other clients in the same industry, but who has had no contact with the current audit engagement. This partner would read the financial statements carefully for proper classification and presentation of items and required disclosures and would, for any questions arising from the study of the financial statements or from knowledge of the industry, determine whether the matters or questions had been appropriately resolved, through discussions with the staff who were directly involved with the engagement or by referring to the working papers. To add further meaning to the purpose of such a review, it might be likened to a final examination over course material at the end of the semester.

### Overall Practice Review to Maintain Quality Control

The preceding discussion has related to what is generally referred to as engagement review and is an important aspect of quality control—a subject referred to briefly in Chapter 2. The overall question of quality control is broader, however, extending beyond engagement review to the firm's entire audit practice. The purpose of quality control is to provide assurance that every aspect of the firm's audit work is being performed in accordance with generally accepted auditing standards. For those firms that are members of the AICPA's SEC Practice Section or Private Companies Practice Section, two more levels of review are superimposed on the other reviews: the firm's internal practice reviews and the mandatory peer review that was mentioned in Chapter 3.

Internal practice reviews are conducted by the firm's own review teams and involve inspection visits to every office of a firm, generally on a 3-year cycle consistent with the triennial peer reviews. The quality control considerations involved in providing assurance that a firm is practicing in conformance with generally accepted auditing standards were originally set forth in Statement on Auditing Standards No. 4 and are now referenced in Professional Standards at QC Sec. 10. Quality control is stated to cover the following elements, for each of which a firm should establish policies and procedures as appropriate.

*Independence.* A firm should establish policies and procedures to provide assurance that all personnel maintain independence in fact and in appearance in satisfaction of the provisions of Rule 101 of the Rules of Conduct.

*Assignment of Personnel to Engagements.* Staff members assigned to each engagement and to specific tasks within the engagement should have a degree of technical training and proficiency adequate for the assignment and relative to the extent of supervision that is provided.

*Consultation.* There must be assurance that technical assistance on accounting and auditing matters is available through persons having appropriate knowledge and competence and that auditors will seek assistance as necessary.

*Supervision.* Adequate supervision and review should be provided to ensure that all work performed meets acceptable standards of quality.

*Hiring.* Recruiting activities and the selection of personnel to be offered employment should provide assurance that those employed will be competent to perform the work to which they will be assigned.

*Professional Development.* Training and continuing professional education must be provided to ensure that audit personnel will have the knowledge required to fulfill assigned duties and to progress within the firm.

*Advancement.* There should be a system of appraising staff performance to identify personnel capable of being advanced to positions of increased responsibility.

*Acceptance and Continuance of Clients.* Policies and procedures should be established relative to accepting and continuing clients to minimize the possibility of having a client whose management lacks integrity. These policies and procedures would properly include the review of financial statements of prospective clients, and inquiry directed to such persons as previous auditors, bankers, and legal counsel about the reputation of the prospective client. Also, clients should be accepted only if the necessary expertise and staff personnel are available to appropriately handle the engagement.

*Inspection.*   Procedures for inspection, such as by interoffice review teams of the type discussed above, should be established to ensure that the policies and procedures established to maintain the quality of the firm's auditing practice are being applied effectively. Checklists and evaluation forms will generally be useful in ensuring the completeness and adequacy of such inspections.

*Peer Review.*   Although not stated as an element of quality control standards, the peer reviews required by the SEC Practice Section and Private Companies Practice Section of the AICPA are in a sense an aspect of quality control. Peer reviews are designed to provide evidence to the member firm and to others that the firm has appropriate controls to ensure that its audits are being made in accordance with generally accepted auditing standards.

## Questions/Problems

For multiple-choice questions 19-1 through 19-7, indicate the letter of the single answer that *best* completes the statement or answers the question, and justify the choice that you have made.

**19-1.**   A principal purpose of a letter of representation from management is to
  a. Serve as an introduction to company personnel and an authorization to examine the records.
  b. Discharge the auditor from legal liability for his examination.
  c. Confirm in writing management's approval of limitations on the scope of the audit.
  d. Remind management of its primary responsibility for financial statements.

(Uniform CPA Examination)

**19-2.**   An auditor performs interim work at various times throughout the year. The auditor's subsequent events work should be extended to the date of
  a. A post-dated footnote.
  b. The next scheduled interim visit.
  c. The final billing for audit services rendered.
  d. The auditor's report.

(Uniform CPA Examination)

**19-3.** Which event that occurred after the end of the fiscal year under audit but prior to issuance of the auditor's report would *not* require disclosure in the financial statements?

a. Sale of a bond or capital stock issue.

b. Loss of plant or inventories as a result of fire or flood.

c. A major drop in the quoted market price of the stock of the corporation.

d. Settlement of litigation when the event giving rise to the claim took place after the balance-sheet date.

(Uniform CPA Examination)

**19-4.** The auditor learned of the following situations subsequent to the issuance of his audit report on February 6, 19X6. Each is considered important to users of the financial statements. For which one does the auditor have responsibility for appropriate disclosure of the newly discovered facts?

a. A major lawsuit against the company, which was the basis for a "subject to" auditor's opinion, was settled on unfavorable terms on March 1, 19X6.

b. The client undertook merger negotiations on March 16, 19X6, and concluded a tentative merger agreement on April 1, 19X6.

c. On February 16, 19X6, a fire destroyed the principal manufacturing plant.

d. A conflict of interest situation involving credit officers and a principal company supplier was discovered on March 3, 19X6.

(Uniform CPA Examination)

**19-5.** The first standard of field work recognized that early appointment of the independent auditor has many advantages to the auditor and the client. Which of the following advantages is *least* likely to occur as a result of early appointment of the auditor?

a. The auditor will be able to plan the audit work so that it may be done expeditiously.

b. The auditor will be able to complete the audit work in less time.

c. The auditor will be able to better plan for the observation of the physical inventories.

d. The auditor will be able to perform the examination more efficiently and will be finished at an early date after the year end.

(Uniform CPA Examination)

**19-6.** Engagement letters are widely used in practice for professional engagements of all types. The primary purpose of the engagement letter is to

a. Remind management that the primary responsibility for the financial statements rests with management.

b. Satisfy the requirements of the CPA's liability insurance policy.

c. Provide a starting point for the auditor's preparation of the preliminary audit program.

d. Provide a written record of the agreement with the client as to the services to be provided.

(Uniform CPA Examination)

19-7. The objective of quality control mandates that a public accounting firm should establish policies and procedures for professional development that provide reasonable assurance that all entry-level personnel

a. Prepare working papers that are standardized in form and content.

b. Have the knowledge required to enable them to fulfill responsibilities assigned.

c. Will advance within the organization.

d. Develop specialties in specific areas of public accounting.

(Uniform CPA Examination)

19-8. In a *first audit* of a client that has been in business for several years:

(a) What accounts would be affected by cutoff errors that occurred at the beginning of the year being audited?

(b) For what accounts will the auditor's examination extend to events and entries *prior* to the beginning of the year being audited? Why?

19-9. "By obtaining a representation letter from the client's officers and ascertaining that the financial statements are in agreement with assertions made in the representation letter, an independent auditor is absolved of any liability for incorrect or misleading information in the financial statements, if the information was intentionally misrepresented to the auditor in the representation letter." Do you agree? Explain.

19-10. A CPA has been asked to audit the financial statements of a publicly held company for the first time. All preliminary verbal discussions and inquiries have been completed between the CPA, the company, the predecessor auditor, and all other necessary parties. The CPA is now preparing an engagement letter.

Required:

List the items that should be included in the typical engagement letter in these circumstances and describe the benefits derived from preparing an engagement letter.

(Uniform CPA Examination)

**19-11.** Retail Corporation, a 10-store men's haberdashery chain, has a written company policy which states that company buyers may not have an investment in nor borrow money from an existing or potential supplier. Chan, the independent auditor, learns from a Retail employee that Williams, a buyer, is indebted to Park, a supplier, for a substantial amount of money. Retail's volume of business with Park increased significantly during the year. Chan believes the debtor-creditor relationship of Williams and Park constitutes a conflict of interest that might lead Williams to perpetrate a material fraud.

Required:

(a) Discuss what immediate actions Chan should take upon discovery of the above facts.

(b) Discuss what additional actions Chan should take to be satisfied that Retail has no significant inventory or cost of sales problems as a result of the weakness in internal control posed by the apparent conflict of interest. Identify and discuss in your answer the specific problems, such as overstocking, which Chan should consider.

(Uniform CPA Examination)

**19-12.** The major written understandings between a CPA and his client, in connection with an examination of financial statements, are the engagement (arrangements) letter and the client's representation letter.

Required:

(a) 1. What are the objectives of the engagement (arrangements) letter?
2. Who should prepare and sign the engagement letter?
3. When should the engagement letter be sent?
4. Why should the engagement letter be renewed periodically?

(b) 1. What are the objectives of the client's representation letters?
2. Who should prepare and sign the client's representation letters?
3. When should the client's representation letters be obtained?
4. Why should the client's representation letters be prepared for each examination?

(c) A CPA's responsibilities for providing accounting services sometimes involve his association with unaudited financial statements. Discuss the need in this circumstance for:

1. An engagement letter.
2. Client's representation letters.

(Uniform CPA Examination)

**19-13.** Millard & Hans, CPAs, has been engaged for several years by Happy Toys, Inc., to perform the "usual" examination of its financial statements and provide other accounting services. The understanding was oral, and the fee was based on an annual retainer.

Millard & Hans regularly prepared unaudited quarterly financial statements and examined and reported on Happy Toys' annual financial statements. During the current year's examination Happy Toys decided to go public and requested that Millard & Hans assist in preparing all the necessary financial statements and other financial information and supply the independent auditor's reports as necessary for inclusion in a registration statement to be filed with the Securities and Exchange Commission (SEC). Millard & Hans is independent in accordance with SEC rules and regulations. Millard & Hans complied with Happy Toys' request and subsequently submitted a bill to Happy Toys for $15,000 for the additional work performed in connection with the SEC filing. Happy Toys refused to pay, claiming the additional work was a part of the "usual" engagement and was covered by the annual retainer.

Required:

1. If Millard & Hans sues Happy Toys for its $15,000 fee, who is likely to prevail? Explain.
2. Discuss how Millard & Hans can avoid similar problems in the future with Happy Toys and other clients.

(Uniform CPA Examination)

**19-14.** In connection with his examination of Flowmeter, Inc., for the year ended December 31, 19X3, Hirsch, CPA is aware that certain events and transactions that took place after December 31, 19X3, but before he issues his report dated February 28, 19X4, may affect the company's financial statements.

The following material events or transactions have come to his attention.

1. On January 3, 19X4, Flowmeter, Inc., received a shipment of raw materials from Canada. The materials had been ordered in October, 19X3 and shipped FOB shipping point in November, 19X3.
2. On January 15, 19X4, the company settled and paid a per-

sonal injury claim of a former employee as the result of an accident which occurred in March, 19X3. The company had not previously recorded a liability for the claim.

3. On January 25, 19X4, the company agreed to purchase for cash the outstanding stock of Porter Electrical Co. The acquisition is likely to double the sales volume of Flowmeter, Inc.

4. On February 1, 19X4, a plant owned by Flowmeter, Inc., was damaged by a flood resulting in an uninsured loss of inventory.

5. On February 5, 19X4, Flowmeter, Inc., issued and sold to the general public $2,000,000 in convertible bonds.

Required:

For each of the above events or transactions indicate the audit procedures that should have brought the item to the attention of the auditor, and the form of disclosure in the financial statements, including the reasons for such disclosures.

Arrange your answer in the following format.

| Item No. | Audit Procedures | Required Disclosure and Reasons |
|----------|------------------|---------------------------------|
|          |                  |                                 |

(Uniform CPA Examination)

**19-15.** You have been engaged in an audit of the financial statements of the Hayhurst Company for the year ended March 31. Field work was completed on May 4, and you are now preparing a list of potential adjustments and disclosures for the financial statements. To do this, you must evaluate the following points raised in the course of the audit:

1. A review of accounts payable vouchers for April and May disclosed the following items which were not recorded until April or May and were listed for evaluation as possible unrecorded liabilities:

   (a) Voucher 4-07 to Albion Supply Co. for saleable merchandise; FOB destination, shipped March 22, received March 28; merchandise was included in the physical inventory on March 31—$1,200.

(b) Voucher 4-13 to Skyview Office Management; payment due April 1 for April rental of office space—$450.

(c) Voucher 4-28 to Albion Supply Co. for saleable merchandise; FOB destination, shipped March 26, received April 2; merchandise was not included in physical inventory on March 31—$650.

(d) Voucher 4-81 to Hoosier Equipment Co. for the final payment on a new machine that went into service in late March—$3,450. (Two previous payments of $3,450 each were charged to the Property, Plant and Equipment account in March.)

(e) Voucher 5-01 to Acme Services for janitorial services in the months of March, April and May—$1,800.

(f) Voucher 5-06 to Phelps and Cox, Attorneys at Law, for invoice dated May 2 for retainer fee for March and April at $750 per month—$1500.

2. Cash collections of $144,000 were made during the period April 1 to May 4 for accounts receivable outstanding as of March 31.

3. On April 15, a payment of $17,000 was made to retire currently maturing serial bonds. This amount was recorded on a March accounts payable voucher and included in the balance of accounts payable at March 31. Serial bonds of $20,000 will mature on April 15 of the following year; these have been included among current liabilities for the March 31 balance sheet.

4. Emory Company, a debtor, filed for bankruptcy on April 5. Full provision had been made as of March 31 in estimated uncollectibles for the $2,000 account receivable.

5. As a result of the general economic recovery and a later Easter season, sales of the Company's products in April were $5,500 higher than in April the year before.

6. The Company has been informed by the Second National Bank that Gregory Supply Co. failed to pay a $30,000 note due May 1. Hayhurst had provided an accommodating endorsement for this note. As of May 4, Gregory's financial status was uncertain.

7. The company owed $25,000 on a note payable on demand to the Second National Bank. The note is presented in the March 31 balance sheet as a current liability, but Company officials indicated the note probably would not be called or paid during the succeeding year.

8. The Company began using an accelerated depreciation method for both income tax and financial reporting on all property additions after April 1, which meet Internal Revenue Service requirements. Prior to April 1, only the straight-line method was used.

9. At its April 5 meeting the board of directors authorized:
   (a) The doubling of plant capacity to be financed by issuing bonds and additional common stock. (Contractual arrangements for a $300,000 building program were concluded on April 26, and the Company plans to expend an additional $400,000 on equipment during the next two years.)
   (b) The extension from April 30 to April 30 of the following year of the maturity date of a $10,000 loan by the Company to its president. (The loan has been presented in the balance sheet as a current asset.)
   (c) An extension of ten years of the Company's lease pertaining to its primary manufacturing site from its scheduled expiration four years hence.

10. March raw materials issue slips of $14,000 were misplaced and not found until after the process costing entries for March had been completed. These slips were then included with the April issues. Raw materials inventory records are maintained on a perpetual basis, and no physical inventory was taken at the end of March. Of the goods manufactured in March using these raw materials, 50 percent were still in work in process and finished goods inventory at March 31.

11. A $13,000 check for an interbank transfer of Company funds was listed in the March 31 bank reconciliation as a deposit in transit to one bank and as an outstanding check to another bank. This check cleared both banks during April.

12. A letter from Phelps and Cox, Company attorneys, disclosed the following:
   (a) The Company is defending itself against a patent infringement suit in which a competitor is seeking $1,000,000 in compensatory damages and an injunction to stop Hayhurst's production and sale of the competing product. The attorneys state in writing that Hayhurst will prevail with no loss to the Company. (The $120,000 cost of developing the new product is being written off over a 10-year period.)
   (b) Legal fees of $6,500 accumulated to March 31 by Phelps and Cox for defending the patent infringment suit have not been billed to the Hayhurst Company.

(c)   The Company has been sued for $76,000 by a former executive under an employment contract which has an expiration date of January 1 two years hence. The executive's services were termintated on January 1 of the current year. The Company has offered to settle for $15,000 and expects that this will be accepted by the former executive.

(d)   The Company has been sued for $200,000 in connection with personal injury from a February accident involving one of the Company's trucks. The Company is fully insured.

(e)   An examination of the Company's federal income tax returns by revenue agents is in progress for the past three years. It is believed that all potential deficiencies are fully provided for in the federal income tax liability account.

(f)   At March 31, Phelps and Cox had not been paid the $750 due on the retainer for regular legal services for the month of March.

Unless otherwise noted, no provision has been made for any of the above items in the accounts of the Hayhurst Company to March 31.

Required:

The points discussed above have been listed in abbreviated form on the schedule shown on the next page. Complete this schedule of proposed adjustments and disclosures as follows:

•   If an adjusting journal entry is appropriate, show the effects of this entry in the proper column(s).

•   If footnote disclosure is advisable, place a check mark in the appropriate column. You should indicate this only if you feel a footnote is necessary for adequate disclosure. Footnote disclosure may be used either as supplementay explanation of an adjustment to the financial statements or when no adjustment is required.

•   If the item requires no adjusting journal entry or footnote disclosure, place a check mark in the No Further Consideration column.

•   Formal footnote disclosures and journal entries not required.

(Uniform CPA Examination)

**Table 19-1.** Work Sheet for Problem 19-15

### Hayhurst Company Schedule of Proposed Adjustments and Disclosures March 31
Adjusting Journal Entries—Debit (Credit)

| Item Number | Description | Current Assets | Other Assets | Current Liabilities | Other Liabilities | Stockholders' Equity | Income Statement | Footnote Disclosure | No Further Consideration |
|---|---|---|---|---|---|---|---|---|---|
| 1. | Accounts payable vouchers | | | | | | | | |
| a. | Vo. 4-07 Albion | | | | | | | | |
| b. | Vo. 4-13 Skyview | | | | | | | | |
| c. | Vo. 4-28 Albion | | | | | | | | |
| d. | Vo. 4-81 Hoosier | | | | | | | | |
| e. | Vo. 5-01 Acme | | | | | | | | |
| f. | Vo. 5-06 Phelps and Cox | | | | | | | | |
| 2. | Collections of accounts receivable | | | | | | | | |
| 3. | Current maturities of serial bonds | | | | | | | | |
| 4. | Emory bankruptcy | | | | | | | | |
| 5. | Increase in April sales | | | | | | | | |
| 6. | Gregory note | | | | | | | | |
| 7. | Note payable to Second National Bank | | | | | | | | |
| 8. | Change in depreciation method | | | | | | | | |
| 9. | Actions by board of directors | | | | | | | | |
| a. | Expansion plans | | | | | | | | |
| b. | Loans to company president | | | | | | | | |
| c. | Lease extension | | | | | | | | |
| 10. | March issue slips | | | | | | | | |
| 11. | Interbank transfer | | | | | | | | |
| 12. | Legal letter | | | | | | | | |
| a. | Patent infringement suit | | | | | | | | |
| b. | Legal fee on above suit | | | | | | | | |
| c. | Suit on employment contract | | | | | | | | |
| d. | Personal injury suit | | | | | | | | |
| e. | Revenue agents' examination | | | | | | | | |
| f. | March retainer fee due | | | | | | | | |

# Chapter 20

# AUDIT REPORTING STANDARDS I

The Standard (Short-Form) Report;
Circumstances Necessitating
Report Modification

Our study of audits and auditors began with reference to the central importance of the auditor's report. Now, having considered the audit process through which evidence is gathered to provide the basis for that report, this text returns to an intensive consideration of the channel through which the auditor communicates the findings and conclusions of the audit. Of first importance are the four standards of reporting that must be observed in every reporting situation, as referenced at Professional Standards, AU Sec. 150.02:

1. The report shall state whether the financial statements are presented in accordance with generally accepted accounting principles.

2. The report shall state whether such principles have been consistently observed in the current period in relation to the preceding period.

3. Informative disclosures in the financial statements are to be regarded as reasonably adequate unless otherwise stated in the report.

4. The report shall contain either an expression of opinion regarding the financial statements, taken as a whole, or an assertion to the effect that an opinion cannot be expressed. When an overall opinion cannot be expressed, the reasons therefore should be stated. In all cases where an auditor's name is associated with financial statements, the report should contain a clear-cut indication of the character of the auditor's examination, if any, and the degree of responsibility he is taking.

### Implementation of the Reporting Standards

To fully implement these standards and to avoid misuse or misinterpretation of the auditor's report, each of the following points should be observed in connection with the preparation and delivery of a report on an audit engagement:

1. The report should be dated. The dating establishes the termination of the auditor's responsibility for discovering and disclosing events occurring subsequent to the balance sheet date and will ordinarily represent the date that the field work was completed in the client's office. In the case of registration statements filed with the Securities and Exchange Commission, the responsibility for disclosure extends to the effective date of the registration statements.

2. The report should be addressed to the client. When the client is a corporation, the report may be addressed to the stockholders, to the board of directors, or to both.

3. The report should disclose the exact name of the audited entity, which in the case of a corporation would be the name specified in the corporate charter, including any abbreviations, such as "&," "Co.," "Corp.," or "Inc.," In addition, it is desirable to disclose the legal form of the business entity to which the financial statements pertain. The disclosure can be made parenthetically, subsequent to the name of the entity given in the opening sentence of the report, as for instance:

The Wheat State Produce Co. (A Kansas Corporation)
or
Sigel & Co. (a partnership)

4. The report should identify each statement (balance sheet, income statement, statement of retained earnings, statement of changes in financial position) to which the report pertains and the exact date of the statement or the period covered by the statement.

5. The report should indicate that the auditor's examination was made in accordance with generally accepted auditing standards, or that assertion should be modified if the standards have not been observed; further, an explanatory paragraph should be added to the report.

6. The report should state that in the auditor's opinion the financial statements present fairly the financial position of the entity and the results of operation and changes in financial position in conformity with generally accepted accounting principles applied on a basis consistent with that of the preceding year. Conversely, the opinion must be modified and an explanatory paragraph added to the report if

   a. The auditor is uncertain about any material item in the financial statements or about the financial statements as a whole.
   b. The statements are not in conformity with generally accepted accounting principles.
   c. The accounting principles have not been consistently applied.

7. The financial statements must be entirely self-explanatory through the use of captions, classifications, descriptive information, and footnotes.

8. The informative disclosures in the financial statements, including the notes thereto, must satisfy generally accepted accounting principles and thus include the statement of changes in financial position and a description of all significant accounting policies of the reporting entity. In addition, the following disclosures are required for certain publicly held companies: earnings per share of common stock; segment information about operations in different industries, foreign operations, export sales, and major customers; and supplementary information about quarterly operating results (SEC registrants only) and the effect of changing prices in terms of constant dollars and current costs.

9. Supplementary information that is required to be presented in financial statements by the FASB, the SEC, or another authoritative body and that is not required to be audited must be clearly marked as "unaudited" unless the client elects to have the supplementary information audited. If the required supplementary information is unaudited but is not so marked, the auditor's report must include a statement that the information has not been audited and that no opinion is expressed

on the supplementary information. Such required information that is unaudited must, however, be subjected to certain review procedures as stated in Professional Standards at AU Sec. 553.

10. The financial statements are the representations of management, and consequently the auditor is precluded from making any changes in the statements without the consent of management.

11. Footnotes may not be used to correct errors or misstatements within the basic financial statements (for example, financial position and results of operations would not be fairly presented if inventories were shown at cost, but a footnote disclosed that the market value of the inventories was substantially less than cost).

12. If an unqualified opinion cannot be expressed, an auditor is not permitted to supplement the report with a statement intended to give "negative assurance." Thus, if the auditor had not observed the taking of the physical inventory and was thereby unable to be fully satisfied that inventories were fairly stated, it would not be permissible to add a comment that "nothing came to our attention that would indicate that inventory quantities were not fairly stated." (Note, however, that, it is permissible to give negative assurance in connection with "review" services, as discussed in the next chapter,)

13. The auditor's report preferably should bear the manual signature of the auditor or the auditing firm, but printing the name is acceptable.

14. The statements and the auditor's report should be bound in such a fashion that the statements and report cannot be separated and used individually without mutilating the paper on which they are presented.

15. When financial statements and the auditor's report are printed in another document, such as the company's annual report to its stockholders, the auditor should compare the printer's proof with the statements and the report that the auditor rendered to the client to be certain that the two documents are in complete agreement. Further, comments and schedules in the client's portion of the report should be reviewed for any inconsistencies with the audited financial statements.

If the auditor's examination has been made in accordance with generally accepted auditing standards, and if the statements are in conformity with generally accepted accounting principles, and if the accounting principles have been applied on a basis consistent with the preceding year, then the standard short-form audit report may be rendered, provided that each of the above fifteen points has been observed. On the other hand, if the requirements of auditing standards or accounting principles have not been satisfied in all material respects, then the standard report must be modified to disclose the deviation from those requirements and to convey the effect of such deviation on the opinion that is being expressed. The extent of the discussion of these modifications in the next section and the precision of the language used in the illustrative examples should be taken as an indication of the importance of unerring communication with readers of the auditor's report. The report should state in unmistakable terms exactly what the situation is and the extent of responsibility, if any, that the auditor is accepting for statement presentations through the opinion expressed in the auditor's report.

### Modifications of the Standard Report

As discussed in Professional Standards at AU Sections 504-561, modifications of the standard report will be necessary under any of the following circumstances, with the resulting report generally expressing either a *qualified* opinion, an *adverse* opinion, or a *disclaimer* of opinion.

a. The auditor is not independent.

b. The auditor's opinion is based in part on the opinion of another auditor, and the principal auditor wishes to disclose the shared responsibility. (This would not be considered a qualified opinion.)

c. The scope of the auditor's examination was limited, and as a consequence the auditor was unable to obtain the desired assurance that certain information in the financial statements is fairly stated.

d. There is an uncertainty about the outcome of certain matters that may have a material effect on the financial statements.

e. The financial statements reflect a departure from a generally accepted accounting principle or a principle promulgated by the Financial Accounting Standards Board or other body designated by AICPA Council to establish such principles.

f. The accounting principles followed in the preparation of financial statements have not been applied on a consistent basis.

g. The auditor's report pertains to comparative financial statements.

h. Required supplementary information to the financial statements has been omitted.

### *Auditor Not Independent*

Inasmuch as the auditor's report will typically be used and relied upon by third parties, independence and objectivity are of inestimable importance, as recognized in the second of the general or personal standards and in Rules 101 and 102 of the AICPA Code of Professional Ethics. Given that importance—and the obvious conclusion that an independent opinion cannot be expressed if the auditor is not independent—in the situation where the auditor is not independent, any audit procedures undertaken would not be in accordance with generally accepted auditing standards, and any expression of opinion on the client's financial statements would be meaningless at best and a fraudulent misrepresentation in the worst case. Accordingly, an accountant who is not independent and who is in any way associated with an entity's financial statements must report the lack of independence and disclaim an opinion with respect to those financial statements. The accountant who is not independent may, however, along with the disclaimer assume and indicate responsibility for having provided a compilation service, as discussed in the next chapter.

The report on the financial statements when the accountant is not independent should not state the reason for lack of independence, and no indication should be given of any procedures that have been performed. The report that follows appropriately reflects these matters.

> I am not independent with respect to Blank & Co., and I have not audited the accompanying balance sheet as of December 31, 19__ or the related statements of income and changes in financial position for the year then ended. Accordingly, I do not express an opinion on those financial statements.

## Opinion Based in Part on the Report of Another Auditor

For a variety of reasons an auditor may utilize the work and reports of other independent auditors who have examined the financial statements of one or more subsidiaries, branches, components, or investee companies that are included in the financial statements on which the principal auditor is reporting. If the auditor who is to report on the financial statements (referred to as the principal auditor) practices from a single office, and if part of a client's operations are conducted at a distant location, it might be more economical and equally satisfactory to engage another auditor who is located nearby to examine the operations at that location. Similarly, even though an accounting firm has practice offices throughout the United States, it might be uneconomical to travel abroad to audit a branch or subsidiary located in a different country. As another possibility, the principal auditor's client may have acquired another company with the understanding that the acquired company will be permitted to retain its present auditor.

In any of these situations the accounting firm serving as the principal auditor must decide whether its participation is sufficient to permit reporting on the financial statements of the client entity. That participation would obviously be insufficient, for example, if the firm is engaged by a multibank holding company but most of the operating banks are examined by other auditors. In deciding whether the principal auditor's participation is sufficient, matters to be considered would include the materiality of the portion of the financial statements examined by the principal auditor relative to the portion examined by other auditors, and the extent of the principal auditor's overall knowledge of the financial statements.

*No Reference to the Report of the Other Auditor.*   A decision that it is appropriate to report as the principal auditor necessitates a second decision: whether to make reference in the report to the examination of the other auditor. No reference would ordinarily be made under any of the following circumstances:

a.  The other auditor was engaged by the principal auditor, and the audit work was performed under the principal auditor's guidance and control.
b.  The other auditor serves in the capacity of an associated or correspondent firm—an arrangement that would be preceded by an investigation of the professional standards and competence of the other firm.
c.  The principal auditor has reviewed the work of the other auditor and is satisfied that there is adequate basis for including the accounts that the other auditor has examined in the statements on which the principal auditor is to express an opinion.
d.  The portion of the financial statements examined by the other auditor is not material to the financial statements as a whole.

*Reference Is Made to the Report of the Other Auditor.*   If the above conditions are not present, if it is not possible to be satisfied as to the other auditor's examination, and if the components of the financial statements examined by the other auditor are material in relation to the statements as a whole, then the principal auditor should modify the audit report by making reference to the examination of the other auditor. The modifications would involve adding explanations such as the following to the scope and opinion paragraphs of the report:

> We did not examine the financial statements of Subsidiary Corp., a consolidated subsidiary representing 22 percent of the assets and 26 percent of the revenues of the consolidated financial statements. The statements of Subsidiary Corp. were examined by other auditors (Note—the other auditors should not be named, except with their express permission and provided that their report is included along with the report of the principal auditor) whose report has been furnished to us, and our opinion as expressed below, insofar as it relates to amounts pertaining to Subsidiary Corp., is based solely on the report of the other auditors.
>
> In our opinion, based on our examination and the report of the other auditors, the accompanying financial statements present fairly . . .

Such a modification of the standard audit report to make reference to other auditors should not be interpreted as a qualification of the principal auditor's opinion or an inferior report in any way, but rather as indicating a division of responsibility for performance of the examination. In all cases, of course, sole responsibility rests on the other auditor for the work that was done and the report rendered on that work.

Regardless of whether the reliance on the work of another auditor is disclosed in the principal auditor's report, the principal auditor is required to make inquiries concerning the reputation and independence of the other auditor and to adopt measures to ensure coordination of the work of both auditors and the proper handling of any matters affecting the combining of accounts in the financial statements. An important aspect of the reputation of the other auditor is membership in the American Institute of Certified Public Accountants (or in a comparable foreign professional organization) and the applicable state society of certified public accountants and/or the local chapter of that professional organization.

### Limited Scope of Examination

Because an auditor can express an unqualified opinion only on the basis of an examination conducted in accordance with generally accepted auditing standards that accordingly included all auditing procedures that the auditor considered necessary in the circumstances, any limitation on the scope of the auditor's examination may affect the opinion to be expressed. Limitation of the scope of the examination may result from such matters as

a. The timing of the work, as when the auditor is appointed after the physical inventory has been taken.
b. Inadequacy of the client's accounting system and the internal controls related to that system.
c. Restrictions on the scope of the examination imposed by the client.

Any limitation on the scope of the auditor's examination will in turn limit the confidence that the auditor is able to attain that related financial statement information is fairly stated. The desired confidence, of course, will almost always be less than 100 percent as a result of the economic necessity of relying on a sampling approach rather than complete inspection of all supporting information, and consequently the starting point for considering the effect of a scope limitation will be something less than 100 percent. As we have noted, the actual confidence level sought or attained is strictly a matter of professional judgment and must consider the perceived risk that the information in question may not be fairly stated.

If the achieved confidence on any aspect of the financial statements is less than the auditor has concluded is necessary in the circumstances, it is incumbent upon the auditor to modify the standard report to convey clearly and unequivocally how the scope of the auditor's examination has been affected and the impact of the scope limitation on the opinion being expressed on the financial statements that are involved. Three identifiable modifications of the report are required:

1. The sentence in the scope paragraph that refers to generally accepted auditing standards should be introduced with the qualifying phrase, "Except as explained in the following paragraph, our examination . . ."
2. An explanatory middle paragraph should be added that discloses the scope limitation that has dissuaded the auditor from expressing an unqualified opinion on the financial statement(s) with respect to financial position, results of operations, or changes in financial position.
3. The opinion should be *qualified* to read, "In our opinion, except for (the effect on the financial statements of the scope limitation discussed in the explanatory middle paragraph) . . ." Alternatively a *disclaimer* of opinion may be necessary as discussed below.

*Qualified Opinion When Scope Limited by Circumstances.* Of critical importance with respect to the above modifications when the auditor concludes that the scope limitation is such that an unqualified opinion cannot be rendered is whether the opinion should be qualified, or if instead the auditor should disclaim an opinion on the financial statements. Determining which of these two alternatives is applicable will depend on the materiality and pervasive effect of the statement item in question. For example, in the audit of a charitable organization that receives a substantial amount of unsolicited contributions, the auditor may be unable to determine whether all contributions received have been properly recorded and accounted for, because there is inadequate control over the receipt and recording of the contributions. If the auditor is satisfied that all *recorded* contributions have been properly accounted for and there is *some assurance* that there are no material amounts of unrecorded contributions, the explanatory paragraph should state the circumstances and indicate that the auditor was unable to determine the amount, if any, of contributions received but not accounted for in the reported receipts of the organization. The auditor's opinion would then be qualified by a statement such as, "In our opinion, except for the amount, if any, of contributions received but not accounted for. . ."

*Disclaimer of Opinion When Scope Limited by Circumstances.* In contrast to the limited probable effect of unrecorded contributions, consider a situation in which a client engaged in manufacturing has a December 31 fiscal year but takes a physical inventory in May, when the plant is closed down during the seasonal low point in its manufacturing operations. Assume that the auditor observed the physical inventory taking and made other appropriate tests at May 15, but was unable to be satisfied through additional procedures that the inventory was fairly stated at December 31. Note that if the auditor cannot be satisfied that inventory is properly stated, and assuming that inventory would be a material item for a manufacturing concern, there would also be a question about the following figures that would be affected by inventory: cost of sales, gross margin, net income, income tax expense and liability, current assets, total assets, retained earnings, and total equities. In recognition of so pervasive an effect of a possible inventory misstatement, it would not be appropriate merely to qualify the auditor's opinion with respect to inventory, but rather, the auditor should disclaim any responsibility for the financial statements as a whole. Thus, the scope paragraph should state a qualification with respect to generally accepted auditing standards and the inability to apply all auditing procedures considered necessary, the explanatory paragraph should identify the inventory amount and explain the audit deficiency, and the disclaimer of opinion should then appear somewhat as follows:

> Since, as noted in the preceding paragraph, the company did not take a physical inventory at December 31 and we were unable to apply adequate alternative procedures, the scope of our examination was not adequate to permit us to express, and we do not express, an opinion on the financial statements referred to above.

A similar consequence would result if the client's records and/or internal control were so inadequate that little reliance could be placed on the information in the records and if it was not feasible to compensate for these deficiencies by expanding the substantive auditing procedures that were applied.

*Restrictions on Scope Imposed by Client.* When a material amount on the financial statements is involved and the scope of the auditor's examination is significantly limited as a result of a restriction imposed by the client, the auditor generally should issue a disclaimer of opinion on the financial statements. Possible examples of restrictions of such consequence would include instructions by the client that receivables not be confirmed or that physical inventory taking not be observed; the client's refusal to request that the client's attorney confirm information about legal claims that have been or may be asserted against the client; or the client's denying the auditor access to minutes of board of directors' meetings. Professional Standards at AU Sec. 509.12 state that when client restrictions significantly limit the scope of an audit, the auditor generally should disclaim an opinion on the financial statements. In such cases not only would there be insufficient information to support an unqualified or qualified opinion, but the client's intervention raises the possibility that the client may be seeking to prevent the auditor from obtaining information that would raise a question about the fairness of the financial statements.

### Uncertainties

The inability to develop adequate confidence that financial statements present fairly a client's financial position or results of operations, as a result of a limited scope of examination, is one form of uncertainty with which the auditor must cope, with such uncertainty possibly leading to a qualified opinion or a disclaimer of opinion. Uncertainty and similar outcomes can also result when the auditor is unable to determine with sufficient confidence the reasonableness of any of the material estimates that are inherent in the preparation of periodic financial statements. For example, companies that own and lease computer equipment are subject to such uncertainties whenever a new generation of computers or other major advance in hardware design is imminent. Those developments typically result in reduced cycle execution times, lower cost per executed instruction, and increased storage capacity—factors that can have a marked economic obsolescence effect on existing equipment. That effect may be quite indeterminate, however, depending on the actual cost reductions that are achievable with the new equipment, the availability and order lead times of the new equipment, reprogramming costs that may be necessary, the unwillingness of present computer lessees to make a change, and other variables that may be equally difficult to assess.

*Uncertainties Involving Specific Matters.*   The computer leasing illustration is an example of an uncertainty about a specific matter in which the possible effects on the financial statements can be isolated and assessed accordingly. Other examples would include the outcome of an assessment of additional income taxes that is being appealed, and the amount that may become collectible or payable in relation to litigation that is in progress. Depending on the materiality and the likelihood of the outcome of such uncertainties, the auditor may conclude that it would be appropriate to issue an unqualified opinion, or instead that a qualified opinion or a disclaimer of opinion would be more appropriate. If the decision is that the auditor's opinion should be qualified, the client should disclose the uncertainty in a note to the financial statements, an explanatory paragraph should be added to the auditor's report describing the uncertainty as completely as possible and referring to the note to the financial statements, and the opinion qualification should be in the form of a "subject to" modification, as for example:

> In our opinion, subject to the effects, if any, on the financial statements of any changes in the economic life of the computer equipment owned for leasing purposes as discussed in the preceding paragraph, the financial statements referred to above present fairly . . .

In the discussion of uncertainties at AU Sec 509.25 the Auditing Standards Board states that appropriate explanation of uncertainties and qualification of the auditor's opinion should adequately inform financial statement users of the presence of an uncertainty and its possible effects. Hence, in the opinion of the Board, the materiality of an uncertainty should not necessitate moving from a qualified opinion to a disclaimer of opinion. Nevertheless, by footnote the Board points out that the position it has taken is not intended to preclude an auditor from disclaiming an opinion if the auditor concludes that a disclaimer is more appropriate.

Two other aspects of the uncertainty of a specific matter require comment. If resolution of an uncertainty is unlikely to materially affect the financial statements, it should not be necessary to modify the auditor's opinion, provided that the client has disclosed the uncertainty in a note to the financial statements if the circumstances so require. The second aspect of the problem is that if the auditor disagrees with management's determination of the likely effects of an uncertainty, the qualification expressed must not be in terms of the uncertainty, but rather should be a qualified or adverse opinion on the basis of a departure from generally accepted accounting principles, as discussed in a subsequent section.

*Multiple Uncertainties and Indeterminate Impact.* When an entity has experienced recurring operating losses and attendant cash flow problems, including possible failure to comply with terms of a loan agreement, continued operation and existence of the entity may be called into question. In those instances an explanatory paragraph and a "subject to" opinion qualification are required as a minimum, with the qualification pertaining to the possible effect on the financial statements should the entity become unable to continue as a going concern. A typical problematical situation would be where there have been recurring losses and the business is in dire need of additional financing, but obtaining the financing is questionable because of the financial crisis brought about by the past losses.

Of course, if it is relatively certain that the needed financing will *not* be obtainable, the going concern assumption of generally accepted accounting principles would be inapplicable, and the only financial statement that would be meaningful would have to be a statement of affairs prepared on a liquidation basis. If the client insists on retaining the statements on a going concern basis under those circumstances, the auditor's response and recourse would have to be the issuance of an adverse opinion. But what if the probable outcome is not that clear? As a minimum, if information about the situation is adequately disclosed in a note to the financial statements, the appropriate response would involve an explanatory paragraph and a "subject to" opinion. On the other hand, given the consequent effect on the financial statements should the business fail, it might seem that a disclaimer of opinion would be more appropriate.

But it is important to recognize the consequences of disclaiming an opinion even though those consequences ought not be permitted to influence the auditor's decision to qualify or to disclaim an opinion. The problem is that a disclaimer for the reasons stated is likely to become a self-fulfilling prophecy, for additional credit or capital are not likely to be forthcoming if the auditor elects the disclaimer alternative. However, the qualified opinion would perhaps be only slightly less damaging to the concern's future prospects.

At issue in such cases is the matter of what is sometimes referred to as information risk versus business risk for the person using the financial statements. Information risk would seem to be appropriately minimized if the concern's financial problem is fully disclosed in the notes to the financial statements, for the uncertainty of the accounting measures and the reliability of the resulting figures should be apparent through analysis of the concern's financial position, coupled with disclosure of the uncertainty of obtaining additional financing. At that point the sole remaining question is the business risk of the concern's future prospects, and that would not appear to be a problem that calls for the auditor's evaluation. Consequently, it has been argued that no modification of the auditor's report should be necessary under those circumstances, but that if the auditor nevertheless believes that it is desirable to make reference to the situation in the auditor's report, a qualified opinion should be adequate to dissipate any remaining information risk. The stronger, more unfavorable disclaimer of opinion in those circumstances would seem to represent an incursion into the matter of assessing business risk—a matter that is essentially outside the auditor's province.

SAS No. 34, The Auditor's Considerations When a Question Arises about an Entity's Continued Existence (Professional Standards Sec. 340), discusses these problems more fully and points out that generally accepted auditing standards do not require that the auditor search for evidential matter relating to the entity's continued existence. In the absence of information to the contrary, an entity's continuation is usually assumed in financial accounting, but the auditor should be alert to any indication that the entity's continued existence may be in question. If such indications become apparent, the auditor should consider the underlying conditions that brought about the question of continued existence and any mitigating factors pertaining to the situation, including management plans to cope with the situation.

### Departure from Generally Accepted Accounting Principles

If financial statements are materially affected by a departure from generally accepted accounting principles, the auditor's opinion should be qualified on that account, or if the effect on the financial statements is *very material*, an *adverse* opinion should be expressed. A qualified opinion states that the financial statements are presented in conformity with generally accepted accounting principles *except for* the reason stated, whereas an adverse opinion states that the financial statements are *not presented* in conformity with generally accepted accounting principles for the reason stated. The question of the materiality of a departure in determining whether an unqualified, qualified, or adverse opinion is appropriate involves both quantitative considerations pertaining to the particular amounts affected and the pervasiveness of the effect on other items in the financial statements. These points may be illustrated using a large retail chain as the basis for an example. Assume that 100 stores and four warehouse distribution centers are involved and that the company owns all of the stores and three of the four distribution centers. The lease for the fourth distribution center is accounted for as an operating lease, whereas the auditor has determined that it should be accounted for as a capital lease. It would appear that changing the concern's accounting to a proper basis for the capital lease would have only a nominal effect on the balance sheet and income statement, so that an unqualified opinion would appear to be appropriate, even though the client declined to change the method of accounting for the lease.

*Qualified Opinion.* By contrast, however, if all four of the distribution centers were leased on terms that required treatment as capital leases, the effect on both the balance sheet and the income statement would probably be sufficiently material to necessitate a qualified opinion and the inclusion of an explanatory paragraph. The added paragraph should indicate the effect on assets, liabilities, and retained earnings of capitalizing the leases, and also the effect of the change on net income and earnings per share. The opinion paragraph should then be changed to read:

> In our opinion, except for the effects of not capitalizing lease obligations, as discussed in the preceding paragraph, the accompanying financial statements present fairly. . .

The qualitative aspects of materiality would be involved if there is inadequate disclosure of loans to officers or an illegal act has been committed.

*Adverse Opinion.* If we reverse the situation pertaining to the stores and distribution centers, so that it is the retail stores that are leased rather than the distribution centers, it would appear likely that the effect on the assets, liabilities, and retained earnings in the balance sheet and the replacement of lease expense with interest and depreciation expense in the income statement would be so significant and pervasive that only an adverse opinion would be appropriate. In that event an explanatory paragraph similar to the one described above for the qualified opinion would be used. The opinion paragraph might then read:

> In our opinion, because of the effect of not capitalizing lease obligations, as discussed in the preceding paragraph, the accompanying financial state-

ments do not present fairly, in conformity with generally accepted accounting principles, the financial position of Blank Stores as of January 31, 19X5 or the results of its operations and changes in its financial position for the year then ended.

Professional Standards at AU Sec. 509.44 point out that the adverse opinion should contain no reference to consistency because a reference to consistency could be misinterpreted to imply that generally accepted accounting principles had been applied, thereby tending to negate the adverse opinion.

*Inadequate Disclosure.* As stated in the listing of reporting requirements at the beginning of this chapter, informative disclosures in the financial statements must be adequate to convey all significant financial and operating information pertaining to the reporting entity. Professional Standards at AU Sec. 509.17 require that if a client declines to disclose essential matters in the financial statements, the auditor should, if practicable, provide the information in the audit report and express a qualified or adverse opinion on the financial statements because of the departure from the disclosure aspect of generally accepted accounting principles. The reference to "if practicable" is taken to mean that the information is reasonably obtainable from the client's accounts and records, but that the information need not be developed by the auditor. Specific exemption from the requirement to provide the absent information that necessitated the qualified or adverse opinion is granted by Professional Standards with respect to the omission of the statement of changes in financial position and segment information.

*Departure from a Promulgated Accounting Principle.* As previously discussed, Rule 203 of the AICPA Code of Professional Ethics states that an AICPA member shall not express an opinion that financial statements are in conformity with generally accepted accounting principles if the statements contain a material departure from an accounting principle promulgated by an officially recognized body unless it can be demonstrated that because of unusual circumstances the financial statements would otherwise have been misleading. In such a case an explanatory middle paragraph of the auditor's report must describe the departure, its approximate effect, and the reasons why compliance with the principle would result in the financial statements being misleading. No modification of the opinion paragraph would then be necessary.

*Omission or Unacceptable Presentation of Required Supplementary Information.* The Financial Accounting Standards Board and the SEC have required that certain supplementary information be presented outside the basic financial statements because the information is considered to be an essential part of financial reporting. Information on the effect of changing prices, the amount of oil and gas reserves, and quarterly operating results are examples of such information. A later section discusses reporting standards for such information, but for the moment we consider only the effect on the auditor's report if such required information is omitted or if the measurement or presentation of the information is materially at variance from guidelines prescribed by the FASB. The required exception reporting in such circumstances should be by the addition of a middle paragraph of the report, such as is illustrated below. The first example deals with an omission, the second with a material variance from FASB guidelines. No modification of the opinion paragraph of the auditor's report would be necessary, because the supplementary information is not a required part of the basic financial statements.

> The company has not presented information on the effect of changing prices that has been determined by the Financial Accounting Standards Board to be necessary information to be provided as a supplement to the basic financial statements.

> The information on the effect of changing prices presented on page XX is required by the Financial Accounting Standards Board to be presented as supplementary information. The information is not a required part of the basic financial statements and we did not audit the information nor do we express an opinion on the information. We have, however, applied certain limited procedures to the information, principally inquiries of management concerning the methods of measurement and presentation of the supplementary information. As a result of these limited procedures, we have concluded that the information on changing prices is not in conformity with guidelines established by the Financial Accounting Standards Board because replacement cost figures have not been reduced to the lower of the realizable values for the assets involved.

### Accounting Principles Not Consistently Applied

When a client changes the application of an accounting principle, the effect of the changes must be included in a note to the financial statements, and the auditor's opinion must be qualified because accounting principles have not been applied on a consistent basis. If the change is to an accounting principle that is not generally accepted, the auditor must, of course, render a qualified opinion on the basis that the principle is not generally accepted. Thus, the absence of a qualification on conformity with generally accepted accounting principles can be taken to indicate that the auditor concurs with the change as being to an acceptable accounting principle, but AU Sec. 546.01 states that in order to be more informative, the auditor should make such concurrence explicit by adding the phrase, "with which we concur" when qualifying the opinion for a change from one acceptable accounting principle to another acceptable principle. Further with respect to changes, Accounting Series Release No. 177 of the SEC requires a letter from the registrant's independent accountant stating whether a change is to a preferable principle. Preferability is addressed by the FASB in Statement No. 32, which designates the accounting principles contained in AICPA accounting and auditing guides as preferable in deciding whether an accounting change is appropriate, until such time as the accounting and audit guides have been reviewed by the FASB and reissued as financial accounting and reporting standards.

Provided that a change of accounting principle is to a method that is generally accepted, the fact that the principle from which the change was made was not generally accepted would require no further modification of the auditor's opinion. It is important to note, however, that the consistency qualification does not require an explanatory middle paragraph if the auditor concurs with the change and if the effect of the change is properly disclosed in a note to the financial statements.

Appropriate reporting of an opinion qualified on the basis of consistency would be as follows:

> . . . in conformity with generally accepted accounting principles which, except for the change, with which we concur, in the method of computing depreciation as described in Note X to the financial statements, have been applied on a basis consistent with that of the preceding year.

*Initial Examination.*  In the first year in which the financial statements are examined for an entity that was in existence for the prior year, the independent auditor should undertake such procedures as are practicable and reasonable to gain assurance that the accounting principles employed are consistent for the current and the preceding year. When the auditor has obtained appropriate assurance on the matter of consistency, no modification of the audit report is necessary. In the audit of the financial statements for the first year of an entity's existence, reference to consistency would be meaningless, and hence the opinion should omit the phrase related to consistency.

### Reports on Comparative Financial Statements

When comparative statements are presented and the auditor has examined the statements for both years, the scope paragraph of the report should identify the statements for both years and indicate that the statements for both years have been examined. The opinion paragraph should likewise refer to the statements for both years and the reference to consistency should be modified as follows:

In our opinion, the financial statements referred to above present fairly the financial position of X Corp. as of December 31, 19X1 and December 31, 19X2, and the results of operations and changes in financial position for the years then ended, in conformity with generally accepted accounting principles applied on a consistent basis.

A report in this form is considered to be an updating of the previously issued report, and any information of which the auditor becomes aware that would affect the previous financial statements must be considered with reference to the updated report.

*Prior Year Statements Unaudited.* If comparative financial statements are presented and the statements for the prior year were unaudited, they should be clearly marked as "unaudited," and a separate paragraph added to the report to indicate the responsibility (if any) assumed for the financial statements of the prior period. If no services were provided with reference to those statements, the separate paragraph could read:

The accompanying balance sheet for December 31, 19X1 and the related statements of operations and changes in financial position for the year then ended were not audited by us and accordingly we do not express an opinion on them.

If the statements being reported on are those of a nonpublic entity and the prior year statements were compiled or reviewed by the auditor (see discussion of compilation and review services in the following chapter), the separate paragraph should indicate the services that were performed and what responsibility consequently has been assumed for those statements. If the prior year statements were reviewed, the following paragraph would be appropriate:

The 19X1 financial statements were reviewed by us, and our report thereon dated February 20, 19X2 stated that we were not aware of any material modifications that should be made to those statements for them to be in conformity with generally accepted accounting principles. Such a review is substantially less in scope than an audit and does not provide a basis for the expression of an opinion on the financial statements taken as a whole.

If the prior year statements were compiled, the following paragraph could be used:

The 19X1 financial statements were compiled by us and our report dated February 20, 19X2 stated that we did not audit or review those statements and accordingly we do not express an opinion on them.

*Prior Year Statements Audited by a Predecessor Auditor.* If the predecessor auditor's report is not to be presented in conjunction with the audited statements from the successor auditor's report, the successor auditor's report should be modified by adding a sentence such as the following at the end of the scope paragraph:

> The financial statements of Blank Corp. for the year ended December 31, 19X1 were examined by other auditors whose report dated February 20, 19X2 expressed an unqualified opinion on those statements.

The opinion paragraph would then refer only to the statements for 19X2 audited by the successor auditor. The result is essentially the same as the shared responsibility discussed earlier in this chapter.

### Other Information in Documents Containing Audited Financial Statements

The discussion in this section is subdivided according to whether the document that is involved is prepared by the auditor—in other words, the auditor's report—or is a client-prepared document, such as a printed annual report that contains audited financial statements.

*Auditor-Prepared Documents.*   The auditor's standard report in an auditor-prepared document covers the basic financial statements and the description of accounting policies, the notes to the financial statements, and any schedules or explanatory material identified as being part of the basic financial statements. The document submitted to the client may also include, however, certain supplementary information required by the FASB or the SEC, and also supplementary information supplied at the auditor's or the client's option and intended to assist in the interpretation of the basic financial statements by providing additional details, as discussed in the following sections.

*Supplementary Information Required by FASB or SEC Pronouncements.* Supplementary information required by the FASB is considered to be an essential part of financial reporting for certain entities, and the FASB has established guidelines for the measurement and presentation of the information. Given the FASB position, the auditor is required by Professional Standards AU Sec. 553.06-.07 to apply certain limited procedures to such information and to report any omission or deficiencies regarding such information. The following procedures have been specified as required:

1.   Make inquiries of management concerning whether the information is measured and presented within the FASB guidelines and whether the measurement and presentation have been changed relative to the prior period. Request information about significant assumptions or interpretations underlying the measurement or presentation.

2.   Compare the information for consistency with the responses of management to the above inquiries, the audited financial statements, and other knowledge obtained in the course of the examination.

3.   Consider including representations concerning the above information provided by management in the specific written representations obtained from management.

Because supplementary information is not audited, and if it is appropriately labeled as unaudited, the auditor is not required to expand the report on the audited financial statements to refer to the supplementary information or to the limited procedures that were applied. The report must be expanded, however, to point out the problem if the required supplementary information is omitted or if the information departs materially from the FASB measurement and presentation guidelines, or if the auditor has been unable to complete the prescribed procedures. Similar considerations apply to SEC-required information such as quarterly data, which now can be reported outside the financial statements.

*Supplementary Information Not Required by the FASB.*   Supplementary information not required by the FASB will generally be submitted in what is referred to as a long-form report, one of the topics covered in the following chapter on reporting. There are certain criteria that must be satisfied regarding such optional supplementary information:

1.   The basic financial statements and related matter identified as being part of the basic statements must be entirely self-sufficient. Any optional supplementary data that might support a contention that the basic financial statements are misleading because of inadequate disclosure of material facts must be presented as a part of the basic financial statements. Such information must therefore be made part of the statements and would thereby be covered by the auditor's standard report.
2.   The supplementary data must not be susceptible to a contention that they constitute exceptions or reservations to the audited financial statements—in other words, the information must be strictly explanatory and supplementary.
3.   Nothing in the supplementary data should support a contention that it constitutes a factual representation with respect to financial statement information.

To conform to the fourth standard of reporting, the following guidelines should be followed (see AU Sec. 551) in reporting on supplementary information not required by the FASB that accompanies the basic financial statements:

1.   The report should state that the examination was made in order to form an opinion on the basic financial statements as a whole.
2.   The accompanying information should be identified by title or page numbers in the report.

3. It should be stated that the accompanying information is presented for purposes of additional analysis and is not a required part of the basic financial statements.
4. The report should include either
   a. An opinion that the accompanying information is fairly stated in all material respects in relation to the basic financial statements taken as a whole, or
   b. A disclaimer of opinion if the information has not been subjected to the auditing procedures applied in the examination of basic financial statements.

Following is an example of an appropriate middle paragraph to be added to the standard report expressing a positive opinion.

Our examination was made for the purpose of forming an opinion on the basic financial statements taken as a whole. The information on pages __ through __ is presented for the purpose of additional analysis and is not a required part of the financial statements. The information has been subjected to the auditing procedures applied in the examination of the basic financial statements and, in our opinion, is fairly stated in all material respects in relation to the basic financial statements taken as a whole.

*Client-Prepared Documents.*   Audited financial statements and the auditor's report may appear in a document such as a printed annual report to stockholders or to contributors to a charitable organization. An auditor's responsibility does not extend beyond the financial information identified in the auditor's report, and consequently there is no obligation to perform any procedures to corroborate other information contained in the client-prepared document. The auditor should, however, read the other information and consider whether the information or the manner of its presentation is materially inconsistent with information appearing in the financial statements. If there is a material inconsistency, the auditor should first consider whether the financial statements or the auditor's report require revision. If no revision of either of these is required, then the auditor should request that the client revise the other information. If the client declines to revise the other information appropriately, the auditor should add an explanatory paragraph to the auditor's report describing the inconsistency, or if more appropriate, withdraw from the engagement and prohibit use of the auditor's report.

## Questions/Problems

For multiple-choice questions 20-1 through 20-14, indicate the letter of the single answer that *best* completes the statement or answers the question and justify the choice that you have made.

**20-1.** An opinion as to the "fairness" of financial statement presentation in accordance with generally accepted accounting principles is based on several judgements made by the auditor. One such judgement is whether the accounting principles used

    a. Have general acceptance.
    b. Are promulgated by the AICPA Auditing Standards Board.
    c. Are the most conservative of those available for use.
    d. Emphasize the legal form of transactions.

(Uniform CPA Examination)

**20-2.** A limitation on the scope of the auditor's examination sufficient to preclude an unqualified opinion will always result when management

    a. Engages an auditor after the year-end physical inventory count.
    b. Refuses to furnish a representation letter.
    c. Knows that direct confirmation of accounts receivable with debtors is not feasible.
    d. Engages an auditor to examine only the balance sheet.

(Uniform CPA Examination)

**20-3.** If the auditor believes that required disclosures of a significant nature are omitted from the financial statements under examination, the auditor should decide between issuing

    a. A qualified opinion or an adverse opinion.
    b. A disclaimer of opinion or a qualified opinion.
    c. An adverse opinion or a disclaimer opinion.
    d. An unqualified opinion or a qualified opinion.

(Uniform CPA Examination)

**20-4.** A CPA who is not independent and is associated with financial statements should disclaim an opinion with respect to those financial statements. The disclaimer should

    a. Clearly state the specific reasons for lack of independence.
    b. Not mention any reason for the disclaimer other than that the CPA was unable to conduct the examination in accordance with generally accepted auditing standards.
    c. Not describe the reason for lack of independence but should state specifically that the CPA is not independent.
    d. Include a middle paragraph clearly describing the CPA's association with the client and explaining why the CPA was unable to gather sufficient competent evidential matter to warrant the expression of an opinion.

(Uniform CPA Examination)

**20-5.** In a first audit of a new company the auditor's report will

    a. Remain silent with respect to consistency.

    b. State that the accounting principles have been applied on a consistent basis.

    c. State that accounting principles have been applied consistently during the period.

    d. State that the consistency standard does not apply because the current year is the first year of audit.

                         (Uniform CPA Examination)

**20-6.** Which of the following four events may be expected to result in a consistency exception in the auditor's report?

    a. The declining balance method of depreciation was adopted for newly acquired assets.

    b. A revision was made in the service lives and salvage values of depreciable assets.

    c. A mathematical error in computing the year-end LIFO inventory was corrected.

    d. The provision for bad debts increased considerably over the previous year.

                         (Uniform CPA Examination)

**20-7.** When financial statements are prepared on the basis of a going concern and the auditor believes that the client may not continue as a going concern, the auditor should issue

    a. A "subject to" opinion.

    b. An unqualified opinion with an explanatory middle paragraph.

    c. An "except for" opinion.

    d. An adverse opinion.

                         (Uniform CPA Examination)

**20-8.** A company issues audited financial statements under circumstances which require the presentation of a statement of changes in financial position. If the company refuses to present a statement of changes in financial position, the independent auditor should

    a. Disclaim an opinion.

    b. Prepare a statement of changes in financial position and note in a middle paragraph of the report that this statement is auditor-prepared.

    c. Prepare a statement of changes in financial position and disclose in a footnote that this statement is auditor-prepared.

    d. Qualify his opinion with an "except for" qualification and a description of the omission in a middle paragraph of the report.

**20-9.** When an adverse opinion is expressed, the opinion paragraph should include a direct reference to

a. A footnote to the financial statements which discusses the basis for the opinion.

b. The scope paragraph which discusses the basis for the opinion rendered.

c. A separate paragraph which discusses the basis for the opinion rendered.

d. The consistency or lack of consistency in the application of generally accepted accounting principles.

(Uniform CPA Examination)

**20-10.** It is less likely that a disclaimer of opinion would be issued when the auditor has reservations arising from

a. Inability to apply necessary auditing procedures. *disclaimer*

b. Uncertainties.

c. Inadequate internal control. *Limitation of scope —disclaimer*

d. Lack of independence. *disclaimer*

(Uniform CPA Examination)

**20-11.** Stone was asked to perform the first audit of a wholesale business that does not maintain perpetual inventory records. Stone has observed the current inventory but has not observed the physical inventory at the previous year-end date and concludes that the opening inventory balance, which is not auditable, is a material factor in the determination of cost of goods sold for the current year. Stone will probably

a. Decline the engagement.

b. Express an unqualified opinion on the balance sheet and income statement except for inventory.

c. Express an unqualified opinion on the balance sheet and disclaim an opinion on the income statement.

d. Disclaim an opinion on the balance sheet and income statement.

(Uniform CPA Examination)

**20-12.** Jerome has completed an examination of the financial statements of Bold, Inc. Last year's financial statements were examined by Smith, CPA. Since last year's financial statements will be presented for comparative purposes without Smith's report, Jerome's report should

a. State that the prior year's financial statements were examined by another auditor.
b. State that the prior year's financial statements were examined by Smith.
c. Not refer to the prior year's examination.
d. Refer to Smith's report only if the opinion was other than unqualified.

(Uniform CPA Examination)

**20-13.** The auditor's best course of action with respect to "other financial information" included in an annual report containing the auditor's report is to

a. Indicate in the auditor's report, that the "other financial information" is accurate by performing a limited review.
b. Consider whether the "other financial information" is accurate by performing a limited review.
c. Obtain written representations from management as to the material accuracy of the "other financial information."
d. Read and consider the manner of presentation of the "other financial information."

(Uniform CPA Examination)

**20-14.** Under which of the following circumstances may audited financial statements contain a note disclosing a subsequent event that is labeled unaudited?

a. When the subsequent event does not require adjustment of the financial statements.
b. When the event occurs after completion of fieldwork and before issuance of the auditor's report.
c. When audit procedures with respect to the subsequent event were not performed by the auditor.
d. When the event occurs between the date of the auditor's original report and the date of the reissuance of the report.

(Uniform CPA Examination)

**20-15.** How would the standard audit report be affected if the client:

(a) Switched from straight line to accelerated depreciation for tax purposes and provided for income tax expense on the basis of the amount of taxes payable?
(b) Switched from straight line to accelerated depreciation for tax purposes and applied income tax allocation?
(c) Switched from straight line to accelerated depreciation for both book and tax purposes?

**20-16.** Public utilities, such as gas or electric companies, ordinarily do not accrue the revenue arising from services supplied to customers but not yet billed to them.

(a) Does this situation warrant any modification of the short-form audit report? Explain.

(b) Should there be any modification of the short-form report if a utility following the above plan switched from monthly to bimonthly billing? Why?

**20-17.** You are engaged in the examination of the financial statements of Rapid, Inc. and its recently acquired subsidiary, Slow Corporation. In acquiring Slow Corporation during 19X1, Rapid, Inc. exchanged a large number of its shares of common stock for 90 percent of the outstanding common stock of Slow Corporation in a transaction that was accounted for as pooling of interests. Rapid, Inc. is now preparing the annual report to shareholders and proposes to include in the report combined financial statements for the year ended December 31, 19X1, with a footnote describing its exchange of stock for that of Slow Corporation. Rapid, Inc. also proposes to include in its report the financial statements of the previous year as they appeared in Rapid, Inc.'s annual report along with a 5-year financial summary from Rapid's prior annual reports, all of which had been accompanied by your unqualified auditor's opinion.

Required:

(a) Discuss the objectives or purposes of the standard of reporting that requires the auditor's report to state whether generally accepted accounting principles have been consistently observed over the past two periods.

(b) Describe the treatment in the auditor's report of interperiod changes having a material effect on the financial statements arising from:
1. A change to an alternative generally accepted accounting principle.
2. Changed conditions which necessitate accounting changes but which do not involve changes in the accounting principles employed.
3. Changed conditions unrelated to accounting.

(c) 1. Would the financial reporting treatment proposed by Rapid, Inc. for the 19X1 annual report be on a consistent basis? Discuss.
2. Describe the auditor's report which should accompany the financial statements as proposed by Rapid, Inc. for inclusion in the annual report.

(Uniform CPA Examination)

**20-18.** Upon completion of all field work on September 23, 19X1, the following "short-form" report was rendered by Timothy Ross to the directors of The Rancho Corporation.

> To the Directors of
> The Rancho Corporation:
>
> We have examined the balance sheet and the related statement of income and retained earnings of The Rancho Corporation as of July 31, 19X1. In accordance with your instructions, a complete audit was conducted.
>
> In many respects, this was an unusual year for The Rancho Corporation. The weakening of the economy in the early part of the year and the strike of plant employees in the summer of 19X1 led to a decline in sales and net income. After making several tests of sales records, nothing came to our attention that would indicate that sales have not been properly recorded.
>
> In our opinion, with the explanation given above, and with the exception of some minor errors that are considered immaterial, the aforementioned financial statements present fairly the financial position of the Rancho Corporation at July 31, 19X1, and the results of its operations for the year then ended, in conformity with pronouncements of the Accounting Principles Board and the Financial Accounting Standards Board applied consistently throughout the period.
>
> Timothy Ross, CPA
> September 23, 19X1

Required:

List and explain deficiencies and omissions in the auditor's report. The type of opinion (unqualified, qualified, adverse, or disclaimer) is of no consequence and need not be discussed. Organize your answer sheet by paragraph (scope, explanatory, and opinion) of the auditor's report.

(Uniform CPA Examination)

**20-19.** The CPA firm of Martinson, Brinks & Sutherland, a partnership, was the auditor for Masco Corporation, a medium-sized wholesaler. Masco leased warehouse facilities and sought financing for leasehold improvements to these facilities. Masco assured its bank that the leasehold improvements would result in a more efficient and profitable operation. Based on these assurances, the bank granted Masco a line of credit.

The loan agreement required annual audited financial statements. Masco submitted its 19X1 audited financial statements to the bank which showed an operating profit of $75,000, leasehold improvements of $250,000, and net worth of $350,000. In reliance thereon, the bank loaned Masco $200,000. The audit report that accompanied the financial statements disclaimed an opinion because the cost of the leasehold improvements could not be determined from the company's records. The part of the audit report dealing with leasehold improvements reads as follows:

Additions to fixed assets in 19X1 were found to include principally warehouse improvements. Practically all of this work was done by company employees and the cost of materials and overhead were paid by Masco. Unfortunately, fully complete detailed cost records were not kept of these leasehold improvements and no exact determination could be made as to the actual cost of said improvements. The total amount capitalized is set forth in note 4.

In late 19X2 Masco went out of business, at which time it was learned that the claimed leasehold improvements were totally fictitious. The labor expenses charged as leasehold improvements proved to be operating expenses. No item of building material cost had been recorded. No independent investigation of the existence of the leasehold improvements was made by the auditors.

If the $250,000 had not been capitalized, the income statement would have reflected a substantial loss from operations and the net worth would have been correspondingly decreased.

The bank has sustained a loss on its loan to Masco of $200,000 and now seeks to recover damages from the CPA firm, alleging that the accountants negligently audited the financial statements.

Required:

Answer the following, setting forth reasons for any conclusions stated.

(a) Will the disclaimer of opinion absolve the CPA firm from liability?

(b) Are the individual partners of Martinson, Brinks & Sutherland, who did not take part in the audit, liable?

(c) Briefly discuss the development of the common law regarding the liability of CPAs to third parties.

(Uniform CPA Examination)

**20-20.** You are completing an examination of the financial statements of the Hilty Manufacturing Corporation for the year ended February 28, 19X1. Hilty's financial statements have not been examined previously. The controller of Hilty has given you the following draft of proposed footnotes to the financial statements:

The Hilty Manufacturing Corporation
NOTES TO FINANCIAL STATEMENTS
Year Ended February 28, 19X1

Note 1.  Because we were not engaged as auditors until after February 28, 19X0, we were unable to observe the taking of the beginning physical inventory. We satisfied ourselves as to the balance of physical inventory at February 28, 19X0, by alternative procedures.

Note 2.  With the approval of the Commissioner of Internal Revenue, the Company changed its method of accounting for inventories from the first-in, first-out method to the last-in, first-out method on March 1, 19X0. In the opinion of the Company the effects of this change on the pricing of inventories and costs of goods manufactured were not material in the current year but are expected to be material in future years.

Note 3.  The investment property was recorded at cost until December 19X0, when it was written up to its appraisal value. The Company plans to sell the property in 19X1, and an independent real estate agent in the area has indicated that the appraisal price can be realized. Pending completion of the sale, the amount of the expected gain on the sale has been recorded in a deferred credit account.

Note 4.  The stock dividend described in our May 24, 19X0, letter to stockholders has been recorded as a 105 for 100 stock split-up. Accordingly, there were no changes in the stockholders' equity account balances from the transaction.

Note 5.  For many years the Company has maintained a pension plan for certain of its employees. Prior to the current year pension expense was recognized as payments were made to retired employees. There was no change in the plan in the current year, but upon the recommendation of its auditor, the Company provided $64,000, based upon an actuarial estimate, for pensions to be paid in the future to current employees.

Required:

For each Note, 1 to 5, discuss:

(a)  The note's adequacy and needed revisions, if any, of the financial statements or the note.

(b)  The necessary disclosure in or opinion modification of the auditor's report. (For this requirement assume the revisions suggested in part "a," if any, have been made.)

Complete your discussion of each note (both parts "a" and "b") before beginning discussion of the next note.

(Uniform CPA Examination)

**20-21.** Presented below are three independent, unrelated auditor's reports. The corporation being reported on, in each case, is profit oriented and publishes general-purpose financial statements for distribution to owners, creditors, potential investors, and the general public. Each of the following reports contains deficiencies.

### Auditor's Report I

We have examined the consolidated balance sheet of Belasco Corporation and subsidiaries as of December 31, 19X1, and the related consolidated statements of income and retained earnings and changes in financial position for the year then ended. Our examination was made in accordance with generally accepted auditing standards and accordingly included such tests of the accounting records and such other auditing procedures as we considered necessary in the circumstances. We did not examine the financial statements of Seidel Company, a major consolidated subsidiary. These statements were examined by other auditors whose report thereon has been furnished to us, and our opinion expressed herein, insofar as it relates to Seidel Company, is based solely upon the report of the other auditors.

In our opinion, except for the report of the other auditors, the accompanying consolidated balance sheet and consolidated statements of income and retained earnings and changes in financial position present fairly the financial position of Belasco Corporation and subsidiaries at December 31, 19X1, and the results of its operations and the changes in its financial position for the year then ended, in conformity with generally accepted accounting principles applied on a basis consistent with that of the preceding year.

### Auditor's Report II

The accompanying balance sheet of Jones Corporation as of December 31, 19X1, and the related statements of income and retained earnings and changes in financial position for the year then ended were not audited by us; however, we confirmed cash in the bank and performed a general review of the statements.

During our engagement, nothing came to our attention to indicate that the aforementioned financial statements do not present fairly the financial position of Jones Corporation at December 31, 19X1, and the results of its operations and the changes in its financial position for the year then ended, in conformity with generally accepted accounting principles applied on a basis consistent with that of the preceding year; however, we do not express an opinion on them.

### Auditor's Report III

I made my examination in accordance with generally accepted auditing standards. However, I am not independent with respect to

Mavis Corporation because my wife owns 5% of the outstanding common stock of the company. The accompanying balance sheet as of December 31, 19X1, and the related statements of income and retained earnings and changes in financial position for the year then ended were not audited by me; accordingly, I do not express an opinion on them.

Required:

For each auditor's report describe the reporting deficiencies, explain the reasons therefor, and briefly discuss how the report should be corrected. Each report should be considered separately. When discussing one report, ignore the other two. Do not discuss the addressee, signatures, and date. Also do not rewrite any of the auditor's reports. Organize your answer sheet as follows:

| Report No. | Deficiency | Reason | Correction |
|---|---|---|---|
|  |  |  |  |

(Uniform CPA Examination)

**20-22.** Roscoe, CPA, has completed the examination of the financial statements of Excelsior Corporation as of and for the year ended December 31, 19X1. Roscoe also examined and reported on the Excelsior financial statements for the prior year. Roscoe drafted the following report for 19X1.

March 15, 19X2

We have examined the balance sheet and statements of income and retained earnings of Excelsior Corporation as of December 31, 19X1. Our examination was made in accordance with generally accepted accounting standards and accordingly included such tests of the accounting records as we considered necessary in the circumstances.

In our opinion, the above mentioned financial statements are accurately prepared and fairly presented in accordance with generally accepted accounting principles in effect at December 31, 19X1.

Roscoe, CPA
(Signed)

Other information:

- Excelsior is presenting comparative financial statements.
- Excelsior does not wish to present a statement of changes in financial position for either year.
- During 19X1 Excelsior changed its method of accounting for long-term construction contracts and properly reflected the effect of the change in the current year's financial statements and restated the prior-year's statements. Roscoe is satisfied with Excelsior's justification for making the change. The change is discussed in footnote number 12.
- Roscoe was unable to perform normal accounts receivable confirmation procedures, but alternate procedures were used to satisfy Roscoe as to the validity of the receivables.
- Excelsior Corporation is the defendant in a litigation, the outcome of which is highly uncertain. If the case is settled in favor of the plaintiff, Excelsior will be required to pay a substantial amount of cash, which might require the sale of certain fixed assets. The litigation and the possible effects have been properly disclosed in footnote number 11.
- Excelsior issued debentures on January 31, 19X0, in the amount of $10,000,000. The funds obtained from the issuance were used to finance the expansion of plant facilities. The debenture agreement restricts the payment of future cash dividends to earnings after December 31, 19X6. Excelsior declined to disclose this essential data in the footnotes to the financial statements.

Required:

Consider all facts given and rewrite the auditor's report in acceptable and complete format incorporating any necessary departures from the standard (short form) report.

Do not discuss the draft of Roscoe's report but identify and explain any items included in "Other Information" that need not be part of the auditor's report.

(Uniform CPA Examination)

20-23. Various types of "accounting changes" can affect the second reporting standard of the generally accepted auditing standards. This standard reads, "The report shall state whether such principles have been consistently observed in the current period in relation to the preceding period."

Assume that the following list describes changes which have a material effect on a client's financial statements for the current year.

1. A change from the completed-contract method to the percentage-of-completion method of accounting for long-term construction-type contracts.

2. A change in the estimated useful life of previously recorded fixed assets based on newly acquired information.

3. Correction of a mathematical error in inventory pricing made in a prior period.

4. A change from prime costing to full absorption costing for inventory valuation.

5. A change from presentation of statements of individual companies to presentation of consolidated statements.

6. A change from deferring and amortizing pre-production costs to recording such costs as an expense when incurred, because future benefits of the costs have become doubtful. The new accounting method was adopted in recognition of the change in estimated future benefits.

7. A change to including the employer share of FICA taxes as "Retirement benefits" on the income statement from including it with "Other taxes."

8. A change from the FIFO method of inventory pricing to the LIFO method of inventory pricing.

Required:

Identify the type of change which is described in each item above, state whether any modification is required by the auditor's report *as it relates to the second standard of reporting*, and state whether the prior year's financial statements should be restated when presented in comparative form with the current year's statements. Organize your answer sheet as shown below.

For example a change from the LIFO method of inventory pricing to the FIFO method of inventory pricing would appear as shown.

| Item No. | Type of Change | Should Auditor's Report be Modified? | Should Prior Year's Statements be Restated? |
|----------|----------------|--------------------------------------|---------------------------------------------|
| Example | An accounting change from one generally accepted accounting principle to another generally accepted accounting principle. | Yes | No |

(Uniform CPA Examination)

**20-24.** Pace Corporation, an audit client of yours, is a manufacturer of consumer products and has several wholly owned subsidiaries in foreign countries which are audited by other independent auditors in those countries. The financial statements of all subsidiaries were properly consolidated in the financial statements of the parent company and the foreign auditors' reports were furnished to your CPA firm.

You are now preparing your auditor's opinion on the consolidated balance sheet and statement of income and retained earnings for the year ended June 30, 19X1. These statements were prepared on a comparative basis with those of last year.

Required:

(a) How would you evaluate and accept the independence and professional reputations of the foreign auditors?

(b) Under what circumstances may a principal auditor assume responsibility for the work of another auditor to the same extent as if he had performed the work himself?

(c) Assume that both last year and this year you were willing to utilize the reports of the other independent auditors in expressing your opinion on the consolidated financial statements but were unwilling to take full responsibility for performance of the work underlying their opinions. Assuming your examination of the parent company's financial statements would allow you to render an unqualified opinion, prepare (1) the necessary disclosure to be contained in the scope paragraph and (2) the complete opinion paragraph of your auditor's report.

(d) What modification(s), if any, would be necessary in your auditor's opinion if the financial statements for the prior year were unaudited?

(Uniform CPA Examination)

# Chapter 21

# AUDIT REPORTING STANDARDS II

**Special Reports:
Compilation
and Review Services;
Other Special Reports;
Long-Form Reports**

Until 1978, when the newly formed Accounting and Review Services Committee of the AICPA issued its first Statement on Standards for Accounting and Review Services, accountants in public practice reporting on financial information with which they were associated stated either that the information had been audited or that it was unaudited and a disclaimer of opinion was issued. During that period, however, it came to be recognized that any association of a public accountant with financial information carried with it some relatively undefined responsibility that the information was actually what it purported to be.

As an example, auditors were cautioned that a disclaimer of opinion would be an improper response in a situation where the auditor disagreed with the manner in which unaudited financial statement information was developed or presented. Statement on Auditing Procedure No. 31 issued in 1961 marked the introduction of the adverse opinion as a more appropriate response than the disclaimer of opinion in those instances when the auditor did in fact have an opinion—namely, that information was not fairly presented in conformity with generally accepted accounting principles. The adverse opinion was, however, anticipated in the discussion in *Generally Accepted Auditing Standards* published by the AICPA in 1954 wherein it was stated (p. 48) "In such cases (where the accountant has reached a definite opinion that financial statements do not fairly present financial position or results of operations), he should be satisfied that his report clearly indicates his disagreement with the statements presented."

Subsequently, Statement on Auditing Standards No. 2 issued in 1974 (as codified in Professional Standards at AU Sec. 509.25) pointed out that "If the auditor believes that the financial statement items affected by uncertainties reflect the application of accounting principles that are not generally accepted, he should also modify his report to state his reservations regarding departures from generally accepted accounting principles." One outgrowth of these developments was that public accountants began to recognize some limited responsibility for unaudited financial statements with which the accountant was associated and which would be accompanied by a disclaimer of opinion.

### How To "Unaudit" Financial Statements

Statements on Auditing Procedure No. 23 (Revised) issued in 1949 pointed out that ". . . when financial statements prepared without audit are presented on the accountant's stationery without comment by the accountant, a warning, such as *Prepared from the Books Without Audit*, appearing prominently on each page of the financial statements is considered sufficient." It is perhaps as an outgrowth of the use of this proviso supplemented in later years by the requirement that the accountant also report a disclaimer of opinion, that accountants who were engaged to prepare unaudited financial statements from a client's accounting records sought to undertake some limited review procedures with respect to those statements. In the July, 1976, issue of *The Journal of Accountancy*, Alan Winters reported that of a group of accounting firms surveyed, only 3 percent of the firms never performed any review of unaudited financial statements with which they were associated. Of the review procedures utilized by the other 97 percent of the surveyed firms, the following review procedures were regularly followed by 90 percent or more of the firms:

> Ensure the clerical accuracy of the financial statements
> Ascertain that the financial statements are supported by and agree with the books of account
> Determine if bank reconciliations are prepared

The reasons for the first two procedures in connection with unaudited financial statements are fairly obvious. No accountant with any sense of professionalism would deign to be associated with statements that did not foot, and the assertion that the statements had been "Prepared from the books without audit" suggest that the accountant ought to know whether the statements were in agreement with the books of account. The third procedure offers some basis for determining the likelihood that the critical cash account, through which most transactions eventually pass, is properly stated. A similar procedure, ascertaining that subsidiary records agree with their control account, was a required procedure in nearly 80 percent of the firms and would further indicate that the accounting records had been properly maintained. Many typical auditing procedures were reported to be used as well, with 40 percent of the responses indicating that inventory test counts were an optional procedure.

### Limited Assurance

Given that there existed varying degrees of limited assurance that could be derived from such unaudited financial statements, and that preparation of unaudited financial statements for many smaller clients was an important aspect of accounting and tax services provided by small and medium-sized accounting firms, the AICPA formed in 1977 a committee to establish standards for nonaudit services that involve the preparation and presentation of financial statements. This new committee, the Accounting and Review Services Committee, was granted authority comparable to that of the Auditing Standards Board, and issued Statement on Standards for Accounting and Review Services (SSARS) No. 1 in December, 1978 (SSARS are referenced in AICPA Professional Standards at Section AR). That statement pertains to all instances in which unaudited financial statements are submitted to a nonpublic entity[1] and identifies two levels of service that may be provided:

> Compilation of financial statements
> Review of financial statements

Little or no assurance is provided by reports on compilation services. More assurance is provided by reports on review services, but of course the level of assurance is less than that provided by unqualified reports on audit engagements, which we have recognized as providing maximum assurance but less than 100 percent assurance that would be tantamount to a guaranty. It is impossible to quantify these levels of assurance other than to state that they are greater than zero and less than 100 percent and that the assurance levels relate to each other as stated above.

SSARS No. 1 further points out that the standards relate only to the two newly identified services and that the statement does not establish standards for such other accounting services as preparing working trial balances, assisting a client in the preparation of adjusting journal entries, maintaining accounting records, or preparing tax returns. The term *financial statements* is defined to include not only the customary three statements, but also statements of cash receipts and disbursements, statements of assets and liabilities, statements pertaining to segments of a business, and other forms of formal presentation of accounting data.

## Compilation of Financial Statements

SSARS No. 1 indicates that the compilation of financial statements involves presenting in statement form financial information that is the representation of management or owners, without endeavoring to express any assurance with respect to the statements. However, on the basis of the guidance offered for the performance of compilation services, it is evident that a third party would be justified in placing more reliance on financial statements prepared as a result of a compilation engagement performed in accordance with SSARS No. 1 than if the statements had been prepared directly by management.

In performing a compilation service, the accountant should adhere to the following standards set forth in SSARS No. 1:

1. The accountant should be knowledgeable about the accounting principles and practices of the industry (including not-for-profit organi-

---

[1]A nonpublic entity is defined as one whose securities are not traded in a public market and are not registered with the SEC.

zations) in which the client operates, in order to be able to compile financial statements that appropriately reflect financial and operating results.

2. The accountant should obtain a general understanding of the client's operations and its business transactions, its accounting records, the competence of its accounting personnel, and the accounting basis on which the statements are to be prepared (for example, cash basis, accrual basis, modified accrual). In this connection the accountant should consider whether appropriate adjusting entries have been prepared and if not, advise and assist the client in developing the appropriate adjustments.

3. No inquiries or corroboration or review procedures other than those stated above are required to be performed, but if in performing procedures related to the compilation or any other services provided to the client the accountant becomes aware that information in the client's records is incorrect or incomplete, the accountant should obtain additional or revised information. Should the client refuse to correct or supply the information in question, the auditor should withdraw from the engagement.

4. The accountant should study the financial statements to be included in the compilation report for the purpose of becoming satisfied that the statements appear to be appropriate in form and free of any obvious errors.

### Reporting on a Compilation

The report to be rendered should state that

- The financial statements have been compiled by the accountant.
- The compilation is limited to presenting in statement form information that is the representation of the client.
- The financial statements have not been audited or reviewed and no opinion or other assurance is expressed on the statements.

In addition, each of the following reporting considerations should be observed:

- Each page of the financial statements included in the report should refer the reader to the accompanying accountant's report.
- The report may include only the statement(s) requested by the client—for example, only a balance sheet.
- The client may request that the financial statements omit the disclosures required by generally accepted accounting principles, and the accountant may comply with the request *provided* 1) that there is no indication of an

intent to mislead users of the financial statements, and 2) that the omission of substantially all disclosures is referred to in the accountant's report.

- If the statements have been compiled on a comprehensive basis of accounting other than generally accepted accounting principles, the basis used must be disclosed either on the financial statements or in the accountant's report.

A report reflecting the above matters is given in the following example:

The accompanying balance sheet of Blank and Blank as of December 31, 19XX, and the related statement of income for the year then ended have been compiled by me on the modified accrual basis used by Blank and Blank for income tax purposes.

A compilation is limited to presenting in financial statement form information that is the representation of the owners. I have not audited or reviewed the accompanying financial statements and, accordingly, do not express an opinion or any other form of assurance on them.

The partners of the firm have elected to omit the statement of changes in financial position and substantially all other disclosures required by generally accepted accounting principles. If the omitted disclosures had been included in the financial statements, they might influence the user's conclusions about the company's financial position and results of operations. Accordingly, these financial statements are not designed for those who are not informed about such matters.

## The Role of Compilation Services in an Accounting Practice

Compiling financial statements for clients has long been an important segment of accounting practice, particularly for individual practitioners and smaller firms that serve primarily smaller client organizations. Compilation would be involved if the accountant provides a full accounting service to clients, preparing accounting records manually or with the use of a computer, from transaction details supplied by the client. Financial statements would have to be compiled from the records in these circumstances in order to communicate effectively to the client the financial and operating results that were achieved. In other cases accounting records would be maintained by minimally trained client employees and then monthly the accountant would take a trial balance, make adjustments that might be necessary, and prepare statements for the client.

Until SSARS No. 1 there were no standards for such compilation services, and the accountant was required to report only that the statements prepared by the accountant were unaudited. As we have seen, SSARS No. 1 instituted standards to be followed in providing such services and in reporting the compiled information to the client. It is important to recognize, however, that regardless of the type of service supplied by an accountant in public practice, the accountant has no control over the client's use of information that the accountant has provided. Consequently, if a bank or other credit grantor does not insist on audited information, any accountant-prepared financial statements are customarily supplied to satisfy the request for information on which to base credit decisions. It is in recognition of this common situation that the various caveats discussed previously have been specified for inclusion in a compilation report, for ordinarily the client should already have been made aware of any omitted information and of any comprehensive basis of accounting being followed other than generally accepted accounting principles.

### *Review of Financial Statements*

In recognition of a need for a service that is midway between a compilation of financial statements and an audit of financial statements, both in level of assurance and cost of the service, SSARS No. 1 introduced the *review* of financial statements of a nonpublic entity. The review service is especially fitting in situations where a bank customer is personally known to the lending officer, so that a full audit of financial statements submitted with an application for credit may not be considered necessary and yet there is a desire for more assurance than is offered by statements prepared by the customer or compiled by a public accountant. The review service has proved to be popular whenever such limited assurance is desired and cost constraints are an important consideration.

The standards for conducting a review engagement set forth in SSARS No. 1 are essentially as follows:

1. As in the case of compilation service, the accountant must be knowledgeable about the accounting principles and practices of the industry in which the client operates, in order to be able to utilize information obtained in the course of the review to ascertain whether material modifications should be made in the financial statements to bring them into compliance with generally accepted accounting principles or another comprehensive basis of accounting.

2. The accountant should obtain a general understanding of the client's organization and operating characteristics, and of the nature of its assets, liabilities, revenues, expenses, and any material transactions with related parties.

3. The accountant should inquire about a) the entity's accounting principles and practices, and the method of applying them, and b) the entity's procedures for recording, classifying, and summarizing transactions and accumulating information for disclosure in the financial statements. (In this connection an appendix to SSARS No. 1 gives a comprehensive list of illustrative inquiries, such as "Have inventories been

physically counted?" "What costing method is used?" and "Have market values been appropriately considered?")

4. Analytical procedures should be applied to identify items and relationships in the financial statements that appear unusual. In applying the analytical procedures, comparison should be made with financial statements for comparable prior periods and with anticipated results in any budgets or forecasts that have been prepared.

5. The accountant should inquire into actions taken at meetings of stockholders, board of directors, committees of the board of directors, or any comparable group that might affect the financial statements.

6. Through carefully reading the financial statements and considering any information coming to the accountant's attention, the accountant should determine whether the financial statements appear to conform with generally accepted accounting principles.

7. If significant components of the client entity have not been reviewed by the principal accountant, reports should be obtained from other accountants engaged to audit or review the financial statements of those components.

8. Inquiry should be made of persons having responsibility for financial and accounting matters for the client concerning a) whether the financial statements have been prepared in conformity with generally accepted accounting principles that have been consistently applied, b) any changes in the entity's business activities or accounting practices, c) any matters about which questions have arisen in the course of making the review, and d) events subsequent to the date of the financial statements that would materially affect the financial statements.

9. Although a review does not involve a study of internal accounting control or tests of evidence to corroborate the accounting records or the responses to inquiries, additional procedures should be performed if there is any indication that information coming to the accountant's attention is incorrect, incomplete, or unsatisfactory in any way. The procedures should provide such limited assurance as the accountant may deem to be necessary that no material modifications should be made to the financial statements in order for them to conform with generally accepted accounting principles.

10. It will generally be desirable to obtain a representation letter from the owner, manager, or chief executive officer of the client, and from the chief financial officer if there be such a person who would be knowledgeable about the representations to be made.

### *Reporting on a Review of Financial Statements*

The report on a review engagement should cover the following matters:

- The review was performed in accordance with standards established by the American Institute of Certified Public Accountants.
- All information in the financial statements is the representation of the (owners, management, officers, as appropriate) of the entity.
- A review consists principally of inquiries made of company personnel and analytical review procedures applied to the financial data.
- A review is substantially more limited in scope than an audit, and accordingly no opinion is expressed on the financial statements.
- The accountant is unaware of any material modifications that should be made to the financial statements in order for them to be in conformity with generally accepted accounting principles.

The following reporting considerations should also be observed in a review engagement:

- Each page of the reviewed financial statements should include the reference, "See Accountant's Review Report."
- If the accountant is unable to complete the inquiry and analytical review procedures considered necessary for a review engagement as a result of circumstances or a client restriction, a review report should not be issued. These limiting conditions must also be considered in determining whether a compilation report would likewise be inappropriate.
- In determining whether it would be appropriate to change an audit engagement to either a review or a compilation engagement, or to change a review engagement to a compilation engagement, the accountant should take into consideration

    The reason for the client's request that the change in the engagement be made, particularly the implications of a restricted scope imposed by the client or by circumstances.

    The additional audit effort and cost necessary to complete the original engagement. If these are insignificant, a question is raised about the propriety of changing the enagement to a lesser service.

    The possibility that the information affected by the scope restriction may be incorrect or incomplete. Thus, if the client will not permit an auditor to correspond with the client's legal counsel or refuses to sign a client representation letter, the only appropriate course of action ordinarily would be to withdraw from the engagement.

- If the accountant concludes that it is appropriate to change the engagement to a lesser level, as for instance if there was a misunderstanding concerning the nature of the service originally contracted for, the report that is issued should make no reference to the original engagement or to any audit procedures that may have been performed.

Following is an illustrative report on a review engagement in which a modification is made as a result of an exception:

We have reviewed the accompanying balance sheet of Blank, Inc. as of May 31, 19XX, and the related statements of operations, retained earnings, and changes in financial position for the year then ended, in accordance with standards established by the American Institute of Certified Public Accountants. All information included in these financial statements is the representation of the management of Blank, Inc.

A review consists principally of inquiries of company personnel and analytical procedures applied to financial data. It is substantially less in scope than an examination in accordance with generally accepted auditing standards, the objective of which is the expression of an opinion regarding the financial statements taken as a whole. Accordingly, we do not express such an opinion.

Based on our review, with the exception of the matter described in the following paragraph, we are not aware of any material modifications that should be made to the accompanying financial statements in order for them to be in conformity with generally accepted accounting principles.

As disclosed in note B to the financial statements, generally accepted accounting principles require that inventories be valued at the lower of cost or market. Management has informed us that inventories are stated in the accompanying financial statements at average cost, without consideration of the market value of those inventories, and that the effects of this departure from generally accepted accounting principles on financial position, results of operations, and changes in financial position have not been determined.

## Reporting When the Accountant Is Not Independent

Because a compilation service is not intended to convey any assurance with respect to the compiled financial statements, it is not necessary that the accountant providing the service be independent. Lack of independence must, however, be disclosed by including the following statement as the last paragraph of the report: "I am not independent with respect to Blank & Blank." The reason for the lack of independence should not be described.

The AICPA has stated in Interpretation 101.3 relative to Rule 101 of the Code of Professional Ethics that independence is not necessarily impaired if the accountant provides bookkeeping or data processing service to the client. This position is contrary to the position of the SEC with respect to registered public companies, which is that an accountant will not be considered independent if bookkeeping or data processing services are provided. However, corporations of a size that would turn to the capital markets for funds would reasonably be expected to have an in-house accountant, and the SEC views the audit of the financial statements by an accountant who had no responsibility for the preparation of the accounting records or the financial statements as a factor that increases assurance about the statements. Such added assurance would appear to be desirable in the impersonal relationships inherent with respect to publicly traded securities.

For smaller, nonpublic business entities, not only is it fairly common to turn to a public accountant for bookkeeping service, but if statements compiled by a CPA are made available to outside parties, the reputation of the particular CPA and of CPAs in general are matters likely to be known to the third parties using the financial statements. Furthermore, professional ethics require the CPA to be independent in fact and thus objective in providing services to clients.

Thus, if a CPA is otherwise independent of a client, the provision of bookkeeping or data processing service should not preclude providing compilation or review services; but if a CPA is not independent, as stated above the lack of independence must be stated as a final paragraph of a compilation report. Because assurance is intended to be conveyed by a review report, however, a review report should not be issued if the CPA is not independent; only a properly qualified compilation report would be permissible.

### Review of Interim Financial Information

The SEC considers interim information to be highly important for investors as an early indication of new developments and changes in financial position and operating results. As a minimum, the SEC requires that annual financial statements be supplemented by unaudited quarterly information that is to be reviewed by the company's independent auditor, thereby seeking to constrain registered companies from reporting inaccurate or misleading information by providing a subsequent reference point against which the originally released quarterly information can be checked. The SEC also encourages (but does not require) registered companies to have current interim information reviewed by their independent auditors before it is publicly released. The Auditing Standards Board set forth standards for the review of interim information in SAS No. 10, issued in 1975, but authorized reporting on the limited review only to the client's board of directors. In 1976, however, in SAS No. 13 the Board authorized reporting on the results of a limited review to stockholders and other interested parties, including regulatory agencies. The two statements were subsequently superseded by SAS No. 24, issued in 1979 and reported in Professional Standards at AU Sec. 721, and then by SAS No. 36 issued in 1981 when the SEC changed its required reporting of quarterly information to permit presentation as a supplement to audited financial statements as an alternative to presentation as a note to such statements.

*Procedures for the Review.* SAS No. 24 points to the more extensive need for estimates in the interim reporting of costs and expenses, some of which cannot be determined with customary accuracy until the year end, as in the case of estimates of inventory shortages and income taxes. Review procedures to be applied to interim information are essentially similar to the procedures set forth for review services in SSARS No. 1

and thus emphasize inquiries and analytical review procedures. Notably different, however, is the fact that typically interim information is reviewed in association with an audit of the annual financial statements, and the review must encompass inquiries about internal control and changes in the internal control system, as well as inquiries about the manner in which transactions are recorded in the accounting system. Also, minutes of the meetings of stockholders and of the board of directors and its committees are to be read rather than inquired into for actions that may affect the financial statements, and a client representation letter is required rather than recommended.

*Reporting on Interim Financial Information.* As in the case of an audit, modifying the report to be issued may be necessary under various circumstances, but if restrictions imposed by the client or by conditions (as for example, internal control weaknesses that make it impossible for interim information to be reported in conformity with generally accepted accounting principles) preclude completing the review, the accountant should not permit use of the accountant's name, or of the report that was issued, in any client-prepared communication setting forth financial information. Following is an example of a report on a review without any of these problems. Each page of the accompanying reviewed financial information should be clearly marked as "unaudited."

> We have made a review of the balance sheet of Blank Consolidated Corp. as of June 30, 19XX, and the statements of operations and changes in financial position for the three-month and six-month periods then ended. Our review was made in accordance with standards established by the American Institute of Certified Public Accountants.
>
> A review of interim financial information consists principally of obtaining an understanding of the system for the preparation of interim financial information, applying analytical review procedures to financial data, and making inquiries of persons responsible for financial and accounting matters. It is substantially less in scope than an examination in accordance with generally accepted auditing standards, the objective of which is the expression of an opinion regarding the financial statements taken as a whole. Accordingly, we do not express such an opinion.
>
> Based on our review, we are not aware of any material modifications that should be made to the accompanying financial statements for them to be in conformity with generally accepted accounting principles.

When reviewed interim information is presented in summary form as an unaudited supplement to the annual financial statements, the accountant's report on the interim review need not accompany the audited financial statements unless the scope of the review was restricted or the interim information does not appear to be presented in conformity with generally accepted accounting principles.

Underwriters are customarily engaged in connection with the public offering of securities to ensure that the expected proceeds from the issue are obtained and to effect sale of the securities. The Securities Act of 1933 imposes on underwriters, and other parties such as attorneys who are associated with securities that must be registered, certain responsibilities in connection with a registration statement for financial information that has not been "expertised" by independent accountants or other parties who have consented to be named as experts. The responsibility relative to any such nonexpertised financial information is intended to further protect investors by imposing a responsibility on underwriters for a duty of diligence to ascertain that the information is not misleading and that no significant information has been omitted.

In order to discharge this responsibility adequately, underwriters customarily turn to independent accountants as being most knowledgeable about such unaudited information and, with the consent of the company seeking to register securities (since the company will have to bear the added cost), request the independent accountants to perform a "reasonable investigation" of the unaudited information and to report on the results of that investigation. The letter to the underwriter reporting on the investigation is typically referred to as a "comfort letter," pertaining to the assurance provided relative to the underwriter's responsibility for making a reasonable investigation, as discussed at AU Sec. 631. The letter will often cover matters in addition to the unaudited information that the accountant has been engaged to examine, and will in general include the following:

1. A statement affirming the independence of the accountant with respect to the client.

2. An opinion that the audited financial statements and schedules in the registration statement are in conformity with applicable accounting requirements of the Securities Act and published rules and regulations under the Act.

3. An indication of the procedures applied to the specified unaudited information that has been examined.

4. Negative assurance (permissible in a report directed to a knowledgeable party) That "Nothing came to our attention as a result of the specified procedures that would cause us to believe that the specified information does not comply as to form in all material respects with applicable accounting requirements of the Securities Act and regulations thereunder, or that the unaudited information is not fairly presented or summarized consistent with generally accepted accounting principles as applied to the audited financial statements."

5. Negative assurance as to whether, during a specified period following the date of the audited financial statements, there has been any change in capital stock or long-term debt or any decrease as compared with the corresponding period in the preceding year in sales, net income, or other specified financial statement items.

It should be noted in this connection that a registration statement must include a balance sheet as of a date within ninety days of the date that the registration statement is filed. If the filing date is more than ninety days after the close of the company's fiscal year, the latest balance sheet may be unaudited, provided that an audited balance sheet as of the end of the most recent fiscal year is also included. A summary of earnings and changes in financial position for the period preceding the "ninety-day" balance sheet for the current and preceding years must also be included with the unaudited balance sheet. It is to these unaudited financial statements and events following the date of the latest balance sheet included in the registration statement that the auditor's comfort letter to the underwriters is primarily directed.

There are no professional standards pertaining to the matters to be covered in a comfort letter or to the procedures to be applied in the accountant's investigation, although the approach will be similar to that discussed earlier for a review engagement. Exactly what information is to be covered by the comfort letter and what procedures are to be applied are matters to be decided by the parties involved and should be detailed in an engagement letter.

### Reports on Financial Statements Prepared in Accordance with a Comprehensive Basis of Accounting Other Than Generally Accepted Accounting Principles

Although in most instances financial statements are prepared in conformity with generally accepted accounting principles, in some instances the statements may be prepared on the basis of some other comprehensive basis of accounting. Examples would include financial statements that must comply with regulations of an agency to which they are to be submitted (for example the Interstate Commerce Commission or a state insurance commission); statements that reflect the basis of accounting elected for use in filing income tax returns; a cash- or modified-cash-basis of accounting; or a basis that has substantial authoritative support, such as a price-level basis of accounting. Under these circumstances the auditor must consider whether the financial statements reported on are suitably titled. Thus a statement of financial position on a cash basis might be titled "Statement of Assets and Liabilities Arising from Cash Transactions." A sample report that conforms to AICPA standards for reporting on an alternative comprehensive basis of accounting is here presented:

> We have examined the statements of assets, liabilities, and partners' capi-tal—income tax basis, of Blank and Partners as of December 31, 19XX, and the related statements of revenue and expenses—income tax basis, for the year then ended. Our examination was made in accordance with generally

accepted auditing standards and, accordingly, included such tests of the accounting records and such other auditing procedures as we considered necessary in the circumstances.

As described in Note 2, it is the policy of the partnership to prepare financial statements on the basis of accounting that is used for income tax purposes; consequently, revenue is recognized at the time that cash is received and certain expenses are recognized when paid. Accordingly, the accompanying financial statements are not intended to present financial position and results of operations in conformity with generally accepted accounting principles.

In our opinion, the financial statements referred to above present fairly the assets, liabilities, and partners' capital of Blank and Partners as of December 31, 19XX, and its revenues and expenses for the year then ended, on the income tax basis of accounting as described in Note 2, which basis has been applied in a manner consistent with that of the preceding year.

Because the statements do not purport to present financial information in accordance with generally accepted accounting principles, there should be no reference to presentation of financial position or results of operations, and it is not necessary to refer to the omission of a statement of changes in assets, liabilities, and partners' capital.

### Reports on Specified Elements of a Financial Statement

An accountant may be called upon to report on one or more specified elements, accounts, or items of a financial statement, either in conjunction with an examination of financial statements or as a separate engagement. In either case the examination should be made in accordance with generally accepted auditing standards, but materiality should be evaluated in terms of the item being reported on, rather than the relation to the statements as a whole. Consequently, the examination of an item to be reported on separately would ordinarily be more extensive than when the same information is being examined as a part of an examination of the financial statements as a whole.

In a report on an engagement to examine a specified account or item of a financial statement, the first standard of reporting is not applicable inasmuch as a specified item is not considered to be a financial statement. AU Sec. 621.10 states that the second standard of reporting dealing with consistency is applicable if the item on which the auditor is to report is stated in accordance with generally accepted accounting principles. If the item has been accounted for in accordance with the provisions of a contract, a law, or a government regulation, an assertion that the item has been accounted for in accordance with those terms should suffice, and consistency with prior years would be self-evident.

When an adverse opinion or disclaimer of opinion has been reported on a client's financial statements, a report on a specified element or elements should not accompany the financial statements, and the report should not encompass a majority of the elements of the financial statements so as to suggest that the report is actually what is known as a piecemeal opinion. Piecemeal opinions are now prohibited because they may tend to overshadow or contradict an adverse opinion or disclaimer of opinion concerning the statements as a whole.

The following sample report reflects the standards of reporting in the common situation where lease payments are computed on the basis of sales volume and the sales figures are to be audited. The report would be addressed to whichever party contracted for the engagement.

> I have examined the accompanying schedule of net sales for Stores, Inc. for the year ended June 30, 19YY. My examination was made in accordance with generally accepted auditing standards and, accordingly, included such tests of the accounting records and such other auditing procedures as I considered necessary.
>
> In my opinion, the above mentioned schedule presents fairly the net sales of Stores Inc. for the year ended June 30, 19YY, and has been prepared in conformity with the provisions of the lease agreement dated July 1, 19XX, between Stores, Inc. and Shopping Center Operators & Co.

### Financial Information Presented in Prescribed Forms

Some government agencies or other bodies require that financial information be furnished on a specified form, such as a tax return, that includes a report to be signed by the accountant/auditor who prepared the form. If the printed form calls for the preparer to make assertions that an independent auditor concludes cannot reasonably be made, the auditor should either reword the report on the form or attach a separate report that is consistent with the reporting requirements of generally accepted auditing standards.

### Reporting on Internal Control

Previous mention has been made of the SEC-induced disclosures of corporate bribes and illegal or questionable payments in the United States and abroad that resulted in the enactment of the Foreign Corrupt Practices Act in 1977. The Act included provisions related to internal accounting control that were obviously based on AICPA pronouncements, the purpose of these provisions being to require registered companies to maintain systems of internal accounting control that will provide assurance that company transactions and dispositions of assets are accurately and fairly reflected in the company's books and records. The internal accounting control provisions are intended to prevent any questionable or improper payments from being made on an unauthorized basis or from being hidden or disguised in the accounts. To increase the effectiveness of the Act's internal control provisions, the SEC proposed that the management of registered companies be required to report to stockholders and other interested parties whether the company's internal accounting control system satisfies the requirements of the Act's control provisions. The SEC also proposed that a company's independent auditors report on whether management's reported opinion was consistent with the auditors' own evaluation of the internal accounting control system, and whether the opinion was reasonable with respect to ensuring that material transactions would be fairly reflected in the company's financial statements. In 1980 the SEC withdrew these proposed requirements, presumably because of the negative response of the business community relative to the cost/benefit aspects of the proposal. In withdrawing the proposal, however, the SEC urged voluntary action by corporations and the accounting profession to accomplish the objectives of the proposal, stating that the SEC would review the situation and what had been voluntarily accomplished after three years.

The AICPA Auditing Standards Board began considering the problem of reporting on internal control shortly after the SEC proposals were announced, and in July, 1980, issued SAS No. 30, Reporting on Internal Accounting Control. This new statement, referenced in Professional Standards at AU Sec. 642 susperseded Sections 640 and 641 and is equally applicable to mandatory and voluntary reporting. The provisions of SAS No. 30 are in addition to the continuing requirement of SAS No. 20 that material weaknesses in internal accounting control be reported to senior management and the board of directors.

*Scope of an Engagement to Express an Opinion on an Entity's System of Internal Accounting Control.* SAS No. 30 indicates that the engagement to express an opinion on internal accounting control can be in addition to an examination of financial statements, but it can also be a separate engagement involving an accountant who is not examining the financial statements. The scope of an engagement to express an opinion on internal accounting control is stated to include

- Consideration in planning the scope of the examination of such factors as
    - Nature of the client's operations
    - Client's organizational structure
    - Principal financial and operating reports used for planning and control
    - Management actions to monitor internal controls, including the development of an internal audit function, and an evaluation of the internal audit function
    - Competence of personnel
    - The effect of changes in the system during the period being reviewed
    - Relative significance of various assets and types of transactions

Any relevant information gained through examinations of the client's financial statements

Available documentation of the system in the form of flowcharts, procedural write-ups, instruction manuals, or other forms

- Review procedures to form an opinion whether control procedures are suitably designed to achieve the objectives of internal accounting control:

Obtain an understanding of the flow of transactions through the accounting system.

Ascertain specific control objectives that relate to points in the system where errors or irregularities could occur.

Evaluate the specific control features and techniques that have been adopted to achieve the specific control objectives, including any administrative controls that contribute to the achievement of the objectives of internal accounting control.

Test compliance with prescribed procedures over the period to be reported on.

Evaluate results of the review and compliance testing, including identification of material weaknesses in the system that result in more than a relatively low risk of material irregularities or errors occurring without being detected and corrected.

Obtain management's written representations acknowledging management's responsibility for establishing and maintaining the system of internal accounting control, stating whether management has disclosed all material weaknesses of which it is aware and any irregularities that have occurred, and stating any changes subsequent to the period being reported on that would significantly affect the system of internal accounting control.

*Reporting on a System of Internal Accounting Control.* An auditor's report may express an unqualified opinion, a qualified opinion because of material weaknesses or because of restrictions on the scope of the engagement imposed by the client or by conditions, or a disclaimer of opinion if the effect of restrictions on the scope of the examination is sufficiently material to necessitate that response. The following example illustrates the appropriate language for a report expressing an unqualified opinion:

We have made a study and evaluation of the system of internal accounting control of Blank Corp. in effect at December 31, 19XX. Our study and evaluation was made in accordance with standards established by the American Institute of Certified Public Accountants.

The management of Blank Corp. is responsible for establishing and maintaining a system of internal accounting control. In fulfilling this responsibility, estimates and judgments by management are required to assess the expected benefits and related costs of control procedures. The objectives of a system are to provide management with reasonable, but not absolute, assurance that assets are safeguarded against loss from unauthorized use or disposition, and that transactions are executed in accordance with management's authorization and recorded properly to permit the preparation of financial statements in accordance with generally accepted accounting principles.

Because of inherent limitations in any system of internal accounting control, errors or irregularities may occur and not be detected. Also, projection of any evaluation of the system to future periods is subject to the risk that procedures may become inadequate because of changes in conditions, or that the degree of compliance with the procedures may deteriorate.

In our opinion, the system of internal accounting control of Blank Corp. in effect at December 31, 19XX, taken as a whole, was sufficient to meet the objectives stated above insofar as those objectives pertain to the prevention or detection of errors or irregularities in amounts that would be material in relation to the financial statements.

An internal control engagement and the resulting report can also cover a period of time rather than a point in time, as in the preceding example. As an alternative, the auditor can issue a report on internal control based solely on the study and evaluation of internal control made as a part of an audit of financial statements; but in that case the report must be restricted to use by management.

## Reporting on Financial Forecasts

The SEC has over the years substantially modified its position on financial forecasts. At one time the SEC prohibited the inclusion of forecast information in registration statements, but now forecasts are permitted and even encouraged in recognition of the important role that future expectations play in investor decisions. However, an inclination on the part of the SEC to completely reverse its position and *require* the inclusion of forecast information has been resisted by the business community, largely out of trepidation over possible legal claims arising out of forecasts that are not achieved, through no fault of those who prepared them.

The AICPA has also had a continuing interest in forecasts, but for a different reason than in the case of the SEC. The AICPA has been concerned that the association of CPAs with so subjective a matter as forecasts might tend to detract from the reputation of the profession for objectivity in dealing with the relatively greater certainty of financial statements. Consequently, the AICPA has had a long-standing rule of conduct, currently listed as Rule 201(E) of the Code of Professional Ethics, stating that an AICPA member's name is not to be used in conjunction with any forecast of future transactions in a manner that may lead to the belief that the member vouches for the achievability of the forecast.

More recently, however, the Auditing Standards Division of the AICPA, in recognition of the public demand for the unique services of

CPAs in adding credibility to financial data, has issued the guide, *Review of a Financial Forecast*. As the title of this 1980 publication indicates, an accountant in public practice would perform a *review* of a financial forecast, not an audit, and hence the report on such an engagement would afford only limited assurance to the user of a reviewed financial forecast.

*Procedures for the Review of a Financial Forecast.*　The objective of the review is to determine the reasonableness of the assumptions on which the forecast is based, that the forecast was properly prepared on the basis of the stated assumptions, and that it is presented in conformity with the recommendations of AICPA Accounting Standards Divison SOP 75-4, "Statement of Position on Presentation and Disclosure of Financial Forecasts." The scope of the review of a forecast is not unlike that of the review of financial statements, except that in addition to a knowledge of the business, the accountant should take into consideration management's forecasting experience.

In the review of assumptions the accountant should consider whether management has developed assumptions with respect to the key factors on which the client's financial results will depend, and consideration should also be given to the forecast's sensitivity to variations in the key factors on which the assumptions are based. The remaining aspect of the review should cover the preparation and presentation of the forecast based on the review of the underlying assumptions, with mathematical accuracy and generally accepted accounting principles being important considerations. The SEC has issued a "safe harbor" rule that protects projections that are made on a reasonable basis and in good faith, by placing the burden of proof on the plaintiff to show that a projection later found to be wrong had no reasonable basis.

*Reporting on a Review of a Financial Forecast.*　An example follows of a standard report that reflects the recommendations of the AICPA Review Guide, assuming that the reporting accountant is satisfied that the forecast is reasonable. Modifications of the report would be necessitated by uncertainty of the outcome of an assumption, for example whether or not a major contract for which a bid has been entered will be received; or when an adverse report should be rendered because the accountant believes one or more significant assumptions are not reasonable or because the forecast does not conform to the guidelines of SOP 75-4. The example of a standard report:

> We have reviewed the accompanying financial forecast of ABC Corp., which consists of a forecasted balance sheet as of December 31, 19XX, and forecasted statements of operations and changes in financial position for the year then ending, including the related summary of significant assumptions. Our review was made in accordance with the guidelines of the American Institute of Certified Public Accountants for such reviews and accordingly

included procedures to evaluate the assumptions used by management as a basis for the financial forecast, and to evaluate the preparation and presentation of the financial forecast.

A financial forecast is management's estimate of the most probable financial results of a future period and reflects management's judgment based on present circumstances of the most likely set of conditions and its most likely course of action. Forecasts are based on assumptions about circumstances and events that have not yet taken place and are subject to variations. There is thus no assurance that the forecasted results will be attained.

We have no responsibility to update this report for events and circumstances occurring after the date of this report.

Based on our review, we believe the accompanying financial forecast has been prepared using assumptions that are reasonable as a basis for management's forecast, and is presented in conformity with applicable guidelines established by the American Institute of Certified Public Accountants for presentation of a financial forecast.

### Long-Form Reports

In situations where owners, managers, or third parties may desire more extensive information, analysis, and interpretation than is available internally or through audited financial statements, the auditor may submit a long-form report to meet that need. Such an extended report may include additional details of items in the financial statements, statistical data, explanatory comments, comparative analyses, or other informative material including nonaccounting related information. Especially useful in such a report is information on how well a company is performing in comparison with its competitors. Helpful comparative information can be obtained from averages compiled by trade associations; the Small Business Administration; or Dun & Bradstreet. The long-form report may also include information about specific auditing procedures that have been applied. Preferably, the supplementary material will be presented in conjunction with the standard short-form report on the client's financial statements, but in any case the auditor has a responsibility to report on all information in any auditor-submitted document. That reporting responsibility extends to a clear description of the character of the auditor's examination and the degree of responsibility, if any, that the auditor is taking for the accompanying information.

Any supplementary information included in a long-form report or other auditor-prepared document must be just that: supplementary, and hence should not be necessary for the presentation of financial position, results of operations, or changes in financial position in conformity with generally accepted accounting principles. Hence, there is no obligation to apply auditing procedures to the supplementary information, although the auditor may choose to modify or redirect certain procedures applied in examining the basic financial statements so that an opinion may be expressed on the supplementary information. The measurement of materiality for the supplementary information, unlike the measurement when reporting on specified elements of a financial statement, is the same as that used in forming an opinion on the financial statements as a whole. Accordingly, audit procedures need not be as extensive as if an opinion were to be expressed on the information when stated and reported on separately.

If the auditor elects to extend the examination and express an opinion on the supplementary information, the auditor's report on the information could read as follows:

> Our examination of the financial statements of Blank Inc. was made for the purpose of forming an opinion on the basic financial statements taken as a whole, as we have reported on page X. The supplementary information presented on pages XX through YY is presented for the purposes of additional analysis and is not a required part of the basic financial statements. Such information has been subjected to the auditing procedures applied in the examination of the basic financial statements and, in our opinion, is fairly stated in all material respects in relation to the basic financial statements taken as a whole.

If the auditor disclaims an opinion on all or part of the supplementary information, the information should be marked as unaudited or should include a reference to the auditor's disclaimer of opinion. The following report would be appropriate if the disclaimer applies to all of the information:

> Our examination of the financial statements of Blank Inc. was made for the purpose of forming an opinion on the financial statements taken as a whole, as we have reported on page X. The supplementary information presented on pages XX through YY is presented for the purpose of additional analysis and is not a required part of the basic financial statements. Such information has not been subjected to the auditing procedures applied in the examination of the basic financial statements, and, accordingly, we express no opinion on it.

*Organization and Content.* The following table of contents is presented to suggest the possible content and arrangement of a long-form report:

Independent auditor's report on examination of financial statements
Balance sheet
Statement of capital changes
Statement of operations
Statement of changes in financial position
Independent auditor's report on supplementary information
Financial and operating highlights

Organization, nature of business, and history
Cash in banks and on hand
Marketable securities
Trade receivables
  Credit terms
  Aging analysis
  Comparative turnover statistics
Inventories
  Product classifications and detail of cost elements
  Turnover statistics
Property plant and equipment
  Asset acquisitions and retirements
  Accumulated depreciation—additions and eliminations
Accounts payable classified by due date
Other current liabilities
Long-term debt
  Notes payable—equipment purchases
  First-mortgage bonds
Capital stock
Retained earnings and dividends
Sales and gross margin by product lines: 5-year comparison
Selling expenses
General and administrative expenses
Federal and state income taxes
  Investment credit
  Deferred taxes
  Reconciliation of tax expense and taxes payable
Schedule of insurance coverage

A unique approach to the preparation of long-form reports has been taken by McGladrey, Hendrickson & Co., a national CPA firm headquartered in Davenport, Iowa. The firm has developed a standard format for their long-form reports, based on the annual financial report for "Model Corporation." By standardizing on this format, the firm has reduced the time required to prepare such reports, and bankers and other third parties to whom clients send copies of the reports find the standardization helpful in ensuring that all desired information will be included and in knowing exactly where in the report the information can be found and in what form.

## Questions/Problems

For multiple-choice questions 21-1 through 21-11, indicate the letter of the single answer that *best* completes the statement or answers the question, and justify the choice that you have made.

**21-1.** Which of the following procedures is *not* included in a review engagement of a nonpublic entity?

a.   Inquiries of management.

b.   Inquiries regarding events subsequent to the balance sheet date.

c.   Any procedures designed to identify relationships among data that appear to be unusual.

d.   A study and evaluation of internal control.

*(Uniform CPA Examination)*

**21-2.** Which of the following would *not be* included in a CPA's report based upon a review of the financial statements of a nonpublic entity?

a.   A statement that the review was in accordance with generally accepted auditing standards.

b.   A statement that all information included in the financial statements are the representations of management.

c.   A statement describing the principal procedures performed.

d.   A statement describing the auditor's conclusions based upon the results of the review.

*(Uniform CPA Examination)*

**21-3.** A CPA has audited financial statements and issued an unqualified opinion on them. Subsequently the CPA was requested to compile financial statements for the same period that omit substantially all disclosures and are to be used for comparative purposes. In these circumstances the CPA may report on comparative compiled financial statements that omit such disclosures provided the

a.   Missing disclosures are immaterial in amount.

b.   Financial statements and notes appended thereto are not misleading.

c.   Accountant's report indicates the previous audit and the date of the previous report.

d.   Previous auditor's report accompanies the comparative financial statement.

*(Uniform CPA Examination)*

**21-4.** A report based on a limited review of interim financial statements would include all of the following elements *except*:

a.   A statement that an examination was performed in accordance with generally accepted auditing standards.

b.   A description of the procedures performed or a reference to procedures described in an engagement letter.

c.   A statement that a limited review would *not* necessarily disclose all matters of significance.

d. An identification of the interim financial information reviewed.

(Uniform CPA Examination)

**21-5.** A CPA should *not* normally refer to which one of the following
subjects in a "comfort letter" to underwriters?

a. The independence of the CPA.

b. Changes in financial-statement items during a period subsequent to the date and period of the latest financial statements in the registration statement.

c. Unaudited financial statements and schedules in the registration statement.

d. Management's determination of line of business classifications.

(Uniform CPA Examination)

**21-6.** The term "special reports" may include all of the following *except* reports on financial statements

a. Of an organization that has limited the scope of the auditor's examination.

b. Prepared for limited purposes, such as a report that relates
to only certain aspects of financial statements.

c. Of a not-for-profit organization which follows accounting
practices differing in some respects from those followed by
business enterprises organized for profit.

d. Prepared in accordance with a cash basis of accounting.

(Uniform CPA Examination)

**21-7.** Which of the following statements with respect to an auditor's
report expressing an opinion on a specific item on a financial
statement is correct?

a. Materiality must be related to the specified item rather than
to the financial statements taken as a whole.

b. Such a report can only be expressed if the auditor is also
engaged to audit the entire set of financial statements.

c. The attention devoted to the specified item is usually less
than it would be if the financial statements taken as a whole
were being audited.

d. The auditor who has issued an adverse opinion on the financial statements taken as a whole can never express an
opinion on a specified item in these financial statements.

(Uniform CPA Examination)

**21-8.** A CPA's report accompanying a cash forecast or other type of
projection should

a. Not be issued in any form because it would be in violation
of the AICPA Code of Professional Ethics.

b. Disclaim any opinion as to the forecast's achievability.
c. Be prepared only if the client is a not-for-profit organization.
d. Be a qualified short-form audit report if the business concern is operated for a profit.

(Uniform CPA Examination)

21-9. If an auditor's report on internal control is distributed to the general public, it must contain specific language describing several matters. Which of the following *must* be included in the specific language?
   a. The distinction between internal adminstrative controls and internal accounting controls.
   b. The objective of internal accounting controls.
   c. The various tests and procedures utilized by the auditor during the review of internal controls.
   d. The reason(s) why management requested a report on internal controls.

(Uniform CPA Examination)

21-10. Which of the following best describes the difference between a long-form auditor's report and the standard short-form report?
   a. The long-form report may contain a more detailed description of the scope of the auditor's examination.
   b. The long-form report's use permits the auditor to explain exceptions or reservations in a way that does not require an opinion qualification.
   c. The auditor may make factual representations with a degree of certainty that would not be appropriate in a short-form report.
   d. The long-form report's use is limited to special situations, such as cash basis statements, modified accrual basis statements, or not-for-profit organization statements.

(Uniform CPA Examination)

21-11. Nonaccounting data included in a long-form report have been subjected to auditing procedures. The auditor's report should state this fact and should explain that the nonaccounting data are presented for analysis purposes. In addition, the auditor's report should state whether the nonaccounting data are
   a. Beyond the scope of the normal engagement and therefore, *not* covered by the opinion on the financial statements.
   b. Within the framework of generally accepted auditing standards, which apply to the financial statements taken as a whole.
   c. Audited, unaudited, or reviewed on a limited basis.

    d.  Fairly stated in all material respects in relation to the basic financial statement, taken as a whole.

(Uniform CPA Examination)

**21-12.** How much responsibility should the auditor assume for the fairness or accuracy of supplementary information or statistical analyses included in a long-form report?

**21-13.** In accordance with a provision in the bond indenture underlying your client's outstanding bonds, the client is not permitted to reduce working capital below $250,000 at any time, and you are required to include in your report a statement as to whether the client has complied with this requirement. What steps would be necessary in order for you to determine whether the client has complied with this requirement?

**21-14.** Write a comment to be included in your client's report explaining why dividend payments on the capital stock have not kept pace with the increase in income in recent years. Your client is a typical manufacturing concern, with total assets of $2,500,000, and its experience has been typical.

**21-15.** A company seeking a short-term bank loan will normally be expected to present a plan for the liquidation of the loan. Would it be proper for the auditor to assist a client in preparing a cash forecast to show the company's plans for repaying the loan? Should the forecast be included in the auditor's long-form report to be presented to the bank? Explain.

**21-16.** Jones and Todd, a local CPA firm, received an invitation to bid for the audit of a local, federally assisted program. The audit is to be conducted in accordance with the audit standards published by the General Accounting Office (GAO), a federal auditing agency. Jones and Todd has become familiar with the GAO standards and recognizes that the GAO standards are not consistent with generally accepted auditing standards (GAAS). The GAO standards, unlike GAAS, are concerned with more than the financial aspects of an entity's operations. The GAO standards broaden the definition of auditing by establishing that the full scope of an audit should encompass the following elements:

    1.  An examination of *financial* transactions, accounts, and reports, including an evaluation of *compliance* with applicable laws and regulations.

    2.  A review of *efficiency and economy* in the use of resources, such as personnel and equipment.

    3.  A review to determine whether desired results are effectively achieved *(program results)*.

Jones and Todd has been engaged to perform the audit of the program, and the audit is to encompass all three elements.

Required:

(a) Jones and Todd should perform sufficient audit work to satisfy the *financial* and *compliance* element of the GAO standards. What should such audit work determine?

(b) After making appropriate review and inquiries, what uneconomical practices or inefficiencies should Jones and Todd be alert to, in satisfying the *efficiency* and *economy* element encompassed by the GAO standards?

(c) After making appropriate review and inquiries, what should Jones and Todd consider to satisfy the *program results* element encompassed by the GAO standards?

(Uniform CPA Examination)

**21-17.** Rose & Co., CPAs, has satisfactorily completed the examination of the financial statements of Bale & Booster, a partnership, for the year ended December 31, 1979. The financial statements which were prepared on the entity's income tax (cash) basis include footnotes which indicate that the partnership was involved in continuing litigation of material amounts relating to alleged infringement of a competitor's patent. The amount of damages, if any, resulting from this litigation could not be determined at the time of completion of the engagement. The prior years' financial statements were not presented.

Required:

Based upon the information presented, prepare an auditor's report which includes appropriate explanatory disclosure of significant facts.

(Uniform CPA Examination)

**21-18.** The financial statements of the Tiber Company have never been audited by an independent CPA. Recently, Tiber's management asked Anthony Burns, CPA, to conduct a special study of Tiber's internal control; this study will not include an examination of Tiber's financial statements. Following completion of his special study, Mr. Burns plans to prepare a report that is consistent with the requirements of Statement on Auditing Procedure No. 49, "Reports on Internal Control."

Required:

(a) Describe the inherent limitations that should be recognized in considering the potential effectiveness of a system of internal control.

(b) Explain and contrast the review of internal control that Mr. Burns might make as part of an examination of financial statements with his special study of Tiber's internal control, covering each of the following:

1. Objectives of review or study.
2. Scope of review or study.
3. Nature and content of reports.

Organize your answer for part b. as follows:

| Examination of Financial Statements | Special Study |
|---|---|
| 1. Objective | 1. Objective |
| 2. Scope | 2. Scope |
| 3. Report | 3. Report |

(c) In connection with a loan application, Tiber plans to submit the CPA's report on his special study of internal control, together with its latest unaudited financial statements, to the Fourth National Bank.

Discuss the propriety of this use of the CPA's report on internal control.

(Uniform CPA Examination)

**21-19.** Charles Burke, CPA, has completed field work for his examination of the Willingham Corporation for the year ended December 31, 19XX, and now is in the process of determining whether to modify his report. Presented below are two independent, unrelated situations which have arisen.

Situation I

In September, 19XX, a lawsuit was filed against Willingham to have the court order it to install pollution-control equipment in one of its older plants. Willingham's legal counsel has informed Burke that it is not possible to forecast the outcome of this litigation; however, Willingham's management has informed Burke that the cost of the pollution-control equipment is not economically feasible and that the plant will be closed if the case is lost. In addition, Burke has been told by management that the plant and its production equipment would have only minimal resale values and that the production that would be lost could not be recovered at other plants.

Situation II

During 19XX, Willingham purchased a franchise amounting to 20 percent of its assets for the exclusive right to produce and sell a newly patented product in the northeastern United States. There has been no production in marketable quantities of the product anywhere to date. Neither the franchisor nor any franchisee has conducted any market research with respect to the product.

Required:

In deciding the type-of-report modification, if any, Burke should take into account such considerations as follows:

- Relative magnitude
- Uncertainty of outcome
- Likelihood of error
- Expertise of the auditor
- Pervasive impact on the financial statements
- Inherent importance of the item

Discuss Burke's type-of-report decision for each situation in terms of the above and other appropriate considerations. Assume each situation is adequately disclosed in the notes to the financial statements. Each situation should be considered independently. In discussing each situation, ignore the other. *It is not necessary for you to decide the type of report which should be issued.*

(Uniform CPA Examination)

**21-20.** You are preparing your long-form report in connection with the examination of State Gas Company at December 31, this year. The report will include an explanation of this year's increase in operating revenues.

The following information is available from the company records:

|  | Last Year | This Year | Increase (Decrease) |
|---|---|---|---|
| Average number of customers | 27,000 | 26,000 | (1,000) |
| MCF sales ................. | 486,000 | 520,000 | 34,000 |
| Revenue ................. | $1,215,000 | $1,274,000 | $59,000 |

To explain this year's increase in operating revenues, prepare an analysis accounting for the effect of changes in:

(a) Average number of customers
(b) Average gas consumption per customer
(c) Average rate per MCF sold (MCF = thousand cubic feet)

(Uniform CPA Examination)

**21-21.** To obtain a more realistic appraisal of his investment, Martin Arnett, your client, has asked you to adjust certain financial data of The Glo-Bright Company for price level changes. On January 1, 19X5, he invested $50,000 in The Glo-Bright Company in return for 10,000 shares of common stock. Immediately after his investment the trial balance appeared as follows:

|                                             | Dr.       | Cr.       |
| ------------------------------------------- | --------- | --------- |
| Cash and receivables......................  | $ 65,200  |           |
| Merchandise inventory ...................... | 4,000     |           |
| Building .....................              | 50,000    |           |
| Accumulated depreciation—building........    |           | $  8,000  |
| Equipment .....................             | 36,000    |           |
| Accumulated depreciation—equipment .....     |           | 7,200     |
| Land .....................                   | 10,000    |           |
| Current liabilities.....................     |           | 50,000    |
| Capital stock, $5 par .....................  |           | 100,000   |
|                                             | $165,200  | $165,200  |

Balances in certain selected amounts as of December 31 of each of the next three years were as follows:

|                               | 19X5      | 19X6      | 19X7      |
| ----------------------------- | --------- | --------- | --------- |
| Sales .........................  | $39,650   | $39,000   | $42,350   |
| Inventory ..................... | 4,500     | 5,600     | 5,347     |
| Purchases.....................  | 14,475    | 16,350    | 18,150    |
| Operating expenses (excluding depreciation) ..................... | 10,050 | 9,050 | 9,075 |

Assume the 19X5 price level as the base year and that all changes in the price level take place at the beginning of each year. Further assume that the 19X6 price level is 10% above the 19X5 price level and that the 19X7 price level is 10% above the 19X6 level.

The building was constructed in 19X1 at a cost of $50,000 with an estimated life of 25 years. The price level at that time was 80% of the 19X5 price level.

The equipment was purchased in 19X3 at a cost of $36,000 with an estimated life of ten years. The price level at that time was 90% of the 19X5 price level.

The Lifo method of inventory valuation is used. The original inventory was acquired in the same year the building was constructed and was maintained at a constant $4,000 until 19X5. In 19X5 a gradual buildup of the inventory was begun in anticipation of an increase in the volume of business.

Arnett considers the return on his investment as the dividend he actually receives. In each of the years 19X5, 19X6 and 19X7, Glo-Bright paid cash dividends in the amount of $8,000.

On July 1, 19X6, there was a reverse stock split-up of the Company's stock in the ratio of one-for-ten.

Required:

(a) Compute the 19X7 earnings per share of common stock in terms of 19X5 dollars.

(b) Compute the percentage return on investment for 19X5 and 19X7 in terms of 19X5 dollars.

(Uniform CPA Examination)

21-22. The president of your client, the Collins Manufacturing Corp., has asked that you prepare a detailed report for him to be used at the next meeting of the board of directors. The report is to be addressed to the board. The president states that he is not interested in details concerning your examination, but in an analysis of the company's operations. He is particularly interested in having you show why the company had to borrow from the bank in the face of increased profits over the preceding year. Condensed balance sheets and income statements for the company are presented below, along with certain additional information. The statements need not be reproduced in your report.

**Table 21-1.** Collins Manufacturing Corp. Comparative Balance Sheets, December 31

| Assets | This Year | Last Year |
|---|---|---|
| Cash ............................... | $ 93,628 | $ 87,425 |
| Receivables ....................... | 275,931 | 241,639 |
| Inventories ....................... | 421,658 | 336,918 |
| Plant and equipment ................ | 384,123 | 406,831 |
| Less accumulated depreciation ....... | (204,963) | (215,869) |
| Other assets ....................... | 15,629 | 13,804 |
| | $986,006 | $870,748 |

| Equities | This Year | Last Year |
|---|---|---|
| Bank Loan ......................... | $ 50,000 | $ — |
| Accounts payable.................... | 165,913 | 148,319 |
| Accrued liabilities ................. | 76,904 | 68,419 |
| Capital stock ...................... | 400,000 | 400,000 |
| Retained earnings .................. | 293,189 | 254,010 |
| | $986,006 | $870,748 |

**Table 21-2.** Collins Manufacturing Corp. Comparative Income Statements, Year Ended December 31

| | This Year | Last Year |
|---|---|---|
| Sales | | |
| Gimmicks ....................... | $ 463,807 | $428,931 |
| Doodads ....................... | 604,361 | $321,173 |
| Total ....................... | $1,068,168 | $750,104 |

**Table 21-2.** Collins Manufacturing Corp. Comparative Balance Sheets, December 31 (Continued)

| | This Year | Last Year |
|---|---|---|
| Expenses | | |
| Cost of sales—gimmicks............. | $ 329,686 | $301,873 |
| Cost of sales—doodads ............. | 334,956 | 182,939 |
| Administrative expenses ........... | 52,316 | 43,281 |
| Selling expenses................... | 113,814 | 84,616 |
| Interest .......................... | 1,241 | — |
| Income taxes...................... | 136,976 | 73,904 |
| Total ......................... | $ 968,989 | $686,613 |
| Net Income ...................... | $ 99,179 | $ 63,491 |
| Depreciation included in expenses..... | $ 27,555 | $ 24,316 |
| Dividends declared and paid ......... | 60,000 | 60,000 |
| Cost of fully depreciated machinery retired................................ | 38,461 | — |

# Chapter 22

# TAX, MANAGEMENT ADVISORY, AND OTHER PUBLIC ACCOUNTING SERVICES

As accounting experienced its early development in the fourteenth and fifteenth centuries, there were relatively few persons who understood its precepts and were knowledgeable about its practice. Most of these few were the early public accountants—practitioners who, as the name implies, were engaged primarily in providing to others services related to accounting. They were the teachers who showed others how to become accountants, and they kept the books for some merchant traders and others engaged in business activities. For others they set up simple record systems and showed the entrepreneurs how to keep their own records. Other accounting-related activities included the teaching of penmanship and occasionally performing audits of the records maintained by others.

From these simple beginnings have developed the huge international accounting firms as we know them today, but to refer to them as firms of accountants belies their main form of activity, which is auditing. In its study of the public accounting profession, the U.S. Senate subcommittee chaired by then Senator Metcalf ascertained that for the eight largest firms, auditing services accounted for between 62 percent and 74 percent of the revenues of these firms; tax services for 15 percent to 24 percent of the revenues, and management advisory services for 5 percent to 16 percent of the revenues. At the other extreme, AICPA studies have shown the income of CPAs practicing as individuals to have been derived from the following sources, based on averages:

| | |
|---|---|
| Auditing | 22 percent |
| Taxes | 30 percent |
| Management advisory services | 12 percent |
| Other services, including compilation and review services, bookkeeping, and data processing | 36 percent |

### Tax Services

Client assistance on tax matters in the United States is largely an outgrowth of the first income tax legislation in 1913, for accountants were obviously in a favored position to develop the figures on which this new and seemingly innocuous tax was based. Today tax services encompass federal and state tax return preparation for audit clients and others, plus the vital area of tax planning as a basis for minimizing taxes to be paid in the future. In connection with tax planning, which provides the greatest opportunity to demonstrate the value of an accountant's services in a tangible manner, the client should be encouraged to consult the accountant before entering into any important contracts or transactions. Tax considerations always exist in such matters, and often a transaction can be handled in a way that will effect substantial tax savings.

Although corporate and individual income taxes represent the bulk of the tax activity, estate, inheritance, and gift taxes are also significant elements of tax practice. Large corporate clients typically have a tax department that handles most corporate tax matters, but a company's auditors may be engaged to provide for corporate officials and for expatriate employees of concerns with foreign operations such services as tax return preparation and financial planning.

As was noted earlier, it is generally advisable to have audit income tax accrual working papers reviewed by the tax department of the firm. Such services would, however, be billed as audit services rather than tax services. Also, of course, if difficult or questionable matters arise in connection with reviewing a tax accrual, tax specialists will conduct the necessary research to resolve those matters. Recommendations for tax-saving alternatives may also be an important ancillary benefit of the accrual review.

To provide these tax services, many accounting firms will have one or more persons on their tax staff with specialized training such as a masters in taxation or a law degree. Legal training has proved to be especially useful in tax practice because knowledge of the law and court decisions frequently have an important bearing on tax questions. The presence of lawyers on the staffs of CPA firms and the fine line that divides accounting practice and legal practice in tax matters has led to occasional conflict between the legal profession and the accounting profession. Local bar associations have sometimes sought to restrict the tax work being done by accountants through test cases in the courts. In an effort to resolve some of the conflict that developed, a National Conference of Lawyers and Certified Public Accountants was formed, and the conference prepared a "Statement of Principles Relating to Practice in the Field of Federal Income Taxation." This statement of principles has been quite successful in accomplishing its intended purpose and in general sets forth the areas open exclusively to lawyers or to CPAs, as well as the areas in which both may properly practice. The statement also points out the importance of having both a lawyer and a CPA serve the client in tax matters that involve both law and accounting. A lawyer on the staff of a public accounting firm should not, however, endeavor to provide legal services to the firm's clients.

Although no AICPA rule specifically prohibits the joint practice of law and accounting by a person who is qualified in both fields, such joint practice is generally discouraged. Furthermore, the two fields are so complicated and subject to constant change that one person can hardly maintain satisfactory proficiency in both fields, and any attempt to do so would seem to be at the expense of the quality of service rendered to clients. Nevertheless, some lawyer-CPAs conduct a dual practice, and they have formed their own professional organization, the American Association of Attorney-Certified Public Accountants.

### Ethics in Tax Practice

A CPA in tax practice is expected to follow the Rules of Professional Conduct with the following exceptions. Rule 101 on independence is applicable only to situations where the practitioner is expressing an opinion on financial statements, and Rules 202 and 203 on auditing standards and accounting principles apply only to audit situations. Also, Rule 302 on contingent fees specifically exempts tax matters inasmuch as final determinations on tax matters are made by the Internal Revenue Service or a judicial body and not by the accountant who is providing the service.

More to the point with respect to tax practice, the AICPA has formed a Federal Tax Division, within which a Responsibilities in Tax Practice Subcommittee issues Statements on Responsibilities in Tax Practice. In general, these Statements, which are referenced in Professional Standards at Sec. TX, point out that preparation of a tax return by a CPA requires an understanding of the information in the return to be obtained through inquiry or investigation of the client's records. The preparer has no responsibility, however, for determining that all taxable income has been reported or for substantiating the amount of deductible expenses other than to pursue any matters that appear questionable based on the preparer's knowledge or responses to inquiries. Statements on Responsibilities in Tax Practice issued to date cover such matters as

- When a tax return should bear the accountant's signature as a preparer.
- The responsibilities assumed when a tax return is reviewed and the reviewer elects to sign as the preparer.
- The proper course of action when one or more questions that are part of the tax return have not been answered.
- The use of estimates.
- How to proceed if an accountant becomes aware of an error in a previously filed tax return when the accountant is engaged in preparing a current return or in representing a client in an administrative proceeding.
- The appropriate action when tax advice has been provided to a client and subsequent developments affect the advice previously provided.
- How to proceed in the preparation of a tax return when taking a position that is contrary to interpretations of the Internal Revenue Code by the Treasury Department or the Internal Revenue Service.

### Management Advisory Services

The third major area of client services provided by CPA firms is that of management advisory services. As the term indicates, these are services directed to assisting management in carrying out its reponsibilities, and the services should be advisory and hence should not involve direct assumption of responsibility for the execution of management functions. Thus these are essentially consulting services and address typical management problems in such areas as accounting and data processing, internal control, organization and administration, internal reporting, financial planning, actuarial benefit determinations, operations research, and production control.

Both interest in providing management advisory services and the extent of those services have grown steadily over the years, with that growth largely attributable to the following factors:

1. Development of such highly specialized techniques as operations research, statistical sampling, electronic data processing, and production control has made it difficult for many businesses to maintain staffs with competence in all of these areas. Under these circumstances businesses have naturally

sought outside assistance as they have become interested in these advanced techniques, and for reasons to be explored shortly, public accountants have been a logical choice to provide the desired assistance.

2. In periods of continued prosperity businesses become more expansive in their thinking and more willing to accept the risks of experimentation with new ideas. Coincidentally, profitable operations provide funds that can be used for such experimentation.

3. The education and training of the people entering public accounting have broadened, thus facilitating the entrance of public accounting firms into the field of business consultation.

4. Consulting services in the management field are a natural outgrowth of the auditing work performed for clients.

5. The fees for consulting work are attractive because they are based in part on the savings or other benefits produced.

## Public Accountants a Logical Choice for Management Services

There are various reasons why management may reasonably be expected to turn to the public accounting firm that conducts the annual audit when seeking consulting assistance. Perhaps most importantly, the auditing firm and the quality of its work are already known to management as a result of an extended period of contact. An outside management consulting firm can be judged only on the basis of its own assertions as to its competence or on the recommendation of others who may have engaged the firm and were satisfied with the results.

Another reason for securing management consulting services from the public accounting firm that conducts the regular audit examination is the familiarity that the firm will already have gained with the client's organization, operations, and problems. A firm that does only management consulting work would have to acquire a similar amount of background information, but acquiring the information would entail added expense and inconvenience to the client.

Management advisory services are also often a natural outgrowth of performing the auditing function—particularly if a "constructive auditing" approach has been employed. As discussed more fully later in this chapter, a constructive approach yields suggestions to management for improving organization, operations, or accounting and related internal controls. Management then frequently turns to the accounting firm for assistance in implementing the suggestions that have been made.

Perhaps one of the major factors pointing to the choice of a concern's public accountants for management consulting service is the presence of what amounts to a practical guarantee that the work will be satisfactory. A management consulting firm is engaged on a one-time basis, and after it has presented its recommendations and collected its fee, its responsibility tends to cease. The public accounting firm, however, has to "live with its recommendations," for it will not willingly risk losing an audit client as a result of faulty management advisory services. Its representatives will therefore be returning under a corresponding pressure to remedy any shortcomings that might appear as the recommendations by management services personnel are implemented.

Another desirable feature of engaging a concern's auditors or any firm of CPAs is the fact that such firms operate under a strict code of ethics intended to ensure the quality of the services to be provided.

### Introduction of Nonauditing Services into Public Accounting

At the turn of the century the auditing profession in the United States was still largely engaged in a routine mechanical form of figure checking, and the typical auditor who was performing such work had only a limited horizon that seldom included a recognition or understanding of the problems of management. The obvious familiarity of the practitioner of that day with accounting systems did, however, frequently lead to engagements to design and install accounting systems. As the amount of such work and the size of accounting firms increased, the opportunity arose for individuals within firms to specialize in systems work, and from such a beginning has developed the more comprehensive activity of management advisory services.

It is interesting to note that although accounting systems work was performed by accounting firms well in advance of the introduction of the first income tax law in 1913, tax services expanded more quickly and soon exceeded systems work as a source of fee income. Taxes were more compatible with the earlier public accountant's penchant for detail, and there was no other group so well qualified to assist with problems arising from the new tax based on income. By contrast, management engineering firms stood ready to aid the company that needed help with its accounting system, and these engineering firms aggressively sought such engagements. There was also a widely held belief that accounting systems were merely one branch of the whole field of systems, which was considered essentially as being the engineer's province. World War II marked a major turning point in the situation as a result of such wartime developments as operations research, electronic computers, and statistical quality control and inspection techniques. Business concerns sought an increasing amount of outside assistance, and accounting firms began to employ specialists to aid in the increasing variety of services being performed, with a resulting rapid growth in the management advisory staff and the services being provided.

### Professional Developments: Practice Standards

In 1953 the AICPA appointed a Committee on Management Services to explore this area of service to clients, to develop ways of furthering recognition of CPAs as competent advisers to management, and to assist

CPAs in providing more competent management advisory services. In 1956 this committee released a pamphlet entitled *A Classification of Management Services by CPAs*, which was designed to show the broad scope of the field of management services. The pamphlet included a list of services intended primarily to be illustrative, but representing services that had actually been performed by CPAs. The 6-page list was classified under eight major headings covering the principal functional areas of business, plus the overall area of general management and administration. Included under these headings were such services as assistance in developing management policies, development of complete plans of internal reporting, advice as to sources of capital and types of securities to be issued, assistance in long-range financial planning, survey of production planning and methods of production and quality control, advice on product prices, and assistance in preparing job classifications and job evaluations. These services in turn have been grouped according to the type of service involved:

Organizational matters

Data processing

Control (including profit planning, responsibility reporting, budgets, standard costs, production and inventory control)

Management science (quantitative problem-solving techniques)

Cost reduction

The AICPA has in various ways provided assistance to its members in developing and increasing competence in the multifaceted aspects of management services. A major publication in this connection is *Management Advisory Services by CPAs*, which reports on the results of a survey to determine the various types of knowledge that an MAS practitioner should have and discusses the overall characteristics of MAS practice.

Standards of practice have also been set forth by the Management Advisory Services Executive Committee of the AICPA. The standards have been published in the booklet *Statements on Management Advisory Services* and are referenced in *Professional Standards* at MS Sec. 101 through 180. The eight standards, which are further elaborated and discussed in the indicated MS Sections, are as follows:

1. *Personal Characteristics.* In performing management advisory services, a practitioner must act with integrity and objectivity and be independent in mental attitude.
2. *Competence.* Engagements are to be performed by practitioners having competence in the analytical approach and process, and in the technical subject matter under consideration.
3. *Due Care.* Due professional care is to be exercised in the performance of a management advisory services engagement.
4. *Client Benefit.* Before accepting an engagement, a practitioner is to notify

the client of any reservations that may be held regarding anticipated benefits.

5. *Understanding with Client.* Before undertaking an engagement, a practitioner is to inform the client of all significant matters related to the engagement.

6. *Planning, Supervision, and Control.* Engagements are to be adequately planned, supervised, and controlled.

7. *Sufficient Relevant Data.* Sufficient relevant data is to be obtained, documented, and evaluated in developing conclusions and recommendations.

8. *Communication of Results.* All significant matters relating to the results of the engagement are to be communicated to the client.

The above standards of practice, plus certain limitations on the provision of management advisory services set forth in a following section of this chapter on professional considerations, have largely been incorporated in the exposure draft for the first of a new series of Statements on Standards for Management Advisory Services to be issued by the AICPA Management Advisory Services Executive Committee. The AICPA has accorded to these statements on standards to be issued by the committee status comparable to the Statements on Auditing Standards issued by the Auditing Standards Board, and hence the standards will be enforceable under the AICPA Rules of Conduct. The exposure draft differentiates MAS engagements and MAS consultations, with the latter not involving the analytical approach and process applied in a formal study or project, but rather involving less formal advice to management that is based largely on existing knowledge of the client and the technical matters in question. The proposed statement on standards is to be equally applicable to both categories of management advisory services, with a proposed January 1, 1982 effective date.

### MAS Practice Guidelines

To further assist CPAs in providing MAS services to clients, the following AICPA Guidelines Series booklets have been issued:

No. 1 *Guidelines for Administration of the MAS Practice*

No. 2 *Documentation Guides for Administration of MAS Engagements*

No. 3 *Guidelines for Systems for Preparation of Financial Forecasts*

No. 4 *Guidelines for the Development and Implementation of Computer-Based Application Systems*

No. 5 *Guidelines for Cooperative Management Advisory Services Engagements*

No. 6 *Guidelines for CPA Participation in Government Audit Engagements to Evaluate Economy, Efficiency, and Program Results*

No. 7 *Interpretations of Management Advisory Services Practice Standards*

In addition, these special reports have been issued:

*Operational Review of the EDP Function*
*Energy Conservation Studies Including Energy Audits*
*Environmental Cost/Benefit Studies*

Through its Continuing Professional Education Division the AICPA provides resident-type courses in all areas of professional practice, including management services, and also offers a wide variety of individual study materials pertaining to MAS and all other areas of professional practice.

### Professional Considerations in Providing Management Services

Management services may extend into areas that are quite unrelated to accounting, but the extension of the accountant's services beyond the area of accounting should cause no concern, provided that the following limitations are not violated:

1. There must be competence in all engagements that are undertaken, both on the part of staff employees performing the work and on the part of the principal of the accounting firm responsible for supervising the work.
2. Engagements should not extend into areas that are legally forbidden, such as law or medicine.
3. The rules of professional conduct applicable to the practice of accounting in general must also be observed in such nonaccounting work.
4. Services should not extend beyond the presentation of recommendations or the giving of advice; making actual decisions for management would jeopardize the independence of the practitioner in performing independent auditing services.

The independence question has been widely discussed in recent years, with those who are critical of accounting firms entering the management services area maintaining that the activity amounts to participation in the management of the client concern, thereby causing a loss of independence in the provision of auditing services to the concern. The contention is that even though the accounting firm does not make actual decisions, the firm still becomes hopelessly enmeshed in the management function. Its consultants participate in all of the preliminary steps in the decision process, short of the final choice from among alternatives, and in most instances the consultants' choice in making recommendations becomes the management choice as well. (Should management choose otherwise, the soundness of the consultants' recommendations is automatically open to question.) Furthermore, in providing management advisory services, the accounting firm of necessity assumes the role of advocate, and third-party interests are of no concern. Finally, independence could suffer by reason of the firm's financial involvement in the outcome of its recommendations. It is conceivable that in a subsequent examination of operating results, the firm providing consulting services might be influenced in accepting accounting figures that would reflect favorably on the efficacy of its management services advice. The problem is especially trenchant in the occasional instances of advising on acquisitions of other companies.

These arguments tend to carry little weight with either individual public accounting practitioners or their professional association, the AICPA and its officers, boards, and committees. The profession's desire to maintain its role in the field of management services is readily explained by the fact that it has developed a vested interest in the provision of these wanted and needed services to its clients, it feels that it is in the best position to satisfy these needs, and it has developed in the management services area a highly attractive source of income. To sustain this position, the profession argues that its independence is not in jeopardy because major consulting engagements are invariably performed by professional staff who have no relationship to the provision of audit services. When consulting services are performed by audit staff on an incidental basis to audit activities, the record established over many years shows no resulting loss of independence. Finally, independence is essentially a state of mind, and the ability to maintain an independent state of mind has been demonstrated over the entire history of the profession in the face of dependence on clients for the payment of fees for audit services that have been provided.

### The Scope of Services Issue

The Securities and Exchange Commission, as we have noted, places primary reliance on independent auditors' reports for assurance that the financial and operating information available to investors in registered companies will be complete and reliable. The cornerstone of that reliance is the independence of the accountants who examine and report on the financial statements of those registered companies, and the SEC has long been concerned about the possible effect on independence when the auditor of a registered company provides MAS services to the company.

The SEC has addressed the problem in two of its Accounting Series Releases. ASR No. 250 requires a registered company to disclose in its proxy statement a description of any nonaudit services rendered by the firm that has been engaged to examine its financial statements. Also required is disclosure of whether before each professional service was rendered, it was approved by the board of directors or its audit committee and whether the possible effect of providing the service on the accounting firm's independence was considered. Further, for any services for which the fee exceeded 3 percent of the audit fee, the percentage relationship of the fee for the service to the audit fee is required to be reported in the proxy statement. Clearly the purpose of these requirements is to promote careful consideration of the independence issue whenever significant nonaudit services are to be obtained from the accounting firm serving as the company's auditor. The required reporting of the nature of the nonaudit services provided and their significance relative to the audit fee are intended to permit interested investors to make their own appraisal of the propriety of the services rendered and the possible effect on independence if the services were significant relative to the audit fee.

In this regard the results of a study of disclosures by 4,319 proxy statements for the period October 1, 1978 through June 30, 1979, as reported by Scott S. Cowen in *Journal of Accountancy*, December, 1980, are interesting. For the companies represented in the survey, tax services averaged 10 percent of the audit fee and MAS services 8 percent. For 50 percent of the companies the total nonaudit fees ranged from 4 percent to 25 percent of the audit fees, and for 10 percent of the companies the nonaudit fees exceeded 50 percent of the audit fee. For the Fortune 1,300 companies covered by the survey, the following services were reported by the indicated percentages of the companies:

| | |
|---|---|
| Management planning and organizational controls | 29 percent |
| Financial and accounting systems and controls | 22 percent |
| Data systems consulting | 18 percent |
| Human resource systems | 16 percent |
| Operational systems and controls | 10 percent |
| Actuarial services | 2 percent |

### Other SEC Initiatives

At about the same time that ASR 250 was issued, the SEC encouraged the public accounting profession to consider whether certain nonaudit services should be proscribed as potentially harmful to audit independence—what has come to be known as the scope of services issue. In response to the questions raised about the scope of services the Executive Committee of the SEC Practice Section of the AICPA Division for CPA Firms acted to proscribe the provision of executive recruiting services to SEC audit clients and to limit the performance of primary or exclusive actuarial services that have an effect on the financial statements of insurance company audit clients. With respect to these two services, however, it should be noted that the proscription applies only to a firm's audit clients, and at least one of the largest international accounting firms has announced that it stands ready to provide executive search services to companies that are not its audit clients.

Subsequently the Public Oversight Board of the SEC Practice Section was requested to study the scope of services issue and in 1979 issued a report, "Scope of Services of CPA Firms." In its report the POB recognized the many potential benefits of permitting auditors to perform management advisory services for audit clients and recommended that such benefits not be denied without a strong showing of actual or potential detriment. The Board also supported the Executive Committee proscriptions regarding executive recruiting services and certain actuarial services, but urged that mandatory limitations on scope of services be based only on the possible impairment of a firm's independence in rendering an opinion on the fairness of financial statements. In that connection the POB looked with disfavor on prohibitions based on a presumption that the services may be incompatible with the profession of public accounting, that they may impair the image of the profession, or that they do not involve accounting- or auditing-related skills. Thus the POB did not endorse proscriptions in the original Organization Document of the SEC Practice Section pertaining to psychological testing, conducting public opinion polls, merger and acquisition work for a finder's fee, marketing consulting, and plant layout.

Instead of such specific proscriptions not directly related to the independence questions, the Board recommended that compliance with the MS provisions set forth in Professional Standards and the AICPA Code of Professional Ethics be made a condition of membership in the SEC section, and that the mandatory peer reviews of member firms be extended to include tests of compliance of MAS engagements with those standards as they pertain to independence. Also, to provide further information about the relative significance of MAS services provided by SEC Practice Section members, the POB recommended that the firms be required to include in their annual disclosure statements filed with the Section the gross fees for MAS and tax services expressed as a percentage of total fees billed for the reporting period.

These recommendations and changes did not, however, entirely satisfy the SEC, as evidenced by the Commission's issuance of Accounting Series Release No. 264, "Scope of Services by Independent Accountants." Although the release imposed no specific rules, the SEC said it wished to "sensitize the profession and its clients to the potential effects on the independence of accountants of performance of non-audit services for audit clients." In Fall 1981, the SEC staff recommended that ASR No. 264 be withdrawn along with ASR No. 250. As the matter stands, there are no specific SEC restrictions on the provision of accounting-related management-advisory services, but both accountants and their clients are under pressure to avoid any situations that might be construed to lead to possible impairment of auditor independence. Subject to proper precautions, however, clients may continue to realize the benefits of MAS services provided by their regular accounting firm as being the firm that would be most knowledgeable about the client and its operations, and audit engagements may continue to benefit from the additional knowledge to be gained about the client and its operations as a result of providing those MAS services to management.

### Management Advisory Services for the Nonpublic Client

Audits serve a vital function for third parties and for society as a whole by increasing the credibility of financial statements, but the benefits of an audit to the *client* tend to be limited to facilitating the procurement of capital funds. Under these circumstances the entrepreneurs and managers of nonpublic enterprises who find it necessary to obtain an audit may be prone to consider the auditor as somewhat of a parasite— an attitude that can be readily altered if the auditor takes a "constructive auditing" approach to the engagement. This approach merely involves utilizing the intimate knowledge of the client's operations and affairs gained in the course of the auditor's examination to identify problems that the client has encountered and to offer possible solutions to those problems via the management letter that has been referred to previously. Possibilities would relate to such matters as internal controls over liquid funds, processing of customers' orders and recording the resulting revenues, credit and collection policies and procedures for accounts receivable, and authorizing and recording the disbursement of funds. There may also be unexplored or alternative sources of financing that can be suggested for additional funds or reduced costs, and of course the tax area is likely to be an especially fertile field for money-saving suggestions.

From the standpoint of the client an examination undertaken with the constructive auditing approach can serve much the same purpose as a regular medical checkup, with the auditor being somewhat of a "business physician" who is prepared to diagnose and prescribe remedies for the ills that may be detected and diagnosed. Also, of course, from the identification of problems and the suggestion of solutions can come opportunities to assist the client in a management advisory services capacity. The following disguised excerpts from actual management letters are presented to suggest the breadth, depth, and intensity of the recommendations that might be made and how the information can be presented.

Blank & Co.
Certified Public Accountants

Mr. S. J. Nannell, President,
Nannell Industries, Inc.:

This memorandum has been prepared as a result of the work we have performed in connection with our initial examination of the company's financial statements. This examination has afforded us the opportunity to observe and study the accounting policies and procedures and the organization of the company, and to become familiar with certain of the company's basic operating and financial problems. The knowledge gained in this process has enabled us to present various suggestions to the company with respect to taxes, controls, and procedures during the course of our work. It also prompted our proposal to make a highspot review of procedures at three of the principal plants in order to obtain a better understanding of the problems which we felt were present with respect to inventory control and production scheduling, and to develop specific suggestions for more effective management control.

We found the company's accounting system to be fundamentally sound and generally well organized to provide essential information to management for effective operating and financial control of the company's business. At the same time we observed certain areas where procedural modifications or revisions might facilitate the development of information, provide additional information or enable management to perform its function to better advantage.

Although certain of the suggestions previously offered to the company were formalized in memorandums, many suggestions have been made verbally during conferences with various members of the company's management. It is appropriate that the more significant suggestions be summarized for the information and use of the entire management of the company. This memorandum has been prepared for this purpose, as well as to offer certain suggestions not previously presented.

It should be recognized that our suggestions for the most part represent by-products of observations made during the audit. Accordingly, in most instances, we have made no detailed review of them, since this was not contemplated in the work being performed. Consequently, even though we consider each of these suggestions to have merit, they should be evaluated carefully and studied further in reaching final decisions regarding their disposition.

We would welcome the opportunity to discuss any of these suggestions with you in more detail.

Very truly yours,
Blank & Co., CPAs


### Summary of Results of Highspot Review

Before the completion of our examination, arrangements were made for qualified personnel of our management services staff to make a highspot review of the operating divisions located in Kansas City, Wichita, and Springfield. The specific objectives of this review were—

1. To supplement the information obtained during the audit by affording these people an opportunity to obtain firsthand knowledge of the operating characteristics and problems of each division and to obtain a more thorough understanding of the policies and practices governing each division.
2. To determine the methods and procedures used for data processing and reporting.
3. To evaluate the information obtained in this review and to pass on our observations to management for further consideration.

Our observations have been discussed with management, and a tentative draft of our comments delivered. This portion of the memorandum will be used to finalize these comments. The points discussed in this section are—

I. The greatest potential for improving operations of the company lies in the area of inventory control and production scheduling. Because of customer service, unbalanced inventories, and high setup costs, the Instruments Division has the most acute problem.

II. There appear to be potential savings to the company in the data processing field. The potential lies in two areas:
   (a) Streamlining the existing system.
   (b) Centralizing data processing.

The company apparently has not decided in which of these areas to concentrate. Management should make this decision so the efforts of all concerned can be directed toward a common goal; however, substantially the same evaluation process is necessary to streamline the existing procedures as is required to study the feasibility of centralized data processing. Management should consider that a properly executed feasibility study will produce—

   (a) The basis for making a decision as to whether or not to centralize.
   (b) The information essential for streamlining the system regardless of the outcome of the decision.

III. Summary techniques could be utilized to reduce the volume and increase the usability of top management reports.

I. Inventory Control

   Of all the areas reviewed, inventory control offers the greatest potential for savings to the company. These savings could be in the form of clerical cost reductions and reduced inventories for given levels of operation.

   The inventory control systems used have certain characteristics which impair their effectiveness. These characteristics can be summarized as follows:

   1. Selective controls are not used for various kinds of inventory. This generates clerical effort which does not produce control.
   2. Management policy in respect to inventories is not adequately defined. As a result, inventory decisions are made at a fairly low level; in many cases, the clerical level.
   3. Inventory status information is not available for management to use in—
      (a) Reviewing the effectiveness of policy and revising where necessary.
      (b) Assuring itself that the established policies are being followed.

## Selective Controls

"Selective Controls" in inventory is a term used to describe techniques which apply the principle that the dollars and effort spent in controlling inventories should be in direct ratio to the value of the inventory being controlled. Generally, in a manufacturing organization, an analysis of the inventory will show—

> 70% of the value in 10% of the quantity of items;
> 25% of the value in 25% of the quantity of items;
> 5% of the value in 65% of the quantity of items.

By concentrating control on only 35 per cent of the items in inventory, 95 percent of the dollars can be effectively controlled, and the majority of the items which represent the least value can be controlled by less expensive methods.

II. Data Processing⎫ ⎡These detailed comments and
III. Management Reporting⎭ ⎣recommendations have been omitted.⎤


Excerpt from the management letter to "Consolidated Utilities, Incorporated"—

### Materials and Supplies

The investment of $1,500,000 in operating and construction materials and supplies represents 57 percent of the total current assets of the company at September 30. Assuming the cost of money to be 12 percent, the company is paying, in interest alone, a total of $180,000 per year to maintain this stock. Interest, of course, is only one factor of the expense involved.

A comparison of the percentage of materials and supplies to utility plant with two other decentralized utility companies in this area follows:

|  | Consolidated Utilities, Incorporated | Company A | Company B |
|---|---|---|---|
| Investment in utility plant .. | $47,445,000 | $146,584,000 | $36,416,000 |
| Investment in materials and supplies ........... | 1,500,000 | 1,471,000 | 490,000 |
| Percentage of materials and supplies to plant ... | 3.16% | 1.00% | 1.35% |

Although the necessary investment for any company in materials and supplies must be determined by that company's individual situation, the above comparison indicates that the company's investment in materials and supplies may greatly exceed the amount required for efficient operation. If materials and supplies on hand could be reduced to an amount comparable to those of Company A and Company B above, a substantial amount of funds could be released for investment in revenue-producing properties and would tend to further defer the necessity of additional financing.

### Control of Investment by Centralized Accounting

An effective method of controlling the investment in operating materials and supplies is the use of centralized stores accounting. With stores records centralized and converted to automated data processing, it would be possible for the purchasing department to have current information available at all times as to the quantities of each type of material on hand at each location, thus permitting transfers of materials in oversupply at one location to eliminate shortages in other locations. With the present decentralized system it is much more difficult to avoid ordering additional materials when an adequate supply is already on hand at another location.

### Issue Tickets Should Be Prepared at the Time Materials Are Issued

In those divisions which we have visited in the last two years the major variations between stores items on hand and the perpetual records have been caused by failure to prepare issue tickets for material taken out on jobs. The reason for this situation is that in some instances line foremen wait until the close of a job to prepare issue tickets, instead of doing this at the time material is removed from stores. The delay in preparing issue tickets by line foremen and other personnel responsible causes difficulty in both stores and plant accounting, because frequent adjustments to work orders occur in connection with:

1. Physical counts of materials and supplies to reflect materials actually on hand.
2. Field inventories of completed projects to reflect issues equal to the number of units actually installed.

A rigid program of requiring issue tickets to be prepared when material is taken from stores would:

1. Assure proper distribution of material costs.
2. Reduce the size and number of physical inventory adjustments.
3. Eliminate the large differences which occur when completed projects are inventoried.
4. Allow maximum use of perpetual inventory records.

For smaller clients a management letter could address more elementary matters such as the following if the practitioner approaches engagements with what has been referred to as a "public controllership" point of view:

1. Developing a good classification of accounts to ensure adequate and useful operating and financial information.
2. Attaining maximum internal control commensurate with the limited number of employees.
3. Instituting simple cost-saving clerical procedures such as "write-it-once" systems, whereby several forms are prepared with a single writing (paycheck, earnings statement, employee earnings summary, and payroll register, for example), supplemented by such basic types of simple machines as cash registers, electronic printing calculators, and stencil-type addressing equipment.
4. Inaugurating basic inventory control records involving the retail inventory method or Kardex unit inventory records.
5. Developing a simple cost accounting system that can aid in cost control and yield useful product cost information.
6. Instituting elementary budgeting and cash forecasting procedures.
7. Assisting in financial planning and obtaining needed financing.
8. Utilizing the capabilities of a microcomputer for any of the above matters that involve repetitive operations or calculations.

## Accounting Services

The largest public accounting firms usually avoid performing accounting services (sometimes referred to as "write-up work") for their clients because their organization and mode of operation are not well adapted to providing such services. Also, the remuneration for these services tends to be substantially less than for most other public accounting services because less professional skill is required. On the other hand, many smaller accounting firms and individual practitioners are likely to have a certain amount of such work. Often, these services may represent the backbone of the accountant's practice during the early stages of the development of a practice.

Accounting services usually involve the preparation of adjusting entries and monthly statements, but often the accountant will also prepare the books of original entry and post the general ledger as well. The goal of every practitioner should be to spend as little time as possible on such services for clients, from the standpoint of both practice development and service to clients, for the well-qualified practitioner can be of greater service to clients in a multitude of other ways. One solution to the problem is for the CPA to employ clerical help with bookkeeping training or experience to do the work, so that supervision can be limited. As increased volume may warrant, microcomputers and packaged programs that require only some skilled clerical assistance for the input of data to perform complete bookkeeping operations and the preparation of financial statements may be utilized to perform the services more efficiently and accurately, and with improved appearance of results.

## In Conclusion

Services that members of the public accounting profession provide to their clients have been the subject of this chapter, and indeed of the entire book. Supplementing the discussion of the three principal services: auditing, tax planning and compliance, and management consulting, the book has considered the intraorganizational branch of auditing that includes internal auditing and governmental auditing. In each of these areas the focus has been on the nature of the various activities, how the activities are carried out, and especially on why each activity is necessary and why it should be carried out in a certain way. In the auditing area, the framework of the discussion of why and how has been in terms of objectives—the objectives of internal control as a major determinant of the scope of a systems-based audit, and the objectives of the audit activities themselves. An overriding consideration has been the various quality control measures introduced by the profession to assure the competent discharge of the responsibilities associated with its service activities—responsibility to third-party users of audited financial information, responsibility to clients, and responsibility to the general public. It is the author's wish and hope that the reader's pursuit of these matters has proven fruitful and rewarding.

## Questions/Problems

For multiple-choice questions 22-1 through 22-8 indicate the letter of the single answer that *best* completes the statement or answers the question, and justify the choice that you have made.

**22-1.** When a CPA prepares a federal income tax return for an audit client, one would expect
   a. The CPA to take a position of client advocacy.
   b. The CPA to take a position of independent neutrality.
   c. The taxable net income in the audited financial statements to agree with taxable net income in the federal income tax return.
   d. The expenses in the audited financial statements to agree with the deductions in the federal income tax return.

   (Uniform CPA Examination)

**22-2.** In accordance with the AICPA Statements On Responsibilities In Tax Practice, where a question on a federal income tax return has not been answered, the CPA should sign the preparer's declaration only if
   a. The CPA can provide reasonable support for this omission upon examination by IRS.
   b. The information requested is *not* available.
   c. The question is *not* applicable to the taxpayer.
   d. An explanation of the reason for the omission is provided.

   (Uniform CPA Examination)

**22-3.** What action should be taken by Washington, CPA, when he discovers that Mr. Madison refuses to answer certain questions on his federal income tax return because a truthful answer would probably prompt an IRS audit of the return?
   a. He should sign the preparer's declaration on the tax return.
   b. He should himself write the answers on the tax return and then sign the preparer's declaration.
   c. He should sign the preparer's declaration on the tax return and attach a statement that he is not responsible for the questions on the tax return.
   d. He should refuse to sign the preparer's declaration on a tax

return that is incomplete as to questions for which answers are available.

(Uniform CPA Examination)

**22-4.** Upon discovering irregularities in a client's tax return that the client would *not* correct, a CPA withdraws from the engagement. How should the CPA respond if asked by the successor CPA why the relationship was terminated?

a. "It was a misunderstanding."
b. "I suggest you get the client's permission for us to discuss all matters freely."
c. "I suggest you ask the client."
d. "I found irregularities in the tax return which the client would not correct."

(Uniform CPA Examination)

**22-5.** A CPA firm's primary purpose for performing management advisory services is to

a. Prepare the CPA firm for the changing needs and requirements of the business community.
b. Establish the CPA firm as a consultant, which will enable the CPA firm to ensure future viability and growth.
c. Provide advice and technical assistance which will enable a client to conduct its business more effectively.
d. Enable staff members of the CPA firm to acquire the necessary continuing education in all areas of business.

(Uniform CPA Examination)

**22-6.** Which of the following is *not* a Management Advisory Service Practice Standard?

a. In performing management advisory service, a practitioner must act with integrity and objectivity and be independent in mental attitude.
b. The management advisory services engagement is to be performed by a person or persons having adequate technical training as a management consultant.
c. Management advisory service engagements are to be performed by practitioners having competence in the analytical approach and process, and in the technical subject matter under consideration.
d. Before undertaking a management advisory service engagement, a practitioner is to notify the client of any reservation regarding anticipated benefits.

(Uniform CPA Examination)

**22-7.** The AICPA Committee on Management Services has stated its belief that a CPA should *not* undertake a management advisory service engagement for implementation of the CPA's recommendations unless

    a.   The client has made a firm decision to proceed with implementation based on a complete understanding and consideration of alternatives.

    b.   The client does *not* understand the nature and implications of the recommended course of action.

    c.   The client does *not* have sufficient expertise within its organization to comprehend the significance of the changes being made.

    d.   The CPA withdraws as independent auditor for the client.

(Uniform CPA Examination)

**22-8.** During the course of an audit, the client's controller asks your advice on how to revise the purchase journal so as to reduce the amount of time his staff takes in posting. How should you respond?

    a.   Explain that under the AICPA Code of Professional Ethics you cannot give advice on management advisory service areas at the same time you are doing an audit.

    b.   Explain that under the AICPA Statement on Management Advisory Services informal advice of this type is prohibited.

    c.   Respond with definite recommendations based on your audit of these records, but state that you will not assume any responsibility for any changes unless your specific recommendations are followed.

    d.   Respond as practicable at the moment and express the basis for your response so it will be accepted for what it is.

(Uniform CPA Examination)

**22-9.** Indicate the areas within which CPAs have performed management services.

**22-10.** What limitations should a CPA observe in extending services outside the area of accounting?

**22-11.** How can a public accounting firm utilize the services of a highly trained mathematician in the management services area if the mathematician has had little experience in business?

**22-12.** Your client expenses all office and factory supplies as they are purchased. The supply rooms are open to those who need supplies, and they select whatever is needed. Would you consider a recommendation to your client that the system of handling supplies be changed in any way? Explain.

**22-13.** What reasons would you advance to your client for changing the fiscal year closing from a calendar year basis to a natural business year basis?

**22-14.** Suggest the advantages to your client (a department store) of preparing and mailing customers' statements on a cycle basis rather than at the end of the month.

**22-15.** What advantages and disadvantages would have to be weighed in reaching a decision on whether to recommend that a public utility client change from monthly to bimonthly billing?

**22-16.** Shortly before the due date Daniel Burr requested that you prepare the 19X1 federal income tax return for Burr Corporation, a small closely held service corporation that he controlled. Burr placed a package on your desk and said, "Here is all the information you need. I'll pay you $300 if you prepare the return in time for filing by the deadline with no extension—and if the tax liability is less than $2,000 I'll increase your fee to $500." The package contained the Corporation's bank statements and paid checks, prior years' tax returns prepared on the accrual basis, and other financial and tax information. The books of account were not included because they were not posted up to date.

You found that deposits shown on the bank statements substantially exceeded Burr's sales figure, and the expenses listed seemed rather large in relation to sales. Burr explained that he made several loans to the Corporation during the year and expenses just seemed to "mount up."

Required:

(a)  1.  What ethical issues should you consider before deciding whether or not you should prepare the federal income tax return for Burr Corporation?
    2.  If you prepare this return, must you sign it? Explain.
    3.  If you sign the return, what does your signature imply?

(b)  Assume that you prepared the Corporation's federal income tax return. Shortly thereafter Burr came to your office and requested that you prepare financial statements for the Corporation solely from the data on the federal income tax return you prepared. The statements are to be submitted to a creditor. Discuss the ethical implications of your preparing the financial statements on:

    1.  Your stationery.
    2.  Plain paper.

(Uniform CPA Examination)

**22-17.** As part of his relationship with his client, a CPA often is asked to prepare or review the client's federal income tax return.

Required:

(a)   In each of the following independent cases:

1. State the CPA's obligation, if any, with respect to signing the preparer's declaration on the federal income tax return.
2. Explain or justify the position taken.

### Case 1

The tax return of Rogers, Inc. was prepared by the Company controller, a recognized expert in the field of taxation. The president of Rogers asks the independent CPA to review the return and sign the preparer's declaration.

### Case 2

The CPA prepares the client's tax return, signs the preparer's declaration and forwards the return to the client for signature. The client requests that the CPA prepare a revised return and sign the declaration; the revision involves certain changes which are unacceptable to the CPA.

### Case 3

At his wife's request, the CPA prepares the tax return for his brother-in-law. The only compensation received for this engagement is reimbursement for secretarial typing services.

(b)   In the course of the preparation of a client's federal income tax return, it is discovered that certain data which must be included in the tax return are not available. These data can be estimated to complete the return.

1. Explain and illustrate the circumstances under which the CPA may prepare federal tax returns involving the use of estimates.
2. Discuss the CPA's responsibilities with respect to the manner of presentation and disclosure of estimates which are used in a tax return that he prepares.

(Uniform CPA Examination)

**22-18.** The following cases relate to the CPA's management of his accounting practice.

### Case 1

Tom Jencks, CPA, conducts a public accounting practice. In 19X1 Mr. Jencks and Harold Swann, a nonCPA, organized Electro-Data Corporation to specialize in computerized bookkeeping services. Mr. Jencks and Mr. Swann each supplied 50 percent of Electro-Data's capital, and each holds 50 percent of the capital stock. Mr. Swann is the salaried general manager of Electro-Data. Mr. Jencks is affiliated with the Corporation only as a stockholder; he receives no salary and does not participate in day-to-day management. However, he has transferred all of his bookkeeping accounts to the Corporation and recommends its services whenever possible.

### Required:

Organizing your presentation around Mr. Jencks' involvement with Electro-Data Corporation, discuss the propriety of:

(a) A CPA's participation in an enterprise offering computerized bookkeeping services.

(b) The use of advertising by an enterprise in which a CPA holds an interest.

(c) A CPA's transfer of bookkeeping accounts to a service company.

(d) A CPA's recommendation of a particular bookkeeping service company.

### Case 2

Judd Hanlon, CPA, was engaged to prepare the federal income tax return for the Guild Corporation for the year ended December 31, 19X2. This is Mr. Hanlon's first engagement of any kind for the Guild Corporation.

In preparing the 19X2 return, Mr. Hanlon finds an error on the 19X1 return. The 19X1 depreciation deduction was overstated significantly— accumulated depreciation brought forward from 19X0 to 19X1 was understated, and thus the 19X1 base for declining balance depreciation was overstated.

Mr. Hanlon reported the error to Guild's controller, the officer responsible for tax returns. The controller stated: "Let the revenue agent find the error." He further instructed Mr. Hanlon to carry forward the material overstatement of the depreciable base to the 19X2 depreciation computation. The controller noted that this error also had been made in the financial records for 19X1 and 19X2 and offered to furnish Mr. Hanlon with a letter assuming full responsibility for this treatment.

### Required:

(a) Evaluate Mr. Hanlon's handling of this situation.

(b) Discuss the additional action that Mr. Hanlon should now undertake.

### Case 3

Fred Browning, CPA, has examined the financial statements of the Grimm Company for several years. Grimm's president now has asked Mr. Browning to install an inventory control system for the Company.

Required:

Discuss the factors that Mr. Browning should consider in determining whether to accept this engagement.

(Uniform CPA Examination)

**22-19.** Savage, CPA, has been requested by an audit client to perform a nonrecurring engagement involving the implementation of an EDP information and control system. The client requests that in setting up the new system and during the period prior to conversion to the new system, that Savage:

> Counsel on potential expansion of business activity plans.
> Search for and interview new personnel.
> Hire new personnel.
> Train personnel.

In addition, the client requests that during the three months subsequent to the conversion, that Savage:

> Supervise the operation of new system.
> Monitor client-prepared source documents and make changes in basic EDP-generated data as Savage may deem necessary without concurrence of the client.

Savage responds that he may perform some of the services requested, but not all of them.

Required:

(a) Which of these services may Savage perform, and which of these services may Savage not perform?

(b) Before undertaking this engagement, Savage should inform the client of all significant matters related to the engagement. What are these significant matters?

(c) If Savage adds to his staff an individual who specializes in developing computer systems, what degree of knowledge must Savage possess in order to supervise the specialist's activities?

(Uniform CPA Examination)

**22-20.** Although your client has not discussed the problem with you, you have concluded that the business is in dire need of additional liquid funds. You have noted that payables are being liquidated well after discount dates have expired and that most equipment is being leased, rather than being purchased as is customary in most businesses of this type. The problem is being aggravated by a continued comfortable increase in volume, which has necessitated carrying larger inventories and receivables and leasing additional equipment at rates well in excess of normal depreciation charges and interest. The owner of the business has already invested all his available liquid funds in the business. Suggest possible recommendations that you might make to aid your client, and indicate other possibilities that seem inapplicable in this situation, stating your reasons for concluding that they are inapplicable.

**22-21.** The Standard Mercantile Corporation is a wholesaler and ends its fiscal year on December 31. As the Company's CPA you have been requested in early January, 19X2, to assist in the preparation of a cash forecast. The following information is available regarding the Company's operations:

1. Management believes the 19X1 sales pattern is a reasonable estimate of 19X2 sales. Sales in 19X1 were as follows:

| | |
|---|---:|
| January | $ 360,000 |
| February | 420,000 |
| March | 600,000 |
| April | 540,000 |
| May | 480,000 |
| June | 400,000 |
| July | 350,000 |
| August | 550,000 |
| September | 500,000 |
| October | 400,000 |
| November | 600,000 |
| December | 800,000 |
| Total | $6,000,000 |

2. The accounts receivable at December 31 total $380,000. Sales collections are generally made as follows:

| | |
|---|---|
| During month of sale | 60 percent |
| In first subsequent month | 30 percent |
| In second subsequent month | 9 percent |
| Uncollectible | 1 percent |

3. The purchase cost of goods averages 60% of selling price. The cost of the inventory on hand at December 31 is $840,000, of which $30,000 is obsolete. Arrangements have been made to sell the obsolete inventory in January at half of the normal selling price on a C.O.D. basis.

The Company wishes to maintain the inventory as of the 1st of each month at a level of three months sales, as determined by the sales forecast for the next three months. All purchases are paid for on the 10th of the following month.

Accounts payable for purchases at December 31 total $370,000.

4. Recurring fixed expenses amount to $120,000 per month including depreciation of $20,000. For accounting purposes the Company apportions the recurring fixed expenses to the various months in the same proportion as that month's estimated sales bears to the estimated total annual sales. Variable expenses amount to 10% of sales.

   Payments for expenses are made as follows:

   |  | During Month Incurred | Following Month |
   |---|---|---|
   | Fixed expenses......... | 55% | 45% |
   | Variable expenses ...... | 70% | 30% |

5. Annual property taxes amount to $50,000 and are paid in equal installments on December 31 and March 31. The property taxes are in addition to the expenses in item "4" above.

6. It is anticipated that cash dividends of $20,000 will be paid each quarter on the 15th day of the 3rd month of the quarter.

7. During the winter unusual advertising costs will be incurred which will require cash payments of $10,000 in February and $15,000 in March. The advertising costs are in addition to the expenses in item "4" above.

8. Equipment replacements are made at the rate of $3,000 per month. The equipment has an average estimated life of six years.

9. The Company's income tax for 19X1 is $230,000. A Declaration of Estimated Income Tax was filed for 19X1. The Declaration estimated the Company's total 19X1 tax as $210,000, and payments of $110,000 were made as prescribed by income tax regulations. The balance of the tax due will be paid in equal installments.

   For 19X2 the Company will file a Declaration estimating the total tax as $220,000.

10. At December 31, 19X1, the Company had a bank loan with an unpaid balance of $280,000. The loan requires a principal payment of $20,000 on the last day of each month plus interest at ½% per month on the unpaid balance at the first of the month. The entire balance is due on March 31, 19X2.

11. The cash balance at December 31, 19X1, is $100,000.

12.  The client understands that the ethical considerations involved in preparing the following statement will be taken care of by your letter accompanying the statement. (Do not prepare the letter.)

Required:

Prepare a cash forecast statement by months for the first three months of 19X2 for the Standard Mercantile Corporation. The statement should show the amount of cash on hand (or deficiency of cash) at the end of each month. All computations and supporting schedules should be presented in good form.

(Uniform CPA Examination)

# INDEX